NANCY MEDINA

D0442164

Essential Psychopathology and Its Treatment

SECOND EDITION
REVISED FOR DSM-IV

A NORTON PROFESSIONAL BOOK

Essential Psychopathology and Its Treatment

SECOND EDITION
REVISED FOR *DSM-IV*

Jerrold S. Maxmen, M.D.
Nicholas G. Ward, M.D.

W. W. NORTON & COMPANY • *NEW YORK* • *LONDON*

The American Psychiatric Association has kindly granted permission
to reprint material from *Diagnostic and Statistical Manual of Mental Disorders,
Second Edition (DSM-II)*, © 1968, and from *Diagnostic and Statistical Manual of
Mental Disorders, Fourth Edition (DSM-IV)*, © 1994.

Printed in the United States of America

Second Edition

Composition by Bytheway Typesetting Services, Inc.
Manufacturing by Haddon Craftsmen, Inc.

Library of Congress Cataloging-in-Publication Data

Maxmen, Jerrold S.
    Essential psychopathology and its treatment / Jerrold S. Maxmen,
Nicholas G. Ward. — 2nd ed.
        p.   cm.
    Rev. ed. of: Essential psychopathology. 1st ed. © 1986.
    "A Norton professional book."
    Includes bibliographical references and index.
    ISBN 0-393-70173-5
    1. Psychology, Pathological. 2. Psychiatry. I. Ward, Nicholas
G. II. Maxmen, Jerrold S. III. Title.
    [DNLM: 1. Mental Disorders—diagnosis. 2. Mental Disorders—
therapy. 3. Psychopathology.   WM 141 M464EA 1995]
RC454.M3   1995
616.89—dc20   94-38839 CIP

W. W. Norton & Company, Inc., 500 Fifth Avenue, New York, NY 10110
W. W. Norton & Company, Ltd., 10 Coptic Street, London, WC1A 1PU

4   5   6   7   8   9   0

To the memory of Jere, whose spirit lives on
in those whom he knew, and whose words
and thoughts live on in his books

To the memory of my brother, Jeff,
and my father, who were my
first guides and teachers

–NGW

Contents

Preface

UNTIL RECENTLY, psychiatric diagnosis was ridiculed by social critics and downplayed by most professionals: At best, diagnoses were meaningless categories; at worst, denigrating labels. But in 1980, psychiatric diagnosis suddenly became the cornerstone for *all* clinical practice. During the 1970s, major developments in psychiatric epidemiology and drug therapy spurred the development of something American psychiatry never had: a clinically useful nosology. (A "nosology" is a system for naming and classifying diseases.) In July 1980, the American Psychiatric Association published this nosology as the third edition of the *Diagnostic and Statistical Manual of Mental Disorders*, or *DSM-III*.

This volume became this century's greatest advance in psychiatric diagnosis. Instead of merely tinkering with old categories or adding nosological blubber, *DSM-III* introduced major conceptual and practical shifts and, for the first time in making diagnoses, favored scientific evidence over theoretical speculation. *DSM-III* respect for rigorous scientific thought has spread throughout clinical practice. Psychotherapy, once a strictly intuitive affair, is now researched with standards similar to other sciences. Since *DSM-III*, meetings of mental-health professionals have undergone a mind-boggling transformation: Participants now ask such once ill-mannered questions as: "Where's the evidence?" and "What's the data?" No longer are things true simply because Professor X says so. Today, diagnostic common-sense necessitates proof. Scientifically, *DSM-III* had its deficiencies, but these stem far more from gaps in scientific knowledge than from inadequacies in *DSM-III* itself.

These deficiencies, real and dubious, motivated a 1987 revision (*DSM-III–R*) and a 1994 update (*DSM-IV*); both presented clinical and scientific advances. *DSM-IV* is also intended to be a cross-cultural and political advance. In much of the world, a diagnostic system called ICD (International Classification of Diseases) is used for psychiatric diagnosis. The most recent version, ICD-10, was released in 1993. *DSM-IV* attempts to be harmonious with ICD-10, so that when clinicians from different countries discuss a particular diagnosis, they are really talking about the same disorder or disease.

Some people consider a *scientific* psychiatry to be a dehumanized psychiatry. We could not disagree more. As long as therapists treat *people*-with-illnesses, instead of *illnesses*-that-happen-to-be-in-people, clinical practice necessitates artistry, intuition, philosophy, ethics, and science—each with its own contribution. The distinct contribution of science is that, when properly conducted, it yields the most likely predictions, and therefore affords patients the greatest chance of receiving treatments most likely to work. Offering patients anything less is hardly humanistic.

There is, of course, far more to proper clinical assessment than diagnosis, and any clinician who evaluates a patient's condition *solely* in terms of whether it meets *DSM-IV* criteria is gravely misinformed. (Such a misapplication of *DSM-IV* reflects a disturbing misunderstanding of the diagnostic process.) Proper clinical assessments must address the patient's context, including his family, friends, upbringing, genetic patterns, physical health, current stressors, psychodynamics, and so on. Still, good care begins with accurate diagnosis.

DSM-III (now *DSM-IV*) is the first nosology widely applied by *all* mental-health disciplines. This is fortunate, for the essentials of psychopathology should be understood not just by psychiatrists, but by physicians, psychologists, nurses, social workers, psychotherapists, and counselors. In 1994, *conservative* estimates established that mental and addictive disorders afflicted between 40 and 50 million Americans. Aside from the emotional toll, these disorders annually cost the nation $20 billion in direct health-care expenditures and another $165 billion in the indirect costs of social services, crime control, lost productivity, etc. These amounts are similar to those for heart disease and cancer, which strike 45 million and 6 million Americans, respectively. Of all patients with mental disorders, about half (54.1%) are treated by primary-care physicians, a quarter (24.4%) by mental-health professionals, and another quarter (21.5%) go untreated. Thus, recognizing and healing psychopathology is an everyday task for every helping professional. *Essential Psychopathology and Its Treatment* presents the current, collective thinking of experts. Although stressing the new, the book does not abrogate the old. Time-tested concepts and practices are included. When our opinions differ from the experts' consensus or from *DSM-IV*, or when no consensus exists, the book says so. It examines some of these disagreements so that students learn to view psychiatric diagnosis as open to question, feisty, and fluid, not embedded in stone. Robert Spitzer, the chief architect of *DSM-III*, insists that was far from the last word in diagnosis, and when I (J.M.) asked him, "What happens if a clinician doesn't want to diagnose using *DSM-III* criteria?" Spitzer replied, "Then don't! It's a free country. *People* wrote *DSM-III*, not God."

Essential Psychopathology and Its Treatment is a "no-nonsense" book. Many psychiatric texts are written as if students were idiots, not to be "subjected" to anything more than the "most basic facts." As for concepts, forget it! "Everybody knows" that students are "antipsychiatry," and therefore, to prevent students from being turned off to psychiatry, these texts should be as simple-minded as possible. Again, we disagree. This text will not pander. Diagnostic psychopathology is essential to clinical evaluation, and if students don't wish to learn the subject and know it well, they might wonder why they are choosing to provide inferior care.

The "essential" in *Essential Psychopathology and Its Treatment* does not refer to the "essence" of psychiatry or to "all the psychiatry you'll ever need to know." Reality dictates that in psychiatry, as in everything else, choices must be made—choices which eliminate some good stuff in the process. For better or worse, the "essential" in *Essential Psychopathology and Its Treatment* reflects these choices: Some information is *relatively* more critical than other information. To save space, smaller type is used for less important material and only references to questionable material are provided. The downside of this "essential trimming" is that major works in diagnostic psychopathology don't appear, significant details are omitted, and text choices still remain.

In this book, people with *major* mental disorders will be called "patients" instead of "clients." Referring to patients with *severe* mental disorders as "clients" is not only euphemistic, but may unwittingly trivialize the burden of having a disorder like schizophrenia. Calling these people "patients" is purely descriptive and certainly no sign of disrespect. In contrast, those who seek help for problems other than serious mental disorders (e.g., adjustment reactions, marital difficulties) are called, quite properly, "clients." This book will employ "he" and "she" randomly, except when discussing a mental disorder more common in men or women.

This text aims to be concise, to give students of all ages and levels of experience a brief, relatively jargon-free, and readable blend of the newest and most fundamental information in this rapidly evolving field. We hope that *Essential Psychopathology and Its Treatment* fascinates students about the subject, encourages them to question whatever they read, to pursue the topic further, to chuckle every now and then, and most of all, to help their patients.

A word of caution: Do yourself a big favor and avoid self-diagnosis. With "medical student's disease," future physicians "catch" diabetes while studying medicine, cancer while studying surgery, and schizophrenia while studying psychiatry. Everybody has some features of a mental disorder, but that hardly means one has a mental disorder. Hemophiliacs bruise, but everyone who bruises isn't a hemophiliac. So too with mental disorders. If you are concerned that you, or a loved one, has a mental disorder, consult an expert.

To respect patients' confidentiality, we have changed their names, ages, sex, religion, city, occupation, and marital status, as well as presenting composites of real people and events. When altering the truth to protect confidentiality, we've tried to maintain the spirit of that truth. Any resemblance between the pseudonyms we've assigned to patients and to actual individuals with the same name is purely coincidental.

Acknowledgments

As THE QUINTESSENTIAL professional, Susan Barrows Munro belongs to that disappearing handful of editors who've produced the major works in our field; seeing her edit this book shows us why. The deficiencies in this text are ours, and only ours. To paraphrase Montaigne, "It's only a fool who never suspects he could be foolishly mistaken."

Perhaps I (J.M.) should thank my friends and relatives for their essential psychopathology, but instead I would like to thank, most genuinely, Drs. Marc Galanter, Steve Hyler, Fred Kass, Ron Rieder, Lawrence Sharpe, Michael Sheehy, and Andrew Skodal for their invaluable suggestions on parts of this text.

I (N.W.) would also like to thank Dr. Gary Tucker for his advice, encouragement, and support, and Drs. Andrew Saxon, Ralph Pascually, and Dorcas Dobie for their excellent suggestions and critiques. Robert Spitzer and Janet Williams were very helpful and kind in providing *DSM-IV* updates before the final draft was published. Paula Milligan and Leslie McEwen provided expert and tireless support and manuscript preparation. Last, but not least, I thank my family for their support, patience, and understanding.

Diagnostic Psychopathology

CHAPTER 1

Psychopathology

> Such is man that if he has a name for something it ceases to be a riddle.
> —I. B. Singer, "Property"

AT 58, AMY'S LIFE stopped. Although cancer-free for five months since her mastectomy, she remained paralyzed by depression and insomnia. Amy had withdrawn from family and friends, quit work, become addicted to sleeping pills, and contemplated suicide. Once a film buff, now she hid in bed ruminating about "it" (she was afraid to say *cancer*). Diligently, she attempted relaxation exercises to overcome insomnia, yet she was unable to concentrate—the harder she tried, the more she failed, and the less she slept. Her demoralization pervaded all.

After all, the reasons for her symptoms were understandable and Amy "knew" that only time could heal. To be sure, having cancer and a mastectomy is an understandable reason for sadness and insomnia. But this misses the point: Amy had an additional problem—a mental disorder called "major depressive disorder."

Only after Amy's psychopathology was recognized and the proper antidepressant medication prescribed did her life return to normal. She still worried about her mastectomy—who wouldn't?—but she worried as a "normal" person, not as a depressed one. Now, at least, she could get her mind off of cancer. Without major depression impeding her concentration, she was able to perform the relaxation exercises, stop taking sleeping pills, sleep well, socialize, and return to work. No matter how "understandable" her symptoms, Amy was helped only *after* her major depression was diagnosed.

Critics would charge that to diagnose Amy's condition is to label and thus to dehumanize her. Yet it was only after a therapist recognized that

3

Amy was suffering from more than the normal post-mastectomy demoralization that her humanity returned. Explained Amy, "For months I'd assumed there wasn't *really* anything wrong with me, and that if I only had the 'right' attitude, I'd feel fine. After all, other women get over their mastectomies. Why couldn't I? It had to be my fault—or so I thought. As soon as I learned there really *was* something wrong with me, and that it had a name, my self-blame vanished. At last, something could be done: My depression could be treated. But you can't treat what you can't name." When used with clear goals in mind, psychiatric diagnosis avoids the pitfalls of labeling, the meaninglessness of academic exercise, and the distortions of an arrogant clinician's ego. Indeed, when diagnostic evaluation is thus abused, the culprit is the therapist, not the process.

THE PURPOSES OF A PSYCHIATRIC DIAGNOSIS

Psychiatric diagnosis serves two main purposes (Spitzer, 1976). The first is to *define clinical entities* so that clinicians have the same understanding of what a diagnostic category means. Patients with a particular (medical or psychiatric) diagnosis need not exhibit identical features, although they should present with certain cardinal *symptoms*. The disorder should have a similar *natural history*—a typical age of onset, life course, prognosis, and complications. A diagnosis should reflect the *etiology* and *pathogenesis* of the condition. (*Etiology* refers to the origins of a disorder; *pathogenesis* refers to its course of development.) Although the same disorder can arise in more than one way, a diagnostic category should indicate whether the disorder consistently runs in families, is genetically transmitted, initiated by psychosocial forces, and exacerbated or aggravated by specific biological and environmental conditions.

The second goal of psychiatric diagnosis is to *determine treatment*. Having diagnosed Amy's condition as "major depression," the clinician knew to provide antidepressants; if the diagnosis had been unhappiness and insomnia, she would not have prescribed antidepressants. Diagnosis not only influences biological treatments, but also shapes the choice of particular psychotherapies.

How well a diagnosis defines a disorder and guides treatment depends on its validity and reliability. When a diagnostic category represents a genuine entity—that is, when patients with the same diagnosis have similar clinical features, natural histories, etiologies, pathogeneses, and responses to treatment—the category is said to have high *validity*. The more clinicians agree on a diagnosis when examining the same patient, the greater its interrater *reliability*. It is possible for a diagnostic category to have high validity without reliability, and vice versa. For example, a professor could conceive of the "Abominable Snowman Syndrome" with very specific diagnostic features. It then would be easy to get clinical agreement (high reliability) on who did or did not fit the diagnosis—but the diagnosis itself is meaningless (low validity) as a syndrome. The diagnostic category of "codependent personality" exemplifies the reverse situation: Such people probably exist and share clinical features, history, etc. (high validity), but the diagnostic criteria are so vague or varied that clinicians have trouble agreeing on who has it (low reliability). Prior to the *DSM-III* diagnostic manuals, the standard joke was that if ten psychiatrists examined the same patient, they would come up with 12 different diagnoses—another example of very low reliability!

DEFINING PSYCHOPATHOLOGY

> Who in the rainbow can draw the line where the violet tint ends and the orange tint begins . . . so with sanity and insanity.
> —Herman Melville, *Billy Budd*

Psychopathology is defined as the *manifestations* of mental disorders. (It also refers to the *study* of mental disorders—their problems, causes, and processes.) Psychopathology involves *impairments*, *deviance*, and *distress*, but not all impairments, deviance, and distress are psychopathology. Being ugly (not gorgeous), inefficient (not active), and thoughtless (not considerate) are all impairments, but not psychopathology. Being an atheist, punker, crook, or drag queen is deviant, but not psychopathological. Being starved, broke, or lonely is distressing, but not psychopathological.

Distinguishing psychopathology from normality is usually easy, although on occasion it can be difficult. Critics like Thomas Szsaz argue that because the line between psychopathology and normality is hazy, psychopathology is a myth. That's nonsense. Day and night clearly exist, even though at dusk it is hard to know which it is. Psychopathology is no less real for its relativity. The definition of a mental disorder in the *DSM-IV* does not suggest that there are sharp distinctions between psychopathology and normality or between different mental disorders. According to *DSM-IV*, mental disorders must produce clinically significant *impairment* or *distress* in one's personal, social, or occupational life. Biological changes may or may not be involved. *DSM-IV* states:

> . . . each of the mental disorders is conceptualized as a clinically significant behavioral or psychological syndrome or pattern that occurs in an individual and that is associated with present distress (e.g., a painful symptom) or disability (i.e., impairment in one or more important areas of functioning)

or with a significantly increased risk of suffering death, pain, disability or an important loss of freedom. In addition, this syndrome or pattern must not be merely an expectable and culturally sanctioned response to a particular event, for example, the death of a loved one. Whatever its original cause, it must currently be considered a manifestation of a behavioral, psychological, or biological dysfunction in the individual. Neither deviant behavior (e.g., political, religious, or sexual) nor conflicts that are primarily between the individual and society are mental disorders unless the deviance or conflict is a symptom of a dysfunction in the individual, as described above. (pp. xii–xxi)

DSM-IV classifies *mental disorders*; it does not classify *individuals* with mental disorders. Patients who receive the same diagnosis are not the same in every important respect. Just as the only similarity among diabetics is having symptoms of diabetes, the only similarity among schizophrenics is having symptoms of schizophrenia. Otherwise, some schizophrenics are delightful, some obnoxious, some brilliant, and some stupid. When, for the sake of brevity, a patient with schizophrenia is called a "schizophrenic," it should be done with the understanding that a disorder is an attribute of a person, and never his or her totality.

Many terms resemble "mental disorder." A *syndrome* refers to any cluster of signs and symptoms. Clinicians often use *mental disease* and *mental illness* as synonyms for mental disorder, especially for the more severe ones clearly involving biological changes, such as schizophrenia and bipolar disorder. Technically, this usage is inaccurate. In medicine, *disease* refers to the specific physical disturbances of a condition, whereas *illness* refers to the total experience of a condition, including physical disturbances. In *DSM-IV*, diagnostic categories are always called *disorders*.

Lay people often use terms such as *insanity* and *nervous breakdown* to mean mental disorder. Neither term has psychiatric meaning. *Insanity*, which is a legal term (the definition of which varies between states), establishes a defendant's lack of criminal responsibility due to a mental disorder or defect. *Nervous breakdown* is a popular term for any severe incapacitation due to emotional or psychiatric difficulties.

The term *problems in living* is often a euphemism for mental disorder. To have a mental disorder is surely a problem in living, but it is far more than that, and to equate the two is to err in categorization and to trivialize the pain of mental disorders. "Problems in living" connote the difficulties of everyday life: losing a job, squabbling with children, undergoing a divorce, fearing rejection, evading the bill collector, dealing with low self-esteem. Problems in living can be miserable, yet they are vastly different in magnitude and type from mental disorders. Problems in living consist of *"issues,"*[1] whereas mental disorders consist of psychopathology.

---

[1] This use of the term *issues* is the authors' and not part of the standard psychiatric lexicon.

Symptoms, Signs, and Issues

Psychopathology manifests as *symptoms* and *signs*. Symptoms are experienced subjectively, cannot be observed, and must be reported by the patient; signs can be observed and documented objectively. Symptoms include pain, hallucinations, appetite loss, paranoid thinking, and anxiety, whereas signs include phobic behavior, restlessness, weight loss, and paranoid speech. Depressed mood is a symptom, crying a sign; chest pain is a symptom, heart failure a sign. Mental-health professionals sometimes ignore this distinction and refer to signs as symptoms. (For literary convenience, this book does likewise, except when lumping them together clouds clinical thinking.)

People may have a symptom (e.g., anxiety, insomnia) without having a mental disorder. By itself, a symptom rarely constitutes a mental disorder. A symptom only reflects a mental disorder when it is a part of a specific symptom constellation. Most symptoms exceed the boundaries of routine experience; unlike issues (or problems in living), symptoms are not everyday occurrences. Everybody contends with issues, only some with symptoms. Patients with mental disorders have both symptoms *and* issues, whereas clients with problems in living have only issues.

Issues contain ideas; symptoms do not. However, just as mail transmits ideas, symptoms can express issues. The ideas patients communicate when they manifest symptoms reflect the issues concerning them. For instance, two men with the severe mental disorder of major depression may have the symptom of overwhelming hopelessness. The first, an elderly, devout Catholic, insists he is hopeless "because I sinned 20 years ago by cheating on my wife." The second, a young up-and-coming actor, feels equally hopeless because "I'm not a star." Both patients have psychopathology—that is, hopelessness—yet, since their issues are so different, each expresses hopelessness quite differently.

As very broad generalizations, *biological factors* primarily cause symptoms, whereas *psychosocial factors* primarily determine issues. Because most symptoms usually arise from an altered *brain*, biological therapies usually correct them; because issues mainly derive from an altered *mind*, psychosocial therapies usually rectify them. Since patients with mental disorders present with both symptoms and issues, their treatment frequently involves medication as well as psychotherapy. Since clients with problems in living present with issues but not symptoms, they only receive psychotherapy. Psychological symptoms such as negative thinking in depression or panic reactions in panic disorder fall in-between these two: They often stem from a combination of psychological and biological causes and are effectively treated by medication and/or psychotherapy.

Phenomenology is the aspect of psychopathology that deals with a person's consciously reported experiences (Jaspers, 1923/1972). It is also a branch of philosophy that posits that behavior is determined not by an objective external reality, but by a person's subjective perception of that reality. Phenomenology is an important aspect of both existential and descriptive psychiatry.

TWO DIAGNOSTIC APPROACHES

There are two major approaches to diagnostic psychopathology. The first is called *descriptive* because diagnoses are based on relatively objective phenomena that require nominal clinical inference; these phenomena include signs, symptoms, and natural history. The second is called *psychological* because diagnoses are based primarily on inferred causes and mechanisms. The psychological approach also considers descriptive phenomena, but as merely superficial manifestations of more profound underlying forces.

The descriptive approach focuses on the *what* of behavior, the psychological on its *why*. Amy's case illustrates the common mistake of confusing the two. *What* was wrong (major depression) had been ignored because people focused on *why* things were wrong (having cancer and a mastectomy). Failing to distinguish the *what* from the *why* of psychopathology is the novice's first big mistake. An example: A hallucinating, disheveled youth, convinced he was Jesus Christ, told beginning medical students that his parents stifled his creativity, poisoned his food, and stole his Nintendo. Once he left the room, the students were asked, "What do you think is wrong with him?" "Nothing," they replied, "the problem is that he has lousy parents." Yet, even assuming he has dreadful parents (the why), he is no less delusional and hallucinatory (the what).

Both descriptive and psychological approaches are valuable, since each addresses a different aspect of psychopathology. Take a delusion. The descriptive approach would detail its characteristics: Is it fixed? Vague? Paranoid? Circumscribed? The psychological approach would focus on inner mechanisms (e.g., projection), which produce the delusion.

Emil Kraepelin (1856–1926) is virtually synonymous with descriptive psychiatry—sometimes called "Kraepelinian psychiatry"—because he devised the first major psychiatric nosology based on descriptive criteria (Kraeplin, 1915/1921). Examining thousands of delusional and hallucinating patients, he divided those without obvious brain damage into two groups according to prognosis and age of onset. The first he diagnosed as "dementia praecox": *dementia* referred to the progressively downhill course of the disorder and *praecox* referred to the appearance of symptoms during the teens or twenties. He diagnosed the second group as "maniacal depression"—today called "bipolar disorder." These patients typically returned to normal and were initially hospitalized in their thirties and forties. Thus, in creating a descriptively-based nosology, Kraepelin added natural (or longitudinal) history to current (or cross-sectional) symptoms. His textbook is *the* classic in descriptive psychiatry and his approach has dominated European psychiatry to this day.

The psychological approach was launched by the Swiss psychiatrist Eugen Bleuler (1857–1939). In *Dementia Praecox, or the Group of Schizophrenias* (1911/1950), Bleuler introduced the term *schizophrenia* to signify the disorder's basic defect of splitting of psychic functions — that is, disorganization and incongruency between thought, emotion, and behavior (not a split or multiple personality, as popularly believed). Bleuler believed these splits gave rise to the fundamental symptoms of schizophrenia: flat or inappropriate *affect*, profound *ambivalence*, *autism*, and disturbed *associations* of thought — the "4A's." These splits are inferred psychological mechanisms of causation and thus fundamentally different from Kraepelin's observed, descriptive criteria.

Until *DSM-III* (1980), the psychological approach dominated American psychiatry, largely because it dovetailed with Freudian thought, which has always enjoyed more popularity in the United States than anyplace else. Indeed, Bleuler's psychological approach paved the way for diagnoses based on psychoanalytic criteria, such as "poor ego boundaries," "oral regression," "polymorphous perversity," "projection," and "primary process." The more psychiatrists focused on these inferred phenomena, the more they recognized that *everybody* had them to various degrees. This belief helps to explain three key differences between psychological and descriptive diagnoses.

First, the psychological view holds that, as a price for civilization, everyone has some degree of psychopathology; with the descriptive approach, only a minority has psychopathology. Second, psychologically-derived diagnoses follow a *unitary model*, in which there is essentially one mental disorder, whose name is a matter of degree, not type — from the least severe to the most: neuroses, personality disorders, manic-depression, and schizophrenia. As in physical medicine, the descriptive approach follows a *multiple model*, in which disorders are distinct and numerous. Third, the psychological view often considers patients to have more severe psychopathology than does the descriptive view. Patients diagnosed as "neurotic" by psychological criteria might have "no mental disorder" by descriptive criteria, whereas those diagnosed as "schizophrenic" by psychological criteria might be diagnosed as "manic" or "depressive" by descriptive criteria.

THE DESCRIPTIVE REVIVAL

A purely psychological approach pervaded *DSM-I* (1952), the first official psychiatric nomenclature for the United States. (All *DSM*s, or *Diagnostic and Statistical Manual of Mental Disorders*, are created by the American Psychiatric Association.) *DSM-I* diagnoses were loosely defined and emphasized psychological etiologies in the terminology ("schizophrenic reactions," "paranoid reactions," and "psychoneurotic reactions," etc.)

The main reason for writing *DSM-II* (1968) was to rectify *DSM-I*'s failure to conform to the World Health Organization's *International Classification of Diseases*. *DSM-II* eliminated "reactive" from most diagnostic labels, thereby inching away from an etiologically-based nosology. Yet in trying to be flexible, *DSM-II*'s diagnostic categories were often vague, idiosyncratic, and susceptible to bias. For example, studies revealed that patients with the same clinical features would receive the more benign diagnosis of manic-depression if they were Caucasian but the more ominous diagnosis of schizophrenia if they were African-American. Without objective diagnostic standards, a nosology based on inferred psychological phenomena often said more about the clinician's orientation than about the patient's attributes. *DSM-II* suffered from low interrater reliability. The "US/UK" study (Cooper et al., 1972) showed that, unlike the descriptively-oriented British psychiatrists, American psychiatrists frequently reached different diagnoses after observing the same videotape of the same patient being interviewed by the same psychiatrist. *DSM-II*'s diagnoses also lacked validity: The categories did not define disorders having predictable symptoms, natural histories, or responses to treatment. In theory, the chief virtue of the psychological approach was that it indicated a disorder's cause, but since the etiologies of most mental disorders were unknown, American psychiatry was moving away from the psychological tradition and returning to Kraepelin.

Additional factors contributed to this descriptive revival and to the emergence of *DSM-III*. Different classes of medications were discovered that alleviated or eliminated symptoms of one disorder but not of another. As a result, correct diagnosis became essential for choosing the correct medication. Researchers increasingly applied the same scientific methods (e.g., standardized interviews, double-blind conditions, matched controls, statistical proof) used in other branches of medicine to study mental disorders. Data began to show which mental disorders ran in families, which had predictable life courses, which afflicted various populations, which improved with specific therapies, etc. To make sure they were studying patients with similar disorders, researchers devised explicit, readily verifiable, and specific diagnostic criteria, which, after adjustment for clinical purposes, became *DSM-III*'s most distinctive innovation.

The latest nosology, *DSM-IV* (1994), continues the descriptive approach of *DSM-III* and *DSM-III–R* (1987). Changes in criteria that have occurred with the two revisions since *DSM-III* have been based largely on field testing of diagnostic criteria for validity, reliability, and stability. Each diagnostic manual is a work in progress that incorporates changes based on new information.

DSM-III AND *DSM-IV*: INNOVATIONS AND LIMITATIONS

DSM-IV (and *DSM-III*) differ from the earlier diagnostic manuals in seven major ways:

1. Whenever possible, *scientific evidence*, not theoretical hypotheses, determines diagnostic categories.
2. A *descriptive* rather than psychological approach is the foundation for diagnosis. Consequently, *DSM-IV* employs a largely nonetiological framework and a multiple rather than a unitary nosological model.
3. Diagnoses are defined by clearly delineated, objective, and readily verifiable criteria.
4. The diagnostic definitions of *DSM-IV* recognize that most patients with the same mental disorder do not have identical clinical characteristics. Patients usually share one or two core features, but beyond that, have a variety of different symptoms that are all consistent with the disorder. Thus, *DSM-IV* diagnoses often require some core diagnostic criteria, but offer a choice among others.
5. *DSM-IV* presents multiaxial diagnosis, allowing separate listings for the personality disorders, contributing medical diagnoses, etc.
6. Technical terms are defined.
7. *DSM-IV* was extensively field-tested prior to publication.

To illustrate some of these innovations, Table 1–1 shows how *DSM-II* and *DSM-IV* define what is essentially the same kind of moderate depression: *DSM-II* calls it a "depressive neurosis," *DSM-IV*, a "major depressive disorder, recurrent."

Whereas *DSM-II* indicates only that depressed patients are depressed (!), *DSM-IV* specifies the symptoms of this type of depression and shows how major depression differs from normality (criteria A–C) and from other mental conditions (criteria D–E). Because *DSM-IV* criteria (e.g., decrease in appetite, insomnia) are relatively objective and explicit, they are far easier for clinicians to identify and agree on; in contrast, *DSM-II*'s inferred psychological mechanisms (e.g., internal conflict) produce a much lower interrater reliability. Whether or not *DSM-IV* criteria for a major depression are optimal or valid can be disputed; yet because they are pre-

TABLE 1–1
DSM-II* and *DSM-IV* Definitions of a Moderate Depression

[Note: This book's clarifications are in brackets, the *DSM*'s, in parentheses.]

DSM-II: DEPRESSIVE NEUROSIS

This disorder is manifested by an excessive reaction of depression due to an internal conflict or to an identifiable event such as the loss of a love object [i. e., a person] or cherished possession.

DSM-IV: MAJOR DEPRESSIVE EPISODE AND MAJOR DEPRESSIVE DISORDER RECURRENT

Major Depressive Episode

A. Five (or more) of the following symptoms have been present during the same 2-week period and represent a change from previous functioning; at least one of the symptoms is either (1) depressed mood or (2) loss of interest or pleasure.

   Note: Do not include symptoms that are clearly due to a general medical condition, or mood-incongruent delusions or hallucinations.

   (1) depressed mood most of the day, nearly every day, as indicated by either subjective report (e.g., feels sad or empty) or observation made by others (e.g., appears tearful). **Note:** In children and adolescents, can be irritable mood.
   (2) markedly diminished interest or pleasure in all, or almost all, activities most of the day, nearly every day (as indicated by either subjective account or observation made by others)
   (3) significant weight loss or weight gain when not dieting (e.g., a change of more than 5% of body weight in a month), or decrease or increase in appetite nearly every day. **Note:** In children, consider failure to make expected weight gains.
   (4) insomnia or hypersomnia nearly every day
   (5) psychomotor agitation or retardation nearly every day (observable by others, not merely subjective feelings of restlessness or being slowed down)
   (6) fatigue or loss of energy nearly every day
   (7) feelings of worthlessness or excessive or inappropriate guilt (which may be delusional) nearly every day (not merely self-reproach or guilt about being sick)
   (8) diminished ability to think or concentrate, or indecisiveness, nearly every day (either by subjective account or as observed by others)
   (9) recurrent thoughts of death (not just fear of dying), recurrent suicidal ideation without a specific plan, or a suicide attempt or a specific plan for committing suicide

B. The symptoms do not meet criteria for a Mixed Episode.

C. The symptoms cause clinically significant distress or impairment in social, occupational, or other important areas of functioning.

D. The symptoms are not due to the direct physiological effects of a substance (e.g., a drug of abuse, a medication) or a general medical condition (e.g., hypothyroidism).

E. The symptoms are not better accounted for by Bereavement, i.e., after the loss of a loved one, the symptoms persist for longer than 2 months or are characterized by marked functional impairment, morbid preoccupation with worthlessness, suicidal ideation, psychotic symptoms, or psychomotor retardation.

TABLE 1–1
(Continued)

Major Depressive Disorder, Recurrent

A. The presence of two or more Major Depressive Episodes.

   Note: To be considered separate episodes, there must be an interval of at least 2 consecutive months in which criteria are not met for a Major Depressive Episode.

B. The Major Depressive Episodes are not better accounted for by Schizoaffective Disorder and are not superimposed on Schizophrenia, Schizophreniform Disorder, Delusional Disorder, or Psychotic Disorder Not Otherwise Specified.

C. There has never been a Manic Episode, a Mixed Episode, or a Hypomanic Episode. **Note:** This exclusion does not apply if all of the manic-like, mixed-like, or hypomanic-like episodes are substance or treatment induced or are due to the direct physiological effects of a general medical condition.

DSM-II, p. 40; *DSM-IV*, pp. 327, 345.

cise, when a therapist states that "patient X meets *DSM-IV* criteria for major depressive disorder," clinicians know what is meant.

Despite the exactness of *DSM-IV* criteria, their application still necessitates clinical judgment. In criterion "A" for depressive episode, for instance, how much sleep loss (#4) constitutes "insomnia"? How much diminished interest or pleasure is "marked" (#2)? In practice, as clinicians gain experience, they develop internal norms to answer such questions. In addition, both recent history—e.g., two-week requirement in criterion "A" for an episode and past history, two or more episodes in criterion "A" for major depressive disorders, recurrent—are included. *DSM-II* says nothing about time.

In regard to etiology, *DSM-IV* is largely atheoretical. Except in obvious cases (e.g., "cocaine abuse," "adjustment reaction"), its diagnostic criteria are free of etiological considerations—be they biological, psychoanalytic, social, or behavioral. In contrast, *DSM-II* requires an internal conflict or major loss to define depressive neurosis.

DSM-III adopted, and *DSM-IV* continues, a *multiaxial* system, so that a diagnosis could reflect more than a primary clinical syndrome, such as schizophrenia or phobic disorder. *DSM-IV* uses five axes, as described in Table 1–2. Axes I–III are required; axes IV and V are optional.

The major reason *DSM-III* introduced *multiaxial* diagnosis was to underscore the distinction between mental and personality disorders or traits. *Personality*, or *character*, refers to a person's longstanding, deeply ingrained patterns of thinking, feeling, perceiving, and behaving. Everybody has personality *traits*, which are prominent behavioral features and not

TABLE 1–2
***DSM-IV* Multiaxial Diagnostic System**

AXIS	CONTENT	EXAMPLE
DIAGNOSTIC AXES:		
I.	Clinical disorders	Major depressive disorder, recurrent
	Other conditions that may be a focus of clinical attention	
II.	Personality disorders	Obsessive-compulsive personality disorder
III.	General medical conditions	Diabetes
OTHER DOMAINS FOR ASSESSMENT:		
IV.	Psychosocial and environmental problems	Problems with primary support group—divorce
V.	Global Assessment of Functioning (GAF)*: currently and at highest level the past year	Current GAF: 55* Highest GAF past year: 80*

*Appendix C

necessarily psychopathological. In contrast, only some people have *personality disorders*—that is, when personality traits are so excessive, inflexible, and maladaptive that they cause significant distress or impairment. Mental disorders (Axis I) tend to be more acute, florid, and responsive to treatment than personality disorders (Axis II), which are more chronic, consistent, developmental, and resistant to treatment. When patients manifest both mental and personality disorder, the multiaxial system helps clinicians focus on the diagnostic and therapeutic differences between the disorders.

Despite its many advances, *DSM-IV* is not diagnostic dogma, but a *guide*. Remember—many who just finished *DSM-IV* are already formulating *DSM-V*. Controversies rage over whether some of *DSM-IV*'s diagnostic categories describe genuine disorders in people or are nothing more than meaningless labels on paper. Nosologies other than *DSM-IV* do exist, and on occasion this text will draw on them.

Although *DSM-IV* diagnoses have improved treatment planning, they remain insufficient, partly due to their variable validity. Yet, even if totally valid, no psychiatric (or medical) diagnosis would be sufficient by itself to establish the treatment. Other factors must be considered: the patient's ability to introspect, his or her defenses, family relationships, current stressors, compliance with therapy, etc. Clinical evaluations that ignore such factors in favor of checklists of *DSM-IV* criteria cannot lead to effective treatment plans, since they overlook that it is patients, not diagnoses, who are being treated. This text certainly stresses diagnosis, but clinical assessment clearly entails more than a diagnosis.

AN OVERVIEW OF PSYCHIATRIC EPIDEMIOLOGY

Psychiatric epidemiology is the science that studies the frequency and distribution of mental disorders within various populations. By identifying the presence or absence of a mental disorder in a specific group, defined by age, sex, race, socioeconomic class, inpatient status, health, diet, other illnesses, etc., the epidemiologist compiles clues about a disorder's etiology, pathogenesis, prevention, and treatment.

Most often cited are measures of *incidence* and *prevalence*. For a specific time interval and population, incidence refers to the number of *new* cases, whereas *prevalence* refers to the number of *existing* cases. These terms are usually expressed as percentages and calculated as follows:

$$\text{Incidence rate} = \frac{\substack{\text{\# persons} \\ \text{developing the disorder}}}{\text{Total number at risk}} \; / \; \text{Per unit time}$$

$$\text{Prevalence} = \frac{\substack{\text{\# persons with disorder} \\ \text{during a period of time}}}{\text{Total number in group}}$$

If 2,000 new cases of a disorder arise in one year in a population of 100,000, the *incidence* rate is 2% (2,000/100,000). *Prevalence* reflects how widespread a disease or disorder is during a specified period of time, which can vary from a moment (called "point prevalence"), to one year ("one-year prevalence"), to a lifetime ("lifetime prevalence").

Incidence and prevalence can convey very different pictures of a disorder's frequency. Treatment does not affect incidence (new cases), but it *does* affect prevalence (existing cases). Unlike incidence, prevalence is a factor of a disorder's duration, frequency of recovery, and death rate. That's why acute disorders generally have a higher incidence than point prevalence, whereas for chronic disorders it is just the reverse. For example, if an average person gets three colds per winter, the six-month incidence rate may be over 90%; however, the point prevalence rate for a cold may only be 20%. For AIDS, a long-lasting illness, the point prevalence rate (existing cases) is much higher than the 6- or 12-month incidence rate (new cases).

The frequency of a mental disorder varies enormously depending on how the disorder is defined, which populations are polled, and which assessment instruments are employed. For instance, pre-*DSM-III*, mental disorders had been defined so variously that older surveys generated prevalence rates from 11% to 81%.

The value of an epidemiologic study depends on the sensitivity and specificity of its diagnostic instruments. A test is *sensitive* when it accurately detects the *presence* of a disorder in a person who *has* the disorder. A test is *specific* when it accurately detects the *absence* of a disorder in a person who does *not have* the disorder. Remember when a "handwriting expert" would examine a person's writing and then say, "Underneath you have feelings of insecurity"? Of course he has some feelings of insecurity! Who doesn't? This test demonstrates high sensitivity but low specificity.

More accurate epidemiologic investigations resulted from a major advance in defining mental disorders. Feighner et al. (1972) first listed specific signs and symptoms as diagnostic criteria. Called the "Feighner criteria," they were used primarily by researchers. Adding duration, severity, and life course, Spitzer and colleagues (Spitzer, Williams, & Skodal, 1980) refined Feighner's criteria into the Research Diagnostic Criteria (RDC). These two diagnostic tools led to the more clinically-oriented *DSM-III*.

The Feighner and RDC approaches developed *structured interviews* that greatly facilitated data collection. A series of preset, standardized questions systematically determined if the subject met specific diagnostic criteria. Two structured interviews widely applied in research are the "Schedule for Affective Disorders and Schizophrenia" (SADS) and the *DSM-III*-based "Diagnostic Interview Schedule" (DIS).

Using the DIS, researchers from the National Institute of Mental Health (NIMH) interviewed almost 20,000 adults to establish the one-year and lifetime prevalences of 30 mental disorders (Robins & Regier, 1991). This project, known as the Epidemiologic Catchment Area (ECA) study, is referred to throughout this book. In a newer study (Kessler et al., 1994), the National Comorbidity Survey (NCS) researchers interviewed 8,098 adults to establish one-year and lifetime prevalences of 17 "common" mental disorders. The NCS used *DSM-III–R* diagnoses and an improved version of the DIS that had more thorough lists of symptoms than the ECA. The NCS yielded much higher rates of mental disorders than the ECA. Trained clinicians interviewed a subset of the respondents and found that most of the diagnoses were accurate.

The ECA and NCS reported that mental disorders affected 20–30% of adult Americans during the preceding year and 32–50% of them throughout life. Table 1–3 presents each disorder's one-year and lifetime prevalence rates for both the ECA and NCS. Using the one-year figures, anxiety disorders were most common (14.4–17.2%), followed by substance abuse (8.8–11.3%), mood disorders (4.3–11.3%), cognitive impairment (5.9%), and schizophrenic (1.0% ECA only) disorders. Because people who have one disorder frequently (about 80% of the time) have two or more disorders, the total percentage for classes of disorders in Table 1–3 is less than the sum of each separate disorder. Tobacco use (36%) and psychosexual disorders (24%), measured in an earlier study (Robins et al., 1984), are even higher than anxiety disorders.

During a lifetime, 36–48% of males and 30–47% of females had a psychiatric disorder, and during the preceding year, 20–30% of both men and women had experienced mental illnesses. Which gender had more lifetime mental disorders depended on the disorder: Women had at least twice as

TABLE 1–3
Prevalence of Specific Mental Disorders

DISORDERS	LIFETIME in percent		ESTIMATED NO. OF ADULT AMERICANS			Sex#	
			ACTIVE (one year) in percent		ACTIVE (one year) (in millions)*	F	M
	ECA	NCS	ECA	NCS	ECA		
Major depressive episode	6.4	17.1	3.7	10.3	6.8	LA	—
Manic episode	0.8	1.6	0.6	1.3	1.1	—	—
Dysthymia	3.3	6.4	α	2.5	6.1†	—	—
ANY MOOD DISORDER (NCS)	α	19.3	α	11.3	20.9	LA	—
Phobia	14.3	b	8.8	b	14.3	A	—
Panic	1.6	3.5	0.9	2.3	1.7	A	—
Generalized anxiety	8.5	5.1	3.0	3.1	5.5	A	—
Obsessive-compulsive	2.6	α	1.7	α	3.1	L	—
ANY ANXIETY DISORDER (NCS)	α	24.9	α	17.2	31.8	LA	—
Alcohol abuse/dependence	13.8	23.5	6.3	9.4	11.6	—	LA
Drug abuse/dependence	6.2	11.9	2.5	3.6	4.6	—	A
ANY SUBSTANCE USE DISORDER (NCS)	α	26.6	α	11.3	20.9	—	LA
Cognitive impairment: mild or severe	α	α	5.0	α	9.2	—	—
Cognitive impairment: severe	α	α	0.9	α	1.7	—	—
Somatization	0.1	α	0.1	α	0.2	LA	—
Antisocial personality	2.6	3.5	1.2	α	2.2	—	LA
Schizophrenia Ψ	1.5	0.7	1.0	0.5	1.8	—	—
ANY NCS DISORDER	α	48.0	α	29.5	54.5	—	—

*Based on 1989 population of Americans 18 years and older. NCS data used for summary categories.

#Prevalence ratios are greater than two for lifetime (L) or active (A) disorders.

α Not ascertained.

b Phobias not grouped in NCS.

†Lifetime prevalence.

Ψ Includes schizophreniform in ECA and all non-affective psychoses in NCS.

ECA findings from Robins, L. E., & Regier, D. A. (Eds.). (1991). *Psychiatric disorders in America: The epidemiologic catchment area study* (pp. 343–350). New York: Free Press.

NCS findings from Kessler, R. C., et al. (1994). Lifetime and 12-month prevalence of *DSM-III–R* psychiatric disorders in the United States. *Archives of General Psychiatry, 51*, 8–19.

many depressive, obsessive-compulsive, and somatization disorders; men had at least twice as many antisocial personality disorders and the highly prevalent alcoholism. Those who were younger, less educated, and unmarried (especially after multiple separations or divorces) were more likely to have a DIS diagnosis. The ECA also confirmed that most mentally ill patients were treated by non-psychiatrists: general practitioners, internists, psychologists, nurses, and social workers.

That almost half of all Americans suffer or have suffered from some type of mental disorder is startling. What both studies make clear is that the essentials of psychopathology should be understood by health-care professionals of all fields.

CHAPTER 2

Assessment

WOULD A PATIENT with severe stomach pain undergo surgery or be given medication without obtaining an evaluation? Hopefully not. Yet in psychiatry, this questionable procedure had been the norm: Many patients had chosen and received specific treatments without being formally assessed or diagnosed. The unitary model of mental illness rendered diagnosis almost academic and, since there was basically one "decent" treatment — psychoanalytic psychotherapy — the "prescription" was a foregone conclusion. If performed at all, assessments blended imperceptibly into psychotherapy. Today, however, the growing number and efficacy of contemporary biological and psychosocial treatments demands that *every* patient must receive a formal diagnostic assessment (evaluation) *before* treatment begins.

Assessment may be defined as *a time-limited, formal process that collects clinical information from many sources in order to reach a diagnosis, to make a prognosis, to render a biopsychosocial formulation, and to determine treatment.* This definition emphasizes that assessment is a specific task that is distinct from therapy. Indeed, some superb therapists are lousy diagnosticians, and vice versa. Clinicians continue to reassess patients as treatment proceeds, but the *formal* assessment ends before *formal* treatment begins.

The patient interview is usually the principal source of data, but it is not the only source. Information can be gathered from friends, family, physical examinations, laboratory tests, psychological studies, staff observations, standardized interviews, and brain-imaging techniques. Patient interviews generally require one to three hour-long sessions, although for patients with impaired concentration, sessions should be shorter and more frequent. Conversely, for healthier outpatients, the initial meeting is often 90 minutes.

19

The primary objective of these initial interviews is to obtain information that will determine the patient's diagnosis, prognosis, psychodynamics, and treatment. These interviews should also make the patient feel comfortable, foster trust, and develop the expectation that psychiatric treatment will help. With these ingredients, a therapeutic alliance can begin to form.

How a clinician seeks, selects, and organizes all the facts, figures, and fears patients present is no easy task. The art of asking the right questions is an important skill.[1] Essential for mastering this task is to find a standardized format; flexibility and following patients' leads are fine, chaos is not. As when learning to play the piano or to dance, students learn the basic formal aspects before improvising. Psychiatric assessment typically consists of eight steps (though the sequence for *conducting* and *reporting* these steps varies to some extent): (1) obtaining a *history*, (2) evaluating the patient's *mental status*, (3) collecting *auxiliary data*, (4) summarizing *principal findings*, (5) rendering a *diagnosis*, (6) making a *prognosis*, (7) providing a *biopsychosocial formulation*, and (8) determining a *treatment plan*. Table 2–1 outlines these steps and presents a method for reporting the formal assessment.

Whether oral or written, the report given to the patient should be clear, succinct, and systematic. Although the exhaustively detailed history, or *anamnesis*, is still used in psychoanalysis, most patients will benefit more from a briefer history, since it is more likely to be read. A major challenge in reporting a patient's evaluation is to convey the germane data in the fewest words. Chapter 6 illustrates a recorded assessment.

THE HISTORY

The patient's history begins with eliciting *identifying information* (II) about the patient, followed immediately by his or her *chief complaint* (CC). The II is the patient's age, sex, marital status, occupation, religion, race, and if pertinent, nationality, ethnic group, and sexual orientation. The CC is a sentence or two describing the *patient's*, not the therapist's, view of the main problem, preferably in the patient's exact words. If the patient's CC is senseless (e.g., "I need a new dress"), the therapist can add his or her own version of the CC (e.g., for three weeks the patient heard auditory hallucinations).

---

[1]A useful booklet on this subject is Mark Zimmerman's "Interview Guide for Evaluating *DSM-IV* Psychiatric Disorders and the Mental Status Exam" (Psych Products Press, 1994).

TABLE 2–1
An Outline of the Psychiatric Assessment

I. HISTORY
  A. Identifying information (II)
  B. Chief complaint (CC)
  C. History of present illness (HPI)
  D. Past psychiatric and developmental history (Table 2–2)
  E. Family psychiatric and medical history (FH)
  F. Medical history (MH) (Appendix D) and physical examination

II. MENTAL STATUS EXAMINATION (MSE)
  A. Appearance
  B. Behavior (including impulse control)
  C. Speech
  D. Emotion
    1. Mood
    2. Affect
    3. Mood congruency
  E. Thought processes and content
    1. Word usage
    2. Stream of thought
    3. Continuity of thought
    4. Content of thought
  F. Perception
  G. Attention
  H. Orientation
    1. Time (date, time of day)
    2. Place
    3. Person
  I. Memory
    1. Immediate
    2. Recent
    3. Remote
  J. Judgment
  K. Intelligence, information, and abstraction
  L. Insight

III. AUXILIARY DATA
  A. Interviews with relatives and friends
  B. Complete medical history and physical examination
  C. Laboratory tests (Table 2–3)
  D. Standardized interviews
  E. Psychological tests (Table 2–4)
  F. Brain-imaging studies

IV. SUMMARY OF PRINCIPAL FINDINGS

(*continued*)

TABLE 2–1
(*Continued*)

V. DIAGNOSES (*DSM-IV*) (Appendix A)
  A. Axis I: Mental disorder
  B. Axis II: Personality disorder/trait
  C. Axis III: General medical conditions
  D. Axis IV: Psychosocial and environmental problems
  E. Axis V: Global Assessment of Functioning (GAF)

VI. PROGNOSIS

VII. BIOPSYCHOSOCIAL FORMULATION

VIII. PLAN
  A. Additional data gathering (e.g., interviews, tests, consultations)
  B. Treatment goals (immediate, short-term, long-range)
  C. Treatment plan
    1. Immediate management
    2. Short-term interventions
    3. Long-term therapies

History of Present Illness (HPI)

The history of the present illness consists of the major symptoms, issues, and events that brought the patient to treatment. For each major problem, the HPI chronicles when it began, what initiated or exacerbated it, what escalated or diminished its severity, what problems concurrently existed, what effect it had on the patient's functioning, how the patient tried to resolve it, when it ended, why it ended, and the patient's subjective view of it. When a problem emerged gradually, estimate the time of onset. If the patient has had the same disorder repeatedly, the history should start with the most recent episode.

Any and all "entrances" and "exits"—that is, people or events entering a patient's life (e.g., a newborn) or exiting from it (e.g., a child leaving for college)—are noted. Changes are always important to identify, even ostensibly good ones. For instance, after obtaining a long-desired promotion to vice-president of a major corporation, a man became severely depressed—now he bossed his former peers, traveled in a faster social crowd, and faced a wife demanding fur coats.

The therapist should ask why the patient has come for help *now*. A 37-year-old single designer sought treatment for, as she said, "an inferiority complex." When asked why she had come for treatment at this particular time, she answered that a friend suggested it. By pursuing the "Why now?" question, the therapist discovered that the day after the patient's mother had married her fifth husband, the patient had wondered, "What's wrong with me?" That is when the patient had followed the friend's advice to seek help.

The clinician should never assume that the patient's use of a technical term is the same as his or her own: Patients will say *anxiety* but mean *depression, paranoia* but mean *embarrassment, nervousness* but mean *hallucinations.* If a clinician is at all unsure of what a patient means by a word, the patient should be asked to describe it more fully or to give an example.

During intake interviews, clinicians notoriously avoid asking about three immediate and critical issues: (a) drug and alcohol use, (b) suicidal tendencies, and (c) violent or homicidal tendencies. The reasons for this avoidance vary. Without realizing it, a therapist may avoid inquiring about these problems because, if they do exist, the therapist might not know how to intervene — it's "safer" not to ask in the first place! A therapist may also fear that such questions would embarrass the patient. This embarrassment, however, is the therapist's more than the patient's: Most patients expect clinicians to ask "embarrassing" questions — it's the clinician's job — and if the clinician doesn't, some patients will feel the clinician is being slipshod or not taking their case seriously. In any event, tactfully posed questions rarely offend patients.

Be sure to ask about present and past use/abuse of alcohol, drugs, and prescription medications. Don't assume that the middle-class suburban homemaker in front of you would never use all those terrible substances. Anyone can. Regarding prescription drugs, an easy question is, "Have you ever used more than the amount prescribed?" Obtain drug names, amount, frequency, and duration used, use of IV drugs, whether needles were shared, and finally, complications and problems related to drug/alcohol use, such as periods of abstinence/sobriety, withdrawal symptoms, lost jobs, etc. Many patients with alcohol problems, when asked if they are alcoholic, respond with "No, I only drink beer," or "No, I only get drunk on weekends." A careful, compassionate approach works best.

Suicide must be evaluated, or at least considered, with *every* patient. Not only is suicide the eighth leading cause of death in America, but its incidence is skyrocketing among all age groups, especially among youth, where it has become the second most frequent cause of death. Although officially, 30,000 Americans kill themselves each year, 100,000 is a more realistic figure.[2] (More people die from suicide than from homicide.) If there is any

---

[2]These statistics are from the National Center for Health Statistics.

question of suicide, the clinician *must* ask. The questions can be posed in a progressive manner, starting with passive suicidal ideation: "Have you ever felt that you would be better off dead, that if you died tomorrow, it wouldn't matter?" If the answer is yes, then active suicidal ideation can be determined by inquiring, "Have you thought about harming or, perhaps, killing yourself?" Questioning patients about committing suicide does *not* make people commit suicide or "introduce suicidal thoughts into their head." A patient who has been depressed, miserable, anxious, and without sleep, when asked, "Have you considered suicide?" will not respond, "Gosh, doctor, that's a good idea, I never thought of that. Thanks for the suggestion." Most potentially suicidal patients are relieved when a therapist raises the subject. Contrary to myth, people who talk about suicide *do* commit suicide. Because 80% of those who have killed themselves previously mentioned their problem to somebody, clinicians should take these patients seriously.

The risk of suicide escalates as the patient's suicidal *thoughts* intensify and become more frequent. Almost everyone has had fleeting suicidal thoughts; only the suicidal ruminate about it. More dangerous is when the patient has a *plan*, especially if he or she has settled on one plan, can detail it, and has begun implementing it. People who *attempt* suicide are more likely to commit suicide; the more serious the past attempt, the greater the risk of eventual suicide. A patient is at greater risk of suicide if a past attempt used a more lethal (in the patient's, not the clinician's mind) method, occurred after long planning rather than impulsively, did not allow much chance of discovery afterwards, and was not prefaced by a signal for help.

Almost 95% of patients who attempt or commit suicide suffer from a mental disorder: 80% of them have depression, 10% have schizophrenia, and 5% have delirium. Alcohol, especially with depression, increases the rate of death; 15% of alcoholics commit suicide. Patients abusing drugs also kill themselves; the frequency depends on the specific drug, with IV-use being especially high. As has been suggested previously, psychotic depression and bipolar disorder may not increase the suicide rate (Black, Winokur, & Nasrallah, 1988). Hopelessness is an experience common to many with mental disorders. Significant hopelessness is a strong predictor of ultimate suicide (Beck, Brown, Berchick, Stewart, & Steer, 1990).

The suicide rate, although greatest for men over 45 and women over 55, has been rising dramatically for teenagers, and especially for males between the ages of 15 and 24. Gun availability certainly helps; firearms kill 66% of American teens versus 6% in Great Britain. The major risk factors for a suicidal patient are being male, older, unemployed, unmarried, living alone, having a chronic illness, and being in a culturally alienated group. Additional risk factors include: (a) a threatened financial loss; (b) being unreligious in the formal sense; (c) a recent loss or death (a particularly higher risk factor for alcoholics); (d) a family history of suicide; (e) suddenly giving away prized possessions (Motto, Heilbron, & Juster, 1985).

Menninger (1938) observed that patients who commit suicide do so from three, not one, possible wishes: the wish to die, the wish to kill, and the wish to be killed. Many people might want to die, yet few are prepared to kill, and even fewer, to be killed; the latter two require a degree of violence, anger, and physical pain that only the "truly" suicidal could endure. Impulsive and angry people who are depressed have a higher risk for suicide and homicide.

Knowing all of these risk factors only tells you the statistical risk of suicide in the future. They can help predict the chances of suicide in the next year or two, but won't necessarily tell you what this particular patient will do in the next few days or week. Two more personal questions can help. Assuming the patient hasn't recently made an attempt, ask, "You have been feeling suicidal but you haven't acted on it — what stopped you?" Answers that suggest low risk include, "I'm a mother and I would never leave my children with a legacy of suicide. I could never do that," or "My religious beliefs [or values] would never let me commit suicide. I don't believe in it." A high-risk answer would be something to the effect of, "So far, I've been chicken, but I'm working up the courage." A second helpful question to ask is, "Why do you want to live?" Patients who are trying to conceal their suicidal feelings often can deny feeling suicidal but have a harder time making up believable reasons for living. They might say, "Because my parents don't want me to kill myself" (a high-risk answer) instead of, "I'm smart and kind. I want to see what I can do to help people" (a lower-risk answer).

The presence of violent tendencies in a patient must always be evaluated. Never assume that the mild mannered "Clark Kent" patient in front of you would not hurt a fly. Asking, "How do you handle your anger?" is a benign introductory probe that then can be followed with, "Have you ever broken things or hurt others when you were angry?" Violent tendencies tend to be expressed via two broad patterns: ongoing suppression or repression punctuated by sudden eruptions; and routine, regular outbursts of anger and destructive behavior. Some individuals are regularly violent towards a certain person or persons (such as a spouse), but to no one else and are probably safe on voluntary inpatient units.

The history of the present illness often ends with ascertaining "significant negatives" — those symptoms, issues, experiences, or events that have *not* occurred, even though they frequently accompany problems like those of the patient. For example, significant negatives for a severely depressed patient might include a denial of suicidal thoughts, the absence of recent losses, an unchanged libido, and no family history of bipolar disorder. When significant negatives are omitted from the report, other professionals cannot tell whether these negatives are truly absent or the interviewer simply forgot to ask about them.

Past Psychiatric History (PH)

The developmental history can be integrated with past psychiatric history or social history or presented separately (whichever is clearer.) The PH describes previous episodes in the patient's life that resemble the current episode, including each episode's duration, treatment, and outcome. The PH presents the patient's longstanding personality traits and characteristic ways of dealing with problems. In setting treatment goals it helps to determine the patient's highest level of functioning during his or her life *and* during the past year. The patient's level of functioning prior to the onset of the current episode is sometimes called *baseline functioning* and is an important reference point in deciding if the patient is better (i.e., back to normal for him or her).

Social and Developmental History (DH)

The social history can begin with the present by elaborating on "identifying information." It should include information on the present family situation, residential setting, occupation, and financial status. Although an exhaustive developmental history is usually unnecessary, it is valuable to cover the highlights, especially when they illuminate the present illness. Table 2-2 lists possible topics in the developmental history. Two quick ways to elicit critical information is to ask the patient (a) to name the three or four crucial turning points in his or her life and (b) to describe the most significant or memorable event during each developmental period.

It is also important to ask if there is a history of physical, sexual, or emotional *abuse*. If there is, do not assume that the patient is devastated. A majority of people who have been abused function normally as adults. Also do not assume that questions about abuse will somehow damage the patient. The questioner's level of comfort with these questions is often the key to establishing rapport. Ask the patient in a gentle, accepting way. For example, "Many people with emotional problems were abused as children and as adults. Has that happened to you?" If the patient becomes very

TABLE 2–2
The Developmental History*

I. PRENATAL
—Pregnancy: Planned? desired?
—Health of mother
—Complications during pregnancy and birth
—Full-term?

II. INFANCY to ADOLESCENCE
—Physical illnesses
—Temperament (especially compared to siblings and social attachments): Shy? friends? family relations?
—Developmental milestones: Walking, talking, reading, grades, learning impairments, menstruation, puberty, furthest grade level completed?
—Family: Stable? abusive? neglectful?
—Earliest and most vivid memories
—Symptoms or phobias: Enuresis? nightmares? cruelty to animals? fire-setting? oppositional? drug or alcohol misuse? identity problems?
—Sexuality and gender identity: Orientation? development?

III. EARLY and MIDDLE ADULTHOOD
—Occupations: First job? dates of each job? repeated performance patterns? likes and dislikes? work disabilities? discrepancies between ability, education, and present work? ambitious? current job and economic circumstances?
—Military service: Combat experience? type of discharge? disability benefits?
—Social: Dating? recreation? activities?
—Family of origin: Separated from? If so, when and how?, If not, why not? Feelings toward them?
—Marriage: When? why? how many? quality of relationship? quality of sex life? money—who manages it? disputes over? "faithfulness"? divorce?
—Children: Dates of miscarriages, including abortions; names, dates of birth, personalities of, and feelings toward, children
—Religion: Its effect, if any, on the patient; conversion? exacerbates or alleviates psychiatric problems? spiritual beliefs?
—Standards: Moral, political, social, atheistic, ethical

VI. LATE ADULTHOOD
—The "seven losses": How the person prepares for, adapts to, or surmounts each of them:
(a) loss of work (unemployment);
(b) loss of financial security (insecurity);
(c) loss of familiar surroundings, including home and community (dislocation);
(d) loss of physical health and ability to function (incapacitation);
(e) loss of mental abilities (incompetence);
(f) loss of people, especially spouse (isolation);
(g) loss of life (death)

*This table suggests topics for inquiry; it is not a comprehensive outline of development.

hesitant, she or he can be told, "Does talking about this right now make you too uncomfortable? You don't have to talk about it right now. You can wait until you feel ready."

Family History (FH)

Some clinicians prefer to put information about family functioning in the social developmental history and reserve the category of family history for family psychiatric problems.

In modern psychopathology all data regarding a family history of mental disorders is of great importance. Special emphasis should be placed on first-degree relatives. Ask about the past presence of alcoholism, drug abuse, antisocial behavior, depression, schizophrenia, "nervous break-downs," suicide, and psychiatric treatment. Because diagnoses by professionals (especially before 1980) were based on criteria different from those in *DSM-IV*, and because laymen do not employ diagnostic terms in the way professionals do, therapists should place little weight on diagnoses ascribed to family members and rely more on the ill relative's objective characteristics (such as speaking incoherently or being hospitalized). In general, patients under-report psychiatric diagnoses in family members (Andreasen, Rice, Endicott, Reich, & Coryell, 1986). A family member with major depressive disorder or generalized anxiety disorder is more likely to report the same disorder in relatives than a member who does not have this diagnosis (Kendler et al., 1991). Since response to medication is genetically transmitted, to some extent, if a mentally ill relative received medication, the clinician should inquire about the type, duration, and results.

Through a *genogram* (McGoldrick & Gerson, 1985) or a traditional narrative, the clinician indicates the "dramatis personae" and how they are related, employed, and involved with the patient. A full genogram can be quite time-consuming and may not be completed on the initial interview. The FH specifies who in the family the patient lives with (if anyone), sees the most, trusts the most, and depends on the most in a crisis. A description of routine family functioning may include information about who plays which roles in the family, who manages the money, who sets the day-to-day rules, and who makes decisions. Family snapshots are valuable as much for how they are selected and discussed as for what they portray. Then, considering the family as a system—that is, as a totality in which each member's actions affect all others—how does the patient normally perpetuate or try to alter the family patterns, and how does the family as a whole contend with crises?

The FH documents how the patient's family members have influenced and been influenced by the patient's illness. The clinician's opinion about these influences is reported in the biopsychosocial formulation; only the opinions of relatives, whether "correct" or not, are reported here. How the relatives (or friends) have tried to solve the patient's difficulties should also be mentioned.

In gathering the FH, the clinician should note if information from family members varies depending on whether the patient is present. Although the clinician should never assume that one family member speaks for all, many families will present a united front, unless the therapist explicitly asks each member to state his or her own view of the problem. Finally, psychiatric crises are highly traumatic for family members; avoid drawing derogatory conclusions about family members' typical behavior based on how they act during a crisis.

The Medical Assessment

The medical assessment consists of the patient's medical history, a physical examination, and laboratory tests (Table 2-3). The chief goals of this stage of psychiatric evaluation are to detect medical causes for psychiatric symptoms, to identify physical states that may alter how psychiatric medications are prescribed, to discover previously undiagnosed medical diseases (which are disproportionately high among psychiatric patients), to alert therapists to substance abuse, and to monitor blood levels of various psychotropic agents.

Most internists agree that there is no such thing as a "routine" lab test. Too often they are ordered on a "you never know what might be wrong and anyway the patient has a good lawyer" basis. Clinical judgment, not a standard checklist, should determine which tests are ordered. The only consistently underutilized tests in psychiatry are urine drug screens (which need to be obtained within 48 hours of ingestion of most drugs in order to be effective). High blood levels in patients who are mildly intoxicated indicate drug tolerance. In a young, well-nourished adult who has no health complaints or risk factors, none of the other lab tests should be regarded as routine. (The GGT is the most sensitive of liver function tests and can detect early signs of alcoholism. However, it is often *too* sensitive, detecting something abnormal when nothing is wrong. Careful interviewing about alcoholism has been shown to detect this disease more efficiently than any lab test.) Lab tests should be ordered on the basis of presumed diagnosis. For example, a patient with significant unexplained anxiety may need to be

TABLE 2–3
Laboratory Tests for Psychiatric Assessment

A. Frequently ordered screening tests:
 1. Complete blood count
 2. Urinalysis (protein, glucose, microscopic exam for bacteria, blood cells)
 3. Electrolytes (sodium, potassium, bicarbonate, chloride, phosphate, calcium, and glucose)
 4. Hepatic and renal function tests
 5. Thyroid function tests (T-4, T3U, and/or TSH [best screen for hypothyroidism])
 6. FTA-ABS (98% sensitivity) or MHA-TP (95% sensitivity) for neurosyphilis (not VDRL or RPR, insensitive for tertiary syphilis)
 7. Toxicology screen of urine (and blood alcohol, if indicated)
 8. Urine pregnancy test (women of childbearing potential)
 9. Serum albumin, total protein (nutritional status)

B. Relatively inexpensive, low-yield tests:
 1. Sedimentation rate (Westergren)
 2. Skin testing (for infectious diseases)
 3. Stools for occult blood
 4. EKG
 5. Chest and skull x-rays
 6. B-12 and folate levels (geriatric)

C. With evidence of cognitive or neurological disorders:
 1. EEG (including sleep tracings)
 2. CT or MRI scan
 3. Lumbar puncture (CSF protein, glucose, cells, gram stain cultures)

D. Serum levels of psychotropic drugs (when appropriate)

evaluated for hyperthyroidism; an elderly depressed patient who is eating poorly might be evaluated for malnutrition.

Whether the medical assessment should be done by the patient's psychiatrist or family physician depends on several factors, one being who is the most qualified to perform it. In most cases, the family practitioner or internist is the first choice. All psychiatric inpatients are required to receive a complete medical assessment, but whether all outpatients should receive one remains controversial. Commonly used guidelines for requesting a medical assessment are: any patient with signs of cognitive impairment (see Chapter 7), psychosis, or incapacitation; all patients over the age of 50 should have a medical examination once a year; those under 50, every three to five years. Clinicians of mental- and medical-health disciplines may wish to have all new patients fill out a questionnaire, such as the "Medical-Psychiatric History Form" in Appendix D.

THE MENTAL STATUS EXAMINATION

The mental status examination (MSE) describes the patient's appearance, behavior, speech, emotions, and cognitive and perceptual processes. (Perhaps the term *psychological status* would more aptly describe this part of the evaluation.) Whereas the psychiatric history is a *subjective* account given by the *patient* about *past* events that *have not been witnessed* by the therapist, the MSE is an *objective* report of the patient's *current* mental state as *observed* by the therapist. Although history of the patient can usually be reconstituted at future times, the MSE provides a profile of the patient that can only be obtained in the present moment. Because it is collected firsthand, the MSE is the most reliable part of the assessment; consequently, *every* patient's mental status must be ascertained.

There are two types of MSEs—*informal* and *formal*. Clinicians gather the informal MSE while taking a history; for most patients, these observations will suffice. The *formal* MSE is given to all patients with possible organic or psychotic disorders; to his or her informal observations, the therapist adds a series of standardized questions that assess memory, thought processes, attention span, and so on.

In reporting a MSE the clinician should present concrete illustrations to justify every conclusion. It is not sufficient to state that a patient is delusional; report the content of the delusions: "The patient is convinced that penguins read his mind." Saying a patient has a depressed mood is a conclusion and as such requires experienced substantiation: "The patient moved slowly, cried throughout the interview, and never laughed. The patient also said he felt sad most of the time."

This last statement illustrates how some information in the MSE could fit into a variety of categories. Should the description of this forlorn patient belong in the category of "Appearance," or "Behavior," or "Speech," or "Emotion," or should it be split among all of them? No single answer exists. *Where* information is reported is less important than *how* it is reported: It should be well-organized, coherent, and clear.

This section on the MSE, as well as the glossary of signs and symptoms in Appendix E, presents much of the language of psychopathology. Although technical terms do give professionals a shorthand for communication, they can also be abused. Jargon can mislead one into a false sense of knowledge and expertise. To know the definition of catatonia does not mean that the clinician knows anything else about catatonia. In reporting the assessment, descriptions in non-jargony language are often more informative and less ambiguous than professional terminology.

At the same time, technical terms are not mere words; they also represent concepts, and so when terms are used carelessly, concepts get muddled. For instance, when clinicians interchange the terms "shame" and "guilt," they're missing an important conceptual distinction: Shame is an *interpersonal* phenomenon involving embarrassment; guilt is an *intrapsychic* phenomenon involving the violation of one's conscience or superego. Given this different focus, when therapists overlook this distinction, assessment and treatment suffer. As Wittgenstein (1958) observed, "Philosophical problems arise when language goes on a holiday" (p. 3).

Once acquired, a professional vocabulary can shape how a professional thinks. That is to be expected — and cautioned against as well. Terms become mental categories, and being human, clinicians will fit their observations into these categories and tend to adjust their observations when they don't quite fit. With a clinical vocabulary, one is more likely to see the world *solely* through the lense of psychopathology. People no longer forget things, they "repress" them; shy persons are now "schizoid"; people aren't even people — they're "objects." The dangers far exceed the rudeness of "psychobabble" and "psychoanalyzing" everybody: To view people only in terms of their psychopathology is to ignore all their other qualities — and that is not only bad manners, it's bad psychiatry. Therapists do not treat psychopathology, but *people* with psychopathology.

Appearance

This section of the MSE reports how the patient looks: clothes, posture, bearing, grooming, apparent age, etc. Clothes are a type of language; what people wear is a form of communication. The patient's degree of alertness should be described (is the patient in a coma, a stupor with clouded consciousness, or alert?). "Palm reading" may reveal if the patient is frail, a hard laborer, or a nail-biter. Shaking hands with the patient at the outset of the interview does more than convey respect: It provides data. Is the patient's handshake crushing, firm, or weak? Are the palms sweaty? Are the hands rough or smooth?

Behavior

This category on behavior refers to the patient's motor activity: gait, gestures, stereotyped movements, other muscular movements such as twitches or tics, and impulse control. Psychomotor agitation and retardation, including extreme manifestations such as catatonia, are described here. Problems with impulse control refer to how the patient handles immediate aggressive, sexual, and suicidal wishes. If difficulties with impulse control arise during the interview (as opposed to only being reported in the history), they also should be reported here. Examples: A patient smashes the clinician's desktop with a fist when the interview is interrupted by a telephone call; a patient dashes from the office on hearing a distressing comment.

Speech

This category describes the manner (volume, rate, coherence) but not the content of speech. Speech can be loud, rapid, pressured, slowed, soft, hesitant, slurred (i.e., dysarthria), monotonous, latent, etc. Latency, a delay in responding and initiating speech, often occurs in depressed patients. Pressured or rapid speech that cannot be interrupted is a cardinal sign of mania. Slightly pressured speech can occur with anxiety. Reporting of foreign or regional accents occurs here.

Mood and Affect

The phenomenology of emotion is discussed psychiatrically in terms of *mood* and *affect*: Mood is a pervasive and subjectively experienced feeling state; affect refers to instantaneous, observable expressions of emotion. In psychopathology, affects are overt and moods are covert. Moods are what people tell you they feel and affects are what you see them feeling. Moods influence how people feel about themselves and their world; affects do not. People complain about their moods, but not about their affects. Moods persist, affects don't.

In reality, distinguishing moods from affects can be difficult. For example, is anger a mood or an affect? It could be either, and which it is doesn't matter all that much unless there is incongruence. *What does matter is that the clinician provides clear, specific descriptions of the patient's emotions.* "He states that he feels angry while smiling and appearing calm" (incongruent or inappropriate). "He cries one moment and laughs the next" (labile). "His expression never varies" (flat). "He says he feels 'like an emotional robot . . . the living dead'." "When first mentioning his wife, he pounded the table." As in this last example, what is occurring or being discussed during an emotional display may be worth reporting.

A normal range of affect is labeled "broad." Other affective ranges include "flat," "blunt," "constricted," "labile," and "inappropriate." A normal mood is called "euthymia." Moods can also be high or low. On the up side, as one gets higher, moods go from "elevated," to "euphoric," to "expansive." On the down side, "dysphoria" is any mood the patient finds unpleasant, including anxiety, apprehensiveness, dysthymia, and irritability. "Dysthymia" will be used throughout this text to mean the *symptom* of depression, as distinguished from the various *syndromes* of depression. *Relatedness* refers to the ability to express warmth and interact with the interviewer. *Mood-congruency* refers to whether a patient's behavior, affect, delusions, and hallucinations are consistent with his stated mood. If he constantly smiles while talking about his sadness and losses, his affect is incongruent with his stated mood. A depressed person who believes that she is evil and that Satan has destroyed her soul has a mood-congruent delusion. If she believes that extraterrestials have programmed her to infiltrate the FBI, she has a mood-incongruent delusion.

Thought Processes and Content

Since no one can directly know another's thought processes, therapists must infer them from the patient's speech and behavior. A patient may *say* he is God, which doesn't necessarily mean he *thinks* so; the style and context of delivery will determine if the assertion is deceptive or delusional. Whenever pathological thought is reported, the clinician should also include examples.

Psychiatrists traditionally used the term *thought disorder* to describe any communication arising from pathological thought processes. However, because the term is so nonspecific, *DSM-IV* discourages its use in favor of more descriptive categories: word usage, stream, continuity, and content of thought.

1. *Word usage* includes abnormalities such as neologisms and word approximations. Neologisms ("I need a flamis to binkle my bed") are most often seen in schizophrenia. Word approximations ("I know the time by the thing that goes around") may be a sign of brain disease.

2. *Stream of thought* refers to the quantity of thoughts (e.g., overabundant, slowed). When the patient's speech is restricted to a few words or syllables, it is called "poverty of speech" and should be described in the speech section of the MSE. This should be distinguished from "poverty of content of speech," which is discussed below. Interruption of a train of speech before a thought has been completed is called "thought blocking." These blockages can last seconds to minutes and may suggest a psychotic process.

3. *Continuity of thought* refers to the associations among ideas. Some of the disturbances in this category are always pathological, such as clanging, echolalia, neologisms, perseveration, and "word salad." When a patient has improved moderately, the flight of ideas will make much better sense. For example, a psychotic patient who was with a group of other patients talking about being abandoned by their families, said, "I've slept in trees before. Sleeping in trees is uncomfortable. Family trees are the worst."

4. *Content of thought*, when disturbed, can result in delusions, overvalued ideas, illogical thinking, and magical thinking. Delusions in which the patient experiences his actions, thoughts, feelings, and perceptions as not

his own or somehow imposed on him are called Schneiderian First Rank Symptoms (FRS) after Kurt Schneider, who first identified the phenomenon. Common examples include experiencing thought insertion or broadcasting, thought removal, and getting special messages from the TV or radio. Although no longer considered pathognomonic[3] of schizophrenia, FRS are often found in schizophrenia and are sometimes observed in mania.

Illogical thinking is another disturbance in thought content. One patient wrote: "People's bodies conform to the shape of their clothes so that my mother's body must be a rectangle because she's wearing a chemise and when my brother wears bell-bottoms, his legs become large, double-edge razors." This patient also said that by getting dressed, he could induce his father, via telepathy, to take a shower (delusional and magical thinking.) A psychology student who says, "I put a textbook by my pillow and learn by osmosis" is also demonstrating magical thinking; however, this is probably not delusional, but instead an overvalued idea or a joke.

Whereas in "poverty of speech" the patient utters only a few words or syllables, in "poverty of content of speech" the patient's words are sufficient and individual sentences may even make sense, but the total communication remains meaningless. (While usually pathologic, this phenomenon may also be observed in political speeches and bureaucratic reports.) For example, when asked what religion meant to him, a patient replied: "All that church stuff. Amazing Grace, Amazing Grace. 'I know that my redeemer liveth, and that he shall stand at the latter day upon the earth.' (Job 19:25) It is personal, very personal. I understand what you mean, you who live in God's grace."

Incoherence is a general, but often useful, term to describe incomprehensible speech in which the specific type of disturbed thinking is difficult to identify, or in which there is a mixture of the thought disturbances mentioned above. Incoherence describes the response of a patient who was asked, "Do you fear anything specific?":

> That's just it. A doctor told me not to put a stamp on me. The Secretary of the Treasury is not part of it. People say to you, "Isn't it too bad that you're sick." It feels like I was very obstreperous. I couldn't communicate at any level. My inside couldn't make sense of my outside. All the anxieties, and all the (pause), and all the rococo themes of psychiatric uh, uh, uh (pause) illness played back upon me again and again.

---

[3]A sign or symptom is *pathognomonic* if it exists in only one disorder.

Obsessions, which are persistent, unwanted *thoughts*, are another type of disturbed content. Because compulsions are "senseless," repeated *deeds*, they are behaviors, but since they arise from obsessions, the two can be reported together.

Perception

This category describes fundamental abnormalities in the five senses — hearing, seeing, touching, tasting, and smelling. These abnormalities, which include hallucinations, illusions, depersonalization, derealization, and déjà vu, are often, but not always, psychopathological. Technically, dreams are hallucinations, but they are not reported as perceptual disturbances. Most people have brief experiences with derealization, depersonalization, and déjà vu.

Although some patients will readily admit when they are hallucinating, many will not. Patients may be hallucinating when their eyes dart from side to side, when they stare at nothing, or when they seem preoccupied, as if they were listening to voices. Ask, "Do you see or hear things that other people do not?" Because some patients will refer to their own thoughts as voices, the clinician should ask if the voices come from inside or from outside her head. If from the inside, ask if the voice is the patient's or someone else's.

In general, only auditory and visual hallucinations occur in psychiatric disorders, whereas these and olfactory, tactile, and other hallucinatory phenomena occur in disorders caused by drug use or medical conditions. The hallucinations of patients with mood disorders tend to be mood-congruent; those of schizophrenics, mood-incongruent.

Attention and Concentration

Attention is the ability to sustain a focus on one task or activity. Impaired attention — distractibility — can usually be detected during a routine interview by observing if a patient's focus is frequently directed to unimportant or irrelevant external stimuli. If attention seems impaired and its immediate cause is unclear (e.g., due to anxiety, hallucinations, or to other psychotic preoccupations), formal clinical testing should be performed.

The most widely used test is "serial 7's," whereby the patient is asked to substract 7 from 100 without stopping as far as possible. The patient's educational background or infrequent use of mathematics may interfere with performance. A more informative test is "serial 1's," in which the patient is asked to "count backwards by

1's from 57 and stop at 22." Because it requires no math skills, this is a purer test of concentration, and by noting if the patient stops at 22, the clinician also tests immediate memory.

Orientation

As patients become progressively disoriented, they are unable to indicate the current time, then their current location (place), and last, their own name. To test for orientation to time, the clinician ascertains if patients can identify the date, the day of the week, the time of day, or how long they have been hospitalized. Failing these questions, they are asked to identify the season and part of the day (e.g., morning, afternoon, evening). Therapists may be astonished to discover a seemingly normal patient who, when asked directly, says the current year is 1953.

Disturbances in orientation, memory, and judgment usually suggest the presence of organic dysfunction, which may arise from substance abuse or from medication toxicity (especially possible with tricyclic antidepressants and phenothiazines that have anticholinergic side effects, or the hypnoanxiolytics that have sedative side effects). Impaired orientation very rarely occurs in schizophrenic, paranoid, psychotic, or mood disorders, but more commonly in dissociative disorders. Impaired memory and judgment may occur in each of these disorders.

Memory

In the MSE, memory is categorized as *remote*, *recent*, or *immediate*. Remote memory refers to many years ago, recent memory to the past several days to months, and immediate memory to the past several minutes. When people begin to lose their memories, immediate memory usually goes first, remote memory, last.

Remote and recent memory can be assessed by how well patients recall historical and current events. Immediate memory is best evaluated by formal testing: For example, clinicians name three single-word objects (e.g., book, umbrella, elephant), and then have patients immediately repeat the words to ensure they registered. Clinicians then tell patients that in five minutes, they will be asked to repeat the three objects. Most patients can recall two out of three; one or zero suggests organic factors.

Sensing their failing memory and disorientation, many patients with neurologic dysfunction feel embarrassed and try to conceal the loss by *confabulating*. One example: A 63-year-old professor with a slow-growing brain tumor had become adept at bluffing by using his charm to hide his inability to remember simple facts. When asked to name the year, he replied, "The year, well, it is the year of our discontent. Who cares about the year? It's but time, and time is relative."

Judgment

This category evaluates patients' abilities to exercise judgment in dealing with social situations, which includes acting appropriately during the interview and understanding the consequences of their actions. Although judgment is largely assessed by observing patients during the interview, if the clinician remains uncertain about the evaluation, patients can be asked what they would do in hypothetical situations: "What would you do if you found a stamped, addressed envelope lying on the street?" or, "What would you do if you were the first one in a theater to see a fire?"

Intelligence and Information

The only precise measure of intelligence comes from an IQ test, such as the Wechsler Adult Intelligence Scale (WAIS). IQ tests were originally developed to predict school performance, and they do this fairly well. However, they *don't* do as well when used for other purposes, such as to predict a person's ability to fix a car, run a company, or win a Nobel prize. Because there are different forms of intelligence and no one global entity, IQ intelligence can be thought of as "scholastic potential." By definition, IQ is whatever an IQ test measures, the average IQ being 100. Most people reading this book will not know anyone in their personal lives with an IQ below 90. The diagnosis of mental retardation requires a tested IQ of below 70 (see *DSM-IV*, p. 46). High IQ scores may reflect the cultural enrichment of a person's inborn biological potential.

The assessment of intelligence includes examining the patient's general fund of information, which is why intelligence and information are usually linked in the MSE. Both are affected by culture, education, performance anxiety, and psychopathology, especially the presence of organicity. Because the initial interview can only reveal gaping deficits, intelligence can be clinically tested by having patients perform simple math (e.g., "multiply 7 × 12") or by having them read something and then tell the examiner what it meant. Evaluating patients' informational resources involves questioning their general knowledge and awareness of current events. Such questions should be geared to the patient's background. "Who wrote Hamlet?" "Who won last week's election for governor?"

Another important aspect of intelligence is the ability to abstract—to think symbolically, to generalize, and to conceptualize. This ability is frequently absent with a functioning IQ under 90 or with schizophrenia. Patients' behavior during the interview usually provides enough data to determine their ability to abstract. If there is any reason to question this ability, especially with evidence of psychosis or organicity, two clinical tests should be performed. Before describing these specific tests, a cautionary note: Too much stock should not be placed in any single answer or on clinical tests in general, since at best they are only rough measures of patients' abilities. They do, however, provide some relatively objective data. (Whenever formal clinical testing is done, clinicians should record not only their conclusion — e.g., "the patient's similarities were concrete" — but also what the patient actually said.)

The first test of abstractive ability determines whether patients can recognize *similarities*. Questions are asked such as, "What is the similarity between a poem, novel, and sculpture?" Or, "What is the similarity between a table, desk, and chair?" To the latter question, a properly abstracted answer would be, "They are all furniture." A concrete answer would be, "All are made of wood"; even more concrete would be, "I don't see any similarity." A bizarre answer would be, "They're all more human than humans."

The second test involves patients' abilities to interpret *proverbs*. Ideally, the proverbs given to patients should contain words and ideas within the parameters of their educational and cultural backgrounds, and *not* be ones that have been heard many times before. If patients already know the proverb, asking what it means may test prior learning but not the capacity to abstract. An example: "The opera's not over till the fat lady sings." An abstract response would be, "Nothing is resolved until everybody does their thing." A concrete response would be, "An opera is never finished until a fat woman sings." A bizarre response would be, "Fatso opera singers like sex." A personalized response would be, "I'm not fat!"

Insight

In the MSE *insight* refers to patients' awareness of their chief problem. A delusional patient who claims she came for treatment to get Ma Bell to stop the ringing in her ears lacks insight. Insight can range from (a) a complete denial of illness, (b) a dim and fleeting admission of illness, (c) an awareness of illness, but with accusations that others are causing it, (d) an intellectual recognition of problems and that they stem from within, to (e) a convincing awareness of the disorder and its internal sources. The patient's level of insight is a rough predictor of how much he will cooperate with treatment and benefit from insight-oriented psychotherapy; the latter can be predicted further by offering the patient several interpretations during the assessment, not for therapeutic purposes, but to see how the patient reacts to an interpretation.

AUXILIARY DATA

Information gathered outside the patient interview is considered auxiliary data; typically, this auxiliary data constitute a tenth to a third of the information needed to determine the patient's diagnosis and treatment. Sometimes with uncooperative or very disorganized patients, outside information is central. As discussed already, two major sources of auxiliary data are interviews with friends or relatives and results from the medical assessment.

Psychological and Neuropsychological Tests

Psychological tests are most often used to quantify personality, intelligence, and the presence, degree, and type of neuropsychological brain dysfunction. Psychological tests can add valuable information that complements the interview. The best tests are *objective* measurements that utilize standardized questions, scoring, and interpretation. The reliability and validity of psychological tests vary. These tests, like laboratory tests, should not be used routinely but to address *specific* questions, the answers to which may alter the patient's treatment. (Patients must not be intoxicated or going through drug withdrawal at the time of testing.) Specific questions might be: "What is the patient's IQ?" "How tenuous is the patient's contact with reality?" "Which conflicts most trouble the patient?" "How much control does the patient have over aggressive impulses?" "Does the patient have neuropsychological (e.g., frontal lobe damage) impairment? If so, which functions are affected and to what extent?" Table 2–4 outlines the most commonly used psychological tests.

Most psychological tests were developed before *DSM-IV* and some still reflect a psychological, rather than descriptive, diagnostic approach. As a result, patients are more likely to be diagnosed as schizophrenic and borderline by psychological tests than by *DSM-IV* criteria. With these reservations in mind, the clinician should formulate specific questions and then ask the testing psychologist whether they can be answered. The choice of tests is the psychologist's, not the referring clinician's.

Amytal Interviews

Although popularly known as "truth serum," amytal does not make people tell the truth; some patients even confabulate while receiving it, and malingerers can continue to malinger. Consequently, amytal interviews have little place in the routine assessment. On occasion, they may be helpful

TABLE 2–4
Psychological Tests

I. *Achievement tests*: Also known as "proficiency tests," they try to measure the outcome of systematic education and training.

II. *Aptitude tests*: They try to measure potential ability in specific areas, such as music, medicine, and accounting.

III. *Intelligence tests*: These tests include the WAIS–R, commonly used for adults, and the Wechler Intelligence Scale (WISC) for children. The Stanford-Binet is sometimes used. In addition to measuring IQ, the tests can detect psychotic and organic impairments. The WAIS and WISC yield verbal (which also includes arithmetic), performance (spatial abilities), and full-scale scores. Education tends to affect the verbal more than the performance score; in dementia, performance often declines more than verbal.

IV. *Personality tests*: These assess personality traits and are of two general types:
   A. *Structured*. In these largely quantitative tests, the patient's response is compared to a "right" or "normal" response. The Minnesota Multiphasic Personality Inventory (MMPI) is the most widely used objective personality test. It has 550 true-false questions covering a wide range of subject matter (e.g., "I like parties and socials"; "I'm afraid of the germs on doorknobs.") It also has validity scales that measure tendencies to portray oneself in a favorable or pathological manner and measures of defensiveness.
   B. *Projective*. In these largely qualitative tests, there is no "correct" answer, only the subject's projections. Projective tests include the Rorschach ("inkblot"), the Thematic Apperception Test (TAT), and the Figure Drawing Test.

V. *Neuropsychological tests*: These tests, such as the Halstead-Reitan Battery and a variety of scales from the WAIS and WISC, specifically evaluate brain impairment, determining if cerebral damage exists and whether it is diffuse or localized. Many tests can be used to assess specific types of brain functioning:
   A. abstract reasoning and problem-solving
   B. memory
   C. orientation
   D. perceptual (auditory, visual, tactile), motor, visuomotor, tactile-spatial, and visuospatial tasks
   E. language (receptive and expressive)
   F. flexibility of thinking and speed of response
   G. attention and concentration

in retrieving lost memories, in differentiating neurologic from psychiatric disorders (Ward, Rowlett, & Burke, 1986), in distinguishing schizophrenic from mood disorders, and in unblocking a stuck psychotherapy. They will not help in detecting a malingerer.

Neuroendocrine Batteries

A variety of neuroendocrine tests has recently emerged, which occasionally may help in differentiating depression from other disorders (details are discussed in Chapter 10 on mood disorders). At present, most psychiatrists believe these neuroendocrine tests lack the sufficient sensitivity and specificity to be useful and valid in the routine assessment.

SUMMARY OF PRINCIPAL FINDINGS

After the history, MSE, and auxiliary data are reported, the clinician's next task is to highlight the major findings in a paragraph or two. This summary must indicate if there is an immediate threat to life (via suicide, assaultiveness, or homicide) and does *not* include the patient's diagnosis, prognosis, biopsychosocial formulation, or treatment plan: These are all conclusions (of sorts) based on the findings summarized in this section.

CHAPTER 3

Diagnosis and Prognosis

> Di-agnostic? . . . Lessee . . . agnostic means "one what don't know"
> . . . an' di is a Greek prefix denotin' two-fold — so the di-agnostic team
> don't know twice as much as an ordinary agnostic . . . right? — Pogo,
> *New York Post*, August 11, 1966

ON THE PUBLICATION of *DSM-III*, its chief architect, Robert Spitzer
(Spitzer et al., 1980, p. 151), began summarizing its major accomplishments
by citing this unimpeachable source: Pogo knows that diagnostic labels may
imply more knowledge than actually exists. Despite increased reliability and
validity, the diagnostic categories of *DSM-III* are not eternal truths, but
state-of-the-science hypotheses. Further revisions — *DSM-III–Revised* and
now *DSM-IV* — are proof that these diagnostic categories are not immuta-
ble. They are to be used with caution, but used nonetheless, for unless the
clinician makes the correct diagnosis, no effective treatment can be
launched and no accurate prognosis can be estimated.

Considering that *DSM-IV* entails over 200 diagnoses, making a diagnosis has
become an increasingly complex task, if only because the number of diagnoses has
skyrocketed. In 1840 there was but one psychiatric diagnosis: idiocy (or insanity).
In 1880 there were seven: mania, melancholia, monomania, paresis (syphilis of the
brain), dementia, dipsomania, and epilepsy. Over the next 100 years, the number of
psychiatric diagnoses has risen at an average rate of two per year. This is progress.

DEFINITIONS

Differential diagnosis is the process of choosing the correct diagnosis
from conditions with similar features. Traditionally, differential diagnosis

began with two general questions: (a) Was the patient's condition caused by a known medical condition or a drug? (b) Was it a psychosis, nonpsychosis, or personality disorder? In large measure, the first question addresses an *etiological* distinction; the second, a *descriptive* distinction.

Disorders caused by general medical conditions were originally called *organic mental disorders*. This term was dropped in *DSM-IV* because it implies that other psychiatric disorders do not have a biological basis. The remaining disorders were called "functional disorders" because no organic cause was known and the prime etiology was assumed to be psychosocial. Because research on schizophrenia, manic depression, and other so-called functional disorders has revealed a strong biological component, the term *functional* has been eliminated.

Psychosis exists when reality testing is grossly impaired; *reality testing* is the ability to evaluate the external world objectively and to distinguish it from inner experience. Delusions, hallucinations, and massive denial are indicative of impaired reality testing and, therefore, of psychosis. Minor distortions of reality are not considered psychotic, such as a person experiencing transitory derealization or a man overestimating his attractiveness to women. Psychosis is usually inferred when a patient's behavior is grossly disorganized, characterized by incoherent speech, "senseless" violence, and total inattentiveness to the environment. Psychosis may be experienced as distressful and alien (i.e., ego-dystonic) or as an acceptable and integral part of the self (i.e., ego-syntonic).

Neurosis, a nonpsychotic and ego-dystonic syndrome, can be very disabling, but in general does not paralyze the individual's functioning or violate social norms. It is purely a descriptive term, without etiological or theoretical associations. *Neurotic process* refers to the unconscious mechanisms that are believed to produce neurotic symptoms.

Personality disorders are longstanding conditions, beginning in adolescence or early adulthood, and characterized by inflexible and maladaptive patterns of sufficient severity to cause either clinically significant functional impairment or subjective distress. Unlike psychoses and neuroses, personality disorders are *always* chronic, even though their intensity may fluctuate. As a rule, they are nonpsychotic and ego-syntonic, but exceptions exist. Exemplifying the rule is antisocial personality disorder, a nonpsychotic state in which the patient doesn't mind his thievery, but his victims do. Two exceptions are the painful shyness seen with avoidant personality disorder and the transient psychosis of the borderline personality disorder. The rages of borderline personalities may be distressing to themselves and others but are usually egosyntonic because they are considered acceptable and integral parts of the individuals.

TWO BASIC DIAGNOSTIC PRINCIPLES

DSM-IV stresses two fundamental principles: *parsimony* and *hierarchy*. The principle of parsimony recommends that clinicians seek the single most elegant, economical, and efficient diagnosis that accounts for *all* the available data; when a single diagnosis is insufficient, the fewest number of diagnoses is sought. The principle of hierarchy is that mental disorders generally exist on a hierarchy of syndromes, which tend to decline in severity: Medical or pharmacologic > psychotic > mood > anxiety > somatic > sexual > personality > adjustment > no mental disorder. Thus, when a patient's symptoms could be attributed to several disorders, but are entirely explainable by the most severe disorder, the most parsimonious diagnosis belongs to the disorder in that category. The "decision tree" in Figure 3–1 illustrates how these two principles guide differential diagnosis. In essence, a decision tree is an algorithm, or flow chart, which uses branching logic to hone in on the most likely diagnosis.

Without the use of these principles, the diagnosis of a patient with auditory hallucinations, persecutory delusions, apprehensiveness, and somatic preoccupations could range from schizophrenia to a paranoid, generalized anxiety, and somatoform disorder. *With* these principles, there is but one diagnosis — schizophrenia — because it is the highest ranking disorder on the hierarchy that accounts for *all* the symptoms. However, more than one diagnosis is sometimes justified. If this person has other clusters of symptoms that are not completely explained by the diagnosis of schizophrenia, then the clinician would proceed down the decision tree in Figure 3–1. For example, if this person also has panic attacks during remission, then panic disorder might be added to the diagnosis.

The decision tree is also a guide to establishing treatment priorities. A patient with substance abuse, a mood disorder independent of substance abuse, and an avoidant personality disorder is likely to be treated in a hierarchical fashion, with the substance abuse being the first priority of treatment.

SEVEN STEPS FOR PSYCHIATRIC DIAGNOSIS

Among the several perfectly good ways of reaching an Axis I or Axis II diagnosis is the following procedure involving seven somewhat overlapping steps. The first two, *collecting data* and *identifying psychopathology*, are performed during the assessment and were discussed in Chapter 2.

3. *Evaluating the reliability of data*: Not all information is equally reliable and not all informants are equally reliable. Present information is more reliable than past information, since memories fade and current

FIGURE 3–1
An Overview of Differential Diagnosis*

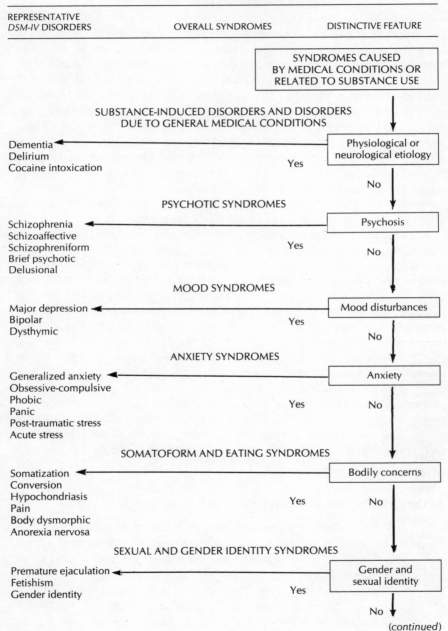

REPRESENTATIVE
DSM-IV DISORDERS   OVERALL SYNDROMES   DISTINCTIVE FEATURE

SYNDROMES CAUSED
BY MEDICAL CONDITIONS OR
RELATED TO SUBSTANCE USE

SUBSTANCE-INDUCED DISORDERS AND DISORDERS
DUE TO GENERAL MEDICAL CONDITIONS

Dementia
Delirium
Cocaine intoxication

Yes

Physiological or
neurological etiology

No

PSYCHOTIC SYNDROMES

Schizophrenia
Schizoaffective
Schizophreniform
Brief psychotic
Delusional

Yes

Psychosis

No

MOOD SYNDROMES

Major depression
Bipolar
Dysthymic

Yes

Mood disturbances

No

ANXIETY SYNDROMES

Generalized anxiety
Obsessive-compulsive
Phobic
Panic
Post-traumatic stress
Acute stress

Yes

Anxiety

No

SOMATOFORM AND EATING SYNDROMES

Somatization
Conversion
Hypochondriasis
Pain
Body dysmorphic
Anorexia nervosa

Yes

Bodily concerns

No

SEXUAL AND GENDER IDENTITY SYNDROMES

Premature ejaculation
Fetishism
Gender identity

Yes

Gender and
sexual identity

No

(continued)

46

FIGURE 3–1
(*Continued*)

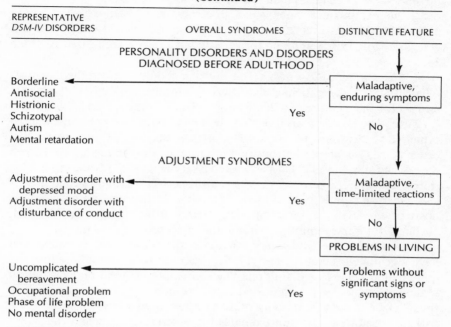

REPRESENTATIVE *DSM-IV* DISORDERS	OVERALL SYNDROMES	DISTINCTIVE FEATURE

PERSONALITY DISORDERS AND DISORDERS
DIAGNOSED BEFORE ADULTHOOD

Borderline
Antisocial
Histrionic
Schizotypal   Yes
Autism
Mental retardation

Maladaptive, enduring symptoms

No

ADJUSTMENT SYNDROMES

Adjustment disorder with
  depressed mood
Adjustment disorder with   Yes
  disturbance of conduct

Maladaptive, time-limited reactions

No

PROBLEMS IN LIVING

Uncomplicated
  bereavement
Occupational problem   Yes
Phase of life problem
No mental disorder

Problems without significant signs or symptoms

*In placing the differential diagnosis of *DSM-IV*'s 200+ categories into a manageable perspective, this overview contains some inaccuracies and oversimplifications. The left column presents sample *DSM-IV* diagnoses. The middle column lists general syndromes, which are clusters of signs and symptoms. The right column indicates the most distinctive overall feature of each syndrome. Some syndromes (such as sleep, impulse, dissociative, eating, and factitious disorders) do not fall neatly into this hierarchy and for simplicity are omitted.

moods often color past recollections. Information garnered during a crisis must be evaluated cautiously. Signs are more reliable than symptoms, because signs can be observed. Objective findings are more reliable than intuitive, interpretive, and introspective findings. Observations such as, "The patient seems to be concealing a depression," or "I'm feeling manipulated by the patient," may be true and worth pursuing, but they are far less useful in making a reliable diagnosis than more readily verifiable observations, such as crying, slow gait, and incoherence.

4. *Determining the overall distinctive feature*: The clinician should try to identify the patient's most prominent symptom cluster, such as those listed in the right-hand column of Figure 3–1. If one general category of distinctive features does not stand out, pick two; the next two steps will resolve uncertainty.

5. *Arriving at a diagnosis*: Following the principles of parsimony and hierarchy, the clinician systematically considers every *DSM-IV* mental disorder that exhibits the patient's overall distinctive feature. This task is not easy: *DSM-IV* lists over 200 diagnoses, which are divided into 16 general categories for Axis I, and one for Axis II; all 17 are summarized in Table 3-1.

6. *Check diagnostic criteria*: The clinician should confirm the diagnosis by verifying if the patient's characteristics meet the *DSM-IV* diagnostic criteria for the disorder. To demonstrate: Table 3-2 lists *DSM-IV*'s criteria for generalized anxiety disorder. (Note how criteria D and F illustrate the principle of hierarchy.) Criterion D illustrates that generalized anxiety disorder (GAD) is at the bottom of the anxiety disorder hierarchy. (Some have even referred to GAD as a "wastebasket diagnosis.") Criterion F illustrates the hierarchy of other disorders above GAD. It is not a rigid hierarchy; a person with alcohol abuse and/or a mood disorder can have a diagnosis of GAD if the symptoms are present after the person has been abstinent for a few months and not in the midst of the mood disorder.

These criteria are guides, not laws. A patient, for instance, might well have a genuine generalized anxiety disorder even if her condition does not quite match *DSM-IV*'s definition. The six symptoms listed under criterion C do not include "an exaggerated startle response" or "nausea and diarrhea," and yet these commonly occur in generalized anxiety disorder. If a patient's condition only approximates the criteria, the clinician can write: "The patient meets *DSM-IV* criteria for generalized anxiety disorder, but has had only five months of excessive anxiety and worry and only two symptoms in criterion C." By using *DSM-IV* as a reference point, clinicians speak the diagnostic language of their colleagues, while not being locked into its use. If clinicians have reason not to use *DSM-IV*, they should specify which criteria is being used (e.g., Feighner, RDC).

7. *Resolve diagnostic uncertainty*: If at this stage, one diagnosis (per axis) does not suffice, or if some evidence is inconsistent with other data, or if the diagnosis remains unclear for any reason, the most likely culprits are (a) inadequate data, (b) premature closure, (c) atypical presentations, or (d) multiple disorders.

Inadequate data may reflect missing information which, once obtained, clarifies the diagnosis. For instance, *DSM-IV*'s brief psychotic disorder must be "at least one day and no more than one month" in duration, but the patient, previously normal, manifested psychotic symptoms every three or four days and then returned to normal. Additional data solved the puzzle: When the patient's urine tested positive for amphetamines, his diagnosis was changed to substance-induced psychotic disorder. Sometimes data

TABLE 3-1
DSM-IV General Diagnostic Categories*

AXIS I

1. *Disorders Usually First Diagnosed in Infancy, Childhood, or Adolescence*
   This category includes most, but not all, of the disorders that arise before adolescence, such as attention deficit disorders, autism, and mental retardation listed under Axis II.

2. *Delirium, Dementia, and Amnestic and Other Cognitive Disorders*
   These disorders are temporary or permanent dysfunctions of brain tissue caused by neurologic diseases, general medical conditions, or chemicals.

3. *Mental Disorders Due to a General Medical Condition*
   This category primarily refers to catatonic disorder and personality changes that are caused by a general medical condition. This section does not include disorders such as major depression and panic disorder that are listed elsewhere but are caused by a general medical condition. In these cases they are listed under the appropriate disorder, e.g., mood disorder due to a general medical condition.

4. *Substance-Related Disorders*
   This category refers to the maladaptive use of drugs and alcohol. Mere consumption and recreational use of substances are not disorders. This category necessitates an abnormal pattern of use, as with alcohol abuse and cocaine dependence.

5. *Schizophrenic and Other Psychotic Disorders*
   The schizophrenic disorders are characterized by psychotic symptoms (e.g., grossly disorganized behavior, nonmood-congruent delusions and hallucinations) and by over six months of behavioral deterioration. The delusional disorders are characterized by delusions in the absence of other psychotic symptoms. In general, these patients are less impaired than schizophrenics. This section also includes a grab-bag of psychotic disorders that usually have a briefer course and better prognosis than delusional and schizophrenic disorders. This category includes schizophreniform disorder, brief psychotic disorder, and schizoaffective disorder.

6. *Mood Disorders*
   The cardinal feature of these disorders is disturbances of mood. Patients may or may not have psychotic symptoms; when they do, delusions and hallucinations are usually mood-congruent. These disorders include major depression, bipolar disorder, and dysthymic disorder.

7. *Anxiety Disorders*
   These disorders are characterized by physiologic signs of anxiety (e.g., palpitations) and subjective feelings of tension, apprehension, or fear. Anxiety may be acute and focused (panic disorder) or continual and diffuse (generalized anxiety disorder). This category also includes phobic, obsessive-compulsive, and post-traumatic stress disorders.

(continued)

TABLE 3–1
(Continued)

8. *Somatoform Disorders*
   These disorders are dominated by somatic symptoms that resemble physical illness but cannot be fully accounted for by disease or a pathophysiological mechanism. There must also be strong evidence that psychological factors have an important role in the genesis of these symptoms. This category includes somatization and (hysterical) conversion disorders, hypochondriasis, pain disorder, and body dysmorphic disorder.

9. *Factitious Disorders*
   In these disorders (e.g., Munchausen syndrome), physical or psychological symptoms are produced voluntarily for no apparent (or ulterior) motive other than being ill.

10. *Dissociative Disorders*
    These disorders all feature a sudden, temporary alteration or dysfunction of memory, consciousness, identity, and behavior, as in dissociative amnesia, fugue, identity disorders, and depersonalization disorder.

11. *Sexual and Gender Identity Disorders*
    This category includes sexual desire and arousal disorders, orgasm disorders, sexual pain disorders, gender identity disorders, and paraphilias (in which bizarre imagery or acts are required for sexual excitement, e.g., necrophilia).

12. *Eating Disorders*
    These disorders involve significant problems in regulating eating. Included are anorexia nervosa and bulimia nervosa.

13. *Sleep Disorders*
    This category covers problems with sleep regulation and the dyssomnias, including primary insomnia, primary hypersomnia, narcolepsy, breating-related sleep disorder, and circadian rhythm sleep disorder. Also included are problems that occur during sleep (the parasomnias) including nightmares, sleep terrors, and sleep walking disorders.

14. *Impulse-Control Disorders Not Elsewhere Classified*
    These disorders involving poor impulse control include pathological gambling, kleptomania, pyromania, trichotillomania, and intermittent explosive disorder.

15. *Adjustment Disorders*
    These relatively mild disorders occur within three months of a clearly identifiable psychosocial stressor. Disorders are classified according to the predominant symptom, such as adjustment disorder with depressed mood or adjustment disorder with disturbance of conduct.

(continued)

TABLE 3–1
(Continued)

16. *Other Conditions That May Be a Focus of Clinical Attention*
    This category covers psychological factors affecting a medical condition, medication-induced movement disorders, marital and other relational problems, or problems related to abuse or neglect.

AXIS II

17. *Personality Disorders*
    These disorders are patterns of personality traits that are longstanding, maladaptive, and inflexible and cause either impaired functioning or subjective distress. Examples include: borderline, schizoid, and avoidant personality disorders.

*DSM-IV, p. 26.

are inadequate because the therapist has not talked to the right people. After conducting two months of stalemated couples treatment, the therapist insisted on seeing the couple's five-year-old daughter as part of a family assessment. Until then, mother and father had colluded in a secret, which in pure childhood innocence, their daughter revealed when she asked, "How come Daddy stumbles around every night after he comes home?"

Premature closure amounts to "to jumping the diagnostic gun," without proper differential diagnosis. A common trap is the "five-minute diagnosis": After interviewing a patient for five minutes, the therapist "unconsciously" reaches a diagnosis and then inadvertently distorts, converts, and selectively seeks information that confirms this initial diagnosis. Call it human nature, but *every* clinician is prone to see what he or she wants to see. What distinguishes the skilled professional is the willingness to double-check a diagnosis by repeating the previous six steps.

One of the author's (J.M.) lesser professional moments came when he diagnosed a patient in the emergency room as having a major depression. The diagnosis seemed obvious: The patient's face was blank, his gait slow, his movements agitated; he felt sad and lonely. He even *said* he was depressed. Yet soon after the patient was admitted, the author was called by a supervisor who said the patient's diagnosis was Parkinson's disease, not depression. The author's mistake was that he saw a depressed-looking person and stopped thinking: He assumed the patient was depressed, did not perform a systematic differential diagnosis, and only saw what he expected to find.

Although *atypical presentations* cause diagnostic confusion, some patients simply do not conform to classic textbook descriptions. For instance, patients with major depression usually feel sad, yet some don't feel sad at

TABLE 3–2
DSM-IV **Criteria for Generalized Anxiety Disorder***

A. Excessive anxiety and worry (apprehensive expectation), occurring more days than not for at least 6 months, about a number of events or activities (such as work or school performance).

B. The person finds it difficult to control the worry.

C. The anxiety and worry are associated with three (or more) of the following 6 symptoms (with at least some symptoms present for more days than not for the past 6 months). **Note:** Only one item is required in children.

    (1) restlessness or feeling keyed up or on edge
    (2) being easily fatigued
    (3) difficulty concentrating or mind going blank
    (4) irritability
    (5) muscle tension
    (6) sleep disturbance (difficulty falling or staying asleep, or restless, unsatisfying sleep)

D. The focus of the anxiety and worry is not confined to features of an Axis I disorder, e.g., the anxiety or worry is not about having a Panic Attack (as in Panic Disorder), being embarrassed in public (as in Social Phobia), being contaminated (as in Obsessive-Compulsive Disorder), being away from home or close relatives (as in Separation Anxiety Disorder), gaining weight (as in Anorexia Nervosa), having multiple compaints (as in Somatization Disorder), or having a serious illness (as in Hypochondriasis), and and the anxiety and worry do not occur exclusively during Posttraumatic Stress Disorder.

E. The anxiety, worry, or physical symptoms cause clinically significant distress or impairment in social, occupational, or other important areas of functioning.

F. The disturbance is not due to the direct physiological effects of a substance (e.g., a drug of abuse, a medication) or a general medical condition (e.g., hyperthyroidism) and does not occur exclusively during a Mood Disorder, a Psychotic Disorder, or a Pervasive Developmental Disorder.

**DSM-IV, pp. 435–36.*

all, but complain primarily of bodily aches and pains. Another advantage of using *DSM-IV* decision trees is that they often detect these atypical cases.

Multiple diagnoses—that is, more than one diagnosis per axis—may be indicated after first attempting to ascribe a patient's symptoms to a single diagnosis. Just as medical patients can have more than one disorder, so can psychiatric patients.

If a diagnostic uncertainty persists, the clinician should use the most applicable *DSM-IV* label: "diagnosis deferred," "unspecified mental disorder," "[class of disorder] not otherwise specified" or "specific diagnosis (provisional)." Finally, the patient may have "no mental disorder," a most underutilized diagnosis.

MULTIAXIAL DIAGNOSIS

In 1947, multiaxial diagnosis was first proposed in Sweden. Although it was rejected, five years later Danish psychiatrists officially adopted a biaxial system that separated symptoms from etiology. After two decades of promotion by the World Health Organization, the concept surfaced in United States in 1975, when John Strauss suggested a multiaxial approach with an axis for social functioning. In 1980, *DSM-III* incorporated multiaxial diagnosis in order to clarify the complexities and relationships of biopsychosocial difficulties and thereby facilitate treatment planning. *DSM-IV* uses five axes:

Axis I: Clinical syndromes (e.g., mental disorders); developmental disorders; other conditions that may be a focus of clinical attention
Axis II: Personality disorders/traits; mental retardation
Axis III: General medical conditions/symptoms that pertain to current problem
Axis IV: Psychosocial and environmental problems
Axis V: Global Assessment of Functioning (GAF)

The main advantage of separating Axes I and II is to prevent the typically more florid presentations of Axis I mental disorders from overshadowing or becoming confused with the more chronic and subtle Axis II personality disorders. Distinguishing between these axes may clarify what therapy can reasonably accomplish, since treatment is more likely to alleviate Axis I than Axis II disorders. Therapists (and clients) who fail to separate mental from personality disorders are frequently disappointed, however unjustifiably, when only the former remits with brief treatment.

Axis III lists only general medical conditions that are "potentially relevant to the understanding or management of the case." It is unfortunate that some nonphysicians are reluctant, or believe it is inappropriate, to list an Axis III diagnosis, since a patient's diagnosis should be complete. When writing an Axis III diagnosis, many nonphysicians like to add in parentheses the source of this diagnostic information (e.g., the patient's doctor, the patient, the chart). For example:

Axis I: Panic disorder
Psychological factors affecting physical condition

Axis II: No personality disorder
Axis III: Crohn's disease (Dr. Sachar)
Axis IV: Occupational problem (job loss, acute)
             Problems with primary support group (failing marriage, chronic)
Axis V: Global Assessment of Functioning = 65

In its dry way, Axis IV attempts to include all of Shakespeare's "slings and arrows of outrageous fortune." It lists the psychosocial and environmental problems that may affect prognosis of mental disorders (Axes I and II). Stressors may involve jobs, finances, living situations, health, social support, family conflicts, and negative life events. Even "positive" stressors should be listed, if they are problematic. For example, the author (N.W.) got the contract to revise this book (Good News! Hooray!) but had only seven months to do it (Bad News! Worry!). All relevant problems should be listed, including those that *contributed to* the disorder(s) and those that *resulted from* the disorder(s). In general, this list is confined to problems in the past year. However, earlier problems should be listed if they clearly contribute to the present diagnosis or have become a focus of treatment; for example, post-traumatic stress disorder, rape, childhood sexual and physical abuse, or combat experience could all be listed. Problems that have become the primary focus of treatment should not only be recorded in Axis IV but also in Axis I (other conditions that may be a focus of clinical attention). For example, if the therapy only focuses on "bad hair" and it really is bad, it might be listed in Axis I. However, the astute clinician in this situation might also want to consider body dysmorphic disorder.

Axis V indicates the patient's current overall level of social, psychological, and occupational functioning. Physical functioning and limitations are not included here but may be listed in Axis IV. The Global Assessment of Functioning (GAF) scale in Appendix C is generally recommended for rating Axis V.

Usually this rating is done to ascertain the patient's level of functioning in the present. This current rating, together with the Axis I diagnosis, help clinicians decide if patients should be immediately hospitalized or live in a group home. Clinicians may also want a rating of patients' highest level of functioning in the past year, which helps to determine prognosis and treatment (since patients who previously functioned at a higher level usually recover at a higher level). To illustrate: With everything else being the same, and with Tom and Jerry being equally delusional — one's certain he's a cat, the other, a mouse — if before becoming ill Tom had a solid marriage, good job, and satisfying hobbies and Jerry did not, then after recovery Tom would probably function better than Jerry. Treatment goals should reflect these different expectations.

PROGNOSIS

In different ways, each *DSM-IV* axis sheds light on prognosis. A patient's prognosis or outcome is a product of several factors: (a) the natural course of the particular disorder; (b) the patient's highest prior level of functioning (see above); (c) the duration of the present illness (the longer the duration, the bleaker the outlook); (d) the abruptness of onset (the more acute the onset, the better the prognosis); (e) the age of onset (the earlier in life, the poorer the outcome); (f) the availability of effective treatments; (g) the patient's compliance with treatment; and (h) the presence of a supportive social network.

It is worth noting that how disturbed a patient is during an acute episode is *not* always a good predictor of long-term outcome. A 20-year-old patient who has deteriorated over a period of six years from schizophrenia and who now displays social withdrawal and flat affect has a far worse long-term prognosis than a 50-year-old patient who functioned well until a month ago when she became acutely manic, insisted she was the reincarnation of Queen Victoria, threw hundred-dollar bills out the window, and spoke nonstop. Clinicians should be clear about *which* prognosis they are determining: Is it for a short-term (e.g., post-hospitalization) or a long-term (e. g., a year after discharge) outcome? Is it for an Axis I or an Axis II disorder? Is it a forecast of something more specific, such as relapse, suicide, assault, social functioning? When clinicians dispense prognostic information to patients and their families, they should describe these various types of outcomes instead of indicating a single, and less meaningful, prognosis.

Warnings About *DSM-IV*

Rote memorization of *DSM-IV* criteria is a long and pointless endeavor to be avoided; learning specific criteria occurs most effectively through clinical experience. However, when this text presents a disorder, students should still examine its *DSM-IV* criteria in order to (a) obtain an overall picture of the disorder, (b) learn its defining characteristics, (c) become familiar with its common symptoms, (d) understand the meanings of the technical terms that describe it, and (e) learn which features differentiate it from other *DSM-IV* disorders.

DSM-IV is based on a categorical approach to diagnosis. As in medicine, this type of approach works best for disorders that have homogeneous characteristics and clear boundaries differentiating them from other disorders. A stroke and a myocardial infarction are examples of such discrete medical categories. This categorical approach does not work as well for disorders that exist on a continuum — those that can be better described by dimensions and have great variability within the diagnostic classification category. Anemia and vitamin deficiency are medical examples of dimensional-continuum types of disorders. Because the diagnosis of anemia depends on a hematocrit (a red blood cell count), what count constitutes anemia is always open to debate. Some people function normally with "low" hematocrits, while others with "low-normal" do not. Diagnosing psychopathology presents the same problems, since every disorder has both categorical and dimensional aspects. Autistic disorder is an example of a diagnosis that fits a pure categorical approach relatively easily. However, other disorders have many continuous dimensional qualities. For example, antisocial personality traits might range from a persistent breaking of parking laws (a not uncommon quality in the general populace) to killing with no remorse (a much rarer characteristic). How to establish hyperactivity in attention-deficit/hyperactivity disorder is equally difficult. In response to the dimensional complexities in a categorical approach, the Task Force on *DSM-IV* recommends:

> In *DSM-IV*, there is no assumption that each category of mental disorder is a completely discrete entity with absolute boundaries dividing it from other mental disorders or from no mental disorder. There is also no assumption that all people described as having the same mental disorder are alike in all important ways. The clinician using *DSM-IV* should therefore consider that individuals sharing a diagnosis are likely to be heterogeneous even in regard to the defining features of the diagnosis and that boundary cases will be difficult to diagnose in any but a probabilistic fashion. This outlook allows greater flexibility in the use of the system, encourages more specific attention to boundary cases, and emphasizes the need to capture additional clinical information that goes beyond diagnosis. (p. xxii)

CHAPTER 4

Etiology

AFTER REPORTING THE history, mental status, diagnosis, and prognosis, the clinician presents a *biopsychosocial formulation* — that is, a discussion of the etiology and pathogenesis of the patient's current problems. In general, *etiology* refers to the *origins* of a disorder, whereas *pathogenesis* refers to *all the mechanisms* that ultimately produce it. In this chapter, the term *etiology* encompasses pathogenesis and includes everything that has caused the patient's presenting difficulties.

Etiology plays an unusual role in psychiatry, since psychiatry is the *only* medical specialty that, virtually by definition, treats disorders without clearly known causes (or definitive cures). At the turn of the century, the most prevalent mental illness was general paresis (i.e., syphilis of the brain). Other common psychiatric disorders were "myxedema madness" (a type of hypothyroidism), the epilepsies, and psychoses due to vitamin deficiencies and brain infections. As soon as the cause for each of these conditions was discovered, the job of treatment shifted to physicians *other* than psychiatrists, such as internists and neurologists. The fact that psychiatrists don't know the cause of mental illness is less an indictment of psychiatrists than a reflection of how medicine assigns disease among its specialists.

Indeed, a major reason *DSM-III* (and now *DSM-IV*) switched to a nosology based on descriptive instead of on etiological criteria was because the etiology of most mental disorders is idiopathic.[1] Exceptions exist, as when a disorder's etiology is both obvious and inherent to its definition,

---

[1]*Idiopathic* refers to unknown causation, whereas *iatrogenic* refers to physician-induced illness (e.g., drug side effects).

such as the role of amphetamines in amphetamine intoxication, or the role of psychosocial stressors in producing a post-traumatic stress disorder. Otherwise, *DSM-IV* eschews all etiological hypotheses — biological as well as psychosocial.

Although the etiologies of most mental disorders are unknown, more is understood about etiology today than ever. Most dramatic have been advances in psychobiology and epidemiology; less heralded (but equally important) has been the growing appreciation of how intrapsychic, familial, and social influences interact with biology to produce mental disorders. As a result, the clinician's "*psychodynamic* formulation" has been superseded by the "*biopsychosocial* formulation; the former was limited to psychological, largely intrapsychic, influences, whereas the latter is a synthesis of *bio*-logical and *psycho*-logical factors — including psychodynamic, cognitive, emotional, and behavioral aspects — together with *social* factors — familial and interpersonal etiologies (see Engel, 1977).

THE DIMENSIONS OF "CAUSATION"

To speak of "*the* cause" of a mental disorder is naive; it is akin to patients who enter treatment and say, "I want to get to the *root* of my problem." This "root myth" assumes that a single factor has caused the problem and that unearthing it will result in cure. Unfortunately, there is no such thing as *the* root to a problem; at most, there are root*s*, with many sprouting, variegated phenomena. Formulations, therefore, should consider diverse etiological influences, such as the following:

What *initiates* a disorder usually differs from what *perpetuates* it. Many teenagers begin smoking to feel grown-up. However, if they are still smoking when they reach 30, the reason is no longer to feel like an adult; at this point, they are smoking from habit. What originates and maintains a problem may also differ from what *exacerbates* a disorder; for example, stress may rekindle a smoking habit in somebody who previously stopped.

Another factor in causation is *predisposition*: a latent susceptibility to a disease or disorder, which may be activated under certain conditions such as stress. A predisposition may be "disorder-*specific*" (e.g., a gene producing a vulnerability to a particular disorder) or "disorder-*nonspecific*" (e.g., broken families during childhood produce a vulnerability to almost every mental disorder).

When determining causation, clinicians should be careful to delineate these four levels: predisposition, initiation, perpetuation, and exacerbation. Many theories of mental illness are originally proposed as initial causes of a disorder, whereas subsequent data indicate that these theories are more relevant to what maintains or aggravates a disorder. For instance, the hypothesis that "double-bind communication" causes schizophrenia has been largely refuted, yet growing evidence suggests that double-bind communication may perpetuate and exacerbate schizophrenia. (An example of double-bind communication would be "for a fat kid, you are pretty good looking.")

Clinicians should also distinguish between what is *inherent* to a disorder and what is a *consequence* of it: Both factors feed into one another and may profoundly affect the patient. The importance of this distinction becomes apparent by carefully examining the sequence of events. For example, a novice may err by assuming that a job loss caused a depression, whereas in reality it was the patient's depression — and concomitant low energy, indecisiveness, and poor concentration — that caused the job loss.

Causes can be categorized as (a) necessary and sufficient, (b) necessary but not sufficient, or (c) facilitating or predisposing but neither necessary nor sufficient. Few diseases have causes that are necessary and sufficient; one example is Huntington's Chorea, a progressive and fatal dementia, in which having the gene is all that is needed to produce the illness. Alcoholism illustrates the second type; although alcohol is necessary for the disorder, other factors are required to produce it, since not everyone who drinks becomes an alcoholic. These other factors may include psychonoxious environments and predisposing genes. Many causes fall into the third category; loss of parents during childhood fosters most mental disorders, even though such a loss is neither necessary nor sufficient to produce any of them. Consequently, the harmful effects of a disorder may be reduced or prevented by rectifying the facilitating or predisposing causes (e.g., poverty, stress), even when they are not necessary or sufficient causes.

Because mental disorders have multiple rather than singular causes, and because some of these causes are facilitating or predisposing, *multicausality* has been misconstrued as *omnicausality*: that is, anything can cause anything, as long as there is a tenuous connection. If a passive father has a schizophrenic son, then passive fathers are deemed a cause of schizophrenia. This line of thinking is stupid; it's like saying milk is a cause of schizophrenia because a schizophrenic drank milk. Omnicausality falters because it equates a *casual* with a *causal* association between two events, a confusion that can only be clarified by studying the matter with scientific *controls* (Goodwin & Guze, 1989).

Some diagnostic categories, such as schizophrenia, consist of not one but several psychiatric entities, which all share similar cardinal features. The entities may be defined by the most prominent symptom, as in the various *subtypes* of schizophrenia (paranoid, catatonic, etc.). Each subtype may involve different etiological factors. Conversely, entities which present with the same clinical picture may have arisen via different etiological routes. For instance, genetics clearly produces some depressions, but not others; many antihypertensive medications induce some major depressions, bereavement triggers others, and "learned helplessness" causes others. The reason these depressions may present with the same symptoms is because, no matter what their origins, at some point a specific series of changes was launched within the brain—that is, a "final common pathway" that produced the characteristic symptoms of major depression.

Symptoms and *issues* usually arise from different causes. Symptoms may be hallucinations or insomnia, while issues contain the meaning of symptoms and reflect how patients cope, how they feel toward authorities, and so on (see Chapter 1). Symptoms and issues, although related, are of a different order. Goodwin (1985) aptly quoted Donald Hebb's observation on whether intelligence was due to heredity or environment: "Each is *fully* necessary. . . . To ask how much heredity contributes to intelligence is like asking how much the width of a field contributes to its area" (p. 171).

For 15 years a middle-aged man occasionally had the delusion that people were sneaking itching powder into his food. Since his divorce of 20 years ago, homosexual urges had frightened him. When he felt close to another man—or to use his words, "got the itch for somebody"—his delusion would arise. The man's symptom was a delusion; many patients have delusions. The man's issues about itching powder and homosexuals were idiosyncratic; they derived from his life experience, were symbolically meaningful to him, and erupted in circumstances stressful for him.

Symptoms have *form* while issues have *content*. Symptoms are to issues what videotape is to programming. For instance, two patients may present with major depression; both complain of severe guilt, hopelessness, and insomnia. Their symptoms are the same, yet their issues vary. The first patient, a young, successful TV executive, insists that her sleeplessness stems from her being "a total failure," while the second, a retired Baptist postal clerk, is sure his sleeplessness is a punishment from God. Both patients suffer from the biologically-induced insomnia of major depression. Yet the issues the patients bring to their insomnia—that is, what it means to them and how they deal with it—differ according to their life experiences.

In general, biology determines symptoms and psychosocial influences shape issues. How patients express a mental disorder greatly depends on their personalties. When drunk or "stoned," some people giggle, some babble, some dance, some cry, some withdraw, some get the munchies, and others become violent. They all have a drug-induced mental syndrome, yet how it manifests varies according to the individual's personality. (The same holds for medical illness. For example, coronary patients contend with heart attacks in many different ways depending on their personality. Arthur Kleinman [1988] makes a similar distinction for all medical disorders: There is a *disease* that may be caused by a virus, bacteria, etc., with *symptoms*, such as fever and abdominal pain; and there is the *illness* and with it, *illness behavior*—going to a doctor, having a shaman exorcise the demon, trying to make spiritual sense out of the fever-induced hallucinations.)

Like intoxication, mental disorders tend to magnify personality traits. During a major depression, a lifelong worry-wart frets nonstop, a chronically suspicious man becomes downright paranoid, and a mild hypochondriac becomes a severe one. Consequently, the cause of a patient's behavior can never be fully attributed to either psychology *or* biology. Both are responsible for behavior, albeit in different ways—a truism recognized long ago by Hughlings Jackson: "There is no physiology of the mind anymore than there is a psychology of the nervous system." As long as people have minds *and* brains, it is hard to imagine how one could function without the other!

Given that mental disorders neither overpower personality nor make it disappear, being mentally ill or taking LSD, PCP, or alcohol neither explains nor justifies committing antisocial acts. (Mental illness is no excuse for bad manners.) Statements like, "Peter beat up Sally because he was drunk," or "Darlene's schizophrenia caused her to drown her child," imply that the patient/criminal is not responsible for the act, as if the drug or the mental illness *made* him or her commit the crime. As a group, schizophrenics are no more or less violent than any other group; being schizophrenic *per se* does not make one violent. Being acutely psychotic may diminish normal social restraints or magnify pre-existing violent tendencies, but that's quite different from dissociating the person from his crime by totally blaming the illness. It is akin to the old defense: "The devil made me do it."

VOLITION

"Volition" means the act of willing. How much a patient "wills" or determines his or her behavior during a mental disorder may be difficult to discern. The first question, to be blunt, is "Can people fake mental illness?" The answer is "Yes, but not for long." If there are any doubts, try it! Actors can fake madness for three hours a night and twice on Wednesdays and Saturdays, but not much longer. Only those with mental disorders can pace for hours, shadow box for days, and dwell on rotting bladders and stinking bowels. It's too exhausting to sustain. Nor can one hallucinate at will, except with the help of certain chemicals or a sensory-isolation chamber.

Nevertheless, the question of people faking mental illness stubbornly persists, partly because some patients seem to respond to the environment according to what's "convenient" or "necessary." When clinicians must decide whether to permit a floridly psychotic inpatient to attend the funeral of a loved one, they find that most patients pull themselves together, go to the funeral, and do just fine. How come? Because, like the intoxicated, the mentally ill can still modify their behavior depending on the situation and the severity of their illnesses. When a tipsy student receives a telephone call from his parents, he can "get his act together," as long as the call is not too long and he is not too drunk. Likewise, if they are not too ill and not required to act "properly" for too long, the mentally ill are often able to "normalize" their behavior. Therefore, highly disturbed psychiatric patients are not helpless automatons, for they can exert some control over their disorder.

Conversely, just as being intoxicated makes it extremely difficult to perform routine tasks, so does being mentally ill. Like everyone else, the mentally ill must contend with problems in living, but unlike everyone else, they must do so with the added burdens of psychiatric symptoms. Interviewing for a job is hard enough; feeling certain that the interviewer is Satan doesn't help. Writing a term paper can be stressful, but imagine doing so with racing thoughts and taunting hallucinations. Mental illness makes everything harder. Simple chit-chat isn't easy when you're sure a bomb is going to explode in your stomach. Given all their symptoms, what amazes is not how poorly the mentally ill do, but how well.

EXPLAINING VERSUS UNDERSTANDING

In the formulation, the clinician should seek to understand as well as to explain the patient's difficulties. Unfortunately, many clinicians are unaware of the difference between "explaining" and "understanding." In this context, understanding is not being used in the *explanatory* sense of "I understand *why* Jim hates his mother," but rather in the *descriptive* sense of "I understand *how* Jim hates his mother."

To explain is to view from the outside; to understand is to view from within. Explaining relies on logic and intellect, understanding on experience and empathy. Explanations should be objective, whereas understandings can only be subjective. Explanations address the "why" of behavior, understanding, the "what." For different reasons, both explaining and understanding are crucial for clinical care. One is not better than the other; they are simply different.

Clinicians often say they are understanding when actually they are explaining. Consider Karen, a psychiatric inpatient, who was convinced she had no legs. When her psychiatrist went on vacation, she walked up to the staff and complained, more intensely than ever, of having no legs. Every time this occurred, her substitute therapist replied, "You're walking, so that proves you have legs. But even so, you're obviously worried about having no legs because your doctor is on vacation." Karen was infuriated; she claimed that the staff "doesn't understand me." The staff responded, "But we do understand: Your psychiatrist has gone away and you're understandably upset." Patient and staff were talking past each other. The patient accurately felt she was being "explained away." The staff mistakenly believed they were showing understanding, when they were actually giving a correct explanation. Another psychiatrist demonstrated empathic understanding when he said to Karen, "You must feel like a paraplegic. It's frightening to feel you have no control over your legs, or that they don't work properly, or that they don't belong to you. No wonder you're upset!" Feeling that somebody was finally on her "wavelength," Karen was ready to consider the explanation about her therapist's absence.

It's not that clinicians never understand their patients; to various degrees, they all do. Yet to the degree that clinicians do understand, it's more a product of their being *people* than of their being *professionals*. Therapists are inherently no better or worse than anyone else at understanding people. Indeed, a good novelist reveals a thorough understanding of a character's psychology without using a single psychological term. The ability to understand can be improved with experience and training, but it doesn't originate in the reading of books or articles.

In contrast, by learning etiological theory, clinicians are far more adept at explaining behavior. They can learn how the unconscious does this and how the id does that; they can learn how the brain's chemicals affect this and how the person's environment affects that. Although clinicians are experts at explaining, but not necessarily at understanding, both explanation and understanding are important and both belong in the formulation. The following sections introduce explanatory theories, since they, unlike understandings, lend themselves to didactic presentations.

NEURONS AND NEUROTRANSMITTERS

The fundamental unit of biologically-derived behavior is the nerve cell or *neuron*. The brain has one trillion neurons; each neuron consists of a microscopic *cell body* (or "head"), which trails off into an *axon* (or "tail") with an extremely narrow width but a length of up to several inches or feet. By definition, axons transmit electrical impulses *away* from the cell body, whereas *dendrites* transmit them *toward* it. Electrical impulses originate in cell bodies and run through these axons, until they are conveyed to hundreds, or even thousands, of other nerve cells.

Neurons are the only cells in the body that are anatomically separate from one another. Therefore, to reach a nearby neuron, electrical impulses do not travel over continuous tissue, but flow across the spaces between neurons. As illustrated in Figure 4–1, this passage is accomplished by chemicals called *neurotransmitters*, which transmit messages over these tiny spaces called *synaptic clefts*.

Neurotransmitters are synthesized inside the neuron and actively trans-

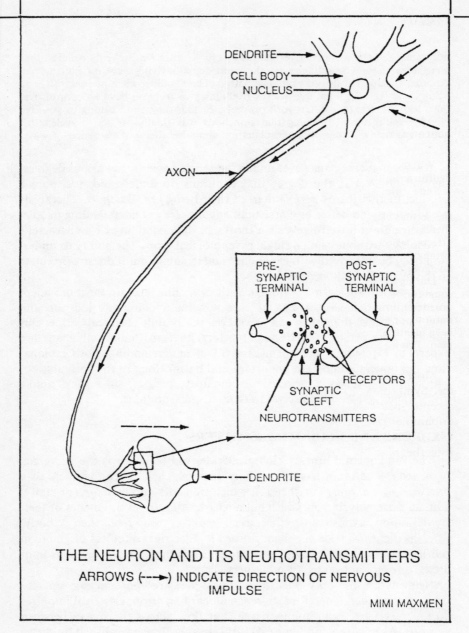

DENDRITE

CELL BODY

NUCLEUS

AXON

PRE-
SYNAPTIC
TERMINAL

POST-
SYNAPTIC
TERMINAL

RECEPTORS

SYNAPTIC
CLEFT

NEUROTRANSMITTERS

DENDRITE

THE NEURON AND ITS NEUROTRANSMITTERS

ARROWS (---➤) INDICATE DIRECTION OF NERVOUS
IMPULSE

MIMI MAXMEN

FIGURE 4–1
The Neuron and Its Neurotransmitters*

*From Maxmen, J.S. (1986b). *The new psychiatry: How modern psychiatrists think about their patients, theories, diagnoses, drugs, psychotherapies, power, training, families, and private lives.* New York: Mentor, p. 141.

ported to the axon's end or *presynaptic terminal*; from here, neurotransmitters swim across the synaptic cleft and bind onto *receptors* that are located on the membranes (or edges) of adjacent dendrites or cell bodies. By doing so, neurotransmitters can trigger or inhibit the receptor's ability to fire. The nerve cell acts like a wet sponge: When it fires, it releases its fluids of neurotransmitters; when not firing, it expands and reabsorbs them.

Whether a nerve cell fires mainly depends on the quantity and arrangement of neurotransmitters reaching its receptors at any instant. Other determining factors include variations in the rate of synthesis and release of a neurotransmitter from the first cell; increases and decreases in the sensitivity and numbers of the receptors on the second cell; inhibition of the first cell's ability to reabsorb neurotransmitters, thereby increasing their concentration at the second cell's receptors. Drugs also exert effects. In pharmacology, *agonists* are substances that enhance or potentiate the firing of a neuron, whereas *antagonists* are drugs that block or reduce the effects of an agonist.

During the past decade many types of receptors have been discovered, including some for benzodiazepines, the group name for diazepam (Valium) and chlordiazepoxide (Librium). Since the body does not produce its own benzodiazepines, the natural purpose of these receptors is unknown. Receptors for endorphins have also been identified, the body's own opiate-like narcotics for mediating the perception of pain. The jogger's "high" may partly reflect a buildup of these endorphins.

Most receptors are affected by one type (or subtype) of neurotransmitter. Symptoms of mental disorders appear to arise from changes in these receptor-neurotransmitter systems, of which six seem especially influential: dopamine (DA), norepinephrine (NE), serotonin (SE), acetylcholine (AC), histamine (H), and gamma-aminobutyric acid (GABA). Table 4–1 lists the *primary precursors* (major chemical antecedents) and *primary*

TABLE 4–1
Neurotransmitters: Precursors and Metabolites

NEUROTRANSMITTER	PRIMARY PRECURSORS	PRIMARY METABOLITES
Dopamine (DA)	Tyrosine L-Dopa	Homovanillic acid (HVA)
Norepinephrine (NE)	Tyrosine L-Dopa	Methoxyhydroxyphenylglycol (MHPG)
Serotonin (SE) or (5-HT)	Tryptophan	5-Hydroxyindoleacetic acid (5-HIAA)
Acetylcholine (AC)	Choline	No specific metabolite
Histamine (H)	Histidine	No specific metabolite
Gamma-aminobutyric acid (GABA)	Glutamic acid	Succinic acid

metabolite (major breakdown product). Dopamine and norepinephrine are *catecholamines*; serotonin is an *indoleamine*.

Although a great deal more research is needed before it is clear how neurotransmitters contribute to mental disorders, some of the more widely touted hypotheses are as follows: Schizophrenia seems to involve excessive activity in the dopamine-receptor systems. The "catecholamine hypothesis" of depression holds that a functional underactivity of norepinephrine causes severe depression, whereas a functional overactivity of this neurotransmitter causes mania. Other theories contend that depression stems from a high ratio of acetylcholine to catecholamine (e.g., dopamine or norepinephrine), whereas mania erupts with the ratio reversed. Sleep and perhaps mood are affected by changes in the serotonin-receptor system. When stimulated, GABA receptors inhibit neurons and induce calm; thus, anxiety increases when this system becomes less active. Abrupt opiate (and sometimes tobacco) withdrawal apparently accelerates the firing of norepinephrine from the *locus coeruleus* — a densely populated area of neurons that produces most of this neurotransmitter.

PSYCHOENDOCRINOLOGY

Psychoendocrinology is the study of interrelationships among the brain, hormones, neurotransmitters, and behavior. Unlike neurotransmitters, which act close to their locus of origin, *hormones* are produced by glands, secreted into the blood stream, and often act far away from their locus of origin. Until recently, psychoendocrinology focused on hormonal actions outside the brain. Now, more sophisticated technologies have made it possible to study the *pituitary*, a "window" into the brain, by examining how neurotransmitters, hormones, and the brain interact to produce mental disorders.

The *hypothalamus* is located directly above the pituitary gland; considerable psychoendocrine activity transpires along this "hypothalamic-pituitary axis." For example, the biological or vegetative signs of depression (e.g., disturbances in sleep, appetite, sex) are partially mediated in the hypothalamus, the chief connecting station where neurotransmitters and hormones affect each other. An underactive thyroid can cause depression and too many thyroid hormones can induce depression, mania, or psychosis. Conversely, during many cases of major depression, the adrenal gland releases excessive amounts of cortisol.

TECHNOLOGY AND ETIOLOGY

Throughout history, etiological knowledge has been only as advanced as the methods available to study it. For example, psychodynamic etiologies have always reflected the patients and the society that were investigated. Freud revealed the pathogenic power of repressed sexuality in a sexually repressive society; Jung's patients were not sexually inhibited but religiously troubled, and his theories focused on philosophical, cosmic, and religious themes. Adler, not surprisingly, uncovered the inferiority complex when dealing with ambitious, middle-class patients (Wender & Klein, 1981).

More recently, an explosion in biomedical technology has uncovered alterations in the brain's anatomy, chemistry, and physiology that were previously undetectable. Introduced in 1973, *computerized tomography* (CT) provides a two-dimensional anatomical image by contrasting the specific gravities of various brain tissue. Even newer is *magnetic resonance imaging* (MRI), in which images reflect the chemical properties of tissues by measuring the resonances of a particular atom (e.g., phosphorus) within those tissues. At present, because of technical limitations, MRI cannot measure neurotransmitter and metabolic defects, but unlike the CT scan, it can distinguish brain tissues with similar densities but different chemistries (e.g., white matter versus gray matter, a tumor versus normal brain tissue, a multiple sclerosis plaque versus white matter). *Positron emission tomography* (PET) measures the metabolic activity of a compound (e.g., glucose) at various sites in the brain. By labeling a psychotropic drug, such as haloperidol, PET can measure the number and alterations of dopamine receptors.

This "new alphabet technology" is helping to invalidate the traditional Cartesian distinction between *organic* and *functional* disorders by demonstrating that many "functional" disorders involve changes in fine neuronal tissues and in cerebral ventricles; altered glucose metabolism and neurochemical changes are also coming to light. Because the organic-functional distinction has little basis in fact, *DSM-IV* has dropped this distinction.

"ENVIRONMENTAL BIOLOGY"

"Environmental biology," the authors' neologism, is the study of the two-way relationship between environment and biology in the production of mental disorders. Three of these relationships deserve comment: (a) biological trauma from the environment, (b) psychosocial trauma inducing biological changes, and (c) genotypes and phenotypes.

Biological Trauma From the Environment

Environmental stress and psychosocial stress are *not* synonymous, since the environment can also generate biological stress. During pregnancy and afterward, viruses, drugs, malnourishment, physical abuse, or premature birth can produce mental disorders in children or, at least, predispose them to one. In comparison to normals, schizophrenics have a higher rate of birth complications and some evidence points to a ("slow") virus as the culprit in a few of these cases.

Light—natural and artificial—appears to be another biological (or physical) force that contributes to mental disorders. Some patients with mood disorders, especially bipolar disorders, become depressed every fall and winter and recover every spring and summer. These patients' depressions improve with prolonged exposure to bright artificial light. The antidepressant effect of light is given further credence by the finding that people are more likely to have depressions the farther they live from the equator (Rosenthal et al., 1984).

Psychosocial Trauma Inducing Biological Changes

Biological changes do not necessarily have biological origins; they may be generated psychosocially. Kandel (1983), for instance, has demonstrated how psychosocial stress can alter the brain's anatomy and biochemistry to produce anxiety. He uses the marine snail *Aplysia* in his research, because it has a relatively simple nervous system with large and easy-to-visualize brain cells.[2] By conditioning the *Aplysia* and then photographing its neurons, Kandel recorded the actual anatomical changes in a brain cell caused by a specific psychosocial environment.

The brain does not mature independently of the environment and, once developed, it continues to be influenced by the environment. Being continually unable to cope—"learned helplessness"—can induce biological changes resulting in depression. As another example, patients with advanced Parkinson's disease who can hardly walk will race to the exit if they are in a movie theater that catches on fire. They *do* have brain disease, yet how their diseased brains function depends on the environment.

Genotype and Phenotype

Having a gene, and having it produce visible effects, are two different things. The gene itself is a *genotype*; whether the gene is expressed—that is, if it becomes manifest—is a *phenotype*. If there is a gene (or genotype) for an ulcer, whether it develops into an ulcer (the phenotype) depends on environmental factors such as diet, stress, and smoking. Because of this interrelationship, to ask whether a mental disorder is caused by genes *or* environment is naive. When a person inherits the genotype for a mental disorder, how the environment affects that gene determines the degree, form, and existence of the disorder.

---

[2]The *Aplysia* weighs up to 4 pounds, consists of only 20,000 cells, and has the largest neurons in the animal kingdom—up to 1 mm in diameter. Whereas a simple human behavior typically involves hundreds of thousands of brain cells, simple behaviors of an *Aplysia* involve less than 50.

Genetic theory is not equivalent with behavioral predestination. If a person inherits the genotype for a mental disorder, biological and psychosocial interventions can still alleviate or prevent it.

THE GENETICS OF MENTAL DISORDERS

Genetic factors are prerequisites for most, but certainly not all, cases of schizophrenia and manic-depression, and somewhat less, for major depression. Heredity partly contributes to panic and obsessive-compulsive disorders, but does not appear to be implicated in generalized anxiety disorders. These conclusions derive mainly from researching twins and adoptees.

Twin Studies

By comparing identical or *monozygotic* (MZ) twins with fraternal or *dizygotic* (DZ) twins, investigators have assessed the relative contributions of nature and nurture in causing certain mental disorders. Identical twins have identical genes; the genes of fraternal twins are like those of any other pair of siblings. A *concordance rate* is the percent of twins who both exhibit the same phenotype. Because MZ and DZ twins usually share the same environment, the difference in concordance rates between MZ and DZ twins largely reflects genetic influences.

For example, on average the concordance rate for schizophrenia among MZ twins averages 45%; this means that when one twin of a MZ pair has schizophrenia, 45% of the time the other twin does also. In contrast, DZ twin-pairs have a concordance rate of 10% for schizophrenia (Weiner, 1985). (If one sibling is schizophrenic, other siblings have a 10% chance of becoming schizophrenic.) The statistically significant difference between 45% and 10% suggests that genes transmit schizophrenia. At the same time, these figures also demonstrate an important role for nongenetic factors. If genes alone were involved, one would expect that if one member of a MZ pair were schizophrenic, then the twin *must* also be schizophrenic. In other words, the MZ concordance rate would be 100%. But it's not; it's only 45%.

Geneticists attribute this 55% difference to *penetrance*, a term used to account for why the genotype does not become the phenotype 100% of the time. Penetrance may occur because the abnormal genes were too weak or were impeded by other genes; spontaneous genetic mutations, viral infections, and *in utero* difficulties may also explain penetrance.

A potential limitation of twin studies might be that their concordance rates might be altered if identical twins were treated differently from fraternal twins. However, two findings do not support this contention. First, MZ twins who were physically dissimilar showed the same concordance rates as those who looked the same. Second, identical twins who grew up with everybody (themselves included) assuming they were fraternal twins showed concordance rates of identical twins.

Adoption Studies

To further clarify the nature/nurture question, various studies of adoptions have been conducted. The first major adoption studies of mental disorders occurred in 1963. They were conducted in Denmark, because the government had a register of every adoption, including those infants who were separated from their biological parents when less than three months old and then legally adopted.

As illustrated in Figure 4–2A, one method of using these records for research purposes is to compare the biological and adoptive parents of adult schizophrenic adoptees. Because biological parents gave away the child so early in life, their psychosocial influence on the schizophrenic

FIGURE 4–2A
Comparison of Schizophrenia Frequency Between
Biological and Adoptive Parents

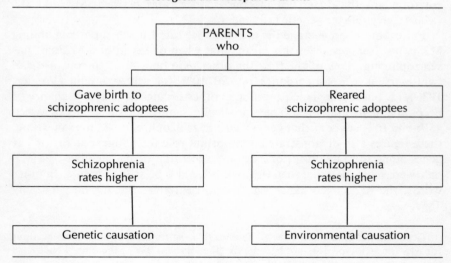

adoptee was probably nil; only genetic influences would persist. Therefore, if schizophrenia were genetically transmitted, the biological parents should have a much higher incidence of schizophrenia than the adoptive parents. On the other hand, if schizophrenia were produced psychosocially, just the opposite should occur. The results were striking: Repeatedly, the schizophrenic adoptee's biological parents were schizophrenic, whereas the adoptive parents were "normal."

In another adoption strategy (Figure 4–2B), children of schizophrenic biological parents were reared by adoptive parents and contrasted to a matched control group of adoptees whose biological parents had no family history of mental disorders. Once again, genetic interpretations prevailed, since schizophrenia-like disorders were far more common among the offspring of biologically ill than among those of "normal" parents. These and similar findings have provided overwhelming evidence that, in most cases, genetic factors are a principal cause of schizophrenia.

Subsequent research has suggested that what is genetically transmitted

FIGURE 4–2B
Comparison of Schizophrenia Frequency
Between Adoptees

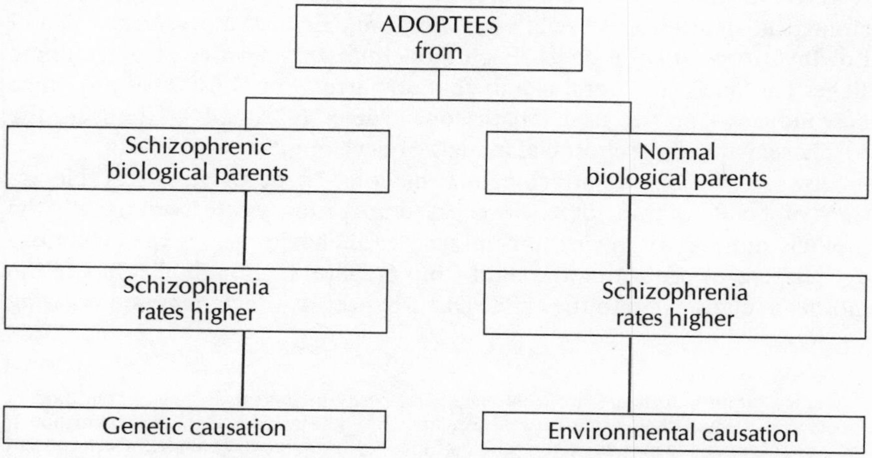

may not be a single gene for schizophrenia, but a gene for "schizophrenic-spectrum disorders." Besides schizophrenia, this spectrum includes several disorders that are similar, but not identical to, schizophrenia, such as the schizotypal personality disorder. The concept of *genetic spectrum disorders* also may apply to other syndromes. For example, evidence indicates that there may be a gene for "depressive-spectrum disorders," which may include major depression, bipolar disorder, alcoholism, drug abuse, panic disorder, phobia, and antisocial personality disorder.

Finally, even when genes are implicated, this concept of spectrum disorders underscores the need to specify *what* is being inherited. Is it a predisposition to one disorder or to a series of disorders? Is it a particular trait, such as shyness or the inability to synthesize information? Or is it a vulnerability to certain psychosocial stressors such as a chaotic family life, loss, or intense emotions? Some of these answers may involve psychosocial influences.

PSYCHOSOCIAL THEORIES

Numerous psychological and social factors influence the course of a mental disorder, and the many ways they do so can be divided into seven general models[3]:

1. *Developmental models.* Three developmental models are of particular etiological significance: Freud's *psychosexual*, Erikson's *psychosocial*, and Bowlby's *attachment* models. Each model presents a series of overlapping stages (or "passages") and claims that an "arrest" or "crisis"[4] at any stage may induce associated psychopathology. Tables 4–2A and 4–2B outline the psychosexual and psychosocial models of development respectively.

Bowlby considered "attachment behaviors" to be those observable actions of a child that facilitate closeness to the primary caregiver, usually the biologic mother. In theory, this attachment behavior serves the evolutionary purpose of protecting the child from predators. "Bonding" refers to the mother's relationship to the child. Disturbances in attachment and bonding

---

[3]Some important models are not mentioned here, partly because their direct application to diagnostic psychopathology has (as yet) been limited. These include (a) the *existential* model, which focuses on the purpose and meaning of life, (b) the *humanistic* model, which concentrates on fulfilling or actualizing one's potential, and (c) Piaget's *cognitive* model, which portrays the stages of development of a child's thought processes.

[4]A developmental *crisis* is not a catastrophe or an emergency; it is the normal developmental challenge posed by each psychosocial stage, which becomes a "necessary turning point, a crucial moment, when development must move one way or another, marshalling resources of growth, recovery, and further differentiation" (Erikson, 1968, p. 16).

TABLE 4–2A
Freudian Psychosexual Development*

AGE (Years)	STAGE	RESOLUTION	
		SUCCESSFUL	PATHOLOGICAL
0–1	ORAL Primary gratification from mouth, lips, and tongue.	Self-reliance; self-trust; trust in others; capacity to give and receive without dependence and envy.	Needy; demanding; dependent on others for self-esteem; pathological optimism or pessimism; jealousy; immature and image distorting; [narcissistic].
1–3	ANAL Primary gratification from sphincter control; aggressive, sadistic, and libidinal impulses.	Autonomy; independence; capacity to cooperate.	Excessive orderliness, stubbornness, and willfulness; miserly; heightened ambivalence; obsessive-compulsive; [immature and neurotic].
3–6	PHALLIC Primary gratification from genital area; oedipal issues.	Basis for sexual identity; drives constructively redirected; superego established.	Castration fear in boys, penis envy in girls; failure to identify with same-sexed parent; neurotic disorders; [neurotic].
6–12	LATENCY Relative quiescent sexual drives.	Integration and consolidation of prior psychosexual gains; basis for love, work, and play.	Lack of or excessive inner controls; poor sublimation; precociousness; premature closure of personality; neurotic disorders; [neurotic].
12–18	GENITAL Reawakening of libidinal drives; sexual maturation.	Full and satisfying genital potency; consolidation of prior accomplishments; [mature].	Any of the above problems; impaired ability to love and work; neurotic disorders; [neurotic].

*General class of defense mechanisms, as categorized by Perry and Cooper (1989) and Vaillant (1971, 1986), are shown in brackets. (See specific defenses in Table 4–3.)

may produce insecurity, anxiety, dysthymia, distrust, fear of loneliness, etc. A significant loss during childhood, usually of a parent, may be of special etiological significance, especially in depression.

Development does not stop with adolescence; it continues through life. The patient's presenting problems may result not only from an immediate precipitant, but also from a phase-of-life, or developmental, crisis. A 40-

TABLE 4–2B
Eriksonian Psychosocial Development

AGE (years)	PERIOD	TASKS	VALUES
0–1	Infancy	Trust vs. mistrust	Hope
1–3	Toddler	Autonomy vs. shame	Will and doubt
3–6	Pre-school	Initiative vs. guilt	Purpose
6–12	School-age	Industry vs. inferiority	Skill and competence
12–20	Adolescence	Identity vs. identity diffusion/confusion	Fidelity
20–30	Young adulthood	Intimacy vs. isolation	Love
30–65	Adulthood	Generativity vs. stagnation	Care
65+	Late adulthood	Integrity vs. despair/disgust	Wisdom

year-old man may be fired and develop acute, overwhelming anxiety. Losing his job is clearly the primary precipitant, yet why he was fired and why he is *that* devastated may be secondary to a "midlife crisis."

2. *Defense mechanisms*. Sometimes called "coping mechanisms," defense mechanisms are relatively involuntary patterns of feelings, thoughts, or behaviors that arise in response to an internal or external perceived psychic danger in order to reduce or avoid conscious or unconscious stress, anxiety, or conflict. Whether a defense mechanism is adaptive depends on the defense and the circumstance. Projection is almost never adaptive, whereas sublimation is always adaptive; denial is usually maladaptive, but when the person is dealing with an overwhelming, acute stress, denial may help to maintain psychic equilibrium. Table 4–3 describes the major defense mechanisms and indicates their degree of maturity: "immature," "image-distorting," "neurotic," and "mature." Immature and image-distorting defenses are primitive and usually pathological.

3. *Intrapsychic conflict*. Freud divided the *topography* of the mind into three levels: the *unconscious*, whose mental content is rarely in awareness; the *preconscious*, the mental content of which is not immediately in awareness, but can be readily recalled by conscious effort; and the *conscious*, the mental content of which is in awareness. Freud also proposed three psychic

TABLE 4–3
Defense Mechanisms*

Acting-out is the direct expression of impulses without any apparent reflection, guilt, or regard for negative consequences. (Whereas "acting-*up*" is a lay term for misbehavior, acting-*out* is a misbehavior that is a response to, and a way of coping with, stress or conflict.) After breaking up with his girlfriend, a teenager acts-out by impulsively overdosing. [Immature]

Altruism is when people dedicate themselves to the needs of others, partly to fulfill their own needs. [Mature]

Denial is the lack of awareness of *external* realities that would be too painful to acknowledge. It differs from repression (see below), which is a denial of *internal* reality. Denial operates when a woman says, "I'm sure this lump in my breast doesn't mean anything." [Immature] Denial may be temporarily adaptive or more extreme and pathological. For example, the same woman says, "I don't really have a lump on my breast." [Image-distorting]

Devaluation is the demeaning of another or oneself by the attribution of exaggerated negative qualities. By constantly ridiculing his competence, a patient devalues a therapist to avoid facing her sexual feelings toward him. [Image-distorting]

Displacement is the discharge of pent-up emotions, usually anger, onto objects, animals, or people perceived as less dangerous than those which originally induced the emotions. A man comes home after a bad day at work and kicks the dog. [Neurotic]

Fantasy is the excessive retreat into daydreams and imagination to escape problems or to avoid conflicts (also called "autistic fantasy" or "schizoid fantasy"). [Immature]

Humor is the use of irony or amusing, incongruous, or absurd associations to reduce what otherwise might be unbearable tension or fear. An example: the character of Hawkeye Pierce in M*A*S*H, or Seinfeld. [Mature]

Idealization is the unwarranted praise of another or oneself by exaggerating virtues. "Better" to idealize a spouse than to see the jerk for what he is and be a very lonely divorcée. [Image-distorting]

Identification is the unconscious modeling of another's attributes. It differs from role modeling and imitation, which are conscious processes. Identification is used to increase one's sense of self-worth, to cope with (possible) separation or loss, or to minimize helplessness, as with "identification with the aggressor," as seen in concentration-camp prisoners who assumed the mannerisms of their Nazi guards. [Immature]

(continued)

TABLE 4–3
(Continued)

Intellectualization is the overuse of abstract thinking, which, unlike rationalization (see below), is self-serving only in its aim to reduce psychic discomfort. Alcoholics use intellectualization when they quibble over the definition of alcoholism as a way of avoiding their drinking problem. [Neurotic]

Introjection is the incorporation of other people's values, standards, or traits to prevent conflicts with, or threats from, these people. Introjection may also help a person retain a sense of connection to a lost loved one, as when people adopted John Kennedy's accent after his death. [Immature]

Isolation of affect is the compartmentalization of painful emotions from the events associated with them, thus allowing the experience or recollection of an emotionally traumatic situation, without the anxiety customarily or originally experienced. A soldier may kill without experiencing the terror or guilt he would otherwise feel. [Neurotic]

Projection is the unconscious rejection of unacceptable thoughts, traits, or wishes by ascribing them to others. [Image-distorting when delusional; immature otherwise]

Rationalization is the self-serving use of plausible reasons to justify actions caused be repressed, unacceptable emotions or ideas. Psychotherapist: "I charge a high fee so that therapy will be meaningful to the patient." [Neurotic]

Reaction formation prevents the expression or the experience of unacceptable desires by developing or exaggerating opposite attitudes and behaviors. "The lady doth protest too much." [Neurotic]

Regression is retreat under stress to earlier or more immature patterns of behavior and gratification. On hearing terrible news, an adult begins sucking his thumb. [Immature]

Repression is the exclusion from awareness of distressing feelings, impulses, ideas, or wishes. Repression is unconscious, suppression (see below) is conscious. A man is unaware that he resents his more successful wife. [Neurotic]

Somatization (hypochondriasis) is an excessive preoccupation with physical symptoms in response to psychologically stressful situations. [Immature]

Splitting is the viewing of oneself or others as all good or all bad, as opposed to being a mixture of positive and negative attributes. In splitting, the person frequently alternates between idealization and devaluation. [Image-distorting]

(continued)

TABLE 4–3
(*Continued*)

Sublimation is the gratification of a repressed instinct or unacceptable feeling by socially acceptable means. Better a surgeon than a sadist. Better a therapist than a voyeur. [Mature]

Suppression is the conscious and deliberate avoidance of disturbing matters: Scarlett O'Hara: "I'll think about it tommorrow." [Mature]

Turning against the self is when the person takes a hostile thought or impulse aimed at another and inappropriately redirects it inward. Less distress is experienced by blaming, hurting, or even mutilating the self than by feeling guilty for being furious at the other person. [Immature]

Undoing is the use of behavior or thoughts to cancel or eradicate the effect of a previous act or thought associated with a painful idea, event, or emotion. After arranging a murder, Lady Macbeth washed her hands, which had no blood on them, and said, "Out, out damn spot." [Image-distorting when delusional; otherwise neurotic or mature, depending on circumstances]

*As indicated in brackets, defense mechanisms reflect various levels of psychological organization, which Vaillant (1971), Vaillant, Bond, and Vaillant, (1986), and Perry and Cooper (1989) have categorized from the least to the most mature: immature, image-distorting, neurotic (intermediate), mature.

structures: the *id*, which harbors instinctual sexual and aggressive drives; the *superego* or conscience; and the *ego*, which mediates between these psychic structures and between the person's inner needs and the environment. Defense mechanisms are ego functions. Intrapsychic conflict involves struggles between these various levels and structures of the mind.

4. *Stress*. The body's response to any demand for adaptation is called *stress*, and the demand, a *stressor*. By itself, stress is neither good nor bad: Without stress, people stagnate or atrophy; with too much stress, they become overwhelmed. A stressor can be acute or chronic. When it is acute and severe, people react in a series of steps as depicted in Figure 4–3; these reactions may be normal or pathological, but even when normal, they may temporarily impair functioning. One need only recall the morning the Challenger exploded to remember how most people immediately reacted with either "outcry" or "denial." Chronic stressors, such as a failing marriage, though less severe at any one moment, may eventually "wear a person down" and lead to a deteriorating mental state.

5. *Behavioral*. Traditionally, the behavioral (or learning) model focused exclusively on how identifiable environmental forces influenced the production of observable behaviors. This model has expanded to include "inner behaviors" that are environmentally-induced, yet nonobservable, such as thoughts and feelings. Cognitive-behavioral and rational-emotive therapy

FIGURE 4–3
Sequential Responses to Trauma*

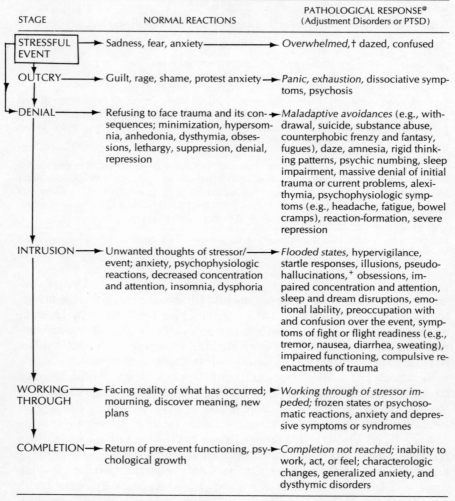

STAGE	NORMAL REACTIONS	PATHOLOGICAL RESPONSE@ (Adjustment Disorders or PTSD)
STRESSFUL EVENT	Sadness, fear, anxiety	*Overwhelmed,†* dazed, confused
OUTCRY	Guilt, rage, shame, protest anxiety	*Panic, exhaustion,* dissociative symptoms, psychosis
DENIAL	Refusing to face trauma and its consequences; minimization, hypersomnia, anhedonia, dysthymia, obsessions, lethargy, suppression, denial, repression	*Maladaptive avoidances* (e.g., withdrawal, suicide, substance abuse, counterphobic frenzy and fantasy, fugues), daze, amnesia, rigid thinking patterns, psychic numbing, sleep impairment, massive denial of initial trauma or current problems, alexithymia, psychophysiologic symptoms (e.g., headache, fatigue, bowel cramps), reaction-formation, severe repression
INTRUSION	Unwanted thoughts of stressor/event; anxiety, psychophysiologic reactions, decreased concentration and attention, insomnia, dysphoria	*Flooded states,* hypervigilance, startle responses, illusions, pseudo-hallucinations,+ obsessions, impaired concentration and attention, sleep and dream disruptions, emotional lability, preoccupation with and confusion over the event, symptoms of fight or flight readiness (e.g., tremor, nausea, diarrhea, sweating), impaired functioning, compulsive reenactments of trauma
WORKING THROUGH	Facing reality of what has occurred; mourning, discover meaning, new plans	*Working through of stressor impeded;* frozen states or psychosomatic reactions, anxiety and depressive symptoms or syndromes
COMPLETION	Return of pre-event functioning, psychological growth	*Completion not reached;* inability to work, act, or feel; characterologic changes, generalized anxiety, and dysthymic disorders

*Modified from: Horowitz, M. J. (1985). Disasters and psychological responses to stress. *Psychiatric Annals,* 15, 161–167.
@Pathological variations also include unusually intense or prolonged "normal" reactions.
†Main features are italicized.
+Pseudohallucinations are fantasized reactions in which people intensely experience something as real, despite intellectually knowing otherwise. These may be the "felt presence" of a dead grandfather or an "out-of-body" experience.

approaches use this expanded model, and some behaviorists are attempting to integrate psychodynamic with behavioral principles. Even still, behaviorism focuses on how the environment creates, shapes, changes, or alters the frequency of a behavior. A behavioral formulation would indicate whether the patient's difficulties are/were encouraged (*positively reinforced*), or discouraged or punished (*negatively reinforced*) by the environment. Often the internal environment of the person's thoughts provide their own reinforcement and punishment.

6. *Family systems.* In this model, the family is viewed as a *system*, which is a complex of interacting elements. Systems theory holds that one cannot fully understand a system (e.g., organization, family, person) by examining only its parts. What happens in one part of a system eventually reverberates and affects the others; no person is an island. In the family systems model, the patient's behavior is viewed less as the product of an intrapsychically-induced mental disorder and more the result of intrafamilial disturbances. This approach does not necessarily deny the existence of mental illness, but suggests that the confluence of forces within the family maintains, exacerbates, and perhaps even initiates it.

7. *Sociocultural.* The pathogenic role of social, cultural, political, economic, religious, racial, and gender aspects are often given shortshrift, partly because ideology tends to overwhelm the few facts that exist. Sociologists examine these matters, but usually lack training in psychopathology to place them in context, whereas mental-health professionals usually lack sociological sophistication. Therefore, clinicians should be especially careful when attributing mental pathology to social pathology (or even social normality). On the other hand, when specific social factors are responsible, their influence (for good or ill) should be recorded in the patient's biopsychosocial formulation.

CHAPTER 5

Treatment

THE MOST IMPORTANT factor in deciding treatment is the patient's diagnosis. Other factors—psychological, medical, sociocultural, ethical, intellectual, financial—influence the choice and conduct of treatment, but except for emergency interventions, no treatment should begin without a diagnosis. Conversely, although diagnosis may serve other ends, its chief purpose is to help determine treatment. Therefore, when clinicians debate a patient's diagnosis, it is important to know how a change in diagnosis will alter the patient's treatment.

WHAT DO TREATMENT PLANS INCLUDE?

Every patient should have a *treatment plan*—that is, an organized program of one or more treatments for helping the patient achieve specified objectives. The clinician should indicate the type, amount, focus, goals, and timing of each treatment.

1. The *types* include group therapy, psychoanalysis, recreational therapy, medication, "suicide precautions," "seclusion room," "school consultation," and so on. These should be specified.

2. The *amount* of treatment refers to its frequency and duration. Will psychotherapy sessions occur once or thrice a week? Will therapy continue for six weeks or six months? The dose, frequency, and duration of medication should also be indicated.

3. The *focus* refers to the specific problem(s) that treatment will address. Treatment does not, and cannot, concentrate on everything; choices and priorities must be set. Is it better to focus on a patient's alcoholism or depression? Should the etiologic focus be on childhood trauma, ongoing familial problems, or precipitating stressors?

4. The *goals* (or objectives) of each treatment should be specified; otherwise, clinicians and patients cannot know *where treatment is going, when it should end*, and *whether it has succeeded*. A goal of "helping the patient function better" is too vague, because it does not specify the areas in which the patient should function better. To report that chlorpromazine (Thorazine) is being prescribed to "treat the patient's schizophrenia" borders on poverty of content. Is the goal to eliminate hallucinations or to stop the patient from telling everyone about his hallucinations? Is it to stop delusions, elevate mood, diminish agitation, increase social interactions, make it possible to leave the hospital, or function at work? No drug should be prescribed without first specifying its target symptoms and functions.

At times, the objectives are clear, but unrealistic: "To help the patient enjoy her (thoroughly obnoxious) mother." In establishing goals, two generalizations should apply: (a) the briefer the treatment, the less ambitious the goals; and (b) the more recent the problem, the fuller and faster it will improve with treatment.

Outlining treatment goals *on paper* helps clinicians sharpen their awareness; if they can't articulate the goals clearly, they don't really know what the goals are. Discussing goals with patients before treatment begins helps patients make a more informed judgment about entering treatment and reduces unrealistic expectations of therapy. (Overexpectations of therapy may be the greatest preventable cause of malpractice suits.) When patients and therapists explicitly agree on the goals of treatment, both are more likely to be on the same "wavelength" during treatment. Clearly delineating goals also minimizes the possibilities of inpatient staff working at cross-purposes, as when an individual psychotherapist tells a teenager "to liberate himself from parental domination," while the family therapist tells his parents "to set limits on their kid."

5. The *timing* of therapies—that is, when, and in what sequence—generally follows these guidelines: Treatment should rectify biological changes before psychosocial influences, symptoms before issues, acute crises before chronic problems, and psychosis before neurosis; psychotic patients should receive supportive psychotherapy; only later, when nonpsychotic, can they benefit from insight-oriented psychotherapy. The hierarchy of *DSM-IV* diagnosis listed in Figure 3–1 can also be used as a guide to determine to which diagnosis/problem should be treated first.

Treatments cannot happen all at once, nor should they. For instance, patients with severe major depression view all information in the worst possible light; they use insights not for self-improvement but for self-punishment. During insight-oriented psychotherapy, a very proper 55-year-old woman recalled a long-forgotten affair from 30 years earlier. But instead of using this insight to unburden herself of a long-repressed guilt (as would "normal" people), she berated herself: "This proves I'm a whore and deserve to die." Like most severely depressed patients, she could benefit from insight only *after* antidepressant medications had alleviated her symptoms.

The inpatient treatment of anorexia nervosa further illustrates the importance of timing. These self-starving young females (see Chapter 16) are usually admitted because their weight has become medically precarious; since 10–15% of these patients who are hospitalized die prematurely, regaining weight is a medical necessity and the first goal of treatment. Yet, on first meeting these patients, clinicians are often struck by their "goodie two-shoes" personae that conceal highly-charged feelings about their mothers. So startling are these issues that clinicians are tempted to explore them immediately, but when immediately addressed, patients usually become so distressed, they actually lose weight. Only after their weight is stabilized can patients benefit from examining these issues.

THREE LEVELS OF TREATMENT

Psychiatric treatment occurs in three stages: biological, psychosocial, and moral-existential. First, if needed, the psychiatrist prescribes medication to rectify *biological* abnormalities. Second, the therapist performs psychotherapies to address *psychosocial* problems. Third, the therapist uses the clinician-patient relationship to demonstrate that he or she values the patient as a person—the *moral-existential* dimension of therapy (Abroms, 1983).

This three-stage model holds that biological and psychosocial treatments are both valuable, albeit in *different* ways. To argue that talk therapy is better than drug therapy (or vice versa) is pointless; they serve different functions. Group therapy frequently helps diabetics cope with their illness, yet nobody would suggest that such groups regulate blood sugar; conversely, insulin regulates blood sugar, yet nobody would suggest it helps diabetics cope with their illness. Just as group therapy and insulin help patients with diabetes in different ways, so do psychotherapies and biotherapies help patients with mental disorders. Excellent therapists can have very different interests (e.g., psychoanalysis, medications), but still appreciate that each treatment serves a distinct purpose.

In general, biological therapies eliminate or alleviate *symptoms*, such as a depressive's insomnia, a schizophrenic's delusions, or a manic's spending sprees; psychosocial therapies usually address *issues*, such as coping with job losses, a failed marriage, medical condition or psychiatric disorder. When used properly, biological and psychosocial therapies do not impede, but facilitate, one another. Repeated evidence has shown that medications do not increase patients' passivity, decrease motivation, or diminish involvement in psychotherapy. Correctly medicated patients gain more from psychotherapy. Wildly hallucinating schizophrenics feel so bombarded by stimuli that they cannot focus sufficiently to benefit from psychotherapy; once medicated, they can.

Conversely, psychotherapies can accomplish what drugs cannot. They can teach patients about their mental disorders—their symptoms, dangers, causes, and precipitants. Psychotherapies can alert patients to situations that are likely to retrigger an illness, help patients understand what their conditions mean to them, improve patients' willingness to adhere to the psychiatric treatment plan (e.g., taking medication), facilitate social adjustment, interpersonal relationships, leisure-time pleasures, and occupational skills, heighten self-esteem, guide ambition, and enhance well-being. Finally, psychotherapeutic investigation can reveal how previous experiences affect current difficulties. A patient who cannot figure out why terrible things keep happening to her—why people are rude to her, why men avoid her, why nobody will hire her—can be shown why these events happen, what she can do about them, and how she can regain control over her life.

The moral-existential aspects of therapy do not involve particular treatments or occur during specified periods. Instead, they prevail throughout therapy, pervading both biological and psychosocial treatments. To quote Abroms (1983), moral-existential interventions involve the "realm of pure value, where the ultimate aim is integrity of the person. . . . [They entail] moral qualities of trust and gratitude, of loyalty and devotion, and above all, of respect . . . the therapist becomes firm in the resolve to stand by the patient, even to tolerate a measure of moral failure." While therapists may not condone their patients' behaviors and choices, they accept patients for who they are. Once patients fully understand what their choices are, they must make an existential decision. Sometimes they may decide not to change, or at least not at this time. Therapists must learn to accept such decisions.

OVERALL GUIDELINES FOR SELECTING TREATMENTS

Treatment selection should be based primarily on pragmatic, rather than on etiologic, considerations. Some of the major difficulties of linking treatment with an etiological theory are as follows: (a) The cause of most mental disorders is unknown. (b) The treatment must then be consistent with the theory, which may determine what can and cannot be treated. For example, Freud's early feelings about schizophrenia excluded this illness from the scope of psychoanalytic therapy. (c) A total commitment to any single etiological theory and its accompanying treatments limits the therapist's

range of interventions. (d) The goals of therapy often become the fulfill-
ment of a theory rather than what the patient actually needs or desires. (e)
Even if a disorder's etiology were known, therapies addressing it are unlikely to rectify the patient's current disorder. For example, a man who is
chronically depressed because he was deprived (or depraved) as a child
might find that further insight into his childhood cannot alter the many
self-destructive patterns that he has developed over the years. When theory
prevails over pragmatism, a therapist may insist that a patient who feels
and functions substantially better has not "really" improved because the
patient has not accepted the origins of his problem and that, as long as he
continues to "resist," he will never improve. In other words, the patient
can't get better unless he "buys" the therapist's theory.

To serve up pragmatically-based treatments, one should follow (Bill)
Tilden's Law: "Never change a winning game." If a treatment works, don't
change it; if a treatment doesn't work, do change it. Tilden's Law does not
mean that clinicians should alter treatments every time patients have set-
backs, but it does mean that if patients fail to improve following an ample
trial with a particular treatment, another treatment should be tried. For
example, even if a patient "should" respond to antidepressant medications,
if she doesn't, she doesn't, and a different treatment should be attempted.
Or, if a patient has failed to improve after three trials of insight-oriented
psychotherapy with three different therapists, chances are that a fourth trial
of insight-oriented therapy won't help; however, another treatment, such as
behavior, cognitive, or drug therapy, might help.

When pragmatically-chosen treatments are based on *scientific evidence*
instead of on intuition or theory, they have the greatest chance of being
effective. For instance, studies show that if a patient's biological relative
has improved with a particular drug, so will the patient. "Scientific," however, is not synonymous with "biological"; although medications are more
amenable to scientific investigation, over 400 well-controlled, quantified
studies have evaluated psychotherapy.

Scientific studies of social relations can also guide the treatment of patients. For
example, before discharging inpatients, staff must decide how much patients should
change their lives during the immediate post-hospital stage. One investigation
(Breier & Strauss, 1984) indicated the answer was "very little." This research reported that discharged psychotic patients go through two stages: First, a period of
convalescence, in which they mainly see themselves as "ex-patients" and maintain
contacts with hospital staff and former patients. During the second stage of *rebuilding*, these patients view themselves more as members of society and less as "ex-
patients"; key relationships are formed with people in the community instead of
with former hospital associations. In general, patients fare much better when ther-

apy fosters stability during the convalescence stage and does not encourage patients to make changes until they enter the rebuilding stage.

Most acutely psychotic patients benefit more from psychotherapeutic contacts that are relatively simple, clear, and brief. These patients are frequently overwhelmed by external stimuli, have trouble distinguishing reality from fantasy, often confuse their outer with their inner world, and have short attention spans. Thus, insight-oriented therapies rarely help, but frequently harm, the acutely psychotic; reality testing is more beneficial. If a patient says, "I'm the worst sinner on earth," the therapist can empathize with the patient's emotional state, but still test (or clarify) reality: "I understand how miserable you feel, but I don't think you're a sinner." Sessions should be shorter and more frequent: An extremely psychotic patient with a short attention span may profit more from five, 10-minute contacts a day, than from the classical, once-a-day, 50-minute hour.

Acutely ill patients should also be discouraged from making any important life decisions, especially if the decisions are irreversible. This does not mean that therapists should run their patients' lives, nor that *all* patients in therapy should place major decisions on hold. Therapists should only intervene when a patient's judgment is severely impaired by a mental disorder.

Every axis in *DSM-IV* highlights a key issue for planning treatment. In setting treatment goals, clinicians distinguish between Axes I and II, since diagnoses on Axis I usually respond more readily to treatment than those on Axis II. Treatment plans address the stressors in Axis IV and use the highest level of functioning on Axis V for determining treatment goals.

Axis III disorders should not be overlooked, especially by nonpsychiatrists: Depending on the study, physical problems are the *chief* cause of psychiatric symptoms among 9% to 18% of psychiatric outpatients and among 5% to 28% of psychiatric inpatients; an additional 25% of patients have medical problems which *aggravate* their psychiatric problem; as many as 42% of psychiatric outpatients and over 50% of psychiatric inpatients are physically ill. In comparison to the general public, not only are psychiatric patients afflicted by more medical problems, but more of these problems go undiagnosed, and for many reasons: Psychiatric patients give poorer medical histories, have more trouble using medical resources, and if they look sloppy or crazy, physicians are less likely to examine them closely. What's more, when it comes to psychiatric patients, mental- and medical-health professionals tend to ignore physical problems (Hoffman & Koran, 1984).

PSYCHOLOGICAL CLUES

During assessment, clinicians should sprout antennae for seven psychopathological clues that facilitate both biological and psychosocial treatments.

1. *Locus of responsibility*: Patients who always view others as responsible for their difficulties — so-called "externalizers" — do poorly in psychotherapy and are less cooperative in taking medication. Patients can change themselves much more readily than they can change others.

2. *Habitual view of "helping" figures*: How patients feel about other "helping" figures — doctors, nurses, teachers, parents — may predict how they will behave toward the therapist. Some patients are highly suspicious of helping figures. The paranoid wonders, "What's the *real* reason this therapist claims he likes me and wants to help?" With suspicious patients, therapists should keep a safe psychological distance to prevent what patients might experience as phony intimacy. These patients are also allergic to interpretations that are too frequent or probing, viewing them as too intrusive and the therapist as "playing with my head." Conversely, for patients who view helping figures as omnipotent, unending sources of gratification and dependency, therapists should avoid becoming swamped by their needs by limiting phone calls and not scheduling too many sessions at the outset of treatment. (Sessions can always be added.)

3. *Defense mechanisms and coping patterns*: Patients who rely on more immature defense mechanisms, such as projection and massive denial, are more likely to not benefit from, and to be harmed by, insight-oriented psychotherapy. Because past behavior is the best predictor of future behavior, therapists should ask, "How have you handled major problems and stresses in the past?" Therapists can then decide if patients have used avoidance, denial, overcompensation (i.e., reaction formation), or intellectualization. These responses often predict "flights into health," in which after several sessions, patients dramatically improve and want to stop therapy; this first blush of relief quickly pales as they discover that their old problems remain.

4. *Patient expectations of treatment*: Although knowing what patients expect of therapy affects treatment planning, there is surprisingly little evidence confirming the popular assumption that therapeutic outcome is directly related to these initial expectations (Bloch, Bond, Qualls, Yalom, & Zimmerman, 1976; Wilkins, 1973a, 1973b). Thus, just because patients anticipate a treatment won't work, that doesn't automatically mean it will fail. (Of course, negative expectations are no guarantee of success!)

If the patient or therapist is unsure if psychotherapy holds promise, the clinician may recommend an initial *trial period* of (roughly) six weekly sessions. Each party can see if the "chemistry" between them is likely to be therapeutic. A formal trial period allows both parties to begin therapy without feeling committed to years of treatment. As long as therapists do not make patients feel as if they are "on trial," a trial period allows each person a graceful way to terminate treatment. This approach is particularly helpful with certain male patients who are fearful of establishing a dependency relationship like therapy and are quite uncomfortable talking about their feelings.

5. *Follow the affect*: By noting what is being discussed *when* the patient's affect abruptly changes, the therapist can discern, from among many issues, the ones of prime import to the patient. For instance, a man claims he's gotten over a divorce yet breaks down and weeps when mentioning his former wife. Usually nonverbal, these telltale affective switches may be subtle—a tear is shed, a cigarette lit, a leg moved, a body tensed. Therapists can gain considerable information by sensitively pursuing any topic that suddenly triggers an intense affect.

6. *Follow the associations*: When patients jump to apparently unrelated topics, or when they keep returning to the same topic, that topic deserves attention. To illustrate: While continually harping about his daughter's failure to apply to medical school, a 65-year-old man kept raising the topic of his own retirement. Initially, the connection between these two concerns was unclear; but exploring the association revealed the man's rage at his daughter for "giving up." Realizing this, he stopped being angry at his daughter and could more objectively consider retirement.

7. *The therapist as "emotional barometer"*: How a therapist feels toward a patient is often, though not always, a reliable indication of how most people feel about the patient. If the therapist is constantly irritated by a patient, even if the therapist doesn't know precisely how or why, the patient is probably irritating. (If the therapist is irritated by *all* her patients, then the problem lies with the therapist, not the patient. In psychoanalytic terms, this is called *countertransference* and it means the therapist might need therapy.) The therapist's reactions to a patient are not irrelevant feelings but germane clinical data. For instance, when a paranoid patient emotionally attacks a therapist, the patient may be conveying, however unconsciously, how he always feels under attack in the "real" world. In many cases, the therapist picks up the patient's feelings. The task is to use these feelings as data about what the patient is experiencing, what the world looks like through his eyes.

A SUMMARY OF PSYCHIATRIC TREATMENTS

Despite the ever-increasing number of therapies—over 250 by one recent count—in reality, the commonly used treatments of any enduring importance have not changed very much over the years. These treatments are listed in Table 5–1 and briefly described below.

TABLE 5–1
Modern Psychiatric Treatments

I. BIOLOGICAL THERAPIES

  A. Medication
    1. Antipsychotics (e.g., chlorpromazine, haloperidol)
    2. Antidepressants
      a. Tricyclics (TCAs) and multicyclics (e.g., imiprimine, amitriptyline)
      b. Selective serotonin re-uptake inhibitors (SSRIs) (e.g., fluoxetine, sertra-line, paroxetine, fluvoxamine)
      c. Monoamine oxidase inhibitors (MAOIs) (e.g., phenelzine)
      d. Atypical (e.g., trazodone, bupropion, venlafaxine)
    3. Anticycling agents (e.g., lithium, carbamazepine, valproic acid, and cal-cium channel blockers)
    4. Hypnoanxiolytics (e.g., benzodiazepines)
      a. Antianxiety agents (e.g., diazepam, alprazolam)
      b. Hypnotics (e.g., flurazepam, temazepam)
      c. Atypical anxiolytics—azapirones (e.g., buspirone)
      d. Atypical hypnotics (e.g., zolpidem)
  B. Electroconvulsive Therapy (ECT)

II. PSYCHOSOCIAL THERAPIES

  A. Individual Treatments
    1. Psychoanalysis
    2. Insight-oriented psychotherapy
    3. Supportive psychotherapy/counseling
    4. Short-term psychotherapies
    5. Cognitive and cognitive-behavioral therapies
  B. Group Treatments
    1. Psychotherapy
    2. Self-help (e.g., Alcoholics Anonymous, Recovery)
  C. Couples and Family Treatments
    1. Counseling
    2. Therapies
    3. Multiple family (or couples) group therapy

III. BEHAVIOR THERAPIES

    1. Biofeedback
    2. Relaxation (e.g., progressive relaxation)
    3. Systematic desensitization
    4. Operant conditioning (e.g., token economy)

IV. HYPNOTHERAPY

VI. NO TREATMENT

BIOLOGICAL TREATMENTS

There are four major classes of psychiatric (i.e., psychotropic) medications: antipsychotics, antidepressants (tricyclics, heterocyclics, selective serotonin re-uptake inhibitors, monoamine oxidase inhibitors), lithium, and hypnoanxiolytics.[1] (Appendix G lists the names and doses of the most frequently prescribed medications; Appendix H, their side effects.)

Modern psychopharmacology began in 1954 with the release of chlorpromazine (Thorazine), an antipsychotic. Before then, only hypnoanxiolytics (mainly barbiturates) were used. Most hypnoanxiolytics have virtually the same effect on everyone: They calm people, quell anxiety, and induce sleep. Except for the new, purer, atypical agents, buspirone (only for anxiety) and zolpidem (only for sleep), they can be used interchangeably for sleep or anxiety. On occasion, hypnoanxiolytics have a disinhibiting effect (of the four major types of psychotropic medications, only hypnoanxiolytics are addictive). In contrast, the other three classes of psychoactive drugs affect *specific* symptoms of mental disorders. For example, unlike hypnoanxiolytics, chlorpromazine eliminates hallucinations and delusions. Similarly, heterocyclic antidepressants, such as imipramine (Tofranil) and SSRIs, help patients with major and bipolar depressions, but they do not make normal people feel happier or alleviate everyday human sadness. When "normals" take lithium, they notice little effect, yet when manics take lithium, their frenetic activity and grandiosity diminish. Thus, the value of psychotropic agents is restricted to particular symptoms of particular mental disorders.

In general, antipsychotics treat psychoses seen in schizophrenia, delusional disorders, medical conditions, substance abuse, and mania. Heterocyclic antidepressants, selective serotonin re-uptake inhibitors, and atypical antidepressants treat major and bipolar depressions; they also prevent panic attacks and phobias. Monoamine oxidase inhibitors (MAOIs) help patients with major and atypical depressions, panic attacks, and social phobias. SSRIs, one tricyclic (clomipramine), and the MAOIs can reduce symptoms of obsessive-compulsive disorder. Lithium, carbamazepine, and valproic

---

[1]Some of these classes go by other names: Antipsychotics are also known as "neuroleptics" and "major tranquilizers," the latter term being a misnomer since tranquilization is not their chief function, and many of them do not even tranquilize. Hypnoanxiolytics are also called "minor tranquilizers," which falsely implies they are a less powerful version of "major tranquilizers." Sedative-hypnotic is another common name, but this implies only a sedating effect rather than a purer anxiolytic effect. When used as anxiolytics during the day, the sedating effects wear off in 7 to 14 days. The pharmacological distinction between typical antianxiety agents and hypnotics is slim; because they can be used interchangeably for sleep and anxiety, the term *hypnoanxiolytic* is used in this book.

acid prevent and attenuate the highs and lows of bipolar disorder. All three agents work better on the highs than the lows and take effect in five to 10 days. Hypnoanxiolytic agents reduce anxiety, induce sleep, and decrease nocturnal awakenings. Electroconvulsive therapy treats severe depressions and can stop a severe mania.

Despite the many anecdotal claims that enormous doses of vitamin C, niacin, pyridoxine, and vitamin B_{12} do wonders for mental illness, unfortunately all the controlled scientific studies refute these assertions (American Psychiatric Association, 1973) (*unfortunately*, because it would be wonderful to cure mental illness with relatively harmless vitamin treatments). Occasionally, a pyridoxine (B_6) deficiency, caused by agents such as estrogen in oral contraceptives, may cause depression, which will then respond to pyridoxine supplements.

PSYCHOSOCIAL TREATMENTS

This text defines psychosocial treatments as the informed and systematic application of techniques based on established psychological principles, by professionals who are trained and experienced to understand these principles and to apply these techniques to modify feelings, thoughts, and behaviors deemed maladaptive.

With so many psychosocial treatments (and so many defended passionately), one can easily overlook their similarities. Both explicitly and implicitly, psychosocial treatments all involve a contract and a degree of rapport and trust between a supposed expert and a patient or client with emotional or behavioral problems. Whether or not the patient has symptoms, all treatments seek to combat demoralization by restoring the patient's sense of mastery; and they all derive from a particular theory or set of principles in which both parties have some faith. Most therapists are not exclusive practitioners of one particular school of therapy, but instead combine approaches depending on the patient's needs.

In preparing patients for psychotherapy—whatever particular treatments are utilized—two questions should be answered before therapy is formally begun: (1) Are there realistic goals that can be reached? (2) What is this therapy all about; how should I act and how will you act? The activity of agreeing on realistic goals can be therapeutic in itself. The patient may feel better now that this "great blob of bad feeling" is being sorted out by somebody who seems to understand. Almost all patients have unspoken misconceptions about therapy that can be corrected. At this stage, unrealistic expectations such as, "I really want to learn how to change my mother," or "You are wise, just tell me what to do," can be dealt with before they undermine the therapy. A patient may come to agree on a preliminary goal such as, "I can only change myself," or "I am not here to attain enlightenment but rather to control my negative thoughts." Later, more specific goals can be established. Preparing patients for what to expect in therapy has been shown to reduce the duration of therapy and result in better outcomes (Yalom, 1985). Too often patients are told to say whatever comes to mind, only to find that talking about the weather and baseball scores wasn't the idea. Patients need to be told how they can behave in order to get the most out of treatment and what they can expect from the therapist.

Individual Psychotherapies

There are three basic types of psychotherapies that involve a single patient: psychoanalysis, insight-oriented psychotherapy, and supportive psychotherapy. (For clarity, the distinctions between these therapies drawn below are somewhat overstated.)

Psychoanalysis. "Free association" is the cardinal rule of psychoanalysis — that is, without self-censorship, the patient should say whatever comes to mind, including dreams, fantasies, early memories, current experiences, or feelings about the analyst (i.e., transference). Psychoanalysis aims to heal by uncovering as much as possible about how the patient's mind functions. The patient reclines on a couch; the analyst sits behind the patient so that no nonverbal signals influence the patient's free associations. By deliberately acting as a "blank screen" and not as a "real person," the analyst assumes that everything the patient attributes to him or her are projections of the patient rather than qualities of the analyst.

Psychoanalysis requires three to five meetings a week. It is prescribed for "problems in living," and for mild to moderate depression, anxiety, and obsessiveness, which does not interfere with more than one of the three main areas of functioning — familial, occupational, and recreational. The patient must be bright, introspective, usually under the age of 50, a good abstract thinker, nonpsychotic, and in general, able to pay roughly $14,000/year. For most, this treatment is an expensive luxury. It is like having a car that isn't running quite right overhauled, when a tune-up might have been enough.

Insight-oriented psychotherapy. In what is also called *psychodynamic* or *psychoanalytic psychotherapy*, clinicians address the patient's difficulties by primarily relying on insight — bringing unconscious or unclear material into sharp awareness. In comparison to psychoanalysis, the patient sits face-to-face with the therapist, has one or two sessions a week, does not free associate, and pays more attention to the realities of current life than to dreams and childhood recollections. The patient should be nonpsychotic, introspective, intelligent, and capable of abstract thought.

Psychodynamic psychotherapy is best used for problems in living, neurotic symptoms, and ego-dystonic character traits. Like psychoanalysis, a successful insight-oriented therapy does not eliminate every problem or bestow "perfect mental health." Problems are inherent to the human condition and perfect mental health does not exist. By therapy's end, however, the patient should have developed more realistic and flexible ways of dealing with and reconciling personal needs and environmental demands; psychic pain, especially when the patient produces it "unnecessarily," should be reduced; the patient should leave understanding why "bad things" were happening and how to avoid similar pitfalls in the future; lastly, the patient should have acquired a framework for continued self-reflection and problem solving.

Supportive psychotherapy/counseling. Whereas psychodynamic psychotherapy stresses insight, supportive psychotherapy emphasizes advice, education, persuasion, reason, and other appeals to conscious processes to alleviate current and practical life difficulties. This is generally what is meant by the term *counseling.* The therapist supports the patient's more mature defenses and adaptive capacities and discourages immature defenses and maladaptive behaviors. To benefit, patients need not be particularly introspective, intelligent, or able to think abstractly, but they do need to have a willingness to change, to examine themselves, and to show up for usually one to four sessions a month.

During an acute psychosis, supportive psychotherapy is the verbal therapy of choice; it provides reality testing, emotional comfort, and help in distinguishing between sensible and senseless ideas, feelings, and actions. After an acute episode, supportive psychotherapy can show patients how to prevent a relapse by avoiding situations that are likely to precipitate symptoms. For instance, after enduring several bouts of major depression, many patients become so adept at identifying the earliest symptoms that they can avert a full-fledged (9–12 months) relapse by calling their psychiatrist, resuming medication, and examining their concerns with the help of professional perspective.

Short-term therapy. This is a time-limited treatment (usually 8–20 sessions) that focuses on a clearly delineated problem which has erupted recently (within the past two months), and the goals of which are specified and agreed on from the outset. There are numerous models of short-term therapy, including behavioral, cognitive, interpersonal, and insight-oriented. These therapies often focus on the same goals and problem areas but differ in the type and timing of interventions (Ursano & Hales, 1986).

Depending on whether it suppresses or provokes anxiety, short-term psychotherapy may stress support or insight. When supportive, short-term psychotherapy helps people get over acute problems and maintain the psychological status quo. When educational, patients may learn about thoughts and behaviors that interfere with their functioning and how to replace them with more adaptive ones. An example: A patient procrastinates responding to a complaint and the complainer gets increasingly angry. In educational therapy, the patient learns how to respond to the complaint, which makes her less anxious and less likely to delay responding. When combined with other biological or psychosocial treatments, this therapy becomes part of a crisis intervention program. Insight-oriented, short-term psychotherapy typically examines a "focal conflict"—a recent and well-defined wish that conflicts with the person's enduring traits. For instance, Ernest Borgnine's ("What are we going to do tonight?") Marty suddenly faces a focal conflict when he meets a woman and must choose between Mom or marriage. Anxiety-provoking short-term psychotherapy would focus on this choice, but not on other related yet more peripheral issues in Marty's life, such as his painfully low self-esteem. The brevity of this therapy helps keep the patient more intensively focused.

Cognitive therapy. Cognitive therapy blends elements of psychotherapy and behavior therapy. "Cognition" means "the process of knowing or perceiving." Cognitive theory assumes that patients' faulty perceptions and attitudes about the world and themselves precede and produce pathological moods—anxiety, depression, worry, guilt, etc. In cognitive therapy, whether a glass is half-empty or half-full all depends on one's glasses (rose-tinted or gray?).

The cognitive therapist identifies the habitual ways in which patients distort information. They make mountains out of molehills, project their own fears onto others, or see things in the worst possible light. These patterns, which are called "automatic thoughts," are accompanied by "automatic emotions" such as dread, worry, and tension. The cognitive therapist teaches patients to recognize their usual patterns of automatic thoughts, the emotions that go with them, the situations that produce them, and then how to view the same information in more rational and healthy ways.

Cognitive therapy is used most often to treat mild to moderately severe depressions, anxiety, panic attacks, and phobias (Beck, Rush, Shaw, & Emery, 1979). Throughout the typical 10 to 25 weekly sessions, patients record episodes at home that led to troublesome feelings and thoughts, and at the following session, the cognitive distortions creating them are examined. It is frequently and effectively combined with behavior therapy (to be described).

A student social worker entered cognitive therapy for a moderate depression that intensified when she started her placement on a psychiatric inpatient service. A typical exchange between her and the therapist:

PATIENT: [situation] On my very first day on the ward, a patient asked me if his medication should be changed. I freaked.
THERAPIST: When you were freaking, what did you think about?
PATIENT: [automatic thoughts] I felt like an idiot. That I can't even answer a

simple question, and if I can't do that, then maybe I shouldn't be a therapist. [automatic emotions] I felt terrible, filled with shame and guilt.

THERAPIST: [Pointing out a more rational thought]: But you're a social work student, not a trained physician. Why should you know about this medication?

PATIENT: [Automatic thought] Maybe, but then the patient asked me when he'd be discharged and I felt like a fool for not knowing the answer.

THERAPIST: In retrospect, do you believe your feeling was justified?

PATIENT: [Rational thought] No. That's silly! Why should I know when he'd be discharged: I had just arrived on the ward two hours earlier. He's not even my patient!!

Behind this is a bigger thought: "I should know everything. If I don't, that means I'm stupid and everybody will think I'm stupid."

Group Treatments

Group psychotherapy. More than any other treatment, group therapy is ideally suited to address *interpersonal* difficulties (Yalom, 1985). Methods vary, but generally patients learn how they affect others and practice better ways of relating to people. Once patients have become comfortable using these new behaviors in the safety of the group, they can try them out in the "real" world. A typical session lasts 60–90 minutes, occurs once a week for outpatients (three to five times a week for inpatients), has six to ten members, and is led by one or two therapists.[2]

Surveyed patients claim that groups help most by giving them a sense of belonging and by showing them they are not the only ones in the world facing difficulties. However, psychotic patients and people who are extremely sensitive to personal slights or to feelings of persecution are likely to panic or become further disorganized if the group becomes too intense. Narcissistic, paranoid, or rigidly moralistic patients generally do poorly in therapy groups and are quickly ostracized by other patients.

Self-help groups. Alcoholics Anonymous, Recovery, and various drug programs run self-help groups that focus on a single problem and are led by the group members themselves. Some psychiatrists criticize these groups for their dubious efficacy, evangelistic nature, lack of trained leadership, and avoidance of scientific scrutiny. Nonetheless, many self-help groups assist patients who are alcoholics and drug addicts, whom many therapists don't like or can't help.[3]

---

[2]Group psychotherapy differs from (a) *encounter groups*, which help normals with consciousness-raising and self-actualization, and (b) *T-groups* (the *T* stands for *training*), which teach normals how groups function (group process) by having them participate in the group.

[3]To obtain information about any self-help group, contact the National Self-Help Clearinghouse, 33 West 42nd St., New York, NY 10036 (212) 354-8525.

Couples and Family Treatments

With these treatments, a convenient distinction is made between "counseling" and "therapy." Couples and family *counseling* is used if the psychopathology mainly resides within the patient, or if the couple or family had been functioning normally but now are doing poorly as a result of a crisis. If the psychopathology is enduring and resides within the couple or family, couples or family *therapy* should be used. Changes in behaviors and interpersonal interactions are the goal.

Whether or not the family has played a major role in producing the disorder, counseling is based on the assumptions that there is a patient with a mental disorder who disrupts the family members, and who, in turn, may act "neurotically," unwisely, or harmfully. Family members are not viewed as victimizers. In a sense, everybody is a victim. Counseling usually helps family members to solve problems, to minimize psychological trauma to other family members, and to deal more constructively with the patient's disorder. Family members, for example, might learn to stop telling a depressed member to "pick yourself up by your bootstraps," but that it *is* okay to ask her to do a few chores or join the family on an outing.

In family therapy, clinicians think of patients as the "identified patient," implying that the real patient is the family and that the identified patient is merely its most vulnerable member. In this view, the family is as much an unwitting victimizer as a victim. Therapy tries to rectify distorted communications and relationships within a couple or a family as a means of helping the entire family, including the "identified" patient.

Multiple family group therapy. This format of group therapy generally consists of four to seven families meeting with two or more therapists for 60 to 90 minutes. These families typically have a hospitalized relative on the same unit. The meetings occur once or twice a week and usually include the hospitalized patients.

In many respects, multiple family group therapy offers something other treatments cannot: It affords relatives a chance to see that they are not alone in the world, to share mutual problems with a uniquely sympathetic audience, to learn how other families cope with similar problems, and to feel more hopeful by observing other patients' improvement. Conversely, this group format enables inpatients to see what other patients' families are like; as a result, when patients talk to one another outside of the multiple family group—informally or in group therapy—they can speak with firsthand knowledge of their families.

BEHAVIOR THERAPIES

Behavior therapy is any treatment that attempts to alter quantifiable behavior, whether external (e.g., smoking) or internal (e.g., thoughts, feelings), by systematically changing the environment that produces the behavior. Generally speaking, in behavior therapy changed behaviors are believed to lead to changed feelings (and attitudes), whereas in psychotherapy changed feelings (and attitudes) are believed to lead to changed behaviors. A simplified example of a patient with an elevator phobia can be used to illustrate the difference between the two approaches. In behavior therapy, the patient is led gradually into an elevator, first mentally and then physically, and *after* each step, he discusses his new feelings and attitudes. In insight-oriented therapy, the same patient would explore how he feels about elevators, understand what riding in them unconsciously represents (e.g., independence), and only then begin to ride in an elevator.

The distinctions between behavior therapies and psychotherapies are more semantic than real, more professional than clinical. Psychotherapies emerged from a medical (and thus, psychiatric) tradition, whereas behavior therapies have their origins in experimental psychology. In any effective therapy new behavior always changes feelings, and vice versa. To varying extents, all psychotherapies address behavior and all behavior therapies address feelings. As the fields of behaviorism, psychoanalysis, and even psychobiology increasingly influence each other, techniques are often called "behavioral" more from tradition than from anything else.

In *biofeedback*, an electronic instrument informs the patient about changes in one or more physiologic variables that she does not normally perceive, such as brainwave activity and blood pressure. A patient with tension headaches, for example, can identify tension in her facial muscles by the sound of beeps from a biofeedback machine, which reflect the degree of this tension. She then experiments with different mental activities (e.g., fantasizing lying on a beach, deep breathing, humming "Oooooooooommmmm") to see which decreases the frequency of beeps, indicating diminished facial tension and headaches. Biofeedback is mainly used to treat psychophysiologic disorders.

In *relaxation* techniques, such as "progressive relaxation," a patient learns how to systematically contract each muscle group in his body and then fully relax it. These exercises, which resemble meditation techniques, can reduce anxiety and induce sleep. They are also used in conjunction with another behavioral technique for treating phobias, *systematic desensitization*, in which the patient is gradually exposed to a hierarchy of feared images. If the patient is phobic about cats, the therapist might say after the patient relaxes, "Picture a cat 100 yards away — that is, the full length of a football field." Once the patient can do this without becoming tense, the therapist might say, "Now imagine this cat 75 yards away." This progressive desensitization process is continued so that, after the patient is able to imagine touching a cat, he may be exposed to cats in photos, and then to cats in real life (*in vivo*). It is this *in vivo* step that is critical for success. In fact, some patients can skip the progressive relaxation step and go straight to the *in vivo* part when accompanied by a trusted person.

Operant conditioning is a process of systematically rewarding and reinforcing positive behaviors. An *operant* is a behavior shaped by its consequence. *Positive reinforcement* is a procedure that uses consequences for increasing operant behaviors. For example, by repeating a routine, a stand-up comic learns which jokes elicit laughs and which do not: The audience's laughter, which is a consequence, positively reinforces certain jokes, which become operants.

With her behavior therapist, a bulimic may discover that bingeing and vomiting reduces anxiety or boredom, thus reinforcing the harmful behaviors. The behavior therapist helps the patient find other activities that reduce anxiety or boredom (such as taking a warm shower, going for a walk, calling a friend). Substitution of the benign activities helps reduce the frequency of binges.

Token economies are programs that systematically apply operant conditioning. They are used most often to prepare chronically hospitalized schizophrenic patients or mentally retarded people for living in the community. When these patients display adaptive behaviors, they receive tokens, which they can exchange for desired goods (e.g., candy) and privileges (e.g., watching TV). This positive reinforcement supposedly conditions patients to perform adaptive behaviors (operants) in response to society's natural rewards (e.g., praise) without needing tokens.

HYPNOTHERAPY

Hypnosis is a state of hypersuggestibility in which the patient is relatively oblivious to everything except the hypnotist's voice. Hypnosis is *not* sleep, but a form of intense, restricted alertness. The "power" of hypnosis lies within the subject, not the hypnotist. When a person says, "You can't hypnotize me," he is correct. Psychological (and probably neurological) variables affect the patient's ability to enter a trance (Pettinati et al., 1990). The hypnotist cannot "control" the patient. [4]

Although the public often views hypnosis as a magic potion that, without any time or effort, will remedy every human affliction, its clinical efficacy is far more limited. Nonetheless, hypnosis can be helpful in treating habits such as overeating and smoking. When psychotherapy with a patient becomes "stuck," hypnosis can be used to accelerate information-giving. Hypnosis is generally ill-advised for patients who are currently or potentially psychotic.

NO TREATMENT

"All that's therapy isn't therapeutic." This dictum of Thomas Detre's receives too little attention. All treatments, including psychosocial treatments, have side effects. Abraham Kardiner (1977) wrote, "Freud was always infuriated whenever I would say to him that you could not do harm

---

[4]Most people have experienced hypnosis without realizing it. In driving long distances at night on a highway, the driver will "glaze over" and then suddenly jerk awake to attention. When "glazed over," the driver is in a light hypnotic trance, focused on the road and oblivious to everything else.

with psychoanalysis. He said, 'When you say that, you also say that it cannot do any good. Because if you cannot do any harm, how can you do good?'" (p.69) Clinical experience confirms Freud's observation: An upsurge of repressed thoughts or primitive feelings can exacerbate psychotic, neurotic, and affective symptoms. Patients can become overly dependent on therapists or "addicted" to therapy; they may substitute therapists for friends and therapy for living. For some patients, insight becomes an excuse to avoid change, while others misuse it as punishment, not learning. Thus, in devising treatment plans, clinicians should weigh a therapy's potential hazards and benefits, and for certain patients conclude that "no treatment" is the prescription of choice.

Sometimes no treatment is the best treatment, not because therapy would harm, but because it would most likely fail. Many patients with psychosomatic problems are not helped by therapy, nor are those with the personality disorders (especially antisocial personality disorder). Too often, somaticizing patients emerge from therapy "psychologizing" their problems — and newly equipped with a whole new list of symptoms and issues. The same often applies to the "unmotivated,"[5] and to those seeking compensation, disability, or a lawsuit. Some people, like those seen during bereavement or an acute crisis, will improve without therapy if they have supportive friends. Thus, don't assume that every patient needs, or will benefit from, treatment, and don't forget that a failed treatment hurts more than no treatment.

DOES THERAPY WORK?

Strange how people say, "I don't believe in psychiatry." No one says, "I don't believe in surgery." That's because everyone knows that surgery helps sometimes, but not at other times: It depends on the patient, the illness, the goals of surgery, and the surgeon. The same holds true for psychiatric treatment: Whether it helps depends on the patient, the disorder, the goals of treatment, and the therapist.

Also strange is asserting, "I don't believe in psychiatry," as if it were a matter of theology, as in "I don't believe in God." Patients should evaluate their therapy by trusting their own judgment, not as a question of faith. They can ask themselves if, given reasonable expectations and sufficient time, treatment seems to be helping or not.

---

[5]Clinicians should think twice when explaining a failed treatment because the patient was "unmotivated." The patient may be unmotivated, but after all, it is the therapist's job to motivate — that's what makes a treatment successful!

What is meant by the assertion, "I don't believe in psychiatry"? Surely, people do believe that psychoactive drugs can treat some problems, and surely they believe that talking to a relatively neutral, objective, and skilled professional who's uninvolved in the patient's personal life can affect how the patient views herself and the world.

To ask, "Does psychotherapy work?" is akin to asking, "Does a restaurant work?" No one would compare McDonald's with Maxim's. Each is splendid at what it does. The same is true for psychotherapy. It does what it does, as long as what's expected of it is appropriate, and as long as the therapist, like the restauranteur, knows her stuff. And just as whether a restaurant "works" depends on who's making the judgment, so too with therapy. In evaluating if a patient has improved, who's the best judge? The patient? The therapist? A researcher? A family member? A friend?

Therefore, the proper question is not, "Does psychiatry work," but "Which treatments work for which disorders, in which patients, toward which goals, under which conditions, and according to whom?" In evaluating if a particular therapy is effective, all valid research now compares the effects of an active treatment (e.g., cognitive therapy, imipramine) with an inactive or placebo treatment (e.g., supportive contact, placebo pill). The patients, and when possible the clinicians, are "blind" to (uninformed about) which treatment is active or, if it's medication, which treatment the patient is receiving. (When only patients are blind, it is called a single-blind study; when both clinicians and patients are kept uninformed, it is a double-blind study.) Part II presents some of the results from this type of research.

CHAPTER 6

Sample Case History: Sherlock Holmes

In *The Seven-Per-Cent Solution*, Nicholas Meyer revealed that Sigmund Freud had evaluated Sherlock Holmes, yet not until now has Freud's initial writeup of the case come to light. Quite remarkably, Freud's presentation illustrated the standard approach used 100 years later![1]

2 June 1891

IDENTIFYING INFORMATION

The patient, Mr. Sherlock Holmes, is a 41-year-old, white, single, Protestant private detective, referred for cocaine misuse, depression, and bizarre behavior by his friend and colleague, Dr. John H. Watson. (*Informant*: Quotations are from the patient, while all other information, unless specified to the contrary, is from Dr. Watson, a reliable historian.)

CHIEF COMPLAINT

"I have applied all my will to banishing this (cocaine) habit and I have not been able to do so. . . . once a man takes the first false step, his feet are set forever on the path to his destruction."

---

[1]This case history is modified from one composed by Drs. Lawrence Sharpe and Jerrold S. Maxmen, based partly on material from Meyers, N. (1993). *The seven-per-cent solution*, New York: W.W. Norton.

HISTORY OF PRESENT ILLNESS

The patient was apparently well until 24 April 1891, when late at night he snuck through the back door of Watson's home, appearing agitated, perspiring, gaunt, and pale. His eyes roved restlessly, but nothing seemed to register. He started to close and bolt every shutter in the room, but suddenly stopped and began to pace until Watson persuaded him to sit. Holmes then launched into a rambling story that people with air guns were after him because he had penetrated the defenses of a Professor Moriarity, an ex-University professor of mathematics with "incredible mental prowess and hereditary diabolic tendencies." He insisted that Moriarity is the "Napoleon of crime, the organizer of half the evil in the world, and the center of a web of malefactors."

After an hour of standing, sitting and pacing, Holmes' excited speech slowed into inarticulate mutterings, followed by whisperings. He slept for two hours and awoke with a blank stare. He did not recognize the name Moriarity when it was mentioned, but insisted that before he slept he was discussing an entirely different subject. Although earlier Watson had mentioned that his wife was away, Holmes requested that she be thanked for an excellent dinner (which had never been eaten).

The next day, Holmes would not admit Watson to his room, fearing he was Moriarity in disguise. Holmes questioned Watson about items that only Watson would have known. Once inside, Watson noted there were new shutters of heavy iron and new locks on the doors. Holmes rambled on about Moriarity.

Later that day, Watson was approached by Professor Moriarity, who taught math at a small school, but had privately tutored Holmes and his older brother Mycroft when both were children. Moriarity claimed that for the previous five weeks, Holmes had been harassing him by standing outside his house all night, dogging his footsteps, telling his superior that he was a master criminal, and sending him telegrams with warnings such as, "Your days are numbered." The Professor was contemplating legal action to prevent this harassment, but was dissuaded from doing so by Watson's reassurances.

Mrs. Hudson, Holmes' landlady of many years, told Watson that around the end of February, Holmes began spending his days locked in his study-bedroom; he would barricade the doors, bolt the shutters, see no one, and refuse all meals. Late at night, he'd sneak out to spy on the professor.

Watson believes that Holmes has episodically snuffed cocaine for at least five years, but that only recently has this use escalated to where it totally impairs occupational and social functioning. He now intravenously injects himself with unknown (but increasing) amounts of a 7% solution of cocaine three to four times a day. Holmes only makes wild accusations about Moriarity during cocaine intoxication; at other times on cocaine Holmes becomes grandiose, saying such things as, "It is very dangerous for me to leave London for any length of time. It generates in the criminal classes an unhealthy excitement when my absence is discovered." He denies and conceals his cocaine use, but without his usual meticulousness and caution — syringes are left in open drawers, his shirt sleeves are rolled up, thereby exposing puncture marks, etc.

Two weeks ago, at Watson's insistence, Holmes stopped cocaine, and within a day, felt extreme despair, gloom, and boredom — extreme even for Holmes. He has stopped working on any other case, believing that no other criminal in Europe is clever enough to bother with. He has lost all interest in his usual activities, has no appetite, has shed ten pounds, looks pale, and stays in bed most of the day. Watson has never heard Holmes speak of suicide. Being concerned about his worsening state, Dr. Watson, in collusion with Mycroft Holmes and Professor Moriarity, tricked the patient into leaving London for treatment here in Vienna.

PAST HISTORY – DEVELOPMENTAL, PSYCHIATRIC, DRUG AND ALCOHOL, AND FAMILY

Little is known about the patient's early childhood. His mother was involved in an illicit love affair, which Holmes' father discovered. He then shot her to death. Moriarity, then Holmes' tutor, was the one who told the patient the news. There is no information as to his behavior prior to, or immediately after, this catastrophe. Sherlock was an intelligent child and went through college with high grades. His income derives from family landholdings and a thriving detective practice.

Watson thinks the patient's father died years ago, but knows nothing of the circumstances. The patient's sole living relative is his older brother Mycroft, who is also a bachelor. Watson claims that Mycroft is even more intelligent, reclusive, and eccentric than the patient, living in London's highly traditional Diogenes Club, the main qualifications for membership of which are shyness and misanthropy, and whose main distinction is that members' chairs are positioned back-to-back so that nobody speaks with another. Watson is unaware of any mental illness in the family.

Watson describes the patient as a "deeply private person, whose reclusivity reaches major proportions" at times and who behaves "as a 'thinking machine,' impassive, aloof, and austere and not in direct contact with the sordid realities of physical existence." Holmes once observed, "Watson, I am a brain." Nonetheless, Watson contends that underneath this bravado, Holmes is a deeply compassionate man, who regards his emotions as interfering with his mental processes. He tries, Watson maintains, to suppress his emotions by indulging in intellectual pursuits, such as chemical experiments and violin improvisation for hours on end, or by practicing shooting at the walls of his room. Except for a brief attraction to Irene Adler, women have been conspicuously absent in the patient's life.

Watson considers Holmes to be an ill-mannered eccentric, who is easily bored when not confronted with an interesting problem to solve. Holmes confirmed this by saying, "I abhor the dull routine of existence, I loathe stagnation." On occasion, he becomes demoralized, sad, and hopeless; he lacks energy, sleeps 10 to 12 hours a day (normally he sleeps under five hours a day), socially isolates himself, loses interest in everything. These depressive periods occur once or twice a year, last from several days to weeks, but no longer than two to three months. Some of these periods end when Holmes gets a new and challenging case, some end for no apparent reason, and some because Holmes binges on cocaine for a week or two. When confronted with an interesting problem, he would stop cocaine, but return to it when bored or depressed. Except for some prior experimentation with morphine injections, Holmes has not used any drug except cocaine.

MEDICAL HISTORY AND PHYSICAL EXAMINATION

Although a physical exam was not performed, the patient was observed to be malnourished, had dilated pupils, puncture marks on both arms, and a weak pulse.

Mental Status Examination

[Formal testing not performed.]

Appearance: Gaunt, sallow, malnourished, tired-looking, and appeared to have lost weight. He continued to wear his only double-visored hat indoors.

Behavior: Entered office slowly, weak handshake, dry palms, and sat throughout the 80-minute consultation. His movements were a bit slow, although when speaking of Moriarity, he became fidgety and spoke with more animation.

Speech: He said very little and only spoke when asked a direct question. His speech was hushed, moderately slow, but not slurred.

Emotion: Patient said he was despondent, had no interest in things, and that nothing brought him pleasure. His facies was glum, his general look, bored. His affect and mood were appropriate to what was said. There were no signs of anxiety.

Thought processes and content: During the middle of the interview, he said that he thought I was Moriarity in disguise, and that his brother and Watson had concocted a sinister plot to deliver him into the clutches of his enemies. Yet, when confronted, Holmes abandoned this idea and apologized. When asked if he still believed that Moriarity was a master criminal, he said he would rather not discuss the matter. Despite these apparently overvalued ideas, there is no evidence of actual delusions, ideas of reference, incoherence, phobias, obsessions, or compulsions. His thinking was goal-directed. He denied suicidal ideation.

Perception: Although not specifically tested, there were no indications of a perceptual disturbance.

Attention: His mind seemed to wander on occasion, but not while speaking.

Orientation: Knew the date, time, place, his name, Watson's name, and my name.

Memory: Excellent immediate, recent, and remote memory.

Judgment: No apparent functional disturbance.

Intelligence, information, and abstraction: Extremely high.

Insight: On confrontation, he admitted to cocaine addiction and acknowledged that it was a serious problem.

DIAGNOSIS

Axis I:	292.84 Cocaine abuse; substance-induced mood disorder
	292.0 Cocaine withdrawal (Provisional, rule out)
	296.30 Major depression (Provisional, rule out)
	296.80 Bipolar disorder (Provisional, rule out)
Axis II:	301.40 Obsessive-compulsive personality disorder (Provisional, rule out)
	Schizotypal personality disorder (Provisional, rule out)
	Paranoid personality disorder (Provisional, rule out)
Axis III:	None
Axis IV:	Psychosocial and environmental problems: None elicited
Axis V:	Global Assessment of Functioning (GAF)
Current:	GAF 35; impairment in reality testing and impairment in mood, judgment
	Highest in past year: GAF 70; excellent work functioning, but few relationships

PROGNOSIS

Guarded prognosis for cocaine abuse, especially in view of (a) the disorder's natural course and the patient's (b) history of depressive symptoms, (c) current reluctance to abandon cocaine, and (d) characteristic unwillingness to place himself under the care of others.

BIOPSYCHOSOCIAL FORMULATION

The patient's heavy cocaine abuse produces grandiosity, persecutory, and overvalued ideas and agitation. Holmes' particular choice of cocaine may be partly to self-medicate an underlying depression (especially given his unusual intolerance of boredom), and partly because he is very attracted to the sense of sharpened intellect cocaine affords. Stopping cocaine brings on and/or aggravates depressive symptoms, especially dysthymia, anhedonia, hypersomnia, psychomotor retardation, and social isolation. Why the patient's use of cocaine sharply increased late last February remains unclear, since no precipitant has been identified.

The diagnosis of cocaine abuse is firm. In addition, in light of current information, the patient's symptoms strongly suggest a mood disorder, even though they frequently fall short of meeting *DSM-IV* criteria. The episodes lasting two weeks after cocaine use strongly suggest a substanced-induced mood disorder. Because his depressive symptoms are episodic, a dysthymic disorder is highly unlikely, whereas a major depression is a distinct possibility. Slightly more probable would be bipolar disorder, since his periods of enormous energy, even when not on cocaine, resemble hypomania and his hypersomniac depressive intervals suggest bipolar depression. Because we lack information, a family history of mood disorder or substance abuse is impossible to make. In view of his longstanding meticulousness, perfectionism, excessive use of logic and intellect at the expense of emotion, and mild self-righteousness and suspiciousness, an obsessive-compulsive personality disorder should be considered. A schizotypal or paranoid personality disorder should also be considered. The patient's belief in having a "sixth sense" for criminals, his odd appearance, always wearing his special hat, and his frequent social anxiety support a schizotypal diagnosis. His brother Mycroft probably has a schizotypal personality disorder, a disorder that has strong genetic components. The patient's paranoid ideas and social anxiety that tends to paranoia support a paranoid diagnosis. The patient's ability to have close friends other than relatives, the appropriateness of being suspicious as a professional detective, and the variability of his overvalued ideas (which may fluctuate with cocaine use) argue against a diagnosis of schizotypal or paranoid personality disorder.

Psychodynamically, *repression*, supplemented by other defenses, appears to have played a major role in shaping Holmes' preoccupations and behavior. His *repressed* rage at his father for killing his mother seems to have been *displaced* onto Moriarity, the man who informed Holmes of the murder. *Introjecting* rage intended for his father may have compounded Holmes' depression. His repressed rage at his mother's unfaithfulness, and her subsequent "abandonment" of young Sherlock may have contributed to his disinterest in women—his viewing them as untrustworthy, immoral, and not dependable. By *sublimation*, Holmes excelled in detective work "to punish the wicked and see justice done."

PLAN

1. Withdrawal from cocaine.
2. Observation; look for hidden cocaine use.
3. Evaluation of mood and personality disorders.
4. Encourage involvement in pursuits that usually bring him pleasure, such as violin playing, attending Wagnerian opera, chasing criminals.
5. Next appointment: Tuesday, 16:00.

Sigmund Freud, M. D.

SECTION II

Mental Disorders

CHAPTER 7

Delirium, Dementia, Amnestic, and Other Cognitive Disorders

"LIKE TREES, WE grow old from the top," says Gore Vidal's Emperor Julian. Although most would agree, they're barking up the wrong tree: Dementia—or what is commonly called "senility"—is *not* inherent to aging, but a set of illnesses that strikes 15% of elderly Americans. To assume that "growing old from the top" is natural and inevitable stereotypes the elderly and causes many curable dementias to go untreated.

As the number of elderly in the population increases, so does the importance of dementia. In 1970, Americans over the age of 65 numbered 20.1 million and comprised 9.8% of the population; by the year 2000, these figures will climb to 34.9 million and 13%, respectively. In 1980, three million people were afflicted with dementia; by the year 2000, four million will have it. Dementia afflicts 58% of the 1.2 million elderly now residing in nursing homes, at a cost of $12 billion a year. Over half of all hospitalized elderly mental patients have dementia, and over half of those with dementia have Alzheimer's disease—the fourth or fifth leading cause of death in the United States. All in all, about 1% of adults have some type of cognitive disorder.

The *DSM-IV* term *cognitive disorder* is used in this chapter to describe what was formerly called *organic brain syndrome*. The term *organic* was dropped because it implied a false dichotomy between physical and mental disorders. The cardinal symptoms of the cognitive disorders are recent

109

memory impairment, disorientation, poor judgment, confusion, and a general loss of intellectual functions. Also common are hallucinations, illusions, delusions, personality changes, and secondary emotional reactions (e.g., depression and persecutory ideas). The cognitive disorders are proven (or reasonably presumed) to be produced by a medical, neurological, or biochemical alteration in the brain's structure or function.

This chapter examines three types of cognitive disorder: *delirium*, whose primary characteristic is a clouding of consciousness (a reduced awareness of the environment); *dementia*, whose chief feature is a deterioration of intellectual functions; and *amnestic disorders*, whose cardinal symptom is memory impairment.

Two other types of cognitive disorder, *intoxication* and *withdrawal*, are discussed in the chapter on substance abuse. Other disorders caused by a *general medical condition* or *substance use*, such as psychotic disorder and anxiety and mood disorder, are discussed in related chapters.

DELIRIUM

Clinical Presentation

Delirium — from the Latin *delirare*, meaning to rave, to be crazy — is characterized by a clouding of consciousness, disorientation, and recent memory loss. These signs arise abruptly (e.g., several hours to days), fluctuate wildly, often become worse at night or in the dark (i.e., "sundowning"), and rarely persist for more than a month. Often appearing frightened and agitated, delirious patients frequently have illusions, hallucinations (in any of the five senses), incoherent speech, and disrupted sleep-wake cycles. The *DSM-IV* diagnostic criteria for delirium are listed in Table 7–1.

Disorientation to time usually comes first: At midnight, the patient may say it's noon, or that the year is 1948. As delirium worsens, the patient becomes disoriented to place (e.g., thinks he's at a country club when he's sitting in his bedroom), and later to people (e.g., misidentifies his spouse); immediate memory dwindles first, followed by intermediate (10-minute), and then by remote, memory. If either disorientation or recent memory loss is absent, the diagnosis of delirium is doubtful. Lucid intervals, with symptoms becoming worse at night, are usually diagnostic of delirium.

Clinical Course and Complications

Any time there is a sudden, unexplained behavioral change or psychosis, delirium must be suspected. Early detection of delirium is extremely important because it can lead to death. Delirium usually arises quickly, from

TABLE 7-1
DSM-IV Criteria for Deliria*

Common Criteria for Deliria

A. Disturbance of consciousness (reduced clarity of awareness of the environment) with reduced ability to focus, sustain, or shift attention.

B. Change in cognition (such as memory deficit, disorientation, language disturbance) or the development of a perceptual disturbance that is not better accounted for by a pre-existing, established, or evolving dementia.

C. The disturbance develops over a short period of time (usually hours to days) and tends to fluctuate during the course of the day.

Additional Criterion for Delirium Due to a General Medical Condition

D. There is evidence from the history, physical examination, or laboratory findings that the disturbance is caused by the direct physiological consequences of a general medical condition.

Additional Criteria for Substance Intoxication Delirium

D. There is evidence from the history, physical examination, or laboratory findings of either (1) or (2):

(1) the symptoms in Criteria A and B developed during Substance Intoxication.
(2) medication use is etiologically related to the disturbance.

Note: This diagnosis should be made instead of a diagnosis of Substance Intoxication only when the cognitive symptoms are in excess of those usually associated with the intoxication syndrome and when the symptoms are sufficiently severe to warrant independent clinical attention.

Additional Criterion for Substance Withdrawal Delirium

D. There is evidence from the history, physical examination, or laboratory findings that the symptoms in Criteria A and B developed during, or shortly after, a withdrawal syndrome.

Note: This diagnosis should be made instead of a diagnosis of Substance Withdrawal only when the cognitive symptoms are in excess of those usually associated with the withdrawal syndrome and when the symptoms are sufficiently severe to warrant independent clinical attention.

Additional Criterion for Delirium Due to Multiple Etiologies

D. There is evidence from the history, physical examination, or laboratory tests that the delirium has more than one etiology (e.g., more than one etiological general medical condition, a general medical condition plus Substance Intoxication or medication side effect).

DSM-IV, pp. 123, 129, 131–33.

several hours to days, depending on its cause. The onset may be dramatic, as when patients begin thrashing about, tearing out IVs, or fighting. When the onset is subtle and the symptoms are exaggerations of normal personality traits, delirium may go undetected. For instance, a normally perfectionistic physician recovering from heart surgery started to cuss at nurses for not washing their hands. Initially the staff said, "Everybody knows doctors make the worst patients," and missed the delirium, until his behavior became frankly psychotic. At first, delirious patients may simply appear a bit confused, mistake a night nurse for a relative, or not find their rooms. Nurses' and families' reports may be the first clue to a delirium when they describe a calm patient by day and a confused one by night ("sundowning"). Frequent, around-the-clock mental-status testing is often needed to detect a delirium.

Accidents are common in delirium. The patient may fall out of bed or step in front of a truck. The longer delirium continues, the greater the chance of permanent brain damage. Delirium rarely persists for over a month — by then, the patient is either demented or dead.

Etiology and Pathogenesis

Most delirious patients have an underlying medical, surgical, chemical, or neurological problem; it may be an infectious disease, drug intoxication or withdrawal, congestive heart failure, fluid and electrolyte imbalance, or stroke. Sometimes the first sign of a medical illness will be a delirium. Drug-induced delirium is most often secondary to anticholinergic toxicity. Psychotropic drugs, especially tricyclic antidepressants, low-potency antipsychotics, and antiparkinsonian medications, frequently cause delirium because of their substantial anticholinergic properties. Hypnoanxiolytic agents can also cause delirium at high blood levels. The elderly are especially susceptible, since they are highly sensitive to anticholinergics and hypnoanxiolytics. Fortunately, most of the newer antidepressants (selective serotonin re-uptake inhibitors and bupropion) and antiparkinsonian agents are not anticholinergic. Unfortunately, several drugs for blood pressure, heart malfunction, ulcers, emphysema, and inflammation have significant anticholinergic effects (Tune, Carr, Hoag, & Cooper, 1992).

Another cause of delirium is sensory isolation, which can occur in intensive and cardiac care units (ICU/CCU psychoses). The monotony of a strange and unfamiliar setting may cause patients to see walls quiver, mistake technological noises for human voices, hallucinate taps on their shoulders, etc. How much patients' deliria stem from sensory isolation or from the disease, medical complications, and treatment which brought them to an ICU or CCU is often unclear and varies depending on the circumstances.

Differential Diagnosis

Accentuated *normal personality traits* are part of patients' past history and persist with minimal fluctuation, whereas personality in delirium often has wild fluctuations between normal (during lucid intervals) and abnormal and out of character (during confused intervals). Unlike *dementia*, delirium is characterized by an abrupt onset, a fluctuating course, and a clouding of consciousness. Sometimes the strokes in vascular dementia cause abrupt deterioration, but they almost always have accompanying neurological deficits. When delirium is superimposed on dementia, it appears as a sudden, unexplained worsening with much fluctuation.

When *schizophrenia* erupts, the patient's hallucinations and apparent confusion can resemble a delirium, but the patient will not have the disorientation, memory loss, and diurnal pattern seen in delirium. *Generalized anxiety disorder* and delirium may both present with agitation, yet the former is without disorientation, confusion, and memory loss.

Management and Treatment

The first priority is to keep the patient alive; a close second is to prevent brain damage; third is to prevent the patient from inflicting self-harm. A thorough history from family, friends, past caregivers, and charts may reveal similar confusional periods with a known cause (i.e., hypoglycemia in diabetes or drug overdose) that immediately suggests a present cause and possible treatment. Quickly identifying a delirium and then referral to a physician to determine its cause are critical to these goals. Careful nursing care is also essential and often lifesaving. Because medically hospitalized delirious patients fall out of bed, wander off, trip, break bones, develop concussions, rip out IVs, hurl IV bottles, and so on, these patients need constant observation and, sometimes, physical restraints.

Delirious patients should be frequently oriented. Health-care professionals' contacts with the patients should be brief and numerous (e.g., three minutes four times an hour), always telling the patient the date, the place, the staff member's name, and what he or she is doing. The patient should be reassured as to her safety and repeatedly oriented. Pictures of family members, a clock, and a calendar showing the date should be visible to the patient. The best treatment for an ICU psychosis is removal from the ICU. If that is medically unsafe, all the above measures should be taken.

Before the underlying cause of the delirium is rectified, the patient may be helped initially by small doses of antipsychotic drugs (such as haloperidol, 2 mg). Some authors (Wells & McEvoy, 1982) claim that antianxiety agents (e.g., diazepam 5 mg to 10 mg, chlordiazepoxide 25 mg to 50 mg, oxazepam 15 mg to 50 mg) are as helpful and safe as antipsychotics, while other authors (Goodwin & Guze, 1989) opine that many delirious patients become even more agitated and disorganized on antianxiety drugs and, therefore, they recommend antipsychotics. However, these drugs risk the added complications of dystonia and/or neuroleptic malignant syndrome. The elderly should receive one-half to one-third of these hypnoanxiolytic doses. They may benefit most from benzodiazepines (such as oxazepam or lorazepam) that are not conjugated into other medically active compounds, have a relatively short half-life, and accumulate less.

More important than the choice of drug is the dose: Too little, and the delirium worsens and becomes more dangerous; too much, and more delirium, coma, and respiratory depression may follow. Because errors on either side of this delicate balance can lead to death, remember that *more* of a drug can always be given, but not *less*! If the initial doses mentioned above are insufficient or wear off, they may be repeated hourly, as long as the patient is checked before each new dose is administered.

DEMENTIA

Clinical Presentation

Dementia—from the Latin *demens*, meaning "out of one's mind"—is characterized by a loss of intellectual abilities, especially memory, judgment, abstract thinking, and language skills—together with marked changes in personality and impulse control. Most dementias begin gradually (months to years), but may erupt suddenly, as after a cracked skull. Unlike delirium, dementia occurs without a clouding of consciousness. Table 7–2 lists *DSM-IV* diagnostic criteria for dementia.

Initially, there is *memory loss* for recent events: Ovens are left on, keys misplaced, conversations forgotten. Later, episodes of getting lost while driving in once familiar locations begin; questions are repeated because the question and the answer are quickly forgotten. Retained, and often dwelled on, are details from childhood (e.g., "Rosebud"). *Personality changes* are often intensifications or exact opposites of pre-existing character traits. A gregarious grandfather retreats to a corner and daydreams. A mildly suspicious and self-righteous woman begins calling the police every night, accusing her neighbors of performing abortions in their basements. *Impaired judgment* and *poor impulse control* are common: Patients may start speaking crudely, exhibit genitals, or shoplift. A normally cautious businessman has three car accidents in six months because he impulsively passes cars on hills and swerves back and forth between lanes "to get ahead of the traffic."

Intellectual abilities deteriorate. Patients may have trouble naming objects (agnosia). They may have difficulties understanding language (aphasia); speech becomes stereotyped, slow, vague, and filled with irrelevant detail as these patients increasingly are unable to concentrate, to follow

TABLE 7–2
DSM-IV* Criteria for the Dementias

Alzheimer's, Vascular, Substance-Induced, or Due to a General Medical Condition

Common Criteria for the Dementias

A. The development of multiple cognitive deficits manifested by both

  (1) memory impairment (impaired ability to learn new information or to recall previously learned information)
  (2) one (or more) of the following cognitive disturbances:

    (a) aphasia (language disturbance)
    (b) apraxia (impaired ability to carry out motor activities despite intact motor function)
    (c) agnosia (failure to recognize or identify objects despite intact sensory function)
    (d) disturbance in executive functioning (i.e., planning, organizing, sequencing, abstracting)

B. The cognitive deficits in Criteria A1 and A2 each cause significant impairment in social or occupational functioning and represent a significant decline from a previous level of functioning.
C. The deficits do not occur exclusively during the course of a delirium.

Additional Criteria for Dementia of the Alzheimer's Type

D. The course is characterized by gradual onset and continuing cognitive decline.
E. The cognitive deficits in Criteria A1 and A2 are not due to any of the following:

  (1) other central nervous system conditions that cause progressive deficits in memory and cognition (e.g., cerebrovascular disease, Parkinson's disease, Huntington's disease, subdural hematoma, normal-pressure hydrocephalus, brain tumor)
  (2) systemic conditions that are known to cause dementia (e.g., hypothyroidism, vitamin B_{12} or folic acid deficiency, niacin deficiency, hypercalcemia, neurosyphilis, HIV infection)
  (3) substance-induced conditions

F. The disturbance is not better accounted for by another Axis I disorder (e.g., Major Depressive Disorder, Schizophrenia).

With Early Onset: if onset is at age 65 years or below
With Late Onset: if onset is after age 65 years

Additional Criteria for Vascular Dementia

D. Focal neurological signs and symptoms (e.g., exaggeration of deep tendon reflexes, extensor plantar response, pseudobulbar palsy, gait abnormalities, weakness of an extremity) or laboratory evidence indicative of cerebral vascular disease (e.g., multiple infarctions involving cortex and underlying white matter) that are judged to be etiologically related to the disturbance.

(continued)

TABLE 7–2
(*Continued*)

Additional Criteria for Dementia Due to Other General Medical Conditions

D. There is evidence from the history, physical examination, or laboratory findings that the disturbance is the direct physiological consequence of one of the general medical conditions listed below.

Dementia due to HIV disease, head trauma, Parkinson's disease, Huntington's disease, Pick's disease, or Creutzfeldt-Jakob disease.

Dementia due to ([Indicate the general medical condition not listed above], e.g., normal-pressure hydrocephalus, hypothyroidism, brain tumor, vitamin B_{12} deficiency, intracranial radiation).

Additional Criterion for Substance-Induced Persisting Dementia

D. There is evidence from the history, physical examination, or laboratory findings that the deficits are etiologically related to the persisting effects of substance use (e.g., a drug of abuse, a medication).

E. The deficits do not persist beyond the usual duration of Substance Intoxication or Withdrawal.

Additional Criterion for Dementia Due to Multiple Etiologies

D. There is evidence from history, physical examination, or laboratory tests that the disturbance has more than one etiology (e.g., head trauma plus chronic alcohol use, Dementia of the Alzheimer's Type with the subsequent development of Vascular Dementia).

DSM-IV, pp. 142–43, 146, 151–52, 154–55.

conversations, or to distinguish the germane from the trivial; words are misused, chosen more by sound than by sense. Patients cannot perform simple motor tasks (apraxia); driving, cooking, handling money, and using tools become too complicated. They find it hard to draw a simple house, copy the placement of four matchsticks, or assemble blocks. Often the severity of these symptoms is not recognized until the patient is observed in a new place (where inability to learn new information is a tip-off), or until the spouse dies and family members become aware of how sick their parent is for the first time. Initially they blame this deterioration on grief but then realize it has been going on much longer.

In response to these impairments, patients most commonly use denial and seem not to notice these major problems, or less commonly, they become ashamed, anxious, demoralized, irritable, and dysthymic; hypochondriasis increases; energy and enthusiasm decline. Some patients display "catastrophic reactions" or "emotional incontinence"—they respond to stimuli by excessive laughing, hostility, or weeping, or by suddenly becoming dazed, evasive, or immobile. Also common is *confabulation* (the fabrication of stories to conceal memory loss); so, too, are suspiciousness and paranoid ideation, especially when the patient has trouble hearing or seeing. Fear invades the memory vacuum: Forgetting where he left his wallet, the patient assumes it was stolen and may accuse others, including loved ones, of the crimes.

The patient's deterioration may go unrecognized for months or even years, because intellectual decline is usually insidious. Memory loss is dismissed as the natural result of normal aging or of not paying attention. The patient's impaired judgment and poor impulse control are explained by stereotyping ("Old folks naturally get crusty and cantankerous with age"). If granddad starts making lewd gestures to teeny-boppers, he's a fun-loving "dirty old man." (Dirty old women don't exist?) Inappropriate jocularity, which arises from impairments of the brain's frontal lobe, is dismissed as "simply being in good spirits." The patient's loss of intellectual sharpness or wit may be too subtle or gradual to be noticed. The patient does "all the right things," but on scrutiny, he's a beat behind: Grace notes become eighth notes.

When presenting clinically, demented patients may move slowly or fidget. They may look glum, bored, or tense. On a formal mental status examination, they show recent memory loss and disorientation and usually have difficulties subtracting serial 1's or 7's and performing abstractions.

The Mini Mental State Exam (See Appendix F) is a widely used screening test for dementia. It does not detect very early, mild dementias, but is effective at detecting dementias that are mild to moderate or worse. (A score of 24 or below indicates probable dementia.)

Subtypes

There are four major subtypes of dementia: (a) *Alzheimer's disease* (in *DSM-IV*, "dementia of the Alzheimer's type") is the most common type and accounts for almost 50% of all dementias. (b) *Vascular dementia* (formerly called "multi-infarct dementia") accounts for 9–15% of dementias and is mainly caused by hypertension or emboli.[1] Contrary to popular belief, vascular dementia is not directly caused by arteriosclerosis ("hardening of the arteries"). (c) *Dementia due to other general medical conditions* accounts for 20–30% of the dementias. This category includes dementias

---

[1]Emboli are small blood clots that break off from the heart or a carotid artery in the neck, flow to the brain, block part of the blood supply, and cause the death (or infarct) of those brain cells.

that are primarily caused by neurological diseases or by systemic illnesses. Parkinson's disease is included because 20–30% of patients with this disease develop dementia. Two very rare, rapidly progressive dementias, Pick's and Creutzfeldt-Jakob diseases, and the rare, slowly progressive Huntington's disease ("Woody Guthrie" disease) are also included here. HIV dementia is more complicated because it can include dementia from HIV itself or treatable dementias from secondary infections. Toxoplasmosis, a protozoan infection, has been identified as a cause of dementia in HIV-positive patients. (d) *Substance-induced persisting dementias* produce 7–9% of the dementias, with alcoholic dementia accounting for most. Table 7–3 lists the frequency of diagnoses in dementia compiled from three major medical centers: the Nashville Veterans Administration Hospital, National Hospital, and Middlesex Hospital.

Unlike AD and vascular dementia, many secondary dementias are treatable (see Table 7-4). Patients who present with dementias *must* receive thorough medical and neurological examinations to determine if they are among the roughly 25% of demented patients who can be treated and sometimes cured, either medically or surgically. Table 7–5 describes how the evaluation of the dementia is conducted. The "big four" — each accounting for about 6% of dementias that are treatable — are *normal pressure hydrocephalus, chronic drug toxicity, resectable brain masses,* and *major depression.* During the first year of abstinence, alcoholic dementia improves some but seldom completely. By preventing further strokes, low-dose aspirin therapy may arrest or slow the progress of vascular dementias.

TABLE 7–3
Summary of Dementia Evaluation from Three Centers*

	NO. OF PATIENTS		NO. OF PATIENTS
Treatable Disease Uncovered-Total	51 (26%)	Definable But Untreatable Disease Uncovered-Total	53 (27%)
Normal pressure hydrocephalus	15 (8%)	Vascular dementia	18 (9%)
Chronic drug toxicity	9 (4.5%)	Alcoholic dementia	14 (7%)
Resectable mass lesions	7 (3.5%)	Huntington's chorea	7 (3.5%)
Depression	12 (6%)	Other	14 (7%)
Other	8 (4%)		
		Unknown disease (atrophy)	93 (47%)

*The Nashville Veterans Administration Hospital, National Hospital, and Middlesex Hospital.

TABLE 7–4
The Treatable Dementias

CAUSE	TREATMENT
A. INFECTIONS	
1. Abscesses	Antibiotics
2. Encephalitis	Antibiotics, antiviral
3. Meningitis, chronic	Antibiotics
3. Syphilis of the brain	Penicillin
4. AIDS with secondary fungal, bacterial, viral, or protozoal infection	Antibiotics, antifungal, antiviral, antiprotozoal agents
B. LUPUS ERYTHEMATOSUS	Steroids, anti-inflammatory
C. MECHANICAL DISORDERS	
1. Normal pressure hydrocephalus	Ventricular shunt
2. Chronic subdural hematoma	Surgery
3. Vascular (cerebral aneurysm, AV malformation, vasculitis)	Surgery
D. METABOLIC DISORDERS	
1. Porphyria	Hematin
2. Hypothyroidism (myxedema)	Thyroid replacement
3. Hyponatremia (low sodium)	Treat underlying disease (#3-9)
4. Hypo- or hypercalcemia (low or high calcium)	
5. Hyperadrenalism	
6. Wilson's disease	
7. Uremia (kidney failure with toxicity)	
8. Hepatic encephalopathy (liver failure with toxicity)	
9. Pulmonary failure	
E. NEOPLASMS	
Benign tumors	
1. Gliomas, meningitis	Surgery
2. Other brain tumors	Surgery
Not benign	
1. Primary and metastatic	Irradiation, chemotherapy, surgery

(*continued*)

TABLE 7–4
(*Continued*)

CAUSE	TREATMENT
F. CHRONIC INTOXICATION AND POISONS	
1. Alcohol	Remove exposure and remove poison
2. Barbiturates	(#1–8)
3. Anticholinergics	
4. Bromides	
5. Carbon monoxide	
6. Metals (e.g., mercury, lead, arsenic, manganese)	
7. Organic phosphates	
8. L-dopa	
G. PSEUDODEMENTIA	
1. Major depressive disorder	Antidepressants
2. Psychoses	Antipsychotics, electroconvulsive therapy
H. VITAMIN DEFICIENCIES	
1. B_1 (Wernicke's encephalopathy)	Replace vitamin (#1–4)
2. B_{12} (pernicious anemia)	
3. Folic acid	
4. Niacin (pellagra)	

About 50% of patients with normal pressure hydrocephalus improve with the help of a brain shunt that diverts cerebrospinal fluid. There are also many less common treatable dementias (see Table 7–4).

On her 70th birthday, widowed, modest Mrs. Kass moved to Miami. Quite unlike her "normal self," she launched her first of many sexual flings "for the hell of it." As she informed relatives, "life is short." Hotly debated was whether Mrs. Kass belonged in a motel or a mental hospital. While the family was paralyzed by worry, Mrs. Kass was thrilled and active. She'd laugh at anything, so much so that one night a policeman noticed her on a fishing pier, lost, confused, and giggling. When he asked her where she was, she burst into "Swanee River," until she forgot a lyric and began weeping all the way to the hospital. Her dementia, initially attributed to Alzheimer's disease, was due to a benign (frontal lobe) brain tumor, which was surgically removed. After a full recovery, she regained her normal temperament and settled down with a retired businessman.

Clinical Course

Although it usually appears after age 65, early-onset Alzheimer's disease (AD) can emerge during the forties, as it did in the case first described by

TABLE 7–5
Useful Studies in the Clinical Evaluation of Patients with Dementia

Initial Studies Performed on All Patients:

—Detailed history and physical examination
—Chest x-ray
—Complete blood count with red cell indices and erythrocyte sedimentation rate
—Serum VDRL
—Urinalysis
—CAT or MRI

Additional Studies Tailored to Individual Patients:

If a metabolic cause is suspected
—Serum electrolytes, calcium, bilirubin, SGOT, BUN
—Thyroid function tests
—Serum vitamin B_{12} level
—Serum drug levels
—Urine heavy metal screen
—Urine porphyrins

If an infectious cause is suspected
—Lumbar puncture with thorough CSF evaluation including glucose, protein, cell count, India ink, VDRL, cultures (bacterial, TB, fungal, viral), protein electrophoresis
—Evaluation of possible systemic infection

If a structural or neoplastic cause is suspected
—CAT scan or MRI
—Cerebral arteriogram
—CSF cytology

Other Helpful Studies in Some Patients:

—Electroencephalogram (metabolic, degenerative, or structural processes)
—Intrathecal cisternogram (normal pressure hydrocephalus)
—Antinuclear factor (vasculitis)
—Serum copper and ceruloplasmin (Wilson's disease)

the German neuropsychiatrist Alois Alzheimer in 1906. Its stealthy onset typically manifests with memory loss and intellectual decline. In about 15–20% of these cases, the initial complaints are personality change with "negative" symptoms—apathy or withdrawal—or "positive" symptoms—agitation, irritability, suspiciousness, or moodiness. In general, Alzheimer's patients in the milder stages deteriorate gradually and do not have marked diurnal changes. Difficulties with speech (finding the right words) and getting lost in familiar places are early signs. Aphasia, apraxia, or agnosia typically appear after several years. Hallucinations and delusions become more common as the disease progresses.

During the endstage of AD, memory is almost totally gone. Patients cannot recognize their closest relatives; everyone becomes a stranger. Speech is reduced to a phrase or two; they cannot dress or feed themselves; bladder and bowel control fail; muscles deteriorate and insomnia plagues. At the very end, full nursing care is required, as patients are bedridden, disoriented, oblivious, and incoherent. They may become mute, stop eating, and lose the ability to swallow. They frequently aspirate food into their lungs and get pneumonia. Alzheimer's patients may survive up to 15 years, but they usually expire in seven to ten years, dying most often from malnutrition, dehydration, infections, pneumonia, or heart failure.

Vascular dementia usually occurs in patients with histories of strokes and cardiovascular disease, causing "patchy" focal neurological signs such as inarticulate speech, small stepped gait, abnormal reflexes, and specific weak muscles. These neurological signs are rarely seen in mild to moderate Alzheimer's disease and are reliable clues for vascular dementia. In contrast to the slow, generalized deterioration of AD, vascular dementia may begin abruptly and progress in a stepwise, individual fashion. In people with many microinfarcts, this disease may appear to progress gradually, as in AD. For unknown reasons, this stepwise worsening is also seen in other dementias and is therefore not a reliable symptom in diagnosing vascular dementia.

Although many dementias look alike in their early stages, several develop very specific symptoms that can be used to make a differential diagnosis. These include vascular dementia, Parkinson's disease, normal pressure hydrocephalus, Huntington's chorea, Wernicke-Korsakoff, and the very rare contagious (only if you eat or handle their brains or body fluids) Creutzfeldt-Jakob disease. Table 7–6 lists the causes and symptoms of these quite recognizable dementias.

In the late stages of dementia, reflexes last seen in infancy reappear. When touched on the mouth or cheek, the patient shows a *rooting reflex* in which the mouth, face, or head moves toward the touch. This is an adaptive reflex in breast- and bottle-feeding babies. When an object is put in the patient's mouth or on the lips, a *sucking reflex* is often seen. Passively moving the patient's limbs elicits a semipurposeful resistance called *paratonia* or *gegenhalten*. The very demented patient may show *perseveration*, the continued repetition of a verbal or motor response that is no longer required (e.g., "Good morning! Oh boy! Oh boy! Oh boy!"). The same answer may be given to a series of different questions. A variation on this is perseveratory groping in which the patient constantly and aimlessly picks at bed

TABLE 7–6
Dementias with Specific Diagnostic Clues

DISEASE	CAUSE	DIAGNOSTIC CLUES
Normal pressure hydro-cephalus	Increased fluid in lateral ventricles	Incontinence, gait disturbance
Huntington's chorea	Genetic	Writhing, choreiform movements
Wernicke-Korsakoff	Thiamine (B_1) deficiency from alcoholism and poor nutrition	Diplopia, ataxia
Creutzfeldt-Jakob	Prions (smaller than viruses, contagious)	Rigidity and myoclonic jerks, abnormal EEG, fatal in months
Vascular dementia	Multiple infarctions (strokes) from emboli, thrombosis, or rupture of small vessels; hypertension most common cause	Focal neurological signs, abnormal reflexes, specific weak muscles
Parkinson's	Destruction of dopamine-containing cells	Slow, shuffling gait, bradykinesia, "pill-rolling" hand tremor, lack of facial expression

sheets or clothing. The apparent opposite of this is *motor impersistence*, the inability to continue a simple action like extending a hand; within seconds, the patient drops his hands into his lap.

Complications

Dementia is a life-shortening illness. Demented patients are susceptible to medical illness and delirium. Their work and social functioning gradually decline, and as their condition worsens, they may get lost wandering away from home. If a patient's mind wanders, he may fall off a ladder or trip on a curb; if he smashes his head and loses consciousness, he may suffer a potentially fatal subdural hematoma.[2] Although dementia often induces

---

[2]A subdural hematoma is a sudden or gradual bleeding under the outer lining (or dura) of the brain. The patient may lose consciousness immediately, yet more often there is a fluctuating course of drowsiness, headache, and confusion that persists for weeks to months, until the patient finally loses consciousness.

severe despair and depression, it rarely leads to suicide. Major depression occurs in 15–20% of patients with Alzheimer's disease; it is more common in the early milder stages because insight about what is lost is still intact.

Epidemiology

The incidence of Alzheimer's disease increases with age, arising most often in people between the ages of 70 and 80 years. The prevalence of dementia in the over-65 group is 6–7%. At age 65, about 5% have AD; by age 80, about 20%; and by age 90, about 25–30% have it. Women may be more affected than men. At present, more than two million Americans have AD. In 50 years, with more people surviving to old age, the prevalence of this disease is expected to triple.

Etiology and Pathogenesis

In general, the biological factors that produce a dementia vary according to the subtype of dementia, whereas the psychosocial influences depend more on the individual's personality and circumstances. For example, Huntington's chorea is caused by an autosomal (comes from either sex) dominant gene. In contrast, vascular dementia has numerous biological causes that are not so directly related genetically.

As noted, during the early stages of most dementias, patients respond with either exaggerations of their normal personality traits or their exact opposite. As discussed later, those close to the patient may also influence the patient's experience and quality of life. During the later stages, most dementias "take over" personalities, irrespective of psychosocial influences.

Genetic. First-degree relatives (e.g., brother, mother, daughter) of patients with Alzheimer's disease demonstrate three to four times the prevalence of this disease as the general population. The incidence is even higher among relatives of those few who develop AD before age 60. Some researchers believe that an autosomal dominant gene is *a* (not *the*) culprit. In some families, if one parent has the gene, the child has a 50% chance of having AD; this likelihood increases to 75% if both parents have the gene. Children in these families tend to manifest the disease at the same age their parents did. In other cases, genetic vulnerability to AD is less clear. In some cases, a dominant gene may express itself late in life so that only some live long enough to show the disease. Estimates vary from 30–80% of the disease as being genetically-induced. In many of these cases, a sporadic or polygenetic transmission is the cause. Most think AD represents a variety of diseases; Down's syndrome is also a predisposition. An autosomal dominant gene definitely causes Huntington's chorea ("Woody Guthrie's disease").

Medical. In addition to the etiologies of treatable dementias listed in Table 7–4, some untreatable dementias are probably due to "slow" viruses or prions (infectious particles that lack nucleic acid) and immunologic deficiencies. Alcohol aggravates all dementias. High-risk factors for vascular dementia include hypertension, cigarette smoking, obesity, and heart disease.

Physiological. In normal aging, although the blood supply to the brain decreases, the brain extracts oxygen more efficiently. In AD, however, the brain's blood supply is also diminished, but the brain extracts both *less* oxygen and glucose. Moreover, the enzymes that both synthesize and metabolize acetylcholine are deficient. Ultimately, most neurotransmitters are affected. On autopsy, inside the neurons of Alzheimer's patients are twisted clumps of protein called "neurofibrillary tangles," which are probably microtubules. Coating the outside of blood vessels are remnants of nerve-cell endings called "neuritic plaques" (not neurotic!) around a core of beta-amyloid protein. These occur in the normal aging process, but in AD there are usually more than ten times as many. There is a high correlation between the number of these plaques and tangles and the severity of the dementia. Beta-amyloid precursor protein (BAPP) is ubiquitous in the normal brain. Some think that in AD this amyloid protein is not broken down normally and leaves behind neurotoxic or nonsoluable amyloid fragments that interfere with the brain's functioning and cause dementia.

Differential Diagnosis

As discussed earlier, dementia must be distinguished from *delirium*. Because delirium presents with disorientation and memory loss, dementia cannot be diagnosed until *after* a delirium clears. Agnosia, apraxia, and aphasia are much more common in Alzheimer's dementia than in delirium. In *normal aging* there is a 10–15% loss in neuropsychological functioning. This includes some memory loss; names and dates are forgotten, papers misplaced, new learning comes harder, thinking becomes slower, and problem-solving gets tougher. Much of the loss in function is due to slowed performance speed. (Give the seniors enough time and they come much closer to their abilities.) These changes do not substantially interfere with occupational or social functioning, whereas the changes from Alzheimer's disease and other dementias do. In Alzheimer's, the decline in neuropsychological functioning is typically over 85%. Some intellectual deterioration may occur in *chronic schizophrenia*, but it is milder than in dementia, specific neurological abnormalities are not usually found, and there usually is a clear history of schizophrenic symptoms.

The second most important fact about dementia is that it may be confused with "pseudodementia," a sign of *major depression* that is highly treatable. From 10–33% of old people with major depressive disorder are misdiagnosed as having dementia, because both disorders may present initially with the same symptoms of memory loss, confusion, disorientation, apathy, and hypochondriasis. To further complicate matters, about 15–20% of patients with dementia also have a major depressive disorder. For patients with pseudodementia, antidepressants may completely improve the "dementia" and in depressed demented patients, antidepressants may improve the dementia.

Surprisingly, patients with depression are more likely to complain about memory problems than patients with *real* memory problems. Patients with dementia are often brought in by their families. For example, Aunt Maude, who has Alzheimer's disease, was brought in by her family after burning the pots on the stove three nights in a row. She wonders what the fuss is all about and doesn't complain about memory problems. In contrast, the depressed patient paces the floor, complaining that he can't remember all the stocks he owns and that he has forgotten his friend's phone number.

Another symptom, the *anhedonia* seen in depression, differs from the normal *narrowing of interest in activities* seen in dementia. When a depressed patient is asked what she enjoys doing, she might say, "Nothing." The patient with dementia might say, "I like picking up the mail, reading large-print books, and watching my TV shows." A typical interviewer who has a wide range of interests might mistakenly conclude that the demented patient is depressed, because *she* (the interviewer) would feel depressed with so few activities. The demented patient can't do the more complex ones, such as cooking, gardening, or handicrafts, but still likes to do the few left that she is still able to do. Depressed patients frequently respond to questions with silence or by saying, "I don't know"; demented patients answer with near-misses. In depression, the cognitive problems develop relatively abruptly within days to two months. True dementia usually evolves much more slowly. Unlike dementia, pseudodementia does not have accompanying neurological symptoms such as aphasia, apraxia, or agnosia. Disorientation to time, getting lost easily, and difficulties with dressing are also much more common in dementia (Reynolds et al., 1988). In the patient who has both depression and dementia, dementia symptoms are present before depression symptoms.

Patients with cognitive decline associated with depression often have a prior, or family, history of mood disorder. Although the CAT or MRI scan is more likely to show cortical atrophy and enlarged ventricles in dementia than in depression, 20% of the time the CAT or MRI scan may be misdiagnosed (Charatan, 1985). Up to 70–80% of depressed elderly patients have abnormal MRI scans; a significant number of normal elderly have abnormal imaging studies. The diagnosis is therefore clinical, not radiological, the key test being whether the patient improves with biological treatments such as antidepressants or ECT.[3]

Antidepressants must be used with caution because demented patients are prone to becoming delirious on them. Antidepressants that are low in cognitive side effects, such as SSRIs and low anticholinergic TCAs (desipramine, nortriptyline), are preferred. The prognosis for cognitive decline associated with depression is not entirely rosy. Many patients develop true dementia several years later (Emery & Oxman, 1992). Major depressive disorder can be viewed as a physiologic stressor that brings out a nascent dementia that later will show itself on its own. Fortunately, many patients with pseudodementia do not develop true dementia.

Management and Treatment

Biomedical Interventions

After the treatable dementias are treated, there may be residual dementia. In Alzheimer's disease there is a deficiency of acetylcholine along with other neurotransmitters. Cholinesterase inhibitors (e.g., tacrine) increase brain acetylcholine by preventing its breakdown and are sometimes used to help these patients. A few improve significantly but most patients improve minimally or not at all with these drugs. Management is the main goal. A majority of people with Alzheimer's develop at least one psychotic symptom. Very low doses of neuroleptics (e.g., haloperidol 0.5–3 mg) are usually effective for this, as well as for the agitation that may accompany the psychosis. Common clinical mistakes include using higher doses, more anticholinergic antipsychotics, or using hypnoanxiolytics, all of which can worsen the dementia. Parkinson's-related dementia is also not really treatable, but adequate treatment of the disease itself can improve cognition.

For calming agitation and alleviating insomnia, psychoactive drugs should be used cautiously, since they can also aggravate the patient's confusion and generate intolerable side effects. The patient, and especially his family, should be questioned about other drugs used medically or surreptitiously that might compound (or produce) symptoms. Anticholinergic ιgents, including those sold over-the-counter or prescribed for glaucoma, are common culprits. Drugs that show some promise of calming agitation in dementia without increasing confusion include trazodone, buspirone, and propranolol.

---

[3]That electroconvulsive therapy *increases* instead of diminishes the memory of patients with pseudodementia suggests that it does not harm brain cells.

If the patient has a vascular dementia, then removing the risk factors of hypertension (cigarette smoking, etc.) is essential. Low-dose aspirin may reduce the risk of new infarcts.

Psychosocial Interventions

Because the care of the demented falls mainly to loved ones and custodians, they must become partners in the patient's treatment plan. For family members, being a caretaker is usually a novel but highly stressful experience; it is difficult and draining, demoralizing and devastating. Relatives need support and practical instruction, and a major task of the physician or therapist is to provide both.

Patient care. The primary goal is to make the demented patient's life as comfortable as possible. The environment should be kept simple and helpful. Clocks, calendars, labels, lists, familiar routines, short-term tasks, brief walks, and simple physical exercises (to prevent muscle atrophy) — such are the elements that improve the patient's quality of life and foster self-respect. In a majority of Alzheimer's patients, memory for facts is much worse than memory for how to do things; they may still enjoy activities like golf as long as someone else keeps score.

Patients should be allowed and encouraged to do what they can, but *only* what they can. Pressing too hard — for example, trying to preserve memory by exercising it — only leads to frustration and resentment. Demented patients dislike abdicating familiar tasks such as handling money, driving, cooking, and later on, the self-care of bathing, dressing, using the toilet, and living alone. It is helpful to break tasks down into small steps and keep possessions simple and organized. Attempts to help may be greeted with insults, complaints, annoying questions, tears, or rage. Responding with hostility is pointless and harmful; distracting and calming patients works better. When these patients lose things and then blame others for stealing them, instead of refuting the accusation, which is pointless, offer to look for the lost items. Reassurance repeated several times each hour is never too much. Later, as words fail, touch may still reassure. Sleeping areas should be made safe, since patients are likely to become more confused at night, wander about, and hurt themselves.

Moving patients to a senior citizen's apartment, sheltered housing, or a nursing home is usually necessary when they become dangerous to themselves, hallucinate, lose bowel or bladder control, or make life impossible for their caretakers. The reasons for such a move should be calmly reiterated; patients will forget the content of the explanations, but the *repeated reassurance* is what counts. Caretakers often feel guilty for "putting Mom away." They have an image of residential living being a warehouse for broken souls—people left alone to stare at the floor. While a few still are like the dreaded nursing homes of old, caretakers need to recognize that many facilities today provide very positive environments. After successful placement, most caretakers state, "I waited too long to do this. I now see I should have done this much sooner."

Family counseling. When dementia is first diagnosed, some relatives deny the patient's illness (e.g., "Everybody grows old"), others blame the patient for being "deliberately difficult" (e.g., "She remembers when she wants to!"), while others are relieved to have an explanation for the patient's difficult behavior. In time, the family members feel overwhelmed and helpless. They may become angry at professionals for "not doing enough"; they may vent their frustrations on each other, and latent family tensions may surface under the strain of caring for a demented relative. A son or daughter may feel guilty about resenting the demented mother or father; the children may be ashamed of the parent or think he or she would be better off dead. The professional must care for the caretakers, who must be told that caring for the demented is an impossible, no-win, and thankless task, over which the family members must not destroy themselves. Thorough education about dementia and how to manage it is critical in order to prevent the many destructive approaches families may use. Loved ones often benefit from a self-help group such as the Alzheimer's Disease and Related Disorders Association (919 North Michigan Avenue., Suite 1000, Chicago, IL 60611-1676; 1-800-272-3900). Caretakers should be encouraged to take advantage of day-care facilities and respite beds, so that they can have several hours to a couple of days off from their responsibilities.

By diagnosing and treating depression and reversible dementias, by removing risk factors, and by helping families help the patient, today's clinicians can offer enormous assistance to these patients and their families.

AMNESTIC DISORDERS

Clinical Presentation

Amnesia, Latin for "forgetfulness," may occur by itself. The patient with an amnestic disorder may have profound difficulty remembering anything from yesterday or from one hour ago, but can converse sensibly with clear awareness and reasonable judgment. Only memory is affected. The *DSM-IV* criteria for amnestic disorders are listed in Table 7–7.

TABLE 7–7
DSM-IV* Criteria for Amnestic Disorder

Common Criteria for Amnestic Disorder

A. The development of memory impairment as manifested by the inability to learn new information or the inability to recall previously learned information.

B. The memory disturbance causes significant impairment in social or occupational functioning and represents a significant decline from a previous level of functioning.

C. The memory disturbance does not occur exclusively during the course of a delirium or dementia.

Additional Criterion for Amnestic Disorder Due to a General Medical Condition

D. There is evidence from the history, physical examination, or laboratory findings that the disturbance is the direct physiological consequence of a general medical condition (including physical trauma).

Additional Criterion for Substance-Induced Persisting Amnestic Disorder

D. There is evidence from the history, physical examination, or laboratory findings that the memory disturbance is etiologically related to the persisting effects of substance use (e.g., a drug of abuse, a medication).

DSM-IV, pp. 160, 162.

Clinical Course and Complications

If the memory loss resulted from a single event, such as a stroke in the hippocampus, all events after that date will be vaguely or never remembered. Events prior to the stroke have been stored and still can be recalled. Toxins, including alcohol, can more insidiously cause pure memory loss. Social, intelligent patients may attempt to mask the problem with confabulation: ("Didn't I see you at Harry's Bar last week?") or bunting questions back to the examiner ("What do you usually call this place?"). Those who have had no memory for years will be perplexed each day at how old people around them look, because they only remember how they looked many years ago. In some, remote memory may also deteriorate, but unlike in dementia, other areas of functions remain intact.

Management and Treatment

Removal of risk conditions such as alcohol use, poor nutrition, exposure to toxins, and hypertension can prevent further deterioration. Patients should be kept in familiar environments as long as possible, because new ones may be difficult or impossible for them to learn. As in dementia, memory devices such as clocks, calendars, labels, lists, and familiar routines help. If patients have completely lost the ability to establish new memories, the deficit can be used to their advantage, as the following case illustrates.

A 72-year-old woman with no recent memory had always liked her lifelong work as a cherry picker. She was brought into the hospital after hitting an attendant at a nursing home. When she had asked, "When can I go back to cherry picking?" the attendant had told her, "Never." The attendant later regretted this choice of words. The woman was not usually violent and, in the hospital, continued to ask when she could work. She got increasingly agitated as staff stalled, trying to avoid confrontations. Then one day she sat by a window smiling; this continued for several days. I (N.W.) asked her nurse what had caused this pleasant transformation. The nurse said she realized that the patient never remembered yesterday, so each day she told the patient that she could go cherry picking tomorrow. From then on, she happily anticipated the coming day. Compassion won over truthfulness.

CHAPTER 8

Substance-Related Disorders

SUBSTANCE ABUSE IS as old as the substances abused.[1] Rock carvings in caves from the fourth millennium B.C. display workmen making beer from barley. In 2285 B.C. a gentleman in China was allegedly banished for getting soused on a rice beverage. Individuals and religions of every era have sought to suspend reality and alter moods by the simplest and quickest way possible — "better living through chemistry."

The current frequency of this "better living" is hard to assess epidemiologically: The drug scene constantly changes, users are reluctant to mention their drug-taking, antidrug/alcohol groups have vested interests in exaggerating dangers, definitions of drug misuse vary considerably, and it is unclear which substances are deemed problematic — tobacco? caffeine? alcohol? Having said this, seven facts are worth noting: (a) The ECA survey of substance abuse by adult Americans revealed six-month and lifetime prevalence rates of 6.4% and 19.2% respectively — two-thirds from alcohol, one-third from other drugs. (b) These figures do not include the most frequent substance disorder among Americans, tobacco use disorder, whose lifetime prevalence is 36%. (c) Substance abuse is greatest among 18- to 24-year olds. From 1975–79, about 65% of high-school seniors reported using at least one illicit drug — most often, marijuana. During middle age, alcoholism is more of a problem. (d) After age 44, substance misuse de-

---

[1]"Substance" is a general term encompassing alcohol, recreational drugs, and medications. "Substance," "chemical," and "drugs" are employed interchangeably. Nonpsychoactive drugs (e.g., insulin) are also abused, but like *DSM-IV*, this book solely discusses *psychoactive* substances. Unless otherwise specified, *this* text uses (or abuses!) "misuse" and "abuse" synonymously.

clines for both sexes. (e) Substances are abused more by men than women, more by inner-city residents than country dwellers, more by nongraduates than college graduates. (f) Caucasians and African-Americans have the same overall rate of substance abuse. (g) Psychiatric disorders, including anxiety, antisocial personality, and mood disorders, have greatly increased rates of substance abuse (Christie et al., 1988): 78% of people with drug and alcohol problems have a psychiatric disorder in their lifetime and 65% at a particular time. The most common disorders are antisocial personality disorder, phobias, psychosexual dysfunctions, major depression, and dysthymia. Alcohol, hypnoanxiolytic, and amphetamine abusers have the highest rates of mental disorders (Ross, Glaser, & Germanson, 1988). Table 8–1 presents the generic, brand, and street names of the commonly misused substances.

DEFINITIONS

Intoxication and withdrawal are the most prevalent substance-related disorders. *Intoxication* is a reversible substance-specific syndrome that arises during or shortly after ingesting a substance and often disturbs perceptions, wakefulness, sleep, attention, judgment, emotionality, and movement. Intoxication becomes a disorder when clinically significant maladaptive behavioral changes (picking fights with everyone, driving into a ditch) or psychological changes (alternatively laughing and crying, inability to compute the restaurant bill) occur during or soon after ingestion. All drugs of abuse have an intoxication syndrome. *Withdrawal* is a substance-specific syndrome that follows when a chronic intake of a substance has been abruptly stopped or greatly diminished and usually manifests as restlessness, apprehension, anxiety, irritability, insomnia, and impaired concentration. It becomes a disorder when clinically significant distress or impaired function occur. Not all drugs have a withdrawal syndrome. Table 8–2 lists *DSM-IV* criteria for substance intoxication and withdrawal.

Intoxication and withdrawal involve two pharmacological phenomena: *Tolerance*, which is the need to markedly increase a drug's intake to attain its original effects, or experiencing a markedly diminished effect with continued use of the same amount of the drug; and *cross-tolerance*, which occurs when a drug exhibits tolerance to other drugs, usually in the same class. For example, patients tolerant to diazepam are tolerant to barbiturates, but not to heroin. In general, the greater the tolerance to a drug, the worse the withdrawal and the greater the amount needed to become intoxicated.

DSM-IV subdivides substance use disorders into substance *dependence*

TABLE 8–1
Names of Misused Substances

CATEGORY	TYPE	GENERIC NAME	BRAND NAME	STREET NAMES
Alcohol				
Anticholinergics		atropine belladona benztropine trihexyphenidyl	Butabell Donnatel Congentin Artane	
Cannabis (THC)	Hashish	Cannabis (fe- male) resin		hash, sheesh
	Marijuana	Cannabis leaves, stems, buds		ganja, grass, reefer, pot, bud, weed, smoke
Hallucinogens ("Psyche- delics")	Amphetamine- like Others	DET, DMT, DOM, MDA LSD		businessman's special blotter, acid, sun- shine, purple haze, win- dowpane
		mescaline myristicin psilocybin		peyote, cactus, nutmeg magic mush- room, buttons, shrooms
Hypoanxiolytes				downers, barbs
	Barbiturates	amobarbital pentobarbital phenobarbital secobarbital	Amytal Nembutal Luminal Seconal	blues, lilly yellow jackets purple hearts reds, pink lady
	Barbiturate-like	chloral hydrate		Mickey Finn (with alcohol)
		ethchlorvynol mebrobamate	Placidyl Equinil Miltown Parest	
	Benzodiaze- pines (short- acting)	alprazolam lorazepam oxazepam temazepam triazolam	Xanax Ativan Serax Restoral Halcion	
	(long-acting)	chlordiazepoxide clonazepam clorazepate diazepam flurazepam prazepam	Librium Klonopin Tranxene Valium Dalmane Centrax	libbies pins Vitamin V

(continued)

TABLE 8–1
(*Continued*)

CATEGORY	TYPE	GENERIC NAME	BRAND NAME	STREET NAMES
MDMA		3,4-methylene-dioxymeth-amphetamine		ecstasy, XTC
Opiates		codeine	Empirin with codeine	T-3s
		diphenoxylate	Lomotil	
		heroin		smack, skag, H, snow, horse, dope, boy
		hydrocodone	Vicodin	
		hydromorphone	Dilaudid	Lords, dL's
		meperidine	Demerol	
		methadone	Dolophine	dollys, amidone, done
		methylmorphine	(codeine)	
		morphine		dope, M, Miss Emma, morpho
		opium (tincture of)	Paregoric	PG, licorice
		oxycodone	Percodan	percs
Pentazocine			Talwin	
Phencyclidine (PCP)			Ketamine	angel dust
			Sernyl	killer weed, crystal, hog, peace, pill
Solvents	(Inhalants)	amyl nitrite		amys, pears
		butyl nitrite		rush, locker room
		carbon dioxide		
		ether		poppers, snapper, wippit
		ethyl chloride		Ethel
		nitrous oxide		laughing gas
		toluene		toolie
Stimulants	(Major) Amphetamines	dextroamphetamine	Dexadrine	uppers, speed, dex, brownies, wakeups, black beauties
		dextroamphetamine/amobarbital	Dexamyl	greenies
		dL-amphetamine	Benzadrine	bennies, A's, jelly beans, peaches

(*continued*)

TABLE 8–1
(*Continued*)

CATEGORY	TYPE	GENERIC NAME	BRAND NAME	STREET NAMES
		methamphe-tamine	Desoxyn	meth, crystal ice, crank
	Cocaine			coke, flake, toot, snow, crack, freebase, girl
	Cocaine with heroin			speedball, white tornado
	Misc.	methylphenidate pemoline	Ritalin Cylert	
	(Minor)			
	Caffeine		Vivarin, No Doz, Coke, coffee	
	Nicotine		Marlboro, etc.	

TABLE 8–2
DSM-IV* Criteria for Substance Intoxication and Withdrawal

Substance Intoxication

A. The development of a reversible substance-specific syndrome due to recent inges-tion of (or exposure to) a substance. **Note:** Different substances may produce similar or identical syndromes.

B. Clinically significant maladaptive behavioral or psychological changes that are due to the effect of the substance on the central nervous system (e.g., belliger-ence, mood lability, cognitive impairment, impaired judgment, impaired social or occupational functioning) and develop during or shortly after use of the sub-stance.

C. The symptoms are not due to a general medical condition and not better ac-counted for by another mental disorder.

Substance Withdrawal

A. The development of a substance-specific syndrome due to the cessation of (or reduction in) substance use that has been heavy and prolonged.

B. The substance-specific syndrome causes clinically significant distress or impair-ment in social, occupational, or other important areas of functioning.

C. The symptoms are not due to a general medical condition and not better ac-counted for by another mental disorder.

*DSM-IV, pp. 184–85.

and substance *abuse*. The *consequences* of the substance use define these illnesses. *Drug dependence* is the repeated, nonmedical use of a substance that harms the user or incites behavior in the user that harms others, and involves psychological and/or physical dependence. *Psychological dependence* is characterized by the compulsive misuse of a substance, taking it longer than planned, intense craving, unsuccessful efforts to cut down, and a preoccupation with obtaining it, often at the expense of psychological, occupational, social, medical, or financial considerations. *Physiological dependence* is the repeated use of a drug to avert physical withdrawal reactions or taking larger amounts to get the same effects (tolerance). Psychological and physical dependencies often co-exist. Table 8–3 lists *DSM-IV* criteria for substance dependence.

Substance abuse involves the misuse of a substance resulting in significant impairment or distress *without actually developing substance dependence*. Table 8–4 lists *DSM-IV* criteria for substance abuse. Problems caused by substances include car accidents, demotions or job terminations, divorce, loss of child custody, arrests, and loss of friends. This diagnosis applies to the person who minimizes: "Yeah, sure I've had a few DWI's (driving while intoxicated), paid a few visits to the emergency room for stitches after bar fights, and spent the night in jail once—but I'm no alcoholic. I can stop anytime I want. I always drink the same amount and I never have withdrawal."

According to the "self-medication hypothesis," the original choice of an abused drug is not random, but is partly made to alleviate a specific distressing symptom or affect. At first, narcotics are used to mask pain, hypnotics to induce sleep, cocaine to eliminate depression, amphetamines to "get up," marijuana to join the crowd, or bourbon to rid boredom. No matter how substance abuse begins, however, once it becomes habitual and stopping it causes severe distress, drug dependence has occurred. At this juncture the habit is sustained less from original motives and more to quell a drug-induced biological imperative. Therefore, treating only the initial cause is less effective: Drug dependence must be directly treated, along with the original problems. An example: When hospitalized, a chronic alcoholic was very suspicious. After three weeks of "drying out," his "head cleared" and his suspiciousness disappeared. Only then did it become apparent that marital problems greatly affected his alcoholism.

Many problems, including conditions likely to prompt relapse, cannot be evaluated properly until the substance abuser has been drug-free for 10 days. (Some experts suggest one to three months.) Table 8–5 outlines the major pharmacological effects of psychoactive substances. In general, the substances that have no withdrawal syndromes (such as marijuana) are likely to elicit only psychological dependence. Marijuana and hallucinogens can also induce "reverse tolerance" in the user: The *more* the drug is used, the less is needed to obtain the original effects. Alcohol, barbiturates, opiates, phencyclidine, solvents, and inhalants are most likely to kill in overdose.

TABLE 8–3
***DSM-IV* Criteria for Substance Dependence**

A maladaptive pattern of substance use, leading to clinically significant impairment or distress, as manifested by three (or more) of the following, occurring at any time in the same 12- month period:

(1) tolerance, as defined by either of the following:

 (a) a need for markedly increased amounts of the substance to achieve intoxication or desired effect
 (b) markedly diminished effect with continued use of the same amount of the substance

(2) withdrawal, as manifested by either of the following:

 (a) the characteristic withdrawal syndrome for the substance (refer to Criteria A and B of the criteria sets for Withdrawal from the specific substances)
 (b) the same (or closely related) substance is taken to relieve or avoid withdrawal symptoms

(3) the substance is often taken in larger amounts or over a longer period than was intended

(4) there is a persistent desire or unsuccessful efforts to cut down or control substance use

(5) a great deal of time is spent in activities necessary to obtain the substance (e.g., visiting multiple doctors or driving long distances), use the substance (e.g., chain-smoking), or recover from its effects

(6) important social, occupational, or recreational activities are given up or reduced because of substance use

(7) the substance use is continued despite knowledge of having a persistent or recurrent physical or psychological problem that is likely to have been caused or exacerbated by the substance (e.g., current cocaine use despite recognition of cocaine-induced depression, or continued drinking despite recognition that an ulcer was made worse by alcohol consumption)

Specify if:
With Physiological Dependence: evidence of tolerance or withdrawal (i.e., either Item 1 or 2 is present)
Without Physiological Dependence: no evidence of tolerance or withdrawal (i.e., neither Item 1 nor 2 is present)

DSM-IV, p. 181.

TABLE 8–4
DSM-IV Criteria for Substance Abuse*

A. A maladaptive pattern of substance use leading to clinically significant impairment or distress, as manifested by one (or more) of the following, occurring within a 12-month period:

  (1) recurrent substance use resulting in a failure to fulfill major role obligations at work, school, or home (e.g., repeated absences or poor work performance related to substance use; substance-related absences, suspensions, or expulsions from school; neglect of children or household)

  (2) recurrent substance use in situations in which it is physically hazardous (e.g., driving an automobile or operating a machine when impaired by substance use)

  (3) recurrent substance-related legal problems (e.g., arrests for substance-related disorderly conduct)

  (4) continued substance use despite having persistent or recurrent social or interpersonal problems caused or exacerbated by the effects of the substance (e.g., arguments with spouse about consequences of intoxication, physical fights)

B. The symptoms have never met the criteria for Substance Dependence for this class of substance.

*DSM-IV, pp. 182–83.

TABLE 8–5
DSM-IV Major Substance Diagnoses*

SUBSTANCE	DEPENDENCE	ABUSE	INTOXICATION	WITHDRAWAL
Alcohol	X	X	X	X
Amphetamines	X	X	X	X
Caffeine			X	X[+]
Cannabis	X	X	X	
Cocaine	X	X	X	X
Hallucinogens	X	X	X	
Inhalants	X	X	X	
Nicotine	X		X[+]	X
Opioids	X	X	X	X
Phencyclidine	X	X	X	
Sedatives, hypnotics, or anxiolytics	X	X	X	X
Polysubstance	X			
Other	X	X	X	X

*DSM-IV, p. 177.
[+]Not classified in *DSM-IV* but does exist.

THE ASSESSMENT OF SUBSTANCE MISUSE

Many factors complicate the diagnosis and treatment of substance abusers. For starters, many give unreliable histories. Unlike most patients, their objectives differ from their therapists': Many abusers *want* their habit—or as a heroin addict put it, "If I had to choose between smack and food and sex, I'd take smack." Denial and lying are often their norms; at times, even addicts don't know which they are doing. Outright lying is common to avoid detection and to hasten discharge. On admission, however, already-discovered addicts may exaggerate their intake to garner more of the drug during detoxification. For all these reasons, clinicians should favor objective signs and social behaviors over subjective reports, and corroborate and supplement this information by interviewing family and friends and obtaining a urine drug screen. Because these patients frequently lie and deny, manipulate professionals, and relapse, they habitually frustrate and infuriate clinicians. Therefore, therapists should constantly monitor their own angry and moralistic feelings. Moreover, therapists should not take these patients' provocations and relapses personally: They are part of the natural history of substance abuse.

The best screening questions for alcoholism are in the CAGE questionnaire (Ewing, 1984). The name is an acronym of the four areas probed (*C*ut down, *A*nnoyed, *G*uilty, and *E*ye Opener). The following questions are used:

*C*ut down	1. Have you ever felt you should *C*ut down on your drinking?
*A*nnoyed	2. Have other people *A*nnoyed you by criticizing your drinking?
*G*uilty	3. Have you ever felt *G*uilty about drinking?
*E*ye Opener	4. Have you ever taken a drink in the morning to steady your nerves or get rid of a hang-over?

Two or more positive answers indicate alcohol dependence. This questionnaire accurately determines the presence or absence of alcoholism over 85% of the time (Beresford, Blow, Hill, Singer, & Lucey, 1990); it misses more cases of alcohol dependence in women than it does in men.

After screening patients for substance misuse, Table 8–6 can be used to assess substance intoxication by applying its extensive evaluation guidelines for those who are suspected of having substance-related disorders.

As soon as clinicians get on top of one drug problem, another pops up, resulting in a constant information-lag about drug abuse. More serious is that *polydrug abuse* has increased sharply. In comparison to single-drug abusers, polydrug abusers have

TABLE 8–6
The Assessment of Substance Misuse in Suspected Abusers

Quick Recognition of Substance Intoxication

		Drugs Used	
Eyes	Pupils dilated	Stimulants	Cocaine
		Hallucino-gens	Amphetamines
	Pupils constricted	Opioids	
	Conjuctival injection (bloodshot eyes)	Cannabis, marijuana	
Psychomotor	Unsteady gait, ataxia	Alcohol	Hynoanxiolytics
	Nystagmus (rhyth-mic oscillation of the eyeballs)	Sedatives Anesthetics	PCP Inhalants

I. HISTORY
  A. Substance(s)
      1. Name(s) (e.g., diazepam, cocaine)
      2. Polydrug use: Indicates names and preferred combinations
      3. Special preparations (e.g., freebasing)

  B. Route (e.g., ingestion, inhalation, injection)

  C. Amount
      1. Typical dose, frequency, and duration of drug use
      2. Dose and duration of drug use during past 10 days
      3. The time and amount of the most recent drug use

  D. Patterns of Use
      1. Self-medication: Is it for physical, psychiatric, or emotional problems or "just for fun?"
      2. Identifiable events or stresses that increase or decrease the use of a substance (e.g., drinking before sex, "chipping" heroin before job interviews, smoking after meals)
      3. History: How did substance abuse begin? Why does it continue? Are there conditioned relapses? What began and ended the patient's longest drug-free period?
      4. Timing: How early in the day does the patient first use the substance?
      5. Style (e.g., sneaking drugs, hiding bottles, boasting, running away, using substances with others or alone)

  E. Acquisition
      1. Sources: legal, illegal, prescription, theft, "mobsters," friends
      2. Time and money spent obtaining substances (e.g., illegal activities such as theft, prostitution, and drug dealing)

  F. Network
      1. Family and friends: Which exert beneficial and harmful influences on the patient?
      2. Family history of antisocial personality, substance misuse, and mood disorder?

  G. Functioning
      1. Interference with social, occupational, recreational, academic, and familial functioning
      2. Adverse influence on physical health, appearance, finances, and self-image
      3. Legal problems

(continued)

TABLE 8–6
(*Continued*)

4. How does the patient feel *without* the drug?
5. Impaired organic functioning such as forgetting location of "stash," poor concentration, impaired judgment
6. Does patient become suicidal or assaultive on the drug?

H. History: Medical and Psychiatric
1. Drug-related medical illnesses: hepatitis, infections, insomnia, allergies, cirrhosis, TB, AIDS, epilepsy
2. All recently-taken prescribed and over-the-counter drugs. Does the patient use these medications differently than they were prescribed or intended? Does the patient take or sneak other people's or family member's medications? Does the patient use multiple doctors and pharmacies to avoid detection? (Have family bring all medications in the patient's home.)
3. History of psychiatric symptoms or mental illness prior to substance misuse
4. History of substance-related syndromes: flashbacks, delirium, idiosyncratic intoxication, hallucinosis

I. Prior Treatment
1. Type, duration, degree of participation, including experiences with community agencies and self-help groups
2. Results as seen by (a) the patient, (b) his or her relatives, and (c) his or her therapist

J. Current Motivations to Change
1. Why the patient is seeking treatment *now*?
2. Current threat of jail, divorce, etc.

II. COMMON SYMPTOMS AND SIGNS
[With special signs of abuse by adolescents and teenagers in brackets]

A. Prodromal phase
1. Increased tolerance
2. Sneaking chemicals [frequently odd places during school, such as closets or storage rooms, to take drugs]
3. Temporary amnesia
4. Preoccupation with chemical use
5. Avoids talking about personal use
6. More frequent loss of memory

B. Crucial or basic phase
7. Time lost from work [or changes in school attendance, grades, or discipline]
8. Loss of control (unusual or apparently unmotivated temper outbursts)
9. Alibis [especially about not doing homework]
10. Increased extravagance—time, money, advice; being a "know-it-all"
11. Aggressive or abusive behavior
12. Persistent remorse
13. Periodic abstinence
14. Losing or changing friends
15. Losing clients or position
16. Persistent resentments
17. Diminished self-care and unhealthy appearance
18. Slovenly dress, sunglasses at inappropriate times (to hide dilated or constricted pupils and to diminish glare) and long-sleeved shirts (to hide needle marks)

(*continued*)

TABLE 8–6
(*Continued*)

19. Borrowing money [and theft of small items from school] to buy drugs
20. Escape—geographical, psychological, social
21. Protecting supply [furtive looks to avoid stash being detected]
22. Morning use of chemical(s)

  C. Chronic phase
23. More-or-less continuous use over 10-hour period
24. Ethical deterioration
25. Decreased tolerance
26. Sleeping at inappropriate times
27. Indefinable fears
28. Tangential or incoherent speech; inappropriate remarks
29. Tremors

III. PHYSICAL EXAMINATION
  A. Rectal and pelvic examinations
    1. Should be considered since substance abusers notoriously hide and smuggle drugs in any way possible

  B. Physical signs
    1. Marks: scarring along a vein, tattooing over a vein, abscesses, ulcers, and needle tracks. The quantity and age of needle marks can serve as a rough check on the validity of the patient's history
    2. Nose: Is it dripping? Are nasal membranes infected, swollen, or septum eroded from snorting cocaine?
    3. Pupils: Constricted (miosis) with opiates and PCP; dilated (mydriasis) with amphetamines, anticholinergics, and hallucinogens
    4. Signs of intoxication or withdrawal (Table 8–2)

IV. LABORATORY EXAMINATIONS
  A. Urine screens
    1. Thin Layer Chemistry (TLC): sometimes inaccurate; used only for screening
    2. Enzyme Innuno Assay (EIA) and Radio Immuno Assay (RIA): These two tests have relatively high degrees of sensitivity and specificity; the EIA is a qualitative test, the RIA, quantitative. Detects people who eat poppy seed cake as opiate positive
    3. Gas Chromatography Mass Spectrometry (GC/MS): the most reliable and informative of tests; expensive but the "Gold Standard"

  B. Serum levels
    1. Abused substances (when urine tests are positive or abused substances are already known)
    2. Other psychotropic drugs (e.g., antidepressants)

  C. Liver and renal function tests
    1. GGT: This liver enzyme (gamma glutamyl transerase) is often the first to rise in alcoholism

more severe and complicated withdrawals and bleaker prognoses. They are harder to diagnose and treat, especially in emergencies, since they present a more confounding mix of signs and symptoms than single-substance abusers. Not uncommonly, an inpatient being successfully treated for an opiate intoxication suddenly convulses from barbiturate withdrawal four days later. The lesson: Polydrug abuse must be evaluated for every substance abuser.

In general, withdrawal, intoxication, and dependence should be addressed in this sequence. The most dangerous acute problem (see Table 8–7) is *hypnoanxiolytic* (including alcohol) withdrawal, since this can be lethal, whereas opiate or stimulant (cocaine, amphetamine) withdrawal is uncomfortable, at most. However, some patients with serious medical problems can die from opiate withdrawal. When it is unclear whether patients are intoxicated or withdrawing from hypnoanxiolytic, err by treating withdrawal, since that poses a greater threat than intoxication.

ALCOHOL

There are more English synonyms for "drunk" than for any other word. Benjamin Franklin was the first to publish them — 228; recently Flexner listed 353 synonyms and said that he had just scratched the surface. "Alcohol" comes from the Arabic *alkuhl*, because Arabs were the first to distill it in 600 A.D. The practice spread and so did the problems. Ghengis Khan counseled his troops, "A soldier must not get drunk oftener than once a week. It would, of course, be better if he did not get drunk at all, but one should not expect the impossible" (Goodwin & Guze, 1984, p. 148).

In 1990 per capita alcohol consumption in the United States was 39.5 gallons, mostly beer, costing $1,811 per person (Wortis, 1993). Today, alcoholism is America's most serious drug problem, as it is for every other industrialized nation (it costs New York City alone $1 billion a year). Alcoholism is an illness of "normal" people, not bums. The typical alcoholic is in his middle thirties and has a good job, home, and family. Less than 5% of alcoholics are on Skid Row.

A practical definition of alcoholism would assign it diagnostically "when a person's alcohol consumption repeatedly interferes with occupational or social functioning, emotional state, or physical health." This definition stresses impairment of the individual rather than an arbitrary consumption figure, such as whether the person downs one or five or 50 drinks a week. People with a condition called "idiosyncratic intoxication" often become violent on a single drink; for them, one drink constitutes alcoholism. In the service of denial, patients and relatives will nitpick over alcoholism's definition; by stating that alcoholism exists whenever problems with alcohol

TABLE 8–7
DSM-IV **Criteria for Alcohol, Sedative, Hypnotic or**
Anxiolytic Intoxification and Withdrawal*

Substance Intoxication

A. Recent ingestion of alcohol, sedative, hypnotic, or anxiolytic.

B. Clinically significant maladaptive behavioral or psychological changes (e.g., inappropriate sexual or aggressive behavior, mood lability, impaired judgment, impaired social or occupational functioning), that developed during, or shortly after, alcohol, sedative, hypnotic, or anxiolytic ingestion.

C. One (or more) of the following signs, developing during, or shortly after, alcohol, sedative, hypnotic, or anxiolytic use:

   (1) slurred speech
   (2) incoordination
   (3) unsteady gait
   (4) nystagmus
   (5) impairment in attention or memory
   (6) stupor or coma

D. The symptoms are not due to a general medical condition and are not better accounted for by another mental disorder.

Substance Withdrawal

A. Cessation of (or reduction in) alcohol, sedative, hypnotic, or anxiolytic use that has been heavy and prolonged.

B. Two or more of the following, developing within several hours to a few days after Criterion A:

   (1) autonomic hyperactivity (e.g., sweating or pulse rate greater than 100)
   (2) increased hand tremor
   (3) insomnia
   (4) nausea or vomiting
   (5) transient visual, tactile, or auditory hallucinations or illusions
   (6) psychomotor agitation
   (7) anxiety
   (8) grand mal seizures

C. The symptoms in Criterion B cause clinically significant distress or impairment in social, occupational, or other important areas of functioning.

D. The symptoms are not due to a general medical condition and are not better accounted for by another mental disorder.

Specify if:
With Perceptual Disturbances

DSM-IV, pp. 197, 198–99, 264, 266.

repeatedly arise, the clinician circumvents semantic quibbling. Part of the clinician's job is to teach patients how the diagnosis is made so that they can make it for themselves. Many patients believe the term *alcoholic* only applies to Skid Row bums. For many it is initially easier to agree to having "problems with alcohol."

Clinical Presentation

Although alcoholics vary considerably, in general they suffer from apprehension, agitation, dysphoria, guilt, remorse, despair, hopelessness, futility, self-deprecation, and insomnia. Their symptoms are usually worse in the morning, after not drinking for hours. *The Lost Weekend*—a "must-see" movie for every clinician—portrays with bone-chilling accuracy the "typical" alcoholic's life: obsessed with drink, continually lying about it, hiding bottles, sneaking drinks, and disappearing repeatedly. After "going on the wagon," alcoholics will reexperience anxiety or depression and start drinking again; a vicious spiral of abstinence-dysphoria-drinking escalates until the alcoholic reaches "rock bottom."

DSM-IV lists 13 mental disorders related to alcohol; Table 8-7 enumerates the diagnostic criteria for intoxication and withdrawal. Abuse and dependence are defined the same for alcohol as for any other drug (see Tables 8-3 and 8-4). (The other mental disorders related to alcohol are delirium, persisting amnestic disorder, psychotic disorder [with delusions or hallucinations], mood disorder, anxiety disorder, sexual dysfunction, and sleep disorder.)

Withdrawal is most critical, since 15% of alcoholics who develop delirium tremens ("DTs") die. The first and most common withdrawal symptom is tremulousness, which begins a few hours after stopping, or greatly reducing, alcohol intake. The others are the same for all hypnoanxiolytics (see Table 8-6).

Alcohol is one of the few drugs to cause *"blackouts,"* a temporary (anterograde) amnesia in which short-term (but not long-term) memory is lost, while other intellectual and motor functions remain intact. To illustrate: The day after a "bender" (remaining drunk for several days), an alcoholic surgeon became angry at a nurse for allowing a tracheostomy to be done on one of his patients without notifying him. She reminded the surgeon that he himself had performed the procedure the day before. He apparently had a blackout, since he had no recollection of doing it. As in this case, alcoholics may appear to function normally and even perform complex tasks during a blackout. Research suggests that the forgotten material does not hold special psychological significance, but results from a neurological deficit in retrieving new information. Blackouts scare alcoholics, who are often terrified of having committed violence they can't remember; blackouts are also frightening because they appear to be dramatic proof that alcohol is destroying their brains. In truth, however, blackouts have no prognostic significance.

Clinical Course

A large number of male alcoholics begin heavy drinking during their late teens or twenties, but only in their thirties, after a long and insidious course, do they fully acknowledge their alcoholism. Jellinek's (1952) three phases of alcoholism—prodromal, crucial, and chronic—are outlined in Table 8-8. Recently it has been shown that there are many patterns to drinking and

TABLE 8–8
Jellinek's Three Phases of Alcoholism*

PRODOMAL PHASE	
Palimpsests (blackouts, amnesia not associated with loss of consciousness)	Avid drinking (gulping)
Surreptitious drinking	Guilt
Preoccupation with drinking	Avoiding reference to drinking

CRUCIAL PHASE (Heralded by the onset of increased palimpsests)	
Loss of control	Changes in interpersonal relationships
Rationalization	Geographic escape
Social pressures to quit drinking	Changed family habits
Grandiosity	Unreasonable resentments
Aggressiveness	Protecting the supply
Persistent remorse	Poor nutrition
Remaining abstinent for periods of time	Decreased libido
Setting rules as to when to drink	Morbid jealousy
Dropping friends	Regular morning drinking
Quitting jobs	First hospitalization for alcoholism occurs about here
Alcohol-centered behavior	Loss of interests

CHRONIC PHASE	
Benders (remaining drunk for several days)	Loss of tolerance for alcohol
Ethical deterioration	Undefinable fears
Impaired thinking	Tremors
Psychosis (10%)	Psychomotor inhibition
Decline in social level	Obsessive drinking
Drinking non-potables	Religious desires
Rationalization fails and the patient becomes accessible to treatment	

*Information from Jellinek, 1952.

the above criteria do not always pertain. Several types of alcoholics have been described:

1. The *alcohol dependent drinker* relies on alcohol for relief of stress. There is no loss of control or gross intoxication and little progression in the course of the illness. Gradually there is loss of physical health. These alcoholics are rarely recognized.
2. The *wine drinker* is unable to abstain without withdrawal symptoms and is in a constant state of mild intoxication (especially prevalent in France and Italy).
3. The *compulsive alcoholic* exhibits extreme loss of control and will drink until unconscious (especially prevalent in the United States and Canada).
4. The *secondary alcoholic* drinks secondary to one or more psychiatric disorders (mood disorder, phobic or anxiety states, cognitive disorders, or psychoses).
5. The *periodic drinker* has long periods of sobriety interspersed with binges ("the weekend drunk").
6. The *chronic alcoholic* is the final common path of many alcohol abusers. It is associated with decreased tolerance, physical complications, and social deterioration.

Mortality rates of alcoholics are approximately twice normal in males, three times normal in females, and are especially high in younger age groups. The predominant causes of death in alcoholics are cancer of the upper digestive and respiratory organs, arteriosclerotic heart disease, pneumonia, cirrhosis, ulcers, accidents, and suicides. Selzer (1969) found that of 96 drivers responsible for fatal accidents, 88 were chronic alcoholics. In almost half of fatal auto accidents, the culpable drivers were drunk. Two and a half years after diagnosis of cirrhosis of the liver, 19% of those who continued to drink died; of those who stopped, none died (Rankin, Winkenson, & Santamaria, 1970). Because "spontaneous" improvement is more common than generally realized, if alcoholics can keep functioning when they reach midlife, their long-term prognosis improves considerably. In other words, alcoholism is *not* a hopeless condition!

Complications

Alcoholism is a major factor in 20% of divorces and 40% of problems brought to family court. Half of all police work, hospital admissions, homicides, and automobile fatalities are alcohol-related. One-fourth of all suicides involve alcohol, especially in men over 35 who have suffered a loss in the last six months. Suicide causes 5–27% of all deaths of alcoholics (Berglund, 1984).

Alcoholism assaults every organ; it causes anemia, muscle weakness, gastritis, diarrhea, ulcers, pancreatitis, "fetal alcohol syndrome," and other birth defects. Pregnant women should not drink at all. Combined with poor nutrition, alcoholism may produce a fatty liver and cirrhosis. Three or four beers a day over 15 years results in 18% with cirrhosis (Sorensen et al., 1984). Poor nutrition and alcoholism also cause the rapidly erupting *Wernicke-Korsakoff syndrome* of eye movement disturbances (nystagmus and inability to look laterally in one or both eyes), ataxia, and mental disturbances (confusion, impaired recent memory). If this syndrome is not promptly treated with massive doses of thiamine, in several days the patient may develop *Korsakoff psychosis*—which is not really a psychosis but a potentially permanent dementia characterized by impaired recent memory with lowered ability to think, disorientation, and confabulation (confabulation is not necessary to make the diagnosis). In the less severe cases, complete recovery may occur slowly over a period of months. Severe cases may be left with serious memory deficits. Of patients who have both alcoholic and metabolic or nutritional problems, Wernicke's encephalopathy is seen in 65%, Korsakoff's psychosis in 53%, and alcoholic polyneuropathy in 70%.

Alcohol withdrawal can cause seizures (rum fits), delirium tremens (DTs, or in *DSM-IV* terms, "alcohol delirium with onset during withdrawal"), or alcoholic hallucinosis (*DSM-IV*, "alcohol psychotic disorder, with hallucinations"). *Alcoholic grand mal seizures* usually occur the first day or two after stopping drinking. In about a third of the cases, they are associated with DTs, the seizures preceding the delirium. The best treatment is prophylaxis with Dilantin in patients who are known to be predisposed to seizures. Delirium tremens usually occur within one week (three to four days average) after stopping drinking and usually last three days or less, although more severe DTs may occur with more prolonged drinking. Symptoms of DTs include disorientation, visual hallucinations, wakefulness, tremulous picking motions, and frequently mild temperature elevations. Long-term (5–20 years) alcoholics are most likely to get DTs. In the past, 6–15% of patients with DTs died, usually of head trauma or pneumonia, but rapid diagnosis and treatment has lowered the death rate. Patients with DTs should be hospitalized and given oral fluids and sedation. Keeping someone with the patient and the lights on can help reduce terror and visual hallucinations.

Alcoholic hallucinosis (usually auditory) is a syndrome (somewhat rarer than DTs) in which patients complain of vivid, usually identifiable voices in a clear sensorium. The voices are frequently (60%) unpleasant and patients' behavior is usually consistent with the content of the voices, including fearful attempts to escape and, occasionally, attempted suicide. This syndrome occurs as a withdrawal phenomenon, usually within the first three days after cessation of drinking in alcoholics of long standing. In 90% of Victor and Hope's (1958) 76 cases, the course was benign and transient, usually ending in less than a week. However, in 10%, the syndrome lasted for months or years and retained a clinical similarity to schizophrenia. Of 43 patients followed up, 11 were dead in five years (two by suicide). Only three of these 43 patients were abstinent and working, indicating a profoundly gloomy prognosis for this condition. Treatment should consist of supportive therapy, prevention of convulsions, and antipsychotics, when indicated.

Epidemiology

In the United States approximately 1 out of 10 adults is an alcoholic, for a total of perhaps 14 million alcoholics in the country. One quarter of alcoholics have an onset prior to the age of 20 and 85% have become alcoholic by the age of 40; onset is earlier for African Americans and Native Americans than for Caucasians. Many times (3:1 or greater) more men than women are alcoholic. Women develop alcoholism later but more rapidly than men; in women, approximately 13 years elapse prior to treatment; in men, it is 21 years.

Etiology and Pathogenesis

About half of all hospitalized male alcoholics have a family history of alcoholism. In contrast to nonfamilial alcoholics, these familial alcoholics become alcoholics earlier in life, have greater dependency, bleaker prognoses, fewer nonalcoholic psychiatric problems, and are less able to maintain "controlled drinking." The best predictor of future alcoholism among adolescents is a family history of alcoholism (Goodwin, 1985).

Twin studies generally support this division by showing that hereditary plays a major role in some, but not all, cases of alcoholism. Whether reared by alcoholic biological parents or by nonalcoholic adopted parents, the sons of alcoholics have three to four times the normal rate of alcoholism, whereas daughters have only a slightly higher rate than the general population. Cloninger (1987) described "type 1 alcoholism" as milder, starts after age 25, hits men and women equally, needs environmental factors (e.g., low social class) as well as genetics, and is 20% heritable. "Type 2 alcoholism" is often severe, starts in the teens, hits men only, and is 90% heritable for male offspring of type 2 fathers. Twenty to 35% of sons of alcoholics become alcoholics; 5–10% of daughters become alcoholics. Mood disorders may run in the families of alcoholics, but this remains controversial. There may also be a relationship between anxiety disorders and alcohol problems: Alcohol problems are more likely to follow the onset of agoraphobia and social phobia; alcohol misuse is more likely to precede and perhaps cause panic disorder and generalized anxiety disorder (Kushner, Sher, & Bertman, 1990).

Treatment and Management

The treatment of alcohol dependence is abstinence and Alcoholics Anonymous (or an equivalent recovery program). Since clinicians can't reliably predict the 5–15% of alcoholics who eventually will be able to drink moderately, abstinence should be urged, especially for the first 6–12 months after hospitalization, when 70–90% of patients relapse. The longer patients remain dry, the sharper their thinking and the better their occupational, social, and sexual functioning. Some patients are very tentative about their diagnosis and hence their treatment. It may be useful to elicit their agreement not to drink at all for three or six months, "just to see what abstinence feels like and how it affects them." In advance, patients are told that inability to follow through on this temporary abstinence is proof of alcoholism.

Supervised (but *not* unsupervised) Antabuse (disulfiram) treatment for alcoholism works better than placebo (Brewer, 1993). For the subgroup of alcoholics who sincerely believe in and desire this as an *adjunct* to treatment, Antabuse may be helpful. Cravings are mitigated by the knowledge that drinking within three to five days of taking the drug will produce severe nausea, flushing, tachycardia, and hypotension. The standard dose is 250 mg/day; higher doses offer no more deterrence and, if mixed with alcohol, are potentially lethal. Antabuse usually should not be the sole treatment. For alcoholics who prefer only Antabuse, a compromise might include giving them Antabuse in exchange for attending AA meetings. AA attendance can be monitored by having patients obtain signed vouchers for attendance. Lithium has been reported to help both depressed and nondepressed alcoholics stay abstinent (Fawcett et al., 1987). There is some controversy about these drug approaches because the ability to stay *compliant* with any medication or placebo regime predicts abstinence.

Alcoholics Anonymous (AA) greatly benefits a majority of alcoholics. AA doesn't go into *why* people drink, just that they *do*, and shouldn't; it stresses a "one-day-at-a-time" philosophy, which allows alcoholics to deal with manageable units of time and end a "dry day" with a sense of accomplishment. On a trial basis at least, all alcoholics should attend AA meetings. Clinicians can help by finding a socially appropriate AA chapter for their patients, by not giving in to rationalizations for why they can't attend this or that AA meeting, and by getting patients linked up with an AA member who is on the same "wavelength." Finding sponsors can help patients begin the AA process and find the right meetings. Some meetings are open to drop-ins and beginners while others are closed so that group members can focus on a certain aspect of their recovery. If there are several choices, patients should explore to see which location(s) is the best fit for them. If patients are on medication for a psychiatric problem such as depression, it is important to find AA groups that are supportive of pharmacologic treatments. AA also welcomes people with other drug problems, especially hypnoanxiolytic, marijuana, and cocaine dependence. Polysubstance abusers can also go to more specialized meetings like Narcotics Anonymous. Some patients never feel comfortable with the AA philosophy and do better with alternatives such as Rational Recovery. Women often feel more comfortable at "women only" groups.

The clinician must also attend to the needs of the alcoholic's family. If one member drinks, the others needn't drown. Growing up with an alcoholic parent can be devastating; so is living with a currently alcoholic spouse. The clinician should assure family members that they are not responsible for the alcoholic's drinking, nor do they have any ethical obligation to "reform" the alcoholic. Whether or not the alcoholic goes to AA, the patient's relatives should attend Alanon, a support group for family members, or Alateen, which offers information and assistance to teenage alcoholics and their teenage relatives. For alcoholics who are resistant to diagnosis and treatment, the family can become an invaluable ally in penetrating the denial and rationalizations. In these cases, an "intervention" might be arranged: Significant people in the alcoholic's life get together and in a very firm, direct, and compassionate manner, confront the person regarding the alcoholism. Interventions are best done with the help of an experienced professional. Many recovered alcoholics look back on these dramatic confrontations as the turning points in their lives.

HYPNOANXIOLYTICS

Hypnoanxiolytics quell anxiety, induce sleep, or both. Table 8–1 classifies the hypnoanxiolytics into three groups: barbiturates, barbiturate-like, and benzodiazepines. *Barbiturates* are the prototypic hypnoanxiolytic. The first barbiturate, Veronal—named after the tranquil city of Verona in Italy—was introduced in 1902 as a "safe" replacement for alcohol. *Benzodiazepines* are now the most widely prescribed hypnoanxiolytics in the world. In the United States, 68 million prescriptions were written (in 1978) for benzodiazepines, with diazepam being the nation's fourth most frequently prescribed drug. (Hypnoanxiolytic disorders are described in Tables 8–3, 8–4, 8–5, and 8–7.)

When taken as an overdose, barbiturates are frequently lethal, but benzodiazepines only rarely. Relative to barbiturates, less tolerance develops to benzodiazepines, withdrawal is less frequent, and potentiation by alcohol is less (Goodwin & Guze, 1984). With benzodiazepines, tolerance tends to develop more often to the sedative than to the anxiolytic effects. Benzodiazepines, however, are not innocuous: The elderly are highly sensitive to them and whether they produce birth defects remains unknown. Longer-acting benzodiazepines may accumulate to toxic levels and insidiously retard cognition and movement. Psychological and physical dependence may arise from ongoing use; in one survey, 58% of long-term users admitted they would have "difficulty" without them (Salzman, 1985). Four to six years after being hospitalized for hypnoanxiolytic dependence, 84% of patients were using hypnoanxiolytics, 52% were abusing them, 42% had been rehospitalized for drug misuse, and 12% had withdrawal convulsions (Allgulander, Borg, & Vikander, 1984). Although benzodiazepine withdrawal is usually mild, it can be severe. Withdrawal symptoms are the same as with alcohol (Table 8–7). Benzodiazepines that reach the brain the fastest and produce a "buzz" are most likely to be abused. For example, diazepam (Valium) and chlordiazepoxide (Librium) have similar characteristics, except that Valium is a highly lipid soluble and quickly penetrates the blood-brain barrier, producing a rapid onset of action. On the street, Valium is worth more than Librium.

In most clinic studies fewer than 5% of patients on benzodiazepines meet criteria for abuse or dependence. Many people are so worried about this happening that they under-use these drugs. People with a history of alcohol abuse or a family history of alcohol or hypnanxiolytic abuse are more likely to abuse benzodiazepines (Ciraulo, Barnhill, Ciraulo, Greenblatt, & Shader, 1989). Several patterns in the development of dependence and abuse have been noted. One prototype—the "prescription pill popper"—is that of the middle-class, middle-aged woman who obtains a prescription because of anxiety or insomnia. Later she increases the dose and frequency of use on her own, using the drug to cope with even minor problems. Another pattern involves males in their teens or early twenties obtaining these drugs from illicit sources and using them for their euphorigenic effects. It is common for patients on methadone programs, who have discontinued opiate abuse, to continue to use benzodiazepines sporadically. Cognitive-behavioral approaches or the use of buspirone (a nonhabit-forming anxiolytic) are recommended as the first treatment in these high-risk groups.

When first prescribing any psychoactive agent, but especially a hypnoanxiolytic, physicians should warn patients that, for a week or so, their reflexes might be a tad slow and they should be extra-careful around machines, crossing streets, and cooking. Daytime sedation might last a week. As far as is known, the anxiolytic effect continues indefinitely in most patients. Nonalcoholic patients can drink alcohol while taking hypnoanxiolytics (and other psychotropic drugs), but they should be told that one drink will probably feel like two to three drinks.

Benzodiazepines are classified as "short-acting," "intermediate-acting," or "long-acting," with half-lives of 2–6 hours, 8–12 hours, and over 24 hours, respectively. (A drug's "half-life" is when 50% of it has become pharmacologically inactive.) The chances of withdrawal increase with increased dosage and duration of use. More cases of benzodiazepine withdrawal have been reported with long-term, low-dose use than with short-term, high-dose use. For example, 15 mg of daily diazepam for two years apparently causes more physical dependence than 50 mg of daily diazepam for six weeks.

Longer-acting benzodiazepines are less likely to be abused than short-acting ones. The longer-acting benzodiazepines are eliminated more slowly and gradually, causing less and more delayed withdrawal than the shorter-acting ones. In a sense, they taper themselves. In some people, alprazolam may last only six hours. If their prescription specifies usage every eight hours, this gap may result in three mini-withdrawals a day.

High-potency benzodiazepines may actually have higher withdrawal risks because they are often used in higher dosage equivalents than the older, low-potency benzodiazepines. For panic disorder, alprazolam is commonly used in doses over 3 mg a day, which would be equivalent to over 30 mg a day of diazepam, a dosage almost never used. A majority of panic disorder patients who have taken alprazolam for over one year report withdrawal symptoms, even when gradually tapered off of it, that are worse than the original panic anxiety symptoms. Too often, physicians' decisions in treating patients can increase the chance of addiction. *Fast*, *frequent*, and *forceful* reinforcements are most likely to cause addiction. They often follow many of the principles of "How to Create an Addict":

1. Choose a fast and powerful reinforcer. Pick a substance that has a rapid onset of action and therefore gives a "buzz" or "rush."
2. Make sure the drug has to be used often to get the reinforcement and, better yet, use a drug that has nasty withdrawal symptoms. This will increase the craving to use the drug again to eradicate the withdrawal symptoms and to get the "buzz." The wider the gulf between withdrawal symptoms and the "buzz," the stronger the reinforcement provided. Short-acting drugs work best for this. Secobarbital meets all of these criteria.
3. Prescribe the drug prn (as needed) or schedule with a frequency that precipitates withdrawal before the next dose is taken. For example, if it is prn, tell the patient to take the drug "only when you feel very anxious"; and if it's scheduled, prescribe a drug to be taken every six hours that lasts only four hours.

Unfortunately, the steps that create addiction are too often used in pain and anxiety treatment. For patients who seek help for benzodiazepine dependence, a very gradual withdrawal extending over two to three months is often recommended. High-potency benzodiazepines probably should be substituted with low-potency benzodiazepines. For a gradual, more gentle withdrawal, the longer-acting benzodiazepines such as chlordiazepoxide, clorazepate, and clonazepam are substituted for the shorter-acting ones on which the patient has become dependent. For a comfortable withdrawal in under seven days, carbamazepine (an anticonvulsant) can be used for dependent patients who have taken benzodiazepines in high doses or for a long period of time (Ries, Roy-Byrne, Ward, Neppe, & Cullison, 1989).

STIMULANTS

Cocaine. Sigmund Freud introduced cocaine into mainstream medicine as a safe, non-habit-forming treatment for opium addiction. He frequently used it himself. Today, Americans consume 50 metric tons of cocaine each year. Fifteen percent of high-school students have snorted "coke," while 10% of Americans have taken "even one sniff" of cocaine, as Cole Porter's (1934) lyric goes. Chic in Porter's day, by the mid-1980s, cocaine had so dropped in price that it is now commonly used in all social classes.

With growing use, there is a growing awareness of its hazards. Reflecting Porter's, "Some get a kick from cocaine," its use has dropped in high school and among college students and professionals, but is unchanged among lower-class street users. In addition to abuse and dependence, *DSM-IV* lists criteria for amphetamine and cocaine intoxication and withdrawal that are identical. For practical purposes, these are combined in Table 8–9. Six other disorders related to stimulant use are also listed: delirium, psychotic disorder (with delusions or hallucinations), mood disorder, anxiety disorder, sexual dysfunction, and sleep disorder.

A typical story of cocaine addiction starts when the curious person pays $75–$150 a gram for a white powder ("snow"), which is usually 30% cocaine and 70% adulterants (inactive sugars). After making a thin, two-inch line of the powder, the user snorts it with a straw or rolled-up dollar bill. This launches a 30-minute high, which tapers off in 60 to 90 minutes. The user feels energetic, creative, talkative, attractive, excited, euphoric, motivated, grandiose, and "connected." Initial negative reactions include restlessness, agitation, anxiety, hyperexcitability, and hostility.

Habitual cocaine abusers gradually become obsessed with the drug and securing its supply. Not uncommonly, the user blows over $3,000 a week on the drug. A week, and then a day, cannot pass without that "extra boost." When high, users are unable to sleep, and once asleep, cannot awaken. Smoking "crack" may ensue.[2]

---

[2]Freebasing: highly flammable solvent (e.g., ether) is heated to separate the adulterants. The pure cocaine (crack) is then smoked to produce an intense two-minute high, followed by extreme dysphoria, craving, and often by marathon "coke" binges of 24 to 96 hours, or until supplies run out.

TABLE 8–9
DSM-IV **Criteria for Amphetamine or Cocaine Intoxication and Withdrawal***

Substance Intoxication

A. Recent use of amphetamine or a related substance (e.g., methylphenidate) or cocaine.

B. Clinically significant maladaptive behavioral or psychological changes (e.g., euphoria or affective blunting; changes in sociability; hypervigilance; interpersonal sensitivity; anxiety, tension, or anger; stereotyped behaviors; impaired judgment; or impaired social or occupational functioning) that developed during, or shortly after, use of amphetamine or a related substance or cocaine.

C. Two (or more) of the following, developing during, or shortly after, use of amphetamine or a related substance or cocaine:

(1) tachycardia or bradycardia
(2) pupillary dilation
(3) elevated or lowered blood pressure
(4) perspiration or chills
(5) nausea or vomiting
(6) evidence of weight loss
(7) psychomotor agitation or retardation
(8) muscular weakness, respiratory depression, chest pain, or cardiac arrhythmias
(9) confusion, seizures, dyskinesia, dystonias, or coma

D. The symptoms are not due to a general medical condition and are not better accounted for by another mental disorder.

Substance Withdrawal

A. Cessation (or reduction of) in amphetamine (or related substance) or cocaine use that has been heavy and prolonged.

B. Dysphoric mood and two (or more) of the following physiological changes, developing within a few hours to several days after Criterion A:

(1) fatigue
(2) vivid, unpleasant dreams
(3) insomnia or hypersomnia
(4) increased appetite
(5) psychomotor retardation or agitation

C. The symptoms in Criterion B cause clinically significant distress or impairment in social, occupational, or other important areas of functioning.

D. The symptoms are not due to a general medical condition and are not better accounted for by another mental disorder.

*DSM-IV, pp. 207–209, 224–26.

Fifty to 70% of heavy cocaine users report paranoid episodes, which almost only happen during the high (Satel & Edell, 1991). On crashing (withdrawing), users feel depressed, anergic, and unmotivated. Appetite disappears and weight drops, often to medically precarious levels. Snorters' noses drip and bleed continuously, exhausting endless supplies of gauze. Work is missed, jobs are lost, friends lose patience, and marriages end.

Despite these serious consequences, of those who have called a cocaine hotline (1-800-333-4444), most still preferred to continue their habit because it produced euphoria (82%), diminished boredom (57%), increased energy and self-confidence (48%), and stimulated sexuality (21%). Callers said that cocaine was more important than food (71%), sex (50%), family activities (72%), and friends (64%). Among all the callers, 61% snorted the drug, 21% smoked, and 18% injected it. Half used the drug daily. On average, users spent $637 a week on cocaine (Gold, 1984).

Tentative evidence suggests that tricyclic antidepressants may help some cocaine-dependent patients (Gawin et al., 1989) and that bromocriptine (a dopamine agonist) (0.6255 mg) exerts an anticraving effect in one to two minutes. Early successes with these pharmacologic treatments, used alone without other treatments, have been tempered by relapse rates six months later that are as high as when no treatment is received. However, by helping patients get off and stay off cocaine for some period of time, these drugs might enable abusers to participate more effectively in rehabilitative treatments such as Cocaine Anonymous or AA. As Sherlock Holmes' case illustrates (Chapter 6), cocaine's many "advantages" offer former abusers little incentive to remain drug-free. Therefore, therapy must help patients find or rediscover interests that will "replace" cocaine. One of the best things cocaine-addicts can do is replace cocaine-using friends with abstinent friends (Kandel & Raveis, 1989). A multicomponent behavioral treatment—using money payments for negative urine specimens, significant others to reinforce abstinence, training in recognizing antecedents and consequences of cocaine, and help in developing new alternative activities to cocaine use—has been shown to be superior to traditional drug counseling (Higgens et al., 1993). (Less specific weekly psychosocial therapy does not improve abstinence [Kang et al., 1991]). Eleven percent of the counseling group and 58% of the behavioral group stayed in 24 weeks of treatment. During treatment, 5% of the counseling group and 42% of the behavioral group achieved at least 16 weeks of continuous abstinence. It is not known if these gains persisted after the treatment was completed.

Amphetamines. Intoxication and withdrawal from cocaine and amphetamine are similar. As overdoses, both are potentially fatal. Acute usage of amphetamines causes tachycardia, and with increased dosage, ventricular fibrillation and respiratory arrest may occur. Hyperpyrexia (increased body temperature) is frequent; seizures may occur and deaths have resulted from status epilepticus (continuous seizures). Pseudocholinesterase is the major detoxifier of cocaine, but there have been several reports of deaths associated with congenital deficiencies of the enzyme. The post-use depression may lead to suicide. After a high-dose binge, some users develop a transient psychosis with a mixture of paranoid and manic-like symptoms. Visual and tactile hallucinations may also be present. At other times, a confused toxic psychosis may develop. Anorexia and weight loss are common in regular users. Long-term use of amphetamines is associated with increased morbidity, mortality, criminality, as well as ongoing, diffuse suspiciousness and a chronic delusional syndrome.

Noteworthy differences between cocaine and amphetamines exist. Because of cocaine's short half-life, tolerance may not develop as rapidly as it does to amphetamines: In just three days, "speed freaks" can go from ingesting 15 mg to 2,000 mg a day to obtain the original effects. Whereas the acute effects of a single amphetamine dose lasts four to six hours, those from cocaine rarely extend beyond two hours. Cocaine is typically used in binges, while amphetamines are used more continuously. More often than cocaine, amphetamines trigger a toxic psychosis resembling paranoid schizophrenia.

Seven days before taking the Medical College Admissions Test (MCAT), Darlene was frantic. Night and day she crammed, hourly popping a 5-mg "black beauty" (dextroamphetamine). Darlene was not only awake, she was flying. Never did she feel more alert and focused. After two days of nonstop studying, she began pacing "because I could concentrate better." By day three, she repeatedly told her roommate that the MCATs were "dumb"—an insight that Darlene alone considered brilliant—and by day four, she began shouting this indictment out her apartment window. By nightfall, she was convinced the MCAT people had hired mobsters to break her arms and legs. Already they were playing tricks on her eyes: One moment beetles were crawling in her hair, the next moment they disappeared. The telephone rang, wrong number, surely the MCAT mobsters. To protect herself, she bolted the door. Believing strangers in front of her apartment were also MCAT mobsters, she hurled darts and dishes at them. As typically occurs, Darlene became psychotic on 60 mg a day, remained psychotic for two weeks, and recovered fully. (Six months later she got high scores on the MCATs, but had trouble getting her driver's license renewed because she had been hospitalized for psychosis.)

The mainstay of acute treatment of stimulant abusers is observation, rest, and nutritious food. During the intoxication phase, benzodiazepines may be used to treat significant anxiety and agitation. Propranolol or clonidine are used for sympathetic overactivity. During an acute stimulant intoxication, safety should be ensured and patients should be observed continuously. Physical restraints may be needed. If paranoid, patients' environment should be simplified, as few people as possible should care for them, and anything they deem dangerous should be removed. An increasing body temperature indicates an increasingly dangerous toxicity. Antipsychotic drugs (e.g., haloperidol 2–5 mg orally or IM) are effective in treating intoxication.

Amphetamines have no safe role in dieting and a very limited one in depression. They do have three legitimate medical indications: treating narcoleptic sleep attacks, childhood attention-deficit/hyperactivity disorder, and (occasionally) treatment of resistant depression. Even here they must be used cautiously—or, as rock star Frank Zappa warned, "Speed will turn you into your parents."

Nicotine. There are two "minor stimulants"—caffeine and nicotine. Caffeine's intoxicating effects are presented in Chapter 11 on anxiety disorders and their sources in Table 11–3. Caffeine withdrawal (not officially accepted as a disorder) is often accompanied by headache, lethargy, and dysphoria. It begins within 2 to 24 hours and lasts about one week (Hughes, Oliveto, Helzer, Higgins, & Bickel, 1992). This occurs even when consumption is two to three cups of coffee a day.

Nicotine has always been controversial. The Turkish and German governments once considered smoking in public an offense punishable by death; the Russians preferred castration. Americans, however, have subsidized its growth. *DSM-IV* made nicotine dependence (see earlier table) and withdrawal a mental disorder. Table 8–10 presents *DSM-IV* criteria for nicotine withdrawal.

Historically, men smoke more than women, but women have almost reached parity. Men have been more successful in stopping. The most effective treatment programs combine education, group support, and behavior modification, yet even

---

TABLE 8–10
DSM-IV Criteria for Nicotine Use Disorders*

A. Daily use of nicotine for at least several weeks.

B. Abrupt cessation of nicotine use, or reduction in the amount of nicotine used, followed within 24 hours by at least four (or more) of the following signs:

    (1) dysphoric or depressed mood
    (2) insomnia
    (3) irritability, frustration, or anger
    (4) anxiety
    (5) difficulty concentrating
    (6) restlessness
    (7) decreased heart rate
    (8) increased appetite or weight gain

C. The symptoms in Criterion B cause clinically significant distress or impairment in social, occupational, or other important areas of functioning.

D. The symptoms are not due to a general medical condition and are not better accounted for by another mental disorder.

---

*DSM-IV, pp. 244–45.

here, within a year, 80% of patients relapse. People who have had a history of major depression are most likely to fail attempts at permanent abstinence. Hypnosis, nicotine gum, and gradual substitution with lower nicotine-containing cigarettes help only some smokers. Nicotine patches are more widely accepted and provide a continuous release of nicotine into the blood. The patch increases abstinence, decreases withdrawal symptoms and depressive symptoms associated with withdrawal, and reduces the rewarding effects of smoking (Levin et al., 1994). Behavioral treatment approaches result in a higher rate of abstinence six months following cessation than educational approaches (Goldstein, Niaura, Follick, & Abrams, 1989).

HALLUCINOGENS

In 1938, while investigating ergot preparations for a pharmaceutical firm in Basel, Switzerland, Albert Hofmann first synthesized LSD-25.[3] Five years later, he unwittingly absorbed it through his fingers and experienced a "not unpleasant delirium." Several days later he swallowed 250 micrograms, and in 40 minutes he felt a "mild dizziness, restlessness, inability to concentrate, visual disturbance and uncontrollable laughter." His diary continues to describe "the bicycle trip heard round the world":

. . . on the way home (a four-mile trip by bicycle), the symptoms developed with a much greater intensity than the first time. I had the greatest difficulty speaking coherently and my field of vision fluctuated and was distorted like the reflections in an amusement park mirror. I also had the impression that I was hardly moving, yet later my assistant told me that I was pedaling at a fast pace. So far as I can recollect, the height of the crisis was characterized by these symptoms; dizziness, visual distortions, the faces of those present appeared like grotesque colored masks, strong agitation alternating with paresis [partial paralysis], the head, body and extremities sometimes cold and numb; a metallic taste on the tongue; throat dry and shriveled; a feeling of suffocation; confusion alternating with a clear appreciation of the situation; at times standing outside myself as a neutral observer and hearing myself muttering jargon or screaming half madly.

Six hours after taking the drug, my condition had improved. The perceptual distortions were still present. Everything seemed to undulate and their proportions were distorted like the reflections on a choppy water surface. Everything was changing with unpleasant, predominately poisonous green and blue color tones. With closed eyes multi-hued, metamorphizing fantastic images overwhelmed me. Especially noteworthy was the fact that sounds were transposed into visual sensations ["synesthesias"] so that from each tone or noise a comparable colored picture was evoked, changing in form and color kaleidoscopically. (Coles, Brenner, & Meagher, 1970, pp. 44–45)

---

[3] The number *25* refers to nothing chemical, but to the date (2 May) Hoffman first produced LSD.

Hofmann apparently slept well and the next day felt "completely well, but tired."

Despite some differences (see Table 8–11), most *pure* hallucinogens (or "psychedelics") produce experiences like Hofmann's. "Street acid," however, is rarely pure, usually consisting of anticholinergics (which are hallucinogens in toxic doses), quinine, sugar, and PCP; it might even contain LSD. As a result, clinicians cannot assume that patients on a "bad trip" know what drug they've taken. Therefore, it is safest to "talk patients down" by reassuring them that the trip will end in a few hours, that they are safe, and that they are not going mad, shrinking, or becoming a zombie. Patients should not fight the experience, but "flow with it"; they should be encouraged to become curious about it, and if they wish, to talk about it. If clinicians do not have the time to offer this reassurance, or if patients remain terrified despite it, diazepam 0.5 mg or alprazolam 5 mg, can be given orally every hour until patients are reasonably comfortable or asleep; either drug causes less hypotension and fewer bad drug interactions than antipsychotics. Because antipsychotics increase anticholinergic activity, these drugs can worsen the condition of someone who already has anticholinergic toxicity. A person with an anticholinergic psychosis has been described as "dry as a bone, red as a beet and mad as a hatter." It's quite recognizable, if you know what to look for.

Less than 5% of Americans have ever tried a psychedelic, and if these drugs were legal, only 1% claimed they would take them. Traditionally, hallucinogens have been used more frequently by high-school and college students, the affluent, artistic, and philosophically minded, rather than by the poor or antisocial. Chronic use is uncommon. Hallucinogens can trigger "flashbacks," in which a person off drugs re-experiences an LSD trip days to months and sometimes years after taking it.

What causes flashbacks is unknown. Psychedelics rarely, if ever, cause psychosis *de novo*, but they, as well as PCP and *high* doses of marijuana, can easily re-kindle a pre-existing psychosis. High-risk patients include those with borderline or schizotypal personality disorders, and those with a personal or family history of drug or nondrug-induced psychoses. Clinicians should inform these patients about their increased risk. This is not moralizing; it is giving information.

CANNABIS

The hemp plant, *Cannabis sativa*, grows anywhere it doesn't freeze; marijuana comes from its stems and leaves, while hashish derives from the resin of female plants. (George Washington smoked hemp at a time when it was believed to be a treatment for "catarrh.") The main psychoactive substance in cannabis is THC (delta-9-tetrahydrocannabinol). The botany of THC in cannabis has changed dramatically; THC in hemp doesn't exceed

TABLE 8–11
DSM-IV **Criteria for Hallucinogen Intoxication and
Hallucinogen Persisting Perception Disorder***

Hallucinogen Intoxication

A. Recent use of a hallucinogen.

B. Clinically significant maladaptive behavioral or psychological changes (e.g., marked anxiety or depression, ideas of reference, fear of losing one's mind, paranoid ideation, impaired judgment, or impaired social or occupational functioning) that developed during, or shortly after, hallucinogen use.

C. Perceptual changes occurring in a state of full wakefulness and alertness (e.g., subjective intensification of perceptions, depersonalization, derealization, illusions, hallucinations, synesthesias) that developed during, or shortly after, hallucinogen use.

D. Two (or more) of the following signs, developing during, or shortly after, hallucinogen use:

    (1) pupillary dilation
    (2) tachycardia
    (3) sweating
    (4) palpitations
    (5) blurring of vision
    (6) tremors
    (7) incoordination

E. The symptoms are not due to a general medical condition and are not better accounted for by another mental disorder.

Hallucinogen Persisting Perception Disorder (Flashbacks)

A. The reexperiencing, following cessation of use of a hallucinogen, of one or more of the perceptual symptoms that were experienced while intoxicated with the hallucinogen (e.g., geometric hallucinations, false perceptions of movement in the peripheral visual fields, flashes of color, intensified colors, trails of images of moving objects, positive afterimages, halos around objects, macropsia, and micropsia).

B. The symptoms in Criterion A cause clinically significant distress or impairment in social, occupational, or other important areas of functioning.

C. The symptoms are not due to a general medical condition (e.g., anatomical lesions and infections of the brain, visual epilepsies) and are not better accounted for by another mental disorder (e.g., delirium, dementia, Schizophrenia) or hypnopompic hallucinations.

DSM-IV, pp. 232–34.

1%. Through genetic selection, marijuana leaves have reached 20% THC in "prize" crops. Hashish is in the 10–30% range and hashish oil contains up to 60% THC. Smoking is the primary mode of use. With normal recreational use, marijuana intoxication peaks in 30 minutes, persists for three hours, and sometimes impairs driving for up to six hours. It stimulates appetite ("the munchies"), causes dry mouth, produces bloodshot eyes, elevates mood, intensifies experiences and perceptions, and heightens relaxation and apathy. Table 8–12 presents *DSM-IV* criteria for cannabis intoxication.

Over 60% of American adults and adolescents have smoked "grass" at least once, and relatively few have experienced severe reactions after 24 hours of using the drug. Panic attacks, which account for 75% of all severe *acute* side effects, can last two to six hours. Severe cases can be treated with benzodiazepines. Otherwise, heavier cannabis use can cause toxic delirium represented by the "4 D's": depersonalization, derealization, déjà vu, and dysphoria. Another effect is a cognitive disorder with impairment in goal-directed, memory-dependent behavior and in carrying out multiple-step tasks. The "short attention span theater" becomes a favored form of enter-

---

TABLE 8–12
DSM-IV* Criteria for Cannabis Intoxication

A. Recent use of cannabis.

B. Clinically significant maladaptive behavioral or psychological changes (e.g., impaired motor coordination, euphoria, anxiety, sensation of slowed time, impaired judgment, social withdrawal) that developed during, or shortly after, cannabis use.

C. Two (or more) of the following signs, developing within 2 hours of cannabis use:

   (1) conjunctival injection
   (2) increased appetite
   (3) dry mouth
   (4) tachycardia

D. The symptoms are not due to a general medical condition and are not better accounted for by another mental disorder.

Specify if:
With Perceptual Disturbances

---

*DSM-IV, p. 218.

tainment. Marijuana can also exacerbate a pre-existing psychosis. Its effects are greatly influenced by "set and setting"—that is, by the user's "mind set" or attitudes towards the drug, and the degree of receptivity and safety in the environment. Adverse reactions occur more often among those who smoke because of peer pressure or who have negative expectations of the drug. In the 1980s less than 1% of university students at campuses with high marijuana use developed panic attacks, whereas 25% did so at rural Southern colleges where use of the drug is discouraged.

Longer-term psychological problems associated with marijuana use are relatively few. Only 9% of marijuana users meet *DSM-IV* criteria for cannabis abuse. Marijuana hallucinosis, flashbacks, or transient delusional syndrome may occur. Although an "amotivational syndrome" of laziness, apathy, and a lack of ambition has been attributed to marijuana, this finding derived from biased samples of largely lower-class patients and has not been supported by more recent surveys in countries where marijuana use is extensive (Jamaica, Costa Rica, and Greece). Passive, unmotivated people may choose marijuana for chronic use. Medically, cannabis diminishes respiratory capacity, produces bronchial and pulmonary irritation (more than equal amounts of nicotine, and like tobacco, may result in constrictive pulmonary disease), causes tachycardia, temporarily impairs cognition and recent memory, reduces fertility, harms the fetus, reduces immune response, and impairs driving and school performance.

Two main types of marijuana dependence have been described. In the more severe type users smoke marijuana many times a day and finally seek treatment on their own. In the second type, users smoke it every day or two and end up in treatment only after involuntary drug testing (Tennant, 1986). Both types may produce a withdrawal syndrome days later and have high relapse rates (Tennant, 1986).

Ever since *Reefer Madness* obtained cult-film status, the dominant question has been whether marijuana leads to the abuse of "heavier" illegal substances. The answer is a qualified no. Repeated studies have strongly suggested that the best predictor of illegal drug use is *legal* drug use. In other words, the chief "gateway" drug is not marijuana, but tobacco or alcohol (Rittenhouse, 1982). Moreover, marijuana use, which peaked in 1978, declined in the 1980s. From 1978 to 1984, high-school seniors who had used marijuana during the preceding month dropped from 37% to 25%, while daily usage dropped from 10.7% to 5%. Nevertheless, patients are not statistics, and the hazards of marijuana use must be evaluated in the light of each person's history.

PHENCYCLIDINE

Originally an animal tranquilizer, "hog" or phencyclidine (PCP) became a battlefield anesthetic in Vietnam. It resurfaced as a recreational drug in California during the late sixties, ironically rechristened as "angel dust." PCP produces a euphoric, floating, energized, invincible, other-worldly, and dream-like state in which time is slowed, thinking is quickened, fantasies are dramatic, life is intensified, and reality goes on holiday.

But PCP is *not* the dust of angels. Users may be immobilized and stare blankly. Myoclonic (leg) jerks and confusion are common. On large doses, patients may become stuporous, enter a coma, and convulse with their eyes wide open. If they recover from the coma, they exhibit an agitated delirium marked by persecutory delusions, hallucinations, illusions, disorientation, agitation, and episodic assaultiveness: Asleep or calm one moment, without warning they may become fanatically violent the next. For no apparent reason, users fight with police, wreck cars, commit suicide, kill strangers. This violence may stem from the extreme suspiciousness and persecutory delusions produced by PCP. Being a "dissociative" anesthetic, PCP makes users feel as if they are outside their bodies; users do not perceive pain and are unaware and amnestic for such experiences. This delirium can last a week. Some patients die, usually due to respiratory depression; others are killed in accidents—drowning, automobile crashes, falls, and fires. Medically, PCP intoxication causes ataxia, nystagmus, and muscle rigidity. Whereas hallucinogens produce dilated pupils, PCP produces normal or small pupils. Table 8–13 presents *DSM-IV* criteria for PCP and related substances.

Phencyclidine is often sprinkled on top of marijuana or parsley. When smoked, its effects arise in one to five minutes, peak after five to 30 minutes, remain high for four to six hours, and dwindle over the next 18 hours. Snorting PCP hastens its effects. Intravenous use is uncommon.

Approximately six million people between the ages of 12 and 25 have used PCP; most users are polydrug abusers. They often drink alcohol while on PCP, even though the combination usually makes them dreadfully sick. Despite the drug's horrifying effects, PCP users typically say they take it because "it's the perfect escape." It is as frequently sold as cannabinol, mescaline, LSD, amphetamine, or cocaine.

The treatment of acute PCP overdose includes cardiopulmonary resuscitation, treatment for seizures, acidification of the urine (to hasten the drug's elimination) with 500–1,000 mg ammonium chloride orally every three to five hours, until the urine pH is below 5. Since patients are unpredictably violent and frequently combative, a low sensory environment should be used; physical restraints may be needed until patients have been calm for several hours. Some clinicians recommend (as needed) hourly haloperidol 5 mg IM; others suggest diazepam 10–30 mg orally or IM. Response to aggressive treatment is generally slow. Most experts agree that phenothiazines should be avoided, since they may compound PCP's anticholinergic and hypotensive effects. After the acute psychosis, PCP users often do not remain in drug treatment programs.

TABLE 8–13
***DSM-IV* Criteria for Phencyclidine Intoxication or**
Phencyclidine-Related Disorders*

A. Recent use of phencyclidine (or a related substance).

B. Clinically significant maladaptive behavioral changes (e.g., belligerence, assaultiveness, impulsiveness, unpredictability, psychomotor agitation, impaired judgment, or impaired social or occupational functioning) that developed during, or shortly after, phencyclidine use.

C. Within an hour (less when smoked, "snorted," or used intravenously), two (or more) of the following signs:

   (1) vertical or horizontal nystagmus
   (2) hypertension or tachycardia
   (3) numbness or diminished responsiveness to pain
   (4) ataxia
   (5) dysarthria
   (6) muscle rigidity
   (7) seizures or coma
   (8) hyperacusis

D. The symptoms are not due to a general medical condition and not better accounted for by another mental disorder.

Specify if:
With Perceptual Disturbances

*DSM-IV, p. 258.

MDMA

Also known as "ecstasy" or "XTC," MDMA was synthesized in 1914, but it wasn't until the early 1970s that it quietly became a recreational and psychotherapeutic drug. In 1985, the popularity of this then legal drug was featured in *Time* and *Newsweek* magazines; by June of that year, the Drug Enforcement Agency had "temporarily" made it illegal. Many opposed this decision, claiming that MDMA had been confused with the psychedelic MDA, that harm allegedly due to MDMA was really from adulterants (e.g., Borax!), and that research into a potentially therapeutic drug was being stymied. MDMA is the only drug discussed in this chapter that is not mentioned in *DSM-IV*. Human recreational doses have been reported to be neurotoxic in primates (Barnes, 1988).

In recreational doses of 75–175 mg, MDMA produces a tranquil, floating, introspective, talkative, two-to-four hour "trip." Grinspoon and Bakalar (1985) claim it "invites rather than compels intensification of feelings and self-exploration." Although chemically related to amphetamines and mescaline (a psychedelic), ecstasy exerts no stimulant effects or hallucinogenic alterations of consciousness, perception, movement, or coordination. Unlike with psychedelics, information revealed during MDMA usage is more readily remembered and applied afterwards. The person does not feel "stoned."

The usage pattern of MDMA is unlike that of any other drug. Users tend to wait several weeks between doses, because taking it too soon increases negative effects and decreases positive effects. Because the positive effects seem to decrease over subsequent doses, MDMA probably is not addictive. The mean number of doses taken by users is only 5.4 (Peroutka, 1987, 1989).

Physical side effects, which are dose-related, include dry mouth, increased blood pressure and pulse rate, anorexia, nystagmus, urinary urgency, blurred vision, loss of balance, and jaw-clenching. Fatigue may persist for a day or two. One fatal overdose has been reported. Bad trips, flashbacks, and psychotic reactions are rare; weekly use is also rare. At present, there have been no reports of MDMA-induced craving or withdrawal. Nonetheless, as always occurs with psychoactive agents, a wider use of MDMA is likely to uncover some currently unknown hazards.

OPIOIDS

> Junk is the ideal product . . . the ultimate merchandise. No sales talk necessary. The client will crawl through a sewer and beg to buy. . . . The junk merchant does not sell his product to the consumer, he sells the consumer to this product.
> —William S. Burroughs, *Evergreen Review*, Jan./Feb. 1960

Opioids (also called opiates) are compounds with morphine-like properties. Opium is derived from the Turkish word for juice—juice of the poppy—because opium, the original opioid, derives from the head of the opium poppy *Papaver somniferum*, cultivated mainly in the Middle East, Southeast Asia, China, India, and Mexico. Although growing it in the United States has always been illegal, throughout the 1840s it was the most popular sleep aide in Kansas. Heroin is the only illicit opioid, morphine is the prototypic opioid (see Table 8–1).

Clinical Presentation

In therapeutic amounts, morphine produces analgesia, induces tranquility, constricts pupils, and elevates mood (although some get dysphoria). Anorexia, nausea, and vomiting may occur, as may reduction in sex, aggression, and hunger drives. As Taylor Mead quipped, "Opium is very cheap considering you don't feel like eating for the next six days." Skin itches, constipation develops, and respiratory rate and other vital signs decline. Except for meperidine, opioids do not cause seizures.

Most opioid intoxication comes from shooting morphine or heroin intravenously, which produces a "rush"—a strong, flushing sensation coupled with an orgastic feeling in the belly. Waves of pleasant, floating drowsiness ("the nod") and dreams follow. Tolerance to opioids develops quickly. Tables 8–14 and 8–15 list *DSM-IV* criteria for opioid intoxication and withdrawal and Table 8–16 outlines the overlapping stages or "grades" of opioid intoxication and withdrawal. Morphine withdrawal peaks up to 72 hours after the last dose and subsides slowly. Most opioid withdrawal symptoms disappear within seven to ten days, although some craving, restlessness, weakness, and fitful sleep may persist. Serious medical consequences of withdrawal are rare. Insomnia and dysphoria usually occur throughout the withdrawal. Lacrimation, rhinorrhea, and sweating are early signs. Later, gooseflesh (piloerection, hence "cold turkey"), muscle twitches (hence "kick the habit"), and lack of appetite are experienced. Finally, muscle aches, severe nausea, vomiting, and diarrhea can develop. Opioid with-

---

TABLE 8–14
DSM-IV* Criteria for Opioid Intoxication

A. Recent use of an opioid.

B. Clinically significant maladaptive behavioral or psychological changes (e.g., initial euphoria followed by apathy, dysphoria, psychomotor agitation or retardation, impaired judgment, or impaired social or occupational functioning) that developed during, or shortly after, opioid use.

C. Pupillary constriction (or pupillary dilation due to anoxia from severe overdose) and one (or more) of the following signs, developing during, or shortly after, opioid use:

(1) drowsiness or coma
(2) slurred speech
(3) impairment in attention or memory

D. The symptoms are not due to a general medical condition and are not better accounted for by another mental disorder.

Specify if:
With Perceptual Disturbances

*DSM-IV, p. 250.

TABLE 8–15
DSM-IV **Criteria for Opioid Withdrawal***

A. Either of the following:

    (1) cessation of (or reduction in) opioid use that has been heavy and prolonged (several weeks or longer)
    (2) administration of an opioid antagonist after a period of opioid use

B. Three (or more) of the following, developing within minutes to several days after Criterion A:

    (1) dysphoric mood
    (2) nausea or vomiting
    (3) muscle aches
    (4) lacrimation or rhinorrhea
    (5) pupillary dilation, piloerection, or sweating
    (6) diarrhea
    (7) yawning
    (8) fever
    (9) insomnia

C. The symptoms in Criterion B cause clinically significant distress or impairment in social, occupational, or other important areas of functioning.

D. The symptoms are not due to a general medical condition and are not better accounted for by another mental disorder.

*DSM-IV, p. 251.

drawal is usually not dangerous unless dehydration from vomiting and diarrhea becomes severe. As can be seen in Table 8–16, the speed of the withdrawal syndrome depends on which opioid is being used.

Clinical Course

Although infrequently seen by professionals, many "chippers" use heroin in a controlled fashion. Otherwise, about half of all opioid abusers become opioid dependent. Whether this opioid dependency becomes chronic de-

TABLE 8–16
Opioid Withdrawal in Sequence

	ONSET/ TERMINATION	PEAK	TOTAL
Meperidine	3–5 hours	8–12 hours	4–5 days
Heroin/morphine	6–8 hours	2–3 days	7–10 days
Methadone	1–3 days	4–7 days	10–14 days

pends on the setting. For example, only 2% of American heroin-dependent soldiers in Vietnam continued their habit after returning home; most who continued were heroin abusers *before* Vietnam. Vaillant (1966) found that 98% of (non-Vietnam) patients at the Federal addiction treatment center in Lexington, Kentucky, returned to opioid use within a year of discharge. One of them, Danny, returned to his old New York neighborhood after six months of abstinence. As soon as he passed a street corner where he once had shot heroin, he immediately developed goose bumps, diarrhea, and hot flashes. As with Danny, such *conditioned withdrawal symptoms* often trigger a relapse. A month later, when Danny was asked why he used heroin, he explained, "If I had to be castrated to keep getting heroin, have me castrated."

The annual death rate of heroin addicts under age 30 is 1.6%; for those over age 30, 3%. Addicts usually die from accidental or intentional overdoses, allergic and acute toxic reactions (including pulmonary edema), infections and foreign material from shared unclean needles (hepatitis, AIDS, abscesses in liver, lung and brain, tetanus, septic pulmonary emboli), a lowered immunologic resistance, and from murder. Many addicts, if asked if they "share" needles, will say no, but if asked, "Do you ever *use* other people's needles?" will say yes.

Epidemiology

Although accurate epidemiologic data on opioid misuse are especially elusive, household surveys during the 1970s revealed that under 1% of adults over age 25 had used an opioid at least once for nonmedical reasons. Among high-school seniors, the lifetime prevalence of heroin use had dropped from 2.2% in 1975 to 1.1% in 1979 (Johnston, Bachman, & O'Malley, 1981). In 1984, although 11.2% of high-school seniors had taken opioids other than heroin at least once, only 1.3% had done so during the preceding month (Galantar, personal communication, 1985).

The "demographic" heroin addict is male (four males to one female), from the inner cities of both coasts, nonwhite, and with a teenage history of truancy, poor school performance, and delinquency. Immediate availability of opioids greatly increases the number of *new* cases of heroin misuse, whereas *chronic* misuse depends less on neighborhood access. All the sorrows of social blight and community disorganization—poor housing, lack of sanitation, malnutrition, unemployment, low educational levels, lack of family cohesiveness, and cultural morale—correlate with opioid misuse.

In addition to personality disorders (particularly antisocial), depression and anxiety disorders commonly accompany opioid dependence. Many opioid addicts are polydrug abusers, especially with "downers" like alcohol and hypnoanxiolytics. For heroin addicts, polydrug abuse is a bad prognostic indicator.

Treatment and Management

No single program works for a majority of opiate abusers, and considerable controversy remains over the preferred approach. In general, there are two schools of thought: The "soft" pro-methadone school and the "tough" anti-methadone school. Methadone can be used for withdrawal and later for maintenance.

Methadone is an opioid with a long (12-hour) half-life that exerts pleasant effects when ingested. Because methadone is cross-tolerant with other opioids, once signs of opioid withdrawal begin, clinicians can initiate *methadone substitution* by giving patients roughly 10 mg three times daily, and then withdrawing them by gradually diminishing the dose. A typical schedule would be total daily doses of 30-30-20-15-10-5-0-0 mg. With medical complications—e.g., high fever, cardiac failure—slightly higher and more frequent doses are indicated, such as 45-45-35-25-15-10-5-0-0 mg. Methadone should not be withdrawn at faster than 20% a day. It is rare for more than 15 mg to be needed at any one time. More recently the alpha-2 adrenergic agonist, clonidine, has also been used for this purpose and the detoxification requires 10 to 14 days. Both drugs appear to be equally efficacious, if the level of tolerance is not greater than the equivalent of 30 mg of methadone per day. At higher levels methadone appears to more effectively suppress the abstinence syndrome. For those patients who have achieved considerable rehabilitation with methadone maintenance treatment, detoxification on an outpatient basis over a period of two to six months is reasonably effective. In any given year, less than 10% of chronic opioid abusers participate in community-based treatment programs. Giving up opioid use is a very slow process and most users who have not achieved abstinence by their late thirties probably never will (Hser, Anglin, & Powers, 1993).

During opiate withdrawal, patients should be in a low bed; they can be allowed to smoke (cigarettes!) only if they are observed; they may need assistance walking to avoid injury. Small doses of diazepam may be given temporarily for insomnia. If patients convulse, they are probably also withdrawing from alcohol or hypnoanxiolytics and should be started on benzodiazepine withdrawal.

The loudest argument against methadone substitution is that using it makes withdrawal too easy and therefore fails to "teach the patient a lesson." No scientific evidence indicates that having this "lesson" prevents relapse. As one patient stated, "I've learned to never let myself run out of heroin again."

The rationale for *methadone maintenance*, (MM), which begins following opiate withdrawal, is that ingested methadone usually blocks the euphoria of injected opiates.[4] Because methadone is taken orally and daily, it diminishes addicts' daily search for heroin and their commission of crimes to pay for it; the users become

---

[4]A high enough dose of heroin can override methadone blockade and therefore, to achieve the objective, high doses of methadone are required.

better workers and family members. Without needles, there are far fewer medical complications and deaths.

Although studies repeatedly support these findings and show that MM produces the best overall results, critics charge that one narcotic is merely being replaced for another, that many addicts sell methadone illicitly, that many studies favorable to MM included only patients with initially good prognoses, that some addicts get a high from shooting up on methadone, and that many patients on methadone can overcome the blockade by taking high doses of heroin. These objections are significant, yet studies have indicated that after four years of MM, a majority of ex-addicts live productively, with 94% no longer committing crimes to obtain "smack."

MM continues to be the most reasonable approach for the majority of opioid addicts. The Federal Drug Administration has set very stringent criteria for admission and continued treatment in these programs. Most programs include group and individual counseling as well as vocational rehabilitation and educational guidance.

With or without MM, the usefulness of psychosocial treatments — including self-help groups, therapeutic communities, and drug treatment centers — remains unknown. More people quit restrictive "tough love" programs; less than 10% of addicts are suitable for these programs. Those who do best are highly motivated, have good ego strength, and are legally committed to the programs. The effectiveness of any therapy for opioid dependence varies largely in relation to the characteristics of various subgroups.

Sometimes *antagonist therapy* is used as an adjunct to opioid treatments. It is based on the idea that if a person continues to use opioids without pleasurable effects, the opioid craving will subside over time. The most commonly used opioid antagonist, naltrexone, has been most effective for recently detoxified methadone patients who have made substantial recovery, professional people, and addicts who are court-referred.

CHAPTER 9

Schizophrenia and Related Disorders

OF ALL THE PSYCHIATRIC disorders, schizophrenia devastates as no other, for no other disorder causes as pervasive and profound an impact—socially, economically, and personally. Schizophrenic patients occupy one-quarter of all American hospital beds and, excluding geriatric patients with cognitive disorders, two-thirds of all psychiatric beds. In 1983, schizophrenia cost the United States $48 billion—60% from lost productivity, 20% for public assistance, and 20% for treatment. Conservatively, costs for schizophrenia equal 2% of the nation's gross national product. On any single day, there are two million schizophrenics in the United States, and in any one year, there are two million new cases arising worldwide.

Parents of schizophrenics endure years of uncertainty, guilt, dashed hopes, rage (at, and from, the patient), financial burdens, self-doubt, and futility. Siblings resent the schizophrenic's getting "all" the attention, berate themselves for feeling resentful, and constantly worry if they too will go crazy.

Yet nobody suffers more than the schizophrenic. When Bleuler (see Chapter 1) invented the term *schizophrenia*, he did not mean a "split personality" (i.e., multiple personality), but a *shattered* personality. Whereas patients with other severe mental disorders may have one or perhaps two symptoms of schizophrenia, the curse of the schizophrenic is to be plagued by most of them. (After reading the following typical case, try to imagine— that is, to understand—how such a person might feel about himself and the world and what it might be like for him to negotiate everyday activities.)

173

Case Illustration

David Sebastian, a 24-year-old single, Catholic, ex-divinity student, was hospitalized for "episodes of inappropriate behavior and being out of touch with reality." For 16 hours nonstop, his inappropriate behavior consisted of masturbatory movements accompanied by groans, prayers, flailing limbs, and head-banging. During these episodes, he was totally self-absorbed: If asked questions, he wouldn't respond; all attempts to restrain him (for his own physical safety) were fiercely resisted. Eventually, he slept.

On awakening, he stared and smiled at a nurse, who described him as "Rasputin imitating the Mona Lisa." He accused the Pope of "fornicating nuns," "spreading diarrhea and gonorrhea," and "plotting to assassinate me [David]." He was convinced that St. Christopher, the former patron saint of travel, was removed from the Catholic Church calendar because David was having sexual thoughts while traveling. His thoughts traveled incoherently from topic to topic. When asked if he feared anything, he replied with a flat affect: "Nothing but the Pope wants slivers up his ass or my ass or he's an ass; you know, this is not me talking but a taped recording of how you are today that couldn't communicate at any level as a dialectical incongruence of spiritual sexuality."

About a year ago, David began to change. Before then he was an outstanding biology student, a jogger, a bit of a loner prone to lengthy philosophical and religious discourses, and as his neighbors would remark, "such a sweet boy to live with his parents." At age 23, however, David's grades began to slip and he became far more reclusive. Seven or so months later, and several weeks before his sister's wedding, he spent days and nights making his sister's wedding gift: a stained-glass penis. Two days before the wedding, his father accidentally knocked the gift off a table, and as it smashed into a million pieces, David did too. For the next month he attacked his family for destroying him, turning him into a robot, and sapping his vital fluids.

God's voice accused him of being too preoccupied with sex and proclaimed that becoming a priest was his only salvation. This instruction gave renewed purpose to his life while permitting a rapprochement with his family. He enrolled in divinity school, but a month later he could no longer concentrate. New and unfamiliar voices began discussing his plight, with one saying that "David's prick doesn't work," and the other saying, "If you were a *real* man, you'd go out and use your prick." He did. David picked up a co-ed and went to her apartment. They hopped into bed, but when David was about to enter her, he began praying out loud and banging his head. Horrified, she fled from the room, called the police, and David was admitted.

Repeated neurological exams and tests revealed no physical disorder. He was placed on antipsychotic medication and over the next ten days, his episodes (catatonic excitement alternating with negativism), delusions, hallucinations, incoherence, paranoia, and self-referential ideas gradually disappeared. Three days after admission he joined group therapy, but within minutes he pointed to the nine people in the room and exclaimed, "Eighteen eyes haunting my head, changing its size, televising my mind, eating it, bleeding it, feeding it. You gyrating Judases, how dare. . . . " Suddenly silent, he left the room. Days later he said he had felt besieged by the other members and that he left the room to escape this bombardment and to stop "embarrassing myself further." Once his psychotic symptoms abated, David actively participated in group and supportive individual psychotherapy. In meetings with the entire family, his parents ventilated their frustration, were told "the facts" about catatonic schizophrenia (David's diagnosis), and discussed how they could all live more peaceably together. After three weeks of inpatient care, he was discharged on medication and was to receive weekly psychotherapy.

For three months David worked at his father's grocery store, visited daily with a neighborhood priest, lived at home, read theology, painted a little, and saw friends. Then, when his father suggested that maybe he should live away from home, David stormed out of the house, wandered the streets, and stopped his medication because "it was digesting my sex organ." Within weeks he looked like a rag picker. He kept to himself. Voices began mocking his scrawny figure and sexual inadequacies and insisted he go out with prostitutes. After considerable guilt, he succumbed. Upon entering the prostitute's room, however, he extricated himself as before — by praying out loud and banging his head. The prostitute called the police and David's second admission began. Later he told a therapist that he was in a "no-win" situation: If he did have intercourse, he was committing a sin; if he didn't, his voices were right and he wasn't a man.

David passed through the proverbial "revolving door" for three more hospitalizations; each occurred after a fight at home or a sexual confrontation. When his parents visited, at first he'd accuse them of "warping" his penis; these meetings, however, would eventually calm him down. Whenever the staff tried to separate David from his parents, he would vegetate in a corner, stop talking, and starve himself; one time, he had to be physically restrained from jumping out the window. After six tumultuous months, David returned home: He worked regularly in a bookstore, remained on moderate doses of antipsychotic drugs, and participated in weekly group therapy. He began a theology class, where he befriended a shy young woman who felt nobody would ever like her. David did. Three years later they are still seeing each other ("We'll marry when *he* can afford me!" she laughs). He works at the bookstore and lives at home. He remains on medication ("I go bonkers without it"), and although he stopped the group ("I outgrew it"), he continues to receive individual psychotherapy ("so my crazy ideas don't overwhelm me").

Clinical Presentation

In *DSM-IV* the essential features of schizophrenia are: (a) a history of acute psychosis with delusions, hallucinations, disorganized speech, catatonia, grossly disorganized behavior, or flat affect, (b) chronic deterioration of functioning, (c) duration that exceeds six months, (e) the absence of a concurrent mood disorder, substance abuse, or a general medical condition. Usually, schizophrenia has a chronic, episodically downhill course, but with modern treatment, patients' conditions may eventually stabilize, allowing them to be moderately independent and productive. Table 9–1 lists *DSM-IV* criteria for schizophrenia.

Criterion A indicates that two symptoms of schizophrenia, one of which

TABLE 9–1
DSM-IV Criteria for Schizophrenia*

A. *Characteristic symptoms*: Two (or more) of the following, each present for a significant portion of time during a 1-month period (or less if successfully treated):

   (1) delusions
   (2) hallucinations
   (3) disorganized speech (e.g., frequent derailment or incoherence)
   (4) grossly disorganized or catatonic behavior
   (5) negative symptoms, i.e., affective flattening, alogia, or avolition
   Note: Only one Criterion A symptom is required if delusions are bizarre or hallucinations consist of a voice keeping up a running commentary on the person's behavior or thoughts, or two or more voices conversing with each other.

B. *Social/occupational dysfunction*: For a significant portion of the time since the onset of the disturbance, one or more major areas of functioning such as work, interpersonal relations, or self-care are markedly below the level achieved prior to the onset (or when the onset is in childhood or adolescence, failure to achieve expected level of interpersonal, academic, or occupational achievement).

C. *Duration*: Continuous signs of the disturbance persist for at least 6 months. This 6-month period must include at least 1 month of symptoms (or less if successfully treated) that met Criterion A (i.e., active-phase symptoms) and may include periods of prodromal or residual symptoms. During these prodromal or residual periods, the signs of the disturbance may be manifested by only negative symptoms or two or more symptoms listed in Criterion A present in an attenuated form (e.g. odd beliefs, unusual perceptual experiences).

D. *Schizoaffective and Mood Disorder exclusion*: Schizoaffective Disorder and Mood Disorder With Psychotic Features have been ruled out because either (1) no Major Depressive, Manic, or Mixed Episodes have occurred concurrently with the active-phase symptoms; or (2) if mood episodes have occurred during active-phase symptoms, their total duration has been brief relative to the duration of the active and residual periods.

E. *Substance/general medical condition exclusion*: The disturbance is not due to the direct physiological effects of a substance (e.g., a drug of abuse, a medication) or a general medical condition.

F. *Relationship to a Pervasive Developmental Disorder*: If there is a history of Autistic Disorder or another Pervasive Developmental Disorder, the additional diagnosis of Schizophrenia is made only if prominent delusions or hallucinations are also present for at least a month (or less if successfully treated).

*DSM-IV, pp. 285–86.

must be an active or "positive symptom" (numbers 1–4), must be present for a significant portion of time during a one-month period. The most prevalent of the florid, acute symptoms are delusions of persecution or of control, other bizarre delusions, and auditory hallucinations. Less frequent are incoherence, disturbed affect, and catatonia.

Schizophrenic *delusions* are often bizarre and mood-incongruent. One can readily empathize with the depressive's delusions, but not the schizophrenic's. His are weird, from "The Twilight Zone." They may be Schneiderian (see Chapter 2 and glossary), such as delusions of control in which the schizophrenic announces, "Martians have taken over my body." Persecutory delusions are also common, but unlike when they appear in organic and mood disorders, in schizophrenia the source of the menace is often an ill-defined and remote group — a vague "they."

Hallucinations are reported by 75% of newly admitted schizophrenics; they are usually in one sensory modality, with 90% being auditory and 40% visual. Fifteen percent of hallucinations are Schneiderian (Ludwig, 1985). Voices may whisper or shout, comment on the patient's actions, or demand morally offensive acts ("command hallucinations"). The voices may be from known people (e.g., a dead grandmother) or strangers; they may be verbose, or just one or two words constantly repeated. Because some people refer to their own thoughts as "voices," be sure to ask, "Do the voices come from inside or outside your head," and "Is it your own voice or someone else's?" Visual hallucinations are bizarre, frightening, and/or threatening (snakes crawling out of skulls, blood dripping from dead relatives) and usually occur in conjunction with the auditory hallucinations. Olfactory hallucinations are rare; most often they consist of disgusting smells from the patient's body. Tactile (haptic) hallucinations are also uncommon; the patient may feel bugs scratching his testicles or legions of ants crawling over or under her skin.

Initially, many schizophrenics present with an unshakable belief in their delusions and hallucinations. After months of confusion, they will suddenly come up with a delusion that "explains" everything; this "insight" has enormous personal meaning, while it mystifies everyone else. In normal recovery occurring over several weeks, patients typically gain increasing distance from their psychosis. They will go from assertions that "The telephone company is poisoning my food," to "*It seems like* the telephone company is poisoning my food." As the psychosis melts further, the statement becomes, "I'm not so sure about that telephone-company stuff." And later, "Every so often I think the phone company is poisoning my food. Isn't that crazy!" This process is called "softening" of the delusions. Frequently, however, delusions only partially soften: "I've learned not to pay attention to those ideas about the telephone company. They just get me in trouble."

As the observable symptom, speech abnormalities are caused by defects in cognitive processes and are the best evidence of a *thought disorder*. *Disorganized speech* is the third possible symptom of group A and manifests as incoherence, frequent derailment, loose associations, tangentiality, circumstantiality, and/or illogical thinking. Poverty of content may occur, but more often, patients seem flooded with ideas and are unable to filter the relevant from the immaterial. Such an example unexpectedly occurred when the author (J.M.) answered the phone and, to his astonishment, heard a total stranger say in a monotonously pert voice (the author's responses are in brackets):

> Hello. I'm paranoid schizophrenic from Tampa. Are you the Dr. Maxim [*sic*] who wrote *The New Psychiatry*? [Yes.] Well, I'm 75 years old, but I grew up in the home of the very famous Dr. Zuckerman who graduated from P&S, your school. He was the Dr. Obsessive-Compulsive Neurosis psychiatrist, who was a brilliant cardiologist, and I was his only psychiatric patient, and he never said he was my father, but my mother was a borderline butch-lesbian personality, and Dr. Zuckerman was the first to take me to the Metropolitan Museum of Art because I have a tooth on the right side that's too big, just as in that Picasso painting, and I have a malformed skull, and a right leg also much longer than my left, and my daughter Infanta Marguarita Pequina lives in Chicago, but Dr. Zuckerman didn't rescue me from a terrible marriage from 1948 to 1966 in which a man beat and raped me in the Jewish community—Are you Jewish? [Yes] Dr. Zuckerman didn't end the marriage but I got out of it in 1962 and have been on Mellaril ever since. [What happens if you stop the Mellaril?] My brain waves flash too fast, just as you said in your book, which I'm taking to my clinical psychologist, where I go three times a week, although Dr. Zuckerman studied with A. A. Brill and Dr. Freud and belonged in psychoanalysis, but that couldn't help my skull, which was genetically deformed and made worse by my sadist husband in the Jewish community. Do you see patients?"

When incoherence is milder or first appears, many listeners will "read into" the patient's speech. Consider this example from a term paper written by an acutely disturbed schizophrenic college student:

> we see the stately dimension of godly bliss that marlowe's *dOctOr fAUstUs* dies and lives. lucifer—oh lucy, luck, lackluster, lazy lucifer—devilishly adorns all sanctifarious, all beauty, all evil. our world dissolves into *SACRED* nihilism."

Individually, the sentences might make sense, but collectively, they're nonsense. Punning without intentional humor, as around "lucifer," is typical of schizophrenic speech; so too is the neologism "sanctifarious." The strange punctuation would seem to have a private meaning, a hunch later confirmed by the patient, who explained, "It's all about Christ. Don't you see? Marlowe's first name is Christopher. Christ. Get it?"

Catatonia, or disorganized behavior, presents as stupor or, as in the case of David Sebastian, as excitement.

Negative symptoms are the final criterion in group A; they are distinguished more by what is missing than present. Schizophrenics become *avolitional* and *unmotivated*. In the hospital, our nurses call it "bed flopping." The untrained confuse this behavior with laziness, but it's not. All behaviors are reduced, including fewer or no words spoken ("alogia"). These symptoms may be the consequence of giving attention to internal stimuli, but they can also be experienced as the complete absence of stimuli. As one schizophrenic patient put it, "The light's not on and nobody's home."

Affects, flat and/or inappropriate, typically develop insidiously and persist chronically. At times they arise acutely. However, pathological affects are not diagnostically specific: Depressed mood, drug-induced dullness, and akinesia (a side effect of antipsychotic drugs) can appear as flat affect; brain syndromes often produce inappropriate affects. Flat affect is one of the negative symptoms of schizophrenia. Inappropriate affect is a form of disorganized behavior. A reasonable inference is that inappropriate affects emerge because patients are responding more to internal than to external stimuli. They may cry when talking about the weather or laugh when hearing about a massive airplane crash. When schizophrenics giggle for no obvious reason, the listener's skin crawls. Their "humor" is not funny; it's tragically pathetic.

Clinical Course

In most cases, schizophrenia first manifests during adolescence or early adulthood. It presents either abruptly or slowly. One-fourth of patients have an abrupt onset with active, positive, or group A symptoms (numbers 1–4). The majority have an acute episode only after a slow, insidious onset of chronic or negative symptoms — social withdrawal, markedly impaired functioning, poor hygiene, flat or inappropriate affect, and the beginnings of positive symptoms — vague, rambling speech, odd or magical thinking, ideas of reference, overvalued ideas, persecutory thoughts, and unusual perceptions such as illusions, derealization, or depersonalization. When these chronic symptoms occur before the initial acute flair-up, they constitute schizophrenia's *prodromal phase*; when they occur following this flair-up, they constitute its *residual phase*. During these prodromal and residual phases, patients seem unmotivated and burned out; in public life, they are labeled as "oddballs," "eccentrics," and "weirdos."

To diagnose schizophrenia, active and/or chronic symptoms must be present for at least *six months* (criterion C). This requirement rules out shorter and potentially more benign psychoses, such as schizophreniform disorder and brief psychosis. At some point, the patient's social or occupational functioning must be impaired (criterion B).

For most patients schizophrenia is a chronic illness characterized by exacerbations and remissions. Women tend to have fewer rehospitalizations and shorter stays then men (Goldstein, 1988). Whereas the first several years of the disease are dominated by active symptoms and frequent hospitalizations, the condition eventually evolves into a nonpsychotic state with chronic symptoms of apathy, low energy levels, social withdrawal, and increased vulnerability to stress. At the worst end of the spectrum are schizophrenics who end up in the back wards of state mental hospitals; they can be seen huddled in corners, bodies contorted, picking imaginary flowers and repeatedly mumbling, "Mineral oil, mineral oil, mineral oil . . . " Most schizophrenics, however, function in the community: They marry and work at moderate-to-low-level jobs. As with many chronic disorders, such as diabetes and heart disease, schizophrenia may require episodic rehospitalization.

Roughly half of all schizophrenic patients report depressive symptoms at some point during their illness. They'll complain of feeling depressed or of an affectless state in which they don't feel anything ("I'm empty, numb"). These depressive episodes, which occur most often after an acute psychotic episode ("post-psychotic depression"), are associated with an increased risk of suicide and relapse, poor social functioning, longer hospitalizations, and bleaker outcomes. This is a particularly dangerous period in the schizophrenic's life, for she's apt to feel hopeless, abandon treatment, and kill herself. The first indications of a pending psychotic relapse are often mood disorder symptoms such as decreased sleep, energy, and mood. Whether these depressive symptoms are inherent to schizophrenia or a reaction to it is unclear. In either case, criterion D points out that to qualify as schizophrenia, symptoms of depression (or mania) must not occur concurrently with the active-phase symptoms or, if they do, they are very brief.

How completely patients recover from an acute episode is *not* related to the severity of the psychosis. Instead, better prognoses are associated with (a) an acute onset, (b) a clear precipitant, (c) prominent confusion and disorganization, (d) highly systematized and focused delusions whose symbolism is clear and often related to the precipitating event, (e) being married, (f) good premorbid functioning, (g) a family history of depression or mania, and (h) no family history of schizophrenia, (i) a cohesive, supportive family, and (j) minimal negative symptoms.

Complications

If schizophrenia's symptoms weren't bad enough, its timing couldn't be worse: It strikes just when individuals are trying to establish themselves in the world and to form identities. Schizophrenia interferes with breaking away from home, performing at school, launching a career, and forming relationships. Schizophrenics have fewer children, marry less often (the men far less than the women), divorce and separate more frequently, and have higher rates of celibacy.

Schizophrenia's chief complication is *suicide*. About 10% of schizophrenics eventually commit suicide; about 20% attempt it. Of those who've already made an attempt, half will eventually kill themselves. In general, schizophrenics do *not* commit suicide during a psychosis, but rather in its immediate aftermath; 30% of outpatient suicides occur within three months of hospital discharge, while 50% occur within six months of discharge. Suicides usually occur after patients gain a nondelusional awareness of their illness, feel depressed, think treatment is futile, and believe the future is hopeless. In comparison to schizophrenics who do not commit suicide, those who do have better premorbid functioning and higher levels of education. These patients may have greater expectations of themselves, view schizophrenia as a greater obstacle to achieving their goals, and be less tolerant of a marginal existence. Patients on relatively low doses of medication, those who've abruptly stopped their medication, and those from relatively nonsupportive families are at greater risk. Roughly 75% of these patients are male and usually unemployed, unmarried, isolated, and paranoid (Drake, Gates, Whitaker, & Cotton, 1985).

Most schizophrenics do not commit violent crimes. When schizophrenics are arrested, it's usually for vagrancy, disturbing the peace, urinating in public, and other misdemeanors. However, individuals with schizophrenia, when compared to those with no psychiatric history, more often report using a weapon in a fight (4.2 times more). Unlike virtually any other group, schizophrenic women commit violent crimes as often as the men. The meaning of this data in relation to the disease is complicated by the fact that one-third of people with schizophrenia also have alcohol or drug abuse or dependence—which vastly increases the risk of violence and homelessness. Despite headlines, the insanity defense is used in only 1% of violent crimes that go to court and most of these are not upheld. Schizophrenics are the *victims* of crime at a higher rate than the general populace.

Homelessness is another complication of schizophrenia. Compared to the general populace, schizophrenics have a 15–20 times higher risk of becoming "street people." However, of the homeless, they are a minority. Nationally, 30% of the homeless have severe psychiatric disturbances and 25–40% have substance abuse (Mowbray, 1985).

Subtypes

DSM-IV lists five types of schizophrenic disorders, each based on the patient's most prominent feature. The *disorganized* type is characterized by marked incoherence along with flat, silly, or inappropriate affect. Formerly called "hebephrenic," these patients have an early and insidious onset, poor premorbid functioning, severe social impairment, and a chronic course.

The *catatonic* type, which is becoming rarer, primarily displays psychomotor disturbances. Patients with catatonia tend to have a more sudden onset, a better prognosis, a greater prevalence of mood disorders among first-degree relatives, and respond to electroconvulsive therapy — four features commonly associated with mood disorders. Pointing out that catatonic excitement and stupor may be due to severe psychomotor agitation and retardation respectively, Ries (1985) and others claim that *catatonia occurs more often in bipolar disorders than in schizophrenia*. Other studies have suggested that in some patients who present with catatonia, a mood disorder will be the most common diagnosis, and both *catatonia due to a general medical condition* (a *DSM-IV* diagnosis that is in its own category because nobody could agree where else to put it) and *schizophrenia* will tie for second place.

Paranoid schizophrenics have prominent persecutory or grandiose delusions or hallucinations with similar content. These patients are often unfocused, angry, argumentive, violent, and anxious. Stiff and mistrustful, they assume people can't be trusted and that anybody who likes them must be up to no good. Unsure of their own gender identity, they may project these fears onto others and be terrified of homosexuals. These patients live a "contained," highly structured existence. Relative to the other schizophrenic types, the paranoid type manifests later in life, interferes less with social functioning, and displays a more stable course. The lucky ones have highly encapsulated delusions. For example, a patient might believe that everybody at a certain shopping center is a satanic murderer, but all other locations are safe. This person can live a relatively normal life simply by avoiding that shopping center.

Schizophrenics who do not fit the above three types are diagnosed as *undifferentiated type* if they are actively psychotic, and as *residual type* if, after an active phase, chronic symptoms predominate. The specific *DSM-IV* criteria for the schizophrenic subtypes are listed in Table 9-2.

Epidemiology

The prevalence and incidence of schizophrenia tend to be the same regardless of political system, nationality, or historical time period. Schizo-

TABLE 9-2
DSM-IV Criteria for Schizophrenia Subtypes*

Paranoid Type

A type of Schizophrenia in which the following criteria are met:

A. Preoccupation with one or more delusions or frequent auditory hallucinations.

B. None of the following is prominent: disorganized speech, disorganized or catatonic behavior, flat or inappropriate affect.

Disorganized Type

A type of Schizophrenia in which the following criteria are met:

A. All of the following are prominent:

    (1) disorganized speech
    (2) disorganized behavior
    (3) flat or inappropriate affect

B. The criteria are not met for Catatonic Type.

Catatonic Type

A type of Schizophrenia in which the clinical picture is dominated by at least two of the following:

    (1) motoric immobility as evidenced by catalepsy (including waxy flexibility) or stupor
    (2) excessive motor activity (that is apparently purposeless and not influenced by external stimuli)
    (3) extreme negativism (an apparently motiveless resistance to all instructions or maintenance of a rigid posture against attempts to be moved) or mutism
    (4) peculiarities of voluntary movement as evidenced by posturing (voluntary assumption of inappropriate or bizarre postures), stereotyped movements, prominent mannerisms, or prominent grimacing
    (5) echolalia or echopraxia

Undifferentiated Type

A type of Schizophrenia in which symptoms meeting Criterion A are present, but the criteria are not met for the Paranoid, Disorganized, or Catatonic type.

Residual Type

A type of Schizophrenia in which the following criteria are met:

A. Absence of prominent delusions, hallucinations, disorganized speech, and grossly disorganized or catatonic behavior.
B. There is continuing evidence of the disturbance, as indicated by the presence of negative symptoms or two or more symptoms listed in Criterion A for Schizophrenia, present in an attenuated form (e.g., odd beliefs, unusual perceptual experiences).

*DSM-IV, pp. 287–290.

phrenia's lifetime prevalence is between 0.8% and 1%. With an incidence of 0.3 to 0.6 per thousand people, about 100,000 new cases of schizophrenia arise annually in the United States. The disorder afflicts men slightly more frequently than women (Lewine, Burbach, & Meltzer, 1984), Caucasians and African-Americans about the same, and urbanites more than country folk. Rural, less stressful settings may provoke less severe episodes and allow a place for schizophrenics to function at their ability level. For example, a Wisconsin dairy farmer brought one of his bachelor hired hands to me (N.W.) for evaluation because the man had stopped milking the cows. I asked the farmer if this man heard voices. The farmer said, "Yes, for 20 years, but we didn't mind until he stopped milking the cows."

Lower socioeconomic classes have a disproportionate number of schizophrenics. To explain why, two theories are usually advanced: "social causation" and "drift." The former asserts that poverty causes stress, which in turn causes schizophrenia. The drift theory holds that because schizophrenia devastates social and occupational functioning, schizophrenics migrate to society's lower echelons. Most evidence points to the drift theory. For example, studies in four nations revealed that, whereas the fathers of schizophrenics were equally distributed among social classes, their schizophrenic sons had drifted downward (Goodwin & Guze, 1989).

Etiology and Pathogenesis

The causes of schizophrenia can be summarized as follows: Schizophrenia involves disturbances of the brain's chemistry, anatomy, and physiology, which in turn distort perception and subjective experiences. This disorder should be called "the schizophrenias," because there are probably several causes of the syndrome. Biology produces schizophrenia; environment alters its course. More specifically, genetic and other biological factors create various degrees of vulnerability to schizophrenia; whether, and how severely, the predisposed individual becomes schizophrenic depends on a mix of biological factors (e.g., severity of heredity, prenatal complications, or slow viruses) *and* psychosocial influences (e.g., traumatic childhood). Once the disorder exists, psychosocial factors (e.g., intense, negative intrafamilial communication) substantially affect the extent of recovery, probability of relapse, overall quality of life, and the symbolic meaning attributed to the disorder. These generalizations fit the modern, *DSM-IV* definition of schizophrenia; they are neither "too biological" nor "too psychosocial," and are supported by the following evidence.

Biological Theories

Mothers often observe that their schizophrenic child "wasn't right since birth"; in comparison to their other (normal) children, she was "fussier," "more temperamental," "distant," "tense," "aggressive," or "inhibited." Although one could discount such comments as biased retrospection, considerable data confirm what mothers have been saying all along. For instance, a subgroup of schizophrenics have a higher rate of complications during pregnancy and birth; so do the children of schizophrenic mothers. "Soft" neurological signs (e.g., abnormal reflexes, minor motor and sensory signs, EEG changes) frequently occur in schizophrenia, but rarely in affective disorders. Long before they're diagnosed, preschizophrenic children have more academic difficulties and lower IQ scores than siblings or controls. Thus, mothers know. See below.

Genetic. Schizophrenia runs in families (see Table 9–3). Overall, first-degree relatives of schizophrenics have a 10% chance of becoming schizophrenic, whereas second-degree relatives (e.g., cousin, aunt, grandson) run a 3% chance. Monozygotic twins have roughly three times the concordance rate of dizygotic twins. Adopted-away studies (Chapter 4) provide strong evidence for a genetic transmission of schizophrenia and "schizophrenic-spectrum disorders" (SSD), which usually include schizophrenia, schizotypal personality disorder, and sometimes, borderline and paranoid personality disorders. They reveal that SSD is five to six times more common among biological, than among adoptive, parents of schizophrenic adults. Furthermore, if a schizophrenic adoptive parent rears an adoptee from

TABLE 9–3
Risk for Relatives of a Schizophrenic

SCHIZOPHRENIC PATIENT	PERSON AT RISK	PERCENT OF RISK
General population	Everybody	0.8–1.0
Father	Each child	10–18
Mother	Each child	10–16
Both parents	Each child	25–46
Child	Each parent	5
One sibling	Each sibling	8–10
Second-degree relative	Another second-degree relative	2–3
Monozygotic twin	Other monozygotic twin	40–50
Dizygotic twin	Other dizygotic twin	12–15
Adoptive parents (schizophrenic)	Adoptee with "normal" biological parents	4.8
Biological parents (schizophrenic)	Adoptee reared by "normal" adoptive parents	19.7

biologically "normal" parents, the adoptee's risk of becoming schizophrenic is four times *less* than if the adoptee had a schizophrenic biological parent and was reared by "normal" adoptive parents. The more severe the schizophrenia, the greater its inheritability.

Biochemical. Most widely touted, the *dopamine hypothesis* states that the symptoms of schizophrenia arise from a relative excess of dopamine (DA) and from an overstimulation of DA receptors. This theory does not necessarily contend that excessive DA is the "cause" of schizophrenia, but merely that it plays a role in producing schizophrenia. Snyder (1981) demonstrated a positive correlation between how much an antipsychotic drug blocks DA receptors (in tissue-cultures) and how much it reduces schizophrenic symptoms. Amphetamines, which can produce a paranoid, psychotic state, stimulate the release of DA into synaptic clefts; they also retard the uptake of DA. L-Dopa, a direct precursor of DA, can also trigger paranoid, psychotic symptoms. Both high levels of dopamine and its metabolite, HVA, and more dopamine receptors have been found in subcortical regions of schizophrenics' brains. However, the negative symptom cluster in schizophrenia may be associated with *low* dopamine activity in the prefrontal cortex (Davis, Kahn, Ko, & Davidson, 1991). High activation of the dopamine system may be a nonspecific marker of psychosis. It also occurs in mania and psychotic depression.

Anatomic and physiologic. The recent advances in biomedical technology (see Chapter 4) have uncovered changes in schizophrenia that were previously undetectable. For example, CT scans reveal that a subgroup of chronic schizophrenics, predominantly male, have enlarged lateral, and perhaps third, ventricles. These have been seen in first-break schizophrenics and are therefore unlikely to be a consequence of the illness or its treatment. What is clear is that cerebral atrophy produces these enlarged ventricles, a finding confirmed by magnetic resonant imaging (MRI). PET scans indicate that the frontal lobes of schizophrenics take up and metabolize less glucose, and neuropsychological tests show that schizophrenics have impaired frontal-lobe action. The frontal lobes are our species' last and most advanced evolutionary achievement. Planning, organizing, and anticipating future events and consequences require normal frontal-lobe function. Absence of these functions may lead to the negative symptoms of schizophrenia.

Histological studies show that in schizophrenics, brain cells that normally migrate to the outer layers of the cortex in the second trimester (fourth to sixth month) of pregnancy fail to migrate as far and get stuck at more interior layers. This abnormality could be caused by an error in genetic programming or by a complication such as a viral infection during the second trimester. For unknown reasons, an influenza infection in the fifth month of pregnancy leads to an increased risk of schizophrenia in females but not males.

Psychosocial Theories

With an unusual consistency for scientific investigations of psychosocial influences, one finding stands out: *The amount of tension patients are exposed to within their families is the most critical psychosocial variable affecting the course of schizophrenia.* American and British studies compared families with "high-expressed emotion" (HEE) to those with "low-expressed emotion" (LEE). The high emotion expressed is not positive; HEE families are more openly critical of the patient, display greater hostility and dissatisfaction, convey little warmth or encouragement, and form overprotective and symbiotic relationships. Typical comments from HEE relatives towards the patient are: "You do nothing but bitch"; "I wish you'd just get out of my hair!"; "I worry so much about you, I don't think you should go out tonight."

Nine months after their initial discharge, schizophrenics living with HEE and LEE families relapsed at rates averaging 56% and 21%, respectively (Caton, 1984). Similar results occurred two years following discharge. Those in HEE families who took or didn't take their medication had relapse rates of 66% and 46%, respectively. Patients exposed to HEE families for more or less than 35 hours a week had relapse rates of 69% and 28%, respectively. In LEE families, relapse rates were uniformly low and unaffected by use of medication and duration of contact. Vaughn and Leff (1976) report that patients with the highest nine-month relapse rate (92%) had high exposure to HEE families and did not take their drugs, whereas patients with the lowest relapse rate (12%) took their meds and lived with LEE families.

Differential Diagnosis

Schizophrenia needs to be differentiated from other psychotic disorders such as schizophreniform disorder, schizoaffective disorder, delusional disorder, brief psychotic disorder, shared psychotic disorder (*foie à deux*), psychotic disorder due to a general medical condition, and substance-induced psychotic disorder. Details on differential diagnosis are presented later in this chapter when each disorder is examined. In general, patients with these potential imitators of schizophrenia do not display all the symptoms needed for a schizophrenia diagnosis or they have not had them long enough. The most important clue in distinguishing schizophrenia from a *mood disorder* or a *psychosis* that is caused by substances or a medical condition is: *Between psychotic episodes, schizophrenics do not completely recover from the psychosis; with these other conditions, patients usually do.*

Patients appearing to have schizophrenia, *catatonic type*, are most likely to have a *mood disorder*, but may also have *catatonia due to a general medical condition.* Those with a mood disorder usually have normal baseline function, report previous episodes of depression or mania, and often have relatives with mood disorder, typically bipolar disorder. A sodium amytal interview or a brief trial of benzodiazepine can temporarily "unfreeze" a catatonic stupor and help clinicians elicit more information from patients. Profoundly elevated or depressed mood symptoms associated with mood disorder, and mood congruent delusions without a formal thought disorder (e.g., disorganized speech, loose associations), are clues to a mood disorder diagnosis. Patients with mania may temporarily have all the positive symptoms of schizophrenia, but also have very expansive moods. Disorientation and a worsening with amytal may be clues to a medically caused catatonia. Common medical causes of catatonia are neurological conditions (e.g., cerebrovascular disease, encephalitis) and metabolic conditions (e.g., hypercalcemia, hepatic encephalopathy, homocystinuria, diabetic ketoacidosis). A careful history, physical exam, and laboratory investigation are essential in assessing catatonia. Occasionally, neuroleptic medication can cause dystonias, acute spasms of particular muscle groups that may closely resemble the posturing of catatonia. This side effect is seen soon after starting antipsychotic medications.

Anxiety and somatoform disorders may resemble schizophrenia, but not for long. Obsessive and hypochondriacal patients may become preoccupied with their concerns to a near-delusional intensity. Yet, unlike the schizophrenics, the obsessive patients know their obsessions are "silly" and hypochondriac patients know they are hypochondriacs.

Schizotypical, paranoid, and borderline personality disorders may present as psychosis and resemble the prodromal or acute phase of schizophrenia, but unlike schizophrenia, the psychotic symptoms remit in hours or days. Severe *schizoid personality disorder* may produce a schizophrenic-like social withdrawal; these patients, however, rarely become psychotic. When a personality disorder and schizophrenia co-exist, diagnose each on Axes II and I, respectively.

Management and Treatment

The goal of treatment of schizophrenic patients is usually not to *cure* them, but to improve their *quality of life*—minimize symptoms, prevent suicide, avert relapses, enhance self-esteem, improve social and occupational functioning, and reduce the pain of the patients' relatives. (Similarly, the goal of treating patients with heart disease, diabetes, arthritis, and most physical ailments is not to cure, but to improve their everyday lives.)

Treatments vary depending on the stage of the patient's disorder. This section refers to *acute care*, which is the treatment of florid symptoms; *transition care*, which is treatment given before and after discharge from a psychiatric hospital; and *chronic care*, which is the community-based treatment of relatively stable, albeit impaired, patients.

Biological Treatments

With each of these three stages of treatment, overwhelming evidence demonstrates that the vast majority of schizophrenics benefit from antipsychotic medications. Although a few patients recover without medications and some become worse with them, it's hard to predict these patients in advance. Traditional antipsychotics are most effective in eliminating the schizophrenia's positive active symptoms, but they also diminish the negative symptoms. Newer antipsychotics, such as clozapine and risperidone, which block both dopamine and serotonin-2 receptors more effectively, treat negative symptoms and are also effective in about one-third of patients who exhibit resistance to traditional antipsychotics. When first prescribed, antipsychotics usually take days or weeks to produce significant effects. *Some* neuroleptics also have a *sedative* effect, which manifests in 10 to 15 minutes, peaks around two hours, and subsides by six hours. Antipsychotic actions continue as long as patients are on the drug; sedative effects tend to wear off in seven to ten days.

Acute care. Clinicians' first priorities are to prevent patients from harming themselves or others. If these dangers are imminent, observation, medication, and sometimes physical restraints are essential. Symptoms of aggression and agitation can be reduced most quickly by "rapid tranquilization," during which patients receive a small dose of an antipsychotic (e.g., 5 mg of haloperidol, 25 mg of chlorpromazine) every 30 to 90 minutes until symptoms subside, they fall asleep, or develop an incapacitating side effect (e.g., dystonia, orthostatic hypotension). To avoid excessive dosage, a reasonable target dose (such as 15 mg haloperidol or 400 mg chlorpromazine) is established in advance. Benzodiazepines are often used to control aggression and agitation in patients who remain out of control after receiving their target neuroleptic dose. To avert a hypotensive crisis, (a) blood pressures should be taken lying and standing before each dose, and (b) antipsychotics should be withheld if the patients are dizzy or light-headed on standing.

When a floridly psychotic patient's immediate safety is not at issue, antipsychotic medication should not be given until diagnoses other than schizophrenia have been ruled out. Since these drugs all exert the same antipsychotic effect, the choice of a particular antipsychotic drug depends primarily on its side effect profile. (See Appendix H.) In general, there is an inverse relation between parkinsonian side effects and anticholinergic (e.g., dry mouth) and sedative side effects. For example, the highly sedating thioridazine is the most anticholinergic and sedating and the least parkinsonian of antipsychotics. Thus, if sedation is desired or if patients are at high risk for parkinsonian side effects, thioridazine could be used. Temporarily adding benzodiazepines to a less sedating antipsychotic may be a more specific way of sedating patients. Then when patients no longer need sedation, the benzodiazepines can be stopped and they can comfortably continue on a less sedating antipsychotic. Patients should only receive as much sedation as required to ensure their safety. A patient banging her head against a wall requires sedation, whereas a patient standing rigidly in the corner does not. (However, if patients are catatonic, a modest dose of a benzodiazepine can temporarily mobilize them.) Dosage (Appendix G) must be tailored to individual patients.

Transition care. Patients should be discharged on the same dose and type of medication that proved necessary when they were inpatients; immediately decreasing medication is a mistake. After living in the relative security of a hospital, the discharged patients must suddenly contend with all the environmental stresses that prompted their admission. To face these stresses, patients need all the help they can get, including medication. Since transition involves so many psychosocial changes, if medication is also changed, it's hard to pinpoint which changes account for problems that might arise. If patients continue in full remission for roughly six months after their first hospitalization, their medication should be dropped gradually to prevent rebound tardive dyskinesia (see below).

At no time should clinicians imply that taking medication is a "crutch": That's akin to telling a diabetic that using insulin is a crutch. In reviewing all well-controlled studies, Davis (1975) found that of 3,609 patients sampled over four to six months, 20% relapsed on drug and 53% relapsed on placebo. Davis determined that the probability of this difference being due to chance is less than 10^{-87}. Thus, every effort should be made to ensure that patients receive their medication, which includes educating patients and their families about the medication. If noncompliance is a potential risk, consider using injectable fluphenazine or haloperidol decanoate (which persists for two to four weeks), having parents monitor the nightly intake of antipsychotic in liquid form, or having patients receive their once-a-day dose in front of a nurse.

Chronic care. How long patients should remain on antipsychotic medications following *subsequent* hospitalizations depends on the duration and severity of the illness. Although the beneficial effects of antipsychotic drugs are greatest during the acute stage, they control symptoms for at least a year and decrease relapses for many years.

Unfortunately, this long-term use of antipsychotics creates one of psychopharmacology's darkest problems—*tardive dyskinesia* (TD). From 10–40% of patients who take antipsychotic medication for over two continuous years (though it can be as little as six months) develop involuntary, bizarre movements of the mouth, limbs, and hips. Although 80–90% of cases are mild, severe impairment occurs in 3–5% of all patients. Most often TD appears as "tobacco-chewing," lip-smacking, and "fly-catching" movements of the mouth and tongue; less often, as hip jerks or slow, undulating motions of the hands or feet. When TD is present, these grotesque movements typically erupt within a few days of decreasing or stopping antipsychotics; they subside only when patients sleep or are put back on the medication. The cause of TD is unknown.[1]

Half the time, TD can be reversed if detected early and the medications are stopped. Although other drugs may occasionally counteract it, once TD occurs, there is usually *no* good way to eliminate it. The risk and severity of TD may be reduced by maintaining patients on the lowest possible dose, and by periodically testing if the drug could be discontinued. Because the only way to avoid TD is to avoid antipsychotics, doctor and patient must decide, as with any medication, if the treatment is worse than the disease.[2] At some point, most schizophrenics must choose between risking TD or madness and institutionalization. In reality, this choice isn't as dreadful as it sounds, since slightly increasing the dose will temporarily suppress TD. In time, however, more severe symptoms of TD may emerge, which only higher doses of medication can control; yet, even here, the increase is usually small, the relief, great, and the options, terrifying. For unknown reasons, TD reaches a plateau in most patients, beyond which there is no further worsening, and in some cases, spontaneous improvement.

When patients do not improve sufficiently on antipsychotic medication, the first consideration is whether the drug is being taken and properly absorbed. These questions can be answered by obtaining serum levels. Fluphenazine and haloperidol decanoate can circumvent problems with drug compliance. These are injected and provide antipsychotic control for one to four weeks. Patients may not be improving because of misdiagnosis or because they have developed affective symptoms that might be better treated with antidepressants or lithium.

Psychosocial Treatments

Acute care. When hospitalized, most actively psychotic schizophrenics have a short attention-span, are overwhelmed by stimuli, and cannot easily discern reality; they often feel lost, alone, and frightened. Therefore, contacts with these patients should be no longer than they can tolerate; in one day most patients benefit more from ten, five-minute contacts than from one, 40-minute contact. These frequent contacts should stress reality testing and reassurance, while avoiding psychologically-sensitive material. Schizophrenic patients may not think they need help for their hallucinations or delusions, but they may have problems that both patient and staff can agree on. Treating poor sleep, "worrying" too much (paranoia), or disorganized thinking can become the cornerstones of a treatment alliance. Arguing with

---

[1]One popular theory holds that because antipsychotic drugs block dopamine (DA) receptors, these receptors eventually become "supersensitive" to DA. When antipsychotics are decreased or withdrawn, the receptors are unable to handle the onslaught of DA; as a result, the receptors degenerate, resulting in TD.

[2]Consequently, antipsychotics should be used only in the treatment of schizophrenia and other persisting psychotic disorders. A draconian, but all-too-frequent, error is that of treating chronic anxiety or depression with anitpsychotics for more than five months.

patients about their delusions won't work and can worsen their condition. Contacts should be performed by as few staff as possible. As the patient's psychosis diminishes, the role of psychosocial treatments increases. At some point, individual supportive therapy should identify the stressors that led to hospitalization and prepare patients to contend with similar stressors following discharge.

Hospitalization is also a major crisis for the patient's family. Prior to hospitalization, most relatives deny or "explain away" the schizophrenic's symptoms (e.g., "It's normal for teenagers to lock themselves in a room"; "Kids often fly off the handle"). When the patient is psychotic and finally admitted, the family is shell-shocked: Members might insist "nothing is wrong," telephone the ward 15 times a day, not leave the unit, etc. These are weird but *normal* responses to an acute and severe stress (see Figure 4-3); they are not indicative of the "craziest family on earth." Only *after* the immediate crisis is it possible to assess the family's normal behavior.

Because schizophrenia is a chronic disorder, the family's long-term involvement as an extension of the treatment team is essential. On admission, most families already feel guilty about "creating" a schizophrenic; this guilt is only compounded when therapists blame them, either directly or euphemistically (e.g., "The family has problems communicating"). Not only do attempts to rectify a family's "communication problems" and "pathological relations" reinforce the family's guilt, but they don't work — at least during short-term hospitalizations. Similarly, separating schizophrenic patients from their families is usually harmful. Like surgery, "parentectomy" is a procedure of last resort.

Near the outset of hospitalization, several members of the staff should begin forming a *collaborative* relationship with the family. Nurses should monitor visits to gather information. A new family should be introduced to relatives of other schizophrenics so that the family members feel less alone, embarrassed, and guilty. Since research demonstrates that most acutely psychotic schizophrenic patients do as well, if not better, during three weeks, rather than three months, of hospitalization, discharge planning that *includes* the family should begin the day the patient is admitted. This is even more critical now in this era of "managed care." In many cases, even three weeks has become a luxury; seven to twelve days has become a more typical length of stay. The goal is to begin treatment and stabilize patients enough to allow non-hospital settings to continue treatment.

Transition care. Chance of relapse and suicide are greatest within the first six months, and especially within the first 14 weeks, following discharge. In general, the patients who fare best during these 14 weeks are those who have the most stability in their lives. This transition phase is *not* the time to introduce major alterations in the patient's living arrangements, social life, medications, therapists, and so on. Some changes may be necessary but should be kept to a minimum. Considerable research (Caton, 1984) shows that discharge planning should focus on preventing the five conditions most likely to produce relapse:

1. *The failure to take medication* is the most frequent cause of readmission — and a common prelude to suicide. Because 24–63% of outpatient schizophrenics take less than the prescribed dose, *all* patients and their families should be educated regarding the purpose and importance of medication.
2. *The failure to continue aftercare* stems less from a lack of resources than from patients' refusal to participate in available programs. Dropout rates from aftercare programs are as high as 75%. Effective discharge planning ensures that patients have visited the aftercare facility, know how to travel there, understand the nature and purpose of aftercare treatment, feel comfortable with the outpatient staff, and know the time of their first aftercare appointment.
3. *Inadequate life-support*, especially in housing and income, but also in money-management skills, hygiene, and medical care, should be addressed in occupational therapy.
4. *Inadequate socialization and recreation* often prompt rehospitalization. If a bowler stops bowling, the bowling skills atrophy; so too with the schizophrenic's leisure-time and social skills. Recreational and group therapy should prevent further deterioration of these skills.
5. *The effects of HEE families* can be reduced by using a "psycho-educational approach," whose effectiveness has been repeatedly demonstrated (Anderson, Hogarty, & Reiss, 1980; Cozolino et al., 1988). This approach aims to reduce the guilt, over-responsibility, confusion, and helplessness of families, and although its implementation varies in different settings, it generally involves five steps: (a) The patient and family are given "the facts" about schizophrenia, including information about its symptoms, natural course, genetics, etc. (b) The family and patient are encouraged to express pent-up concerns about the illness and each other, preferably with other families. (c) The family is taught about the psychonoxious effects of HEE environments. (d) Next, family members are trained to contain emotional outbursts, to avoid (or at least delay and mute) criticisms, to praise positive activities, to reduce unrealistic guilt and over-responsibility, and to be less judgmental. (e) If the family is, for whatever reason, an immutably HEE family, than the patient's amount of contact with the family should be reduced. Community-based self-help groups for the families of schizophrenics often provide a kind of psycho-educational approach over the long haul.

The greatest danger during the transition period is suicide, which mostly occurs when patients (a) have a post-psychotic depression, (b) are discouraged about their treatment, (c) believe their future is hopeless, (d) misconstrue a drug-induced akinesia for depression and futility, or (e) stop taking medication. Therapists should be alert to these specific warning signs, tell family members to also be aware of them, and meet frequently with patients to check on them.

Chronic care. Contrary to many long-held assumptions, more therapy is not always better therapy. Hogarty, Goldberg, Schooler, & Ulrich (1974) found that supportive psychotherapy is more beneficial with patients who take medication, more likely to hasten relapse in nonmedicated patients, and more effective the longer the patients have not been actively psychotic.

Even at the very best of facilities (e.g., Chestnut Lodge), however, long-term intensive psychotherapy is ineffective in treating schizophrenia. A 15-year follow-up showed that only 14% of these patients were functioning "good" or better (McGlashan, 1984). Chronically hospitalized patients function better in the community when they are *gradually* released from the hospital, often to halfway houses or to group settings with patients they knew in the hospital.

Despite the severity and chronicity of schizophrenia, modern treatments can enable patients to live relatively satisfying lives. The authors know many patients who, after 5 to 15 years of institutionalization, went on to become independent and productive with the help of sound and sensible treatment. These cases are not rare; patients and families should be made aware of these successes, if for no other reason than to combat demoralization.

SCHIZOPHRENIFORM DISORDER

The *DSM-IV* criteria for schizophreniform disorder and schizophrenia (Table 9-1) are identical, except that schizophreniform disorder has (1) shorter duration (between one and six months) and (2) social or occupational function need not be impaired. This six-month cut-off point and absence of poor functioning were chosen because they appear (for now) to be the best predictors for which patients recover (from schizophreniform) and which become chronic (schizophrenic).

Schizophreniform disorder is further classified in *DSM-IV* as having *good prognostic features* if the patient has two of the following four indicators: (1) onset of prominent psychotic symptoms within four weeks of first noticeable change in unusual behavior or functioning; (2) confusion or perplexity at the height of the psychotic episode; (3) absence of blunted or flat affect; and (4) good premorbid social and occupational functioning.

Roughly half of patients *initially* diagnosed as having schizophreniform disorder will improve or recover substantially; in general, the longer the disorder persists, the worse the prognosis. Although findings conflict, most suggest that there is no increased prevalence of schizophrenia among relatives. The ECA survey (Chapter 1) found a lifetime prevalence of 0.1% for schizophreniform disorder in the general population. The disorder's etiology is unknown.

Schizophreniform disorder differs from *brief psychotic disorder*, which resolves in under one month and does not include negative symptoms as part of the criteria. Brief psychotic disorder often occurs after a major stressor (brief reactive psychosis) and the content of the psychoses often involves the stressor. For example, an intern, after three weeks of substantial sleep deprivation and feeling overwhelmed by his duties, began complaining that the nurses were persecuting him by paging him all the time. The nurses told him that they hadn't paged him in hours. Then he knew there was a plot.

Schizophreniform disorder differs from *schizoaffective disorder*, which has a strong affective component (see below). All the factors for differentiating *medical- and substance-induced syndromes* and *mood disorders* from schizophrenia apply to schizophreniform disorder. Schizophreniform disorder is treated symptomatically, with observation, antipsychotic medication, supportive psychotherapy, suicide precautions, and family involvement.

Mood disorders with psychosis often involve delusions and hallucinations, but they are typically mood-congruent: Delusions of poverty, sin, and disease are common with depression; those of overconfidence and grandiosity are common with mania; patently bizarre, Schneiderian, and nonmood-congruent delusions are more typically schizophrenic. When asked why he is being persecuted, the person with mood disorder is likely to say, "because I deserve it," while the paranoid might say, "I am angry and will seek revenge." Persecutory delusions occur in both mood and schizophrenic disorders. Indeed, distinguishing these two disorders is a frequent and difficult problem, since at some point over half of all schizophrenics have depressive symptoms, and patients with mood disorders can show deterioration, withdrawal, and psychosis. When patients exhibit symptoms of both disorders, the timing and duration of symptoms are critical: Schizophrenia should be diagnosed only if (a) no major depressive or manic episodes have occurred along with the active psychosis, and (b) the schizophrenic symptoms have persisted for six months. In the prodromal or residual phase, these may be only negative symptoms or attenuated positive symptoms. When the two disorders cannot be distinguished and truly occur simultaneously, diagnose *schizoaffective disorder*.

SCHIZOAFFECTIVE DISORDER

In 1933, Kasanin introduced the term "schizoaffective disorder" to describe a psychosis with prominent schizophrenic *and* affective symptoms; since then, the term's use has been equally "schizophrenic" and "affective." Experts disagree whether schizoaffective disorder is an actual disorder: Some claim it is nothing more than a mere label, a fudge-factor, a provisional diagnosis to be used until the patient's *real* diagnosis—schizophrenia

or affective disorder—becomes apparent. Others contend that schizoaffective disorder is a genuine entity that combines features of both disorders.
DSM-IV has added the diagnosis, suggesting that, at least in some patients,
schizoaffective disorder is a genuine entity (see Table 9–4).

By these criteria, Fred, a 24-year old librarian, would seem to have a schizoaffective disorder. At first, over a period of seven months, he developed typical signs of
schizophrenia: He believed a nearby hospital was zapping his brain with X-rays,
thereby controlling his actions. By stringing together the first letter of each book
title returned to the library, Fred uncovered a secret code, which auditory hallucinations later informed him was part of a plot to destroy Dartmouth College. After a
three-week period of hospitalization, including treatment with antipsychotics, Fred
recovered, returned to work, and then secretly stopped his medication. Within a
week his delusions reappeared, but this time accompanied by symptoms of major
depression: insomnia, anorexia, anhedonia, psychomotor retardation, and severe
dysthymia. The delusions and syndrome of major depression continued for six
more weeks. Did Fred have a post-psychotic depression? Probably not, because in
post-psychotic depression the patient feels hopeless, or anergic, or depressed—in
other words, a *symptom*, instead of a *syndrome*, of depression. Fred had the syndrome (Table 9–4), and met criteria for a schizoaffective disorder.

TABLE 9–4
DSM-IV Criteria for Schizoaffective Disorder*

A. An uninterrupted period of illness during which, at some time, there is either a
Major Depressive Episode, a Manic Episode, or a Mixed Episode concurrent with
symptoms that meet Criterion A for Schizophrenia.

   Note: The Major Depressive Episode must include Criterion A1: depressed mood.

B. During the same period of illness, there have been delusions or hallucinations for
at least 2 weeks in the absence of prominent mood symptoms.

C. Symptoms that meet criteria for a mood episode are present for a substantial
portion of the total duration of the active and residual periods of the illness.

D. The disturbance is not due to the direct physiological effects of a substance (e.g.,
a drug of abuse, a medication) or a general medical condition.

Bipolar Type: if the disturbance includes a Manic or a Mixed Episode (or a Manic or
a Mixed Episode and Major Depressive Episodes)

Depressive Type: if the disturbance only includes Major Depressive Episodes

---

DSM-IV, pp. 295–96.

When schizoaffective disorder is used as a temporary diagnosis awaiting further clarification, appending the term "provisional" clarifies the clinician's intention. In Fred's case, however, schizoaffective disorder was diagnosed as a disorder. Little is known about this "true" disorder. It may be a heterogeneous entity with numerous etiologies. Some genetic studies have shown that these patients have an increased family history of alcoholism, affective, and schizophrenic disorders. It appears to occur more in women. Age of onset, degree of recovery, natural history, and prognosis fall between those for schizophrenia and affective disorders. The longer the psychosis, the bleaker the outcome.

Treatment is symptomatic: Schizophrenic symptoms are treated with antipsychotics, manic symptoms with lithium, depressive symptoms with antidepressants. Some "schizo-manic" patients treated with lithium require lower doses of antipsychotics; some, taking both drugs concurrently, become extremely confused or parkinsonian; and some do well on lithium without antipsychotics, which is the most desirable option, since lithium has fewer side effects and does not cause tardive dyskinesia. Because the treatment of schizoaffective disorders often requires two or more drugs, these patients' mental status should be frequently and formally tested. These drug interactions frequently cause confusion.

A history of normal baseline functioning between each psychotic episode and a mood disorder with every psychosis indicates the possibility of an atypical psychotic mood disorder, which has a better prognosis.

DELUSIONAL DISORDERS

Delusions or delusional jealousy lasting over a month are the chief features of delusional disorders, in which the delusions are usually enduring, systematized, interrelated, and internally consistent. Their themes can be single or multiple, simple or complex. In the *persecutory type*, patients may think they are being drugged, poisoned, followed, conspired against, or maligned. In the *grandiose type*, patients may believe they have created a wonderful secret invention, discovered a cure for AIDS, or are confidantes of the president. With *delusional jealousy*, a spouse's "unfaithfulness" is fabricated on issues of "evidence"—a misplaced stocking, a misconstrued remark. A patient with the *erotomanic type* may believe that she is secretly Robert Redford's lover and badger him with phone calls, angry letters of feeling rejected, and perhaps even stalk him. About 80% with erotomanic type are women. The typical erotomanic patient leads a socially empty life, is unmarried, unattractive, and has a low status job. The object of their attention is believed to be, and usually is, of superior status, looks, intelligence, and/or has authority (Segal, 1989). (Unfortunately, many movie and entertainment stars are plagued by people with these erotomanic delusions.)

A patient with the *somatic type* of delusional disorder may believe that he has cancer and is giving it to other people, or that he has a head so small, most people can't see it.

Delusional disorders do not manifest the prominent hallucinations, incoherence, disorganized or catatonic behavior, or negative symptoms seen in schizophrenia. The delusions are not bizarre or Schneiderian, such as thought broadcasting or delusions of control. Delusional disorders, which are rare, are characterized by delusions involving nonbizarre real-life situations in otherwise well-functioning people. *Somatic delusions* need to be distinguished from *body dysmorphic disorder*, which is a preoccupation with an imagined defect in appearance ("My nose is too big,"; "My eyes are too close together"). Somatic delusions are more extreme, far exceeding the magnifications of imperfections normal to adolescence. Table 9–5 presents *DSM-IV* criteria for delusional disorder.

The *persecutory type* of delusional disorder usually begins with a plausible suspicion or grievance against an individual, government agency, or business. As the patient becomes increasingly frustrated in trying to rectify his complaint, he may develop psychotic fantasies as he presses for justice. He may bring legal action, recruit supporters, make public appeals, or send petitions. With growing self-importance and messianic zeal, he often displays the pressured speech seen with manics. Yet unlike mania or schizophrenia, *the psychopathology does not contaminate other areas of functioning*.

Most cases of persecutory delusions arise gradually during middle or late adult life, have chronic and stable courses with few remissions and exacerbations, and disproportionately affect those who are female, married, immigrants, and in lower socioeconomic groups. Paranoia constitutes 1–4% of all psychiatric hospital admissions, with an incidence of first admissions between 1 and 3/100,000 population per year. Its etiology is unknown. Paranoia does not run in families. Social isolation and stress may foster paranoia in the elderly, while projection is its chief defense mechanism.

Because the delusions are usually egosyntonic, patients with delusional disorder seldom seek treatment. If they do—and it's usually under coercion—a trial of antipsychotic medication is indicated, even though they are unlikely to take it. The somatic type may respond to pimozide, an atypical neuroleptic, if ordinary antipsychotics fail. If the somatic or jealousy delusions are mild and it is a preoccupation that dominates, treatments for obsessive-compulsive disorder (such as serotonergic antidepressants) can be tried. The erotomanic type may also require a restraining order to stay away from the love object (Segal, 1989).

TABLE 9–5
DSM-IV Criteria for Delusional Disorder*

A. Nonbizarre delusions (i.e., involving situations that occur in real life, such as being followed, poisoned, infected, loved at a distance, being deceived by spouse or lover, or having a disease) of at least 1 month's duration.

B. Criterion A for Schizophrenia has never been met. **Note:** Tactile and olfactory hallucinations may be present in Delusional Disorder if they are related to the delusional theme.

C. Apart from the impact of the delusion(s) or its ramifications, functioning is not markedly impaired and behavior is not obviously odd or bizarre.

D. If mood episodes have occurred concurrently with delusions, their total duration has been brief relative to the duration of the delusional periods.

E. The disturbance is not due to the direct physiological effects of a substance (e.g., a drug of abuse, a medication) or a general medical condition.

Specify type (the following types are assigned based on the predominant delusional theme):

Erotomanic Type: delusions that another person, usually of higher status, is in love with the individual

Grandiose Type: delusions of inflated worth, power, knowledge, identity, or special relationship to a deity or famous person

Jealous Type: delusions that the individual's sexual partner is unfaithful

Persecutory Type: delusions that the person (or someone to whom the person is close) is being malevolently treated in some way

Somatic Type: delusions that the person has some physical defect or general medical condition

Mixed Type: delusions characteristic of more than one of the above types but no one theme predominates

Unspecified Type

*DSM-IV, p. 301.

BRIEF PSYCHOTIC DISORDER

Occasionally, real psychosis looks like it does in the movies. "Brief psychotic disorder" is just what the director ordered. In a majority of cases the victim was a relatively normal person in whom psychosis developed rapidly (the person "snaps") after a very stressful event. This is accompanied by emotional turmoil with rapid shifts of mood, perplexity, or confusion.

Negative symptoms are not a usual feature. Most recover entirely. In a few cases this is an unusual, abrupt beginning of a schizophrenic disorder. A clinical rule-of-thumb is that the faster the onset of the disorder, the faster the offset. Table 9–6 presents *DSM-IV* criteria for brief psychotic disorder.

Marc, a 30-year-old hotel executive, was at work when a "moderate" earthquake toppled the hotel, killing four occupants and injuring many others. Dazed but physically unharmed, Marc wandered away from the rubble, arrived home hours later, and kept mumbling that he was responsible for the hotel's collapse. Staring into space as if listening to someone, Marc would mumble, "The devil is saying, 'You're to blame, you're to blame. You'll fry in hell.'" At times Marc would sit and sulk, sometimes he was rigid and mute, while at other times he would pace the floor, arguing loudly with the devil. Marc had no previous psychiatric difficulties and his mental state was stable prior to the earthquake.

Marc's wife took him to the emergency room for treatment. His drug screen was

TABLE 9–6
DSM-IV* Criteria for Brief Psychotic Disorder

A. Presence of one (or more) of the following symptoms:

   (1) delusions
   (2) hallucinations
   (3) disorganized speech (e.g., frequent derailment or incoherence)
   (4) grossly disorganized or catatonic behavior

   Note: Do not include a symptom if it is a culturally sanctioned response pattern.

B. Duration of an episode of the disturbance is at least 1 day but less than 1 month, with eventual full return to premorbid level of functioning.

C. The disturbance is not better accounted for by a Mood Disorder With Psychotic Features, Schizoaffective Disorder, or Schizophrenia and is not due to the direct physiological effects of a substance (e.g., a drug of abuse, a medication) or a general medical condition.

Specify if:
With Marked Stressor(s) (brief reactive psychosis): if symptoms occur shortly after and apparently in response to events that, singly or together, would be markedly stressful to almost anyone in similar circumstances in the person's culture

Without Marked Stressor(s): if psychotic symptoms do *not* occur shortly after, or are not apparently in response to events that, singly or together, would be markedly stressful to almost anyone in similar circumstances in the person's culture

With Postpartum Onset: if onset within 4 weeks postpartum

*DSM-IV, p. 304.

negative and his brief reactive psychosis was treated with 5 mg of haloperidol stat and 2 mg tid for the next two days. Marc's symptoms began to recede the day after the earthquake, and three days later, he was back to normal.

Differential Diagnosis

If Marc's symptoms had lasted under two to three hours, his diagnosis would have been *psychotic disorder NOS*; if they had persisted for one month, his diagnosis would have been *schizophreniform disorder*. Gradually increasing psychopathology before the florid psychosis characterizes schizophrenic and schizophreniform disorders, but not brief psychotic disorder. In contrast to *schizophrenia*, brief psychotic disorder usually has an acute precipitant, a rapid onset, delusions and hallucinations that pertain to the stressor, and a quick and complete recovery. However, not all cases have acute precipitants, making them look more like other disorders. If the patient meets the full *DSM-IV* criteria for *mood disorders*, brief psychotic disorder should not be diagnosed. At their worst, *adjustment disorders* and *uncomplicated bereavement* do not usually produce psychosis. Sometimes auditory and visual hallucinations of the deceased can occur in an otherwise normal bereavement. *Malingering* and *factitious disorder with psychological symptoms* must be considered, as should *organic conditions*, especially delirium and psychomotor or *partial complex seizures* that suddenly produce delusions, hallucinations, and repeated automatisms with fluctuating levels of consciousness; a third of these cases are without confusion (McKenna, Kane, & Parrish, 1985). EEG recordings are abnormal in approximately 50% of patients with partial complex seizures. *Petit mal seizures*, which present as absence attacks, may be confused with catatonia, but no other psychotic symptoms are present. Finally, *substance misuse*, especially intoxication or withdrawal, is often the prime suspect and the most important to diagnose promptly.

Management and Treatment

The priorities in treating brief psychotic disorder are: First, prevent suicide attempts or assaultiveness. Second, hasten recovery by prescribing antipsychotics (e.g., perphenazine 4 mg q4h prn). If the patient is imminently suicidal or dangerous, "rapid tranquilization," as well as antipsychotics, may be indicated. Tapering medication should begin only after the patient is clearly recovering. Third, initiate talking therapy that emphasizes reality testing and provides repeated assurances of safety and improvement to the patient. At this point, relatives and therapists should refrain from "psychologizing" the meaning of the psychosis with the patient. (For instance, probing Marc's guilt over the earthquake would have further disorganized him.) Fourth, *after* the psychosis resolves, some patients benefit from psychotherapy that addresses (a) the stressor and its personal meaning, or (b) incompletely resolved issues related to the psychosis. For example, on returning to his wife's grave a year after she died, a well-functioning man developed an acute psychosis that disappeared in a week. Recognizing that his psychotic episode indicated that he was more distressed by his wife's death than he had realized, he entered brief psychotherapy to examine this concern.

The genetics and prognosis of brief psychotic disorder are not clear. Some patients have one or more further brief psychotic episodes. A family history of mood disorder is frequently found in those who experience stress-induced brief psychotic episodes. These patients may have a higher risk of developing a mood disorder.

SHARED PSYCHOTIC DISORDER (*folie à deux*)

This very rare, strange disorder looks like psychosis by contagion, in which one person "catches" another's "delusion virus." However, no virus is involved. The person who "gives" the delusions (the primary case) already has a psychotic disorder with delusions and usually dominates in a very close, long-term relationship with a socially isolated, more passive, initially healthy person who "gets" the delusions. This person acquires the same or very similar delusions as the delusion "donor." Table 9–7 presents *DSM-IV* criteria for shared psychotic disorder.

The delusions in this shared psychotic disorder are usually within the

---

TABLE 9–7
DSM-IV **Criteria for Shared Psychotic Disorder (*folie à deux*)***

A. A delusion develops in an individual in the context of a close relationship with another person(s), who has an already-established delusion.

B. The delusion is similar in content to that of the person who already has the established delusion.

C. The disturbance is not better accounted for by another Psychotic Disorder (e.g., Schizophrenia) or a Mood Disorder With Psychotic Features and is not due to the direct physiological effects of a substance (e.g., a drug of abuse, a medication) or a general medical condition.

DSM-IV, p. 306.

realm of possibility and may stem from common past experiences of the two people. Although this disorder is most commonly seen in relationships of two people (*folie à deux*), cases have been reported involving up to 12 family members. The disorder tends to be chronic, with the recipient typically less impaired because only part of the primary person's delusional system is adopted. Treatment involves either successful antipsychotic medication of the primary person or interrupting the relationship with the primary person.

PSYCHOTIC DISORDER SECONDARY TO A GENERAL MEDICAL CONDITION

This psychotic disorder presents with delusions or hallucinations often accompanied by incoherence and inappropriate or labile affects. In *DSM-IV*, dementia and delirium are not considered to be a general medical condition. Therefore, psychoses with profound confusion, memory loss, fluctuating levels of consciousness, and disorientation would be classified dementia or delirium "with delusions" or "with hallucinations." Schizophrenic hallucinations are most often auditory and frequently visual, but organic hallucinations may involve any of the senses, including olfactory and tactile. Most schizophrenics defend their hallucinations as reasonable and valid, whereas many patients with brain syndromes consider them inexplicable, crazy, and foreign—not their "real selves." Table 9–8 lists *DSM-IV* criteria for psychotic disorder secondary to a general medical condition.

TABLE 9–8
DSM-IV* Criteria for Psychotic Disorder Due to a General Medical Condition

A. Prominent hallucinations or delusions.

B. There is evidence from the history, physical examination, or laboratory findings that the disturbance is a direct physiological consequence of a general medical condition.

C. The disturbance is not better accounted for by another mental disorder.

D. The disturbance does not occur exclusively during the course of a delirium.

With Delusions: if delusions are the predominant symptom

With Hallucinations: if hallucinations are the predominant symptom

*DSM-IV, pp. 309–310.

If there is no family history of *schizophrenia*, or if schizophrenic-like symptoms first arise in a person over 40, the diagnosis is less likely to be schizophrenia. *Complex partial seizure disorder* can simulate schizophrenia, but is usually associated with complete or nearly complete remissions and abrupt recurrences. Many other medical conditions, including *hormone abnormalities* (hypothyroidism, hyperthyroidism), *Cushing's disease* (too much cortisol), and *brain tumor* can be the culprits in causing this form of psychosis.

SUBSTANCE-INDUCED PSYCHOTIC DISORDER

Substance-induced psychotic disorder, especially intoxication from amphetamines, cocaine, hallucinogens, PCP, cannabis, and alcohol, may be indistinguishable from the active phase of schizophrenia, schizophreniform disorder, or acute psychosis. Symptoms are usually temporary and can be confirmed by urine screening. Although *alcoholic hallucinosis* typically stops within 48 hours of withdrawal, it may persist for weeks and facsimilate the early stages of schizophrenia. However, in alcoholic hallucinosis, the hallucinations are exclusively auditory, not visual, and the patient's response to these images is appropriate to their content, e.g., anxiety in response to frightening images. Of course, schizophrenics can also have a superimposed drug-induced psychosis. Amphetamine psychosis can blend into a prolonged and sometimes chronic paranoid state. People who already have risk factors for schizophrenia are more likely to experience this prolonged result; the amphetamines may push the vulnerable person "over the brink." Table 9–9 presents *DSM-IV* criteria for substance-induced psychotic disorder.

Psychosis can also be induced by drug withdrawal. Here lab tests are useless in making the diagnosis, but a history of recent, usually prolonged, drug use may help. Changes in vital signs (e.g., increased blood pressure, heart rate, and temperature), sweating, and shaking frequently accompany serious withdrawal from alcohol and hypnoanxiolytics. Prescribed drugs can also cause psychosis: Corticosteroid, thyroid, and anticholinergics are common culprits. Sleuthing through these substance-induced and medically-induced syndromes makes most psychiatrists glad that they went to medical school!

TABLE 9–9
DSM-IV **Criteria for Substance-Induced Psychotic Disorder***

A. Prominent hallucinations or delusions. **Note:** Do not include hallucinations if the person has insight that they are substance-induced.

B. There is evidence from the history, physical examination, or laboratory findings of either (1) or (2):

    (1) the symptoms in Criterion A developed during, or within a month of, Substance Intoxication or Withdrawal

    (2) medication use is etiologically related to the disturbance

C. The disturbance is not better accounted for by a Psychotic Disorder that is not substance-induced. Evidence that the symptoms are better accounted for by a Psychotic Disorder that is not substance-induced might include the following: the symptoms precede the onset of the substance use or medication use; the symptoms persist for a substantial period of time (e.g., about a month) after the cessation of acute withdrawal or severe intoxication, or are substantially in excess of what would be expected given the type or amount of the substance used or the duration of use; or there is other evidence that suggests the existence of an independent non-substance-induced Psychotic Disorder (e.g., a history of recurrent non-substance-related episodes).

D. The disturbance does not occur exclusively during the course of a delirium.

Note: This diagnosis should be made instead of a diagnosis of Substance Intoxication or Substance Withdrawal only when the symptoms are in excess of those usually associated with the intoxication or withdrawal syndrome and when the symptoms are sufficiently sure to warrant independent clinical attention.

Specify if:
With Onset During Intoxication: if criteria are met for Intoxication with the substance and the symptoms develop during the intoxication syndrome

With Onset During Withdrawal: if criteria are met for Withdrawal from the substance and the symptoms develop during, or shortly after, a withdrawal syndrome

*DSM-IV, pp. 314–15.

CHAPTER 10

Mood Disorders

MOOD DISORDERS ARE the most common disorders seen by outpatient psychiatrists. Mood disorders, principally depression, are far and away the number one cause of suicide. What's more, with each decade in the 20th century, the prevalence of depression and suicide has risen (Klerman et al., 1985). Teenage suicides are increasing at an alarming rate. Most of these suicides, however, *are* preventable, and in doing so, the first step is to learn about their chief cause — depression.

When non-professional people speak of depression, they usually mean the *emotion* of feeling sad, "blue," down-in-the dumps, unhappy, demoralized — i. e., dysthymia. When clinicians speak of depression, they are usually referring to a *syndrome* or mental disorder consisting of many symptoms and signs, including appetite loss, anhedonia, hopelessness, insomnia, and dysthymia. Whereas the emotion of depression affects everyone to some degree, the syndrome afflicts only some — a "mere" 15% of Americans during their lives and a 100 million earthlings every day. (For clarity, in this text *dysthymia* refers to the emotion or symptom of depression while *depression* refers to the syndromes and disorders of depression. *Dysphoria* refers to any unpleasant mood, including dysthymia.)

Mood disorder is the overall category for entities whose predominant symptom is usually a pathological mood: dysphoria, euphoria, or both. In *DSM-IV*, mood disorders that consist solely of "lows" are called "major depression" and its milder version, "dysthymic disorder"; those that combine "highs" and "lows" are called "bipolar disorder" and its milder form, "cyclothymic disorder."

Mood disorders have also been classified according to at least four different conceptual models. First, the *endogenous versus reactive model* considers endogenous depression to be a strictly biological event unrelated to any environmental forces, whereas reactive depression must be psychosocially triggered and devoid of any biological factors. This distinction unjustifiably assumes that a depression's etiology is (a) known and (b) either biological *or* psychosocial. Indeed, many "endogenous" depressions follow environmental stressors and many "reactive" depressions emerge without any obvious precipitant. Second, in the *primary and secondary model depressions*, secondary depressions are preceded by another physical or mental disorder (e.g., alcoholism, hypothyroidism, anxiety disorder), whereas primary depressions are not. Third, in the *unipolar versus bipolar model*, a bipolar disorder exists whenever a manic episode has occurred. Patients with bipolar depression must have a history of mania or hypomania, while those with unipolar depressions don't. Fourth, historically *psychotic and neurotic depressions* were distinguished, with psychotic depressions referring to any severe depression, even when the patients were not psychotic. In *DSM-IV*, however, a "psychotic depression" must display psychosis. Neurotic depressions are roughly equivalent to "atypical depression" or dysthymic disorder.

Clinical Presentation

Major depression. The first essential feature of major depression is *either* severe dysphoria *or* anhedonia — that is, a pervasive loss of interest or ability to experience pleasure in normally enjoyable activities. The dysphoria is usually dysthymia, but it can be irritable or apprehensive. Patients describe this dysphoria as "living in a black hole," "feeling dead," "overwhelmed by doom," or "physically drained." However, many patients with major depression do *not* feel depressed or even dysphoric, but anhedonic. A baseball fan suddenly doesn't care about the World Series; a loving father loses interest in his child; a devoted nurse cares little for her patients. Just because patients don't look unhappy or complain about "being in the dumps," if anhedonic, they might still have a major depression. A majority of patients with major depression look lifeless, boring, or dull, rather than sad and crying. Patients suspected of having a major depression should be asked not only if they feel depressed (or sad, blue, down, etc.), but also if they no longer enjoy things anymore. In medically ill patients, questions about enjoyment should be restricted to things they can still do. For example, a person with back pain may still enjoy reading, watching TV, or even taking walks, but it would be a mistake to ask, "Do you still like bowling?"

The second essential feature of major depression is the presence of three to four other symptoms. The *biological (also called vegetative) signs and symptoms of depression* generally include appetite loss, unintentional weight loss or gain, insomnia or hypersomnia, psychomotor retardation or agitation, a lack of energy or fatigue, and diminished libido. With another common biological sign, "diurnal mood variation," patients feel worse in the morning and slightly better by night; this pattern continues through weekends and is not just a result of facing work or school. Patients typically awake in the middle of the night (middle insomnia) or in the early morning (terminal insomnia), finding it hard or impossible to return to sleep. Patients who have slightly improved may say that their sleep and appetite are okay when both are still abnormal. Continue to probe by asking, "How does that compare to normal?" The psychological signs and symptoms of depression include a diminished ability to think or make decisions, negative thinking about the past (e.g., guilt), present (e.g., low self-esteem), and future (e.g., hopelessness), and thoughts about death and suicide.

As presented in Table 10-1, *DSM-IV* criteria for major depression requires dysphoria *or* anhedonia *and* several biological signs of depression, which must exist nearly every day for at least two weeks. Moreover, as Amy's case of major depression in Chapter 1 illustrated, the *DSM-IV* diagnosis of this disorder is based on symptoms and, after the loss of a loved one, clinical course, and not whether the disorder is produced by environmental stressors.

Everything about patients with psychomotor retardation is slow—walking,[1] talking, thinking, eating, reacting. If asked their spouse's name or their own occupation, it may take them 20 to 30 seconds to answer. For unknown reasons, this latency of response also occurs with psychomotor agitation. Concentration can be so impaired that they may be unable to sit through a sitcom or to read a simple paragraph. Their slowed thinking, impaired concentration, and negative worldview paralyze decision-making. Readily overwhelmed by easy tasks, depressed patients no longer try to do anything. In contrast, patients with psychomotor agitation may fidget, pace, wring their hands and exhibit frenzied preoccupation with somatic concerns. In milder forms, it is important to find out if the psychomotor behavior is a change from normal. Sometimes family members can more accurately determine this than the patient.

Depressed patients view the world through gray-tinted glasses. To them, everything is bleak—their life, their world, their future, and their treatment. "I beg you to shoot me," a depressed woman pleaded, "if they'll put a sick horse out of its misery, why not a person?" They ruminate over personal failures, real or imagined, often making mountains out of molehills. With a nearly delusional conviction, they may feel utterly hopeless,

---

[1]Frame-by-frame analysis of movies shows that, in walking, depressed patients lift their thighs with their lower legs lagging behind, whereas most people propel their lower legs and feet forward.

TABLE 10–1
DSM-IV **Criteria for Major Depressive Episode and Disorder***

Major Depressive Episode

A. Five (or more) of the following symptoms have been present during the same 2-week period and represent a change from previous functioning; at least one of the symptoms is either (1) depressed mood or (2) loss of interest or pleasure.

Note: Do not include symptoms that are clearly due to a general medical condition, or mood-incongruent delusions or hallucinations.

(1) depressed mood most of the day, nearly every day, as indicated by either subjective report (e.g., feels sad or empty) or observation made by others (e.g., appears tearful). **Note:** In children and adolescents, can be irritable mood.

(2) markedly diminished interest or pleasure in all, or almost all, activities most of the day, nearly every day (as indicated either by subjective account or observation made by others)

(3) significant weight loss or weight gain when not dieting (e.g., a change of more than 5% of body weight in a month), or decrease or increase in appetite nearly every day. **Note:** In children, consider failure to make expected weight gains.

(4) insomnia or hypersomnia nearly every day

(5) psychomotor agitation or retardation nearly every day (observable by others, not merely subjective feelings of restlessness or being slowed down)

(6) fatigue or loss of energy nearly every day

(7) feelings of worthlessness or excessive or inappropriate guilt (which may be delusional) nearly every day (not merely self-reproach or guilt about being sick)

(8) diminished ability to think or concentrate, or indecisiveness, nearly every day (either by subjective account or as observed by others)

(9) recurrent thoughts of death (not just fear of dying), recurrent suicidal ideation without a specific plan, or a suicide attempt or a specific plan for committing suicide

B. The symptoms do not meet criteria for a Mixed Episode.

C. The symptoms cause clinically significant distress or impairment in social, occupational, or other important areas of functioning.

D. The symptoms are not due to the direct physiological effects of a substance (e.g., a drug of abuse, a medication) or a general medical condition (e.g., hypothyroidism).

E. The symptoms are not better accounted for by Bereavement, i.e., after the loss of a loved one, the symptoms persist for longer than 2 months or are characterized by marked functional impairment, morbid preoccupation with worthlessness, suicidal ideation, psychotic symptoms, or psychomotor retardation.

(continued)

TABLE 10–1
(Continued)

Major Depressive Disorder—Single or Recurrent Episode

A. Presence of a single Major Depressive Episode.

B. The Major Depressive Episode is not better accounted for by Schizoaffective Disorder and is not superimposed on Schizophrenia, Schizophreniform Disorder, Delusional Disorder, or Psychotic Disorder Not Otherwise Specified.

C. There has never been a Manic Episode, a Mixed Episode, or a Hypomanic Episode. **Note:** This exclusion does not apply if all of the manic-like, mixed-like, or hypomanic-like episodes are substance or treatment induced or are due to the direct physiological effects of a general medical condition.

Specify (for current or most recent episode):
Severity/Psychotic/Remission Specifiers
Chronic
With Catatonic Features
With Melancholic Features
With Atypical Features
With Postpartum Onset

DSM-IV, pp. 327, 344–345.

helpless, worthless, or guilty. A severely depressed man insisted on shock treatment because, he asserted, "I deserve to be punished." (So much for "informed consent!") A self-made millionaire declared that he was a "financial flop" who had "forced my family into the poorhouse." Whereas the unhappiness of everyday life comes and goes, the dysphoria of major depression never leaves. With everyday unhappiness, one can go to a movie and temporarily enjoy it, but with major depression, patients cannot be distracted by a movie. The suicidal preoccupations of depressed patients often arise more from a wish to escape unrelenting dysphoria than to actually die. They frequently do a "Russian history revision" of their past: What was good, average, or at least bearable now becomes terrible and deserving of infinite guilt. In revising their life events, they can be so convincing that the interviewing clinician also feels depressed and becomes convinced that the patient's depression was inevitable.

Virtually diagnostic of major depression is that relatives or others have devoted hours to reassuring the patient, but to no avail; no matter how effective or frequent their pleas, nothing they say "sticks" for more than a minute or two. Depressed patients view all decisions as a choice between something awful and something terrible. Loved ones soon become impatient or even furious at the patient: They realize she's ill, but feel but that she has spurned their advice and does nothing to help herself. Depression is also "contagious": The patient's futility may become the family's futility. People avoid depressed people—they are depressing! Although the withdrawal of others may aggravate the depression, at other times it doesn't really matter, since patients are too self-absorbed to care. For these patients, it feels like No Exit: They can't escape depression; they can't talk about it and they can't *not* talk about it.

Bipolar disorder. Ten to 15% of major depressives eventually exhibit mania or its attenuated version, hypomania. By definition, a bipolar patient is anybody who displays mania, with or without a period of depression. Most patients, however, have both manic and depressive episodes in various sequences and frequencies.

An elevated, euphoric, expansive, or irritable mood is the cardinal feature of mania. These patients are hyperactive, highly distractible, and grandiose. They have flight of ideas, pressured speech, tangentiality, and a diminished need for sleep. They're prickly and quick to anger. As their disorganization worsens, they may develop persecutory and grandiose ideas of reference that often become delusions. Persecutory delusions among schizophrenics frequently are not aimed at anyone or anything specific, whereas manics believe that harm is coming from specific individuals or organizations. Sherlock Holmes' obsession that Professor Moriarty was interfering with his attempt to rid the world of evil was a typical manic persecutory delusion. About a quarter of manics develop hallucinations that are usually auditory or visual and of shorter duration than those in schizophrenia. Disorganization may occur, but more briefly than with schizophrenia. Table 10–2 lists *DSM-IV* criteria for a manic episode.

Manics talk a blue streak, do "20 things at once," and launch outrageous projects. A manic patient spent $100,000 hiring city planners, attorneys, architects, and a guru to construct a 90-story building on one square foot of land. Another manic, a UCLA undergraduate, telephoned Yeltsin to invite him to the Rose Bowl, and although Boris didn't get the message, the student did reach a high Kremlin official (who declined). Manics often resemble fast-talking comics of the Robin Williams genre. People laugh with, not at, manics. They have pressured speech and it's hard to get a word in edgewise. Manics can be supersalespeople. Caught unaware, I (J.M.) was visited by a manic salesman, who almost sold me a set of encyclopedias for my children—but I have no children! On the spur of the moment, a Dartmouth graduate who resided in California jumped on a plane and admitted himself to "the hospital of my alma mater." He arrived with four tennis rackets, three suitcases, a fishing rod, dozens of lollipops, and a

TABLE 10–2
DSM-IV* Criteria for Manic and Mixed Hypomanic Episode

Manic Episode

A. A distinct period of abnormally and persistently elevated, expansive, or irritable mood, lasting at least 1 week (or any duration if hospitalization is necessary)

B. During the period of mood disturbance, three (or more) of the following symptoms have persisted (four if the mood is only irritable) and have been present to a significant degree:

    (1) inflated self-esteem or grandiosity
    (2) decreased need for sleep (e.g., feels rested after only 3 hours of sleep)
    (3) more talkative than usual or pressure to keep talking
    (4) flight of ideas or subjective experience that thoughts are racing
    (5) distractibility (i.e., attention too easily drawn to unimportant or irrelevant external stimuli)
    (6) increase in goal-directed activity (either socially, at work or school, or sexually) or psychomotor agitation
    (7) excessive involvement in pleasurable activities that have a high potential for painful consequences (e.g., engaging in unrestrained buying sprees, sexual indiscretions, or foolish business investments)

C. The symptoms do not meet criteria for a Mixed Episode.

D. The mood disturbance is sufficiently severe to cause marked impairment in occupational functioning or in usual social activities or relationships with others, or to necessitate hospitalization to prevent harm to self or others, or there are psychotic features.

E. The symptoms are not due to the direct physiological effects of a substance (e.g., a drug of abuse, a medication, or other treatment) or a general medical condition (e.g., hyperthyroidism).

Note: Manic-like episodes that are clearly caused by somatic antidepressant treatment (e.g., medication, electroconvulsive therapy, light therapy) should not count toward a diagnosis of Bipolar I Disorder.

Hypomanic Episode

A. A distinct period of persistently elevated, expansive, or irritable mood, lasting throughout at least 4 days, that is clearly different from the usual nondepressed mood.

B. During the period of mood disturbance, three (or more) of the following symptoms have persisted (four if the mood is only irritable) and have been present to a significant degree:

    (1) inflated self-esteem or grandiosity
    (2) decreased need for sleep (e.g., feels rested after only 3 hours of sleep)

(continued)

TABLE 10–2
(Continued)

---

(3) more talkative than usual or pressure to keep talking

(4) flight of ideas or subjective experience that thoughts are racing

(5) distractibility (i.e., attention too easily drawn to unimportant or irrelevant external stimuli)

(6) increase in goal-directed activity (either socially, at work or school, or sexually) or psychomotor agitation

(7) excessive involvement in pleasurable activities that have a high potential for painful consequences (e.g., the person engages in unrestrained buying sprees, sexual indiscretions, or foolish business investments)

C. The episode is associated with an unequivocal change in functioning that is uncharacteristic of the person when not symptomatic.

D. The disturbance in mood and the change in functioning are observable by others.

E. The episode is not severe enough to cause marked impairment in social or occupational functioning, or to necessitate hospitalization, and there are no psychotic features.

F. The symptoms are not due to the direct physiological effects of a substance (e.g., a drug of abuse, a medication, or other treatment) or a general medical condition (e.g., hyperthyroidism).

Note: Hypomanic-like episodes that are clearly caused by somatic antidepressant treatment (e. g., medication, electroconvulsive therapy, light therapy) should not count toward a diagnosis of Bipolar II Disorder.

DSM–IV, pp. 332, 338.

swimsuit; it was winter. Five minutes after his grand entrance, he coaxed all the patients and staff into singing, "The Yellow Rose of Texas." Further demonstrating tangential thinking, he declared that everybody should wear a yellow ribbon and surrender peacefully.

But, eventually, things get out of control in mania. When crossed, or when people don't go along with them, manics become irritable, nasty, and sometimes cruel. They may play the "manic game," in which they are constantly testing everybody's limits; they manipulate others' self-esteem, perceive and exploit people's vulnerabilities, and project responsibility. After wreaking havoc and infuriating everybody, they will blame everyone but themselves. For instance, the Dartmouth grad told a plump, insecure teenage inpatient, "You're a fat pig. No wonder boys don't like you." The girl dissolved in tears, and the other patients, urged on by the manic, rushed to the teenager's defense and blamed *the staff* for allowing her to get so upset. On the slightest whim, manics will call total strangers and amass enormous phone bills. Manics may have no inhibitions. A well-respected "Southern gentleman" was brought into the hospital by neighbors when he was found dancing naked on a pizza in his back yard. He told the staff, "I wanted to raise my spiritual awareness and that was the best way to do it." One staff member dubbed him "Dances with Pizzas."

Manic patients develop reputations as normally being a Dr. Jekyll — upstanding, likeable, and productive — yet sometimes becoming a Mr. Hyde — outrageously excitable, intrusive, and demanding. *Unpredictable* is what some people call them: fine one month, profoundly depressed the next month. Because periods of high energy, creativity, and achievement are not recognized as hypomania, bipolar disorder may go undiagnosed. (Clinicians find that an excellent barometer of these hypomanic periods is the patient's diminished need for sleep.) The adaptiveness of moderate hypomanic behavior allows many bipolar patients to stand with society's most accomplished individuals.

Bipolar disorder is more severe than major depression. Patients with bipolar depressions stay depressed longer, relapse more frequently, display more depressive symptoms, show more severe symptoms, have more delusions and hallucinations, commit more suicides, require more hospitalizations, and experience more incapacitation (Coryell, Endicott, Andreasen, & Keller, 1985). Yet when a patient first presents with a severe depression, it's usually hard to tell if it is bipolar or major (unipolar) depression. However, because prognoses and treatments differ substantially, it's desirable to distinguish these two depressions as soon as possible: When compared to the signs and symptoms of unipolar depression, those of bipolar depression more often include extremely low energy, psychomotor retardation and the reverse vegetative symptoms: hypersomnia, hyperphagia, and mood worsening in the evening. In general, bipolar depressives prefer to remain in bed and have what are termed "laying-down depressions." Bipolar patients are more likely than unipolar patients to have psychotic depressions and many have little insight into past manic episodes. They minimize or deny having poor judgment and acting grossly different from normal. However, they can describe episodes lasting many days or weeks in which they did not need much sleep and still had a lot of energy. Close friends, roommates, or family members are often helpful allies in making the right diagnosis of bipolar disorder. Table 10-3 lists the characteristics that tend to distinguish unipolar from bipolar depressions.

Dysthymic disorder. Formerly called "depressive neurosis," dysthymic disorder presents with a chronic dysphoria or anhedonia that is not severe

TABLE 10-3
Characteristics That Tend to Distinguish Unipolar from Bipolar Depressions

UNIPOLAR DEPRESSION	BIPOLAR DEPRESSION
PRESENTING SYMPTOMS	
Psychomotor agitation or retardation	Psychomotor retardation
Anxiety	Lethargy
Insomnia	Hypersomnia
Anorexia	Hyperphagia
Underweight	Overweight
Feel worse in morning and better as the day goes on	Feel worse in evening and better in morning
("diurnal mood variation")	("reverse diurnal mood variation")
Psychosis less likely	Psychosis more likely
LONGITUDINAL FEATURES	
Less family history of mood disorders	More family history of depression and mania
Premorbidly obsessional, shy, moralistic, insecure	Premorbidly outgoing, active, uninhibited, successful
No prior mania or hypomania	Prior mania or hypomania
No prior hospitalizations	Prior hospitalizations

enough to meet all the criteria for major depression. *DSM-IV* requires that symptoms exist for at least two years. This dysphoria or anhedonia may be continual or episodic; euthymia may exist for several days to weeks, but no longer than several weeks. The diagnosis should not be made if an interval of normal mood lasts for more than a few months. Whereas many patients with major depression are unable to work or to socialize, those with dysthymic disorders function, though not at their peak. By definition, dysthymic disorders never present with delusions or hallucinations. When a major depression is superimposed on a dysthymic disorder, it's dubbed a "double depression." Table 10–4 lists *DSM-IV* criteria for dysthymic disorder.

In contrast to major depression, dysthymic disorder is more relenting and less consuming: Patients may laugh and tell a joke; on occasion, they even enjoy themselves. Although loved ones find dysthymic disorders less infuriating and frustrating than major depressions, others become bored with the dysthymic patient's habitual moaning and complaining. Dysthymic patients often become upset over matters that others take in stride. A woman whose brother had dysthymic disorder described him as having a "garlic depression—he makes everyone around him feel a little worse."

TABLE 10–4
DSM-IV* Criteria for Dysthymic Disorder

A. Depressed mood for most of the day, for more days than not, as indicated either by subjective account or observation by others, for at least 2 years. **Note:** In children and adolescents, mood can be irritable and duration must be at least 1 year.

B. Presence, while depressed, of two (or more) of the following:

   (1) poor appetite or overeating
   (2) insomnia or hypersomnia
   (3) low energy or fatigue
   (4) low self-esteem
   (5) poor concentration or difficulty making decisions
   (6) feelings of hopelessness

C. During the 2-year period (1 year for children or adolescents) of the disturbance, the person has never been without the symptoms in Criteria A and B for more than two 2 months at a time.

D. No Major Depressive Episode has been present during the first 2 years of the disturbance (1 year for children and adolescents); i.e., the disturbance is not better accounted for by chronic Major Depressive Disorder, or Major Depressive Disorder, In Partial Remission.

   Note: There may have been a previous Major Depressive Episode provided there was a full remission (no significant signs or symptoms for 2 months) before development of the Dysthymic Disorder. In addition, after the initial 2 years (1 year in children or adolescents) of Dysthymic Disorder, there may be superimposed episodes of Major Depressive Disorder, in which case both diagnoses may be given when the criteria are met for Major Depressive Episode.

E. There has never been a Manic Episode, a Mixed Episode, or a Hypomanic Episode, and criteria have never been met for Cyclothymic Disorder.

F. The disturbance does not occur exclusively during the course of a chronic Psychotic Disorder, such as Schizophrenia or Delusional Disorder.

G. The symptoms are not due to the direct physiological effects of a substance (e.g., a drug of abuse, a medication) or a general medical condition (e.g., hypothyroidism).

H. The symptoms cause clinically significant distress or impairment in social, occupational, or other important areas of functioning.

Specify if:
Early Onset: if onset is before age 21
Late Onset: if onset is age 21 or older

Specify (for most recent 2 years of Dysthymic Disorder):
With Atypical Features

*DSM-IV, p. 349.

Patients with dysthymic disorder have been shown to have slightly more impairment than those with major depression alone. Only about 50% fully recover from dysthymic disorder alone and, if major depression occurs with dysthymia, only 32% recover (Klein, Taylor, Harding, & Dickstein, 1988).

Carol Campanella, a 40-year-old married woman from a traditional Italian family, sought treatment because, "I'm anxious and shaky most of the time, especially at work. I can't be that way at home, ever since my mother-in-law moved in for good and I have to be on my best behavior when I'm around her." The patient said she'd been unhappy most of her life, but had felt much worse since her mother-in-law camped in five months ago. "She comes from the old country. She expects me to wait on her, but nothing I do ever satisfies her. She complains; otherwise she does nothing. I return exhausted from work and immediately prepare dinner; so what does she say? 'You made the carrots wrong; you should cut them at angles, not up-and-down.' When I ask my husband to do something about *his* mother, all he says is, "You're overreacting." I feel unappreciated and drained. I cry all the time, but only in private: I don't want anybody to see I'm weak."

For the first time, somebody did. Tears and words gushed out, as Carol revealed her darkest fear: "I'm terrified I'm turning into my mother. Our family lived near Rome, which is where my mother was hospitalized for shock treatment, but she was depressed most of her life. She would sit in the corner for hours and say nothing. At other times, she'd act crazy and speak nonsense; she'd talk to the dead and accuse the milkman of stealing. My mother wasn't mean to me; it was more like she was mentally absent. That's when I learned you can't rely on anybody to solve your problems but yourself. . . . When I was 16, my mother began to improve. Suddenly, I had the mother I always wanted. I loved it. Two years later, though, she died of cancer. I still miss her, and I know I can't expect my mother-in-law to replace her, yet sometimes I do, and *that's* nuts. Far worse is that I'm acting like my mother—snapping at people, never laughing, overly serious, avoiding people, not talking, and always hopeless. I'm frightened I'll be crazy like her."

Carol's marriage ("my ticket to America") was sexless and passionless ("all he does is eat"). Because of financial limitations, she quit premed and became a secretary. Over the years, she's been promoted to administrator, but far slower than "other women with less skill." She claimed to have "always" had initial insomnia and poor appetite. During the past year she has shed 25 pounds, felt increasingly sluggish and restless during the day, preferred being alone, and seemed immune to praise. Carol had no history of hypomania or mania, nor did she ever contemplate suicide.

Her dysthymic disorder was treated with an antidepressant, and after two weeks, her sleep and appetite normalized and her dysthymia lifted. She could laugh and enjoy people. Although she still felt just as unappreciated at home and at work, she stopped fretting about it. After a month of treatment, her symptoms abated completely, but Carol refused to have any of her family meet with the therapist, saying simply, "I will handle things myself." (Note: Another example of how Axis-I problems resolve much easier than Axis II problems.) Two months after her first visit, she observed, "I must have been depressed my entire life. Until now, I didn't know what it was like *not* to be depressed. . . . I feel like a new person, and yet I still worry that someday I'll go crazy like my mother." It was only after eight months of psychotherapy that this fear disappeared.

Cyclothymic disorder. Cyclothymic patients have hypomanic *and* dysphoric periods that are not severe enough to qualify as a bipolar disorder. Moreover, whereas bipolar disorder is episodic, cyclothymic disorder is continual; it, like dysthymic disorder, must exist for at least two years without the patient being euthymic for more than three months. *DSM-IV* criteria for cyclothymic disorder are listed in Table 10-5.

Clinical Course

Major depression. The age of onset is equally distributed throughout the adult life cycle; age 40 is the mean, and it can arise during childhood and infancy. Major depression usually appears over days or weeks, but it may

---

TABLE 10–5
DSM-IV **Criteria for Cyclothymic Disorder***

A. For at least 2 years, the presence of numerous periods with hypomanic symptoms and numerous periods with depressive symptoms that do not meet criteria for a Major Depressive Episode. **Note:** In children and adolescents, the duration must be at least 1 year.

B. During the above 2-year period (1 year in children and adolescents), the person has not been without the symptoms in Criterion A for more than 2 months at a time.

C. No Major Depressive Episode, Manic Episode, or Mixed Episode has been present during the first 2 years of the disturbance.

   Note: After the initial 2 years (1 year in children and adolescents) of Cyclothymic Disorder, there may be superimposed Manic or Mixed Episodes (in which case both Bipolar I Disorder and Cyclothymic Disorder may be diagnosed) or Major Depressive Episodes (in which case both Bipolar II Disorder and Cyclothymic Disorder may be diagnosed).

D. The symptoms in Criterion A are not better accounted for by Schizoaffective Disorder and are not superimposed on Schizophrenia, Schizophreniform Disorder, Delusional Disorder, or Psychotic Disorder Not Otherwise Specified.

E. The symptoms are not due to the direct physiological effects of a substance (e.g., a drug of abuse, a medication) or a general medical condition (e.g., hyperthyroidism).

F. The symptoms cause clinically significant distress or impairment in social, occupational, or other important areas of functioning.

DSM-IV, pp. 365–66.

erupt in a day or evolve over months or years. Anxiety, phobia, panic, or dysthymia may predate a major depression. The sequence of events leading to a depression should be precisely determined, since it is a mistake to assume that, for example, a patient's termination from his job caused his depression, whereas it was actually his depression (and poor functioning) that caused the terminations. Some depressions arise out of the blue, some after a precipitant. If untreated, major depression usually persists three to nine months. Within a year, 85% of major depressions have remitted.

Single and recurrent episodes of major depression may be slightly different species. Roughly half of all patients with a major depression never have another episode (Maj, Veltro, Pirozzi, Lobrace, & Magliano, 1992). Of those having a second episode, 50% have a third one, and so on. Patients with recurrent major depressions continue to have a 15% risk of their next episode being manic, no matter how many depressive episodes they have had. They also have more difficulties between depressive episodes. Recurrence rates are greatest during the first four to six months after recovery; thereafter, the further away from the episode, the lower the chance of a recurrence. For patients with major (or bipolar) depression, the risk of future episodes increases if they have a history of dysthymic disorder, a persistent dysthymia after a major or bipolar depression, a substance abuse or anxiety disorder, an older age of onset, or a greater number of previous episodes.

Roughly 15–20% of patients with major depression become chronically depressed; 80% recover fully. Thus, for the vast majority, major depression is an episodic condition; outside of distinct periods of illness, these patients are their normal productive selves. Of those having a recurrence, 22% are depressed for over a year, especially if they delay getting treatment, are elderly, poor, or had a longer prior depressive episode (Keller, Lavori, Rice, Coryell, & Hirschfeld, 1986).

Bipolar disorder. On average, bipolar disorder arises by age 30, although on rare occasions it may begin in octogenarians. First onset mania in the elderly is almost always associated with medical conditions, particularly neurologic disease or medications. Mania more often precedes depression. Whereas most bipolar depressions emerge over days or weeks, mania can erupt suddenly. The most common prodromal symptoms of mania are increased activity, elevated mood, and a decreased need for sleep. On the average, these develop about three weeks prior to the manic episode (Molnar, Feeney, & Fava, 1988). If biologically untreated, bipolar depressions typically persist six to nine months, manic episodes, two to six weeks.

The sequence and frequency of manic and depressive episodes vary: Some patients have three or four depressive periods before exhibiting mania; others alternate between highs and lows. Some have an episode every ten years, whereas others, known as "rapid cyclers," have four or more episodes of either mania or depression in a single year. The episodes of bipolar disorder tend to become more frequent and longer over time.

The term *bipolar* is misleading because it implies that mania and depression are opposites and that euthymia occurs between them. Yet careful observation reveals that mania and depression are closer to each other than to normality. For instance, it's common to see a depressive affect intrude on mania; a patient will be talking a mile-a-minute, when for no apparent reason he cries a eulogy to a long-departed mother, and then just as suddenly, starts imitating Tina Turner. It is also common to see mania and depression alternate, with no intervening period of normalcy. There is also a strange species of mania called "dysphoric mania" or mixed manic-depression, in which people have manic and depressive symptoms at the same time (Post et al., 1989).

Dysthymic disorder. This disorder typically emerges during early adult life, although it commonly occurs in children and adolescents. Its onset is gradual and often hard to pinpoint. Its course is chronic, its symptoms fluctuating.

Cyclothymic disorder. The age of onset for cyclothymic disorder is most often in early adulthood. It begins gradually and persists chronically. Intermixing or alternating hypomanic and dysphoric symptoms may fluctuate within hours, days, weeks, or months. Intermittent euthymic periods may exist for up to two months.

Complications

Suicide is committed eventually by 15% of patients with severe—that is, major or bipolar—depression. (It rarely occurs with dysthymic and cyclothymic disorders.) Men commit suicide at least twice as often as women, while women make suicide attempts more often than men. Some of these differences can be explained by the fact that men are more likely to choose violent, highly lethal methods (e.g., shooting, hanging, crashing), whereas women more often overdose. Major and bipolar depressions account for 50–70% of suicides, making depression the chief cause of suicide. (Alcoholism is second.) Although the evaluation of suicide is discussed in Chapter 2, it's worth repeating that, contrary to myth, those who talk about suicide *are* more likely to commit suicide.

Substance abuse, particularly from alcoholism, is a frequent complication in all mood disorders. Patients will "medicate" their dysphorias with alcohol, cocaine, amphetamines, and less often with marijuana and hypnoanxiolytics. Convinced they're immune from danger and oblivious to their own limitations, hypomanic and manic patients take drugs to remain "up." *Death* from physical illness is four times more prevalent among patients with major depression. In adults, this prevalency is not accounted for by the increased suicide rate, but rather by a large increase in the usual "natural" deaths from illnesses such as cancer and cardiovascular disease (Murphy, Monson, Olivier, Sobol, & Leighton, 1987). The reasons for this increase are unknown, but it is known that impairments in the immune system and disturbances in heart rhythms are more likely to occur during depressive episodes.

Impaired judgment and *lousy decisions* are common. If a depressed patient thinks she's a terrible person or, because of anhedonia, feels "no love," she may try to divorce a loving spouse; if he's sure he's incompetent, he may quit a perfectly good job. Manics may also initiate divorce and quit work, thinking they are too good for their spouse or job. Clinicians should inform patients that their pathological moods are distorting their judgment and that they should postpone major decisions until they've recovered. *Occupational and academic failures* result from poor judgment, and more: Depressed patients function slowly, work inefficiently, and display little effort. Neuropsychiatric tests show that their abstract thinking abilities, attention spans, and short-term (but not long-term) memories are impaired. Depressed and manic patients often trap colleagues into covering for them.

Familial consequences, including an increased rate of marital difficulties, separation, and divorce, occur in major depression. Although the mechanisms are unclear, roughly 40% of children with a depressed parent develop major, longstanding impairments, especially mood, neurotic, and conduct disorders. Targum, Dibble, Davenport, and Gershon (1981) found that after hospitalized bipolar patients and their spouses learned of the increased risk of inheritance and the long-term burdens of the disorder, 5% of patients and about half of the spouses confessed that, if given a second chance, they would not get married or have children.

In summary, major depression has an enormous negative impact on a person's life. When compared with ten major medical disorders, including heart disease, diabetes, and back pain, depression and cardiac disease were tied for having the worst impact on social, occupational, familial, and physical function.

Subtypes

Types and subtypes of mood disorders are important to identify for several reasons: Some require different treatments; some often escape detection (and treatment) because they resemble other disorders; some suggest different etiologies; some of these have research implications. Some have already been mentioned: endogenous/reactive, primary/secondary, unipolar/bipolar, psychotic/neurotic. (Reader beware! The classifications presented above and below are commonly used but not fixed in stone.)

DSM-IV's most important subtypes of major depression are those with "psychotic," "melancholic," or "atypical features." *Major depressive episode with psychotic features* displays either delusions or hallucinations. The delusions and hallucinations may be either *mood-congruent* ("the devil is taking me to Hell") or *mood-incongruent* ("the FBI is trying to program my brain to become an informant"). Depressed patients rarely hallucinate without also having delusions. During the first six months, psychotic depressions are more severe than nonpsychotic depressions. The chief reason for distinguishing psychotic from nonpsychotic depressions is that they benefit from different treatments.

Major depressive episode with melancholic features are dominated by symptoms seen in endogenous depressions, but no attempt is made to include cause or lack of cause as a feature. These patients are both lucky and unlucky; they are *unlucky* because they feel awful, but *lucky* because they have a depression that has an especially good chance of responding to biological treatments (e.g., antidepressants and electroconvulsant therapy) better than to psychotherapy or placebo (Peselow, Sanfilipo, DiFiglia, & Fieve, 1992). Table 10–6 lists *DSM-IV* criteria for melancholic features.

Major depressive episode with atypical features is almost the opposite of melancholic depressions. Atypical episodes display reverse biological signs and an extreme reactivity to environmental events, which often manifest as "rejection sensitivity." The slightest rejection plunges these patients into dark despair, while the slightest good news induces ecstasy.

A typical (excuse me!) exhibition of rejection sensitivity occurred when Mary Rae's fiancé met her at the airport. He casually remarked to Mary Rae that a passerby was "attractive." Mary Rae became incensed, opened her suitcase, threw clothes all over the place, spent 30 minutes screaming at him, and then left the airport by herself. By evening she had calmed down, yet for weeks she pouted that, "The cluck doesn't realize I'm sensitive about my looks. Why couldn't he say something nice about *my* body?"

Patients with atypical features don't respond very well to tricyclic antidepressants or electroconvulsant therapy, but do better on monoamine oxidase inhibitors and selective serotonin re-uptake inhibitors.

Bipolar disorder is divided into "bipolar I," which meets the full diagnostic criteria for a major depressive and manic episode, and "bipolar II," in which there is a major depressive episode and hypomania, not mania; the

TABLE 10–6
DSM-IV Criteria for Mood Disorder with Melancholic or Atypical Features*

Specify if:

With Melancholic Features (can be applied to the current or most recent Major Depressive Episode in Major Depressive Disorder, and to a Major Depressive Episode in Bipolar I or Bipolar II Disorder only if it is the most recent type of mood episode)

A. Either of the following, occurring during the most severe period of the current episode:

   (1) loss of pleasure in all, or almost all, activities
   (2) lack of reactivity to usually pleasurable stimuli (does not feel much better, even temporarily, when something good happens)

B. Three (or more) of the following:

   (1) distinct quality of depressed mood (i.e., the depressed mood is experienced as distinctly different from the kind of feeling experienced after the death of a loved one)
   (2) depression regularly worse in the morning
   (3) early morning awakening (at least 2 hours before usual time of awakening)
   (4) marked psychomotor retardation or agitation
   (5) significant anorexia or weight loss
   (6) excessive or inappropriate guilt

Specify if:

With Atypical Features (can be applied when these features predominate during the most recent weeks of a Major Depressive Episode in Major Depressive Disorder or in Bipolar I or Bipolar II Disorder when the Major Depressive Episode is the most recent type of mood episode, or when these features predominate during the most recent 2 years of Dysthymic Disorder)

A. Mood reactivity (i.e., mood brightens in response to actual or potential positive events)

B. Two (or more) of the following features:

   (1) significant weight gain or increase in appetite
   (2) hypersomnia
   (3) leaden paralysis (i.e., heavy, leaden feelings in arms or legs)
   (4) long-standing pattern of interpersonal rejection sensitivity (not limited to episodes of mood disturbance) that result in significant social or occupational impairment

C. Criteria are not met for With Melancholic Features or With Catatonic Features during the same episode.

*DSM-IV, pp. 384–86.

patient's "highs" do not merit hospitalization. Although bipolar II disorder is generally considered to be a milder version of bipolar I, it may be an intermediate entity between bipolar I and major depression, or a completely distinct entity (Coryell et al., 1985; Dunner, 1973).

In *rapid cycling bipolar disorder*, patients have four or more episodes per year of mania, hypomania, or major depression. Each episode is followed by either remission or a switch into an episode of opposite polarity (Bauer & Whybrow, 1993). This represents a particularly severe form of bipolar disorder in which lithium is less effective than anticonvulsants such as carbamazepine and valproate.

Mood disorder with seasonal pattern, formerly called seasonal affective disorders (SAD) (or "the winter blues," as patients call it), refers to those depressions that invariably occur in the fall and winter; they improve within days of moving from cold to warm climates or from areas with short to long exposures to daylight. When depressed, these patients tend to eat more and sleep longer or later in the morning. SAD seems to be alleviated by artificial, bright (2500 LUX) light, particularly if given in the early morning. If these patients develop hypomania or mania, it's usually in the summer. Clinicians should inquire about seasonal patterns of mood with every patient who presents with any type of mood disorder (Wehr & Rosenthal, 1989).

Epidemiology

Among outpatients, mood disorders are the most common mental disorders psychiatrists treat, comprising 27.6% of their practice in 1980. Whether this pattern occurs with nonmedical psychotherapists is unknown. A large study at Cornell showed that about a quarter of all hospitalized *and* ambulatory patients had mood disorders, a sliver less than the percentage for schizophrenia. Among Cornell patients, 12.8%, 2.7%, and 7.1% had major depressive, dysthymic, and bipolar disorders, respectively.

In the general population, mood disorders rank third (behind anxiety and substance-related disorders), not first. The one-year prevalence rate for mood disorders using *DMS-III-R* is 11.3%, with the rate for major depression at 10.3%, for dysthymic disorder at 2.5%, and for bipolar disorder at 1.3% (Kessler et al., 1994).

In general, mood disorders strike twice as many women as men; however, this ratio varies depending on the disorder. Ninety percent of "atypical depressions" occur in women. Major depression and dysthymic disorder afflict two to three times more women than men. Bipolar disorder is nonsexist, with an equal male-female distribution. During a lifetime, roughly 20% of women and 10% of men will suffer a major depressive episode; about a third of these patients will be hospitalized. Urbanites have twice the rate of depression as rural folks. Patients with recurrent depression have high rates of avoidant (30%), obsessive-compulsive (19%), and dependant (16%) personality disorders (Pilkonis & Frank, 1988). Contrary to popular belief, the elderly do not have an increased risk for major depression. One of the highest risk groups for depression is young women who have children and minimal support in child rearing (Ensel, 1982). Another high-risk group is those who are widowed when young or middle-aged (Zisook & Schuchter, 1991).

It appears that each successive generation since World War II has had an increased rate of depression and an earlier age of onset (Klerman et al., 1985). Simultaneously, the rate of suicide, especially among youth, has also escalated with each generation. For instance, since the 1950s, the suicide rate for 15- to 24-year-olds has tripled, replacing homicide as the second leading cause of death among youth. These increased rates of depression and suicide are distressingly genuine; they are not methodological artifacts. Why depression and suicide have increased is unknown. Nevertheless, despite suicide still being most prevalent among the elderly, more than ever, today's clinician must be alert to teenage suicide.

The prevalence of mood disorders varies widely from culture to culture, being as low as 1% among the Amish. Depression is virtually unheard-of in Kenya and Rwanda, but frequent in Ghana and Nigeria where depressed patients complain that "worms are crawling all over the head." (Suicide is rare in Africa.)

Etiology and Pathogenesis

Some mood disorders arise for no apparent reason; others are triggered by a precipitant. Unless the precipitant is blatantly obvious, clinicians should be cautious about attributing a depression to it. If clinicians look hard enough, they can always find a stressor to "explain" a depression. (Review your past month and you will surely discover some stressor to "account" for why you should be depressed.) Stress is the way of the world; therefore, the path toward depression must involve more than stress.

With or without environmental stressors, major depressions present with similar symptoms.[2] The reason they present the same is because no matter how a depression begins, at some point a *final common pathway* of biological dysfunction is reached. In this way depression may be more like fever, for which there are many causes but a final common pathway and presentation. This commonality may explain why particular biological abnormalities are only seen in subgroups of mood disorders and usually in less than

---

[2]Hirschfeld, Kerman, Andreasen, Clayton, & Keller (1985) compared "situational" (i.e., triggered by an environmental event) with "nonsituational major depressions." Although situational depressives were younger, had fewer depressive episodes, and fewer hospitalizations, both groups had the same overall clinical pictures, types and amounts of stress, premorbid social supports, and family psychopathology.

60% of depressives. The final common pathway may arise from many biological or psychosocial causes: a genetic vulnerability, a "depressogenic" medication, an early loss, a lack of positive reinforcement, and so on.

Biomedical Factors

Genetics. Based on twin and adoption studies, genetics contributes 50–60% of the variance in the pathogenesis of bipolar disorder and 35–50% in unipolar mood disorder. Severe endogenous depression carries a higher genetic loading than milder forms. Females with mild depression have an increased number of female relatives with this kind of depression and male relatives with alcoholism and antisocial personality. Winokur calls this group "depressive spectrum disease," reserving the term "pure depressive illness" for depressives that breed true in males and females (Winokur & Coryell, 1992). Genetic linkage studies have identified different sites of transmission in different families. There is no one depression gene. Because genetic penetrance is incomplete, not all carriers of "depression" genes may get depressed.

Biochemistry. Many studies suggest that during depression, there is decreased serotonergic function and/or dysregulated noradrenergic function in the brain. The dysregulation involves a high basal (tonic) rate of firing but, when stimulated, a low response rate. The result in the noradrenergic system is like a TV with poor reception. There is a lot of "snow" in the picture (high basal rate of firing) and images come in weakly and poorly (low response). Most antidepressants normalize both the decreased serotonergic and dysregulated nonadrenergic function (Charney, Menkes, & Heninger, 1981). It is thought that these abnormalities occur only during the depressive episode. Increased cholinergic sensitivity is found during and after many depressions (Dilsaver, 1986). Many of the relatives of depressed patients have this increased cholinergic sensitivity, including those who have never had depression. This cholinergic sensitivity may create a vulnerability to depression and be a trait abnormality in many depressives.

Abnormalities in endocrine challenge tests (such as the dexamethasone suppression test and the TRH-TSH stimulation test) in patients with major depression occur 40–60% of the time. With a variety of endocrine challenges, a lack of the normal response occurs. If suppression normally occurs, nonsuppression or "escape" is seen, and if stimulation usually occurs, blunting of the stimulation manifests in depression. These probably are state abnormalities that normalize with recovery.

Psychosocial Factors

The *loss of either the mother or father* during the first five years of life, or the loss of the father between the ages of 10 and 14, is associated with increased risk of adult depression. Losses during these time periods are also later associated with increased doctor visits (help-seeking behavior), whether or not the patient is depressed. In adulthood, although many different kinds of stressful events can contribute to depression, losses are most directly associated with increased risk for depression.

Little or no support system leads to a much higher risk for depression. Social support has been shown to mitigate the effects of negative stressors such as losses.

Sexual, physical, and/or emotional abuse leads to a much higher adult rate of major depression as well as to a variety of other psychiatric disorders. Children in environments in which their self-esteem is constantly threatened, or in which a very negative view of life is communicated, are more likely to become depressed as adults.

A biopsychosocial continuum of response vulnerabilities is always present. One person might carry a very high genetic biological risk for depression and need little environmental stress to precipitate the disorder, while another person may have a high psychological risk for depression and need little genetic predisposition. Most individuals are likely to fall between these two poles on the continuum.

Psychosocial Theories

Despite the variety of psychosocial theories of depression, their differences often rest more in language than content. Most of these theories involve the factors of *loss* and *self-esteem*. Many types of losses can trigger depression. Besides the obvious—deaths, separations—depression may occur after the removal of a bodily organ or on the anniversary of a personally-significant loss. A manifestly good development may bring on a depression: For example, after winning a Pulitzer Prize, a once-obscure writer is suddenly inundated with admirers—groupies, money-management types, the cocktail set, publishers—all wanting a "piece" of him. Unable to meet everyone's expectations, dissatisfied with his own inability to write another masterpiece, and missing his old friends, he becomes depressed. Loss can also trigger mania.

Psychoanalytic theories. Freud proposed that an *early severe loss* or trauma during childhood causes a vulnerability to depression. Although subsequent research has tended to support this hypothesis, the research has also raised doubts about how much and how frequently early loss contributes *specifically* to depression. Brown (1961) showed that the loss of a parent during childhood occurred in 51% of adult depressives and in 16% of controls. In contrast, Roy (1985) demonstrated that early parental separation and loss accounted for relatively few additional cases, that ages five to eleven were most crucial, and curiously, that loss of a father was slightly more psychonoxious than losing a mother.

In *Mourning and Melancholia* (1917), Freud observed that the normal mourner accepts both positive and negative feelings about the deceased, whereas the melancholic cannot tolerate or consciously acknowledge any negative feelings toward the deceased; this *"ambivalence toward the lost object"* induces guilt and depression. Mourning is a reaction to a realistic loss, but melancholia may be a reaction to an imagined, or an unconsciously exaggerated, loss.

A controversial yet widely-touted hypothesis is that depression results from "retroflexed anger"—that is, patients turn their rage against a lost object onto themselves. Today, hundreds of therapists hear a similar story: A patient's fiancé suddenly breaks their engagement, but rather than getting angry at the fiancé, the patient becomes depressed and says things like, "This proves I'm unworthy." The concept of retroflexed anger neatly dovetails with the inverse relationship between suicide and homicide; it may also account for the low self-esteem of the depressed, for why some believe they deserve punishment, and for why many are terrified of expressing and experiencing anger. The catch-22 is, the more depressed patients express their fury, the more depressed they become—it's "proof" they're terrible people—and the more likely they are to commit suicide. Retroflexed anger may be germane to some depressions as either a contributor or a consequence; it may be more prominent in people who normally blame themselves for everything.

Ego psychologists initially claimed that many depressed patients were "mourning" more for their *loss of self-esteem* than for the loss of the object itself. Whether the object is a job or a lover, when patients believe their self-esteem is an extension of that lost object, then depression becomes increasingly likely. Later, ego psychologists stressed that depression arose from a discrepancy between the patient's actual and idealized self-esteem.

Behavioral theories. Many behaviorists view depression as a product of *"learned helplessness"*—that is, patients experience themselves as continually trying and failing. Repeated loss of positive reinforcement and concomitant increase of negative reinforcement results in discouragement, giving up (which further reduces rewards), and depression (Abramson, Seligman, & Teasdale, 1978; Beck, Rush, Shaw, & Emery, 1979).

Cognitive theories. The cognitive theory of depression emphasizes the patient's conscious thoughts. Depressed patients display the "cognitive triad": a negative view of oneself, the world, and one's future. They think of themselves as inadequate, their world as unrewarding, their future as hopeless. Cognitive theory claims that these attitudes distort the patient's perceptions of reality and cause depression; however, other studies suggest that the cognitive triad is a consequence of depression.

SUBSTANCE-INDUCED MOOD DISORDER

Drugs That Induce Depression

Before it can be assumed that a drug causes depression, it should be demonstrated that the drug increases the rate for a major depression over the point prevalence in the general population: 3% for men and 5–6% for women. In most reports on drugs "causing" depression, there was no screening for depression when the drug was started.

Oral contraceptives. Women on oral contraceptives (containing 50 mcg. estrogen) in the 1970s appeared to have an increased rate (12%) of depression, with features such as hypersomnia, hyperphagia, and retardation. Half of the depressed women on oral contraceptives had an absolute pyridoxine (vitamin B_6) deficiency, secondary to estrogen's competitive effects with pyridoxine coenzyme systems. When they were treated with pyridoxine 50 mg BID, there was a 90% recovery rate. Women without a deficiency responded to pyridoxine about 30% of the time (placebo response rate). It is not known if the lower estrogen oral contraceptives of the 1990s cause the same problem.

Antihypertensives. Reserpine induces depression in about 15% of cases, probably through its ability to deplete biogenic amines. The beta-blocker propranolol increases the risk of depression two-fold (8–9% rate) or at least creates a depression-like syndrome (insomnia, low energy, apathy). Less lipophilic beta-blockers such as atenolol have a lower depression risk because they don't reach the brain. Methyldopa has also been reported to induce depressions. In some instances, calcium channel blockers and ACE inhibitors have been reported to cause mild improvement in depressive symptoms and may be preferred treatments in people at risk for mood disorders.

Steroids. High doses of corticosteroids (> 80 mg equivalent of prednisone) result in major psychiatric sequelae in about 20% of the cases; depression and mania are frequent among these.

Hypnoanxiolytics. While diazepam and chlordiazepoxide have often been touted to induce depression, there is little convincing evidence of this. Many depressed patients present with anxiety, which treatment with a benzodiazepine may relieve while unmasking the remaining depressive symptoms. In higher doses (> 30 mg equivalent of diazepam) benzodiazepines, barbiturates, and alcohol all probably exacerbate or cause depression. A 25% depression rate has been reported in patients who were started on alprazolam 4 mg a day for panic disorder without depression. Diazepam 30 mg is equivalent to alprazolam 3 mg, clonazepam 1.5 mg, lorazepam 4–6 mg, or beer 5–6 bottles.

Drugs That Cause Mania

Mania can be precipitated by stimulants such as *cocaine* and *dextroamphetamine*. Sometimes patients report frequent manic episodes that are really two-to-four-day cocaine binges. When people abruptly stop using stimulants, they may appear depressed: They sleep a lot, are apathetic, and have extreme psychomotor retardation, but may not actually *say* they are depressed. This phase of stimulant withdrawal usually passes in a few days. Antidepressants can induce mania; TCAs, about 2% of the time and SSRIs about 1%. This rate is much higher in known bipolar patients. A variety of other drugs (such as hallucinogens and corticosteroids) occasionally are associated with manic episodes.

Mood Disorder Due to a Medical Condition

Generally, medical illnesses (e.g., TB, hepatitis, mononucleosis, anemia, hypothyroidism) differ from depression in that fatigue tends to be associated with hypersomnia (rather than the insomnia of depression) and depressed mood increases as the day progresses, rather than peaking in the morning, as is typical in depression. In medical conditions such as cancer that produce several "vegetative symptoms," psychological symptoms such as dysphoric mood, hopelessness, guilt, worthlessness, and suicidal ideation are the best indicators of a major depression. For unknown reasons, pancreatic cancer has much higher depression rates (60%) than other cancers.

Certain medical illnesses have higher depression rates than others. These include:

Neurological conditions such as multiple sclerosis, Parkinson's disease, and strokes (particularly in the frontal left hemisphere). Mania is also more frequent in multiple sclerosis.

Endocrine diseases such as hypothyroidism and Cushings disease are associated with higher depression rates. Cushing's disease and hyperthyroidism have higher mania rates. Women with treatment-resistant depression have higher thyroiditis rates, but may have no other obvious thyroid abnormality.

Autoimmune disorders such as rheumatoid arthritis and systemic lupus all carry higher depression rates than non-autoimmune disorders that have the same degree of disability. For example, rheumatoid arthritis has a higher depression rate than osteoarthritis.

Differential Diagnosis

Uncomplicated bereavement may present with the biological signs and symptoms of depression. In normal grief reactions, self-esteem tends to be preserved and anhedonia fluctuates considerably. Severe motor retardation, diurnal variation of mood, suicidal ideation, and significant disturbance of functioning are more often characteristics of depression. During normal bereavement, mourners episodically fantasize about their own death, berate themselves for not visiting or saving the deceased, or feel guilty that the wrong person died (survivor guilt). But when bereavement evolves into major depression, patients can think of nothing but their loss, themselves, and their depression. Normal mourners acknowledge the deceased's unfavorable traits; depressives idealize the departed and repress their faults. Bereavement with symptoms of depression may be delayed, but it usually emerges within two or three months of the loved one's death. After three months, normal mourners have moments of grief, but gradually return to their usual activities and can sustain thoughts about matters unrelated to the death. In contrast, when bereavement is complicated by depression, the depression often persists for more than three months, may get more (instead of less) severe over time, presents with numerous biological signs, and prevents the patient from getting back into the "swing of things." In about 10% of patients, bereavement becomes major depression. Highest-risk patients are those with no or minimal support systems.

Secondary anorgasmia or *secondary impotence* can occur with depression or as a result of a medical problem such as diabetes. In depressives these two symptoms are a result of the decrease in libido. In men, nocturnal erections can be lost in diabetes; in depression, nocturnal erections usually occur, although in some cases of depression, these will be absent. In diabetes, normal libido is initially present despite the impotence. Women who have had normal sexual desire and been orgasmic may become anorgasmic with depression.

Somatization can be the result of depression or a disorder in its own right. Patients with a somatization disorder by definition have had it since at least age 30. In contrast, depressives often start somatizing only when they get depressed; while depressed, they will double their doctor visits with an average of five to six visits a year. Before the depression and after treatment, somatic complaints and doctor visits return to normal levels. These patients may acknowledge anhedonia but deny depressed mood or blame depression symptoms on their somatic complaint. For these reasons, they are often called "masked depressions."

Alcoholism or hypnoanxiolytic dependence can cause depression or be a result of attempts to self-medicate depression. The diagnosis of depression should not be made until a four-to-six-week trial of abstinence has been completed. Twenty percent of alcoholic women and 10% of men have a primary depression. Binge drinking accompanying episodic depression or depressive symptoms during abstinence are a clue to the depression diagnosis.

Pain occurs in approximately 65% of depressed patients, with headache, back pain or abdominal pain the most common (Ward et al., 1990). About 15–30% of patients presenting with chronic pain have a diagnosis of major depressive disorder. Antidepressants have been reported to be effective in chronic pain with or without depression, particularly if a "pain lifestyle" has not yet been established.

Juvenile delinquents have major depression about 25% of the time. These are the ones who are treatable and much less likely to have antisocial personalities. They manifest classic vegetative signs of depression and, while possibly denying depression, will acknowledge persistent boredom (anhedonia). The girls may be promiscuous, but driven by a need for warmth and affection and not by increased libido. The boys frequently abuse drugs to escape their situation rather than for strictly recreational purposes. Often, these were the good kids in grade school who "went bad." Depressed kids commit antisocial acts in an effort to be accepted by other kids, while antisocial kids behave in this way no matter what the consequences to others.

Anxiety is a presenting complaint for many patients, more than half of whom really have a major depression. All symptoms of depression are present, but patients attribute them to anxiety. Antidepressants are more effective than anxiolytics in treating this combination. Patients who have high anxiety with their depression take longer (a 26-week average) to recover fully than those with low anxiety (13-week average) (Clayton et al., 1991).

Since *schizophrenia* and mood disorders can display psychotic, catatonic, and dysphoric features, the most likely diagnosis is the one which presents first, occurs in first-degree relatives, shows the characteristic natural history, and meets *DSM-IV* criteria. If catatonia is present and the patient is mute, an amytal interview or brief treatment with benzodiazepines may help with the diagnosis by allowing the patient to talk. Psychosis in depression and mania is usually briefer and less bizarre than in schizophrenia. If criteria for schizophrenia are met and there is an additional major depressive or manic episode, than the patient has a schizoaffective disorder (see Chapter 9).

Management and Treatment

The management and treatment of mood disorders employ one or more of the following interventions: (a) suicide prevention, (b) biotherapies, (c) psychotherapies, and (d) family involvement. These interventions tend to be used in this sequence; for example, preventing suicide precedes psychotherapy. These interventions are interrelated; for example, suicide prevention often entails family involvement. Each of these interventions serves a different purpose; for example, biotherapies rectify symptoms by correcting biochemical abnormalities, psychotherapies address issues arising from and contributing to the disorder, and family involvement may be used to support patients or to remedy pathogenic family systems.

Regardless of the intervention, working with affectively disturbed patients is ultimately rewarding, since most patients recover, though in the short-run, treatment may frustrate the most experienced of therapists and evoke considerable countertransference. Depressed patients frequently present with marked dependency, which they themselves disdain, expect others to meet, yet when this occurs, they get furious. Relatives may respond with pity, which patients will overtly reject yet feel they deserve. This dynamic of dependency strivings, anger over deprivation, anticipated rejection, and "entitled pity" leads clinicians to feel guilty, helpless, angry, and drained — feelings therapists should keep in check. While clinicians often feel that nothing they do for these patients is ever enough, they should be careful not to run the patient's life. Therapists should avoid overpromising; they should dispense hope, not saccharine. Especially during the more impaired or serious periods of the disorder, therapists should be warm, "real," and accepting. To quote Sederer (1983):

> The therapist must be able to bear the patient's pain with him; extra time may be needed for this affect to emerge, especially in view of the depressed patient's psychomotor retardation. . . . The depressed patient feels unworthy of and unable to reciprocate excessive warmth and tends to withdraw and feel worse when this is offered. Excessive humor on the part of the therapist denies the patient his grief and is devaluing. (p. 22)

If therapists identify with depressed patients, they will begin to feel depressed and trapped by patients' nihilistic view of the world. Instead, empathy is needed, allowing appreciation and acceptance of patients' feelings, but in the larger context of a more objective viewpoint.

Suicide Evaluation and Prevention

Assessment and management of suicidal feelings/ideation. In a lifetime, 15% of patients with major depression will eventually die by suicide (Guze & Robins, 1970). Approximately 80% of people who kill themselves have seen their physicians in the previous six months, often for symptoms of major depressive disorder (e.g., insomnia, decreased energy, etc.) or exaggerations of ongoing medical complaints. Therefore, all depressed patients should be asked about suicidal ideation. This can be done by approximations. One recommended sequence of questions is:

1. Do you sometimes have a feeling that life isn't worth living, or do you think about death much?
2. Do you sometimes think that if you died tomorrow from an accident or illness, that it just wouldn't matter? (This is *passive* suicidal ideation.)
3. Have you had thoughts of killing yourself? (This is *active* suicidal ideation.)

If patients answer yes to passive but not to active suicidal ideation, for now they are probably low risk, unless they are engaging in high-risk behavior (e.g., auto racing). If patients answer yes to the last question, further risk assessment is in order. Many patients who acknowledge ideation are at minimal risk if they have strong reasons for not committing suicide. Ask patients, "What has kept you from acting on your suicidal ideas?" Patients who respond that they could not actually do it because of their religious beliefs or because of their families are usually low risks. Similarly, patients who experience suicidal ideation as ego alien and frightening are at lower risk. The higher demographic risks are male, over 40, alone, socially alienated, with chronic disease, obsessive-compulsive or perfectionist tendencies, and/or substance abusers. People who have already made a suicide attempt are at higher risks, but only 2–4% kill themselves in the five years after an attempt (Pierce, 1981).

How can actively suicidal patients be managed? Suicidal impulses, like alcoholic impulses, can be managed better one day or one week at a time. Many suicidal patients can agree to go for one or two weeks or a month without killing themselves, but cannot agree to *never* kill themselves. This "no suicide decision," which they make for themselves (and not as a promise to the clinician or anyone else), can help to buy time while treatment is started (Drye, Goulding, & Goulding, 1973). It should also include a "no-escape clause": "no matter what happens." This allows for crisis situations (such as a cocaine-using boyfriend leaving the relationship). Suicidal ideation should be reassessed at least weekly and at the end of the agreed-upon time period, and if patients are still suicidal, a new "no suicide decision" should be made. Patients who are unreliable because of substance abuse, personality disorders, or indicate that a week is too long to defer suicide, require expert evaluation and possible hospitalization.

The clinician's next priority is to prevent suicide, which in most cases entails breaking the patient's "inertia cycle." When they finally seek professional help, most suicidal patients have been mired in painful, unproductive ruminations that have intensified their helplessness. One way to avert suicide and to stop this inertia is to hospitalize the patient. This key decision may depend less on the patient's actual suicide potential and more on his or her network of support. It's crucial to immediately involve the patient's family or close friends, not only to determine how well they can care for the patient, but also to teach them how to be extensions of the treatment team — how to mobilize the patient, what warning signs to look for, what to do with medications, what to discuss (and not discuss) with the patient, and so on.

Interrupting the inertia cycle is the start to treatment, not its end, and a good place to start is to assign patients household chores. No matter how mundane this sounds, patients feel that "at last" something is happening, that they are a part of it, and that they are finally "giving" instead of just "getting." Outpatients should have follow-up appointments within days, not weeks. Until the first appointment, the therapist can have the patient telephone, if only for three minutes a day. Since a 10-day supply of tricyclic antidepressants ingested all at once can be lethal, only a few days worth of pills should be prescribed, or low lethality antidepressants such as SSRIs should be used.

Potentially suicidal patients might also be reminded that "suicide is a permanent solution to a temporary problem," and that depressed patients, after they are successfully treated, invariably stop feeling suicidal.

Biological Treatments

The biological treatment of mood disorders includes heterocyclic antidepressants (mainly tricyclic antidepressants, TCAs), atypical antidepressants (trazodone, bupropion, and venlafaxine), selective serotonin re-uptake inhibitors (SSRIs), monoamine-oxidase inhibitors (MAOIs), lithium, and electroconvulsive therapy (ECT). The names, doses, and side effects of these medications are outlined in Appendices G and H, while their applications are discussed below. Patients need to be told that none of these medications causes physical or psychological dependency.

Heterocyclic and atypical antidepressants and SSRIs. Considering patients with *all* types of major depression, 78% improve with ECT, 70% with heterocyclic antidepressants, atypical antidepressants, or SSRIs, and 23% with placebo. Of the seven well-controlled studies comparing ECT and TCAs, four showed no difference and three favored ECT. Nonetheless, because ECT is more inconvenient to administer and ominous to laymen, antidepressant medications are usually the first biological treatment for major depression.

TCAs. (In the following discussion, if information also pertains to SSRIs and atypical antidepressants, the term *antidepressants* will be used.) In general, patients who benefit from antidepressants have *biological signs* of depression, while those without biological signs do not. The predictors of response to TCA antidepressants include insomnia, anorexia, psychomotor retardation, anhedonia, insidious onset, and one puzzling nonbiological predictor: guilt (Jewish, Catholic, or Protestant guilt — it doesn't matter). It also doesn't matter whether or not the depression has been environmentally triggered, or whether it is "understandable." If a patient lost her job and then developed major depression with its accompanying biological symptoms, antidepressants still work. One or more atypical and reverse biological signs, including hypersomnia, hyperphagia, profound anergy, mood reactivity, rejection sensitivity, and nocturnal worsening of mood, appear to reduce effectiveness of TCAs to 50%, while SSRIs and MAOIs retain their 70% effectiveness.

In order for antidepressants to work, patients must be on the *proper dose* for the *proper duration*. For a typical TCA like imipramine, the proper adult dose is usually 150 to 300 mg/day (a third to half this amount for the elderly). Moreover, the patient's mood doesn't lift until she's been on a full dose for at least 10 to 14 days; some patients require four to six weeks. Patients (and relatives) should be told, "Don't give up because you don't feel better in a day or so. Valium acts right away, but antidepressants don't; they take two to six weeks." Most patients on antidepressants show some improvement before two weeks.

Tricyclic antidepressants such as amitriptyline, imipramine, doxepin, and desipramine are usually begun at 25–50 mg and increased until a 2.5–3.5 mg/kg dosage is reached. Typically, the dose can be increased by 25–50 mg every three to five days as tolerance to side effects develops. Which TCA to prescribe depends on whether one previously helped the patient or a close biological relative and on whether its particular side effects will least bother the patient. After two weeks of taking 150 mg/day of imipramine without improvement, gradually boost the dose toward 300 mg/day. If the patient still hasn't fully recovered in another four weeks, see if the patient's serum level of TCAs is within the therapeutic range. If below it, the drug will be ineffective and if above it, the patient may be enduring unnecessary side effects.

Sedation, orthostatic hypotension, and anticholinergic side effects are the most common side effects for heterocyclic antidepressants. Of the commonly used tricyclics, *amitriptyline and doxepin tend to be the highest* in all of these side effects and *desipramine and nortriptyline tend to be lowest. Sedation* usually decreases over days and weeks and at mild levels may be experienced positively because sleep is facilitated and anxiety lessened. Patients placed on TCAs should be warned that (a) TCAs potentiate alcohol, so that "one drink will feel like two drinks," (b) "at first, drive briefly in a safe place, since your reflexes might be just a tad off," (c) "be extra cautious around machinery, such as a sewing machine, and when crossing streets." *Orthostatic hypotension* is a sudden drop in blood pressure upon standing from a lying or sitting position. Younger patients often compensate by increasing their heart rate (tachycardia), so that orthostatic hypotension is not seen. Older patients don't compensate as well and are at a high risk for falls. If some dizziness is experienced, patients should be told to stand up very slowly and contact their doctor. If the orthostatic hypotension is mild, preventive measures to increase blood pressure to normal, such as increasing fluid (and perhaps salt) intake, exercising, and decreasing other medications that may reduce blood pressure, are recommended.

The *anticholinergic side effects* include dry mouth, constipation, blurred near vision, decreased memory, and urinary retention. When these side effects significantly interfere with function, the dose is lowered or the patient is switched to an antidepressant with lower side effects.

The selective serotonin re-uptake inhibitors (SSRIs, fluoxetine, sertraline, and paroxetine) usually don't have any of the tricyclic or heterocyclic side effects. Furthermore, more often than not, the starting dose is enough to treat a depression. The SSRIs may perform better than the tricyclics in patients with reverse vegetative symptoms and atypical depressions. Their side effects include nausea and diarrhea (about 20–25%), which often disappears in a week to ten days, agitation, anxiety or insomnia, which might not abate, and decreased sexual and orgasmic function (about 13%) in men and women. The side effects of SSRIs are usually infrequent and mild enough that only 15% of patients in SSRI drug studies drop out, compared to 30% of patients in heterocyclic antidepressant trials. Optimal serum levels have not been found for the SSRIs.

Patients should remain on antidepressants until they have been symptom-free for at least 16 to 20 weeks or until stressors in the their lives are down to manageable levels. Discontinuing medication at the time of a child-custody battle would be a bad idea. To encourage staying on medication, patients should be informed that there is a 50% chance of relapse if they stop sooner than six months. Mild symptoms are just as predictive of relapse as major symptoms, so that even when major symptoms have disappeared, the presence of minor symptoms indicates the disorder has not run its full course (Prien & Kupfer, 1986). Antidepressants should be prescribed for longer periods in patients with more frequent depressive episodes, longer depressive cycles, and an older age of onset. If depression is severe and frequent enough, prophylactic, long-term antidepressant therapy may be indicated. TCAs should always be discontinued slowly—no faster than 25 mg/day; they should never be stopped abruptly. If they are, in two to four days patients may have insomnia, nightmares, or nausea and a flu-like syndrome without a fever. Fluoxetine probably can be stopped all at once, because it stays in the blood for weeks. When sertraline and paroxetine are abruptly withdrawn, however, nausea and headache might be seen.

Despite their overall effectiveness, antidepressants do not completely eliminate symptoms in 25% of patients with major depressions. If patients have not begun to improve after four weeks, and if the diagnosis, dose, and serum level have all been rechecked, another medication should be added to, or replace, the antidepressant. These options include: (a) adding lithium or T3 (a thyroid compound) in about 50% of patients can reverse a previously unresponsive depression; (b) changing antidepressants to a heterocyclic, an SSRI, an atypical (e.g., bupropion), or an MAOI; and (c) ECT. Studies favor ECT or combining antipsychotics with antidepressants for *psychotic* depression (Khan et al., 1987). Supplemental low-dose benzodiazepines may initially alleviate anxiety and insomnia.

Monoamine-oxidase inhibitors. While MAOIs have the same efficacy as other antidepressants in treating typical depressions, they do not lose efficacy in depressions with one or more atypical symptoms (hypersomnia, hyperphagia, mood worse at night, severe energy, rejection sensitivity, mood reactivity, or in depression with panic attacks). But MAOIs are rarely chosen first, because if patients on MAOIs ingest tyramine-containing foods (e.g., herring, aged cheese, salami) or sympathomimetic drugs (e.g., cocaine, amphetamines, decongestants), they can develop a "hypertensive crisis"—soaring blood pressure, splitting headache, chest pain, fever, and vomiting. However gruesome this sounds, the actual dangers of hypertensive crises can be substantially reduced. Most patients never develop them, and most who slip up on their diet have relatively minor symptoms.

MAOIs, however, should not be prescribed for patients who are likely to consistently abuse their diet. Patients should learn how to take their own blood pressure, so that if they get a splitting headache or some other ominous symptom, they can find out if it is due to a hypertensive crisis. They can then abort a hypertensive crisis by taking nifedipine, a fast-acting antihypertensive.

Lithium. Lithium is a salt, much like table salt, except that lithium replaces sodium. The immediate predecessor to the beverage 7-Up contained lithium and was marketed as a lithium soda that took the "ouch out of the grouch." Trace amounts of lithium are in the water supply, a tidbit which impresses some patients to reason, "It's okay to take lithium because it is a natural substance and not a drug."

Lithium is best for preventing mania and as effective as antidepressants for preventing bipolar depression. Acute bipolar depression is treated equally well by lithium and antidepressants, whereas acute mania responds best to lithium and the addition of benzodiazepines for agitation or antipsychotics for psychosis. Although lithium usually takes ten days to take effect, the benzodiazepines and antipsychotics can calm manics within hours for up to a few days.

Following the first manic or depressive episode, if there is no other episode for six months, lithium should be stopped. However, there is evidence that with each new episode, the bipolar disorder worsens both in frequency and severity. Some recommend that most patients should stay on lithium for life to prevent this deteriorating course. A patient who gets manic only once a year — for example, in the summer — might need to take lithium from May to September each year; a patient who has had eight years between episodes may only need to take lithium six months at a time. In the rare circumstance in which large doses of antipsychotics cannot contain a life-threatening emergency (e.g., anorexic starvation, driven suicidal behavior), one to three ECTs can be effective.

After a careful medical evaluation, including tests for electrolytes, thyroid, and kidney function, lithium can be started in 300-mg doses thrice daily. The amount is elevated until patients develop either side effects — such as a severe hand tremor[3] or nausea — or reach a serum lithium level of 1.0 to 1.6 meq/L. When lithium is used for prevention, serum levels should fall between 0.6 to 1.2 meq/L, with 0.7 to 0.9 meg/L the norm. Ideally, blood samples for serum lithium should be drawn 12 hours after the last dose. Always treat the patient, not his or her serum level. Even the best laboratories make mistakes. Many a salt-deficient patient will have a serum

---

[3]Nurses and activities therapists are often the first to detect this fine tremor; they'll see the patient spilling coffee, writing sloppily, or missing piano keys.

lithium inside a therapeutic range, yet still be delirious. A normal salt intake will suffice; extra salt is unnecessary.[4] Acutely manic patients usually require 900–2,400 mg/day of lithium; prophylactic doses are usually 600–1,800 mg/day. Overall, 75–80% of bipolar patients substantially improve on lithium.

A common problem, especially with "rapid cyclers," is mania or depression occurring in lithium-treated patients. When this happens, first check serum lithium levels to see if they are actually taking the drug and have a high enough lithium level for an acute episode. Bipolar patients often stop lithium because they miss their highs—can you blame them? Second, check patients' thyroid functioning, since hypothyroidism mimics the symptoms of depression and may result from prolonged lithium therapy. Third, if patients become depressed, add an antidepressant. Although usually helpful, giving antidepressants to depressed bipolar patients may increase the rapidity of cyclic mood changes or "switch" patients to mania. (SSRIs and bupropion may have a lower risk of switching patients.) Fourth, if none of the above works, or if patients cannot tolerate lithium's side effects, use the anticonvulsant carbamazepine (Tegretol) or divalproex (Depakote) (Prien & Gelenberg, 1989). Divalproex sodium can significantly decrease mania in five days.

Antipsychotics. Patients with psychotic depression only respond about one third of the time to antidepressants alone and just under half the time with antipsychotics alone (Khan, 1987; Khan, Noonan, & Healey, 1991). Combining the two treatments results in 65–75% response rates. Failing this combination, ECT is the preferred treatment.

Electroconvulsive therapy. ECT, as it is now administered, is the most effective of all the antidepressant treatments with over 80% responding. Historically, ECT was frightening: Patients would receive over 20 treatments for just about any condition; they'd convulse wildly, fracture spines, lose memories, and be dazed silly. Those days are gone. Today ECT is a safe and effective treatment for severe depressions (and sometimes for life-threatening mania). Usually six to eight treatments, one every other day, are given. Fractures and wild convulsions no longer occur; memory loss and confusion are either nonexistent or minimal and short-lived. Nobody knows why ECT helps, but it may work by massively discharging or releasing all neurotransmitters. (It does not scare patients into getting better, since sham-ECT doesn't work.)

Now patients are given a short-acting anesthetic (about 10 minutes), oxygen, and a temporary muscle paralyzer to prevent fractures. The seizure is monitored with an EEG because often there is no motor seizure to see. The convulsion usually lasts from 25 to 60 seconds. Convulsions less than 25 seconds have less therapeutic

---

[4]Bipolar patients are especially prone to being salt-deficient: They may be too depressed or too manic to eat. Bipolar patients tend to be middle-aged and thus more likely to be taking diuretics or steroids, following low-sodium diets for cardiac or weight problems, or having impaired kidney function. Since lithium replaces sodium within the cell, a serum lithium may not accurately reflect *intracellular* lithium, which is what counts.

effect. Several minutes later patients awaken from the anesthesia with no memory of the shock and without discomfort (Khan, Mirolo, Hughes, & Bierut, 1993).

First-time observers of ECT invariably describe it as "underwhelming." Patients, too, are surprised they don't feel anything, and why should they?—brain tissue is free of pain fibers. A survey of patients who received ECT revealed that two-thirds found going to the dentist more upsetting than getting ECT. The mortality rate from ECT is lower than for tonsillectomy, the former ranging from 0.008–0.05%. Indeed, the most dangerous aspect of ECT is not ECT *per se*, but the anesthesia. The main side effects of ECT are short-term memory loss and confusion; these may not occur or they may be so bad that the patient urinates in public or can't name his or her spouse. These problems, which are greatly minimized by unilateral ECT, significantly decrease within two weeks of the final treatment. When compared to bilateral, unilateral ECT has a slightly lower response rate. ECT does not cause any permanent brain damage or memory loss. Six months later, patients who have had ECT do as well on memory and other neuropsychological tests as do people who have never had ECT.

Psychotherapies

The psychotherapy of mood disorders can help patients to (a) learn the "facts" about their disorder, (b) feel less alone, (c) cope better with their disorder, (d) identify and avert situations likely to rekindle another episode, (e) abort episodes that have just begun by early symptom recognition, (f) view themselves and their world more rationally and constructively, (g) improve interpersonal relations, and (h) address the problems plaguing them.

Which of these goals are pursued depends primarily on patients' current mental state. If they are in an acute manic or depressive episode, psychotherapy should stress support more than insight, since they lack the attention span, abstract thinking abilities, and emotional perspective to use insight appropriately. For example, a man with major depression who "suddenly discovers" his sexual feelings toward his daughter will not apply this realization to understand his marital problem but to "prove his depravity." Patients with melancholia or psychotic depression are especially unable to profit from insight, and if anything, will use it for self-flagellation. Cognitive-behavioral or interpersonal psychotherapies benefit about 70% of patients with mild to moderate depression. These psychotherapies work as well but more slowly than antidepressants. Typically, 12 to 16 weeks are needed. Psychotherapy is indicated if patients with mild to moderate depression prefer this treatment. Patients with severe and/or psychotic depressions or with personality disorders don't do as well with psychotherapy and should be treated with antidepressants first. Among the more commonly used therapies are the following:

Interpersonal psychotherapy (ITP). This therapy is based on the theory that almost all people who become depressed have a major interpersonal problem—conflicts with a significant other, a boss, difficult role transitions, or deficient social skills and social isolation. These problem areas are identified and addressed. Instead of concentrating on intrapsychic material with a goal of personality change, ITP focuses on interpersonal matters, both inside and outside of therapy. Some studies have showed that combining ITP and TCAs yields superior results and lower dropout rates than either treatment alone. By teaching patients how to cope with problems, ITP may reduce the risk of relapse later on (Frank, Kupfer, & Perel, 1989). The conduct of ITP has been detailed in a manual (Klerman, Weissman, Rounsaville, & Chevron, 1984).

Behavior therapies. These approaches assume that depressed patients lack positive reinforcement and would benefit from being taught to identify the relation between events and feelings, to maximize praise from self and others, to avoid self-punishment, to set realistic goals, and to improve social skills. Behavior therapy for depression is detailed in a manual (Lewinsohn, Antonuccio, Steinmetz, & Teri, 1984).

Cognitive therapy (CT). Because CT focuses on more accessible conscious and preconscious material, it can be used by many more depressed patients than can traditional psychoanalytic treatments. The actual technique of CT is summarized in Chapter 5 and its use for depression is best detailed by Beck et al. (1979). It is usually combined with behavioral therapy.

Group therapy. Group behavioral, cognitive, and psychodynamic therapy may be only slightly less effective than their individual versions.

Brief psychodynamic psychotherapy. The goal of this therapy is "to resolve core conflicts based on personality and situational variables." Compared to the other therapies, it may be somewhat less effective for depression. Treatment manuals are available (Luborsky, 1984; Malan, 1979; Sifneos, 1979; Strupp & Binder, 1984).

Marital therapy. Marital therapy may treat both the depression and the marital and family problems (Jacobson, Holtzworth-Munroe, & Schaling, 1989). Marital discord or separation often precedes depression, persists after depression, and frequently precedes relapses. In more than half of distressed couples who are considering or are in the process of separation and divorce, one spouse will be clinically depressed. This form of therapy might be considered as the main psychotherapy or as an adjunct with a depressed patient who has marital discord.

Family Involvement

The importance of involving family members cannot be overemphasized. Like therapists, family members often feel that their advice and support are ignored, but unlike therapists, family members *live* with their depressed relative, and doing so can drain the most caring and resilient of loved ones. Besides the adverse consequences of depression already mentioned, research shows that 12–36 months following their discharge, depressed inpatients had nine times the normal divorce rate seen in the general population. This same study revealed that 54% of depressed inpatients had spouses with a psychiatric disorder (Merikangas, 1984). When bipolar patients on lithium decompensate, it's often because they feel coerced into doing something that entails the family (Lieberman & Strauss, 1984). This is particularly true for early episodes. As bipolar illness continues, it tends to have a life of its own, independent of stressors.

There are three general therapeutic reasons for involving relatives: (a) to support the patient, (b) to support the family, and (c) to treat the family. During acute affective episodes, therapists should employ family members as extensions of the treatment. Relatives should be told the "facts" about mood disorders — their symptoms, natural history, genetic risks, prognosis, and treatment. They should be counseled on how to respond to the patient's disorder. They should be cautioned about getting sucked into the patient's pessimistic views, as well as to understand the limits of what they can do to alleviate their loved one's misery. By helping the family help the patient, the therapist helps support the family.

Citing confidentiality, some depressed patients seek to prevent any family involvement. Although confidentiality is usually respected, when a patient's *judgment is impaired*, maintaining confidentiality may be senseless and harmful. Some depressed patients exclude relatives so that the relatives "won't be contaminated by me"; others "use" confidentiality to deny they are ill and need help; still others invoke confidentiality as a way of avoiding intimacy. In each case, the therapist must assess what information should be shared with the family and what should remain private. That a patient has sexual fantasies about aardvarks is nobody's business; that he's contemplating suicide or selling the family business is!

After a severe episode has passed, there are times when it is best to examine the family's or couple's role in causing or aggravating the patient's depression. This possibility is especially important to consider with female patients, since they tend to assume full responsibility for the problem that is actually the entire family's. As a result, they seek individual treatment when couple's or family therapy would be more appropriate.

Family treatment is also of special use for depressed teenagers, because they often come from families with a low tolerance for individuation and anger. The kid will rebel but succumb in despair. One parent might frequently abuse substances while the other is chronically depressed. A common pattern is for the parents to be furious with each other, yet bait their child by being "injustice collectors" and "grave-diggers" — that is, resurrecting past misdeeds and using them as accusations. Therapists should help these adolescents distinguish their problems from their parents', while also addressing the depression and substance abuse that usually afflict other family members. Depressed adolescents can be very convincing about the utter malevolence of their parents. They often tell their own version of the Cinderella story, with them as the victims and the parents as the evil persecutors. This may be an example of the negative thinking of depression and a face-to-face meeting with the family is needed to see where truth lies.

Finally, in the ultimate tragedy — suicide — clinicians should talk with the family to afford comfort, to prevent others from committing impulsive suicides, to minimize the self-blame of relatives (which might require pointing out to them that suicide is a hostile act because it hurts everyone), and finally, to learn from any therapy mistakes that might have been made. Sometimes lawyers recommend against this, but the chances of lawsuit are much higher if the family sees the clinician as cold, distant, or uncaring.

CHAPTER 11

Anxiety Disorders

A RECENT NATIONWIDE study of the prevalence of mental disorders in the United States revealed the surprising fact that anxiety disorders, not depression, were the most prevalent group of psychiatric diagnoses, affecting 12.6% of the population in a given 12-month period (Narrow, Regier, Rae, Marderscheid, & Locke, 1993). Table 11–1 summarizes the epidemiology of the most frequent anxiety disorders. The majority of these individuals are not seen by mental-health professionals, but present instead to medical-care settings with anxiety-related physical complaints or to substance-abuse treatment settings. In medical settings, anxiety and anxiety-induced insomnia are the most common psychological complaints. People with anxiety-related problems represent approximately 30% of patients seeking help from primary-care physicians. Frequently, these patients complain about somatic symptoms related to anxiety — for example, heart racing, diarrhea, upset stomach, dizziness, chest tightness — rather than about the anxiety itself. When both the patient and physician maintain a strictly somatic orientation, the underlying anxiety frequently goes unrecognized. In the following discussions, it is assumed that anxiety is not a unitary phenomenon but, rather, a complex and variable response that frequently co-occurs with other psychiatric disorders and by itself may define one of five distinct anxiety disorders (panic, phobic, obsessive-compulsive, stress, and generalized anxiety).

Normal Versus Pathological Anxiety

Although everybody experiences anxiety, only some are impaired by it. Anxiety in moderation can be highly adaptive, since optimal learning and adaptation to a variety of problems occur at moderate rather than high

244

TABLE 11–1
Epidemiology of *DSM-III–R/DSM-III* Anxiety Disorders*

DISORDER	LIFETIME %		12-MONTH %	
	MALE	FEMALE	MALE	FEMALE
Panic	2.0	5.0	1.3	3.2
Agoraphobia without panic	3.5	7.0	1.7	3.8
Social phobia	11.1	15.5	6.6	9.1
Simple phobia	6.7	15.7	4.4	13.2
Generalized anxiety	3.6	6.6	2.0	4.3
Obsessive-compulsive**	2.0	3.0	1.4	1.9
Any phobia**	10.4	17.7	6.2	12.8
Any anxiety disorder (does not include PTSD or OCD)	19.2	30.5	11.8	22.6

*DSM-III–R data summarized from Kessler et al., 1994.
**DSM-III data available from Robins & Regier, 1991.

or low levels of anxiety/arousal. Studies in medical settings support this conclusion. In one study (Janis, 1971) surgical patients with moderate levels of preoperative fear experienced after surgery the lowest levels of anger, complaining, and fear, and the most rapid recovery. The low-fear group had the poorest postoperative adjustment. This and other studies suggest that good postoperative adjustment requires some preoperative arousal. In addition to arousal, information about what to expect and how to cope with the situation increases adaptiveness (Ley, 1977). Thus it is not necessarily appropriate for clinicians to provide blanket reassurance or to implore patients "not to worry."

While moderate levels of anxiety may be normal and adaptive, the ability to vary anxiety levels in response to different situations is also desirable. Most people have a characteristic range of anxiety responses that is relatively fixed and can be viewed as a personality trait. This is called "trait anxiety." In clinical settings, when trait anxiety is uniformly high and maladaptive, it is called "chronic anxiety." In contrast to trait anxiety, the anxiety response at a particular time and situation is called "state anxiety"; it is not fixed and is time-limited. In clinical settings, when state anxiety is high and maladaptive, it is referred to as "acute anxiety," which may continue beyond the particular stressful situation and become chronic anxiety.

How is pathological anxiety diagnosed? In diagnosing an anxiety syndrome, the presence of both psychological and physiological symptoms should be ascertained. Psychological symptoms include a subjective sense of apprehension, worry, tension, and uneasiness without a known object or event, or out of proportion to known specific events. Hypervigilance, in which the person becomes excessively attentive to the point of distractibility, irritability, or insomnia, is also frequently seen. Physiological symptoms include motor tension (tremors, twitches, muscle aches, jitters) and autonomic hyperactivity (sweating, heart racing, frequent urination, diarrhea, dizziness, hot or cold spells). These autonomic symptoms are easily set off in most "normal" people without anxiety disorders by the appearance of flashing police car lights in the rear-view mirror, combined with the sound of a siren. Making the diagnosis of anxiety can be difficult when patients present only with physiologic symptoms, since each of these symptoms may stem from a host of other medical disorders. For example, if patients complain only of headache or diarrhea, direct but supportive questioning may reveal additional symptoms of an anxiety syndrome that they have been reluctant to reveal.

It is important to recognize anxiety in patients who are not complaining of it. High levels of anxiety can exacerbate a wide variety of medical conditions, including gastric and duodenal ulcers, ulcerative colitis, asthma, hypertension, hives, hypoglycemia, and some seizure disorders. It may also be an important component in the aggressive, pressured, "Type A" cardiac personality, who is at increased risk for myocardial infarction.

Just eliciting reports of anxiety-related symptoms is not enough, however. Many of these symptoms may exist with normal anxiety. Normal and pathological anxieties are quantitatively and qualitatively different. In anxiety syndromes the anxiety is high and maladaptive; there is decreased functioning because of the anxiety; the physiological symptoms are distressing and disturb normal functioning and/or the psychological symptoms interfere with the individual's ability to cope. Even when complete information is available, diagnosing anxiety is not a simple task. There are no concrete or cardinal signs; rather, clinicians have to exercise considerable judgment, for example, when concluding that the patient's emotional reactions are out of proportion to the situation.

That relatively few people with anxiety disorders seek treatment is unfortunate, since treatment is usually effective, and without it, less than a quarter of these patients fully recover. In general, the earlier in life patients receive treatment, the better their long-term outcome. Thus, early detection matters.

The Causes of Anxiety

Psychodynamic theory. At first, Freud postulated that pathological anxiety resulted from a failure to repress painful memories, impulses, or thoughts. When the psychic energy used for this repression is particularly intense, the repressed material breaks into consciousness in a disguised form. For instance, after "discovering" she was sexually molested as a child, a woman was flooded not with sexual thoughts, but with anxiety, difficulty breathing, hyperventilation, and other symptoms of a panic attack. Later, Freud introduced the concept of "signal anxiety," the experience of which enables the person to avoid dangerous thoughts, impulses, etc., through repression, phobic avoidance, compulsions, etc.

Behavioral theories. In Pavlov's classic experiment, a dog salivated on repeated simultaneous exposure to food and the sound of a bell. When Pavlov removed the food, the dog had become conditioned to salivate on hearing the bell alone. When students walk into a classroom and hear the instructor say, "Surprise exam!", immediately the effects of years of associating exams with anxiety trigger anxiety before the content of the exam is even glimpsed. Watson, Skinner, and most behaviorists view conditioning as essential in perpetuating and intensifying anxiety. In the 1970s and 1980s, Kandel (1983) photographed the actual changes in nerve cells produced by behavioral conditioning.

Although many assume that psychic anxiety causes and conditions somatic anxiety, William James (1893) proposed the opposite: That is, subjectively experienced anxiety is a conditioned response to the physical signals of anxiety such as tachycardia and rapid breathing. When injected with norepinephrine, people report feeling angry if they are watching a fight and more anxiety if they are watching a chase. Here there was no difference in the somatic symptoms but in how they were labeled. Under stress and at rest, anxious subjects have a higher rate of these bodily signals than do controls. Some evidence suggests that patients who report higher levels of psychic anxiety do so, not because they have greater physiologic arousal, but because they are more sensitive to perceiving physiologic arousal, and are more likely to label it anxiety instead of excitement or anger.

Biological theories. Whereas James, in what came to be known as the James-Lange theory, claimed that peripheral symptoms provoked central anxiety, Cannon (1932) argued that anxiety originates in the brain, which in turn produces peripheral symptoms. In Cannon's view, anxiety and panic are not consequences but causes of tachycardia, sweating, rapid respiration, etc. Yet if anxiety and panic tend to go from the brain to the body (and not vice versa), where and how does this originate in the brain?

During the late 1970s, two major discoveries began to address these questions. The first advance (Redmond, 1979) involved the locus coeruleus (LC), a dense cluster of neurons, which produces 70% of the brain's norepinephrine. When the LC is stimulated electrically or by the drug yohimbine, anxiety increases; when the LC is inhibited by drugs called "adrenergic blockers" (e.g., clonidine, propranolol), anxiety diminishes. In addition, benzodiazepines and TCAs slow the LC's firing and reduce anxiety.

The second major advance (Skolnick & Paul, 1983) was the discovery of benzodiazepine (BZ) receptors in the brain. Benzodiazepines (e.g., diazepam) appear to work by augmenting the antianxiety action of the GABA inhibitory system. How do these two biological systems relate? Nobody knows; no relationships are obvious. Many investigators suspect they pertain to different clinical syndromes — the very ones Freud and *DSM-IV* have characterized! — the LC to panic disorder and the BZ receptor to generalized anxiety disorders (GAD). When stimulated, the LC produces the symptoms and intense somatic signs characteristic of panic anxiety. In contrast, the BZ receptors may play more of a role in GAD.

The third major advance was the discovery that several drugs that primarily affect the serotonin system also affect anxiety disorders (Murphy & Pigott, 1990). Buspirone is mainly used for GAD and the SSRIs are effective in panic, obsessive-compulsive disorder, and possibly GAD. The cell bodies of the nucleus raphe (the brain's main group of serotonin neurons) send projections to the LC, limbic system, and prefrontal cortex, all areas involved in anxiety regulation. It is not clear exactly how this serotonin system interacts with the other two main systems. It used to seem simpler and clearer, but each new advance reveals more complexity — we knew more then than we know now!

ANXIETY DISORDER DUE TO A GENERAL MEDICAL CONDITION AND SUBSTANCE-INDUCED ANXIETY DISORDER

One of the first steps in the diagnosis of an anxiety disorder is to determine if it has a known specific cause. If it is caused by a medical condition or is substance-induced, treatment can then be directed at the underlying problem.

The *DSM-IV* criteria for anxiety disorders due to a general medical condition and substance-induced anxiety disorder are listed in Table 11–2.

Several medical conditions can mimic *panic disorder*. These include:

Cardiopulmonary disorders. (a) Recurrent pulmonary emboli (blood clots in the lungs) produce repeated episodes of acute anxiety with hyperventilation or dyspnea (shortness of breath) in conjunction with decreased oxygen concentration in the blood. Functional anxiety is associated with slightly increased oxygen concentrations. (b) Paroxysmal atrial tachycardia starts with a sudden increase in heart rate and then, unlike panic disorder, suddenly decreases. (c) Silent myocardial infarction, which more often

TABLE 11–2
DSM-IV Criteria for Anxiety Disorder Due to a General Medical Condition and Substance-Induced Anxiety Disorder*

Common Criteria for Both Disorders

A. Prominent anxiety, Panic Attacks, or obsessions or compulsions predominate in the clinical picture.

B. The disturbance does not occur exclusively during the course of delirium.

C. The disturbance causes clinically significant distress or impairment in social, occupational, or other important areas of functioning.

Additional Criteria for Anxiety Disorder Due to a General Medical Condition

D. There is evidence from the history, physical examination, or laboratory findings that the disturbance is the direct physiological consequence of a general medical condition.

E. The disturbance is not better accounted for by another mental disorder (e.g., Adjustment Disorder With Anxiety in which the stressor is a serious medical condition).

Specify if:
With Generalized Anxiety
With Panic Attacks
With Obsessive-Compulsive Symptoms

Additional Criteria for Substance-Induced Anxiety Disorder

D. There is evidence from the history, physical examination, or laboratory findings of either (1) or (2):

(1) the symptoms in Criterion A developed during, or within 1 month of, Substance Intoxication or Withdrawal
(2) medication use is etiologically related to the disturbance

E. The disturbance is not better accounted for by an Anxiety Disorder that is not substance induced. Evidence that the symptoms are better accounted for by an Anxiety Disorder that is not substance induced might include the following: the symptoms precede the onset of the substance use (or medication use); the symptoms persist for a substantial period of time (e.g., about a month) after the cessation of acute withdrawal or severe intoxication or are substantially in excess of what would be expected given the type or amount of the substance used or the duration of use; or there is other evidence suggesting the existence of an independent non-substance-induced Anxiety Disorder (e.g., a history of recurrent non-substance-related episodes).

Specify if:
With Generalized Anxiety
With Panic Attacks
With Obsessive-Compulsive Symptoms
With Phobic Symptoms

DSM-IV, pp. 439, 443.

occurs in diabetics, produces palpitations, sweating, and dyspnea in the absence of chest pains. (d) In mitral valve prolapse (MVP), diagnosed by auscultation and echocardiogram, the mitral valve doesn't close properly and produces a murmur or "systolic click." It is associated with panic disorder but is *not* a definite cause of panic. Because patients with panic attacks often think that something is wrong with their heart, they go see cardiologists, who on finding MVP, decide that this caused the panic. The evidence does not support this conclusion. MVP sometimes improves after the panic is satisfactorily treated, suggesting that panic disorder may actually cause some forms of MVP. In others, the MVP remains unchanged, but the panic attacks remain successfully treated. Because the MVP does not need to be corrected in order for the panic attacks to get better, it is unlikely that MVP is the cause of the attacks.

"Temporal lobe" epilepsy. Sudden, paroxysmal episodes of fear accompanied by derealization, depersonalization, and epigastric discomfort often constitute the prodrome of a complex partial seizure in which chewing, lip smacking, or other automatisms occur without the patient remembering. When there is no grand mal seizure component in the patient's history, this can be a difficult differential diagnosis. Information from people living with the patient can be the key to diagnosis.

Pheochromocytoma. This is a rare (less than 1 in 10,000) catecholamine-secreting tumor that produces marked episodic elevations of blood pressure and vasomotor lability in conjunction with a wide array of anxiety symptoms. However, patients with this tumor do not usually complain of the psychologic symptoms of anxiety. Blood pressure rises in panic disorder are modest by comparison.

Other medical conditions can mimic *generalized anxiety disorder (GAD)*. These include:

Hyperthyroidism. In this syndrome, unlike in GAD, a fine tremor and heat intolerance usually accompany symptoms of anxiety.

Hypoglycemia. A constellation of symptoms occur together, including hunger, weakness, headache, sweating, palpitations, and anxiety. The syndrome including anxiety is episodic, predictably occurring several hours after meals. It can be reversed by glucose ingestion (e.g., eating a candy bar). Differentiating anxiety from hypoglycemia is somewhat complicated by the fact that anxiety can worsen glucose tolerance. Generalized anxiety does not have predictable waves of anxiety associated with hunger, and panic attacks come on much faster and stronger. *Hypoglycemia is a very rare cause of anxiety* and is probably grossly over-diagnosed in patients actually suffering from anxiety disorders.

Post-concussion syndrome. Anxiety frequently accompanies this medical condition for several months after the head trauma. This is not just a psychological phenomena. It is seen in people with no memory of the accident (secondary to the concussion) and usually the anxiety is not related to the traumatic event. Anticonvulsants sometimes are effective.

Delirium. Anxiety sometimes is the prominent feature in delirium, but unlike in anxiety disorder, disturbed consciousness and problems in cognitive functioning are also always present.

Several drugs often cause symptoms that mimic generalized anxiety disorder and can worsen all other anxiety disorders. These include:

Alcohol or hypnoanxiolytic withdrawal. Frequently, patients do not recognize alcohol as a cause of anxiety but, rather, see it only as a treatment for anxiety. Direct questioning about alcohol and hypnoanxiolytic use is necessary, as many patients may try to conceal this information. If patients have been using long-lasting medications such as diazepam or clonazepam, withdrawal symptoms might not appear for four to seven days following drug discontinuation. In some anxiety disorders, even the ingestion of small amounts of alcohol can produce severe anxiety several hours later, as blood levels of alcohol fall (a "rebound" from the brief calming effect of alcohol). Thus, "social drinking," not just alcoholism, may cause anxiety.

Caffeine overuse. This is frequently not recognized by patients as the cause of their anxiety symptoms. For example, in the elderly, increased sensitivity to caffeine can precipitate a new anxiety-like syndrome in a person who has maintained a constant intake over the years. Only a reduction in caffeine intake will relieve the symptoms. It has also been shown that patients suffering from certain anxiety disorders are more sensitive to caffeine. Some have discontinued use of caffeinated beverages on their own in an attempt to reduce their symptoms; others, however, remain unaware of the link between caffeine and anxiety. Symptoms of caffeine intoxication—nervousness, irritability, agitation, headache, rapid heart rate, tremulousness, and occasional muscle twitches—can result from ingesting over 250 mg of caffeine a day. These effects can last seven hours. Table 11–3 lists the sources of caffeine.

Other stimulants. Both illegal and legal stimulants can cause significant anxiety. Common legal sources are decongestants, over-the-counter diet pills, and anti-asthmatic medications that rely on beta-adrenergic stimulation. Common illegal sources are methamphetamine and cocaine.

Other drugs. Yohimbine, marijuana, phencyclidine, and organic solvents have all been reported to increase anxiety and induce panic attacks.

PANIC DISORDER

"Worse than anything at Auschwitz" is how a concentration-camp survivor described her panic attacks. Suddenly and without reason, panic attacks

TABLE 11–3
Sources of Caffeine*

SOURCE	AMOUNT OF CAFFEINE (mgs.)
Beverages	
Brewed coffee	100–150 per cup
Instant coffee	86–99 per cup
Tea	60–75 per cup
Decaffeinated coffee	2–4 per cup
Cola drinks	40–60 per glass
Mountain Dew and Mellow Yellow	51 per glass
Dr. Pepper	42 per glass
Regular Sunkist Orange	42 per glass
7-Up, Sprite, Fresca, Diet Sunkist Orange, Fanta Orange, Hires Root Beer, caffeine-free colas	0 per glass
Prescription medications	
Cafergot	100 per tablet
Darvon compound	32 per capsule
Fiorinal	40 per tablet
Migral	50 per tablet
Over-the-counter drugs	
Stimulants:	
No-doz	100 per tablet
Vivarin	200 per tablet
Pain relievers:	
Anacin, aspirin compound, Bromo-Seltzer, Cope, Easy-Mens, Empirin compound, Midol, Vanquish	32 per tablet
Excedrin	60 per tablet
Pre-Mens	66 per tablet
Cold Pills	30 per capsule

*Modified from Maxmen, J. S. (1986a). *A good night's sleep: A step-by-step program for overcoming insomnia and other sleep problems.* New York: Warner, p. 74.

engulf the victim with a sense of imminent doom, death, or destruction. Since most victims have never heard of panic attacks, they fear that they're going mad and won't tell loved ones or physicians about them. Panic attacks may be the most terrifying of all psychiatric symptoms.

Clinical Presentation

The essential feature of panic disorder is a history of *panic attack*. These attacks usually affect women and strike outside the victim's home—most often in a store, sometimes on the street. The woman feels she's in a life-threatening situation from which she must escape — immediately. She might fear an imminent stroke, heart attack, or nuclear explosion. Very often she can't pinpoint what she fears, but knows it's horrendous. Her imagination takes over: She might die right on the spot, go berserk, or be killed, butchered, or maimed. Her heart pounds so, it could bust or burst through her chest. She may scream or look blank, even though she's frozen in fear and unable to move. The woman from Auschwitz, now quite elderly, says she's terrified of falling and clutching onto strangers. Another woman described her arm turning to stone and people appearing miles away. Most patients will gasp for air, hyperventilate, develop parethesias, or feel dizzy and lightheaded. They will race outside and only then will their breathing slow and their attack subside. Most attacks last three to ten minutes, and rarely more than 30 minutes.

Many patients shrug off the first attack, but in several days, unprovoked attacks recur; these may be less intense, but still frightening. Patients begin to dread future attacks. Although the timing of panic attacks is unpredictable, the locations may follow a pattern. A patient may panic in the same bank on three occasions, but not on the fourth nor in any other bank. A patient's attacks usually have their own symptom cluster: Some patients have primarily respiratory distress, some worry about going crazy, some fear death. *DSM-IV* criteria for panic attack and disorder are listed in Table 11–4.

Panic attacks can occur in a variety of anxiety disorders (e.g., panic disorder, social phobia, simple phobia, post-traumatic stress disorder). In determining the differential diagnostic significance of a panic attack, it is important to consider the context in which the panic attack occurs. There are two prototypical relationships between the onset of a panic attack and situational triggers: (1) *unexpected* (uncued) panic attacks, in which the onset of the panic attack is not associated with a situational trigger (i.e., occurring "out of the blue"); and (2) situationally *bound* (cued) panic attacks, in which an attack almost invariably occurs immediately upon exposure to, or in anticipation of, the situational trigger (cue). The occurrence of unexpected panic attacks is required for a diagnosis of panic disorder, while situationally bound panic attacks are most characteristic of social and specific phobias.

Moreover, there are panic attack presentations that do not conform to either of these prototypical relationships. These *situationally predisposed* panic attacks are more likely to occur upon exposure to the situational trigger (cue) but are not invariably associated with the cue. In addition, these panic attacks may not necessarily occur immediately after the exposure. There is some evidence that situationally predisposed panic attacks

TABLE 11–4
***DSM-IV* Criteria for Panic Attack and Panic Disorder With and
Without Agoraphobia***

Common Criteria for Panic Attack

A discrete period of intense fear or discomfort, in which four (or more) of the following symptoms developed abruptly and reached a peak within 10 minutes:

(1) palpitations, pounding heart, or accelerated heart rate
(2) sweating
(3) trembling or shaking
(4) sensations of shortness of breath or smothering
(5) feeling of choking
(6) chest pain or discomfort
(7) nausea or abdominal distress
(8) feeling dizzy, unsteady, lightheaded, or faint
(9) derealization (feelings of unreality) or depersonalization (being detached from oneself)
(10) fear of losing control or going crazy
(11) fear of dying
(12) paresthesias (numbness or tingling sensations)
(13) chills or hot flushes

Common Criteria for Panic Disorder

A. Both (1) and (2):

(1) recurrent unexpected Panic Attacks
(2) at least one of the attacks has been followed by 1 month (or more) of one (or more) of the following:

(a) persistent concern about having additional attacks
(b) worry about the implications of the attack or its consequences (e.g., losing control, having a heart attack, "going crazy")
(c) a significant change in behavior related to the attacks

B. The Panic Attacks are not due to the direct physiological effects of a substance (e.g., a drug of abuse, a medication) or a general medical condition (e.g., hyperthyroidism).

C. The Panic Attacks (and if agoraphobia is present, the anxiety or phobic avoidance) are not better accounted for by another mental disorder, such as Social Phobia (e.g., occurring on exposure to feared social situation), Specific Phobia (e.g., on exposure to a specific phobic situation), Obsessive-Compulsive Disorder (e.g., on exposure to dirt in someone with an obsession about contamination), Posttraumatic Stress Disorder (e.g., in response to stimuli associated with a severe stressor), or Separation Anxiety Disorder (e.g., in response to being away from home or close relatives).

(continued)

TABLE 11–4
(Continued)

Additional Criteria for Panic Disorder Without Agoraphobia

D. Absence of Agoraphobia (defined below).

Additional Criteria for Panic Disorder With Agoraphobia

D. The presence of agoraphobia: Anxiety about being in places or situations from which escape might be difficult (or embarrassing) or in which help may not be available in the event of having an unexpected or situationally predisposed Panic Attack or panic-like symptoms. Agoraphobic fears typically involve characteristic clusters of situations that include being outside the home alone; being in a crowd or standing in a line; being on a bridge; and traveling in a bus, train, or automobile.

Note: Consider the diagnosis of Specific Phobia if the avoidance is limited to one or only a few specific situations, or Social Phobia if the avoidance is limited to social situations.

E. Agoraphobic situations are avoided (e.g., travel is restricted) or else endured with marked distress or with anxiety about having a Panic Attack or panic-like symptoms, or require the presence of a companion.

DSM-IV, pp. 395, 397, 402, 403.

are especially frequent in panic disorder, but may at times occur in specific phobia or social phobia.

In time, instead of returning to their baseline state, most patients develop *anticipatory anxiety* in between panic attacks. This anxiety resembles that seen in GAD and includes continued motor tension, autonomic hyperactivity, apprehension, hypervigilance, and initial insomnia. Patients say this anxiety stems from a terror of having future attacks. This anxiety can be mild or severe; it may be the most dominant symptom, thereby misleading clinicians into diagnosing GAD.

Over time, a majority of patients with panic disorder will also develop situationally bound panic attacks. In some cases, these become the main form of panic attack. Subsequently, some patients—and there's no way of knowing which ones—develop *phobic avoidance*. They may be phobic for situations associated with the panic attacks. This avoidance may be based on the mistaken belief that the situation caused the attack or on the reality that many of the panic attacks have become situationally bound. For example, a patient may avoid driving because she thinks driving caused her to panic. More often, patients avoid situations in which they fear being trapped or unable to get help (e.g., busses, elevators, bridges, department stores). In lectures or movies they may take an aisle seat near the door to assure the possibility of escape. When restrictions on travel away from home significantly impair functioning, the diagnosis of *agoraphobia* is merited. The number of blocks a patient ventures away from home is a simple and reliable measure of impairment.

Clinical Course

Panic disorder usually begins during the late teens and twenties (usually in the twenties) and rarely after age 35. There is usually an initial discrete attack, although chronic anxiety, fatigue, or dizziness may precede it. Most patients originally consult a physician for difficulty breathing or chest discomfort, and less often, for abdominal distress or "irritable colon." In one survey, 70% of the patients had visited more than 10 physicians, 95% had prior psychiatric treatment, and 98% had long trials of hypnoanxiolytics; on average, each patient took over 8,772 doses.

Over time, the intensity of panic attacks, anticipatory anxiety, and phobic avoidance varies. Spontaneous remissions occur for months and sometimes for years. A patient may go five to ten years without an attack, suddenly have three attacks in a month, and then not have another attack for a decade. In general, five to 20 years after the initial attack, 50–60% of patients will recover substantially, while 20% will remain moderately impaired. Some studies suggest bleaker prognoses.

The earlier patients get treatment, the better the outcome. If panic attacks can be squelched relatively early, anticipatory anxiety and phobia may be averted or minimized. Even if the latter stages occur, early treatment can reduce their incapacitations and complications.

Complications

Substance abuse is a frequent complication because patients discover that alcohol and benzodiazepines will temporarily calm their anticipatory anxiety. Misdiagnosis by physicians may also lead to benzodiazepine misuse. Occupational, social, and marital impairments are common, often compounded by the patient's concealment of the attacks and by others not knowing that panic disorder exists.

Depression may affect up to 50% of all patients with panic disorder. These depressions are usually mild, two-thirds last under three months, and most are associated with a precipitating stress, such as a divorce. Yet a third of patients with panic disorder have had a major depression years *before* having their first panic attack. This suggests that for some patients, depression is not a complication of panic disorder, but a second disorder.

Epidemiology

The one-year prevalence of panic disorder is 2.3% and lifetime prevalence is 2.6%. Two to three times more women than men get it, and it is most prevalent between the ages of 16 and 40. During pregnancy, the frequency of panic attacks appears to decline sharply. Severe separation anxiety or sudden object loss during childhood may predispose to panic disorder.

Etiology

Panic disorder runs in families. About 20% of these patients' first-degree relatives have panic disorder, in comparison to about 4.0% of normals' first-degree relatives. Given an MZ to DZ ratio of 5:1 for panic disorder, genetics seem to play a major role in this familial transmission. (Knowing this, parents with panic disorder can spare their children considerable grief by ensuring that their kids know about the disorder and obtain early treatment.)

The initial panic attack, though not triggered by a specific stressor, usually occurs during an unusually stressful period. Relocation to new places commonly precede the onset of panic attacks (Roy-Byrne, Geraci, & Uhde, 1986). First attacks frequently happen in patients with thyroid disorders, during the immediate postpartum period, and after using marijuana, cocaine, or amphetamines. Caffeine produces panic attacks in 71% of patients with panic disorder and stopping caffeine reduces the frequency and intensity of the attacks.

Lactic acid, the stuff causing stiff muscles from exercise, plays a currently unknown role in panic disorder. Intravenous infusions of sodium lactate trigger panic attacks in those with panic disorder but not in controls. Vigorous physical exercise, which produces lactic acid, can trigger panic attacks in some patients (Pitts & McClure, 1967). Yet if patients with panic disorder receive a tricyclic antidepressant (TCA) prior to being infused with lactate, they do not develop an attack. This finding is noteworthy, given that TCAs block panic attacks. Donald Klein has proposed two theories based on the idea that panic attacks are "normal" in little children who have been abandoned and in people of all ages who feel suffocated. The abnormalities that then predispose an adult to panic attacks would be fear of separation or an abnormally low "suffocation" alarm threshold. Lactate can create a sense of breathlessness.

Differential Diagnosis

As discussed earlier, several medical conditions can mimic panic disorder. Differentiating *generalized anxiety disorder* from panic disorder may be complicated because anticipatory anxiety may be the dominant symptom of panic disorder, even when the patient has long-forgotten he or she ever had panic attacks. A history of repeated discrete attacks points to panic disorder. Several anxiety disorders, including *obsessive-compulsive, post-traumatic stress, separation anxiety*, and *social phobia*, have very specific fears that, in severe form, may look like a panic attack. Unlike panic attacks, however, these fears are *only* precipitated by very specific cues related to these disorders.

Sleep panic attacks occur recurrently in 33% of patients with panic disorder and occasionally in 69% (Mellman & Uhde, 1989). It is easy to confuse these with *nightmare disorder* and *sleep terror disorder*, but there are a few important differences. People with sleep panic attacks usually also have panic attacks during the day. Unlike nightmare disorder, there is no nightmare remembered and, unlike sleep terror disorder, the person with a panic attack remembers it well (does not have amnesia) and is quite responsive.

Management and Treatment

From the start, clinicians should help patients and their families have reasonable expectations of treatment. It should be pointed out that panic disorder is not a figment of the patient's imagination, but a genuine illness with biological components that often cause severe impairments. They should be told that panic disorder has a fluctuating course and that patients should not feel that they, or the treatment, has failed if some symptoms persist or recur. They should know that improving the patient's ability to function and to travel are key goals of treatment.

Treatment of mild panic disorder. Patients who have had only a few panic attacks or get them very intermittently but do not have much anxiety between episodes should be given an explanation of how the attacks occur, emphasizing that they are not life-threatening, dangerous to health, or a symptom of impending insanity. New techniques aimed at changing patients' catastrophic thinking about attacks are highly effective in patients with infrequent attacks, especially if there is high anticipatory anxiety between attacks. These cognitive-behavioral therapies have been systematized and are available in manual form (Barlow & Cerny, 1988).

Treatment of moderate and severe panic disorder. If attacks are occurring frequently (five to seven times a week) or there is significant anxiety between attacks and some disability, in addition to the cognitive-behavioral approach there are three classes of medications that can be considered. Imipramine at doses of 150 mg or higher has been show to be effective about 70% of the time. Most other tricyclic antidepressants are probably equally effective, but there are fewer well controlled studies on them. Imipramine, desipramine, or nortriptyline has been the first choice for treating panic disorder. More recently introduced, selective serotonin re-uptake inhibitors (SSRI) such as fluoxetine, sertraline, and paroxetine also appear to be effective and may be more easily tolerated because of a lower side-effect profile. Full response can take six to twelve weeks. Early over-stimulation with exacerbation of panic may occur unless the initial doses are small (10 mg imipramine/5 mg fluoxetine) and titration proceeds slowly.

Monoamine oxidase inhibitors (MAOIs) such as phenelzine appear to be effective in panic disorders about 75–80% of the time and are particularly effective in treatment-refractory cases. Because of the need to stay on a low tyramine diet to avoid hypertensive crisis, these drugs are probably under-utilized by most physicians.

Benzodiazepines in doses two to three times higher than usually used for simple anxiety have been reported to be effective in about 70–90% of panic disorder cases. There are many controlled studies supporting alprazolam's effectiveness and a few for clonazepam, lorazepam, and diazepam. High doses of benzodiazepines present a risk of physical dependence, but nonetheless should be considered in patients who have not responded to or cannot tolerate antidepressants or who may be fearful of taking MAOIs because of the danger of dietary interactions (a significant number of patients, perhaps 30%). Response to benzodiazepines (one to two weeks) is much faster than to antidepressants (three to four weeks). Short-term use (six weeks) during administration of antidepressant treatment may be indicated to prevent early over-stimulation and to provide more rapid relief of panic, especially in patients with occupational or familial dysfunction. Unfortunately, when attempts to withdraw the benzodiazepines are made, patients may not only have a return of the original symptoms but also rebound withdrawal symptoms. During this withdrawal period, patients can have worse symptoms than when they started treatment (Fyer et al., 1987). Beta-blockers have *not* been shown to effectively block panic attacks and are over-utilized for the treatment of anxiety by internists and cardiologists. Other drugs that have been shown to be ineffective include bupropion and trazodone (antidepressants), buspirone, and neuroleptics.

Long-term management of panic attacks. When the *anticipatory anxiety* of having panic attacks continues for months and years, the anxiety that develops in anticipation of these attacks becomes entrenched and resistant to treatment. Although it may seem redundant to the therapist, repeatedly telling the patient that she won't get panic attacks while on her medication goes a long way to quelling anticipatory anxiety. The cognitive-behavioral treatment program for mild to moderate panic disorder can help to prevent further symptoms. Because these drugs have become the patient's "security blanket," stopping medications is usually difficult. Extremely slow decreases are recommended. In the case of benzodiazepines, this is also necessary to minimize withdrawal symptoms. Sometimes patients will get stuck on the last tiny dose which, though they know it is pharmacologically inactive, remains psychologically quite active for them. Finally, they give it up.

The *agoraphobia* that frequently accompanies panic disorder is discussed below. Any treatment that eventually exposes patients to the phobic stimulus is likely to work, whereas any treatment that never exposes them to the stimulus is likely to fail.

PHOBIC DISORDERS

A phobia is an irrational dread of, and compelling desire to avoid, a specific object, situation, or activity. Phobics know their phobias are "crazy," unreasonable, or excessive. Unlike panic attacks, phobias are always anticipated and never happen spontaneously. (Patients with both panic attacks and phobias are diagnosed as having panic disorder.)

The *original phobia* is usually followed by mild to severe *anticipatory anxiety*, although if the phobic stimulus is avoided, some patients will remain anxiety-free. Patients' degree of anticipatory anxiety depends primarily on their confidence in being able to avoid the phobic situation. Patients who are phobic to unusual things, such as snakes, are generally calm in other circumstances; those who dread common things that might suddenly appear, such as pigeons, tend to be chronically anxious unless they're in a safe haven (home).

A set of *avoidant behaviors* often occurs. A fish-phobic is not only uncomfortable around fish, but before visiting new friends, may phone ahead to make sure they won't serve herring and don't have goldfish. If the fish can't be hidden or trashed, the fish-phobic won't visit.

On occasion, virtually everyone, especially children, are bugged by some phobia—mice, snakes, insects, etc. Phobic *symptoms* become phobic *disorders* when they cause undue distress and impair functioning. Roughly 20% of patients with phobic symptoms develop phobic disorders.

Many phobias remit quickly without therapy, but if they endure for over a year, they're unlikely to remit spontaneously. Many childhood phobias vanish within a year; treatment hastens their disappearance. The prognosis is worse in adults: In a five-year span, 50% of patients will improve, but only 5% will be symptom-free.

One medical dictionary lists 275 types of phobia; *DSM-IV* lists three:

Agoraphobia originally meant "fear of the marketplace," but now refers to fear of being in places or situations where escape might be difficult or, in the cases with panic attacks, of being where help is not available (e.g., shops, theaters, streets). The most severe of phobic disorders, agoraphobia accounts for 60% of phobic disorders in clinical practice. *Social phobia* refers to the fear of being scrutinized and judged, as in "stage fright"; social phobias comprise 10% of phobic disorders. *Specific phobia* encompasses irrational fear and avoidance of specific objects or situations not covered by agoraphobia or social phobia. Simple phobias usually involve animals or insects (dogs, spiders, etc.), things (e.g., hypodermic needles), or places (e.g., heights, closed spaces). Whereas social phobias are normally confined to a few stimuli, simple phobias usually involve only one object. In comparison to social phobias, simple phobias begin earlier in life, rarely incapacitate, and have better prognoses. Among the phobias, simple phobias are most common in the population, but agoraphobias are most common in the office. Table 11-4 described criteria for agoraphobia; Table 11-5 presents criteria for specific and social phobias.

Clinical Presentation

Agoraphobia. The public places or open spaces typically feared by these patients include driving a car, riding a bus, crossing bridges, standing in lines, passing through tunnels, walking through crowds, or shopping. Exposure to the phobic stimulus often triggers intense somatic anxiety. Some phobic patients fear going berserk in public—screaming without reason, propositioning strangers, guffawing nonstop, disrobing, or masturbating. Agoraphobia mushrooms: Fears of taking a bus may escalate to fears of going anywhere by any means. Because agoraphobics often become terrified of leaving safe places (e.g., home), of being without a familiar object (e.g., a cane), or of traveling alone, they become highly dependent on others. Unless treated early, patients may increasingly restrict their activities and venture outside only with a trusted companion.

When agoraphobia is not a sequela of panic attacks, it usually arises during the early twenties, even though it may begin at any age. Many patients delay getting treatment for a decade or more. Over time, symptoms typically fluctuate from mild to severe. Spontaneous remissions occur, but uncommonly. Without early treatment or a spontaneous remission, patients tend to get worse.

Complications are frequent. If the patient is home-bound, depression is common. Alcohol and hypnoanxiolytic abuse may result from patients medicating their anticipatory anxiety or from physicians incorrectly treating patients' depressions or anxieties. Many agoraphobics develop compulsions: They cannot leave home, for

TABLE 11–5
DSM-IV Criteria for Specific Phobia and Social Phobia*

Specific Phobia

A. Marked and persistent fear that is excessive or unreasonable, cued by the presence or anticipation of a specific object or situation (e.g., flying, heights, animals, receiving an injection, seeing blood).

B. Exposure to the phobic stimulus almost invariably provokes an immediate anxiety response, which may take the form of a situationally bound or situationally predisposed panic attack. **Note:** In children, the anxiety may be expressed by crying, tantrums, freezing, or clinging.

C. The person recognizes that the fear is excessive or unreasonable. **Note:** In children, this feature may be absent.

D. The phobic situation(s) is avoided or else endured with intense anxiety or distress.

E. The avoidance, anxious anticipation, or distress in the feared situation(s) interferes significantly with the person's normal routine, occupational (academic) functioning, or with social activities or relationships with others, or there is marked distress about having the phobia.

F. In individuals under 18 years, the duration is at least 6 months.

G. The anxiety, Panic Attacks, or phobic avoidance associated with the specific object or situation are not better accounted for by another mental disorder, such as Obsessive-Compulsive Disorder (e.g., fear of dirt in someone with an obsession about contamination), Posttraumatic Stress Disorder (e.g., avoidance of stimuli associated with a severe stressor), Separation Anxiety Disorder (e.g., avoidance of school), Social Phobia (e.g., avoidance of social situations because of fear of embarrassment), Panic Disorder with Agoraphobia, or Agoraphobia Without History of Panic Disorder.

Specify if:
   Animal Type
   Natural Environment Type (e.g., heights, storms, water)
   Blood-Injection-Injury-Type
   Situational Type (e.g., planes, elevators, enclosed places)
   Other Type (e.g., phobic avoidance of situations that may lead to choking, vomiting, or contracting an illness; in children, avoidance of loud sounds or costumed characters)

Social Phobia (Social Anxiety Disorder)

A. A marked and persistent fear of one or more social or performance situations in which the person is exposed to unfamiliar people or to possible scrutiny by others. The individual fears that he or she will act in a way (or show anxiety symptoms) that will be humiliating or embarrassing. **Note:** In children, there must
                                                                          (*continued*)

TABLE 11–5
(*Continued*)

be evidence of capacity for social relationships with familiar people and the anxiety must occur in peer settings, not just in interactions with adults.

B. Exposure to the feared social situation almost invariably provokes anxiety, which may take the form of a situationally bound or situationally predisposed Panic Attack. **Note:** In children, the anxiety may be expressed by crying, tantrums, freezing, or shrinking from social situations with unfamiliar people.

C. The person recognizes that the fear is excessive or unreasonable. **Note:** In children, this feature may be absent.

D. The feared social or performance situations are avoided or else endured with intense anxiety or distress.

E. The avoidance, anxious anticipation, or distress in the feared social or performance situation(s) interferes significantly with the person's normal routine, occupational (academic) functioning, or with social activities or relationships with others, or there is marked distress about having the phobia.

F. In individuals under 18 years, the duration is at least 6 months.

G. The fear or avoidance is not due to the direct effects of a substance (e.g., a drug of abuse, a medication) or a general medical condition, and is not better accounted for by another mental disorder (e.g., Panic Disorder With or Without Agoraphobia, Separation Anxiety Disorder, Body Dysmorphic Disorder, a Pervasive Developmental Disorder, or Schizoid Personality Disorder).

H. If a general medical condition or other mental disorder is present, the fear in Criterion A is unrelated to it, e.g., the fear is not of Stuttering, trembling in Parkinson's disease, or exhibiting abnormal eating behavior in Anorexia Nervosa or Bulimia Nervosa.

Specify if:
   Generalized: if the fears include most social situations (also consider the additional diagnosis of Avoidant Personality Disorder)

*DSM-IV, pp. 410–11, 416–17.

example, without repeatedly checking if the oven is turned off or the back door is locked. Marital and sexual problems may precede or follow agoraphobia.

Social phobia. These patients have an irrational fear of being scrutinized, judged, or humiliated in public. It may be a dread of embarrassing oneself while speaking in public, eating in restaurants, or using public lavatories. Social phobics tend to blush and twitch, whereas agoraphobics become dizzy, faint, short of breath, weak in the limbs, and have ringing or buzzing in their ears (Liebowitz, Gorman, Fyer, & Klein, 1985). Social phobia is diagnosed if the fear or avoidant behavior interferes with occupational or social activities or relationships. The phobia may be discrete (public speaking) or extend to more widespread social situations. In the latter case, it is easily confused with panic disorder, unless patients are asked if they've ever panicked when *not* in social situations.

With a mean age of onset of 19, social phobias usually begin before agoraphobia. Without early therapy, social phobia has an unremitting, chronic course. At some point, a third to a half will have depressive symptoms, a majority will stop work or school, 60% will abuse alcohol or drugs, and about half will avoid all social interaction outside the immediate family (and then may qualify for the diagnosis of avoidant personality disorder).

Specific phobia. The most common, benign, and circumscribed of the phobias, these usually start in childhood or early adolescence and cease within five years in 50% of patients. Simple phobia is the elevation of a specific fear to phobic proportions. Animals and creepy crawlies are the most common phobias for which treatment is sought. The more unibiquitous the phobic object, the more incapacitating phobia. For example, phobias for common household pets are socially inconvenient and discomfort may be excessive and frequent. Animal phobias almost always begin in childhood. Before puberty, simple phobias occur equally in males and females. It is not known why the animal phobias tend to persist in women and not men. Acrophobia (fear of heights) and claustrophobia (fear of closed spaces) are examples of other common simple phobias. Blood/injury/illness phobias are distinguished by their unique physiology (bradycardia, hypotension, and fainting, as opposed to tachycardia and hypertension) and may be encountered more often in medical settings. In the wild, this response obviously protected humans from profuse bleeding.

Epidemiology

Epidemiologic surveys of phobias can yield very different results because what qualifies as a phobia can vary considerably. Is somebody phobic if she's queasy around snakes? Does one count phobias that appear with other disorders? In the general population, the prevalence of phobic *symptoms* is 19–44%, whereas for phobic *disorders*, 5–15%.

Although women have two to three times more agoraphobia and simple phobia than men (Table 11-1), social phobias affect the sexes equally. Adults who are phobic and non-phobic had the same rates (4%) of phobias during their childhoods. Separation anxiety during childhood and sudden loss of a loved one predispose to agoraphobia. Social phobia is a more common psychiatric precursor to schizophrenia than any other psychiatric disorder. Social phobia is also common in some alcoholic populations ("Have a few drinks to help your confidence").

Etiology and Pathogenesis

As a general proposition, it can be said that unknown biological or psychosocial mechanisms cause phobic patients to acquire an ingrained and unconscious stimulus-response association, which generates fear on subsequent exposure to the phobic stimulus. However, why some objects and not others are feared, and why some phobias vanish while others intensify, are unknown. The standard (tautological) explanations are: The phobic object is "chosen" because it carries enormous symbolic importance, of which patients are unaware; and repression and displacement are the chief defense mechanisms that cause phobias.

For example, a woman who was usually punished as a child by being locked in her bedroom may become claustrophobic when fired by her boss. If she has forgotten (or repressed) these childhood banishments, she will be unaware of having been conditioned to associate punishment with being locked in a room, and she will be puzzled by her current claustrophobia. As in any phobia, conditioning or the secondary gain of the "sick role" may extend her claustrophobia into anticipatory anxiety and avoidant behaviors (e.g., not seeking jobs).

Agoraphobia runs in families; most social and simple phobias do not. Nevertheless, some studies show that children specifically phobic to insects and animals are likely to have mothers with similar phobias. This suggests that imitation, indoctrination, or identification may transmit phobias in some cases. Genetic factors may also play a role in the pathogenesis of phobia. Identical twins raised apart have a significantly increased chance of having a phobia and, not only that, but the *same* phobia.

Differential Diagnosis

A phobic disorder should not be diagnosed when another mental or personality disorder better accounts for the phobia. For example, fear of contamination results from *obsessive-compulsive disorder* and fear of a specific past stressor occurs with *post-traumatic stressor disorder*. Yet whereas the feared object leads the obsessive to perform rituals or to block out intrusive thoughts, it primarily induces anxiety in the phobic patient. *Schizophrenia* may produce social withdrawal resembling agoraphobia and social phobia, but schizophrenics have many more symptoms and avoid situations because of delusions, whereas phobics know their phobia is absurd. *Paranoid disorders* can lead to avoidant behavior, but unlike the phobic, the paranoid sees nothing irrational about his or her behavior. Because many patients with *depressive disorders* feel worthless, gradually restrict their activities, and become reclusive, they may appear agoraphobic. However, pervasive symptoms, biological signs of depression, and excessive guilt and shame point to depression rather than to an anxiety disorder. Patients with *dementia* may withdraw to "think clearly," but this phobic-like avoidance is not associated with a specific feared stimulus; MSE testing will eliminate any remaining diagnostic confusion. Phobias commonly occur in patients with *borderline, paranoid*, and *avoidant personality disorders*.

Normal fears of public speaking should be distinguished from social phobia, as should "normal fears" of bugs or snakes from simple phobia. In these cases, the border between "normal" and pathological depends on the degree of distress and disability the phobia generates.

Management and Treatment

> One can hardly master a phobia if one waits till the patient lets the analysis influence him to give it up . . . one succeeds only when one can induce them by the influence of the analysis to . . . go [about alone] . . . and to struggle with their anxiety while they make the attempt. — Sigmund Freud (1919)

Essential in the treatment of phobias is exposing patients to the feared object or situation for an uninterrupted period of time. This applies to all treatments, including psychoanalytic psychotherapy, behavior therapy, hypnosis, and medication. Historically, the preferred treatment for phobias was primarily behavior therapy involving relaxation training, mental rehearsal and exposure, supplemented by supportive individual, family, and group therapy, whenever appropriate. More recently, however, evidence suggests that supportive psychotherapy may be just as effective as behavior therapy, as long as patients encounter the feared situation. Freud believed that because phobias were based on underlying conflicts, just removing the symptom (the phobia), but not the underlying conflict, would result in "symptom substitution"—another symptom popping up. On the contrary, eliminating phobias by "superficial" behavioral or pharmacologic means rarely, if ever, leads to this substitution.

Biotherapies. Most studies show little use for TCAs and MAOIs in phobic patients without panic attacks or social phobia. Social phobias appear to respond well to MAOIs and more modestly to TCAs. In many cases in which the social phobia was so severe that the person developed avoidant personality disorder, a year on MAOIs produced such dramatic improvement that the avoidant personality disorder diagnosis no longer existed. Because beta-adrenergic blockers (e.g., propranolol) diminish somatic (but not psychic) anxiety, they may be useful for some social phobias, such as stage fright, in which somatic anxiety is paramount. Hypnoanxiolytics can be used temporarily to reduce anticipatory anxiety, but their long-term use risks habituation.

Behavior therapies. Live exposure to the phobic stimulus—the essential therapeutic intervention—may be performed in three ways. First is *flooding*, in which patients are directly confronted with the phobic stimulus for sessions lasting from 30 minutes to eight hours. Flooding may also involve bombarding the patient with the feared stimulus. The author (J.M.) cured a man of his pillow phobia by having him sit for two 45-minute sessions in a hospital room stuffed with 127 pillows. Second is a *graduated exposure*, in which patients initially confront the phobic object for a brief time (e.g., 30 seconds to one minute), and then gradually escalate the duration of exposure to over 60 uninterrupted minutes. Marks et al. (1983) have shown that only nominal benefit results from therapist-aided exposure. The third approach is *systematic desensitization*, usually involving *muscle relaxation*, as described in Chapter 5. To be effective, this technique must be followed (at some point) by direct exposure to the phobic object.

Assertiveness training. Modeling, role playing, behavior rehearsal, and *in vivo* homework assignments may also be helpful for social phobics and chronic phobics with marked dependence needs.

Psychotherapies. Individual psychotherapy can supplement behavior therapy by encouraging patients to enter the phobic situation, by addressing any secondary gain that might perpetuate their avoidant behaviors, and by exploring the symbolic meaning of the phobic object. Group psychotherapy may help patients redevelop social skills, foster assertiveness, reduce or distribute dependency, and decrease loneliness. For some patients and their families, self-help groups for phobics are invaluable.

OBSESSIVE-COMPULSIVE DISORDER

Being "obsessive" or "compulsive" is not the same as having *obsessions* or performing *compulsions*. The distinction between "si*ve*" and "si*on*" is more than two letters; it's the difference between a personality *style* with some adaptive features and a mental *disorder* that's often incapacitating.

Obsessions are persistent, disturbing, intrusive, thoughts or impulses, which the patient finds illogical but irresistible. Unlike delusions, patients consider obsessions absurd and actively resist them. Most of us have experienced these in a mild form when we have had an advertizing jingle or catchy little song like "It's a Small World" (get this out of your head at once!) take over our minds for a few hours or days. *Compulsions* are obsessions expressed in action. Obsessions and compulsions are methods for reducing anxiety. True obsessions and compulsions are the essential traits of obsessive-compulsive disorder (OCD), a surprisingly common disorder occurring in almost 3% of the population.

Clinical Presentation

The first and most important point to remember is that people with OCD rarely reveal their symptoms; they are too embarrassed and keep them a big secret. Clinicians usually must ask gently about the most common obsessions and compulsions and not wait for patients to offer the information on their own. *DSM-IV* diagnostic criteria for OCD (Table 11–6) illustrate the many ways obsessions and compulsions can present. Obsessions may appear as *ideas*—words, rhymes, or melodies that annoyingly interrupt normal thought and are often considered nonsensical, obscene, or blasphemous by the patient; they may appear as *images*, which are usually violent or disgusting (e.g., children burning, rape).

Underlying most cases of OCD is some form of pathological doubting— "Something bad will happen unless I do this." If there is any possibility of something bad happening, these patients can rapidly elevate the possibility to a probability and, in many cases, to a near certainty. We all have some fears about contracting disease and even occasionally feel compelled to wash our hands, but a person with OCD is plagued by this dreaded possibility and may wash all day long. All patients with OCD have obsessions and a majority have compulsive rituals based on those obsessions. The compulsive rituals are either directly linked to the obsession (e.g., washing hands to prevent disease) or linked by magical thinking (e.g., "My parents might die if I don't wash my hands").

Most forms of OCD fall into the following five categories (most people with OCD have symptoms in more than one category):

1. *Washers* fear contamination and usually have cleaning compulsions (e.g., "If I don't clean this, something bad will happen").
2. *Checkers* repeatedly check things like ovens being turned off, doors locked, etc. Each time the pathological doubt recurs ("If I left the oven on, the house will burn down"), the person checks it again, up to 20 times a day or more.

TABLE 11-6
TABLE 11-6
DSM-IV* Criteria for Obsessive-Compulsive Disorder

A. Either obsessions or compulsions:

Obsessions as defined by (1), (2), (3), and (4):
(1) recurrent and persistent thoughts, impulses, or images that are experienced, at some time during the disturbance, as intrusive and inappropriate and cause marked anxiety or distress
(2) the thoughts, impulses, or images are not simply excessive worries about real-life problems
(3) the person attempts to ignore or suppress such thoughts or impulses or to neutralize them with some other thought or action
(4) the person recognizes that the obsessional thoughts, impulses, or images are a product of his or her own mind (not imposed from without as in thought insertion)

Compulsions as defined by (1) and (2):
(1) repetitive behaviors (e.g., hand washing, ordering, checking) or mental acts (e.g., praying, counting, repeating words silently) that the person feels driven to perform in response to an obsession, or according to rules that must be applied rigidly
(2) the behaviors or mental acts are aimed at preventing or reducing distress or preventing some dreaded event or situation; however, these behaviors or mental acts either are not connected in a realistic way with what they are designed to neutralize or prevent, or are clearly excessive

B. At some point during the course of the disorder, the person has recognized that the obsessions or compulsions are excessive or unreasonable. **Note:** This does not apply to children.

C. The obsessions or compulsions cause marked distress, are time consuming (take more than 1 hour a day), or significantly interfere with the person's normal routine, occupational functioning, or usual social activities or relationships.

D. If another Axis I disorder is present, the content of the obsessions or compulsions is not restricted to it (e.g., preoccupation with food in the presence of an Eating Disorder; hair pulling in the presence of Trichotillomania; concern with appearance in the presence of Body Dysmorphic Disorder; preoccupation with drugs in the presence of a Substance Use Disorder; preoccupation with having a serious illness in the presence of Hypochondriasis; preoccupation with sexual urges or fantasies in the presence of Paraphilia; or guilty ruminations in the presence of Major Depressive Disorder).

E. The disturbance is not due to the direct physiological effects of a substance (e.g., a drug of abuse, a medication) or a general medical condition.

Specify if:
   With Poor Insight: if, for most of the time during the current episode, the person does not recognize that the obsessions and compulsions are excessive or unreasonable

---

*DSM-IV, pp. 422–23.

3. *Doubters and sinners* fear terrible things will happen if everything is not perfect ("Am I a good Catholic?"; "Did I do this job right?"). They are more likely to be paralyzed into inaction than to have compulsions.
4. *Counters and arrangers* are ruled by magical thinking and superstitions. Obsessions about order, symmetry, and number fuel the counting and arranging. Certain numbers or colors may be "bad" and asymmetry may lead to imagined catastrophes. Pencils all must face north or no work proceeds.
5. *Hoarders* cannot throw anything away because if they do, terrible things might happen. Not all hoarding is based on OCD. Some people are poorly organized and never get around to throwing things out; others intend to sort those piles but don't find the time. The important question to ask a hoarder is, "What would happen if all that stuff were thrown out?" A catastrophic answer suggests OCD. A more banal one—"Oh, well, I needed to get rid of stuff anyway"—suggests procrastination or poor organization.

Clinical Course

Two-thirds of patients with OCD had substantial symptoms before the age of 15 and almost all had some symptoms in childhood. On the average, men develop OCD five years earlier than women. The first psychiatric contact is around age 27 and the first hospitalization (if any), during the thirties. Although it tends to begin gradually, OCD may erupt suddenly after a severe psychosocial stressor. In the average patient it is a chronic life-long illness with waxing and waning of symptoms. Outcome is not related to the content of the obsessions; patients with milder symptoms, no compulsions, briefer duration of symptoms, and higher premorbid functioning have better prognoses.

Complications and Comorbidity

Attempts to resist an obsession or compulsion may produce anxiety of panic proportions; hence the inclusion of this disorder with the anxiety disorders. Depression is the most frequent (80% of patients) complication for these patients, followed by a failure to marry and an inability to sustain interpersonal relations. Although going insane, being totally incapacitated, or permanently incarcerated are all common fears of the obsessional, these fears rarely materialize. Despite much suicidal thinking, less than 1% of these patients commit suicide.

Several uncommon disorders may co-exist with OCD, but are not necessarily a result of it. These include anorexia or bulimia nervosa (13%), trichotillomania (15%), and Tourette's disorder (10–15%). Body dysmorphic disorder (e.g., "My nose is too big, my lips too small")—sometimes called the "Michael Jackson Syndrome"—also occurs with OCD. Underlying many of these is pathological doubting (such as, "I am too fat," in the anorectic).

Epidemiology

The lifetime prevalence of OCD in the general population is 2.6% (see Table 11–1). The sexes are equally affected. OCD is more common among the higher educated, higher socioeconomic groups, and those with higher IQ scores—three interrelated factors. Obsessive-compulsive personality disorder is not particularly more common in OCD, but avoidant and dependent personality disorders are. More recent data suggest that believing the thoughts or behaviors are real or reasonable does not indicate a poor prognosis.

Etiology and Pathogenesis

Freudian psychodynamic theory states that obsessions and compulsions develop in three phases: (a) an internally perceived dangerous impulse, (b) the threat of what would occur if this impulse were acted upon, and (c) the defenses to avert the threat. The most commonly used defenses are repression, reaction-formation, isolation, and undoing.

Biological research indicates that there are abnormalities in the frontal lobes, basal ganglia, and cingulus areas of patients with this disorder (Jenike et al., 1991). Cingulotomy in extreme cases can substantially relieve or cure OCD (Jenike et al., 1991). The basal ganglia is involved in over-learned routine behaviors such as grooming and the prefrontal areas in planning and organizing behaviors. Because drugs that treat OCD all markedly affect serotonin transmission, the serotonin system is probably involved.

Psychopathology in general and obsessions in particular run in the families of obsessionals. Given that concordance rates for OCD are 70% and 50% among MZ and DZ twins, respectively, genetic transmission is involved. A patient with OCD has a 25% chance of having a first-degree relative with this disorder.

Differential Diagnosis

Normal obsessions and compulsions are not resisted or considered ridiculous by the person having them. Avoiding sidewalk cracks and other compulsions are common during childhood, but kids don't mind them; they do mind OCD. Kids have a lot of magical thinking and don't see the senseless-ness of their acts. Adults may feel their obsessive brooding, ruminations, and preoccupations are annoying and excessive, yet they usually think they're meaningful; not being fully ego-dystonic, these are not the true obsessions of OCD. This disorder was once believed to be intimately related to *obsessive-compulsive personality disorder*, but more recent evidence sug-gests no real relationship between the two. The obsessive and compulsive traits in obsessive-compulsive personality disorder are ego-syntonic, where-as they are usually ego-dystonic in OCD; moreover, patients with obsessive-compulsive personality disorder do not have true obsessions or compul-sions. Neither are so-called *"compulsive" gambling, eating, and sexual behaviors* true compulsions; the person usually enjoys doing them, does not imagine any disaster occurring if they are not done, and at least is temporar-ily distracted from unpleasant feelings.

OCD should not be diagnosed when specific obsessions and compulsions arise directly from other disorders. *Schizophrenic delusions* may resemble obsessions, but they are usually ego-syntonic and occur without patients' insight. Obsessions are overvalued ideas, not delusions; patients with OCD usually accept the fact that their obsessions are not realistic. Because *major depression* is often accompanied by ruminative, guilt-ridden, and self-critical obsessions, and since major depression and OCD both have episodic courses, differentiating the two can be difficult. In general, the diagnosis of OCD should be reserved when an OCD clearly precedes a major depression, or when the obsessions are not directly related to the depression. Similarly, in disorders in which preoccupations normally occur, OCD is diagnosed only if the obsessions include other areas of concern.

Management and Treatment

Medication. The only proven effective drug treatment for this disorder are the serotonin re-uptake blocking antidepressants (fluoxetine, sertraline, paroxetine, fluvoxamine) and the highly serotonergic TCA clomipramine. Clomipramine, the chlorinated derivative of imipramine (itself ineffective), must be given in an eventual dose of 150–250 mg after gradual titration. High doses of SSRIs (fluoxetine 60–80 mg, sertraline 150–200 mg, paroxe-tine 40–50 mg) may be required, although one recent study showed that doses traditionally effective for depression do work. Response can take 10 to 12 weeks, so premature termination of medication trials should be avoided. Although 70% of patients respond to some degree, most are left with residual symptoms. Only about 10–15% of patients have full remis-sions. The average partial responder has a 40% reduction in symptoms. In

OCD, however, that may mean three to five more hours of good functioning each day—a big improvement. Most patients stay on medication chronically; about 85% relapse in a month or two after stopping medication.

Behavioral therapy. A combination of behavioral therapy and antidepressants are generally recommended for OCD patients. Behavioral approaches have been moderately successful, particularly with patients who have compulsions. Graded exposure and response prevention are usually used for the compulsions. For example, a hand-washer might be taken into a "contaminated" place and prevented from washing his hands for two minutes. Catastrophic thoughts are identified and the patient may watch his anxiety peak and then subside. In another case, a man who fears contamination if he touches anything without wearing gloves is directed to not wear gloves for half an hour and to touch a variety of feared objects (i.e., food, newspapers, silverware, old sweat socks). Eventually, he becomes desensitized to touching these objects.

Surgery. Cingulotomy has been used occasionally for very severe, very treatment-resistant cases. As noted, about 25–30% of these patients substantially benefit from this (Jenike et al., 1991).

POST-TRAUMATIC STRESS DISORDER

Post-traumatic stress disorder (PTSD) occurs after a severe and extraordinary stressor: a massive fire, hurricane, holocaust, rape, mugging, military combat, or terrorist bombing. The stressful events are usually more than "normal" bereavement, chronic illness, business losses, divorce, etc.

Hours or months following the stressor, patients waver between the two main stages of PTSD: re-experiencing (also called intrusion) and avoidance of the event. Often, *avoidance* or *denial* comes first, with "psychic numbing" dominating. Patients minimize the significance of the stress, forget it happened, feel detached from others, lose interest in life, display constricted affect, daydream, and abuse drugs or alcohol. In the re-experiencing stage, patients are hypervigilant, "on edge," and flooded by intrusive images (e.g., illusions, hypnogogic hallucinations, true hallucinations, nightmares, mental images). They cannot sleep or concentrate; they ruminate about the stressor, cry "without reason," show emotional lability, are startled or upset by the slightest reminders of the trauma, and develop somatic anxiety. Patients compulsively relive the stressful event, are often unable to think about anything else, and fear "going crazy." (In *DSM-IV*'s criteria for PTSD [Table 11-7], the avoidance phase is generally covered under criterion C and the re-experiencing phase under B.)

Normal and pathological responses to traumatic events are usually, but

TABLE 11-7
DSM-IV **Criteria for Posttraumatic Stress Disorder***

A. The person has been exposed to a traumatic event in which both of the following were present:

   (1) the person experienced, witnessed, or was confronted with an event or events that involved actual or threatened death or serious injury, or a threat to the physical integrity of self or others
   (2) the person's response involved intense fear, helplessness, or horror. **Note:** In children, this may be expressed instead by disorganized or agitated behavior.

B. The traumatic event is persistently reexperienced in one (or more) of the following ways:

   (1) recurrent and intrusive distressing recollections of the event, including images, thoughts, or perceptions. **Note:** In young children, repetitive play may occur in which themes or aspects of the trauma are expressed.
   (2) recurrent distressing dreams of the event. **Note:** In children, there may be frightening dreams without recognizable content.
   (3) acting or feeling as if the traumatic event were recurring (includes a sense of reliving the experience, illusions, hallucinations, and dissociative flashback episodes, including those that occur upon awakening or when intoxicated). **Note:** In young children, trauma-specific reenactment may occur.
   (4) intense psychological distress at exposure to internal or external cues that symbolize or resemble an aspect of the traumatic event
   (5) physiologic reactivity upon exposure to internal or external cues that symbolize or resemble an aspect of the traumatic event

C. Persistent avoidance of stimuli associated with the trauma and numbing of general responsiveness (not present before the trauma), as indicated by three (or more) of the following:

   (1) efforts to avoid thoughts, feelings, or conversations associated with the trauma
   (2) efforts to avoid activities, places, or people that arouse recollections of the trauma
   (3) inability to recall an important aspect of the trauma
   (4) markedly diminished interest or participation in significant activities
   (5) feeling of detachment or estrangement from others
   (6) restricted range of affect (e.g., unable to have loving feelings)
   (7) sense of a foreshortened future (e.g., does not expect to have a career, marriage, children, or a normal life span)

D. Persistent symptoms of increased arousal (not present before the trauma), as indicated by two (or more) of the following:

   (1) difficulty falling or staying asleep
   (2) irritability or outbursts of anger
   (3) difficulty concentrating
   (4) hypervigilance
   (5) exaggerated startle response

(continued)

TABLE 11–7
(*Continued*)

E. Duration of the disturbance (symptoms in Criteria B, C, and D) is more than 1 month.

F. The disturbance causes clinically significant distress or impairment in social, occupational, or other important areas of functioning.

Specify if:
    Acute: if duration of symptoms is less than 3 months
    Chronic: if duration of symptoms is 3 months or more
Specify if:
    With Delayed Onset: if onset of symptoms is at least 6 months after the stressor

*DSM-IV, pp. 427–29.

not always, easy to distinguish (see Figure 11-1). Normal responders react with sadness or anxiety and find it harder to acknowledge guilt, rage or shame. They may undergo periods of denial and intrusion. They often go through stages similar to those associated with grief, but without resolution. Indeed, this is one of the few times that producing symptoms is healthy.

There is a very brief (less than four weeks) variation of PTSD called Acute Stress Disorder (see Table 11-8). PTSD disorder has three subtypes: the *acute* form lasts less than three months; the *chronic*, three months or more; and the *delayed-onset* form emerges at least six months past the trauma.

The delayed subtype has the worst prognosis. A study of 26 Vietnam and 10 World War II veterans with delayed PTSD showed that *all* of them had an additional psychiatric disorder during their lives—most often, alcoholism or depression. PTSD arose first in all but four of these cases. Two-thirds of these patients had family members with a psychiatric disorder, usually substance abuse or an anxiety disorder. In both subtypes, encountering a circumstance similar to the original stressor often aggravates or rekindles symptoms. The intensity and duration of symptoms are usually less severe if the trauma is caused by nature (e.g., hurricane) than people (e. g., rape, torture).

After spending four years in a Korean POW camp, an ex-marine returned to his Indiana home. That was April. He felt fine until December, when seeing the first snow unleashed memories of being a POW. He broke into hot and cold flashes, arose screaming from nightmares (of cats with oriental eyes), stared blankly at food, stuttered, and was unable to study. Images of being yelled at, beaten, bleed-

FIGURE 11-1
Sequential Responses to Trauma*

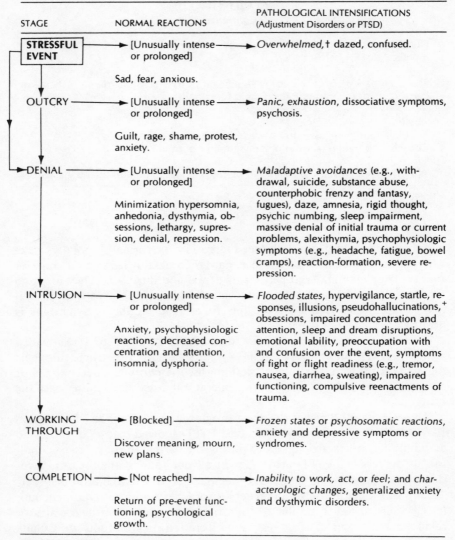

STAGE	NORMAL REACTIONS	PATHOLOGICAL INTENSIFICATIONS (Adjustment Disorders or PTSD)
STRESSFUL EVENT	[Unusually intense or prolonged] Sad, fear, anxious.	*Overwhelmed*,† dazed, confused.
OUTCRY	[Unusually intense or prolonged] Guilt, rage, shame, protest, anxiety.	*Panic, exhaustion*, dissociative symptoms, psychosis.
DENIAL	[Unusually intense or prolonged] Minimization hypersomnia, anhedonia, dysthymia, obsessions, lethargy, supression, denial, repression.	*Maladaptive avoidances* (e.g., withdrawal, suicide, substance abuse, counterphobic frenzy and fantasy, fugues), daze, amnesia, rigid thought, psychic numbing, sleep impairment, massive denial of initial trauma or current problems, alexithymia, psychophysiologic symptoms (e.g., headache, fatigue, bowel cramps), reaction-formation, severe repression.
INTRUSION	[Unusually intense or prolonged] Anxiety, psychophysiologic reactions, decreased concentration and attention, insomnia, dysphoria.	*Flooded states*, hypervigilance, startle, responses, illusions, pseudohallucinations,+ obsessions, impaired concentration and attention, sleep and dream disruptions, emotional lability, preoccupation with and confusion over the event, symptoms of fight or flight readiness (e.g., tremor, nausea, diarrhea, sweating), impaired functioning, compulsive reenactments of trauma.
WORKING THROUGH	[Blocked] Discover meaning, mourn, new plans.	*Frozen states* or *psychosomatic reactions*, anxiety and depressive symptoms or syndromes.
COMPLETION	[Not reached] Return of pre-event functioning, psychological growth.	*Inability to work, act, or feel*; and *characterologic changes*, generalized anxiety and dysthymic disorders.

*Modified from: Horowitz, M. J. (1985). Disasters and psychological responses to stress. *Psychiatric Annals*, 15, 161–167.

†Main features are italicized.

+Pseudohallucinations are fantasized reactions, in which people intensely experience something as real, despite intellectually knowing otherwise. These may be the "felt presence" of a dead granddad or an "out of body" experience.

TABLE 11–8
DSM-IV* Criteria for Acute Stress Disorder

A. The person has been exposed to a traumatic event in which both of the following were present:

    (1) the person experienced, witnessed, or was confronted with an event or events that involved actual or threatened death or serious injury, or a threat to the physical integrity of self or others

    (2) the person's response involved intense fear, helplessness, or horror

B. Either while experiencing or immediately after experiencing the distressing event, the individual has three (or more) of the following dissociative symptoms:

    (1) a subjective sense of numbing, detachment, or absence of emotional responsiveness

    (2) a reduction in awareness of his or her surroundings (e.g., "being in a daze")

    (3) derealization

    (4) depersonalization

    (5) dissociative amnesia (i.e., inability to recall an important aspect of the trauma)

C. The traumatic event is persistently reexperienced in at least one of the following ways: recurrent images, thoughts, dreams, illusions, flashback episodes, or a sense of reliving the experience; or distress on exposure to reminders of the traumatic event.

D. Marked avoidance of stimuli that arouse recollections of the trauma (e.g., thoughts, feelings, conversations, activities, places, people).

E. Marked symptoms of anxiety or increased arousal (e.g., difficulty sleeping, irritability, poor concentration, hypervigilance, exaggerated startle response, motor restlessness).

F. The disturbance causes clinically significant distress or impairment in social, occupational, or other important areas of functioning or impairs the individual's ability to pursue some necessary task, such as obtaining necessary assistance or mobilizing personal resources by telling family members about the traumatic experience.

G. The disturbance lasts for a minimum of 2 days and a maximum of 4 weeks and occurs within 4 weeks of the traumatic event.

H. The disturbance is not due to the direct physiological effects of a substance (e.g., a drug of abuse, a medication) or a general medical condition, is not better accounted for by Brief Psychotic Disorder, and is not merely an exacerbation of a preexisting Axis I or Axis II disorder.

*DSM-IV, pp. 431–32.

ing, and freezing in the snowy camp flooded his mind, despite all efforts to stop them. Four weeks of twice weekly psychotherapy uncovered considerable (irrational) bitterness at his fellow marines for not preventing his capture, and rage at his family and government for not being more sympathetic to his plight as a POW. After some family counseling, his delayed PTSD ended.

In men, military experience is the most common cause of PTSD and in women rape, sexual, and/or physical abuse. Men entering the military who are most likely to get PTSD are younger, have had less military training, were previously emotionally or physically abused, or already have had some psychiatric symptoms. Particularly severe traumas involving witnessing the death or dismemberment of buddies, witnessing or participating in atrocities, repeated endangerment to the self, and physical injury with permanent disability are more likely to cause chronic and severe PTSD (Kulk et al., 1990). Women who have been raped are more likely to develop PTSD if physical force, display of a weapon, or injury to the victim occurred (Bownes, O'Gorman, & Sayers, 1991). They also tend to have more acute guilt, shame, and suicidal ideation (Dahl, 1989). A woman who was sexually abused in childhood by a male is less likely to develop PTSD if she had a supportive mother who intervened and an overall positive family environment. Later, a gentle, caring boyfriend can help a woman desensitize to her trauma and to men in general. Women with PTSD from childhood sexual abuse may display less obvious but highly related symptoms, such as going to bed fully clothed with a night light on, having insomnia until dawn comes, and then sleeping well. These are all understandable responses to being regularly sexually abused at bedtime or during the night. A dissociative disorder more often accompanies PTSD induced by childhood trauma.

This disorder can occur at any age, but children and the elderly general have a more difficult time coping with traumatic events. Studies conducted after the San Fernando earthquake of 1971 and the Chowchilla bus kidnapping in 1976 demonstrated the effects of significant trauma on children. In the latter instance, all 25 kidnapping victims who had been held for 27 hours (16 of those hours, they were buried in their school bus) demonstrated pessimism, shame, increased fearfulness, repeated nightmares, and related symptoms four years after the trauma. Frequently, traumatized children stop thinking about the future, feeling that they have none. Childhood trauma more often results in dissociative experiences, self-injurious behavior, difficulties with impulse control, traumatic reenactments, social isolation, and profound restrictions in emotional responsiveness (Terr, 1991). There are no data on sex ratio, familial pattern, or prevalence of this disorder.

Differential Diagnosis

On one hand, PTSD may go undiagnosed because (a) patients don't report the initial trauma or the subsequent symptoms, (b) substance abuse masks the symptoms, or (c) their traumatic visual imagery is misattributed to schizophrenia, LSD intoxication or flashbacks, temporal lobe epilepsy, or a dissociative disorder. On the other hand, when PTSD is used to justify financial compensation, malingering might be the diagnosis. Differentiating PTSD from *malingering* can be difficult, partly because the patient may no longer be able to distinguish reality from fabrication. People who deliberately malinger may not present with the specific diagnostic criteria in *DSM-IV*, but rather display their own version of what they (or television) consider madness. Careful coaching by an attorney or others may later help them get the symptoms "right." The differential diagnosis includes the other *anxiety disorders, major depression, compensation neurosis,* and *adjustment disorder. Adjustment disorder with anxiety* should not be confused with PTSD. Adjustment disorders are triggered by more ordinary stressors (e.g., exams to graduate from college, a court hearing, or an impending wedding). Over 95% of PTSD patients have a past psychiatric disorder of some kind and over 50% have an additional current diagnosis.

Management and Treatment

Debriefing immediately after the trauma can reduce the victim's chances of developing PTSD. A typical two-hour debriefing includes four stages: (1) disclosure of events; (2) exploration of troubling reactions; (3) identification of practical coping strategies; and (4) exploration of feelings about leaving the disaster, plan of action regarding transition, and requests for referrals (Marmar & Freeman, 1988). Often the trauma victim will accept support only from a person who has experienced a similar trauma. This is based on the mistaken belief that a person who has had the same experience will automatically understand and empathize with the victim. A well-functioning support group can be especially helpful for those temporarily overwhelmed by the trauma by providing practical support reinforcing the victim's reactions as "normal," addressing common fears, concerns, and traumatic memories, increasing the capacity to tolerate disturbing emotions, and sharing strategies for coping (Marmar et al., 1988). In psychodynamic therapy, former adaptive defenses are restored and a safe therapeutic environment is established before traumatic memories are gradually and gently explored. In cognitive-behavioral therapy, exposure approaches are used to reduce fear responses to both the original trauma and present reminders. Cognitive restructuring methods focus on distorted views of the original trauma and subsequent changes in basic life assumptions regarding self-invulnerability, life meaningfulness, and equitability and positive self-esteem (Janoff-Bulman, 1985).

Acute PTSD may remit spontaneously; mild and acute cases may respond to supportive psychotherapy; chronic (more than five months) and severe cases may require more intensive psychotherapy. Individual or group therapy for chronic and severe cases involves active confrontation of feared topics and memories, examining misinterpretation of the events, and developing better methods of coping with the trauma. Most chronic cases do not remit spontaneously and, if untreated, continue for decades or a lifetime and spawn associated substance abuse, mood, panic, or phobic disorders, and occupational and interpersonal impairments. These must also be a focus of therapy. Medications are often indicated, since phobic and anxiety symptoms and major depressive disorder are often dominant features that interfere with psychotherapy.

Medications for PTSD can be used adjunctively for some symptoms. The MAOI phenelzine may be more effective than imipramine in treating PTSD. Both drugs can reduce intrusion symptoms such as nightmares, flashbacks, and intrusive recollections, but phenelzine is better for social withdrawal and numbing. An eight-week trial might be needed to show full effect (Solomon, Gerrity, & Muff, 1992). The anticonvulsant carbamazepine increases behavioral control, particularly for irritability and aggression (Wolf, Alavi, & Mosnaim, 1988). The adrenergic blockers such as propranolol and clonidine can decrease anger and the physiologic components of PTSD (e.g., excessive startle response). Benzodiazepines have not been shown to work and may disinhibit. MAOIs should not be used in substance abusers, because of the risk of hypertensive crisis from a drug-MAOI interaction. Trazodone can be used safely for insomnia in this population.

GENERALIZED ANXIETY DISORDER

Very little is known about generalized anxiety disorder (GAD). Also unknown are GAD's natural history, etiology, and predisposing factors. Not surprisingly, some experts believe that GAD is not a specific disorder, but merely a residual category for the anxiety disorders. Yet in a study of 108 highly anxious patients, those with anticipatory anxiety had phobic or panic disorders, whereas those without anticipatory anxiety were characterized by chronic worry and apprehensive expectation in multiple life situations (Barlow, Blanchard, Vermilyea, Vermilyea, & DiNardo, 1986). Although these findings suggest that GAD is a valid clinical disorder, in practice, patients are frequently assigned to this diagnosis when they have some of the features of the other disorders, but do not meet diagnostic criteria. With these reservations in mind, the ECA study (Robins & Regier, 1991) reported that the lifetime prevalence of GAD is 8.5%; the one-year prevalence is 3.0%. Women had more than twice the one-year prevalence of men.

Clinical Presentation

These patients are chronic worry-warts. During a majority of their days, they are tense, highly distractible, irritable, restless, and so "on edge" that they're often fatigued and mildly depressed. (Unrelenting anxiety is, by itself, very exhausting.) The anxiety is diffuse, unfocused, free-floating, and ongoing; it may or may not be accompanied by prominent physical complaints such as sweating, dizziness, clammy hands, tachycardia. When somatic symptoms dominate, patients tend to consult numerous medical specialists, chiropractors, physiotherapists, or nutritionists, which may lead them to fad diets and substance abuse. GAD also impairs social and occupational functioning. The *DSM-IV* criteria are listed in Table 11-9.

Differential Diagnosis

As discussed earlier, drugs and medical conditions commonly mimic GAD. Patients with early *schizophrenia* with extensive anxiety also manifest disorganized thinking, will be suspicious and distrustful, and may appear to be emotionally remote, with very constricted affect. A *mood disorder* is the most common diagnosis (more than 50%) in patients presenting with anxiety. Differentiating anxiety from *depression* is somewhat difficult. Since the frequency of mixed anxiety and depression is perhaps as high as 50%, patients complaining mainly of anxiety who have definite symptoms of the depressive syndrome should be treated as having depression. Antidepressants have been shown to be more effective than antianxiety agents in this group. While these anxious depressives may not complain of depression, they usually do experience anhedonia, a distinct loss of pleasure in situations that were formerly enjoyable, along with other classic depressive symptoms such as insomnia, anorexia, and fatigue.

Panic disorder is the second most common diagnosis in patients presenting with anxiety. It may be confused with GAD, since chronic anxiety often occurs between panic attacks; yet unlike GAD, panic disorder has distinct episodes of intense anxiety. In *phobic disorder* the patient's anxiety is specific for the phobic stimulus, whereas in GAD it unfocused and continual.

TABLE 11–9
DSM-IV Criteria for Generalized Anxiety Disorder*

A. Excessive anxiety and worry (apprehensive expectation), occurring more days than not for at least 6 months, about a number of events or activities (such as work or school performance).

B. The person finds it difficult to control the worry.

C. The anxiety and worry are associated with three (or more) of the following six symptoms (with at least some symptoms present for more days than not for the past 6 months). **Note:** Only one item is required in children.

  (1) restlessness or feeling keyed up or on edge
  (2) being easily fatigued
  (3) difficulty concentrating or mind going blank
  (4) irritability
  (5) muscle tension
  (6) sleep disturbance (difficulty falling or staying asleep, or restless unsatisfying sleep)

D. The focus of the anxiety and worry is not confined to features of an Axis I disorder, e.g., the anxiety or worry is not about having a Panic Attack (as in Panic Disorder), being embarrassed in public (as in Social Phobia), being contaminated (as in Obsessive-Compulsive Disorder), being away from home or close relatives (as in Separation Anxiety Disorder), gaining weight (as in Anorexia Nervosa), having multiple physical complaints (as in Somatization Disorder), or having a serious illness (as in Hypochondriasis), and the anxiety and worry do not occur exclusively during Posttraumatic Stress Disorder.

E. The anxiety, worry, or physical symptoms cause clinically significant distress or impairment in social, occupational, or other important areas of functioning.

F. The disturbance is not due to the direct physiological effects of a substance (e.g., a drug of abuse, a medication) or a general medical condition (e.g., hyperthyroidism) and does not occur exclusively during a Mood Disorder, a Psychotic Disorder, or a Pervasive Developmental Disorder.

DSM-IV, pp. 435–36.

The somatic complaints of GAD may resemble *hypochondriasis*, but the hypochondriac more gravely exaggerates the danger of his symptoms and is a "specialist" in the fear of disease.

Management and Treatment

Psychotherapies. Several studies show that psychotherapy of various kinds is as effective as medication for all but a minority of patients. All psychotherapies seek to identify the stressors producing the anxiety, offer better means of handling stress, and eliminate dietary or physical sources of anxiety. Insight-oriented psychotherapies will explore the *unconscious* and symbolic meanings of the patient's anxiety and clarify its defensive and "signal" functions. In cognitive therapy, patients identify the precise events or circumstances that trigger *conscious* dysphoric "automatic thoughts" and then develop more rational ways of thinking and feeling in response to the same stressors.

Behavior therapy. Muscle relaxation, meditation, biofeedback, and autogenic training are frequently employed either by themselves or as supplements to the previously mentioned therapies.

Pharmacotherapy. Buspirone, a novel anxiolytic with no sedative or amnestic properties and no risk of dependence, is probably the safest drug for chronic anxiety. Begin with doses of 5 mg TID and titrate up to 20 mg TID. Response takes four to six weeks and the drug may work better in patients with additional symptoms of mild depression and prominent cognitive, ruminative symptoms of anxiety. There is no "buzz" with buspirone; patients should be told that it will take the edge off of their anxiety but will not eliminate it. Benzodiazepines can be used as treatment of acute, paralyzing exacerbations of anxiety. Generally, these should be prescribed for limited durations, such as two to four weeks, to avoid long-term physical and psychological dependence. Patients who are primarily distressed by the physiologic symptoms of anxiety such as increased heart rate or "butterflies" may respond well to beta-blockers. Several studies have reported that both sedating and non-sedating antidepressants are effective for GAD without depression.

A treatment manual for patients and therapists has been developed by Craske, Barlow, and O'Leary (1992) entitled *Mastery of Your Anxiety and Worry*.

CHAPTER 12

Somatoform Disorders

DOCTOR: It's all in your head.
PATIENT: But it's *not* in my head; it's in my stomach.

What the doctor considers reassurance the patient may consider an accusation. The doctor says that nothing is *physically* wrong with the patient, but the patient hears that *nothing* is wrong. Yet there *is* something wrong: The patient's stomach hurts. Even when psychological factors produce the pain, for the patient that pain is just as real and just as miserable. When the physician ignores this central fact, the patient feels accused of being a fake or crazy.

Patients with psychogenic physical symptoms frustrate professionals because they don't have "real" illnesses, don't respond to conventional medical treatments, shop around for doctors, are stubbornly unpsychological, and dwell on their physical complaints. The professional claims the patient's physical problems are psychogenic, and because the patient disagrees, he or she is, in essence, rejecting the professional's expertise.

Consequently, these patients receive lousy care. Not knowing what else to do and succumbing to the patients' demands for medication, physicians often prescribe drugs, expecting them not to work. These medications are frequently hypnoanxiolytics and patients become addicted. (At least now they have a "real" problem!) These patients undergo countless tests, procedures, and operations—mostly useless. In comparison to controls, somatoform disorder patients have three times the weight of body organs removed surgically (Cohen, Robins, Purtell, Altmann, & Reid, 1953). Sensing, often correctly, that doctors consider them "crocks" and "gomers," these patients distrust doctors and don't follow their advice. Yet they also feel helplessly dependent on doctors and glom onto them, causing further alienation. In a "no-win situation," these patients distrust the very doctors they must rely on.

Fortunately, in recent years imprecise labeling and name-calling have been replaced by a relatively valid and helpful system for diagnosis. Also, there are now genuinely effective treatments for many of these conditions. In *DSM-IV*, somatoform disorders are those in which patients have physical symptoms that cannot be fully explained by medical findings or known physiological mechanisms; if there are medical findings, these patients' complaints or impairment exceed what would be expected. There must also be positive evidence, or at least a strong presumption, that psychological factors play an important role in the onset, severity, exacerbation, or maintenance of symptoms. As with ulcers, the presence of psychological factors does not mean the symptoms have no physical basis. Either these underlying physiologic mechanisms are yet to be discovered, or the diagnostic technology to detect already known ones is still lacking.

For example, a 40-year-old lawyer had been plagued by episodic unexpected orgastic feelings running up and down his legs for seven years. After two normal EEGs and three psychotherapies "to resolve psychosexual conflicts," a fine metal electrode was painlessly inserted into his thalamus and revealed that he'd been having sensory seizures. Anticonvulsant medications cured his "psychosexual conflicts."

Somatoform disorders differ from three other psychiatric conditions that generate symptoms resembling physical illness. In *malingering* and *factitious disorders*, patients deliberately make and fake symptoms, whereas in somatoform disorders, symptoms are produced involuntarily. In *psychological factors affecting physical condition*, often called "psychosomatic disorders," emotional factors trigger, aggravate, or exacerbate a clearly existing medical condition, such as ulcers or hypertension, through a known pathophysiologic mechanism, whereas in many somatoform disorders there is no identifiable medical disease nor any known pathophysiologic mechanism to account for the patient's symptoms.

DSM-IV describes six major somatoform disorders: (a) somatization disorder, (b) conversion disorder, (c) hypochondriasis, (d) body dysmorphic disorder, (e) psychogenic pain disorder, and (f) undifferentiated somatoform disorder.

SOMATIZATION DISORDER

Clinical Presentation

Somatization disorder—also named "Briquet's syndrome" after the French physician who first described it in 1859—is a chronic condition featuring multiple, unexplained, somatic symptoms in numerous organ systems. Vomiting, aphonia (inability to produce sounds), painful limbs, muscle weakness, dizziness, painful menstruation, burning sensations in sex organs, paralyses, and conversion symptoms are common. Table 12–1 presents *DSM-IV* criteria for somatization disorder.

As "few" as eight unexplained or excessive symptoms distributed in the

TABLE 12–1
DSM-IV Criteria for Somatization Disorder*

A. A history of many physical complaints beginning before age 30 years, that occur over a period of several years and result in treatment being sought or significant impairment in social, occupational, or other important areas of functioning.

B. Each of the following criteria must have been met, with individual symptoms occurring at any time during the course of the disturbance:

　(1) *four pain symptoms*: a history of pain related to at least four different sites or functions (e.g., head, abdomen, back, joints, extremities, chest, rectum, during menstruation, during sexual intercourse, or during urination)

　(2) *two gastrointestinal symptoms*: a history of at least two gastrointestinal symptoms other than pain (such as nausea, bloating, vomiting other than during pregnancy, diarrhea, or intolerance of several different foods)

　(3) *one sexual symptom*: a history of at least one sexual or reproductive symptom other than pain (e.g., sexual indifference, erectile or ejaculatory dysfunction, irregular menses, excessive menstrual bleeding, vomiting throughout pregnancy)

　(4) *one pseudoneurological symptom*: a history of at least one symptom or deficit suggesting a neurological condition not limited to pain (conversion symptoms such as impaired coordination or balance, paralysis or localized weakness, difficulty swallowing or lump in throat, aphonia, urinary retention, hallucinations, loss of touch or pain sensation, double vision, blindness, deafness, seizures; dissociative symptoms such as amnesia; or loss of consciousness other than fainting)

C. Either (1) or (2):

　(1) after appropriate investigation, each of the symptoms in Criterion B cannot be fully explained by a known general medical condition or the direct effects of a substance (e.g., a drug of abuse, a medication)

　(2) when there is a related general medical condition, the physical complaints or resulting social or occupational impairment are in excess of what would be expected from the history, physical examination, or laboratory findings

D. The symptoms are not intentionally produced or feigned (as in Factitious Disorder or Malingering).

DSM-IV, pp. 449–450.

right way can qualify a person for somatization disorder. This is a little simpler than *DSM-III*, which listed 37 symptoms; women with 14 and men with 12 symptoms qualified for the diagnosis. Still it is not easy to remember all the possible symptoms. For clinical convenience, Othmer and De-Souza (1985) found that the presence of any two out of seven specific symptoms predicted the correct diagnosis of *DSM-III* somatization disorder in 80–90% of cases; they incorporated this finding into the screening test outlined in Table 12–2.

Everyone has physical symptoms, but they mostly ignore them. Not so for patients with somatization disorder. For every ache and pain they will see a doctor, want a complete workup, and expect a prescription. (Any patient who enters a doctor's office with three dozen medications has a

TABLE 12–2
Screening Test for Somatization Disorder*

MNEMONIC	SYMPTOM	ORGAN SYSTEM
S omatization	Shortness of breath	Respiratory
D isorder	Dysmenorrhea	Female reproductive
B esets	Burning in sex organs	Psychosexual
L adies	Lump in throat	Pseudoneurological
A nd	Amnesia	Pseudoneurological
V exes	Vomiting	Gastrointestinal
P hysicians	Painful extremities	Skeletal muscle

Questions used to assess the presence of the seven symptoms of the screening test for somatization disorder:

S. Have you ever had trouble breathing?
D. Have you ever had frequent trouble with menstrual cramps?
B. Have you ever had burning sensations in your sexual organs, mouth, or rectum?
L. Have you ever had difficulties swallowing or had an uncomfortable lump in your throat that stayed with you for at least an hour?
A. Have you ever found that you could not remember what you had been doing for hours or days at a time? (If yes) Did this happen even though you had not been drinking or taking drugs?
V. Have you ever had trouble from frequent vomiting?
P. Have you ever had frequent pain in your fingers or toes?

If any two of the above seven questions are answered affirmatively, this *screening* test is positive; a positive test simply means the patient *might* have a somatization disorder. To confirm the diagnosis, the patient should meet *DSM-IV* criteria for somatization disorder (Table 12–1).

*This table is adapted from Othmer, E., & DeSouza, C. (1985). A screening test for somatization disorder (hysteria). *American Journal of Psychiatry, 142,* 1146–1149.

somatization disorder till proven otherwise.) These patients don't just present symptoms, they dramatize them: "I'm puking like a volcano." "I almost fainted in front of a bus." "I'm breathing so hard, I'm going to suffocate." Hyperbole is their norm: Headaches aren't headaches, they're "the worst headaches ever." Their histories are vague; it's never clear when their symptoms began, why they seek help now, and what they want. On repeated tellings, symptoms "change": One day a backache is dull, the next day it's sharp; one day it began 12 months ago, on the next visit it started a month ago. Symptoms never end; as soon as the clinician thinks he's heard them all, another pops up. However, these histrionics should not mislead clinicians into underestimating these patients' genuine discomfort.

Somatization disorder usually arises during adolescence, but always before age 30. Its course is fluctuating, lifelong, and exacerbated by environmental stressors—a fact deemed irrelevant or accusatory by the patient. Hardly a year passes without intense discomfort and medical treatment. Frequent complications are substance abuse, excessive laboratory tests and surgery (and its complications), work and social impairment, chronic demoralization, dysthymia, anxiety, marital problems, and divorce. The disorder is important to diagnose, if only to reduce these complications. These patients commonly attempt suicide, but rarely commit it.

Epidemiology

Somatization disorder is rarely diagnosed in men. Reported lifetime prevalence rates range widely from 0.1% to 2.0%. The ECA found its prevalence in the general population to be 0.1%. Its frequency among general psychiatric patients is reported to range from 1.1% to 6.0%, whereas among medical/surgical patients referred for psychiatric consultation, it may be as high as 14%. In the United States it occurs more among African-Americans, lower socioeconomic groups, and less formally educated people.

Etiology and Pathogenesis

About 20% of first-degree female relatives of these patients will have a somatization disorder—that's roughly 20 times the normal frequency for women in the general population. Somatization disorder appears to be genetically and environmentally linked to antisocial personality disorder and alcoholism. Adopted children have a higher risk for alcoholism, antisocial personality, and somatization disorder if they have a biological parent or an adoptive parent with any of these disorders.

Family studies reveal a high prevalence of antisocial personality disorder and alcoholism among the *male* relatives of somatization patients. Conversely, there's an increased prevalence of somatization disorder among the *female* relatives of convicted male felons. Many delinquent girls develop somatization disorder as adults, and adult female felons have an increased prevalence of medical contacts (Goodwin & Guze, 1989).

Somatization is often considered a defense mechanism in which the patient unconsciously avoids painful affects by experiencing physical discomfort. Supposedly, the central defense mechanism is somatization and the painful affect, depressive. Indeed, alexithymia, the inability to recognize and express feelings, has been especially associated with somatization disorder. Other studies reveal that patients with somatization disorder are more troubled by confused and negative self-identities (Oxman, Rosenberg, Schnurr, & Tucker, 1985) and have higher rates of childhood sexual abuse. For some, somatization may be learned from a parent with somatization. In others, physical symptoms may have been the only or best way to get attention or escape abuse.

Differential Diagnosis

Hypochondriasis and somatization disorder share many features, including an early and gradual onset. However, in somatization disorder patients focus on *symptoms* of disease, whereas hypochondriacs are preoccupied with a *fear* of disease. Hypochondriasis may appear in somatization disorder, but not as the dominant symptom.

A *schizophrenic* or *psychotically depressed* patient with multiple somatic delusions — "Insects are eating my liver" — may look like a somatization disorder, but true somatization patients specialize only in nondelusional complaints. Patients with *dysthymia*, *generalized anxiety*, *major depression*, and *panic disorder* all complain about physical symptoms more than normal, but they rarely meet full criteria for somatization disorder. Most do not have a pseudoneurological symptom. However, somatization disorder can be diagnosed concurrently with any of these psychiatric disorders. In *factitious disorder* and *malingering*, symptoms are intentionally produced. Certain *medical conditions* mimic somatization disorder and need to be ruled out. For example, multiple sclerosis, systemic lupus erythematosus, porphyria, and hyperparathyroidism can all cause vague, multiple, and confusing somatic symptoms.

Management and Treatment

Since most of these patients are leery of psychiatry, they rely on nonpsychiatric, especially primary-care, physicians. Doctors can greatly help these patients if they remember to do the following: (a) Repeatedly check their own annoyance; since somatization disorders are chronic, lifelong conditions, being angry at these patients for complaining about symptoms is akin to being angry at diabetics for having uncooperative blood sugars. (b) The primary goal of treatment is not to eliminate patients' physical complaints but to improve their functioning. (c) Avoid raising false hopes or promises, such as, "You're going to feel completely better." (d) Protect patients from needless laboratory tests, medical treatments, and surgical interventions. (e) Relate to patients "as they are": Try changing their personality and the only change will be one less patient. (f) Offer positive reinforcement for "noncomplaining behaviors," ignore complaining behaviors, and teach the families to do likewise.

More specifically: On her first visit to the doctor, a patient with somatization disorder should receive a thorough history and physical. Assuming this examination is "negative," the doctor should tell her, "I'm pleased there is nothing *seriously* wrong with you, but I know you're experiencing considerable discomfort. So I want to follow you carefully and see you in a (week, two weeks, or a month—doctor's choice)." An appointment is made, whether or not the patient has symptoms; therefore, the patient doesn't *have* to get sick to see the doctor. The scheduled interval between visits should coincide with doctor-going frequency, but as-needed visits should be discouraged. At the next appointment, the doctor conducts a briefer exam, repeats the same message, and schedules another appointment. Each week, the doctor devotes full attention to the patient for 15 minutes, telling her how marvelously she's doing despite her symptoms, lauds her planned trip to Arizona, restates that she doesn't have cancer and that nothing else is seriously wrong. Eventually, the patient not only *complains* less about symptoms, but actually *experiences* fewer symptoms.

Typically these patients are avoided by all because of their incessant complaining. They then become socially isolated, more miserable, and complain more. This approach can be amplified by having a family meeting to establish a very specific goal: from then on, the patient should not talk to family members or friends about her symptoms but only to an expert, her doctor. For a while she will not know what to talk about, but over time, normal social conversation gradually replaces the medical litany. After a good physician-patient alliance has been established, some instructions about symptoms may help; for example, that everybody has 1.7 weird-but-temporary symptoms a week, and that it is normal.

HYPOCHONDRIASIS

Clinical Presentation

Hypochondriasis is an overwhelming, persistent preoccupation with physical symptoms based on unrealistically ominous interpretations of physical signs or sensations. (The Greeks believed that the seat of these troubles was the *hypochondrion*, the area between the rib cage and the navel.) Hypochondriacs may have a physical disease, but what distinguishes them is their unrealistic and dire interpretation of it. As noted in the previous section, the somatization patients worry about *symptoms*, whereas hypochondriacs *fear* a serious disease—the symptoms being only harbingers. The somatization patient who coughs complains that it hurts; the hypochondriac who coughs concludes he has lung cancer. To the hypochondriac, a skipped heart beat is a heart attack, a headache, a brain tumor. Hypochondriacs may present with many symptoms in many organ systems, or they may have a single preoccupation, as does the "cardiac neurotic." *DSM-IV* criteria for hypochondriasis are listed in Table 12–3.

Hypochondriasis affects the sexes equally and usually begins between ages 20 and 30. Its severity fluctuates over time and it rarely stops completely or permanently. Hypochondriasis may or may not impair occupational and social functioning; it almost always strains patients, however, because needless operations and tests occur.

TABLE 12–3
DSM-IV* Criteria for Hypochondriasis

A. Preoccupation with fears of having, or the idea that one has, a serious disease based on the person's misinterpretation of bodily symptoms.

B. The preoccupation persists despite appropriate medical evaluation and reassurance.

C. The belief in Criterion A is not of delusional intensity (as in Delusional Disorder, Somatic Type) and is not restricted to a circumscribed concern about appearance (as in Body Dysmorphic Disorder).

D. The preoccupation causes clinically significant distress or impairment in social, occupational, or other important areas of functioning.

E. The duration of the disturbance is at least 6 months.

F. The preoccupation is not better accounted for by Generalized Anxiety Disorder, Obsessive-Compulsive Disorder, Panic Disorder, a Major Depressive Episode, Separation Anxiety, or another Somatoform Disorder.

Specify if:
    With Poor Insight: if, for most of the time during the current episode, the person does not recognize that the concern about having a serious illness is excessive or unreasonable

---

DSM-IV, p. 465.

Etiology and Pathogenesis

Little is known about the etiology of hypochondriasis, but it probably arises for a number of reasons: For some patients, secondary gain is crucial; for others the disorder may be a defense against low self-esteem or a fear of being defective; for still others, introjection may be paramount purpose—these patients "prefer" punishing themselves over being angry at others. Given the higher incidence of painful injuries and diseases among close relatives of hypochondriacs, identification may be a key influence on some patients. A previous legitimate medical illness also predisposes to hypochondriasis.

Differential Diagnosis

The differential diagnosis for hypochondriasis is the same as for somatization disorder. Unlike the delusions of *schizophrenia* or *psychotic depression*, in hypochondriasis the patient will entertain the possibility that another interpretation of the symptoms is valid. The hypochondriac has an overvalued idea but not a delusion. In *mood* and *anxiety disorders*, dread or misinterpretation of disease is not a central feature, nor is it usually a longstanding preoccupation.

Management and Treatment

Investigations of treatment for hypochondriasis are few and rarely controlled. Although hypnoanxiolytics diminish somatic symptoms in anxious patients and TCAs diminish somatic complaints in depression, most clinicians find that neither drug lessens hypochondriasis.

Some researchers (Fallon et al., 1993) have redefined hypochondriasis as a variant of obsessive-compulsive disorder: The patient has a symptom, then obsessively thinks about it with catastrophic expectations (obsession), and then goes to the doctor (the compulsion) to receive temporary reassurance. As with OCD, the relief is fleeting. Armed with this theory, patients with hypochondriasis have been successfully treated with high doses of fluoxetine (40–80 mg) given over eight to 12 weeks. As with most OCDs, response speed was slow, but in the end, more than 70% were substantially improved. They still thought about their bodies excessively, but were no longer driven by obsessive fears and the need to see a doctor.

In Kellner's (1982a, 1987) literature review, the beneficial interventions for hypochondriasis were *repeatedly* (a) giving patients the facts about their difficulties, (b) clarifying the difference between pain and the *experience* of pain, (c) describing how emotions affect the *perception* of physical sensations (e.g., "real" pain is experienced as more painful when one is anxious than when one is calm), (d) demonstrating how selective attention and suggestion contribute to overestimating a symptom's seriousness, (e) stressing that "life can go on" despite physical symptoms, (f) conveying acceptance and empathy for the hypochondriasis, and (g) applying the approach described for treating somatization disorder. Several studies indicate that these strategies yield complete or vast improvement in roughly 75% of hypochondriacs for one to three years, and for over three years in a third of the patients. In view of the generally unfavorable prognosis of this condition, these results are striking. Even if these findings reflect nothing more than a more invested physician, if that works, it's nothing to sneeze at.

CONVERSION DISORDER

Clinical Presentation

The cardinal feature of a conversion disorder is an involuntary loss or alteration of a function, which although resembling a physical disorder, appears to arise from psychological mechanisms. Conversion disorders usually consist of a single motor or neurological symptom (e.g., blindness, paralysis). Also common are tunnel vision, seizures, coordination disturbances, akinesia, dyskinesia, anosmia (no smell), anesthesia, and parathesias. A single non-neurological symptom may arise, such as pseudocyesis (false pregnancy). By *DSM-IV* criteria (Table 12–4), if pain is the only symptom, the diagnosis is psychogenic pain disorder; if the only disturbance is psychosexual, a psychosexual disorder is diagnosed.

The strong psychological evidence required for the diagnosis can assume various forms. The conversion symptom may have symbolic meaning to the patient: For example, pseudocyesis may represent a fear of, and wish for, pregnancy. Psychogenic vomiting may symbolize revulsion or disgust. Conversion symptoms may arise from unconscious mechanisms. (Freud was right some of the time.) For instance, a man developed paralysis of his right arm after discovering his wife in bed with his best friend. The arm had normal nerve conduction and muscle tone. During a sodium amytal interview, he told me (NW) that he used to be a fighter but quit after badly injuring a man in a bar fight. I asked him what would happen if his arm still worked. As he thrust his "paralyzed" arm out and nearly decked me, he said, "I'd kill the bastard, but then I could never live with myself."

Often the conversion is a medical impossibility. "Glove anesthesia," in which sensation is felt to stop evenly at the wrist, is neurologically impossi-

TABLE 12–4
DSM-IV* Criteria for Conversion Disorder

A. One or more symptoms or deficits affecting voluntary motor or sensory function that suggest a neurological or general medical condition.

B. Psychological factors are judged to be associated with the symptom or deficit because the initiation or exacerbation of the symptom or deficit is preceded by conflicts or other stressors.

C. The symptom or deficit is not intentionally produced or feigned (as in Factitious Disorder or Malingering).

D. The symptom or deficit cannot, after appropriate investigation, be fully explained by a general medical condition, or by the direct effects of a substance, or as a culturally sanctioned behavior or experience.

E. The symptom or deficit causes clinically significant distress or impairment in social, occupational, or other important areas of functioning or warrants medical evaluation.

F. The symptom or deficit is not limited to pain or sexual dysfunction, does not occur exclusively during the course of Somatization Disorder, and is not better accounted for by another mental disorder.

Specify type of symptom or deficit:
With Motor Symptom or Deficit
With Sensory Symptom or Deficit
With Seizures or Convulsions
With Mixed Presentation

*DSM-IV, p. 457.

ble (unless one's wrist is slashed!), but it conforms to the patient's conception of the nervous system. (Remember Frankenstein?)

Soon after the swine-flu vaccine was found to produce Guillain-Barré syndrome, an ascending paralysis *arising* from the feet, the author (JM) saw three cases of "Guillain-Barré" in the emergency room: These patients had a "paralysis," but they misread the newspapers: Their "paralysis" spread *downward*!

Although conversion patients are often said to have histrionic personalities, many do not. They are also known for displaying *la belle indifference*—a nonchalance to their impairment, which has the paradoxical effect of making the impairment more noticeable. This trait is of little diagnostic value, since it is also found in seriously ill medical patients who are stoic about their situation.

Conversion symptoms may begin at any age, but usually surface during adolescence and early adulthood. An acute psychosocial stressor generally triggers the symptom, which will arise suddenly, last for several days or weeks, and then stop abruptly. Conversion symptoms can persist for months or years. When this occurs, organic pathology must be re-evaluated, since many of these patients turn out to have neurological disease. Long-term conversion symptoms may cause disuse atrophy and muscle contractures. "Psychological contractures" also occur: Patients become so mired in the sick role that after a conversion symptom disappears, work and social functioning may remain impaired.

Epidemiology

Conversion disorder presents far less today than during Freud's time; back then, it mainly afflicted women. Today, it appears more around battlefronts and in military hospitals; its sex distribution is now equal, although globus hystericus (a discomfort in swallowing) is more common in females. Conversion symptoms are reported to be twice as prevalent among African-Americans than Caucasian Americans, they are more common in lower socioeconomic classes, and they occur more commonly in subcultures that consider these symptoms expectable, not crazy.

Etiology and Pathogenesis

A conversion symptom affords patients either *primary gain*—that is, it *protects* them from experiencing a painful underlying feeling—or *secondary gain*—that is, it *gratifies* them by enabling them to receive concern and support from others. For example, a nurse who cared for her dying father became "blind" immediately after his death. The psychological evidence for a conversion disorder was the temporal relation between the death and the symptom's onset. The primary gain from this "blindness" was that it prevented her from seeing her father dead; the secondary gain was the added sympathy she would receive. Moreover, because she interpreted her father's death as a profoundly personal/professional failure, her "blindness" unconsciously relieved her of guilt (primary gain) and protected her from others' blame (secondary gain). In the military, a "paralyzed" hand usually serves a secondary gain—to avoid firing a gun.

Clinicians should be careful in deciding what constitutes psychological evidence. Because environmental stressors occur all the time, only those of obviously substantial impact on the patient should qualify. Furthermore, if clinicians want to find something, almost anything can have unconscious significance. Consider psychogenic vomiting: If the reader tries, he or she surely can find something in his or her psyche to explain psychogenic vomiting.

Differential Diagnosis

Conversion disorder typically involves one symptom, whereas other *somatoform disorders* present with many symptoms in numerous organ systems (except for "undifferentiated somatoform disorder"). Patients with conversion disorders tend to minimize their problems; those with other somatoform disorders dramatize them. Conversion disorders arise suddenly, whereas *somatization disorder* and *hypochondriasis* emerge gradually. Unlike conversion disorders, there is no loss of function in hypochondriasis. Unlike *undifferentiated somatoform disorder*, symptoms tend to be dramatic and discrete, not vague and/or subjective (such as fatigue or loss of appetite).

Physical disorders, especially those with vague, episodic, and hard-to-document symptoms, must be considered, such as *multiple sclerosis* and *systemic lupus erythematosus*. Since it is common for a neurological disorder to be uncovered a full decade after symptoms first present, *all* patients with a longstanding conversion symptom should be evaluated *repeatedly* for underlying medical conditions.

Management and Treatment

Because many conversion symptoms spontaneously disappear within a few weeks to months of their onset, very early treatment may be unnecessary. Therapy aims to temporarily remove patients from the situation that has overwhelmed their usual coping mechanisms, to reassure them that they will soon recover, to minimize any secondary gain which may prolong recovery, and to reinforce alternative coping strategies. Occasionally hypnosis, with post-hypnotic suggestions of recovery, is helpful. Sometimes suggestions without hypnosis can be helpful, such as, "How much better are you today?" or "Let's see how quickly you get better."

BODY DYSMORPHIC DISORDER

Clinical Presentation

Body dysmorphic disorder (BDD), originally called "dysmorphophobia," is the preoccupation in a normal-appearing person with an imagined defect in appearance or a markedly excessive concern with a slight physical anomaly. People with this disorder complain, "My nose is too big," "My mouth is too small," or "My face is crawling with wrinkles."

To separate those with this disorder from the rest of us "normals," the preoccupation must also be very upsetting or impair some important areas of functioning such as a job, marriage, or social situations. People with BDD run to their dermatologist or plastic surgeon, almost never to a psychiatrist. Table 12-5 lists the *DSM-IV* criteria for body dysmorphic disorder.

The focus of concern can be virtually any area of the body or anything on the face. Frequent mirror checking, sometimes consuming hours each day, is common. Others will avoid mirrors with equal passion and consequent distress. Because of embarrassment, it's usually a secret problem, shared only with doctors. Camouflage tactics are common and can include makeup, hats, hands, or hair to cover the imagined defect or countermeasures such as jutting forward a receding jaw.

Clinical Course and Complications

Body dysmorphic disorder affects women slightly more often than men (1.3:1 ratio), often begins in adolescence, can wax and wane for years, and if untreated, can go on for decades. Major depression and dysthymia are associated with this disorder, but probably as complications rather than causes. Usually the depression comes *after*, not *before*, the onset of BDD. Another complication is unnecessary plastic surgery. Obsessive-compulsive disorder has also been reported to travel with BDD. Nobody really knows what causes it. Sometimes it is acutely triggered by a chance remark like, "My, you have a small head," or "You're very handsome considering how big your nose is." Sometimes it comes after a threat to, or breakup of, a relationship.

TABLE 12-5
DSM-IV Criteria for Body Dysmorphic Disorder*

A. Preoccupation with an imagined defect in appearance. If a slight physical anomaly is present, the person's concern is markedly excessive.

B. The preoccupation causes clinically significant distress or impairment in social, occupational, or other important areas of functioning.

C. The preoccupation is not better accounted for by another mental disorder (e.g., dissatisfaction with body shape and size in Anorexia Nervosa).

---

*DSM-IV, p. 468.

Differential Diagnosis

Body dysmorphic disorder shouldn't be diagnosed in people who are concerned about minor defects if their concern is not excessive (e.g., typical adolescents). "Bad hair" days don't count! One study found that 70% of college students had at least some dissatisfaction with their appearance and 46% were somewhat preoccupied with one particular aspect of their appearance (Fitts et al., 1989). If the preoccupation is about weight, it is an *eating disorder*, not BDD. In BDD the belief is not delusional in intensity as it is in a *delusional disorder, somatic type*. Patients recognize the possibility that they have exaggerated the extent of the defect or that there isn't a defect at all. Exaggerated concerns about appearance are common in *major depressive disorder*, *avoidant personality disorder*, *social phobia*, and *narcissistic personality disorder*, but unlike in BDD, they aren't the predominant feature.

Management and Treatment

The literature is full of reported successes and failures, often with the same purported treatment. Plastic surgery usually leads to new problems — the surgery wasn't quite right or there are other parts of the body that aren't right. Some people with BDD undergo as many plastic surgeries as Michael Jackson. *Behavior therapy*, using progressive exposure techniques, audiovisual self-confrontation, and systematic desensitization, has been successful.

A successful result is more often a response along the lines of, "Who cares about my big nose?" rather than an all-out assertion, "My nose is normal." The *serotonergic antidepressants* clomipramine and fluoxetine work in depressed and nondepressed BDD patients and occasionally even in the BDD patient who has crossed the line into delusion. Responses with less selective antidepressants have been mixed. This parallels patterns of treatment response for obsessive-compulsive disorder, leading some to suggest that BDD is a variant of OCD.

PAIN DISORDER

Eighty percent of all patients who consult physicians do so for pain-related problems. Low back pain alone disables seven million Americans and prompts more than eight million doctor visits a year. In 1986, estimated health care and indirect (loss of work days, compensation litigation, and quackery) costs for chronic pain were $79 billion. What percent of these patients have a psychogenic pain disorder is unknown.

Not all patients with psychogenic pain have a pain *disorder*. For instance, among patients hospitalized in a three-week program for chronic pain, 32% had a major depression. Over half had a psychiatric disorder before their chronic pain developed (Katon, Egan, & Miller, 1985). In fact, chronic pain may be a symptom of major depression. In *DSM-IV*, pain disorder is not diagnosed if the pain is due to a mood, anxiety, or psychotic disorder.

Clinical Presentation

Pain disorder is characterized by a predominant complaint of significantly distressing or impairing pain in which psychological factors play an important role. The pain can have a medical cause, but is not totally ex-

---

TABLE 12–6
DSM-IV* Criteria for Pain Disorder

A. Pain in one or more anatomical sites is the predominant focus of the clinical presentation and is of sufficient severity to warrant clinical attention.

B. The pain causes clinically significant distress or impairment in social, occupational, or other important areas of functioning.

C. Psychological factors are judged to have an important role in the onset, severity, exacerbation, or maintenance of the pain.

D. The symptom or deficit is not intentionally produced or feigned (as in Factitious Disorder or Malingering).

E. The pain is not better accounted for by a Mood, Anxiety, or Psychotic Disorder and does not meet criteria for Dyspareunia.

Subtypes:
   Pain Disorder Associated with Psychological Factors: psychological factors are judged to have a major role in the onset, severity, exacerbation, or maintenance of the pain. (If a general medical condition is present, it does not have a major role in the onset, severity, exacerbation, or maintenance of the pain.) This type of Pain Disorder is not diagnosed if criteria are also met for Somatization Disorder.
   Pain Disorder Associated with Both Psychological Factors and a General Medical Condition: both psychological factors and a general medical condition are judged to have important roles in the onset, severity, exacerbation, or maintenance of the pain.

---

*DSM-IV, pp. 461–62.

plainable on a medical basis. Table 12–6 lists *DSM-IV* criteria for pain
disorder. The following case is typical.

Carol, a 45-year-old high school teacher, was standing outside her classroom
when three students began taunting her with lewd remarks. When she objected, one
picked her up, wheeled her around, and threw her to the ground, breaking her left
arm and causing numerous facial contusions. The next day Carol developed sharp
pains radiating up her neck and both arms, across her chest, and toward her pelvis.
After a month, her arm and face had mended, but her radiating pains continued,
even though no medical explanation could account for this pain. Although Carol
was medically approved to return to work and she was eager to do so – she needed
the money – her pain kept her home. She then sued the school for not protecting its
teachers. Carol frequently expressed her rage about these students, not just for
hurting her, but especially because of their sexual innuendos.

On psychiatric examination, Carol wore a neck brace and made sure one noticed
how slowly she sat down. While her flitting forefinger pointed to every radiating
pain in her body, she said, "The pain just zaps you like shock waves. It attacks your
entire body. If I touch anything, it triggers another shooting pain." (She missed the
pun.) Initially she denied any psychiatric problems, but later admitted that for
months before her injury, her boyfriend had been "trying real hard to get me into
the sack, and when I refused he'd always call me a prude." However, since her pains
developed, "he's been a prince – he's stopped pushing me sexually and has been very
considerate."

Carol's case raises three questions: First, is there sufficient physical evidence to
explain her pain? No. Second, is she faking the pain? Probably not. As with many
pain patients, possible compensation suggests malingering, but the apparent genuineness of Carol's pain and her eagerness to return to work suggest otherwise. Third,
is there psychological evidence to account for her pain? Yes. Her pain affords the
secondary gain of cooling her "oversexed" boyfriend while eliciting his support and
affection. There is also temporal and psychodynamic evidence: When she was having sexual conflicts with her boyfriend, the students' sexual insults especially hit
"below the belt," just where her pains were shooting. Therefore, the most likely
diagnosis was pain disorder. With the treatment described below, her pain gradually
disappeared in three months and she returned to school.

Although pain disorder may arise anytime in life, most often it surfaces
during adolescence and young adulthood. Symptoms are usually initiated
by an acute stressor, erupt suddenly, intensify over the next several days or
weeks, and subside when the acute stressor is gone. Less often, presumably
because of secondary gain, the pain persists long after the acute stressor,
waxes and wanes for months or years, worsens under stress, and may continue indefinitely. These patients "doctor-shop," become demoralized,
abuse analgesics, undergo unnecessary surgery and tests, get stuck in the
sick role, restrict social and occupational functioning (some are bedridden

for years), and develop secondary muscle spasms and pins-and-needles sensations around painful areas.

Epidemiology

In the absence of proper epidemiologic study, it appears that pain disorder more often afflicts women and is common in clinical practice. However, surveys might find that after disorders associated with psychogenic pain (e.g., major depression) are eliminated, pain disorders may be less frequent.

Etiology and Pathogenesis

In Katon et al.'s (1985) study of hospitalized patients with all types of chronic pain, about 60% had a first-degree relative with chronic pain, 38% with alcohol misuse, and 30% with a mood disorder. These figures may be high, but many believe they suggest a link — psychological or biological — between chronic pain, alcoholism, and depression. That roughly 50% of patients with chronic pain improve with antidepressants fuels the old speculation that chronic pain is a "depressive-equivalent." However, antidepressants also help chronic arthritis pain and work in a variety of nondepressive disorders such as panic (Ward et al., 1990). Pain patients may repress intense affects and conflicts, or their cognition or perception of internal feeling states may be greatly distorted. Given that pain runs in families, identification with a family member may also play an etiological role for some patients.

Pain disorder may allow some patients to escape an unpleasant situation such as work (secondary gain). People without physical abnormalities who work in dangerous, exhausting jobs (such as coal mining) more often stop working because of a pain disorder then those in less physically taxing jobs.

Differential Diagnosis

The dramatic presentation of organic pain may appear excessive, but this alone does not qualify as a pain disorder. Dramatic presentations may reflect a person's normal or cultural style of communicating. To qualify as a pain disorder, pain must be severe and psychological factors must play an important role. Patients with pain disorder may or may not have a medical condition. If a patient's pain is produced by another mental disorder, pain disorder is not diagnosed.

Management and Treatment

Acute pain management. Among the worst mistakes professionals make is giving *insufficient* narcotics to hospitalized medical or surgical patients in acute pain. Marks and Sachar (1973) found that inadequate doses of narcotics caused moderate to severe distress in 73% of patients. Studies have replicated this finding, even after staff received lectures on the subject (Perry, 1984). The main reasons (rationalizations) doctors and nurses give for underusing narcotics is a fear of "addicting" and "overdosing" patients, even though both are highly unlikely and rarely occur with such patients. Another common excuse is that "patients don't really hurt *that* much." Since nobody can know how much pain another person feels, it's never clear how patients are supposed to *prove* the extent of their pain. Professionals often point to the fact that patients *demand* narcotics as evidence of their being "manipulative." Nonsense. Patients might just want narcotics because they're in pain! And even if the doctor or nurse is "manipulated," that's hardly a calamity, for one hopes the professional's ego will survive.

Next to underusing narcotics, the next biggest error is to dispense them "as needed" instead of on a regular schedule (e.g., every four to six hours). When given "as needed" (or p.r.n.), the drug invariably arrives late (like everything else in a normal hospital) and the patient may become conditioned to associate complaining of pain with getting a drug-induced euphoria. Thus, for hospitalized medical/surgical patients in acute pain, narcotics should be given freely and on a regular schedule, without patients having to ask (or beg) for them.

Chronic pain management. There are few studies of pain disorder *per se*, but many of chronic pain in general. Research demonstrates that patients having all kinds of chronic pain clearly benefit from antidepressants, behavior and activity therapy, couples therapy, and supportive group therapy. Individual psychotherapy seems less useful. These treatments are effective (or ineffective) whether or not the patient's pain has a physical basis.

A wide variety of antidepressants is effective in chronic pain for both depressed and nondepressed patients. For most types of pain the results are modest, with about 50–55% of patients getting 50% (or more) pain reduction (Ward et al., 1990). For migraine and neuropathy, 60–70% response rates are seen. Benzodiazepines afford little benefit. ECT helps in patients with severe depression and chronic pain. Most patients with chronic pain deserve a trial on antidepressants (except trazodone and bupropion, which aren't very effective).

Pain clinics employ a multidisciplinary team to provide antidepressants, behavior therapy, and group psychotherapy. In a typical program, Fordyce et al. (1973) treated 36 patients whose pain had lasted an average of seven years and who did not improve from conventional medical treatments. Patients were hospitalized one to three months and continued as outpatients for another three weeks. The program's aims and methods were: (a) To decrease the patient's use of medication, drugs were given at regular intervals and not "on demand"; over time, drugs were tapered. Frequently, chronic pain improved when hypnoanxiolytics and opiates were stopped. (b) To diminish pain behavior, the staff praised patients for conducting nonpain-related activities; when patients exhibited pain-related behavior (e.g., not going to movies on account of pain), the staff ignored them. (c) To increase functioning, patients were rewarded for participating in a tailored program of gradually increasing physical activity. Rest was contingent on performing the activity, not on complaining of pain. (d) To maintain the patient's gains after discharge, the staff trained relatives to reinforce nonpain, instead of pain, behaviors.

At discharge, there was a 50% increase in time spent sitting, standing, walking, and exercising; most patients were taking little or no medication. At other pain centers, 60–80% of patients have shown similar gains in functional activity, decreased medication, and improved quality of life for at least three to five years. These improvements occurred regardless of whether patients were still in pain. What's more, most patients not only *talked* less about pain, they *experienced* less pain (Ochitill, 1982).

Group therapy for inpatients hasn't been systematically studied, but with outpatients it reduces their perception of pain and their use of medication; dysthymia is alleviated and employment increases. These groups provide support, ventilation, education about pain mechanisms, relaxation techniques to reduce the experience of pain, and reinforcement of nonpain behaviors.

CHAPTER 13

Factitious Disorders

FACTITIOUS DISORDERS ARE RARE conditions in which patients feign physical or psychological symptoms with the sole intent of being a patient. Their "symptoms" so closely resemble known illnesses that they trick doctors into hospitalizing them, conducting numerous tests, and performing unnecessary surgeries. Little is known about these patients, because when they're finally detected,they flee the hospital and are lost to follow-up. They will repeat their charade at many hospitals.

These patients create symptoms *intentionally*, in the sense of feeling that they control their production. Clinicians infer this intentional quality from the adeptness at simulating illnesses. However, although these patients intentionally generate symptoms, they are also driven to do so. Their fakery is compulsive; they can't refrain from subjecting themselves to procedures they know are dangerous and needless. Their illness-feigning behavior is deliberate and purposeful, but their motivations are not; for reasons beyond their control, they are impelled to be a patient.

Factitious disorders lie in the middle of a continuum between the outright fakery of physical symptoms (malingering) and their unconscious production (somatoform disorders). Unlike patients with factitious disorders, *malingerers* fabricate symptoms for reasons other than being a patient, such as draft evasion, drugs, disability payments, or missing classes. The malingerer's behavior *and* motivations are conscious, deliberate, and easily understandable. Unlike patients with factitious disorders, those with somatoform disorders are not consciously faking illness.

DSM-IV divides factitious disorders into those with *psychological signs and symptoms* and those with *physical signs and symptoms*. In both, symptoms can't be explained by another mental disorder, but are often superimposed on one. In the latter, the patient's physical "symptoms" result in multiple hospitalizations. Table 13–1 lists *DSM-IV* criteria for these two factitious disorders.

Clinical Presentation

With Predominantly Physical Signs and Symptoms. Asher (1951) coined the name "Munchausen syndrome" to designate patients who travel from hospital to hospital, dramatically presenting plausible histories and receiving surgery. Their stories are so elaborate that Asher named their condition after Baron Karl Friedrich Hieronymus Freiherr von Munchausen (1720–1797), a German cavalry officer and worldclass liar. *DSM-IV* equates Munchausen syndrome with chronic factitious disorder with physical symptoms.

These patients' "symptoms" are limited only by their creativity and medical knowledge; many work in hospitals as nurses or technicians; some study medical texts and speak medicaleze. Most will dramatically enter an emergency room with a classical description of a disease (e.g., crushing chest pain, sudden loss of breath, convulsions). Once hospitalized, they may insist on narcotics or tell staff which lab tests and procedures to perform.

Their *piéce de resistance* is feigning objective physical signs and abnormal laboratory findings. One patient "raised" his rectal temperature by

---

TABLE 13–1
DSM-IV Criteria for Factitious Disorder*

A. Intentional production or feigning of physical or psychological signs or symptoms.

B. The motivation for the behavior is to assume the sick role.

C. External incentives for the behavior (such as economic gain, avoiding legal responsibility, or improving physical well-being, as in Malingering) are absent.

Subtypes

With Predominantly Psychological Signs and Symptoms: if psychological signs and symptoms predominate in the clinical presentation
With Predominantly Physical Signs and Symptoms: if physical signs and symptoms predominate in the clinical presentation
With Combined Psychological and Physical Signs and Symptoms: if both psychological and physical signs and symptoms are present but neither predominates in the clinical presentation

---

*DSM-IV, p. 474.

relaxing and contracting his anal sphincter. Another swallowed blood, strolled into the ER, and puked. Patients will spit saliva into urine samples to elevate urinary amylase, or they may prick a finger and squeeze a little blood into their urine to "develop" hematuria. Self-injecting insulin will produce hypoglycemia. Fecal bacteria will somehow find their way into urine. Patients have swallowed nails, fish hooks, and paint. By self-inducing disease, some of these patients become genuinely sick, although death is rare.

Factitious patients often spin intriguing yarns ("pseudologia fantastica") — false accounts of famous parents, financial wizardry, or show-biz exploits; they might be still another bastard descendant of Aaron Burr or claim a surgical scar came from battlefield heroics. For all their "accomplishments" or "notoriety," the staff begin to wonder why they have so few visitors, phone calls, or friends. Further clues to this diagnosis are extensive travel, self-mutilation, *la belle indifference* to pain and painful procedures, drug abuse (in 50% of cases), ever-changing medical complaints, and substantial evidence of prior treatment, such as venous cutdown scars, signs of recent cardioversion, or a "gridiron abdomen" from multiple operations (Sussman & Hyler, 1985).

When the staff become suspicious, these patients become increasingly strident and may present new evidence of illness. Any suggestions of a psych consult are angrily rejected. If confronted with their contradictory stories or inconsistent findings, instead of recanting or displaying embarrassment, factitious patients will question the staff's competence or threaten litigation. Once these ploys fail, patients will sign out of the hospital against medical advice or leave surreptitiously. A few days later they may pop up at another hospital, recycling the same saga.

Factitious disorder usually begins during early adulthood, but can start during childhood. Although initially these patients may receive medical care for a real illness, they then develop a pattern of repeated ambulatory treatments and hospitalizations. The prognosis worsens as patients escalate from (a) giving a fictitious history, (b) to simulating signs of illness, to (c) inducing pathological states.

With Predominantly Psychological Signs and Symptoms. Factitious patients will fake several, often psychotic-like symptoms, which laypeople would take as a mental illness, but professionals would realize are inconsistent with any known psychiatric disorder. Patients may complain of hallucinations, erratic memory loss, itchy feet, facial twitches, and episodic blindness — a symptom cluster that, although inventive, doesn't exist. They're also highly suggestible: If told that hallucinating patients don't sleep, these patients don't sleep. When observed, their symptoms get worse. Some are negativistic and refuse to answer questions. Many have a (genuine) border-line personality disorder.

Some present with overwhelming grief instead of psychosis (Phillips, Ward, & Ries, 1983). Invariably, many family members have been killed, usually by dramatic means (train wrecks, murders). Authenticity of the story is rarely questioned because these patients are already enduring enough suffering and need support rather than suspicions. They differ from those really grieving in not having any family members ("they all died") or friends who can be contacted to verify the story. The best way to confirm suspected factitious mourning is to ask for the place and date of the alleged death(s) and call the appropriate coroner.

Others, especially prisoners, may have Ganser syndrome, whose chief symptom is *vorbeireden*—that is, giving approximate answers, near misses, or talking past the point. They appear to understand questions, but to deliberately give false answers: Ask when Santa comes, and they'll say Halloween; ask them to subtract 7 from 100 and they'll respond, "92, 84, 76," etc. *Vorbeireden*, however, is also found in other disorders.

Epidemiology

Factitious disorder is rare, but its true prevalence is unknown: The rate may be underestimated, because patients don't stay around to be detected or counted; or overestimated, since patients move from hospital to hospital and the same patient may be reported many times. One patient had over 420 documented hospitalizations. Epidemiologic figures from university populations may be inflated, since these patients are drawn to these facilities. This might account for why Pope, Jonas, and Jones (1982) found that 6.4% of patients admitted to a psychosis-research service had factitious disorders with psychological symptoms. Males may have more factitious disorders than females, but nobody really knows.

Etiology and Pathogenesis

What causes factitious disorders is unknown, but they probably develop from a confluence of factors, which vary depending on the patient. People with factitious disorder with physical symptoms are more likely to have had physical disorders (often requiring extensive treatment) while growing up; a close relationship with a doctor in the past, such as having a doctor in the family or having been sexually abused by a doctor; or a grudge against the medical profession, sometimes based on bad past medical care. For all types of factitious disorders, a severe personality disorder—often borderline, dependent, or passive aggressive (no longer in *DSM-IV*)—is a predisposing factor.

All patients with factitious disorders are engaging in "inappropriate care-getting behavior." They probably want care and attention but can't or don't get it in usual, healthy ways. Given their self-destructiveness, *masochistic* impulses may feed on a *love-hate relationship* with health-care professionals. If they could say it, their underlying message might be, "Help me, you bastard." These patients often suffer from *childhood deprivation, neglect, and abuse*, which may steer them into dependent roles even as they expect health professionals to make up for lost parenting. This need also might account for factitious disorder "*by proxy*," a rare phenomenon in which a parent induces symptoms in his or her child in order to live vicariously through the child as she or he receives the parental affection of doctors and nurses. Some Munchausen patients *identify* with health-care professionals, while enjoying a *sense of mastery and control* from learning about illness, coping with pain, and outwitting physicians.

Differential Diagnosis

The main reason for identifying factitious disorder is to spare patients from unnecessary hospitalizations and potentially harmful medical procedures and operations. The chief diagnostic problem is to distinguish factitious disorder from *true medical illness*. Factitious disorders should be considered when patients stage their history as high drama, exhibit pseudologia fantastica, disrupt a ward and break hospital rules, argue continuously with staff, show off medical jargon and knowledge, demand narcotics, "advertise" signs of numerous prior medical treatments and surgeries, give contradictory histories, develop frequent or inexplicable medical complications, present new symptoms after every negative workup, and become hostile when questioned about their medical history or personal background.

As discussed previously, factitious disorder should be distinguished from *somatoform disorder* and *malingering*. *Antisocial personality disorder* may be misdiagnosed on account of these patients' pseudologia fantastica, impostership, lying, drug abuse, and few close relations. Sociopaths, however, usually avoid painful tests and hospitals, unless these might get them out of a jail sentence; Munchausen patients "attract" them. Some *schizophrenics* self-induce physical symptoms, but secondarily to a specific delusion or command hallucination.

Diagnosing factitious disorder with psychological symptoms is especially difficult, because most psychological symptoms can't be objectively verified. Whenever symptoms don't fit the pattern of a *known mental disorder*, factitious disorder merits consideration. Factitious disorder with psychological symptoms *and* another mental disorder can both be diagnosed, as long as the factitious symptoms are produced without an ulterior motive (as in malingering). For a malingerer whose motive is as simple as "three hots and a cot" (three meals and a bed), a psychiatric hospitalization with its "painless patienthood" may seem like a good alternative for the patient (but not for anyone else).

Management and Treatment

Wilhelm Kaiser claimed the only requirement for successful therapy is that two people be in a room. And since patients with factitious disorders don't stay in the room, the only thing that's clear about treating them is that nothing is known to work. Failed treatments include hypnosis, medications (of all kinds), ECT, insulin coma, and lobotomy. Several authors advocate psychotherapy, but have too few treatment cases to establish its efficacy. Even when physicians gently confront these patients with their true diagnoses, patients usually react with hostility and reject any offer of help.

Munchausen and somatization disorder patients who stay in one state and whose medical funding comes from that state can be tracked and allowed to go to only one hospital and one doctor. If they go to another hospital, computers pick up their I.D. number and alert everyone. When this was done in Washington state, these patients got better care, almost no unnecessary procedures were performed, and the state saved more than $100,000/year on *each* patient.

Despite the absence of any clearly effective treatment, experts generally recommend that, once the diagnosis of factitious disorder is established, clinicians should: (a) Be careful not to overlook genuine medical disease. (b) Keep patients in the hospital—for once out, always out—to begin to involve them in extended psychiatric treatment. (c) If necessary to ensure safety, commit children with factitious disorders by proxy to hospitals. (d) Carefully check annoyance with these patients, avoid power struggles and public humiliations, and be ever-alert to the behaviors and dynamics (including splitting) commonly associated with borderline personality disorder. (e) If outsmarted by these patients, do not get bent out of shape. The disorder is the patient's, not the staffs'.

CHAPTER 14

Dissociative Disorders

HOW COME DISSOCIATIVE disorders, although relatively uncommon, are of such uncommon interest? *Sybil*, *The Three Faces of Eve*, *The Boston Strangler*, and (if brainwashed) Patty Hearst fascinate many because they are very ordinary individuals who have made an extraordinary transformation. And if these people can become completely different people, then couldn't we? If such strangeness can lurk within them, why not within us?

Dissociative states refer to the "splitting off" from conscious awareness of some ordinarily familiar information, emotion, or mental function. In other words, selected mental contents are removed or dissociated from conscious experience, but continue to produce motor or sensory effects. These are the elsewhere disorders: Part of the person (e.g., memory, identity) is elsewhere and not available at the present time. In dissociative states, people can appear unconscious and focus selectively on the environment (e.g., sleepwalking, trance), act bizarrely (e.g., running "amok," going "berserk"), lose their identity and wander away from home (e.g., fugue), lose memory without wandering away from home (e.g., amnesia), assume an alien identity (e.g., multiple personality, witchcraft, possession), or be brainwashed.

Some dissociative states are not pathological, and to some extent, some are highly adaptive. We all forget things. We all switch states of consciousness, from meditating to sleeping to working to daydreaming, and to do so, sets of memory and attitudes must also switch. Dissociation also may occur in crystal gazing, intense prayer, "mass hysteria," religious revivals, healing ceremonies (e.g., Holy Spirit possession, glossolalia ["speaking in tongues"]), and hypnosis. Amazingly enough, it can even occur during lectures or while reading textbooks (not this one) — "I blanked out on what he said" or — "I spaced out on that page — I'll have to read it again."

Most dissociative states are activated by a psychosocial trigger, arise suddenly, and end abruptly. During normal intervals, people are partly or totally amnestic for their dissociative episodes. For example, using *posthypnotic suggestion*, a hypnotist may instruct a hypnotized subject, "After you awake, when I scratch my head, you'll sing 'God Save the Queen,' but not remember that I told you to." Ten minutes after the subject awakens, the hypnotist scratches and the subject wails "God Save the Queen." Ask why she's singing, she may confess she doesn't know or confabulate, "I thought people would like the music."

Dissociative experiences are common. On the Dissociative Experience Scale, 29% of the general population agreed that the following happened to them in almost one-third of their conversations: "Some people find that sometimes they are listening to someone talk and they suddenly realize that they did not hear part or all of what was said" (Ross, Joshi, & Currie, 1990). In the same study, 5% scored over 30, a score highly associated with having a dissociative disorder. There were no differences in scores based on gender, income, occupation, education, or religion. However, dissociative experiences (like hypnotizability, a phenomenon highly correlated with dissociation [Frischholz, Lipman, Braun, & Sachs, 1992]) decrease with age. Men and women differed only on two items. Men more often endorsed the statement, "Some people find that they have no memory for important events in their lives, for example, a wedding or graduation" (until now, something women had suspected was happening but couldn't prove), while women more often endorsed the statement, "Some people sometimes find that when they are alone, they talk out loud to themselves."

DSM-IV defines dissociative disorders as conditions whose predominant feature is a disturbance or alteration in the normal integrative functions of consciousness, identity, or memory. The type of alteration dictates the type of dissociative disorder: In *dissociative amnesia*, consciousness is altered and significant personal events forgotten. In *dissociative fugue*, identity and motor behavior are altered; patients unexpectedly travel far from home, assume a new identity, forgetting their old one. In *dissociative identity disorder* (multiple personality disorder), numerous identities arise. In *depersonalization disorder*, patients feel as if they are outside of their mind or body, as an observer. Table 14-1 presents *DSM-IV* criteria for these disorders. There's also a residual category, *dissociative disorder not otherwise specified*, which covers *brainwashing* and *trance disorder*.

Clinical Presentations

Dissociative amnesia. These patients are suddenly unable to remember significant personal information, which is far in excess of ordinary forget-

TABLE 14–1
DSM-IV Criteria for Dissociative Disorders:
Dissociative Amnesia, Fugue, Identity, and Depersonalization Disorders*

Common Criteria

A. The symptoms or experiences cause clinically significant distress or impairment in social, occupational, or other important areas of functioning (not criterion for Dissociative Identity disorder).

B. The disturbance is not due to the direct physiological effects of a substance (e.g., a drug of abuse, alcohol intoxication, a medication) or a general medical condition (e.g., partial complex seizures, head trauma).

Dissociative Amnesia—Specific Criteria

C. The predominant disturbance is one or more episodes of inability to recall important personal information, usually of a traumatic or stressful nature, that is too extensive to be explained by ordinary forgetfulness.

D. The disturbance does not occur exclusively during the course of Dissociative Identity Disorder, Dissociative Fugue, Posttraumatic Stress Disorder, Acute Stress Disorder, or Somatization Disorder.

Dissociative Fugue—Specific Criteria

C. The predominant disturbance is sudden, unexpected travel away from home or one's customary place of work, with inability to recall one's past.

D. Confusion about personal identity or assumption of new identity (partial or complete).

E. The disturbance does not occur exclusively during the course of Dissociative Identity Disorder.

Dissociative Identity Disorder (Multiple Personality Disorder)—Specific Criteria

C. The presence of two or more distinct identities or personality states (each with its own relatively enduring pattern of perceiving, relating to, and thinking about the environment and self).

D. At least two of these identities or personality states recurrently take control of the person's behavior.

E. Inability to recall important personal information that is too extensive to be explained by ordinary forgetfulness. **Note:** In children, the symptoms are not attributable to imaginary playmates or other fantasy play.

Depersonalization Disorder—Specific Criteria

C. Persistent or recurrent experiences of feeling detached from, and as if one is an outside observer of, one's mental processes or body (e.g., feeling like one is in a dream).

312

TABLE 14–1
(*Continued*)

D. During the depersonalization experience, reality testing remains intact.

E. The depersonalization experience does not occur exclusively during the course of another mental disorder, such as Schizophrenia, Panic Disorder, Acute Stress Disorder or another Dissociative Disorder.

DSM-IV, pp. 481, 484, 487, 490.

fulness. Patients know they've forgotten something, but don't know what. Often they don't seem to care. Feeling perplexed, disoriented, and purposeless, they're often picked up by the police as lost or for wandering aimlessly. During their amnesia, patients are able to perform relatively simple tasks (e.g., taking a bus) and, less often, more complicated ones (e.g., shopping, cooking).

Most often, patients' amnesias are *localized* to several hours or days during and after a highly disturbing event and are only rarely *generalized* for an entire life. Although most amnesias are total, they may be *selective* for only some events, usually the most traumatic. An uninjured person may remember driving and talking to staff at a hospital, but not the car accident itself. Rare is *continuous* amnesia, wherein patients forget everything from the time of the stress until the present. (Some politicians have been accused of selective amnesia because they seem unable to remember any promises they made from before the election to the present.)

An example of localized amnesia is the case of a photojournalist in Vietnam who, confused and bewildered, strolled into the office of Army Intelligence. He had no recollection of the past three days, but his camera did. It showed photographs of a Buddhist monk immolating himself. Like most dissociative amnesias, his completely cleared within 24 hours of being discovered.

Dissociative fugue. These patients flee from home or their customary locale, forget (or are confused about) their previous identity, and adopt a partial one. During a fugue, patients usually behave with sufficient skill to go unnoticed by most casual observers. Fugues typically are precipitated by an acute stressor and consist of a several-day excursion with minimal social contact. Perplexity and disorientation may occur in some fugues, but if they dominate, the condition is diagnosed as dissociative amnesia and not fugue. Other fugues are more elaborate, lasting weeks to months: Previously quiet and very ordinary people may establish a new residence, fashion a completely new, more gregarious identity, have a full social calendar, and appear no different than any other colorful new arrival in town. Patients have traveled thousands of miles and passed numerous customs officials without detection. A rare few are violent. Afterwards, patients can't remember what transpired during the fugue. In contrast to amnesia patients, who are aware of their memory loss, fugue victims are usually not aware.

Dissociative identity disorder. This new name for "multiple personality disorder" is used because the most common and fundamental alteration in this disorder is the presence of more than one discrete identity, i.e., what the person calls herself and believes herself to be. The quiet, careful guy at the lab who is a "wild man" at parties may look to others like a multiple personality, but he sees these ways of being as different aspects of his identity and does not suffer from dissociative identity disorder.

These patients have two or more distinct identities or personality states, each dominant at a particular moment. Each identity is a complex, integrated being with its own name, memories, behavioral traits, emotional characteristics, social relations, employment histories, mental and physical disorders, and psychological test responses. Even rates of cerebral blood flow and evoked electrical potentials differ between the identities. Needing to eat for three identities, one patient ate nine meals a day! The average number of identities is eight to 13, but more than 50 have been reported. Sybil had 16 personalities, and Eve, 22 faces.

Transitions from one identity to another are usually sudden, follow a stressor, and catch most observers off-guard. They're spooky to watch, since the "new" person seems to have taken over the patient's body and soul. Dress, speech, gait, and facial expressions may change so much the person goes unrecognized. The original (or primary) personality is usually unaware of the other (or secondary) personalities, but most secondary personalities are aware of the primary personality. The secondary personalities generally have some inkling of the others; they converse with each other, protect each other, or one may act while others watch. Secondary personalities are often extreme caricatures of the original personality. A shy, conventional primary personality may have secondary personalities as a whore, drag queen, devil, and social worker. Secondary personalities may have a different sex, race, or age from the original personality.

Clinicians are frequently unaware that they're treating a multiple identity, since these patients are tough to detect. One psychiatrist reported that seven years had passed before he realized his patient had this disorder. Few enter treatment complaining of a multiple personality, and if they come at all, it's usually for depression. These patients may reveal themselves through memory lapses, time distortions ("lost weekends"), using "we" rather than "I" in conversations, being charged for items they don't remember buying (imagine the VISA bills!), and encountering friends who act like strangers and strangers who act like friends. If asked to write their thoughts freely for a half-hour, another personality may emerge. Another personality breaks through half the time in psychotherapy (Harvard, 1985).

Multiple identity, and the proliferation of new identities, often continues for life, making this condition the worst of the dissociative disorders. These patients are frequently depressed, abuse substances, mutilate themselves, attempt suicide, and have psychotic episodes, tension headaches, phobias, conversion symptoms, and hypochondriasis. "Hallucinated" voices in "psychotic" episodes are often one or more other personalities talking.

Depersonalization disorder. Depersonalization is a common perceptual distortion in which the person experiences his body, or mental processes, as if he were a detached, outside observer. The person may feel anesthetized or wooden; a sense of unreality or self-estrangement may confound him. The size and shape of objects may seem altered. Although the person feels, and indeed fears, that he's not in full control, gross reality testing is *not* impaired.

Because temporary depersonalization frequently occurs during normal, psychopathologic, or physiologically altered states, depersonalization *disorder* is only diagnosed in the absence of another mental disorder, a general medical condition, or a direct effect of a substance, and when it's so persistent or recurrent that it significantly interferes with social or occupational functioning. Over time, its severity fluctuates and hypochondriasis is frequent. Nevertheless, the disorder rarely produces lasting impairment.

Dissociative disorder NOS. This category of disorders that don't fit anyplace else includes brainwashing. Three myths about brainwashing abound: (a) that it doesn't exist; (b) that it's no different from education, advertising, and psychotherapy; and (c) that it's an irresistible method that robs people of their beliefs and personalities. Instead, brainwashing can be defined as a "comprehensive, systematic, and total program using psychological techniques, to stress *confession* and then *reeducation* in order to change fundamental beliefs. During confession, the subject admits to past errors and renounces past affiliations; during reeducation, the subject is refashioned to conform to the idealized image of the brainwasher" (Lifton, 1963).

This category also includes derealization without depersonalization and dissociative trance disorder, in which the person feels she has been taken over by a new identity attributed to the influence of a spirit, power, deity, or other person. Running "amok" in Malaysia is an example. To be called a disorder, the patient's symptoms can't be part of a broadly accepted culture or religious practice. Therefore, "speaking in tongues" when "possessed" by the Holy Spirit would not be classified as a disorder if the person is a "Holy Roller"—but might be if the person is a Unitarian!

Epidemiology

Dissociative disorders were once thought to be rare; now it is estimated that 4–5% of the population have had one. Psychogenic amnesia and fugue are common during war and natural disasters. In battle, young males are at highest risk. Away from battle, adolescent and young adult women have slightly more dissociative disorders. In psychiatric populations, multiple personality is reputed to affect four times as many women as men, but if prison populations were included, the sex differential would narrow. Except for the variable age of onset of psychogenic fugue, dissociative disorders rarely begin after the age of 40 and almost never originate among the elderly.

Etiology and Pathogenesis

Because dissociative states induced by substances or medical conditions are excluded by definition, dissociative disorders are produced psychosocially. Most often, the immediate precipitating factor is an imminent threat of injury or death, the performance of a guilt-provoking act (e.g., an affair), or a serious auto accident.

Psychoanalytic theory suggests that dissociative states protect the individual from experiencing painful sexual or aggressive impulses. With amnesia, one forgets what's painful; with fugue, one runs away from it; with multiple personality, one displaces it onto a new identity; with depersonalization, one abandons it.

Almost all patients with dissociative identity disorder report being physically or sexually abused as children (Ross, Miller, et al., 1990). Sybil's mother tortured her as a child; Billy Milligan's father frequently raped him from the ages of nine to 16 and threatened to kill him if he told anybody. These children have been cannon fodder in custody fights, raised as the opposite sex, had their genitals squeezed in a vice, and kidnapped by parents. Dissociation into different identities defends against these trauma by isolating the horror, sectioning off the child's negative self-images, and permitting a modicum of self-control. By compartmentalizing emotions, the child says, in effect, "I can't deny that this is happening, but I can deny that it's happening to me" (Harvard, 1985).

Differential Diagnosis

Neurologic disorders (NDs) can simulate dissociative amnesia, except in NDs, memory loss is more recent than remote and usually unrelated to a specific stressor. Most NDs arise slowly, rarely improve, and are accompanied by other signs, such as confusion, disorientation, attention deficits, and clouding of consciousness. Delirium may arise quickly but will also have all of these other signs and symptoms. Unlike those with dissociative fugue, most patients with neurological disorders who wander off are unable to perform complex, purposeful tasks.

Substance-induced intoxications can produce *hypnoanxiolytic* and *alcoholic "blackouts,"* an amnesia for events occurring while intoxicated. In blackouts, the history of drinking and the lack of a complete recovery exclude psychogenic amnesia. In *alcohol amnestic disorder*, five-minute (not immediate) memory is lost. *"Dissociative" anesthetics*, primarily phencyclidine (PCP), frequently cause depersonalization, but a drug history and urine screen are sufficiently diagnostic.

In *postconcussion amnesia*, patients generally have a retrograde memory loss for the period before the head trauma, whereas in psychogenic amnesia there's generally an anterograde memory loss for the period since the precipitating stress. Hypnosis and amytal interview can usually retrieve lost memories in psychogenic amnesia, but not in concussion. In dissociative amnesias, memory loss tends to be global and total; after concussion, it tends to be spotty and patchy. Patients with concussive amnesia do not form new identities. In psychogenic amnesia patients retain prior skills, have little difficulty conducting current tasks, and apparently benefit from secondary gain; patients with postconcussion amnesia lose some prior skills, have problems coping with present tasks, and do not appear to acquire secondary gain (Ludwig, 1985).

Partial complex seizures (PCC) may cause sudden memory loss and flight, but unlike psychogenic fugue, patients can't perform complex tasks or form a new identity; they often have stereotyped movements, like lip smacking, and about half the time there's an abnormal EEG. Sometimes PCC is hard to distinguish from dissociative amnesia. Because people with severe dissociative disorders often were physically abused as children, including being knocked unconscious many times, they may have both PCC and dissociative amnesia. A trial of anticonvulsants may be useful. Many who exhibit partial complex seizures but have a normal EEG during the seizures (called a pseudoseizure) are found to have dissociative symptoms often precipitated by guilt-laden grief (Ramchandani & Schindler, 1993).

Malingering must always be considered, especially if there's obvious secondary gain. Attorneys are seeing many more claims of multiple identity by criminals. "Hey, judge, it's not *me* who slaughtered the guy, it's that *other* personality." Kiersch (1962) found that of 32 cases of suspects with alleged amnesia who were standing trial, 21 subsequently confessed to lying about their memory loss. Patients with dissociative conditions usually recover during hypnosis and amytal interviews, but malingerers do not. Remember, amytal is not truth serum. Liars can keep on lying under amytal.

Descriptively and psychodynamically, multiple identity often resembles *borderline personality disorder*. Emotional lability, low self-esteem, impulsivity, substance abuse, chronic boredom, identity confusion, temper tantrums, manipulative interpersonal relations, and suicide attempts characterize both disorders. In fact, in one investigation (Horevitz & Braun, 1984), 70% of patients with multiple personality were also diagnosed as borderline. Observing the patient's abrupt personality changes settles the diagnosis.

Distinguishing among dissociative disorders is usually easy. When a person forgets *and* travels to another locale, the diagnosis is psychogenic fugue; when the person "merely" forgets, it's psychogenic amnesia. Patients with dissociative amnesia look more befuddled, rarely conduct complex tasks, and are more readily spotted by lay observers. Awareness of one's original identity is absent in psychogenic amnesia and fugue, but present in multiple personality.

Management and Treatment

Although the literature on treating dissociative disorders is growing, it is still mainly anecdotal. A summary follows:

Dissociative amnesia and fugue. Because of the relatively acute onset, brief duration, and high rate of spontaneous recovery of these states, this sequence of interventions is recommended: (a) *Evaluate* patients, allowing a few days for a spontaneous remission. Suggest that they might find their memory returning slowly day by day. If patients do not fully recover, (b) provide *discussion, support, and persuasion*: Encourage them to talk freely of recent events, periodically suggest avenues for exploration, and gently persuade them to keep looking for lost memories. If these methods are not sufficient, (c) employ an *associative anamnesis* by having patients free-associate to events surrounding the amnesia. (d) Use *hypnosis*; amnestic patients, as most patients with dissociative disorders, are extremely good subjects. Instruct them to give a running commentary of known past incidents, which usually leads to abreaction. Once these emotions calm, patients are told to keep talking and, then, to wake up. When awake, patients are surprised to find themselves recounting past events and their amnesia ends. If it doesn't, (e) administer an *amytal interview* and then gently prod them to review events around the forgotten period. The closer in time to the onset of the amnesia, the more effective the interview. (f) If memory still hasn't returned, reconsider *neurologic causes*, and if none is found, (g) gather a more exhaustive *psychological history* with attennae attuned to possible secondary gain (Coombs & Ludwig, 1982).

Dissociative identity disorder. Only very experienced therapists should treat this disorder. Initially these patients fascinate, but then soon overwhelm and exasperate therapists. As soon as psychotherapy with the primary identity is underway, a secondary identity (often referred to as an "alter") takes over, and then another, and another, and another. Many are hostile, seductive, and manipulative; some will bait the primary identity, try blocking alliances with the therapist, or act out by drug-taking and wrist-slashing. All resist recalling traumatic events. These patients sense the therapist's fascination with the drama and may try to please him or her by exaggerating past horrors, which were already bad enough. Because these patients are very suggestible, leading questions must be avoided, such as,

"Don't you think your parents may have been involved in a Satanic cult?" (something the FBI and police have seldom been able to prove), or "Aren't there many more personalities in there?" Too often, leading questions are experienced as new suggestions which are dutifully followed.

Hypnosis may engage certain personalities, but it should not be introduced too early, since the patient may experience it as an emotional assault. *Group therapy* often backfires (unless all participants share the same diagnosis), because they consider the patient a fraud. An intriguing approach is "internal group therapy" in which the therapist "moderates" a discussion between the patient's personalities and facilitates the quiescent ones to speak via hypnosis. *Videotaping* early in treatment may help personalities get acquainted. *Family counseling* should also be considered. Unless one of the personalities has another mental disorder (e.g., major depression), *medications* have no particular use. Often it is tempting to use neuroleptics for "the voices," but those are other personalities and not usual hallucinations. In a study of the treatment of borderline personality disorder, Marcia Linehan included patients with dissociative identity disorder, but did not alter her approach to them and ignored the different personalities. Later, I (NW) evaluated some of these patients and saw increased or complete fusion of the personalities, despite their being ignored. Perhaps good treatment for the borderline personality disorder is sufficient, although most argue that the treatment of dissociative identity disorder is highly specialized.

CHAPTER 15

Sexual and Gender Identity Disorders

SEX PLAYS A UNIQUELY pervasive role in people's lives; it influences how we think, feel, dress, flirt, play, mate, and love. Maybe that's one reason the ECA found that sexual and gender identity disorders (in *DSM-III*, "psychosexual disorders") will affect one in four adults, making them the second most common group of mental disorders in America (see Table 1–4). These disorders only include sexual or gender identity problems not caused by other mental disorders.

DSM-IV lists six classes of sexual disorders (Appendix A) and one class of gender disorder. *Sexual desire disorders* refer to excessive interest in or aversion to sexual activity. *Sexual arousal disorders* refer to the inability to attain or maintain gender-normal psychophysiologic changes during sexual activity. *Orgasm disorders* involve either delays or absence of orgasm in men and women after normal sexual excitement, or in men, the opposite: premature ejaculation. *Sexual pain disorders* are characterized by the chronic presence of pain during sexual activity. *Sexual dysfunctions due to a general medical condition* or *substance-induced sexual dysfunction* include the preceding four disorders if they are caused by a medical problem (such as diabetes or hypothyroidism). *Paraphilias* are persistent patterns of sexual arousal in response to atypical or bizarre stimuli (e.g., fetishism). *Gender identity disorders* are characterized by discomfort with one's anatomic sex and the adoption of behavioral patterns associated with the other sex, mainly transsexualism.

At the outset, some basic terms and concepts need clarification. A person's *anatomic sex* is his or her biologic sex as determined by whether he has XY, or she has XX, chromosomes. *Gender identity* is the individual's *internal* feelings as to whether he or she is a male or a female. *Gender role* refers to whether a person wishes to be seen by others (or by oneself) as a male or as a female; gender role involves the person's *external* appearance and behavior, including sexual behavior. *Sexual orientation* describes a person's preference for partners of the same (homosexual) or opposite (heterosexual) sex.

Atypical gender role and sexual orientation alone are not listed as disorders because they are not necessarily a result of psychopathologic processes and do not necessarily interfere with functioning. Gender identity disorders are listed because they invariably cause significant distress, or as one patient said, "How would you like to go through life as a woman trapped in a man's body?"

SEXUAL DYSFUNCTIONS

Sexual dysfunctions are disturbances in the human sexual response cycle (Table 15-1). The nine specific psychosexual dysfunctions defined in *DSM-IV* are outlined in Table 15-2. In each of these the problem (1) is persistent or recurrent; (2) does not occur exclusively during the course of another Axis 1 disorder (other than another sexual dysfunction) such as major depressive disorder and is not due to the direct physiological effects of a substance (e.g., a drug of abuse, a medication) or a general medical condition; (3) causes marked distress or interpersonal difficulty. In describing a sexual dysfunction, clinicians also should indicate if it's *lifelong* or *acquired* (with or without previously normal functioning); if it's *generalized* or *situational* (with a particular partner); if it's *conjoint* or *solitary* (with or without [as in masturbation] another partner); or if it's due to *psychological* or *combined* factors. Clinicians should also note its frequency, setting, duration, degree of sexual impairment, level of subjective distress, and effects on other areas of functioning (e.g., social, occupational).

Most sexual dysfunctions arise during young adulthood or with first sexual encounters. The overall clinical course is highly varied; a disorder may be brief, recurrent, smoldering, or permanent. Patients usually delay seeking treatment for three to 12 years and then do so only after several years of a sustained sexual relationship. Dysfunctions also may arise later in life; for males, inhibited sexual desire and excitement is more common in middle adulthood. Women tend to have increasing sexual responsiveness until their thirties and often maintain their responsiveness into old age.

TABLE 15–1
The Human Sexual Response Cycle

NUMBER	PHASE	KEY FEATURES
I.	APPETITIVE	Fantasies about sexual activity and the desire (i.e., libido) to have it.
II.	EXCITEMENT	Subjective sense of sexual pleasure with accompanying physiologic changes in the male leading to erection, and in the female leading to vasocongestion, vaginal lubrication, and swelling of the external genitalia. Mediated by the parasympathetic nervous system, this phase includes the "excitement" and "plateau" stages described by Masters and Johnson (1970) and the "vascular" stage described by Kaplan (1974).
III.	ORGASM	The peaking of sexual pleasure and the release of sexual tension. This phase is mediated by the sympathetic nervous system and called the "muscular" stage by Kaplan. During it, males sense an inevitable ejaculation, which is followed by a single, intense muscular contraction that emits semen. In a more variable response, females contract the outer third of their vagina.
IV.	RESOLUTION	There is a generalized and muscular relaxation, during which males are physiologically refractory to further erection or orgasm, whereas females can respond immediately to additional stimuli.

From peak sexual responsiveness in the teens or early twenties men tend to decrease over the rest of their lives. For pure sex, a 35-year-old woman and an 18-year-old man may be the best match.

Some sexual dysfunctions are associated with specific psychiatric traits. For example, women with histrionic personalities are more likely to have inhibited sexual desire and inhibited orgasm. Men with obsessive-compulsive personalities are prone to inhibited sexual desire and excitement. Anxiety predisposes to premature ejaculation and also impotence.

A patient's dysfunction will involve one or more etiological factors. These may be (a) *intrapsychic*, such as "performance anxiety," guilt, low self-esteem, denial,

TABLE 15–2
***DSM-IV* Sexual Dysfunctions**

SEXUAL DESIRE DISORDERS (Phase I disorders)

Hypoactive sexual desire disorder is a deficiency (or absence) of sexual fantasies and desires for sexual activity. It is more common in women and is often accompanied by other sexual dysfunctions.

Sexual aversion disorder is an extreme aversion to and avoidance of all (or almost all) genital sexual contact with a partner.

SEXUAL AROUSAL DISORDERS (Phase II disorders)

Female sexual arousal disorder and *male erectile disorder* are disorders in which, prior to the sexual act being concluded, there is a partial or complete failure in men to attain or maintain an erection (impotence) or in women to attain the lubrication-swelling response.

ORGASM DISORDERS (Phase III disorders)

Female and male orgasmic disorders are disorders in which there is a delay in or absence of orgasm following a normal sexual excitement phase. *Premature ejaculation* is a disorder in males in which ejaculation occurs with minimal sexual stimulation before, on, or shortly after penetration and before the person wishes it. The clinician must take into account the person's age, novelty of the sexual partner, and the frequency and duration of coitus.

SEXUAL PAIN DISORDERS

Dyspareunia is recurrent or persistent genital pain (usually in women, but sometimes in men) that occurs during or after sexual intercourse.

Vaginismus is recurrent or persistent involuntary muscular spasm of the outer third of the vagina that interferes with sexual intercourse by making penetration difficult, painful, or impossible.

---

and undue self-monitoring; (b) *interpersonal,* such as fear of abandonment, power struggles, lack of trust, failure to explicitly inform partners about one's particular sexual needs and specific pleasures, a "sex manual mentality," or displaced anger; (c) *cultural,* such as sexual myths, insufficient or incorrect information, and negative attitudes about sex learned from parents, religion, or society; (d) *medical,* such as drugs, alcohol, or illness; or (e) *psychiatric,* such as depressive and obsessive-compulsive disorders.

The most common failure in treating sexual dysfunctions is overlooking the presence of a medical illness, another mental disorder, or a drug effect. No matter how obviously emotional problems are affecting the patient, no psychosexual dysfunction should be treated until *after* the patient has had a complete medical workup, preferably by a physician well-versed in the medical causes of sexual dysfunction. A common example is a 55-year-old man with impotence. Diabetes is the most likely cause and loss of nocturnal erections is the best clue. Almost all psychiatric and many nonpsychiatric drugs can cause sexual side effects.

Modern sex therapies are short-term and experiential, aim for symptomatic relief, focus on the here-and-now sexual interactions of a couple, and combine treatments such as education, couples psychotherapy, use of vibrators, homework assignments, desensitization, the squeeze and stop-start techniques, and sensate focusing.[1] Using modern sex therapies, Masters and Johnson (1970) report an 80% overall success rate, with 5% of patients having a recurrence of symptoms within a five-year period. In general, male dysfunctions respond best, with success rates highest for (in declining efficacy) premature ejaculation, retarded ejaculation, secondary impotence, and primary impotence. Treatment is reputed to reverse vaginismus 100% of the time, with less success for generalized unresponsiveness and inhibited orgasm among women. Medications that have been reported, but not yet proven, to enhance responsiveness include testosterone (in men), yohimbine, and cyproheptadine.

PARAPHILIAS

Derived from the Greek meaning "along side of" and "love," a paraphilia is the involuntary and repeated need for unusual or bizarre imagery, acts, or objects to induce sexual excitement. Paraphilias involve either (a) inanimate objects, (b) suffering or humiliation, or (c) sexual activity with nonconsenting partners. To qualify as a disorder, the patient's imagery or actions must produce sexual excitement, orgasm, or relief from nonerotic tension for at least six months. Paraphiliac disorders are rarely diagnosed, but judging from the sales of pornographic magazines, movies, and "aids" that involve paraphilia, they may be more common than we think. They are of unknown etiology and almost always occur in men.

Whether a paraphilia is "normal" or pathological depends on the degree of harm it causes and whether it is the person's preferred or sole way of obtaining sexual gratification. Although some people enjoy their paraphil-

---

[1]The squeeze and stop-start (actually, start-stop) techniques are used mainly to treat premature ejaculation. Clients concentrate on arousal while the penis is stimulated, and then stop stimulation just before ejaculatory inevitability. With stop-start, control quietly returns; with the squeeze, the partner squeezes the penis below the corona until the erection slumps, after which stimulation is resumed. Sensate focusing teaches partners to enjoy sexual activity that is not intended to lead to intercourse.

ias, others feel guilty, develop psychosexual dysfunctions, or end up behind bars. The common paraphilias are described in Table 15–3.

A good way to assess sexual functioning is to ask, "*What is the total number of behaviors in a week that culminate in orgasm?*" Kinsey referred to this number as the "total sexual outlet." Only 5% of men have an outlet of seven or greater, a majority of men with paraphilic disorder have persistent hypersexual desire and tie or exceed this number. A good way to find out what abnormal and normal sexual behaviors are occurring is to ask, "*What are the different ways that you become aroused to the point of orgasm?*" Honest answers to this question will reveal paraphilias and paraphilic-related behavior problems such as promiscuity, dependence on pornography, and compulsive masturbation.

Paraphilic-related problems can cause much distress, wreck marriages, and end jobs. Though sometimes referred to as "sexual addictions," they are classified in *DSM-IV* as "sexual disorders not otherwise specified." Like "real" addictions, these behaviors have a compulsive, repetitious, and ultimately unsatisfying quality. Paraphilic men in stable relationships often have paraphilia fantasies intrude during sexual activity with their partners and paraphilic behaviors replace most normal sexual behaviors. They usually do not specialize in one paraphilia, but rather have two or more during a lifetime. If they have another Axis 1 diagnosis, it is usually dysthymic disorder (but with more libido, not less) or substance abuse (most commonly, the big disinhibitor — alcohol). Not all paraphilias are impulsive. Exhibitionism usually is, but pedophilia is often planned. Arrest for paraphilia typically occurs after the average homosexual pedophile has committed 30 or more molestations and the exhibitionist hundreds of exposures. Pedophilia and transvestic fetishism are discussed in more detail below.

In pedophilia, the erotic stimulus is a prepubescent child (generally age 13 or younger), either of the same or opposite sex. The offender must be at least 16 years old and at least five years older than the child. A late adolescent involved in an ongoing sexual relationship with a 12- or 13-year-old does not count. Pedophiles are almost always male; heterosexual pedophilia is twice as common as homosexual pedophilia. Some pedophiles are homosexual, but the average homosexual is no more likely to be a seducer of children than is the average heterosexual man. Certain subtypes of pedophilia should be noted: (1) Is the *sexual attraction to males, females, or both*? (2) Is the pedophilia *limited to incest*? (3) Is the person *exclusively* or *nonexclusively* attracted to children?

For the most part, the pedophile engages in genital petting or oral-genital contact. Physical aggression against children in such situations is exceedingly rare, although because of the publicity when this happens, the public

TABLE 15–3
The Paraphilias

Any one of these must occur over a period of at least six months and involve recurrent, intense sexual urges and sexually arousing fantasies or behaviors regarding the paraphilia that result in clinically significant distress or impairment in social, occupational, or other important areas of living.

Exhibitionism involves achieving sexual excitement by compulsively and repetitively exposing one's genitals to an unsuspecting stranger. Masturbation may occur, but more often erections can't be obtained. Usually, this behavior is not just a sexual experience but an aggressive act to shock and disgust females. Without the shock value, many exhibitionists get little pleasure. Exhibitionism, which typically begins in the mid-twenties, tends to occur in shy, married, heterosexual males.

Fetishism involves the use of nonliving objects (fetishes), which are not limited to female clothes used exclusively in cross-dressing (transvestism) or to devices solely designed for sexual stimulation (e.g., vibrators). Most fetishes involve clothes, such as women's undergarments.

Pedophilia involves fantasizing about or engaging in sexual activity with a prepubescent child or children (generally age 13 or younger). The pedophile must be at least 16 years old and at least five years older than the child or children molested. Often sexually abused as children, these patients usually turn (on) to pedophilia in midlife during a set-back in marriage or in another close relationship. Most pedophiliacs are male heterosexuals with low self-esteem, who enjoy a sense of mastery and safety when fondling children. Pedophilia is usually a chronic disorder with frequent relapses and resistant to therapy.

Sexual masochism involves real, not simulated, acts of being humiliated, bound, whipped, beaten, or made to suffer in some other way. Masochistic fantasies often arise during childhood, but are not acted on until early adulthood. Normals engage in some sexual masochism, but whether it is pathological depends on the extent of the harm. Some men engage in sexual masochism, but the ratio is 20 females to each male. Unintentional suicides have resulted from sexual masochism.

Sexual sadism involves real, not simulated, acts in which the psychological or physical suffering (including humiliation) of the victim is sexually exciting to the person. The sexual activity may involve a consenting or nonconsenting partner. Mild, consensual, "benignly kinky" sadism that is usually simulated is not a mental disorder. Although sexual sadism may lead to murder and rape, few rapists are sexual sadists.

Voyeurism involves the act of observing an unsuspecting person who is naked, in the process of disrobing, or engaging in sexual activity. Most "Peeping Toms" are more erotically stimulated by watching than by other sexual acts. They don't wish to have sex with the observed and would be frightened if it were offered. They prefer to masturbate while observing or to fantasize about the observed woman feeling helpless, mortified, or terrorized if she knew Tom was observing her.

Frotteurism involves touching and rubbing against a nonconsenting person. It is the touching, not the coercive nature of the act, that is sexually exciting.

TABLE 15–3

(*Continued*)

Transvestistic fetishism involves cross-dressing by a heterosexual male.

Atypical paraphilia not otherwise classified is a residual category for paraphilias not meeting criteria for any of the specific paraphilias. Examples include: smearing feces, *coprophilia*; self-administering enemas, *klismaphilia*; lying in filth, *mysophilia*; exclusive focus on parts of the body (e.g., "all I want is your feet"), *partialism*; sexual activity with animals, *zoophilia*; having sex with a corpse, *necrophilia*; making lewd phone calls, *telephone scatologia*; and a golden oldie, urinating on others, *urophilia*.

has come to associate pedophilia with murderous violence. Probably between a quarter and a third of the sexual offenses committed by adults against children are committed by true pedophiles. Most sexual offenses against children are committed by other types of individuals such as mentally retarded persons, psychotics, men with neurological disease, sociopaths, and occasional males who impulsively approach children while under the influence of alcohol.

In sharp contrast with common belief, most pedophiles are mild mannered and innocuous-appearing men with profound feelings of masculine inadequacy. They are often adults who are unable to relate comfortably to the opposite sex and have turned to children instead. Many were sexually abused as children; as teenagers, they were frequently shy and awkward. In their relations with mature women, they frequently suffer from inadequate sexual performance or impotence, all of which reinforces the individual's profound sense of masculine inadequacy and impaired self-esteem.

Pedophiles are notorious rationalizers, using excuses such as "it has educational value for the child," "the child gets rewarded with sexual pleasure," or "the child was sexually provocative and wanted it." Methods of preventing the child's disclosure range from direct threats to being very generous and attentive to the child's needs.

Management and Treatment

Few paraphilics seek treatment, and if they do, it's usually to extricate themselves from secondary legal or marital difficulties. Many male paraphilics are shy or immature and have difficulty establishing mature heterosexual relations. For them, the paraphilia becomes the main sexual outlet. Therapy attempts to (a) diminish sexual arousal from the paraphilia, (b) increase "normal" heterosexual arousal, (c) teach appropriate assertiveness and social skills (since many of these patients have trouble simply talking to the opposite sex), (d) provide sex education, and (e) correct psychosexual dysfunctions. Behavioral methods such as shock or noxious odors paired with pictures or fantasies of the arousing stimuli and deliberately fantasizing only "normal" sex during masturbation can help reduce the power of the paraphilia.

Cognitive-behavioral treatments focus on relapse-prevention by identifying high-risk thoughts, feelings, and situations. If possible, the patient tries to avoid these, but when this isn't possible, cognitive restructuring strategies are used.

Pharmacologic approaches include drugs that reduce libido such as medroxyprogesterone acetate. This is usually reserved for men who have exhibited violent or illegal paraphilic behavior and is injected every one to three weeks during the first six months of a treatment program. High doses of SSRIs (e.g., 40–80 mg fluoxetine) have been reported to decrease paraphilic fantasies and behaviors while sparing conventional sexual behaviors (Kafka, 1993). The total number of sexual outlets also decreases from hypersexual to "normal" levels.

GENDER IDENTITY DISORDERS

These disorders involve a disturbance in the person's sense of being a man or a woman—that is, a conflict between one's anatomical sex and one's gender identity. By definition, this desire must not be the product of psychosis or of congenital sexual anomalies, such as occurs in a hermaphrodite who has testicular and ovarian tissues. (This latter problem would be called "gender identity disorder not otherwise specified.")

Transvestic Fetishism

Transvestites are heterosexual men who derive erotic pleasure by dressing as women. Usually beginning during childhood or adolescence, the transvestite first experiments with cross-dressing in private (often with masturbation) and then increases the frequency and number of worn items. He may join a transvestite subculture. In time, cross-dressing may no longer provide erotic stimulation, but merely relieve anxiety. When not cross-dressing, transvestites look like regular guys. Although heterosexual, their sexual experiences involve few women and may include an occasional man. Some transvestites claim that during childhood, they were punished and humiliated by mothers or sisters into wearing female attire.

Interfering with this cross-dressing frustrates transvestites and is a useful diagnostic clue. Transvestites differ from *transsexuals* in that the former have male gender identities and do not wish to get rid of their genitals, while the latter have female gender identities and don't receive sexual excitement by wearing women's clothes. When transvestism occurs in conjunction with transsexualism, transsexualism is the diagnosis. When *cross-dressing solely to relieve anxiety* occurs without sexual pleasure, transvestism is not the diagnosis. When *male homosexuals* dress as "drag queens"—for a goof, for masquerade, or for attracting another man—there's no erotic sensation. Neither are *female impersonators* sexually aroused by cross-dressing. *Fetishism* is diagnosed when objects other than clothes stimulate sexual excitement.

Transsexualism (Gender Identity Disorder)

Transsexualism is rare, with a prevalence among men that varies from 1 in 40,000 to 1 in 100,000; among women, prevalence varies from 1 in 100,000 to 1 in 400,000. It can be diagnosed in childhood and adolescence.

Transsexualism, now called "gender identity disorder," is a persistent feeling of severe discomfort with one's own anatomical sex, accompanied by a strong wish to be rid of one's genitals and to live as the opposite sex. (Don't confuse "trans*vest*ism" with "trans*sexualism*": the former changes his vest, the latter, his sex.) Transsexuals usually but not always cross-dress to be in accord with their own gender identity. The patient's family members typically recollect that as a child *he* wanted to be a *she* or vice versa, even as early as three years old. This cross-gender identification confounds relatives and patients alike. While growing up, most transsexuals are scorned and victimized by relatives, peers, doctors, and ministers. This abuse leads to high rates of attempted suicide, antisocial behavior, and self-mutilation (frequently of the genitals). Table 15-4 presents *DSM-IV* criteria for gender disorder

A quiet evening for unsuspecting parents was suddenly interrupted by shrieks from their six-year-old son. They raced to the bedroom to find the walls splattered with blood and their child writhing in pain. Next to their son was a rope—one end was attached to a doorknob, the other to his penis and testicles. Having tied the rope thusly, the child slammed the door shut in a deliberate act of auto-castration. This tragedy is extreme, but the intensity of the unhappiness generating it is frequent for this group of people.

As adults, transsexuals try to live as if they belonged to the opposite sex. Many pull it off (so to speak) even without surgical intervention, and co-workers and friends never know that she is a he (or vice versa). Sexual intimacy is restricted; a majority of transsexuals don't marry, and when

TABLE 15–4
DSM-IV* Criteria for Gender Identity Disorder

A. A strong and persistent cross-gender identification (not merely a desire for any perceived cultural advantages of being the other sex).

In children, the disturbance is manifested by four (or more) of the following:

(1) repeatedly stated desire to be, or insistence that he or she is, the other sex
(2) in boys, preference for cross-dressing or simulating female attire; in girls, insistence on wearing only stereotypical masculine clothing
(3) strong and persistent preferences for cross-sex roles in make-believe play or persistent fantasies of being the other sex
(4) intense desire to participate in the stereotypical games and pastimes of the other sex
(5) strong preference for playmates of the other sex

In adolescents and adults, the disturbance is manifested by symptoms such as a stated desire to be the other sex, frequent passing as the other sex, desire to live or be treated as the other sex, or the conviction that one has the typical feelings and reactions of the other sex.

B. Persistent discomfort with his or her sex or sense of inappropriateness in the gender role of that sex.

In children, the disturbance is manifested by any of the following: in boys, assertion that his penis or testes are disgusting or will disappear or assertion that it would be better not to have a penis, or aversion toward rough-and-tumble play and rejection of male stereotypical toys, games, and activities; in girls, rejection of urinating in a sitting position, assertion that she has or will grow a penis, assertion that she does not want to grow breasts or menstruate, or marked aversion towards normative feminine clothing.

In adolescents and adults, the disturbance is manifested by symptoms such as preoccupation with getting rid of primary and secondary sex characteristics (e.g., request for hormones, surgery, or other procedures to physically alter sexual characteristics to simulate the other sex) or belief that he or she was born the wrong sex.

C. The disturbance is not concurrent with a physical intersex condition.

D. The disturbance causes clinically significant distress or impairment in social, occupational, or other important areas of functioning.

*DSM-IV, pp. 537–38.

they do, the marriages usually fail. Because they experience themselves as members of the opposite sex, they prefer normal heterosexual partners of the same biologic sex. Drugs and talk therapies do not alter the transsexual's cross-gender identification. (However, psychotherapy can alleviate emotional problems arising from the transsexualism.) The cause of human transsexualism is not known, although in animals it can be created by imposing the "wrong" hormone balance in the mother during pregnancy. Once the transsexual clearly decides to switch sexes, professionals should support the patient in going to a sex reassignment clinic to be assessed for the possibility of a sex-change operation. The transsexual no more chooses a gender identity of the opposite sex than the reader chooses a gender identity of his or her own sex. If clinicians have moral qualms about supporting the transsexual's change, they should remove themselves from the case.

A majority of transsexuals wish to change their sex permanently. In America, two to eight times more men than women go to sex reassignment clinics. To qualify for a surgical sex transformation, most centers require that patients live as the opposite sex for at least two years, during which time they should demonstrate good social and occupational functioning, be able to sustain enduring friendships, and be free of major psychopathology. Meanwhile, after obtaining a thorough medical and psychiatric evaluation, they receive estrogen or testosterone. The surgical transformation is more successful for males than females. The man's genitals are amputated, an artificial vagina is constructed from existing fascial planes, and the urethra is moved to its feminine location. Bladder infections are the most common post-operative physical complication. Although many sexual, personal, and occupational problems persist after sex reassignment, most transsexuals never regret having the surgery.

CHAPTER 16

Eating Disorders

IN 1689, DR. RICHARD MORTON described a self-starving 18-year-old female who looked like a "skeleton only clad with skin." He called her condition "nervous consumption"; in 1874, Sir William Gull called it *"anorexia nervosa."* This disorder is characterized by an irrational dread of becoming fat, a zealous pursuit of thinness, massive weight loss, a disturbed body image, and an almost delusional belief of being too fat. *Bulimia*, which wasn't recognized until the 1950s, is characterized by binge-eating and self-induced vomiting. Unlike anorexia nervosa, bulimia usually afflicts normal, or slightly overweight, individuals. Weight preoccupation and pathological approaches to losing weight are shared by the two disorders.

The frequency of eating disorders is rapidly escalating. For example, in Rochester, Minnesota, the incidence of anorexia nervosa among women aged 10–19 jumped a walloping 375% between 1950–1954 and 1980–1984 (Lucas et al, 1991); similar increases have been reported in Zurich and London. These dramatic increases, which have mainly occurred in the most vulnerable group, teen-age girls, are genuine and not merely the result of greater awareness. Anorexia nervosa is also *lethal*, with its mortality rate averaging 5%. The combined prevalence of anorexia nervosa and bulimia in the highest risk group, adolescent and young adult women — mainly upper and middle-class students — ranges between 1–4%.[1]

Although this chapter discusses anorexia nervosa and bulimia, *DSM-IV* describes two other eating disorders under disorders of infancy and childhood: *Pica*, in which children persistently ingest non-nutritive substances (e.g., lead paint chips, hair,

---

[1]See the American Psychiatric Association Practice Guidelines For Eating Disorders (Yager et al., 1993) for a superb review.

x

dirt). (Pica is the Latin word for "magpie," a bird and renowned scavenger.) The other, *rumination disorder of infancy* or merycism, is a rare and sometimes fatal disorder of repeated regurgitation. *Obesity* isn't a *DSM-IV* mental disorder because it lacks a consistent psychological pattern. *DSM-IV* suggests that when psychological forces promote obesity, they should be indicated as "psychological factors affecting physical condition" in the section entitled, Other Conditions That May Be a Focus of Clinical Attention.

ANOREXIA NERVOSA

Clinical Presentation

The essential features of anorexia nervosa are a dread of being fat and a compulsion to be thin, substantial weight loss, refusing to maintain a healthy weight despite being skinny or emaciated, distorted internal and external perceptions of one's body as fat despite being underweight, and in women, amenorrhea. Table 16–1 lists *DSM-IV* criteria for anorexia nervosa.

TABLE 16–1
DSM-IV Criteria for Anorexia Nervosa*

A. Refusal to maintain body weight at or above a minimally normal weight for age and height (e.g., weight loss leading to maintenance of body weight less than 85% of that expected; or failure to make expected weight gain during period of growth, leading to body weight less than 85% of that expected).

B. Intense fear of gaining weight or becoming fat, even though underweight.

C. Disturbance in the way in which one's body weight or shape is experienced, undue influence of body weight or shape on self-evaluation, or denial of the seriousness of the current low body weight.

D. In postmenarcheal females, amenorrhea, i.e., the absence of at least three consecutive menstrual cycles. (A woman is considered to have amenorrhea if her periods occur only following hormone, e.g., estrogen, administration.)

Specify type:
Restricting Type: during the current episode of Anorexia Nervosa, the person does not regularly engage in binge-eating or purging behavior (i.e., self-induced vomiting or the misuse of laxatives, diuretics, or enemas)
Binge-Eating/Purging Type: during the current episode of Anorexia Nervosa, the person regularly engages in binge-eating or purging behavior (i.e., self-induced vomiting or the misuse of laxatives, diuretics, or enemas)

*DSM-IV, pp. 544–45.

No clinician forgets his or her first hospitalized anorectic. The patient looks like a concentration camp victim. This pale, wizened bag of bones prances down the hallway with unrelenting cheerfulness that exhausts onlookers who are riveted in disbelief. Ask why she's skinny and she'll say she's fat. Ask why she's running and dieting, and she'll say it's to lose more weight. The anorectic is childlike in her logic, appearance, and emotions.

In a typical case, a teenager or woman in her early twenties, formerly a "model child," starts dieting for being mildly overweight; this may occur after a stressor (e.g., puberty, a broken romance, a family divorce) or for no apparent reason. After shedding a few pounds, she decides that's not enough. This cycle repeats itself until she virtually stops eating. Only in the most severe stages does she lose her appetite. (Hence, *anorexia* nervosa is a misnomer, since true anorexia doesn't occur until late in the disorder.) Most of the time she has a raging appetite and constantly thinks about food. Unfortunately, her food choices are down to "Romaine versus iceberg lettuce? With or without lemon juice?" She may memorize the calorie-content of foods and prepare meals for everyone but herself. She may hide food, steal it, or play with it. To lose weight, she exercises frenetically, goes on fad diets, abstains from carbohydrates and fats, takes laxatives and diuretics, gorges food and induces vomiting (i.e., bulimic episodes). In time, "Twiggy" resembles the concentration-camp victim.

At first, she's energetic, enthusiastic, and pert, but then depressive symptoms set in, especially dysthymia, insomnia (or hypersomnia), social withdrawal, and decreased libido. She's usually perfectionistic and introverted. She'll have stomach pains, nausea, constipation, cold intolerance, headaches, frequent urination, low blood pressure, and diminished secondary sex characteristics. Vomiting that started intentionally may become automatic. As teenagers, female anorectics may shy away from boys and sex. Normal overt anger is curiously lacking in many anoretics (the restrictors, not bulimics).

The anorectic's family resembles a typical family in a G-rated Disney movie: "As nice as you could find." They frequently speak for the patient: "No, you (to the patient) don't get angry, do you?" They may tell you that she became an extreme vegetarian and now won't eat with the family, in restaurants, or anywhere else in public. Efforts to get her to eat have backfired — she just starves herself more. They proudly tell you that "before this all started, we never fought."

Clinical Course and Complications

Although anorexia nervosa may stop within 12 months, it usually persists for years, punctuated by remissions and exacerbations. About half have bulimic symptoms of binge-eating and purging. Nutritionally, patients usually recover in two to three years, but even then about half continue to have menstrual problems, sexual and social maladjustment, massive weight fluctuations, or disturbed appetite, while two-thirds continue to fret over their weight and body image. In terms of their overall prognosis, on average 44% recover completely (weight 85% or more of recommended weight), 28% improve considerably, 24% remain unimproved or severely impaired (weight never approaches 85% of recommended weight), and 5% die prematurely, usually by cardiac arrest secondary to electrolyte imbalance (from vomiting or purging) or suicide (Hsu, 1986, 1990; Norman, 1984). In the past, death rates reached 20% among patients followed for 20 years (Theander, 1985). A few patients develop osteoporosis leading to pathological fractures, and so complaints of bone or back pain should be investigated. The bone calcium loss may never be regained. Brain mass decreases in 50% of patients, a loss which also may be permanent. Table 16–2 summarizes the medical complications of anorexia.

How anorexia begins has little bearing on its course or outcome. Instead, predictors of a favorable outcome include a good premorbid level of functioning, more education, being single, early age of onset, less weight loss, less denial of illness, overactivity, greater psychosexual maturity, and feeling hunger when hospitalized. Indicators of a poor prognosis are the opposite of above, plus premorbidly disturbed family relationships, perinatal complications, bingeing, self-induced vomiting and purging, longer duration of illness, longer delay in initially obtaining treatment, failure to respond to previous treatment, severe dysthymia and obsessions, and greater exaggeration of body width.

Epidemiology

The typical anorectic is a white, teen-age girl from the middle and upper classes, who will attend college. Given that 90–95% of anorectics are female, the diagnosis should be made extra cautiously in males. Dancers, modeling students, and athletes (e.g., gymnasts, marathon runners) have a higher incidence of anorexia nervosa, but only *after* they began these activities. Eating disorders have also been found in male athletes, especially wrestlers, who learned to starve and vomit "to get down to weight." Male anorectics often don't say they started because they were too fat but rather to get "better muscle definition." All in all, the prevalence of anorexia nervosa is between 0.2–0.3% for females and 0.02% for males. Rates for teen-age girls are around 0.5–0.8%.

Etiology and Pathogenesis

Psychologically, anorectics share two cardinal features: the dread of not being in control and the distorted perception of their own bodies. Before becoming ill, the typical anorectic is a "model child"; afterwards, every-

TABLE 16–2
Medical Complications of Anorexia

Endocrine/Metabolic:
Amenorrhea*
Constipation*
Osteoporosis*
Lanugo hair*
Euthyroid sick syndrome
Decreased norepinephrine secretion
Decreased somatomedin C
Elevated growth hormone
Decreased or erratic vasopressin secretion
Abnormal temperature regulation (hypothermia)*
Hypercarotenemia
Hair loss
Elevated cortisol and abnormal dexamethasone tolerance test
Abnormal glucose tolerance test

Cardiovascular:
Bradycardia*
Hypotension*
Arrhythmias
Impaired cardiac function with normal EKG (with increased sudden death)

Renal:
Increased BUN
Decreased glomerular filtration rate
Renal calculi
Pedal edema (also caused by decreased albumin)

Hematologic:
Anemia*
Leukopenia
Thrombocytopenia

*Most common complications.

thing's a power struggle. Superficially strong and defiant, she's devoid of self-confidence, paralyzed by helplessness, and terrified by her lack of self-control. To compensate, everything is absolute and nothing is relative. The anorectic reacts to gaining a pound with the same distress that the reader might have if she gained 50 pounds overnight. When frantic parents fight with her about eating, they merely feed the patient's stubbornness, since to her, the issue isn't health or even love, but control. (To parents, however, the issue is rejection: "By rejecting my food, she rejects me.")

Struggles over control are inflamed by the patient's internal and external misperceptions of her own body. She minimizes internal stimuli: In comparison to normals, she says she feels less hunger after not eating and feels less exhaustion after exercising. Externally, she sees her body differently from the way others see it. Precise measuring shows that anorectics greatly overestimate their width (often twofold), yet correctly estimate their height, the height and width of female models, and the size of physical objects. Genuinely perceiving her scrawny body as chubby or fat, the anorectic doesn't think she's making herself sick, but merely trying to be attractively thin.

Psychosocial Theories

Biopsychosocial. Our culture has an absurd thinness ideal for females but not for males. This thinness ideal is a historical and cultural aberration, largely confined to Western civilization of the mid- to late-20th century. Prior to this, more rounded and filled-out women were the ideal. Examples include the women in Rubens' paintings in the 1800s and movie stars such as Mae West in the 1920s and 1930s. By today's standards these women would be labeled "too fat." In countries where food is not plentiful, such as China, India, and parts of Africa, being thin means not getting enough food — a condition to be pitied, not admired. Anorexia and bulimia are very rare in these places — a fact that substantially challenges purely biological etiologies of eating disorders.

Unfortunately, our culture has experienced a *shrinking* thinness ideal. Since the 1960s representatives of feminine beauty — Miss America contestants (and winners), *Playboy* centerfolds, movie stars, models, and even department store mannequins have been getting progressively thinner and are now typically below ideal body weight. In modern Western civilization, a woman's appearance tends to be scrutinized and evaluated more than a man's, with a high premium placed on youthfulness and attractiveness. All this is happening during a time when young American women are actually becoming heavier for height, apparently owing to improved nutrition, creating a progressively greater discrepancy between the real situation and the so-called ideal. The pressure to conform to the ideal drives many young women (even prepubescent girls) to diet. In one study of normal-weight adolescents, 80% of the girls "felt fat," compared to 20% of the boys. The women's popular press responds to this pressure by publishing increasing numbers of articles featuring reducing diets (more than 100 per year).

Although there are strong societal influences on the development of eating disorders in women, clearly only a minority of women who are subjected to these influences actually develop eating disorders. Therefore, individual factors in those women must play a role. Adolescents have several daunting developmental tasks to perform including developing and solidifying their own identity, individuating from their family, coming to terms with their sexuality and feeling accepted by peers. Some adolescents are going to have a harder time accomplishing these goals and be more vulnerable to developing anorexia. At highest risk are those with low self-esteem (anorectics have high rates of depression), rigid approaches in dealing with problems (25% of anorectics also have obsessive-compulsive personality disorder), overcontrolling (and, in some cases, undercontrolling) families in which problems don't get worked out, and those with serious conflicts about sexuality. Anorexia becomes a means of dealing with these issues, albeit pathologically. An anorectic girl can define herself in terms of what she is *against* (food! fat!), indirectly fight with her family, temporarily ignore sexuality issues as she loses secondary sexual characteristics, and, in the beginning, but not later, feel more attractive to her peers. In some, the initial massive weight loss may alter their biological homeostatic mechanisms in such a way as to maintain the anorexia.

Psychodynamic. Analysts blame domineering mothers for preventing the anorectic from the two chief psychosocial tasks of adolescence — separating and individuating. Anorectics demand independence even as they cling to their mothers. Yet with these, as with most etiological theories of anorexia nervosa, what's purported to be a cause of the disorder may be both a cause and consequence of it.

Family. Many papers describe the anorectic's father as ineffective, her mother as overbearing, and both parents as intrusive. The family system is out-of-whack and the parents are acting screwy. But how would any "normal" parents behave watching their daughter starve herself to death?

When anorectics are hospitalized, clinicians are often struck by how parents will hover over their daughter and be within an inch of exploding. But once again, is this cause or effect? Amdur, Tucker, Detre, and Markhus (1969) showed it was effect, because the parents' behavior reflected their daughter's condition. For the first six weeks of hospitalization, when patients were at their worst, staff rated parents as unfeeling, intellectualizing, and rigid; during the last six weeks, when patients were recovering, staff rated parents as appropriately emotional, flexible, and supportive of autonomy. This study does not address the original cause of anorexia nervosa; instead, it suggests that once the disorder has arisen, family psychopathology is more a reaction to the patient's difficulties than a cause of them. Such reactions surely aggravate and perpetuate matters and merit treatment.

Biological Theories

A major debate in recent biological research has been whether or not eating disorders share common biological pathways with depression. The affirmative side points to the high frequency of depression in anorectics (40–75%), and the higher prevalence of mood disorders in close relatives of anorectics and especially bulimics. The negative side points out that eating and depressive disorders are more different than alike. Although the question remains open, anorexia nervosa might be a heterogenous disorder, with some cases having, and other cases not having, a biological link to depression.

Genetic. Anorexia nervosa is more prevalent among the first-degree female relatives of anorectic patients. For instance, 6.6% of sisters of anorectics have the disorder. The prevalence of depression and alcoholism, but not schizophrenia, appears greater among family members. Winokur, March, and Mendels (1980) reported mood disorders in 22% of relatives of anorectics compared to 10% of controls.

Biochemical and anatomical. As measuring techniques improve and attention to these disorders increases, neuroendocrine abnormalities in the hypothalamic-pituitary and gonadotropin-ovarian axes keep popping up. Most, but not all, authorities view these changes more as consequences than causes. Similarly, CT scans of anorectics show them to have enlarged third and lateral ventricles in the brain, but this too might be nothing more than a consequence of malnutrition (Datlof, Coleman, Forbes, & Kreipe, 1986).

Differential Diagnosis

Anorexia nervosa is easy to distinguish from other disorders, primarily *schizophrenia* and *depression*, in which massive weight loss is prominent. Besides lacking the common symptoms seen in these disorders, anorectics and bulimics misjudge their body image, misperceive internal body cues, binge and purge, and display hyperactivity, inordinate cheerfulness, a zealous preoccupation with food, and a dread of obesity. These distinctions also apply for *malnutrition* and *starvation* (e.g., *tuberculosis, Crohn's disease, ulcerative colitis, extreme poverty*), as well as various *neurological diseases*, such as *epilepsy* and *brain tumors*. One question can usually distinguish a very thin person from an anorectic: "What is your ideal body weight?" Almost all anorectics will say something less than their current weight, while all others will say, "I need to gain weight, I'm too thin."

Management and Treatment

The legacy of Karen Carpenter, the young pop singer who died from anorexia nervosa, should remind clinicians that the first goal in treatment is always to (a) keep the patient alive. Beyond this, the goals are to (b) establish adequate nutrition, (c) treat physical complications, (d) correct abnormal eating habits, (e) supplant family overinvolvement with more appropriate intrafamilial relationships, (f) enhance self-control, identity, and autonomy, (g) identify and begin correcting dysfunctional thoughts, attitudes, and beliefs, and (h) correct defects in affect and behavioral regulation.

Hospitalization and behavior therapy. If the patient's weight is *medically precarious*, hospitalization is mandatory. Bargaining by the patient — "Please, I beg! I promise to gain weight" — means zilch. If matters have so deteriorated that the patient is in danger of losing her life, professionals must take charge. Family members can't. Once hospitalized, treatment follows the same principles set down in 1874 by Sir William Gull, who named the disorder. Patients should be fed at regular intervals and surrounded by persons who would have moral control over them; relatives and friends generally are the worst attendants.

More specifically, behavior therapy is used first to prevent starvation, restore nutritional balance, and increase weight. Programs vary but, in essence, the patient is told that she must gain about one-fourth to a one-half pound each day above her highest recent weight. It is important to pick only battles that can be won. Cleaning her plate and not exercising are not realistically enforceable. How she gains the weight is her business. There's no fuss, no special diets, no exercise restrictions. If she wants a dietician's advice, that's okay. She may request liquid nutrition supplements because she has difficulty with solid foods. She's weighed every morning in the nude or in a hospital gown, since these patients are pros at sneaking extra pounds in the heels of shoes, hems of nighties, etc. If she drank a gallon of water just before weigh-in, wait about an hour and a half to weigh her. If she doesn't gain her goal weight, in some programs she's tube fed, in others, she's confined to bed all day. If she does gain her weight, she does whatever she wants. Penalties are sometimes built in for bingeing weight gains, e.g., more than one pound a day. This program is continued until the patient reaches medically safe weight, usually within 10% of the norm. Discharging only at an acceptable weight (15% of norm) is risky. If she loses one-half pound the next day, she may have to be rehospitalized. After discharge her doctors, *not her family*, should follow her weight, typically at weekly intervals.

Nurses play a crucial role during this early phase. Besides implementing this regimen, nurses should tell the patient to notify them as soon as she's tempted to stuff her face, and they will stop her from doing so. This is a potent message: It shows they understand her dread of becoming fat; this allies them *with* her, not *against* her, thereby undercutting the rebellious aspect of overeating and circumventing the power struggles that occurred within the family. (Just knowing the nurses are *available* is usually enough for the patient to stop herself.) Nurses must prevent parents from cajoling the patient on how and what to eat.

Family therapy. Early on, parents should not have any responsibility for the patient's care. This diffuses family tension, permits autonomy for the patient, and gracefully lets the parents off the hook. In some programs, either a week after admission or once the patient begins to gain weight, informal lunches with the entire family are held to evaluate family interactions at mealtime, to reduce intrafamily power struggles, and to promote more helpful behavior around the table. These family therapy lunches are continued after discharge to establish more balanced family relationships. Most programs just use traditional family therapy.

Psychotherapy. Individual psychotherapy focuses on helping the patient learn to abandon her self-destructive stabs at autonomy and to find more enduring self-worth and self-control from within. Variations on assertiveness training are helpful so that patients can say "no" in family conflicts without aggression, undercutting, or capitulation. *Group therapy* helps patients re-establish lost social skills and assists them in viewing themselves as "somebody other than an eating freak." Many locales offer self-help groups for patients with eating disorders.

One caveat: Anytime a therapist says, "The patient's making progress in therapy, even though she's losing weight," the patient is in trouble. This statement is the psychiatric equivalent of, "The operation was a success, but the patient died." Psychotherapies are no substitute for proper nutrition and weight gain.

Medication. Many anorectics also have major depression, which sometimes improves with weight restoration. Between 40–60% of patients benefit from antidepressants. Because their blood pressure is already low, employ these medications with caution, since malnourished patients are especially sensitive to drugs. Orthostatic hypotension is the biggest risk with the tricyclic antidepressants. The SSRIs are often recommended as a first choice because they don't cause orthostatic hypotension and have minimal effect on heart rhythms. Nonresponders may improve with the serotonin antagonist, cyproheptadine (Periactin), an appetite enhancer. This only works if they have lost their appetite and can view appetite as a cue to eat and not exercise or play with their food.

BULIMIA NERVOSA

The word *bulimia* is not a misnomer. It means "the hunger of an ox" from the Greek: *bous* = ox, *limos* = hunger. Binge-eating is the central feature of bulimia. Bulimics view their bingeing as pathological, dread their inability to control their eating, and become unhappy and self-deprecating after bingeing. Because they're ashamed, a majority try to hide their problem, the Big Secret, from clinicians. Although self-induced vomiting occurs in 88% of patients, it is not a diagnostic requirement. In contrast to anorexia nervosa, severe weight loss is uncommon and amenorrhea is less common (40%). *DSM-IV* criteria for bulimia are listed in Table 16–3.

Eating-binges last a few minutes to two hours; on average they're an hour. Bulimics may binge twice a week or over ten times a day. Always ask what the person means by a binge. An anorexic once told me (NW) that her "binge" was three carrots. Dysphoria usually precedes a binge and is relieved by it. Patients usually give more than one reason for bingeing: feeling anxious or tense (83%), craving certain foods (70%), feeling unhappy (67%), "can't control appetite" (59%), hunger (31)%, insomnia

---

TABLE 16–3
DSM-IV* Criteria for Bulimia Nervosa

A. Recurrent episodes of binge eating. An episode of binge eating is characterized by both of the following:

    (1) eating, in a discrete period of time (e.g., within any 2-hour period), an amount of food that is definitely larger than most people would eat during a similar period of time and under similar circumstances

    (2) a sense of lack of control over eating during the episode (e.g., a feeling that one cannot stop eating or control what or how much one is eating)

B. Recurrent inappropriate compensatory behavior in order to prevent weight gain, such as self-induced vomiting; misuse of laxatives, diuretics, enemas, or other medications; fasting; or excessive exercise.

C. The binge eating and inappropriate compensatory behaviors both occur, on average, at least twice a week for three months.

D. Self-evaluation is unduly influenced by body shape and weight.

E. The disturbance does not occur exclusively during episodes of Anorexia Nervosa.

Specify type:
    Purging Type: during the current episode of Bulimia Nervosa, the person has regularly engaged in self-induced vomiting or the misuse of laxatives, diuretics, or enemas
    Nonpurging Type: during the current episode of Bulimia Nervosa, the person has used other inappropriate compensatory behaviors, such as fasting or excessive exercise, but has not regularly engaged in self-induced vomiting or the misuse of laxatives, diuretics, or enemas

---

*DSM-IV, pp. 549–550.

(22%).[2] Bulimics are more likely to binge as the day goes on. While gorging themselves, most patients aren't aware of hunger and don't stop even when satiated. They don't chew, they gobble, preferably foods high in calories and easy to devour. Three thousand calories is an average binge, but calorie consumption ranges from 1,200 to 11,500 calories. Bulimics will "pig out" on three pounds of chocolate, popcorn for an army, and four pints of ice cream. Bulimics can spend over $100 a day on food; some steal food. To avoid detection, most binge in private.

Bingeing typically stops when the patient is discovered, falls asleep, develops stomach pain, or induces vomiting. By diminishing abdominal cramps and distention, this self-induced vomiting permits further binges. Besides wishing to lose weight, bulimics continue to binge in order to delay the inevitable postbinge dysphoria. This dysphoria is described as guilt (87%), feeling too full (64%), worried (53%) still hungry (22%). A minority feel relaxed (23%) or satisfied (15%). In therapy, bulimics describe their bingeing as "disgusting" but irresistible. When having a normal meal — on average, a twice-a-week event — they fear bingeing again or gaining weight.

These patients are preoccupied with their appearance, body image, and sexual attractiveness, as well as how others, men especially, perceive and respond to them. By using various techniques — binge eating (100%), fasting (92%), exercise (91%), vomiting (88%), spitting out food (65%), laxatives (61%), diet pills (50%), diuretics (34%), saunas (12%) — bulimics can readily add or shed ten pounds a day. Rarely are bulimics skinny; 5% are overweight. Prior to their bulimia, 14% were underweight, 56% were overweight. They frequently have problems controlling their impulses in other areas. About a third have abused drugs and alcohol and about a fifth have received treatment for it. A minority will steal, mutilate themselves, or attempt suicide. To look thin and sexually attractive — a redundancy to bulimics — and to alleviate sadness, they'll go on clothes-buying sprees ("retail therapy"). Unlike anorectics, they are usually sexually active, and some are promiscuous.

Clinical Course and Complications

Bulimia usually arises a little later than anorexia, during the late teens or early twenties, and rarely, after thirty. The first episode commonly follows a traumatic event or a period of stringent dieting. Bulimia is a chronic disorder, with fluctuating intensity and alternating periods of normal and

---

[2]The percentages given in this section are mostly from Mitchell, Hatsukami, Eckert, and Pyle's (1985) study of 257 bulimics.

binge-eating. Less often, normal eating doesn't occur; the patient cycles between periods of bingeing and fasting. Anecdotally, bulimics generally improve or completely recover. Death, usually from hypokalemia (low potassium), is rare.

During periods of rapid weight gain, bulimics' hands, feet, and ankles often swell from a "refeeding edema." These patients endure weakness (84%), abdominal bloating (75%), stomach pain (63%), headaches, and dizziness. They get sore throats from the vomiting (54%), painful swellings of salivary and parotid glands called "chipmunk" or "puffy" cheeks (50%), dental caries (37%), and finger calluses (on their gagging fingers). Menstrual irregularities are common and 40% have intermittent or sustained amenorrhea. If they use Ipecac to make them vomit, they are at risk of death from cardiomyopathy.

Dehydration is common in underweight bulimics who use diuretics or vomit after bingeing. Electrolyte imbalance, most often hypokalemic alkalosis, occurs in about half of bulimics. It can result from vomiting as well as diuretic and laxative abuse. The hypokalemia can cause patients to feel lethargic and cognitively dulled and may even lead to serious or life-threatening cardiac conduction abnormalities. Because of the problems in thinking, hypokalemia should be corrected before psychotherapy is tried. Patients report problems with intimate or interpersonal relations (70%), family (61%), finances (because of food purchasing) (53%), and work (50%).

Epidemiology

Like the anorectic, the prototypic bulimic is a white, adolescent girl from the middle or upper class, who attends a university (cases of bulimia in African-Americans are uncommon). Ninety to 95% of bulimics are female. In a survey of 257 bulimics by Mitchell, Hatsukami, Eckert, and Pyle (1985), 88% were from social classes I through III; two patients were Native Americans, the rest were white.

The prevalence of bulimia varies enormously depending on the particular subpopulation. Although the prevalence is less than 0.5% in the general population, in a survey of 500 college students, 4.4% had eating disorders; 86% of these had bulimia using the less restrictive *DSM-III* criteria, while only 14% had anorexia nervosa (Strangler & Printz, 1980).

Although eating disorders are clearly on the rise, their frequency is often inflated in the popular press, such as "at least one-half of the women on campuses today suffer from some kind of an eating disorder" (Squire, 1983). Professionals have also been guilty of overestimating their prevalence. A common mistake is to equate binge-eating with an eating disorder. The difference can be substantial. Hart and Ollendick (1985) found binge-eating among 41% of working women and 69% of female university students, but the full bulimic syndrome was seen in only 1% of working, and 5% of college, women.

Etiology and Pathogenesis

Very little is known about the causes of bulimia. Descriptive and biological psychiatrists have noted a relationship between bulimia and other psychiatric disorders. About 75% of bulimics develop major depression; 43% have anxiety disorders; 49% have substance disorders; and 50–75% have personality disorders or trait disturbances (usually in cluster B). First-degree relatives of bulimics have a higher frequency of mood disorder, substance abuse, and obesity (Yager et al., 1993).

Bulimic families appear enmeshed but disengaged. In comparing 105 bulimic and 86 control families, Johnson and Flach (1985) found that the former set high expectations, but placed small emphasis on their daughter's intellectual, cultural, or recreational activities. Despite the fact that the overall structure and rules of bulimic families resembled those in normal families, the bulimic families were more disorganized, showing lack of ability to solve problems, manage crises, or get things done. Although high expectations were also seen in the control families, the disorganization of the bulimic's family and little concern for the patient's activities best correlated with the severity of the patient's symptoms.

Differential Diagnosis

Distinguishing between anorexia nervosa and bulimia is the only common diagnostic difficulty. Few people make a habit of bingeing and vomiting, except for bulimics and 40–50% of anorectics. There is probably a continuum between the two disorders with pure "restricting type" anorectics at one end and pure bulimics at the other. The anorectics who binge and purge are somewhere in-between. Bingeing anorectics (the bulimic subtype) are more akin to normal-weight bulimics than to anorectics who don't binge (the restrictive subtype). In comparison to restrictive anorectics, normal-weight bulimics and bulimic anorectics perceive more family conflict and are more impulsive, outgoing, sexually active, and emotionally disturbed; they may be more prone to depression and have twice as many relatives with mood disorders. Table 16–4 compares anorexia and bulimia.

Management and Treatment

Medical complications. The medical complications associated with bulimia are related to the individual aspects of the illness. These must always be addressed first in evaluation and treatment because several are life-threatening and disabling.

TABLE 16–4
Comparison and Contrast of Anorexia and Bulimia

	Anorexia	Bulimia
Obesity	Uncommon	Common
Sexual activity	Low	Normal
Amenorrhea	100%	40%
Exercise	Excessive	±
Depression	50%	75%
Substance abuse	Rare	Common
Suicidality	10%	40%
Personality disorders/traits	Obsessive-compulsive	Borderline/narcissistic
	Avoidant	Impulsive
	Schizoidal	Demonstrative
Family conflict	Covert	Overt
	Controlled	Disorganized

Electrolyte imbalance occurs in about half of bulimic patients. It can result from vomiting as well as diuretic and laxative abuse. Hypokalemic alkalosis is particularly common. The hypokalemia (low potassium) can lead to serious, even life-threatening cardiac conduction abnormalities. This can cause patients to feel lethargic, weak, and cognitively dulled.

Bulimic patients who use diuretics may experience dehydration and rebound edema as well as the electrolyte disturbances mentioned earlier. Some bulimic patients use syrup of Ipecac to induce vomiting. Its active ingredient, emetine, can produce myopathies, both generalized and cardio-myopathy. This is a particularly insidious complication because the effect of the emetine is cumulative. Bulimic patients who misuse laxatives are at risk for laxative dependency, steatorrhea, protein-losing gastroenteropathy, and gastrointestinal bleeding. Laxatives will cause the bulimic to lose only 3% of calories consumed. Many bulimics, when informed of this, quit this dangerous method. To avoid an atonic bowel, excessive laxatives should be slowly tapered, not stopped abruptly.

Parotid gland enlargement (chipmunk cheeks) is common among bulimic patients, but the mechanism for this is unknown. As many as a third of bulimic patients may have elevated serum amylase levels; however, this does not appear to be correlated to the presence of parotid gland enlargement, and both salivary and pancreatic isoenzyme may be involved. Dental erosion and numerous cavities are common with vomiting. Menstrual irregularities are also common among bulimic patients, even those of normal weight. Gastric or esophageal rupture is a rare complication of binge-eating, whereas acute gastric dilation is a common and a painful result of it.

Hospitalization. Most bulimics are best treated as outpatients, but under what conditions should they be hospitalized? Three conditions warrant this intervention: (1) to manage a medical emergency (electrolyte imbalances, severe orthostatic hypertension, or precipitous weight loss); (2) to break a severe, recalcitrant binge-starve cycle; (3) to evaluate diagnostically or deal with a family crisis.

Medication. Bulimia, or at least bingeing, is moderately responsive to antidepressants (TCAs, SSRIs, and MAOIs) over six to eight weeks (Walsh, 1991). On average, antidepressants decrease bulimics' binge frequencies by 50%, with 20% achieving complete recovery. Both depressed and nondepressed bulimics show equally effective responses. The highest dose (60 mg) of fluoxetine, usually reserved for obsessive-compulsive disorder, works better than the usual antidepressant dose (20 mg). When bulimic patients are treated with antidepressants alone for six months or more, there are many dropouts, and by 12 months, antidepressants do no better than placebo (Walsh, 1991). When antidepressants are combined with therapy, there are fewer dropouts and possibly an additive effect of the therapy (Abbot & Mitchell, 1993). Patients who don't respond to the usual antidepressants still can respond to MAOIs. Antidepressants may be most useful in "jumpstarting" a bulimic's therapy while awaiting the delayed positive effects of psychotherapy. Those who are excellent responders could elect to stay on their medication. The antidepressants could also be reserved for patients who aren't progressing well with psychotherapy. At this time, it is not known how to predict who will do better with antidepressants alone, in combination with psychotherapy, or with psychotherapy alone.

Psychotherapy. Individual and group therapy using either cognitive-behavioral or psychodynamic (particularly, interpersonal) approaches are quite effective in treating bulimia. Generally there are two phases to the treatment. Phase 1 focuses on breaking the binge-purge cycle — a behavioral approach can quickly reduce bingeing and purging. The patient keeps a careful record of food intake, vomiting, purgative abuse, and the context of bingeing (time, place, mood, etc.). The abnormal pattern of eating is then shaped into a more normal pattern by avoiding precipitants of binges and substituting alternative pleasurable activities (showers, baths, walks, talk to a friend on the phone). Patients are also instructed to practice delaying (but not necessarily stopping) vomiting, especially if it happens after normal meals. For example, they may try to wait 30 minutes before vomiting, having succeeded at waiting 25 minutes the day before.

Phase 2 focuses on broad areas of behavior and attitudes — cognitive-behavioral therapy (CBT) appears to be best. CBT is as effective as behavioral and interpersonal therapy at reducing bingeing and depression and

more effective in modifying disturbed attitudes toward shape, weight, dieting, and the use of vomiting to control shape and weight (Agras, 1991).
Patients who participate in CBT show greater overall improvement. Dietary
management helps further. One goal is eating for weight maintenance to
break the binge-fast roller coaster. Group therapy works at least as well
as individual therapy in this phase. Fairburn et al. (1993) reported that
interpersonal therapy is as effective as CBT, but it takes longer.

The five-year mortality rate for bulimia is not known. The overall short-
term prognosis is about 70% reduction in bingeing and purging, with reasonably good maintenance of gains over six years.

CHAPTER 17

Sleep Disorders

ON AN APRIL NIGHT IN 1952, in Chicago, the greatest of all sleep discoveries was made: Non-rapid eye movement (NREM) and rapid eye movement (REM) sleep differ in significant ways (Dement & Kleitman, 1975). Under Dr. Nathaniel Kleitman's direction, a physiology graduate student, Eugene Aserinsky, was instructed to record the floating eyes of sleeping infants. The eyes did float, as expected, but then they suddenly went berserk. Was the baby creeping or was the machine malfunctioning? No—but the weird marks persisted and formed patterns. Could it be that sleep was not one, but two, physiologic entities? It sure was: The slow tracings seemed to be NREM (nondream) sleep, while the erratic ones were REM (dream) sleep.

During NREM sleep, muscles move; during REM sleep, they're paralyzed. Erections spring up in REM sleep and flop in NREM sleep. Throughout NREM sleep, the senses shut off and the person loses touch with the environment; REM sleep reawakens the senses. In NREM "quiet" sleep, cardiac rate, blood pressure, respiration, temperature, and metabolism decrease; REM's more "active" sleep increases them. Snoring appears in NREM, but disappears in REM sleep. Dreaming no longer is seen as REM-only activity; in fact, 20% of dreaming occurs during NREM sleep, but these dreams tend to be mundane and boring, like sitting in class or driving a car—while REM dreams are more often primary process, crazy and exotic.

NREM sleep consumes about three-quarters of all sleep time. At bedtime people doze off into NREM sleep, descending from "light" stages 1 (5% of the night) and 2 (48% of the night) into deep or "delta" stages 3 (7% of the night) and 4 (15% of the night) (Maxmen, 1991). With each stage, brain waves become slower. After 40 to 50 minutes, NREM sleep goes back to stage 2, and at 70 to 80 minutes, the first REM sleep pops up. As the night proceeds, the duration of REM sleep increases so that the initial clip spins for five to 10 minutes, whereas the final movie flutters for 30 to 40 minutes (Maxmen, 1985) (that's why people often wake up from a dream). Four to five NREM-REM sleep cycles complete the night. When not clearly in sleep stages, people are either between sleep stages, awake, or drowsing but not quite asleep. Any awakening under five minutes is usually forgotten the next morning.

Sleep patterns fluctuate throughout the lifespan. Newborns, who dream 80% of the time, nap from 14 to 18 hours each day. By six months, from falling asleep to waking up—that is, total sleep time (TST)—declines to 13.7 hours; REM sleep assumes a third of it. NREM sleep stages emerge by two and reach adult percentages by adolescence. Between ages 20 and 60 the average TST dips a mere 30 minutes—from 7.7 to 7.2 hours—but delta sleep plummets from 23% to 8%. So when the elderly complain about insomnia, their gripe is really with the depth and not the length of their sleep.

How much sleep do people need? Only as much as to feel refreshed the following day. Sleep requirements are individual, be they three, eight, or 12 hours a night. Although it's hard to convince some patients otherwise, there's nothing magical or sacred about eight hours of sleep. Insisting on eight hours is like asserting that since the average adult male is five-feet eight-inches tall, any guy who is five-feet-six-inches is pathological. If sleep invigorates in four hours, the person is an efficient, not a poor, sleeper. (Over 70 years, four less hours/night of sleep would provide 12 added years to read this text and play video games.) If people require 11 hours of sleep, they simply need more sleep. What's more, TST can vary from night to night, as long as the general sleep pattern rejuvenates over time.

Aside from occasional sleeplessness, under 5% of the citizenry complain of chronic fatigue, but an added 15–30% complain of frequent or persistent insomnia. If a questionnaire asks if poor sleep ever bothers subjects, 35% answer positively and 17% consider their insomnia serious. Eighty percent of consultation-liaison patients report poor sleep, 14% tell physicians about it, 21% seek treatment, and at least 11% receive a prescription for it (Maxmen, 1985). Older people, who indicate relatively more sleep problems, mainly suffer from middle and late insomnia, whereas youth have trouble dropping off to sleep. "Sleep problems" are confessed far more than is "insomnia."

The continuous use of prescription sleeping pills (hypnotics) often worsens insomnia. Although they initially knock one out, many hypnotics wear thin in five to 30 days, and with this tolerance, a greater dose is needed to achieve the same effect. Some hypnotics, especially shorter-acting ones such as triazolam and estazolam, can induce a rebound insomnia that flares up in just one to two nights after suddenly halting a normal amount of the drug (Maxmen, 1991). It's tempting to relieve both conditions with more hypnotics, yet that's the worst thing to do: These pills rank among medicine's most addictive.

Three sources can diagnose sleep disorders: patients, bedmates, and sleep clinics. Each has limits. Insomniacs typically overestimate their time falling asleep: For those claiming an hour to doze off, 60% and 44% did so in 30 and 15 minutes, respectively. Only one in six patients who complain of a TST of under five hours was correct; 65% slept for over six hours. Despite these inaccuracies, self-reports clarify how patients experience their predicaments. For some disorders, bedmates can provide key facts that patients can't, such as snoring in sleep apnea.

Sleep clinics, which have mushroomed across the country, have become the insomniac's salvation. These clinics are invaluable, but their usefulness with sleep disorder patients is far from automatic. They should only be involved if there exists a good diagnostic or therapeutic reason. Sleep clinics utilize at least four technological devices: a polysomnograph (PSG) that records brain-wave activity and other variables on an electroencephalogram (EEG); an electromyogram (EMG) that transcribes minute electrical currents from muscle fibers; an electrooculogram (EOG) that charts eye movements, and a finger-pulse oxyimeter (FPO) that measures moment-by-moment oxygen saturation.

Because many diverse factors can disrupt or distort sleep, clinical detectives should track them down in the following sequence (the *DSM-IV* names for the first three, the secondary sleep disorders, are included; diagnostic criteria are in Table 17–1).

1. **Drugs**, such as hypnotics: *substance-induced sleep disorder*;
2. **Medical**, such as pain: *sleep disorder due to a general medical condition*;
3. **Mental**, such as depression: choose either *insomnia* or *hypersomnia* related to whichever Axis I or Axis II disorder;
4. **Primary sleep disorders**, which are divided into two groups: *dyssomnias*, such as *primary insomnia, primary hypersomnia, sleep apnea, narcolepsy, nocturnal myoclonus/restless legs syndrome*, and *circadian rhythm difficulties* (e.g., jet lag); and *parasomnias*, such as bedwetting, sleepwalking, sleep terrors, nightmares, and sleep-talking.

TABLE 17–1
DSM-IV **Criteria for Secondary Sleep Disorders Due to a General
Medical Condition, Substance Use, or Axis I or II Disorder***

Common Criteria

A. A prominent disturbance in sleep which is sufficiently severe to warrant independent clinical attention.

B. There is evidence from the history, physical examination, or laboratory findings that the sleep disturbance is the direct physiological consequence of a general medical condition, or either (1) or (2):

   (1) the symptoms in Criterion A developed during, or within a month of, Substance Intoxication or Withdrawal
   (2) medication use is etiologically related to the sleep disturbance

C. The sleep disturbance causes clinically significant distress or impairment in social, occupational, or other important areas of functioning.

D. The disturbance does not occur exclusively during the course of a delirium.

Additional Criterion for Sleep Disorder Due to a General Medical Condition

E. The disturbance does not meet criteria for a Breathing-Related Sleep Disorder or Narcolepsy.

Additional Criterion for Substance-Induced Sleep Disorder

E. The disturbance is not better accounted for by a Sleep Disorder that is not substance induced. Evidence that the symptoms are better accounted for by a Sleep Disorder that is not substance-induced might include the following: the symptoms precede the onset of the substance use (or medication use); the symptoms persist for a substantial period of time (e.g., about a month) after the cessation of acute withdrawal or severe intoxication, or are substantially in excess of what would be expected given the type or amount of the substance used or the duration of use; or there is other evidence that suggests the existence of an independent non-substance-induced Sleep-Disorder (e.g., history of recurrent non-substance-related episodes).

DSM-IV Criteria for Insomnia or Hypersomnia Related
to an Axis I or Axis II Disorder
Common Criteria

A. The excessive sleepiness (for hypersomnia) or sleep disturbance or dayime sequelae (for insomnia) causes clinically significant distress or impairment in social, occupational, or other important areas of functioning.

B. The hypersomnia or insomnia is judged to be related to another Axis I or Axis II disorder (e.g., Major Depressive Disorder, Dysthymic Disorder, Generalized Anxiety Disorder, Adjustment Disorder with Anxiety), but is sufficiently severe to warrant independent clinical attention.

(Continued)

TABLE 17–1
(Continued)

C. The disturbance is not due to the direct physiological effects of a substance (e.g., a drug of abuse, a medication) or a general medical condition.

D. The disturbance is not better accounted for by another Sleep Disorder (e.g., Narcolepsy, Breathing-Related Sleep Disorder, a Parasomnia) or (for hypersomnia) by an inadequate amount of sleep.

Additional Criterion for Insomnia Related to Axis I or Axis II Disorder

E. The predominant complaint is difficulty initiating or maintaining sleep, or nonrestorative sleep, for at least 1 month that is associated with daytime fatigue or impaired daytime functioning.

Additional Criterion for Hypersomnia Related to Axis I or Axis II Disorder

F. The predominant complaint is excessive sleepiness for at least 1 month as evidenced by either prolonged sleep episodes or daytime sleep episodes occurring almost daily.

DSM-IV, pp. 596–97, 600–601, 606–7.

By definition, dyssomnias are problems in the amount, quality, or timing of sleep, while parasomnias are bothersome events during sleep that don't necessarily affect sleep quality or quantity. Table 17–2 summarizes the PSG findings and treatments for the major sleep disorders.[1]

DYSSOMNIAS THAT CAUSE HYPERSOMNIA: BREATHING-RELATED SLEEP DISORDER

Clinical Presentation

Snoring is boring—except when it kills—and that occurs when especially loud snoring stems from sleep apnea, a common and potentially fatal disease. Patients with sleep apnea stop breathing. Without realizing it, they might not breathe for 30 to 130 seconds, 200 to 400 times a night. Very mild cases may have as few as five episodes an hour. An episode includes two phases: *apnea* lasting 10 or more seconds, and *hypopnea,* which is a decrease in oxygen saturation of at least 4%. What two-thirds of these pa-

---

[1] Patients with any of these disorders and clinicians desiring referral information can contact the American Sleep Disorders Association, 1610 14th St. NW, Rochester, Minnesota 55901, phone (507) 287-6006.

TABLE 17–2
Polysomnograph and Treatment of Sleep Disorders

Diagnosis	Polysomnograph Findings	Primary Treatment
Sleep apnea (obstructive)	EEG micro-arousals, EKG arrhythmias	Weight loss, continuous positive airway pressure, surgery
Sleep apnea (central)	Central sleep apneas, micro-arousals	Acetazolamide, low-flow oxygen, stimulants, stimulating antidepressants, estrogen
Narcolepsy	Repeated sleep onset REM periods (multiple sleep latency test)	Stimulants (e.g., methylphenidate), TCAs for cataplexy
Periodic limb movement disorder; restless legs syndrome	Periodic leg twitches, EEG micro-arousals	Benzodiazepines, carbidopa-levodopa
Circadian rhythm disorders, delayed or advanced type	Delayed: sleep onset and awakening later. Advanced: sleep onset and awakening earlier.	Chronotherapy, bright lights, physical activity
Parasomnias	Partial arousal out of slow-wave sleep	Various behavioral or pharmacologic methods
Primary insomnia	Varies from normal to interrupted sleep continuity	Biofeedback, stimulus control, temporal control, short-term benzodiazepines
Dyssomnias from another mental disorder, such as major depression	Short REM latency, prolonged first REM period, increased REM	TCAs, MAOIs, psychotherapy, benzodiazepines

tients report is that they are exhausted by day; the other third can't fall asleep at night (Maxmen, 1985).

These patients typically surface as medical disasters: They are often overweight and suffering from coronary artery disease and strokes (Phillipson, 1993). Usually hypertensive, sleep-distracted men, sleep apneacs may never mention their snoring — but bedmates will. The *DSM-IV* criteria for breathing-related sleep disorder are listed in Table 17–3.

Subtypes. Sleep apnea can be *obstructive* or *central*. In obstructive sleep apnea, the soft palatal tissue and muscles of the upper airway collapse. Snoring that precedes apnea by many years is the result of a partial collapse. Obesity can contribute to this blockage (Moran, Thompson, & Nies, 1988). Hence an early term for this condition, the Pickwickian syndrome, which was based on the very fat, always

TABLE 17–3
DSM-IV* Criteria for Breathing-Related Sleep Disorder

A. Sleep disruption leading to excessive sleepiness or insomnia, that is judged to be due to a sleep-related breathing condition (e.g., obstructive or central sleep apnea syndrome or central alveolar hypoventilation syndrome).

B. The disturbance is not better accounted for by another mental disorder and is not due to the direct physiological effects of a substance (e.g., a drug of abuse, a medication) or another general medical condition (other than a breathing-related disorder).

*DSM-IV, p. 573.

sleeping and snoring man in Dickens' *The Pickwick Papers.* Hypersomnia is the usual complaint. Alcohol and probably hypnoanxiolytics can convert snoring into apnea. The combination of habitual snoring, witnessed apnea, gasping or choking during the night, and daytime sleepiness are very good indicators of obstructive sleep apnea.

In the central form the respiratory drive is decreased or shuts down. Because apnea doesn't always happen, this is called the *central alveolar hypoventilation syndrome.* These patients don't snore, have more insomnia than hypersomnia, and are less apt to be obese. Frequently both types exist in the same patient. About 50–60% of hypersomniacs have mixed or obstructive types; 10% of persistent insomniacs have the central variety (Moran et al., 1988).

Complications. Adding to their problems, these patients may develop cognitive impairment, memory loss, cardiac arrhythmias, recurrent low oxygen levels, systemic and pulmonary hypertension, right-heart ventricular failure, and erectile dysfunction. They also have two to three times more auto accidents (Moran et al., 1988; Phillipson, 1993). Then they may be cursed by psychiatric problems, including dementia, delirium, hallucinations, and depression. In one study, 20% of male sleep apneacs had depression and 16% abused alcohol (Moran et al., 1988). There may be an association between dementia and central sleep apnea. Correction of the sleep apnea reverses or at least improves most of these problems, including cardiac function.

Epidemiology

Of 30–60-year-old workers, two percent of women and four percent of men have sleep apnea syndrome (Young et al., 1993). The rate increases with age. Half of men with excessive daytime sleepiness *and* hypertension have sleep apnea, as do 35% of obese males over 60. Sleep apnea may contribute to the 10,000 annual deaths from sudden infant death syndrome, which causes more deaths than any disease during the first six months of life (Maxmen, 1991).

Management and Treatment

Diagnosis of sleep apnea requires a PSG and a finger-pulse oximeter (FPO), which usually show hundreds of respiratory pauses lasting from 10 to 120 seconds, typically coupled with severe oxygen desaturation and cardiac arrhythmias, often during REM sleep (Phillipson, 1993). Sometimes FPO is used alone outside the lab, as a less expensive screening test. If an abnormality is found, sleep lab studies follow.

Treatment depends on the condition's severity and type. In milder obstructive forms, weight loss, sleeping on one's side, and avoiding hypnotics and alcohol have improved nighttime breathing. In order to ensure sleeping on one's side, a tennis ball can be sewn into the back of the patient's night garment. (The cost of this medical procedure is usually under $2.) In more hazardous cases, continuous positive airway pressure is the proven preferred treatment. Soft-palate surgery may reduce the number of apneic episodes; a tracheotomy may be a necessity. However, in general, surgery has fewer proven benefits. Central apnea is best helped with low-flow nasal oxygen, diaphragmatic pacing, and medications such as estrogen, stimulating tricyclic antidepressants (especially protriptyline and desipramine), stimulants, or acetazolamide. All sleep apnea patients should be warned of the dangers of using alcohol or hypnotics (Moran et al., 1988).

NARCOLEPSY

Clinical Presentation

REM on a rampage: That's narcolepsy. Instead of taking the usual 90 minutes, narcoleptics immediately descend into REM sleep, causing sleep attacks or cataplexy, combined with either muscle paralysis or hypnopompic or hypnagogic hallucinations.

Sleep attacks are overwhelming episodes of daytime sleepiness. Two-thirds of sleep attacks are related to fatigue, or general drowsiness, as in dozing off during a movie. The other third is characterized by sudden sleep for 10 to 15 minutes. Boredom usually precipitates these events, but they also can occur inconveniently and sometimes dangerously, such as during a bank robbery, scuba diving, auto driving, and even sex.

Cataplexy is an abrupt loss in muscle tone, resulting in anything from mild weakness to total collapse. These episodes can happen as infrequently as every other month or as frequently as a hundred times a day. Although alert during the attack, the patient's cataplexy often erupts after a stressful incident: a tennis player smashes an overhead and plops to the court; a father screams at his son and slumps into his chair; a teen-age girl hears a car backfire and teeters like a drunk. Sleep attacks usually precede cataplexy by two to five years (Moran et al., 1988).

Muscle paralysis is a normal feature of REM sleep, but in narcolepsy it produces a rapid, unexpected inability to move on falling asleep or waking up, which can drag on for several seconds to minutes. Terrified at first, patients soon discover that the paralysis usually vanishes if another person touches them.

Hypnopompic hallucinations are experienced upon awakening, whereas *hypnogogic hallucinations* appear when dropping off. (When either hallucination emerges *without* narcolepsy, it is a benign curiosity that still scares patients into thinking they are crazy. Professionals should tell them that these images are a normal variation of "premature dreaming" or "dreaming while awake." Approximately 10% of the U.S. population has experienced these pre- and post-sleep hallucinations.) Even when the person is alert, narcoleptic hallucinations can be horrifying, such as an actor who was rehearsing *Hamlet* and hallucinated a skull. The *DSM-IV* criteria for narcolepsy are listed in Table 17–4.

Complications

With advancing age, narcoleptics develop extremely fragmented nighttime sleep. In the sleep laboratory, 15–30% exhibit nocturnal myoclonus or

---

TABLE 17–4
DSM-IV* Criteria for Narcolepsy

A. Irresistible attacks of refreshing sleep that occur daily over at least 3 months.

B. The presence of one or both of the following:
   (1) cataplexy (i.e., brief episodes of sudden bilateral loss of muscle tone, most often in association with intense emotion)
   (2) recurrent intrusions of elements of rapid eye movement (REM) sleep into the transition between sleep and wakefulness, as manifested by either hypnopompic or hypnogogic hallucinations or sleep paralysis at the beginning or end of sleep episodes

C. The disturbance is not due to the direct physiological effects of a substance (e.g., a drug of abuse, a medication) or another general medical condition.

*DSM-IV, p. 567.

sleep apnea. Yet of greatest concern is that they have attacks at the wrong time, as when flying a plane or driving a car.

Epidemiology

The United States has half a million narcoleptics. Starting before the age of 30 and typically during adolescence, the disorder affects the sexes equally and is usually inherited. A majority of patients have histocompatibility complex antigens that appear to be genetic markers for narcolepsy.

Differential Diagnosis

Because narcolepsy and sleep apnea both generate fatigue or prolonged sleep, ask patients these two questions: (a) "Do you snore a lot?" (If so, sleep apnea, probably obstructive, is more likely.) (b) "Do you lose control of your muscles or posture when stimulated?" (If true, cataplexy suggests narcolepsy.) To pin down narcolepsy, the PSG must display immediate and repeated outbursts of REM sleep during the transition between wakefulness and sleep.

Bipolar depression and *atypical depression* frequently show hypersomnia, but rarely as a chief complaint. Although *physically ill* patients sleep excessively, they often deem it a relief. Narcoleptic attacks resemble epileptic *psychomotor seizures*, but seizures usually have perserverative motor movements, such as repeated swallowing, hand rubbing, or oddball exercising.

Management and Treatment

Stimulants (e.g., methylphenidate), with or without less sedative TCAs, treat sleep attacks. These patients rarely, if ever, abuse stimulants. Lower doses and drug holidays cut side effects. Cataplexy is remedied best by low TCA doses, gamma hydroxybutyrate, and stimulants. MAOIs and SSRIs are promising, but less proven, approaches. Stimulants assist if tolerance develops to TCAs.

Families need to know about narcolepsy: "Why does Mom plop over in a crowded shop or Dad walk like a zombie?" Kids often assume they provoked the weirdness and benefit from a true and concrete explanation of the mysterious disease.[2]

---

[2]Information can be obtained from the American Narcolepsy Association, 425 California St., Suite 201, San Francisco, CA 94104, phone (415) 788–4793; or the Narcolepsy Network, P.O. Box 190, Belmont, CA 94002, phone (415) 592–7884.

PRIMARY HYPERSOMNIA

Clinical Presentation

To diagnose primary hypersomnia, patients must complain of excessive sleepiness lasting for over a month. A typical patient complains of daytime drowsiness for years that interferes with performance and leads to long, unrefreshing daytime naps (which, on the job, can lead to unemployment). Nights aren't much better. These patients often have *long, undisturbed sleep* and *extreme difficulty awakening*, frequently accompanied by "*sleep drunkenness.*" During the period of sleep drunkenness, they may be disoriented and are sometimes verbally or physically abusive. They try to fight sleepiness as long as they can and, with a blank stare, may engage in semi-controlled automatic behavior that is interrupted by one-to-four-second micro-sleeps. The automatic behavior is usually inappropriate, such as putting the cereal box in the refrigerator after pouring orange juice on the cereal; putting the clothes in the dishwasher and turning it on. Hypersomniacs usually don't remember what they did, but they do remember a period of intense drowsiness. In this way they differ from the occasionally sleepy person who accidently puts salt in his morning coffee. One patient referred to these benign normal episodes as "near-life experiences." The *DSM-IV* criteria for primary hypersomnia are listed in Table 17–5.

Subtypes. There appear to be at least two subtypes of this poorly understood disorder: (1) patients with *partially expressed narcolepsy* will have it for life and usually have relatives with narcolepsy or at least primary hypersomnia; (2) patients who sleep as a response to stress or as a means of withdrawing from life. This subtype of hypersomnia has a more waxing and waning quality, based on the patient's life situation and psychological status, with worsening occurring during periods of boredom, apathy, or stress.

Differential Diagnosis

A sleep disorders center typically can identify a known cause of the hypersomnia in 85% of the cases: 50% have *sleep apnea*, 25% *narcolepsy*, and 10% have *restless legs syndrome* and/or *periodic limb movement disorder*. *Medications* such as hypnoanxiolytics, antihypertensives, and anticonvulsants can cause hypersomnia, as do some *illicit drugs* such as cannabis. Common medical causes of hypersomnia are *post-viral syndrome*, *post-encephalitis syndrome*, and *endocrine abnormalities* such as hypothyroidism. These patients may also be diagnosed as having *chronic fatigue syndrome*, a condition that may continue for months or years but usually finally remits. A long duration and onset before age 30 suggests narcolepsy.

TABLE 17–5
DSM-IV Criteria for Primary Hypersomnia

A. The predominant complaint is excessive sleepiness for at least 1 month (or less if recurrent) as evidenced by either prolonged sleep episodes or daytime sleep episodes occurring almost daily.

B. The excessive sleepiness causes clinically significant distress or impairment in social, occupational, or other important areas of functioning.

C. The excessive sleepiness is not better accounted for by insomnia and does not occur exclusively during the course of another Sleep Disorder (e.g., Narcolepsy, Breathing-Related Sleep Disorder, Circadian Rhythm Sleep Disorder, or a Parasomnia) and cannot be accounted for by an inadequate amount of sleep.

D. The disturbance does not occur exclusively during the course of another mental disorder.

E. The disturbance is not due to the direct physiological effects of a substance (e.g., a drug of abuse, a medication) or a general medical condition.

Specify if:
   Recurrent: if there are periods of excessive sleepiness that last at least 3 days occurring several times a year for at least 2 years

*DSM-IV, p. 562.

Onset in later life suggests sleep apnea. Intermittent hypersomnia suggests psychological or drug causes.

Management and Treatment

The patients who appear to have partially expressed narcolepsy are often treated with stimulants, as are some cases of post-viral syndrome. Stimulating antidepressants have been tried with somewhat less success. Psychotherapy and behavioral approaches (e.g., scheduling activities, beginning vigorous exercise) are often used for hypersomniacs whose conditions appear to have a psychological origin.

DYSSOMNIAS THAT CAUSE INSOMNIA: RESTLESS LEGS SYNDROME AND PERIODIC LIMB MOVEMENT DISORDER

Clinical Presentation

Restless legs syndrome (RLS) (classified under *dyssomnia not otherwise specified*) presents as an uncomfortable, painless, crawling sensation in the deep calves, extending occasionally into the thighs and feet. Restless legs squirm right *before* sleep. The medical word for this is *dysesthesia*. Patients describe RLS as an "inner itch," "ants creeping up and down my legs," or "worms slithering inside my muscles." The feet may fidget by day, but they only take off and prevent sleep at night. Walking temporarily stops these jitters; resting or sitting starts them. Neuroleptic drugs may generate the restlessness of akathisia. This agitation however, remains throughout the day, even while walking.

Periodic limb movement disorder (PLMD) was previously called nocturnal myoclonus (NM).[3] These patients kick and move their arms rhythmically during light sleep every 10 to 60 seconds without realizing it. They often blame their mates for torn bedsheets and are puzzled by their fatigue the next day. More commonly, they kick briefly and suffer insomnia; less frequently, they kick up to 600 times a night and are continually exhausted. Usually it is only the kicked sleep partner who reports the PLMD.

About 50–80% of patients with RLS have periodic limb movement disorder: Since PLMD rarely occurs by itself, it is usually considered to be part of the RLS. Patients with PLMD usually complain of fatigue and hypersomnia, whereas those with RLS alone complain of problems getting to sleep. PLMD arises during sleep and RLS before sleep. When combined, the two usually cause fatigue and insomnia.

Epidemiology and Pathogenesis

RLS may affect 10% of chronic insomniacs who consult sleep clinics. PLMD afflicts men more than women and increases with age, bothering 16–33% of people over 65. Both disorders have unknown etiologies.

Management and Treatment

Keeping precise records is important in assessing effects of treatments of PLMD and RLS. PLMD waxes and wanes; it may be bad one night and absent the next. Usually three nights of observation are needed to assess it. Benzodiazepines are used to soothe the discomfort of RLS and to ensure continued sleep during PLMD. Carbidopa-levodopa (Sinemet) can also reduce the discomfort of RLS, while TCAs or levodopa by itself exacerbate and sometimes cause PLMD. Nothing has been shown to really stop PLMD. The best that can be hoped for is a good night's sleep by the patient and an unbruised bed partner.

---

[3]Because "nocturnal myoclonus" may suggest, albeit falsely, an epileptic trigger, researchers have substituted "periodic limb movements" or "myoclonic sleep" for NM.

Walking RLS off for 10 to 20 minutes may temporarily relieve the dysesthesias, but they reappear within minutes. Good sleep hygiene, including exercise and eliminating coffee and tea, may help RLS. Iron, calcium, folic acid, and vitamin E have all been anecdotally reported to help. When all of these approaches fail, a sleep specialist should be consulted. Without becoming addicted, some patients improve with low doses of opiates prescribed by a sleep specialist.

CIRCADIAN RHYTHM SLEEP DISORDER

Good sleep but at the wrong time can produce circadian rhythm disorder (CRD) (sleep-wake schedule disorders), as seen in shift-changers, long-distance flyers, isolated writers, and street people. With no regular bedtime, their sleep and biological rhythms (e.g., temperature) become disorganized. Yet, because people rarely think about CRD, they often attribute a CRD to a "commonsense" explanation: "Teenagers always oversleep to cut classes"; or, "Toby misses work because she is bone lazy."

At six months of age, a roughly 24-hour (or "circadian") rhythm emerges, which persists until age 14; for a decade it then extends 26 to 30 hours. In other words, the daily circadian rhythm slows down. That's why adolescents typically feel it is 8 P.M. when it is actually 11 P.M.; their longer biological rhythms, rather than stubbornness, are at fault. Waking up is also difficult: Teenagers don't want to. That's because kids experience 7 A.M. as if it were 4 A.M. The wish is not to avoid school (well, maybe); rather, their reluctance largely stems from a dragged-out rhythm. By the late twenties, the cycle's length (fortunately) diminishes to closer to 25 hours. Less fortunately, by their sixties, people's biological rhythms start declining so that they fall asleep (circa 8 P.M.) and awaken earlier (circa 3 A.M.) (Hauri, 1989).

Flatter biological rhythms distinguish the ages further. When teenagers are awake, they are awake; when they are asleep, they are deep asleep. Older people vary less: When they are awake, they are not *that* awake; when they are asleep, they are not *deep* asleep (Dement et al., 1985). The daily shift in body temperature alters by roughly two degrees in adolescents and merely half a degree in the elderly.

If people under 60 are plunked into a cave without any time indicator, their daily biological rhythm expands from 24 hours to 26–32 hours. Nature, therefore, shapes the body's clock. These time indicators are called *zeitgebers*, and they are everywhere: sunlight, clocks, fixed meeting times, disk jockeys, etc.

If there's no sleep problem, don't mess with rhythms, but if a teenager or younger adult has a CRD, the best *zeitgeber* is to wake up at a regular time every morning, including weekends. For older people, the best *zeitgeber* is falling asleep at a regular bedtime, including weekends. Doing both can be very, very difficult: What's needed is considerable family and therapeutic support.

Complicating matters is that people have not one, but two internal clocks. The first is a neurological clock that responds to light through the retina and varies the body's daily temperature. The second clock increases and depletes chemicals, as in the sleep-wake cycle. *Zeitgebers* influence both clocks.

CRDs arise from mismatches between the internal biological and the external environmental clocks. When a day-worker suddenly becomes a night-worker, his inner clocks keep ticking, but the clocks are out-of-whack with his new social clock. This switch dislodges his normal circadian cycle, which disrupts his sleep/wake cycle, temperature, biochemical activity, and leads to poor performance and emotional ups and downs. The *DSM-IV* criteria for circadian rhythm sleep disorder are listed in Table 17–6.

TABLE 17–6
DSM-IV* Criteria for Circadian Rhythm Sleep Disorder

A. A persistent or recurrent pattern of sleep disruption leading to excessive sleepiness or insomnia that is due to a mismatch between the sleep-wake schedule required by a person's environment and his or her circadian sleep-wake pattern.

B. The sleep disturbance causes clinically significant distress or impairment in social, occupational, or other important areas of functioning.

C. The disturbance does not occur exclusively during the course of another Sleep Disorder or other mental disorder.

D. The disturbance is not due to the direct physiological effects of a substance (e.g., a drug of abuse, a medication) or a general medical condition.

Specify type:
    Delayed Sleep Phase Type: a persistent pattern of late sleep onset and late awakening times, with an inability to fall asleep and awaken at a desired earlier time
    Jet Lag Type: sleepiness and alertness that occur at an inappropriate time of day relative to local time, occurring after repeated travel across more than one time zone
    Shift Work Type: insomnia during major sleep period or excessive sleepiness during major awake period associated with night shift work or frequently changing shift work
    Unspecified Type

---

*DSM-IV, p. 578.

Clinical Presentation

CRD has many causes, both *chronic* (e.g., from shift changes) and *acute* (e.g., from jet lag). In both types, patients develop inadequate, fragmented, or excessive sleep and also experience disorientation, uneasiness, overstimulation, irritability, fatigue, incoordination, and poor concentration (Regestein & Monk, 1991). When food accumulates without stomach acid at night, and when acid increases without food during the day, indigestion develops. Workers with chronic CRD ingest more caffeine than do their steady daytime counterparts; 16% of men on variable shifts consumed more than four alcoholic drinks daily; night eating increases. Shift changes often devastate the social fabric: Family contact and recreation are greatly diminished, divorce rates double, job stress accelerates, accidents multiply, and psychiatric problems emerge (Regestein & Monk, 1991). And yet, because CRD is rarely considered, something "must" be wrong with the Joneses: She's always alone, he's never there, and the kids are obnoxious. Suspicions emerge, making a bad situation worse.

For far too long, people have ignored the serious accidents that result from abnormal sleep times. Mistakes and catastrophes are far more common during the night and early morning than in the mid-afternoon. All three nuclear disasters — Three Mile Island, Peachtree, and Chernobyl — happened in the early morning. In North Carolina a semi-trailer crashed into a school bus, killing six students and injuring 12 others: The truck driver had slept a mere 90 minutes during the previous 36 hours. There are countless examples. Labor, management, and government should know more about the problems from altered sleep schedules.

Despite these adversities, the United States is the only Western democracy without legal restrictions on shift work. Brazilian law limits the work week to 36 hours for shift workers; the French limit shift lengths to nine hours and the work week to 39 hours. In Austria, firms with more than 50 shift workers must employ an on-site medical officer and pay employees for added days off. The schedule of airplane crews is highly restricted in Germany. Japanese corporations must afford special sleeping breaks for shift workers. All this legislation "evens the playing field" for companies without impairing competitiveness. Yet because Americans largely assume that chronic CRD is caused psychologically, not biologically and socially, these protective laws don't exist (Regestein & Monk, 1991).

Subtypes

Delayed sleep phase type of CRD occurs when people fall asleep and awaken consistently later than typical; the *advanced sleep phase type* of CRD arises when people retire and wake up earlier than usual. As discussed above, teenagers tend to have the delayed type, older people, the advanced type. The absence of a regular bedtime schedule generates both forms.

Jet lag usually becomes a problem when people fly three time zones east or west. (There is no north-south jet lag.) Age determines the more troublesome direction. The younger, with slower-than-24-hour circadian rhythms, have more jet lag flying east — e.g., California to New York — because their body-clock time is being squeezed into a shorter day. Going west — e.g., New York to California — generates more jet lag for older people. After flying, middle-aged adults need about one day to recover for each time zone crossed going east and about half a day for each time zone going west.

A washed-out or "awake but muddled" feeling may emerge during the one to seven days of jet lag. Many diplomats and professional businessmen are not allowed to render major decisions for at least 24 hours after long flights. Even Henry Kissinger confessed to paying "a psychological price" for losing his temper at a secret Vietnam negotiation after a protracted plane ride.

Epidemiology

Although schedule-induced, CRD affects some folks more than others, and research has yet to determine which people and how often. Poor quality sleep was reported by 20% of non-rotating workers, in contrast to 65% of shift workers who rotated to earlier shifts in the day. When shift work was moved later every 21 days (rather than backward), a plant's production increased by 20%; approximately 20% of 9,000 shift workers reported having trouble adjusting to night work (Regestein & Monk, 1991). As a general rule, 75% of flyers may have transatlantic jet lag.

Management and Treatment

Remedying a CRD caused by shift work is more difficult than most people imagine. For starters, the therapist should inform the entire family about how shift working introduces many hardships. Together they must realize that new time slots must be protected. If Dad now works from 11 P.M. to 7 A.M., a visitor who drops by to chat at nine in the morning is being as rude as a person who drops in at 11 at night. The new night worker should schedule specific times with his kids to do something active, such as going shopping or seeing a night movie, rather than sitting passively, watching the tube. Darken the bedroom; use soundproofing, if helpful. Limit coffee, tea, cola, and caffeine; avoid heavy, spicy, or hard-to-digest foods. Most importantly, ensure that every family member learns that shift working changes life in ways that most people never think about.

Schedule changes also assist. For younger people, who most often experience shift changes, shifts should be moved forward (day to evening to night to day, etc., not backward). Changes should be made slowly — if possible, no faster than one shift every three weeks. When the Philadelphia police force changed shifts for 18 days from counterclockwise to clockwise, poor sleep diminished by more than a third, fatigue dwindled from 40% to 20%, traffic accidents dropped from 50 to 30 per million miles driven, and sleeping pills and alcohol dipped by half (Hauri, 1989). On the other hand, people over 50 probably do better moving shifts counterclockwise.

To correct phase-shift disorders, sleep-time changes — chronotherapy — must be performed slowly; environmental support is nice, but not therapeutic. For younger people with a delayed phase shift, chronotherapy should move sleep time forward, not backward. Suggest to patients that they do so during vacations. On day one, instead of going to bed when tired (e.g., 5 A.M.), patients might retire three hours later (8 A.M.), and sleep as late as they want. On day two, retire three hours later (11 A.M.) and sleep until the late afternoon or whenever. After about a week, the clock has been circled until bedtime sleepiness descends at the typical 11 P.M. or midnight. Unfortunately, although this technique can be quite successful, a majority of patients find it hard to do because they can't restructure their lives.

To facilitate recovery from a shift-phase disorder (as well as from jet lag), bright light — phototherapy — really helps. During phototherapy, patients sit three feet away from a very bright light (2,500–10,000 lux) or walk in the sunshine. Brightness must be intense: ordinary room light, which is 150–200 lux, does not suffice. Summer sunlight can be 100,000 lux. Patients start with a one-hour exposure to the light. This is done at the beginning and/or the end of the "day" (which may really be night) to synchronize the brain with the new day. If a patient's day is phase-delayed (late onset, late wake up) bright light upon waking up will advance it. If phase-advanced, bright light near the new bedtime will help delay it. If a patient is too "hyper" initially, cut down temporarily to 30 minutes; if the effect is insufficient, increase to two hours. Whenever the body feels tired is a good time to get some more bright light. In a few days, sleep and wakefulness should be improved. If phototherapy is stopped, the condition may worsen, it's then best to continue longer and see if the patient accommodates to a new schedule.

If a New York student flies to Paris for two weeks, her sharpness may be dulled for one to six days. For the first few days, she should avoid important meetings. When tired, she should soak up as much sun as possible until jet lag stops. Japan Air Lines has high-lux rooms in San Francisco so that their pilots can reset their body clocks and minimize jet lag more quickly. During the 1970s, the U.S. Army flew its soldiers to Europe, where they worked outdoors and overcame jet lag in two to three days. Their commanders, however, remained indoors: They had jet lag for over two weeks. Physical activity and light are potent *zeitgebers*.

A promising experimental approach when sleep onset is delayed is taking melatonin, a natural brain hormone that dramatically increases during sleep. A 0.5 mg dose taken at the desired bedtime appears to promote normal sleep and resets the circadian clocks.

PRIMARY INSOMNIA

Clinical Presentation

Diagnose primary insomnia if patients can't fall asleep or maintain sleep; feel exhausted or irritable the next day; worry about not sleeping, by night, dread going to bed, fearing that nothing works; by day, unexpectedly doze off at a party or while watching a hockey match. Since anyone can have a bad night's sleep, an insomnia disorder must persist for at least a month and not be caused by a mental disorder, medical condition, or substance use or abuse.

Although stress often initiates this insomnia, sleeplessness by itself may persist long after the stress. Insomnia can be lifelong or it may disappear in a new bed. People who swear they don't sleep are frequently light sleepers. Their EEG won't show shortened sleep, but will show more fragmented sleep and more stage 1 and 2 sleep. If people dream about not sleeping, they may have "pseudo-insomnia." (Showing them the sleep EEG astounds them!) One patient insisted that he had terrible sleep every night except Friday. "Why Friday?" I asked (JM). "That's because," he responded, "it's against our religion to have a medical problem on the Sabbath." Every conceivable planetary force can disrupt sleep. Table 17–7 lists *DSM-IV* criteria for primary insomnia.

Differential Diagnosis

Before primary insomnia is diagnosed, all the specific causes of insomnia mentioned before in this chapter must first be considered and eliminated. Two questions can help pinpoint the causes. The first is: "What prevents

TABLE 17–7
DSM-IV **Criteria for Primary Insomnia***

A. The predominant complaint is difficulty initiating or maintaining sleep, or nonrestorative sleep, for at least 1 month.

B. The sleep disturbance (or associated daytime fatigue) causes clinically significant distress or impairment in social, occupational, or other important areas of functioning.

C. The sleep disturbance does not occur exclusively during the course of Narcolepsy, Breathing-Related Sleep Disorder, a Circadian Rhythm Sleep Disorder, or a Parasomnia.

D. The disturbance does not occur exclusively during the course of another mental disorder (e.g., Major Depressive Disorder, Generalized Anxiety Disorder, a delirium).

E. The disturbance is not due to the direct physiological effects of a substance (e.g., a drug of abuse, a medication) or a general medical condition.

---

*DSM-IV, p. 557.

you from falling asleep and what keeps waking you up?" The answer to this may vary from, "I keep having to pee" (possibly a medical cause such as diabetes) to, "We always argue about politics, religion, and problems in our marriage right before bedtime." The second question is: "What do you do during the day in the areas of exercise, naps, drinking, eating, sex?" Answers to this question might include remarks such as, "I have a little siesta after lunch," or, "I drink a cup of coffee at 4:30 P.M. to wake up a little for the drive home from work." Answers to these questions can help classify the insomnia as a *circadian rhythm sleep disorder* or as an effect of a *medical condition* or *substance use*. Most of the ones left over are all called primary insomnia, except for insomnias caused by disturbing environmental factors (e.g. noise, light, barking dogs) that are diagnosed as dyssomnia NOS.

Epidemiology

The overall prevalence of insomnia may be as high as 30% and rises to 50% in people over 60 years old (it is not known how many of these have *primary* insomnia). Women, particularly married ones, and poorer people are more likely to have it. People with primary insomnia tend to have higher depression, hypochondriasis, and hysteria scales on the MMPI.

Management and Treatment

In many cases, eliminating obvious causes of primary insomnia may be enough. Adding activities that help promote sleep may help even more. Vigorous daytime exercise often improves sleep, but exercise in the hours just before bedtime may actually delay sleep. Pleasurable and satisfying sexual intercourse can help people get to sleep, but unsatisfying sex will delay it. Some people will respond to a metronome or a ticking clock, but it better be slow — around 60 beats/minute or slower — to imitate the beat of a very relaxed human heart. Relaxation exercises can help get people to sleep, but the exercises need to be practiced regularly so that they can be condensed to under five minutes. Doing 45 minutes of relaxation exercises to treat a 35-minute-sleep-onset latency problem doesn't make much sense. To decrease stimulation and increase a soothing environment, things such as ear plugs or calming reading may help.

When all these easy and sensible approaches fail, the person still returning to the practitioner's office is either a born insomniac and/or a "neurotic" insomniac. Neither of these are *DSM-IV* terms, but they describe these individuals well. Both are formidable foes to the clinician's sense of self-efficacy. To treat neurotic insomniacs, you must know how they got that way.

How to Become an Insomniac

1. Keep an unrealistic goal of the number of hours of sleep you should have. If you really only need six or seven hours, make eight or nine the goal. If you are age 65 or over and once needed eight hours but now need only seven hours, ignore that and shoot for eight hours.
2. Catastrophize about not meeting this goal, especially in the middle of the night. For example, think, "I will never be able to function tomorrow unless I get more sleep. I probably will (fail, flunk, get fired — nonsleeper's choice) if I don't sleep enough."
3. Remember, hours of insomnia expand proportionally to the number of hours spent in bed. If you need seven hours of sleep in every 24 hours and spend nine hours in bed, you can guarantee at least two hours of insomnia. Taking a one-hour nap during the day can help increase this to three hours of insomnia. Because you now have had three hours of insomnia, spend ten hours in bed the next night trying to get enough sleep.
4. Spend all of the desperate hours fighting to get to sleep in bed. In Pavlovian fashion, this will make the bed a stimulus for profound upset.
5. Make the bed a center for many other daily activities — reading, writing, TV, etc. The bed then becomes a cue for many more things than sleep.
6. If you have the opportunity, start taking sleeping medications. Over-the-counter antihistaminic ones are best because they are relatively ineffectual, tolerance develops within days, and they suppress REM sleep. Consequently, if you try to stop taking them, you will have vicious REM rebound with many nightmares. Continue to increase the dosage to get enough sleep. The benzodiazepines aren't quite as effective at creating insomnia, but over weeks and months tolerance can develop, some REM rebound can occur, and variations on benzodiazepine withdrawal might also occur, worsening the insomnia.

It is very likely that the person with primary insomnia has tried one or more of the preceding ideas. The sleep hygiene suggestions in Table 17–8 are the antidotes. The hardest task for clinicians is to convince patients with

TABLE 17–8
Good Sleep Habits*

AVOID

A. Excessive noise (wear earplugs if necessary)

B. Caffeine (which can disrupt sleep up to seven hours before bedtime)

C. Cigarettes (since they flatten sleep brain waves)

D. Alcohol (especially "night caps" that disorganize sleep)

E. Napping (the longer people are awake, the faster and deeper they will sleep)

F. Catching an extra wink in the morning (since this fragments sleep and creates fatigue)

G. Upsetting or stressful activities before bedtime

MAINTAIN

A. Temperature in bedroom at 60–65 degrees Fahrenheit

B. Exercise in the afternoon or early evening (morning exercise doesn't work and if shortly before sleep, it stimulates)

C. Satisfying (safe) sex

D. Light snacks (since hunger can aggravate sleep)

E. Warm milk, Ovaltine, or Horlicks before sleep

F. Awaken at the same time every morning (including weekends and even if sleep was poor) and go to bed only when sleepy (waking up at the same period determines the time to fall asleep)

G. Imagine a tranquil place (the beach or mountain lake) and calming sounds (surf, music)

H. If repeatedly awake 20 minutes after retiring, relax in another room, only returning to bed when really tired (don't stare at the clock—*hide* it)

---

insomnia that they might need less sleep than they think; this also entails decreasing the catastrophizing. Finding examples of adequate functioning following a less than adequate night's sleep helps build the case that a little less sleep isn't the disaster they thought it was. For example, I (NW) once worried about insomnia on nights prior to giving big lectures and thereby increased the chances of getting it. During my son's infancy, when he would get sick, a "good night's sleep" for me was four or five hours; three to four hours was the usual. When I slept five or six straight hours, I then would say to myself, "Great, that's a lot more than I thought I would get." When I got four hours of sleep and gave a lecture, the students would still say it was good. Since then I have held on to these two ideas: (1) If I awake in the night after five "straight" hours of sleep I now say, "This is a lot better than it used to be." (2) If I remain awake, I now say, "It would have been nice to get more sleep, but I'll still be able to function adequately tomorrow." I have also discovered that I really needed only six and a half hours of sleep rather than the seven and a half to eight hours that I thought I needed. That discovery eliminated an hour of potential "insomnia" each night. Amazingly, these tips can work for patients as well as clinicians.

If all else fails, one might simply agree with the patient's interesting views (e.g., all people need eight hours of sleep and anything less than that is a disaster) and then compliment him on how well he's doing on less. Reassurance, coupled with any method to diminish the fear of not sleeping, is invaluable.

When cautiously used, medications also have a place in the treatment of chronic insomnia, but nonpharmacologic approaches should be tried first. Unfortunately, 35–40% of hypnoanxiolytics are given to elders who only represent 12% of the population (Moran et al., 1988). Many of these have secondary insomnia that was never detected. The antihistamines (the main ingredient in over-the-counter sleep-aids) and the barbiturate-like drugs should be avoided, because they either don't work or tolerance develops quickly and REM suppression occurs, followed by REM rebound. In most cases, drugs that are used for their sedating side effects are the wrong choice. Questions to ask when evaluating a hypnotic are: (1) How effective is it on the first night? Some accumulate and work better on succeeding nights. (2) How long is it effective? Some, like triazolam, last only four hours. Others, like flurazepam, may last 10 or more hours. (3) Is it still effective after chronic use? (4) What is the immediate effect of withdrawal? (5) How long does the withdrawal last? Flurazepam may show withdrawal days later.

Which drugs are reasonable choices? There are four: the benzodiazepines, zolpidem (a nonbenzodiazepine that works on specific benzodiazepine receptors), chloral hydrate, and possibly trazodone. All of these have relatively modest effects in terms of REM and stage 4 suppression, so that they don't usually cause bad rebound insomnia. If sleep onset is the main problem, pick a drug that reaches the brain quickly. Oxazepam, which takes one to two hours to work, is thus a poor choice to prescribe for sleep unless it is given one and a half to two hours before bedtime. Trazodone and diazepam reach the brain in under a half hour. Some benzodiazepines are marketed specifically as sleepers, but there is nothing to distinguish them from others that are marketed as anxiolytics; in general, they can be used interchangeably. For people who have trouble sustaining sleep, an adequate duration of action (six to nine hours) is needed. Drugs that last longer may cause daytime sleepiness, and if used daily, may reach toxic levels in a few weeks. These should be avoided in the elderly. Shorter-acting benzodiazepines may cause some night rebound anxiety and more antero-grade amnesia (Greenblatt et al., 1989). For more detailed information about these drugs, see Appendix H.

Chloral hydrate tends to wear off in two weeks, while the benzodiaze-pines that have been studied don't cause significant tolerance for over one month. Trazodone is well tolerated by 70–80% of people, with the remain-der feeling drugged or dizzy (orthostatic blood pressure drop) during the daytime. About one in 800 males develops priapism (a sustained, painful, nonsexual erection) with trazodone, so male patients need to be warned about this possibility and told to rush to the emergency room if it happens.

PARASOMNIAS

Parasomnias are distressing events that occur during sleep, but unlike dyssomnias, they are not primarily a disturbance of sleep. Sleepwalking per se is a problem, but usually doesn't result in a significant disturbance of sleep and therefore is a parasomnia; sleep apnea's hypersomnia is more bothersome than sleep apnea itself, and therefore, sleep apnea is a dyssom-nia. The parasomnias that emerge solely from NREM delta sleep — sleep-walking, bedwetting, and sleep terrors — are more common in boys, run in families, are clinically benign, happen usually once a night (unlike night-mares), emerge in the early night, are forgotten by morning, and normally fade out by adolescence. Other parasomnias, such as nightmare disorder, stem from outside deep sleep. *DSM-IV* recognizes three specific parasom-nias — nightmares, sleep terrors, and sleepwalking — and classifies the rest as "parasomnia not otherwise specified." *DSM-IV* criteria for parasomnias are listed in Table 17–9.

Sleepwalking

Sleepwalkers are often confused, bump into things, knock stuff over, coordinate poorly, and walk around objects. If they drive a car, their re-flexes are usually impaired and they crash. Rarely, somnambulists can be

TABLE 17–9
***DSM-IV* Criteria for Parasomnias:**
Nightmare, Sleep Terror, and Sleepwalking Disorders*

Nightmare Disorder

A. Repeated awakenings from the major sleep period or naps with detailed recall of extended and extremely frightening dreams, usually involving threats to survival, security, or self-esteem. The awakenings generally occur during the second half of the sleep period.

B. On awakening from the frightening dreams, the person rapidly becomes oriented and alert (in contrast to the confusion and disorientation seen in Sleep Terror Disorder and some forms of epilepsy).

C. The dream experience, or the sleep disturbance resulting from the awakening, causes clinically significant distress or impairment in social, occupational, or other important areas of functioning.

D. The nightmares do not occur exclusively during the course of another mental disorder (e.g., a delirium, Posttraumatic Stress Disorder) and are not due to the direct physiological effects of a substance (e.g., a drug of abuse, a medication) or a general medical condition.

Sleep Terror Disorder

A. Recurrent episodes of abrupt awakening from sleep, usually occurring during the first third of the major sleep episode and beginning with a panicky scream.

B. Intense fear and signs of autonomic arousal, such as tachycardia, rapid breathing, and sweating during each episode.

C. Relative unresponsiveness to efforts of others to comfort the person during the episode.

D. No detailed dream is recalled and there is amnesia for the episode.

E. The disturbance is not due to the direct physiological effects of a substance (e.g., a drug of abuse, a medication) or a general medical condition.

Sleepwalking Disorder

A. Repeated episodes of arising from bed during sleep and walking about, usually occurring during the first third of the major sleep episode.

B. While sleepwalking, the person has a blank, staring face, is relatively unresponsive to the efforts of others to communicate with him or her, and can be awakened only with great difficulty.

TABLE 17–9
(*Continued*)

C. On awakening (either from the sleepwalking episode or the next morning), the person has amnesia for the episode.

D. Within several minutes after awakening from the sleepwalking episode, there is no impairment of mental activity or behavior (although there may initially be a short period of confusion or disorientation).

E. The sleepwalking causes clinically significant distress or impairment in social, occupational, or other important areas of functioning.

F. The disturbance is not due to the direct physiological effects of a substance (e.g., a drug of abuse, a medication) or a general medical condition.

DSM-IV, pp. 583, 587, 591.

dangerous and leap from windows. A typical episode starts with the patient sitting up and repeating acts, such as picking at pajamas or bedsheets. What follows, aside from walking, are more complicated behaviors, including dressing, munching, and urinating. With blank and staring faces, these patients are rarely affected by those who attempt to contact them.

Episodes typically persist for several minutes to half an hour. If the walking suddenly stops, the waking-up patient may be disoriented for a few minutes. Sometimes patients don't walk but just fret in bed. When they do walk, they may return to bed without recalling their sleepwalking, or they may be surprised to arise from a different bed. Hostility is uncommon among sleepwalkers; if they sleep-talk, they're usually inarticulate.

Most sleepwalking children are psychologically normal. Children fear traipsing around where they are likely to be discovered, as can happen at summer camps or overnight bunking. Sleepwalking parents breed sleepwalking kids.

Sleepwalking typically begins between ages six and 12 and may be stress-related. Customarily, sleepwalkers exhibit other delta-sleep interruptions. At some time, 1–6% of children sleepwalk substantially; 15% do so occasionally. Adult sleepwalking is far less common, usually worse, and more chronic.

Sleepwalking should be distinguished from *psychomotor epileptic seizures*, in which patients are awake at the start but are totally nonresponsive to feedback, frequently recapitulate the same behaviors (e.g., rubbing arms, closing eyes), almost never return to their own bed, and display seizures on EEGs. The two disorders can coexist. Uncommon in children, *psychogenic fugue* typically erupts during wakefulness, lasts hours or days, presents no disturbed consciousness, and exists with other psychopathology. Because sleepwalkers appear vague on arising, their condition may imitate *sleep drunkenness* (very slow awakening); however, belligerence is common in sleep drunkenness and rare in sleepwalking.

Medical assistance—relaxation techniques, biofeedback training, hypnosis, diazepam, or imipramine—helps. Sleepwalkers may need to sleep on the ground floor, have the outside doors securely locked, and have the car keys unavailable.

Sleep Terror Disorder

The scariest of delta-sleep attacks—sleep terrors—forces children to speed their breathing, heart rate, sweating, and movement. Eyes open, screams erupt. Despite this panic, which typically strikes in the early evening, these children remember nothing on waking up or in the morning. They are not having nightmares.

In contrast to nightmares, sleep terrors do not respond to psychotherapy. Low doses (e.g., 2 mg) of diazepam before bedtime often reduce sleep terrors. Try limiting the medication's dose and time—for instance, prescribing the drug only for the summer, during camp. Longer sleep might help. Diagnostically, patients with sleep terrors do not recall anything, whereas those with REM-based nightmares can clearly describe their dreams.

Nightmare Disorder (Dream Anxiety Disorder)

Aside from inspiring novelists (e.g., Edgar Allan Poe), few of us savor nightmares or bad dreams; they stimulate unwelcome physiological changes, such as increasing agitation, sweating, cardiac rate, and breathing. Usually occurring in the early morning when REM sleep dominates, the same nightmare may recur repeatedly or different ones may pop up three times a week. Stress may induce 60% of nightmares. Half of the cases of nightmare disorder appear before age 10 and two-thirds before age 20.

Drugs—e.g., thioridazine, TCAs, SSRIs, benzodiazepines—may trigger nightmares. Suddenly withdrawing REM-suppressant medications and drugs, causing REM rebound, can do likewise. Alcohol, TCAs, and MAOIs suppress REM sleep.

Parasomnias not Otherwise Classified

Sleep-Talking

Like restless legs syndrome, the person complaining of this "disorder" is the bed partner, not the patient. My [JM] wife, who designs costumes for theater, but not for film or TV, launched my sole medical discovery. While perfectly asleep, she sat up and screeched, "I want full screen credit!"

"That's nice," I told her, "but would you please be quiet so I could sleep?"

"Yes, dear," she said, dozing off.

On hearing about her sleep-talking (somniloquy) the next morning, she giggled, yet had no memory of it. I've subsequently suggested to those stuck with sleep-talkers that they simply ask them to be quiet — it works.

People can sleep-talk during REM or delta sleep, although they will remember neither. If they speak in REM sleep, their pronunciation is clear and understandable; in deep sleep, it's apt to be mumbled and unintelligible.

Other disorders listed as parasomnias NOS include *sleep paralysis* during the transition between waking and sleep, and *REM sleep behavior disorder* (often characterized by agitated and violent behavior).

CHAPTER 18

Impulse Control Disorders Not Classified Elsewhere

ON OCCASION, EVERYONE IS IMPULSIVE, many like to gamble, and plenty can't resist chasing fire engines to a fire. Unlike these normal behaviors, however, people with impulse control disorders have three essential characteristics: (a) They *can't resist* an impulse or drive to do something, which they know will be harmful to themselves or others. (b) They experience increasing *tension* before performing the act. (Patients often describe this tension as "pressure," "restlessness," "anxiety," or "discomfort.") (c) They feel enormous *relief*, gratification, or satisfaction when committing the act. As a result, while acting on the impulse is momentarily ego-syntonic, later they might feel guilt, self-reproach, or regret. They act in haste and repent at leisure. However, repenting is not a necessary part of the diagnosis. Patients may or may not be aware of the impulse, and the deed may or may not be premeditated. Patients with impulse disorders tend to portray themselves as weak souls who readily cave into temptation or are easily overwhelmed by external forces. In a way, they're right, in that pathological impulsivity stems less from deliberate intent and more from an irresistible urge to discharge tension. People with impulse disorders share two historical features: (1) onset in childhood, adolescence, or early adulthood (except for gambling, which doesn't start as early as childhood), and (2) *associated psychopathology and family history*—mood disorders and substance-use disorders are frequent (McElroy, Hudson, Harrison, Keck, & Aizley, 1992).

DSM-IV groups impulse disorders in a residual category called, "Impulse

Control Disorders Not Classified Elsewhere," because impulse disturbances also occur in bulimia, mania, substance abuse, and paraphilias, and in borderline and antisocial personality disorders. *DSM-IV*'s residual category lists five specific impulse disorders: pathological gambling, kleptomania, pyromania, intermittent explosive disorder, and trichotillomania (the failure to resist impulses to pull out one's hair, resulting in noticeable hair loss). This chapter highlights pathological gambling as a prototypic impulse disorder; the other impulse disorders are briefly described.

PATHOLOGICAL GAMBLING

Distinguishing "social" from pathological gambling is akin to differentiating the social drinker from the alcoholic. Social gambling, like social drinking, is done for pleasure, with friends, and feels optional. Pathological gambling, like alcoholism, is done because the person can't stop, excludes friends, and feels obligatory. In most respects, pathological gambling, like alcoholism, is an *addiction*.

Clinical Presentation

Gambling addicts feel unable to resist gambling, despite knowing that they'll lose and can't afford it. As one patient explained, "I've placed hundreds of bets, not caring whether I win or lose. Why? Because I love the action. I'm drawn to the excitement. When I bet, I feel good and important. My orgasm is gambling."

Like other addictions, pathological gambling begets further gambling, which goes on to disrupt and damage every aspect of a person's life. Gambling debts take precedence over grocery bills. Forgery, fraud, arrests, tax evasion, excessive borrowing, stealing from friends, defaulting on loans, juggling financial obligations, lying, and forgetting who's owed what—it's all part of the disorder. Obligations to family and friends are supplanted by obligations to loan sharks and pawn brokers. Even when these patients are not gambling, they're preoccupied with gambling. Everything they do is a result of gambling. Like a child, they will sneak away from home to borrow money or to place a bet. Some compulsive gamblers develop a perverse thrill or pride in the creativity of their reasons for why their debts aren't being paid and why their "big winnings" aren't paying off. Short of violence, anything will be done for money. As a "big game" approaches, pathological gamblers reach an intolerable level of tension, which only the game relieves. Winning or losing has no effect on their gambling; they gamble as long as people will let them. Table 18–1 presents *DSM-IV* criteria

TABLE 18–1
DSM-IV Criteria for Pathological Gambling*

A. Persistent and recurrent maladaptive gambling behavior as indicated by five (or more) of the following:

  (1) is preoccupied with gambling (e.g., preoccupied with reliving past gambling experiences, handicapping or planning the next venture, or thinking of ways to get money with which to gamble)

  (2) needs to gamble with increasing amounts of money in order to achieve the desired excitement

  (3) has repeated unsuccessful efforts to control, cut back, or stop gambling

  (4) is restless or irritable when attempting to cut down or stop gambling

  (5) gambles as a way of escaping from problems or of relieving a dysphoric mood (e.g., feelings of helplessness, guilt, anxiety, depression)

  (6) after losing money gambling, often returns another day to get even ("chasing" one losses)

  (7) lies to family members, therapist, or others to conceal the extent of involvement with gambling

  (8) has committed illegal acts such as forgery, fraud, theft, or embezzlement to finance gambling

  (9) has jeopardized or lost a significant relationship, job, or educational or career opportunity because of gambling

  (10) relies on others to provide money to relieve a desperate financial situation caused by gambling

B. The gambling behavior is not better accounted for by a Manic Episode.

DSM-IV, p. 618.

for pathological gambling; the problems listed under criterion A highlight the disorder's chief problems.

The compulsive gambler turns every nongambling situation into a gamble. Explains a pathological gambler: "When a normal person is driving with a quarter tank of gas on a highway and spots a sign saying the next gas station is 50 miles away, she'll stop for gas. The gambler won't. He'll make a bet with himself that he can reach the next station without stopping for gas. This is a typical 'mind bet,' and when I'm not making a real bet, I'm making a mind bet."

Gambling, or talk of gambling, dominates conversation; it's as if every social skill has atrophied, except for gambling or talking about gambling. Damon Runyon's characters might be fiction, but his descriptions of the gambler's mentality are not. For instance, a Runyon character says that whenever Feet Samuels—so-named because his feet are always at 90° angles—stands at a corner, gamblers will bet on which way Feet Samuels will go. In *Guys and Dolls*, Nathan Detroit calls Sky Masterson "the highest player of them all. . . . Another time he was sick and would not take penicillin because he bet his fever would go to 104°."

Generalizations surely, but impulsive gamblers tend to be "big talkers" and "big spenders." Normally overconfident, self-centered, abrasive, energetic, and jovial, their moods reflect their earnings: On winning, they're temporarily elated; on losing, they're moody and anxious.

Clinical Course and Complications

While still teenagers, future pathological gamblers bet socially; their gambling usually becomes serious by early adulthood, often after some modest winnings and during some stressful period. Gamblers Anonymous (discussed later) describes four phases in the deterioration of pathological gamblers. First is the *winning phase*, in which they gamble occasionally, fantasize about winning, escalate their bets, and win big. Next comes the *losing phase*, in which they gamble alone, skip work, lie, borrow heavily, don't pay debts, and return the next day to win back losses ("chasing"). Third is the *desperation phase*, during which they are filled with remorse and their reputation suffers: They become separated from family and friends, get fired, blame others, panic, and steal. Last is the *hopeless phase*, in which they feel utterly futile, get arrested and divorced, drink heavily and abuse drugs, become demoralized and depressed, and on hitting "rock bottom," contemplate or attempt suicide. Pathological gambling is a chronic disorder that waxes and wanes.

Pathological gambling impairs most aspects of the gambler's life: Lost jobs, broken marriages, imprisonment, financial ruin, and attempted suicide are common. While stressing the many similarities between pathological gambling and alcoholism, a "reformed" gambler aptly pointed out a big difference: "If you're an alcoholic with $1,000, you'll drink $50-worth of booze and fall asleep; when you awake, you've still got $950. If you're a druggie and shoot up $400-worth, you'll drift off and still awake with $600. But if you're a gambler, you'll blow all $1,000 and end up with *nothing!*"

Epidemiology

With the growth of legalized gambling in the United States, the number of pathological gamblers has climbed from 4 million in 1976 to 12 million in 1990—which is 2–3% of the population. A parallel pattern has occurred in Great Britain, suggesting that legalized gambling may promote pathological gambling. [1]

In a New York state study (Volberg & Steadman, 1988), 1.4% of the population was classified as pathological gamblers. The men outnumbered the women at least 2 to 1 (most are betting that the odds are even higher). Gambling affects all social classes, though it is more common in those making under $25,000 a year than in those earning more. However, this yearly income figure may be a *result* of gambling and not a cause of it.

---

[1] Nearly two-thirds of Americans patronize legalized gambling: casinos, horse racing, dog racing, church bingo, state-run lotteries, etc. Their promoters don't call it "gambling," but run ads imploring listeners to, "Get where the action is!"—a most telling phrase, given the pathological gambler's thirst for excitement.

Etiology and Pathogenesis

Little is known about the etiology of pathological gambling; a combination of psychological and psychosocial factors is generally cited. The typical impulsive gambler comes from a family in which social gambling was at least condoned, or in which a parent of the same sex was a compulsive gambler or alcoholic. Disturbed childhoods, broken homes, financial difficulties, and materialism characterize the gambler's upbringing.

On the biological side, gamblers may be hooked on their own norepinephrine. Several studies report that physiological arousal reinforces and maintains pathological gambling. High sensation seekers and extroverts may be particularly vulnerable. The trait "sensation seeking" is correlated with bigger bet size and higher heart rate in casino gamblers and also with how extensive their gambling is in general. Pathological gamblers have higher levels of norepinephrine and its metabolites than normals (Roy et al., 1988) and these high levels are also associated with extroversion in the gamblers (Roy, DeJong, & Linnoila, 1989). Maybe for them, a shot of norepinephrine is like a shot of cocaine—while for us it's like a shot of espresso.

Other lines of research suggest that pathological gambling may belong to the depressive spectrum disorders. Pathological gamblers have more first-degree relatives with mood and substance-use disorders (McElroy et al., 1992).

Differential Diagnosis

When a patient's chief complaint is *depression,* pathological gambling can be readily overlooked. If seeking treatment during the desperation or hopeless phases, the gambler may be so ashamed of his "moral weakness" that he avoids the topic, complaining instead of hopelessness, helplessness, suicidal thoughts, insomnia, and other depressive symptoms. Since clinicians rarely ask depressed patients if they gamble excessively, the disorder can elude diagnosis. Unlike people with *antisocial personality disorder*, most pathological gamblers have good work records prior to their serious gambling, and they steal solely to pay debts or to have money for gambling.

Pathological gambling may be confused with *manic* or *hypomanic episodes*, since (a) mania often leads to outrageous betting, (b) both conditions involve poor judgment and little foresight, and (c) euphoria usually follows a gambler's winning streak. The presence of other manic behaviors, however, easily rules out pathological gambling. As previously discussed, pathological gambling should be distinguished from *social gambling*, the kind between friends where limits on losses are decided in advance.

Management and Treatment

Many gamblers will enter treatment simply to get relatives off their back; once things cool down, gambling resumes. If they remain in treatment, four attitudes frequently undermine therapy: (a) Lack of money is seen as *the* problem; (b) an instant or miraculous cure is expected; (c) life without gambling is inconceivable; and (d) repaying debts is desirable but impossible (Custer, 1979). Denying these attitudes during treatment, especially near the beginning, should raise doubts about the authenticity of the patient's commitment to change. Since these patients are often bright and have a gift of gab, place little stock in what they *say* and far more in what they *do*. Treatment should be judged on the duration of gambling-free intervals, on debts being paid, and on developing interests other than gambling.

The last goal, often overlooked, is crucial, since substitute excitements and pleasures must eventually replace gambling; hence, vocational counseling and recreational therapy may be an invaluable adjunct to therapy. Meeting periodically with relatives is also important, as much for the relatives as for the gambler. Clinicians should remind themselves and loved ones that pathological gambling is a *chronic* disorder in which lapses are expected and do not necessarily mean that therapy is a bust.

If the patient is on trial for problems secondary to his gambling, such as tax evasion, the best sentence might involve an extended probation *contingent* on the patient participating fully in therapy, repaying all debts on schedule, not gambling, being employed regularly, and periodically showing financial accountability. Imprisonment is only useful when the gambler doesn't fulfill this program.

Founded in 1957, Gamblers Anonymous (GA) is modeled after Alcoholics Anonymous, claims 12,000 members, and affiliates with Gamonan, which is for relatives of gamblers and similar to Alanon. (Contact: GA's National Service Office, P. O. Box 17173, Los Angeles, CA 90017, 213/386-8789.) Only 5-8% of gamblers who join GA stop gambling, but if GA is combined with comprehensive inpatient care, half who complete the program refrain from gambling for a year, and a third do so for several years (Kellner, 1982a). Given the similarities between gambling and alcoholism and between GA and AA, if a GA chapter isn't available, attending AA is a good substitute.

KLEPTOMANIA

Kleptomania is the recurrent failure to resist impulses to steal objects that are not for immediate use or for economic gain. Kleptomaniacs typically have enough money to buy objects, and once possessing them, they have no use for them; they are likely to give the objects away, return them, or forget them. Unlike other thieves or shoplifters, kleptomaniacs experience mounting tension before stealing and a gratifying relief of tension afterwards; they steal by themselves, spontaneously, and without compatriots. Because they steal to alleviate tension, when that tension becomes unbearable, they're more concerned with discharging anxiety than with taking precautions. Hence, kleptomaniacs make lousy thieves: Their bounty isn't worth much and they're frequently caught. Contrary to myth, kleptomaniacs do *not* want to be caught: What they do want is the thrill of discharging that tension. Table 18-2 presents *DSM-IV* criteria for kleptomania.

Kleptomania is more common among women, seems to wax and wane over time, and often decreases with age. Four percent of apprehended shoplifters are kleptomaniacs. Because most patients aren't kleptomaniacs, the best question to ask to make the diagnosis is, "Why did you do it?" Kleptomaniacs will give their own version of the tension and relief cycle. *Psychotics* will tell you things like, "The CIA made me do it." *Antisocial and conduct disorders* will say, "I wanted it," unless they are also *malingerers* and have learned to give the "right" answers for kleptomania. Then you have to see what was being stolen—pencils, lipstick?—or what really counts—jewelry, money, or valuable electronics items! (*antisocial*). *Manics* will say it was the fun thing to do and have all the other symptoms of mania. Other nonkleptomaniacs may admit doing it out of anger or revenge.

Kleptomania is associated with extraordinarily high rates of other psychiatric disorders. In one study using *DSM-III-R Lifetime diagnosis* (McElroy, 1991), 100% had a mood disorder, 80% had at least one anxiety disorder, 60% had an eating disorder (most often bulimia), 50% had a substance disorder, 45% had obsessive-compulsive disorder, and 40% had some other impulse control disorder.

TABLE 18–2
DSM-IV Criteria for Kleptomania*

A. Recurrent failure to resist impulses to steal objects that are not needed for personal use or for their monetary value.

B. Increasing sense of tension immediately before committing the theft.

C. Pleasure, gratification, or relief at the time of committing the theft.

D. The stealing is not committed to express anger or vengeance and is not in response to a delusion or a hallucination.

E. The stealing is not better accounted for by Conduct Disorder, a Manic Episode, or Antisocial Personality Disorder.

---

*DSM-IV, p. 613.

Similarly high rates of these disorders were found in the patients' families. In a majority of cases, one of the other psychiatric disorders came first.

Almost nothing is known about the specific treatment of kleptomania. However, treating the other disorders associated with it is essential. Bulimia and obsessive-compulsive disorders, and to some extent substance abuse, also share the tension-relief cycle, so approaches to this cycle, such as response prevention, alternative forms of tension release, and antidepressants (particularly the SSRIs) might be helpful.

PYROMANIA

Pyromania is the recurrent failure to resist setting fires, along with an intense fascination with igniting and watching them. Setting fires is gratifying because it discharges mounting tension. Pyromaniacs thrill at seeing flames leap up and destroy things; by definition, pyromaniacs do not set fires for any other reason (e.g., greed, revenge, politics). They rarely feel remorse or regret, despite knowing that they've destroyed property, maimed victims, or even murdered. Even planning arson, which they do far in advance, brings pleasure. This planning feature makes pyromania different from the other impulse disorders. Table 18–3 lists *DSM-IV* criteria for pyromania.

TABLE 18–3
DSM-IV Criteria for Pyromania*

A. Deliberate and purposeful fire setting on more than one occasion.

B. Tension or affective arousal before the act.

C. Fascination with, interest in, curiosity about, or attraction to fire and its situational contexts (e.g., paraphernalia, uses, consequences).

D. Pleasure, gratification, or relief when setting fires, or when witnessing or participating in their aftermath.

E. The fire setting is not done for monetary gain, as an expression of sociopolitical ideology, to conceal criminal activity, to express anger or vengeance, to improve one's living circumstances, in response to a delusion or hallucination, or as a result of impaired judgment (e.g., in dementia, Mental Retardation, Substance Intoxication).

F. The fire setting is not better accounted for by Conduct Disorder, a Manic Episode, or Antisocial Personality Disorder.

*DSM-IV, p. 615.

Case studies show that as children, most future pyromaniacs are fascinated by fires, fire engines, firefighters, and any firefighting equipment. They have pulled many a false alarm and relished the sight of firefighters rushing to the scene; orchestrating this whole to-do may afford children an enormous sense of power, control, and mastery, which they probably lack in other areas of life.

Pyromaniacs are drawn to any huge fire (which is the first place police look to nab a firesetter). Since most pyromaniacs come to psychiatrists via the courts, the literature about them is skewed. They are often diagnosed with alcohol abuse (91%), mood disorder (95%, usually dysthymia), and intermittent explosive disorder (68%). Also associated with pyromania is a higher rate of borderline personality disorder, attention-deficit/hyperactivity disorder, and learning disabilities. In one study, impulsive firesetters were found to be low in serotonin metabolites (Virkkunen, DeJong, Bartko, & Linnoila, 1989). Low serotonin has been correlated with increased aggression and impulsivity. Pyromania is a rare disorder. Firesetters are men 90% of the time; female pyromaniacs tend to set fires in their own homes and to experience marital discord and depression. Pyromania in children differs from *normal childhood fascination with fires*, in that the latter is less frequent, pernicious, and all-consuming. Although patients with *antisocial personality disorders* set fires, their reasons are not limited to being gratified by the fire. Deliberate sabotage, as "paid torches," political terrorism, and good old-fashioned revenge must be ruled out. *Schizophrenics* set fires, but in response to delusions or hallucinations. Unlike pyromaniacs, *demented* patients set fires, although by accident, and always without planning or without realizing the consequences of the act.

There are no controlled studies assessing treatment. Anecdotal reports indicate that most child pyromaniacs recover fully, whereas adult pyromaniacs do not. With the majority having mildly low intelligence and ingrained impulsiveness, few pyromaniacs benefit from insight-oriented psychotherapy. Behavior therapies might be more useful by substituting healthy gratifications and by improving social skills. Perhaps the most useful intervention is to ensure that pyromaniacs don't drink.

INTERMITTENT EXPLOSIVE DISORDER

This very rare disorder is characterized by discrete episodes of violence based on little or no provocation. The outbursts, which start and stop abruptly, usually last several minutes but may be persist for several hours. The person suddenly breaks windows, throws chairs, and so on. The "seizures" or "spells" may be immediately preceded by a rapid mood change, flushing, tachycardia, or altered sensorium (e.g., confusion, amnesia). Patients then describe an "irresistible impulse that comes over" them to smash everything in sight. Afterwards, most will assume responsibility for the act and express genuine remorse. Table 18–4 lists *DSM-IV* criteria for intermittent explosive disorder.

TABLE 18–4
DSM-IV **Criteria for Intermittent Explosive Disorder***

A. Several discrete episodes of failure to resist aggressive impulses that result in serious assaultive acts or destruction of property.

B. The degree of aggressiveness expressed during the episodes is grossly out of proportion to any precipitating psychosocial stressors.

C. The aggressive episodes are not better accounted for by another mental disorder (e.g., Antisocial Personality Disorder, Borderline Personality Disorder, a Psychotic Disorder, a Manic Episode, Conduct Disorder, or Attention-Deficit/Hyperactivity Disorder) and are not due to the direct physiological effects of a substance (e.g., a drug of abuse, a medication) or a general medical condition (e.g., head trauma, Alzheimer's disease).

DSM-IV, p. 612.

This disorder primarily affects men and usually arises during their twenties or thirties. The prototypic patient grew up in a broken home where he was physically abused by an alcoholic parent; he had either attention-deficit/hyperactivity disorder, or suffered encephalitis or perinatal head trauma; as an adult, he's muscular, has alcohol problems, is concerned with his masculine identity, and is usually in prison. Women more often end up in psychiatric facilities.

These patients have been labeled "explosive characters" and "epileptoid personalities" because they frequently display soft neurological signs and because their "attacks" are often triggered by premenstrual tension, bright lights, and loud noises—the same stimuli that trigger epileptic seizures. Despite this, their EEGs are usually normal. The "mean drunk" can look like this, but specializes in violence only when intoxicated. Intoxication with any psychoactive substance and any neurologic condition (such as head trauma) must be ruled out as the cause of the violent episodes. All the *DSM-IV* disorders associated with increased violence and outbursts must be examined to make sure they aren't the main source of the destructive behavior. Keep in mind that many people with intermittent explosive disorder also have a personality disorder; separating out the two diagnoses is no easy task. They also are more likely to be firesetters, and like pyromaniacs, are low in the serotonin metabolites (5-hydroxyindeacitic acid).

There is no clearly effective treatment, although some patients have been helped by anticonvulsant medications (e.g., carbamazepine), beta-blockers (e.g., propranolol, metaprolol), lithium, antipsychotics, and antidepressants. Hypnoanxiolytics may worsen the condition by disinhibiting it. Group therapy is claimed to be more useful than individual therapy.

TRICHOTILLOMANIA

Trichotillomania (besides being hard to say) is the recurrent failure to resist pulling out one's own hair. It's usually not fun. Tension mounts before the moment of plucking and is released during or after the act. The majority specialize in pulling out one hair at a time, concentrate on scalp hair, and say it doesn't hurt. Eyelashes (22%) and eyebrows (8%) are other favored sites. Multiple sites (two on average) are eventually used, and because it's easily concealed, even pubic hair (17%) is included. After pulling out the hair, these patients will put their hair in or around their mouths, including rubbing the hair around the mouth (25%), licking it (8%), and/or eating it (10%) (Christenson, MacKenzie, & Mitchell, 1991). Most patients are females who, for years, have concealed their problems through clever hair styling over bald patches and makeup on their eyebrows and lashes. Hair loss varies from barely noticeable thinning to total loss. Table 18–5 lists *DSM-IV* criteria for trichotillomania.

Many don't come in for treatment. A third of the women who come in the clinic for treatment say that they have had the problem less than a year. A broader, nonclinic study (Christenson et al., 1991) found that most had started the behavior within five years before or after puberty and had had the problem for two decades. Only 18% did *not* have another Axis I disorder. The rest had a lifetime diagnosis of mood disorders (65%), anxiety disorder (57%), eating disorders (20%), and/or substance-use disorder (22%). Within the anxiety disorders, 18% had panic disorder, 10% had obsessive-compulsive disorder, and 18% had obsessions or compulsions but did not meet the full criteria for obsessive-compulsive disorder.

Because people with trichotillomania often keep it secret, a common medical cause of hair loss (in medicalese, "alopecia") is often suspect. With a biopsy, a dermatologist can easily distinguish between the medical condition of *alopecia are-*

TABLE 18–5
DSM-IV* Criteria for Trichotillomania

A. Recurrent pulling out of one's hair resulting in noticeable hair loss.

B. An increasing sense of tension immediately before pulling out the hair or when attempting to resist the behavior.

C. Pleasure, gratification, or relief when pulling out the hair.

D. The disturbance is not better accounted for by another mental disorder and is not due to a general medical condition (e.g., a dermatological condition).

E. The disturbance causes clinically significant distress or impairment in social, occupational, or other important areas of functioning.

---

*DSM-IV, p. 621.

ata and the traumatic loss of hair from trichotillomania. If the patient insists to the clinician that she never pulls out her hair, the dermatologist can verify if this is a lie; then the person really has a *factitious disorder* with physical symptoms. If only one question can be asked, make it, "What makes you pull out your hair, and how do you feel once you've done it?" People with *obsessive-compulsive disorder* will say that they are doing it to prevent or produce some future situation. Kids and adults with *stereotypic movement disorder* will say that they don't know why they do it, they just do, and it doesn't bother them. Fiddling with the hair and occasionally pulling it is normal; no tension-relief cycle is noted. Normals might say, "I barely thought about it — I was spaced out."

Along with behavioral approaches, treatment with antidepressants can be very helpful. As in obsessive-compulsive disorder, serotonin agents like clomipramine and fluoxetine appear to be more effective than standard antidepressants like desipramine. Perhaps trichotillomania is a variant of OCD.

CHAPTER 19

Personality Disorders

"PERSONALITY" OR "CHARACTER" *traits* are ingrained, enduring patterns of behaving, feeling, perceiving, and thinking, which are prominent in a wide range of personal and social contexts. Personality is the psychological equivalent of physical appearance: We grow up with both, and although we can adjust each, they remain essentially the same and affect the rest of our lives. As Heraclitus observed, "A man's fate is his character." Personality features may or may not be adaptive. Compulsiveness in a student is adaptive when it promotes orderly study habits, but it's maladaptive when the student spends hours sharpening pencils instead of studying. Personality traits turn into personality *disorders* when they become (a) inflexible and maladaptive, and (b) significantly impair social and occupational functioning or cause substantial subjective distress. People with personality disorders are not always in significant emotional distress. Often, the people they are living or working with are more distressed. Freud once defined a successful mature adult as someone "who is able to love and to work." People with personality disorders frequently fail at both.

In *DSM-IV*, personality traits and disorders are listed on Axis II, while mental disorders are indicated on Axis I. This separation distinguishes patients' current and more florid mental disorders from their ongoing, baseline, personalities; this distinction should result in more *realistic* treatment goals. Since Axis I mental disorders are more responsive to treatment than Axis II personality disorders, a realistic treatment goal may be to remedy the former but not the latter. For instance, it may be unrealistic to expect a dependent personality who develops a major depression to be rid of both after a brief hospitalization.

Kahana and Bibring (1964) show how identifying medical patients' personality types may alter how clinicians relate to patients. For example, when a doctor pats Mr. Moscowitz on the shoulder and says, "Don't worry, everything will be fine," a dependent patient will be greatly relieved; do the same with a paranoid patient and he'll draw away and think, "How does he know I'll be okay? Why's he being so chummy? How dare he touch me!" Paranoid patients feel safer with clinicians who keep their distance. Thus in many settings, clinicians should not attempt to change the patient's personality, but rather should adjust their own behavior to fit the patient's personality type.

When treatment for a personality disorder is attempted, the goal is not to reverse a constitutional defect but to help the person live more comfortably and efficiently within his or her limitations; treatment can help modify and reduce the defect. The task of therapists who treat individuals with personality disorders is to help them (and others around them) recognize and accept their defects, and having done so, to organize their lives in such a way that their defects are minimized and their remaining talents and strengths maximized.

Understanding a patient's personality traits can guide psychotherapy, medication use, family involvement, nurses' monitoring, etc. To illustrate: During group therapy, Mrs. Grant suddenly asked to see her hospital chart. If Mrs. Grant were a paranoid personality, the group therapist could be fairly sure she wanted to uncover malicious information that the staff were writing about her. However, Mrs. Grant is not paranoid; she has an avoidant personality, and as such, the therapist can reasonably guess that she wanted to know whether the therapist liked her—a proposition he raised for the group's consideration. Another illustration: If during a highly stressful period, a patient asked for a three-day supply of sleeping pills, all things being equal, a patient with a borderline personality would be far more likely to abuse the pills than would a schizoid personality. Or, if a psychiatric nurse has to leave patients in the care of another patient, she would much prefer an obsessive-compulsive to an antisocial personality.

Differential Diagnosis

In general, never diagnose a personality disorder in the midst of an episode of a major psychiatric illness without having information about the person's behavior before this episode. Too often, mole hills in a personality become mountains during an acute psychiatric episode. Minor traits such as dependency may look like full-blown personality disorders during the acute stress.

1. *Neurosis vs. personality disorder*: Patients who develop a neurosis regard their neurotic behavior as uncharacteristic of their usual self, as different for them. In contrast, the pathological behavior exhibited by patients with personality disorders is in character, is usual for them. Neuroses may develop at any time; personality disorders are longstanding. Neurotic individuals are usually uncomfortable with their symptoms, whereas individuals with personality disorders often justify and rationalize their behavior.

2. *Personality trait vs. disorder*: Some people have only one or two characteristics of a disorder, which do not significantly impair functioning as does the full-blown disorder.
3. *Major mood disorders and schizophrenia vs. personality disorders*: Impairment in functioning is seldom as profound in personality disorders as in major mood disorders and schizophrenia. Individuals with personality disorders seldom require hospitalization. They are not psychotic.
4. *Late onset mental disorder*: Late onset (adulthood) personality changes suggest the presence of a major mental or medical disorder.

This chapter summarizes the 10 personality disorders listed in *DSM-IV*. In general, personality disorders first become apparent during adolescence or earlier, persist through life, and become less obvious by middle or old age. The diagnosis is not made until adulthood, since behavioral disorders of childhood and adolescence are frequently transient. Personality disorders are more pronounced during periods of high energy (as in adolescence) and under stressful conditions; they should only be diagnosed when they cause life-long problems, not just discrete periods of dysfunction. Except for schizotypal, borderline, and antisocial personalities, hospitalizations are rare.

In a retrospective chart review, 36% of 2,462 psychiatric patients had personality disorders. Borderline personality disorder was diagnosed most frequently (12% of total); next (at 10%) was *DSM-III*'s residual category of "mixed, atypical, or other personality disorder." The other personality disorders were diagnosed in under 3% of the patients. Substance-abuse disorders were the most common Axis I diagnosis found among those with personality disorders (Koeningsberg, Kaplan, Gilmore, & Cooper, 1985).

DSM-IV divides personality disorders into three clusters: The first consists of paranoid, schizoid, and schizotypal personality disorders, characterized by odd or eccentric behavior. The second includes histrionic, narcissistic, antisocial, and borderline personality disorders, characterized by dramatic, overemotional, and erratic behavior. The third consists of avoidant, dependent, and obsessive-compulsive personality disorders, characterized by highly anxious and fearful affects.

PARANOID PERSONALITY DISORDER

"I only trust me and thee and I'm not so sure of thee."

— Anonymous

The essential features of a paranoid personality disorder (PPD) are: (a) pervasive and unwarranted suspiciousness and mistrust of people, (b) hypersensitivity, and (c) emotional detachment. None of these features should stem from another mental disorder, such as schizophrenia or paranoid disorder. Table 19–1 lists the *DSM-IV* criteria for PPD.

"Paranoids have enemies" mainly because they're paranoid. Paranoid people are very unpleasant, always blaming and suspicious of others. Suspicions may be justified and adaptive, but when contradictory evidence is presented, most people abandon them. Paranoids do not, but rather view the evidence as further proof that the person intends to harm them. The paranoid's world is hostile, devious, and dark, filled with persecutory forces for which the paranoid must be eternally vigilant. On entering a restaurant, he will scan the room to ensure no enemies are present and then sit with his back to the wall so that nobody can sneak behind him. Highly secretive, he may hide behind dark glasses. Paranoids bristle at the slightest contradiction or criticism, distrust people's loyalty, and misconstrue what they say. When a co-worker congratulated a paranoid man on plans to buy a home, the paranoid snapped, "It's mine! You can't have it!" Paranoids may be ambitious and bright, yet stubborn and defensive. They're quick to argue and find fault. They'll seize an alleged injustice, overblow its significance, and distort the facts to fit their suspiciousness.

Table 19–1
DSM-IV Criteria for Paranoid Personality Disorder*

A. A pervasive distrust and suspiciousness of others such that their motives are interpreted as malevolent, beginning by early adulthood and present in a variety of contexts, as indicated by four (or more) of the following:

   (1) suspects, without sufficient basis, that others are exploiting, harming, or deceiving him or her
   (2) is preoccupied with unjustified doubts about the loyalty or trustworthiness of friends or associates
   (3) is reluctant to confide in others because of unwarranted fear that the information will be used maliciously against him or her
   (4) reads hidden, demeaning, or threatening meanings into benign remarks or events
   (5) persistently bears grudges, i.e., is unforgiving of insults, injuries, or slights
   (6) perceives attacks on his or her character or reputation that are not apparent to others and is quick to react angrily or to counterattack
   (7) has recurrent suspicions, without justification, regarding fidelity of spouse or sexual partner

B. Does not occur exclusively during the course of Schizophrenia, a Mood Disorder With Psychotic Features, or another Psychotic Disorder and is not due to the direct physiological effects of a general medical condition.

*DSM-IV, pp. 637–38.

A paranoid English professor discovered that a classroom he had reserved was occupied by another faculty member. The professor became enraged, citing it as "this draconian administration's efforts to drive me from the university." The next day, after learning the university press would not publish his definitive study of Iago, he launched a $3 million law suit against the university. Four months later, the university threatened not to renew his contract. He dropped the suit, but then instigated student protests against the university for "stifling academic freedom."

People keep their distance from paranoids, which merely confirms the paranoid's general distrust. Paranoids are pathologically jealous, tense, rigid, unwilling to compromise, moralistic, always detecting ill-intent and special messages, litigious, humorless, coldly objective, overly rational, haughty, and distant. That's why "paranoids have enemies," have few friends, and fewer, if any, intimate relationships. They have contempt for the weakness in others; disdain the sickly, defective, and imperfect—that is, everybody, but themselves. They think in hierarchical terms: Who's superior to whom; who controls whom. With their egocentricity and exaggerated self-importance, they make a great show of self-sufficiency. They're drawn to politics, history, science, and technology; to them, the arts are for sissies. As unpleasant as the paranoid can be, remember that it's a terribly uncomfortable existence.

PPD is more common in men than women. Social relations and job advancement are often severely impaired. Unlike paranoid disorders and paranoid schizophrenia, paranoid personalities are *not* psychotic. When a person with paranoid disorder is challenged about the certainty of his allegations, he will say, "I'm quite sure," or "It's highly probable." If pushed further about alternative explanations, he might say, "Yes, those alternatives are possible but highly unlikely." The psychotic will say, "It is fact and there are no alternative explanations." People with PPD can become psychotic when highly stressed. A person with PPD has over-valued ideas, not delusions.

These patients seldom come for psychiatric treatment since they do not perceive weakness or faults in themselves. They may be sent by bosses or wives under threat of the loss of a job or marriage, but the relationship they form with a therapist tends to be adversarial rather than collaborative and thus is often doomed to failure. They do, of course, need medical treatment from time to time and when this happens, they interact with their physicians in the same manner as they interact with others. They tend to be guarded in giving information about themselves, suspicious of the intent behind the questions asked, and distrustful of examinations, procedures, and treatments. They often question the training and qualifications of those who treat them. They are particularly apt to bring suit. It is therefore important that clinicians who deal with this group of people do so in an honest and comprehensive fashion. They should be thoroughly informed and their consent obtained for whatever is done. Further, careful documentation of both the information given and the informed consent is advised.

In psychological treatment, the therapist's main task is to minimize the patient's distrust of the therapist and of therapy. It often takes months before the patient feels at all relaxed in treatment. Clinicians should be respectful and business-like, avoiding intimacy and too much warmth, which paranoids experience as invasive. Deep psychological interpretations are verboten, since paranoids are already leery of "shrinks who read people's minds and trick them." Insight to a therapist is "mind-fucking" to a paranoid. In the office, clinicians should *not* sit between the patient and the door; the paranoid feels far less threatened if nobody "blocks" his exitway. What's an office to a therapist is an observation chamber to a paranoid. When clinicians err, they should admit the mistake, apologize, and get on with it; overapologizing fosters distrust. Nor should clinicians ask paranoids to trust them, since to the paranoid, that's like a Nazi guard asking a Dachau inmate to trust him. Being straightforward and "professional" is the most reassuring approach. When starting medications, paranoids should be given detailed and accurate side-effect information. They already expect the worst but feel better knowing about it.

SCHIZOID PERSONALITY DISORDER

The central features of a schizoid personality disorder (SDPD) are: (a) minimal or no social relations, (b) restricted expression of emotion, (c) a striking lack of warmth and tenderness, and (d) an apparent indifference to others' praise, criticism, feelings, and concerns. Unlike schizotypal personalities (see below), schizoid patients do *not* exhibit eccentricities of speech, behavior, or thinking. Table 19–2 lists *DSM-IV* criteria for SDPD.

Patients with schizoid personalities are often "in a fog," absentminded, loners, detached from others, self-involved, "not connected." What appears as aloofness is actually profound shyness. Often dull and humorless, they will disavow feelings of anger or interest in sex; they prefer solitary activities and daydreaming to friendships. Dating is painful, marriage rare. Although SDPD greatly impedes social relationships and professional advancement, these patients can excel if permitted minimal interpersonal contact. The prevalence of SDPD is unknown, though schizoid individuals may be common on skid row.

SDPD resembles *avoidant personality disorder*, since both display prominent social isolation. Yet whereas the avoidant personalities want friends, schizoids don't; whereas avoidants are alone because they're afraid people won't like them, schizoids have no interest in personal involvement. Once considered a prodromal phase of *schizophrenia*, SDPD and schizophrenia are now considered to be unrelated (see below). Few schizoid patients become psychotic.

Little is known about the treatment of this disorder; most persons with this condition probably do not seek professional help or do so only when seeking help for depression, substance abuse, or other problems. Most schizoids undoubtedly lack the insight or motivation for individual psychotherapy and probably would find the intimacy of typical group therapy too threatening. If the patient is motivated, behavioral techniques may be helpful, such as graded exposure to a variety

TABLE 19–2
DSM-IV Criteria for Schizoid Personality Disorder*

A. A pervasive pattern of detachment from social relationships and a restricted range of expression of emotions in interpersonal settings, beginning by early adulthood and present in a variety of contexts, as indicated by four (or more) of the following:

   (1) neither desires nor enjoys close relationships, including being part of a family
   (2) almost always chooses solitary activities
   (3) has little, if any, interest in having sexual experiences with another person
   (4) takes pleasure in few, if any, activities
   (5) lacks close friends or confidants other than first-degree relatives
   (6) appears indifferent to the praise or criticism of others
   (7) shows emotional coldness, detachment, or flattened affectivity

B. Does not occur exclusively during the course of Schizophrenia, a Mood Disorder With Psychotic Features, another Psychotic Disorder, or a Pervasive Developmental Disorder and is not due to the direct physiological effects of a general medical condition.

Note: If criteria are met prior to the onset of Schizophrenia, add "Premorbid," e.g., "Schizoid Personality Disorder (Premorbid)."

*DSM-IV, p. 641.

---

of social tasks. For example, the clinician might encourage the patient to attend a concert, then join a bridge club, and eventually enter a dance class. Long-term group psychotherapy with other schizoidal patients has also been reported to be successful (Yalom, 1975).

SCHIZOTYPAL PERSONALITY DISORDER

In *DSM-IV*, the essential feature of a schizotypal personality disorder (STPD) "is a pervasive pattern of social and interpersonal deficits marked by acute discomfort with, and reduced capacity for, close relationships as well as by cognitive or perceptual distortions and eccentricities of behavior" (p. 645). These patients have few friends because they are very strange and eccentric. They live in The Twilight Zone, filled with weird thoughts, ideas of reference, paranoid ideation, telepathy, and "magical thinking"—e.g., "If I think hard enough, I can make the wind blow"; "My teeth itch." Their speech may be hard to follow, although without loose associations or incoherence. Their affect is flat or inappropriate. Sloppy, unkempt, giggling for no reason, and often talking to themselves, they are hypersensitive to criticism and dreadfully anxious around people, especially if more than three are together. Table 19–3 lists the *DSM-IV* criteria for STPD.

TABLE 19–3
DSM-IV **Criteria for Schizotypal Personality Disorder***

A. A pervasive pattern of social and interpersonal deficits marked by acute discomfort with, and reduced capacity for, close relationships as well as by cognitive or perceptual distortions and eccentricities of behavior, beginning by early adulthood and present in a variety of contexts, as indicated by five (or more) of the following:

(1) ideas of reference (excluding delusions of reference)
(2) odd beliefs or magical thinking that influence behavior and are inconsistent with subcultural norms (e.g., superstitiousness, belief in clairvoyance, telepathy, or "sixth sense"; in children and adolescents, bizarre fantasies or preoccupations)
(3) unusual perceptual experiences, including bodily illusions
(4) odd thinking and speech (e.g., vague, circumstantial, metaphorical, overelaborate, or stereotyped)
(5) suspiciousness or paranoid ideation
(6) inappropriate or constricted affect
(7) behavior or appearance that is odd, eccentric, or peculiar
(8) lacks close friends or confidants other than first-degree relatives
(9) excessive social anxiety that does not diminish with familiarity and tends to be associated with paranoid fears rather than negative judgments about self

B. Does not occur exclusively during the course of Schizophrenia, a Mood Disorder With Psychotic Features, another Psychotic Disorder, or a Pervasive Developmental Disorder.

Note: If criteria are met prior to the onset of Schizophrenia, add "Premorbid," e.g., "Schizotypal Personality Disorder (Premorbid)."

*DSM-IV, p. 645.

Unlike *schizoid* personalities, schizotypal personalities are more likely to (a) display bizarre and peculiar traits, (b) develop fanatic, eccentric, or racist beliefs, (c) become dysthymic and anxious, (d) have an accompanying borderline personality disorder, (e) become transiently psychotic under stress, (f) evolve into schizophrenia, (g) run in families (Baron, Guren, Asnis, & Lord, 1985), and (h) have a schizophrenic relative. Unlike STPD, patients with *schizophrenia, residual type* would have previously displayed a florid schizophrenic psychosis. If schizophrenia develops in a schizotypal patient, the schizotypal diagnosis is dropped. Indeed, schizophrenia should always be suspected in schizotypal patients under 35.

Treatment of schizotypal patients often centers on issues that led them to seek treatment. These issues may include feelings of alienation due to paranoid ideation or ideas of reference. A supportive approach has been recommended, while exploratory and group psychotherapies are felt to be overly threatening. Social skills training may be useful in helping eccentric, odd persons to feel more comfortable with others. Low-dose antipsychotics have been recommended to alleviate some of the intense anxiety and cognitive symptoms such as odd speech and unusual perceptual experience; this approach has some empirical support. However, any enthusiasm for using these medications must be tempered by their tendency to induce troublesome and potentially irreversible side effects. Antipsychotics should not routinely be used with these patients.

HISTRIONIC PERSONALITY DISORDER

"Seeing is believing, but feeling is God's own truth."

—Old Irish Proverb

These individuals are lively, overdramatic, and always calling attention to themselves. Their behavior is over-reactive, with minor stimuli giving rise to emotional excitability such as irrational outbursts or temper tantrums. Histrionics crave novelty, stimulation, and excitement and become quickly bored with normal routines. Though they are often creative and imaginative, they seldom show interest in intellectual achievement and careful, analytic thinking. Table 19–4 lists *DSM-IV* criteria for histrionic personality disorder.

In relationships, histrionics are perceived as shallow and lacking genuineness, though superficially charming and appealing. They are quick to form friendships, but once a friendship is established, they become demanding, egocentric, and inconsiderate. Because of feeling helpless and dependent, they make continuous demands for reassurance and manipulative suicidal threats, gestures, or attempts. Typically attractive and seductive, histrionics attempt to control the opposite sex or to enter into dependent relationships.

TABLE 19–4
DSM-IV Criteria for Histrionic Personality Disorder*

A pervasive pattern of excessive emotionality and attention seeking, beginning by early adulthood and present in a variety of contexts, as indicated by five (or more) of the following:

(1) is uncomfortable in situations in which he or she is not the center of attention
(2) interaction with others is often characterized by inappropriate sexually seductive or provocative behavior
(3) displays rapidly shifting and shallow expression of emotions
(4) consistently uses physical appearance to draw attention to self
(5) has a style of speech that is excessively impressionistic and lacking in detail
(6) self-dramatization, theatricality, and exaggerated expression of emotion
(7) suggestibility, i.e., easily influenced by others or circumstances
(8) considers relationships to be more intimate than they actually are

*DSM-IV, pp. 657–58.

Although flights into romantic fantasy are common, their sexuality is often constricted or unsatisfying. They experience periods of intense dissatisfaction and unhappiness, usually related to external changes such as a break-up with a lover.

This disorder is common and diagnosed more frequently in females than in males. It occurs more frequently among family members than in the general population. A frequent complication is substance-use disorder. A co-diagnosis of narcissistic, dependent, or borderline personality disorder is common. Although the cause of histrionic personality is unknown, the disorder has been linked through family studies to somatization disorder and antisocial personality. Research has suggested that histrionic and antisocial personalities may be sex-typed phenotypic variants of the same underlying genetic diathesis. It has also been suggested that histrionic personality is a sex-biased diagnosis that merely describes a caricature of stereotypic femininity.

If one talks about personality *styles* rather than *disorders*, "hysterics" and "compulsives" are cognitive opposites. Hysterics think in impressions, compulsives in facts. If Holly Go-Lightly, the Hysteric, and Carl Compulsive were to describe a person they recently met, Holly would exclaim, "He's just a darling, and such thrilling eyes. He must've murdered somebody. Either that, or he's poet. Did you see how he looked straight through me? I loved it." Carl would say, "He's about five-feet, eleven-inches tall, weights 160 pounds, has black hair, bushy eyebrows, a Southern accent. . . . " Compulsives present exhaustive, and ultimately boring, details; hysterics make global comments that lack specificity and focus. Compulsives are too mired in detail to make hunches, whereas hysterics base all their decisions on hunches, eschewing logic and information. Most people invoke hunches as temporary hypotheses, but hysterics use them as final conclusions (Shapiro, 1965). Because they so complement each other, it's not uncommon for compulsive professionals to marry histrionic artists. This marriage offers drama for the compulsive and stability for the histrionic.

In clinical interviews, it is very difficult to get detailed information from patients with histrionic personality disorder. It's like trying to nail Jello to a wall. Asking a patient *how long* she has been feeling badly might evoke a response such as, "Forever, a very long time" (in reality, it started 12 days ago). If asked *how badly* she feels, the patient might say, "The worst ever. I can't take the pain." The patient is not deliberately creating a smoke screen or being passive-aggressive; she stores *impressions* in her brain, not details. To adapt to the histrionic's style, clinicians may fare better by using more global wording than usual (most clinicians tend more to the compulsive side). If medications are prescribed, the generalities about side effects may suffice, since the details will be lost anyway.

Interventions have not been clearly studied, but psychoanalytic psychotherapy has a long tradition in the treatment of this and related syndromes, and for that reason is considered by some the treatment of choice. However, others advocate a more supportive, problem-solving approach or a cognitive approach to deal with distorted thinking (i.e., inflated self-image) and to minimize the counterproductive effects of frequent excessive emotional outpouring. Interpersonal approaches tend to focus on uncovering conscious (or unconscious) motivations for seeking out disappointing lovers and being unable to commit to stable, meaningful relationships. Group therapy may be useful in addressing provocative and attention-seeking behavior. Because patients may not be aware of their behaviors, it can be helpful for others to point out these traits to them. A condition that may be related — *hysteroid dysphoria*, described in depressed women who have a history of sensitivity to rejection in relationships — is reportedly responsive to monoamine oxidase inhibitors (e.g., phenelzine).

NARCISSISTIC PERSONALITY DISORDER

> "Please get me a tissue, I have a runny nose."
> — Patient asking a nurse, who is attempting
> to resuscitate a collapsed patient in the hallway.

Narcissus was the mythological Greek youth who fell so in love with his own reflection, that he pined away and died. Several (million) years later, Havelock Ellis (1898) used this myth to describe a case of male autoeroticism. Twelve years later, Freud introduced the term *narcissism*. Although narcissism has been defined in many ways, in *DSM-IV* the essential features for narcissistic personality disorder (NPD) are: (a) grandiose self-importance, (b) preoccupation with fantasies of unlimited success, (c) driven desire for attention and admiration, (d) intolerance to criticism, and (e) disturbed, self-centered interpersonal relations. Table 19–5 lists *DSM-IV* criteria for NPD.

These patients' *grandiosity* manifests as an exaggerated sense of self-importance or uniqueness. Others call them "conceited." They greatly overestimate not only their accomplishments and abilities, but their failures as well. For example, at age 30, Isaac described himself as "the greatest actor since Edmund Kean." When he failed to land a part in a major motion picture, he insisted that "everyone in Hollywood will think I'm washed up."

Fantasies of fame substitute for actual achievements. Everyone daydreams, but true narcissists are preoccupied with brilliance, wealth, ideal love, beauty, copping an Oscar (or two), or whatever. In real life, most

TABLE 19–5
DSM-IV **Criteria for Narcissistic Personality Disorder***

A pervasive pattern of grandiosity (in fantasy or behavior), need for admiration, and lack of empathy, beginning by early adulthood and present in a variety of contexts, as indicated by five (or more) of the following:

(1) has a grandiose sense of self-importance (e.g., exaggerates achievements and talents, expects to be recognized as superior without commensurate achievements)

(2) is preoccupied with fantasies of unlimited success, power, brilliance, beauty, or ideal love

(3) believes that he or she is "special" and unique and can only be understood by, or should associate with, other special or high-status people (or institutions)

(4) requires excessive admiration

(5) has a sense of entitlement, i.e., unreasonable expectations of especially favorable treatment or automatic compliance with his or her expectations

(6) is interpersonally exploitative, i.e., takes advantage of others to achieve his or her own ends

(7) lacks empathy: is unwilling to recognize or identify with the feelings and needs of others

(8) is often envious of others or believes that others are envious of him or her

(9) arrogant, haughty behaviors or attitudes

*DSM-IV, p. 661.

people enjoy reaching these goals, but narcissists don't. Their ambition is driven, their pursuit of recognition is a burden, their accomplishments don't satisfy. Isaac will perform in front of his own mirror, but not at an audition. He only takes roles if his agent gets him one, but even then, he loves the applause but hates the acting.

The narcissistic personality craves *attention* and universal admiration. Appearance is more important than substance. Being seen with the "right" people is more important than liking them. Narcissists are preoccupied with their physical image; they seek not merely to look attractive, but to appear godlike. Isaac's home is a museum studded with photographs of Isaac, mostly in the nude.

Intolerance to criticism arises from narcissists' low self-esteem. When their grandiosity is doubted, they respond with "narcissistic rage": cool disdain, anger, humiliation, extreme boredom, pessimism, negativism, and shame. Depressed moods result when they're rejected, neglected, or frustrated. When Isaac missed a key while playing the piano, he blamed the piano tuner for not doing his job correctly. At a party, Isaac was regaling his audience with show-biz stories, but when another actor joined in, Isaac became stone silent.

Interpersonally selfish, narcissists act with a sense of entitlement, as if they are the masters and everyone else, servants. Arriving an hour late on the set, Isaac doesn't apologize ("Why should I? I rushed like hell to get here. If anything, they should thank me.") Narcissists do not sustain genuine, positive regard for anyone. Some alternate between idealization and devaluation ("splitting"), worshiping an individual one moment and despising him or her the next. While there may be many people in their lives, they are all "insignificant others."

Narcissistic and *histrionic personalities* are both self-centered, but the narcissist is more grandiose, egotistical, arrogant, vigorous, and selfish, whereas the hysteric is more overdramatic, flighty, and apprehensive. *Manics* are grandiose, but episodically and often psychotically, whereas the narcissist's grandiosity is continual and nonpsychotic. Few patients with NPD become psychotic, and when they do, the episodes are brief.

Although NPD's prevalence and sex ratio are unknown, it's been attributed more often to men. Wilhelm Reich (1949/1968) described the "phallic-narcissistic character" whose "penis is not in the service of love but is an instrument of aggression and vengeance" (p. 203). Indeed, some narcissism creates many a business tycoon, surgeon, trial lawyer, politician, movie producer, actor, and orchestra conductor. Great accomplishments require great egos.

At about four years of age, narcissism is quite normal. All boys are "Superman" (or some other hero) and want everybody to watch them do their next stunt. Girls are vying for the highest social standing, all wanting to be the queen or prima donna. The boy's parents either "pound it out of him, so he doesn't get too big for his britches," or the opposite, indulge his every whim so as "not to frustrate and upset him." The girl's parents might constantly tell her she is pretty or cute but pay little attention to her real accomplishments or ignore her because they really wanted a boy. Either approach can warp progress toward a normal narcissism that is healthy and has realistic limits on it: "I am unique and special, but so are others and I need to respect their rights."

Patients with NPD infrequently seek treatment ("Why should I? There's nothing wrong with me.") But when they do, it's usually because depression or a medical illness threatens their grandiosity. Successful short-term management of these patients includes acknowledging their "specialness," setting some reasonable limits, and allowing them to conclude that their therapist or M.D. is also special and therefore able to appreciate their "special" problems. Long-term psychotherapy is usually recommended, even though its chance of inducing major change is low. When their invincibility is exposed, narcissists project their resentment onto their therapists, who should try to respect their patients' exaggerated self-importance while gently placing it into perspective. Group therapy should usually be avoided, because narcissists will monopolize the group until either everybody quits or group members run them out (Yalom, 1985).

ANTISOCIAL PERSONALITY DISORDER

"Why do I rob banks? Because that's where the money is."
— Willy Sutton, professional bank robber

In *DSM-IV*, the essential features of antisocial personality disorder (ASPD) are: (a) continuous and chronic antisocial behavior that violates the rights of others, (b) an onset prior to age 15, (c) a persistence into adulthood, and (d) several years of poor job performance. Table 19-6 lists *DSM-IV* criteria for ASPD. This condition is also called "sociopathy."

Clinical Presentation

Although many sociopaths are charming and resourceful, they're without enduring or intimate relationships. Friendships, even with fellow crooks, are opportunistic alliances to be broken whenever it's convenient. With radar for people's vulnerabilities, sociopaths can readily manipulate,

TABLE 19-6
DSM-IV Criteria for Antisocial Personality Disorder*

A. There is a pervasive pattern of disregard for and violation of the rights of others occurring since age 15, as indicated by three (or more) of the following:

   (1) failure to conform to social norms with respect to lawful behaviors as indicated by repeatedly performing acts that are grounds for arrest
   (2) deceitfulness, as indicated by repeated lying, use of aliases, or conning others for personal profit or pleasure
   (3) impulsivity or failure to plan ahead
   (4) irritability and aggressiveness, as indicated by repeated physical fights or assaults
   (5) reckless disregard for safety of self or others
   (6) consistent irresponsibility, as indicated by repeated failure to sustain consistent work behavior or honor financial obligations
   (7) lack of remorse, as indicated by being indifferent to or rationalizing having hurt, mistreated, or stolen from another

B. The individual is at least age 18 years.

C. There is evidence of Conduct Disorder with onset before age 15 years.

D. Occurrence of antisocial behavior is not exclusively during the course of Schizophrenia or a Manic Episode.

DSM-IV, pp. 649–650.

exploit, control, deceive, and intimidate others. Unlike other criminals, sociopaths enjoy "making suckers" of people. Their sexual relations are thrilling conquests and nothing more—and that includes marriage.

Emotionally shallow, they seem incapable of shame, guilt, loyalty, love, or any persistently sincere emotion; although quick to anger, they don't even sustain hatred. One moment they'll proclaim how deeply they feel about someone, and momentarily, they might believe themselves. These feelings are at most fleeting. Expressions of guilt and remorse don't affect future conduct.

Like addicts crave heroin, sociopaths crave stimulation. Excitement alone medicates their allergies to boredom, depression, and frustration. They can't hold a job; it would be too dull. Sociopaths are always on the move, "making deals," bumming around, picking fights, raping people, or killing them. Sociopaths live solely in the present; the past is a dim memory and the future a fiction. Unconcerned with the consequences of their actions and unable to learn from experience, the threat of punishment affords little restraint. Rewards must come now, not later; gratification cannot be delayed. Sociopaths are said to have "superego lacunae," that is, they are virtually without conscience. Expediency, immediate pleasure, and "stimulus hunger" override all other restraints.

Clinical Course

Antisocial personalities have "always" been up to "no-good"; they are not "good kids" who simply "fell into a bad crowd." *DSM-IV* stresses that ASPD begins before age 15. In boys, it emerges during early childhood, in girls, around puberty.

As children, sociopaths habitually lie, steal, skip school, and defy authority. They conceal feelings and talk to parents only when they want something. Exploiting parental affection, using siblings, running away from home, delighting in forbidden acts, and hanging around with older delinquents are common.

A mother describes her delinquent son: "He's always been different from my others, as if he's possessed. What kind of five-year-old steals from his mother's purse? Once I caught him hammering a squirrel to death, and when I yelled at him to stop, he just smiled. He enjoyed taunting me."

As adolescents, sociopaths abuse substances, gamble heavily, and display unusually early or aggressive sexual behavior. They mock rules, cut class, cause fights, and get expelled; their grades plummet. They're "pathological liars"—they lie without reason. Sociopaths delight in terrorizing others. A delinquent youth pulled out a pistol, aimed it at his teacher's head, and demanded he undress. Once the teacher was nude, the youth nudged the teacher's testicles with his gun, and fired. The gun wasn't loaded. Only the youth laughed.

By age 30, their promiscuity, fighting, criminality, and vagrancy tend to diminish. They "burn out." Some find they no longer have the energy required for a shiftless life and try to go "straight." Some succeed partially but few completely. Some end up on skid row, some are chronic substance abusers, some die by violence; in many prisons up to 75% of the inmates are sociopaths. Many subsist from one low-paying job to another and from one town to another. Only 2% of cases with full-blown ASPD remit after age 21.

Alcoholism and depression are the mental disorders most often affecting sociopaths and, thus, the most common reasons they seek treatment. Sociopaths often have conversion symptoms, especially when stressed or arrested. Many delinquent teenage girls develop somatization disorder as adults. Most sociopaths have low-to-normal IQs; a few have significant mental deficiency (IQ < 70).

Complications

ASPD markedly impairs social and occupational functioning. Plagued by infidelity, jealousy, and child abuse, their marriages usually end in separation and divorce. Sociopaths tend to marry young, beat their wives, and marry other sociopaths. Besides getting murdered, they have unusually high rates of venereal disease, out-of-wedlock pregnancies, injuries from fights and accidents, substance dependence, and gun wounds—which all lead to their shorter life expectancies. Major depression, suicidal threats and gestures are common; about 5% commit suicide.

Epidemiology

In the general population, ASPD affects 5.8% of men and under 1.2% of women (Kessler et al., 1994). Among psychiatric populations, ASPD affects 3–15% of men and 1–3% of women. ASPD is more prevalent in lower socioeconomic groups and among urban dwellers.

Etiology and Pathogenesis

One should distinguish the "habitual" criminal (i.e., ASPD) from the "occasional" criminal. Habitual antisocial behavior stems from genetic *and* psychosocial factors, whereas occasional antisocial behavior seems to arise more from psychosocial causes. This is a big generalization, but in large measure, "habitual" criminals are born and "occasional" criminals are made. This section only discusses the "habituals."

Psychosocial Factors

Sociological. Poverty contributes to ASPD, but it's hardly the sole cause. In a study of Philadelphia inner-city youth, 35% of males under 18 had at least one contact with the police, but only 6% caused half of all delinquencies and two-thirds of all violent crimes. (These data confirm the difference between "habitual" and "occasional" criminals.) While nobody endorses poverty as a lifestyle, these data suggest that despite substantial economic deprivation, the vast majority of the poor do *not* become sociopaths.

Additional evidence demonstrates that factors other than poverty must be involved. First, ASPD also arises in middle and upper socioeconomic groups. Second, ASPD is becoming more prevalent worldwide, even where there's increasing wealth. Third, the childhood behaviors of adult sociopaths are remarkably similar regardless of economic class. Fourth, these childhood antisocial behaviors emerge so early, it's improbable that sociological factors are a primary cause.

Familial. Sociopaths generally grow up amid considerable parental discord (e.g., desertion, separation, divorce, custody fights) and family disruption (e.g., early deaths, frequent moves, brutal discipline). Mothers of sociopaths often do not provide consistent affection or discipline (Glueck & Glueck, 1959; Rutter, 1981). Also common during their childhoods are maternal neglect, indifference, and alcoholism. Instead of the mother, Robins (1966) found that the best predictor of ASPD was having a sociopathic or alcoholic father. The children grew up to become delinquents whether or not their fathers had reared them. Was the father's absence or inconsistency the culprit? Or was sociopathy being inherited from these fathers? The evidence is inconclusive. Many sociopaths are also reared in stable families with loving parents and normal siblings. ASPD probably has multiple etiologies.

Biomedical Factors

On neuropsychological tests, sociopaths frequently do better on performance then on verbal tests. When younger, they have trouble interpreting and abstracting verbal information. Tell a six-year-old-would-be sociopath, "Do not get near the stove," and he will not understand *near* and continue approaching it from different directions until he is told *no*. He may appear to be "testing limits," but in reality he may be trying to figure out what was meant by *near*. It is not a coincidence that many fail reading and writing, but excel at working on their cars or assault rifles.

Studies of male felons, most having ASPD, revealed that 20% of their first-degree male relatives were sociopaths and 33% were alcoholics. Among female felons, half being "habitual" criminals, a third of their male relatives were sociopaths and half were alcoholics. Although most research demonstrates higher concordance rates for ASPD among identical (36%) than fraternal (12%) twins, these different rates are not as eye-popping as those with other mental disorders. Adopted-away research suggests that genetic factors play some etiological role, but that environmental factors are also important.

Differential Diagnosis

ASPD should be diagnosed *unless* the antisocial behavior only occurs during the course of *schizophrenia* or a *manic episode*. Schizophrenia pre-empts ASPD because it's hard to know what is producing the antisocial conduct. Mania is easy to differentiate because its antisocial behavior is episodic, time-limited, and rarely occurs during childhood. Sociopaths often abuse drugs and alcohol, but a *substance-use disorder* should only be diagnosed when the patient meets the full *DSM-IV* criteria for it. Some people with substance-use disorder displayed no antisocial behavior before they became addicted (Gerstley, Alterman, McLellan, & Woody, 1990). Now they lie, steal, and kill for their drugs. Treating the addiction in some cases may reverse this behavior.

Management and Treatment

No psychotherapy has been found to help sociopaths. ASPD is ego-syntonic; sociopaths have no desire to change, consider insights excuses, have no concept of the future, resent all authorities (including therapists), view the patient role as pitiful, detest being in a position of inferiority, deem therapy a joke and therapists as objects to be conned, threatened, seduced, or used.

A "tough love" approach reduces some of these problems by showing that the therapist cares but is not a patsy. It is important to remember that sociopaths are human beings with feelings. Frequent confrontation is expected. Sociopaths want to do things for themselves; they need to see that the way they are doing things isn't working. If they finally "burn out" or become depressed, they may become willing to try the "straight" way.

Judges are as stuck as psychotherapists. They know that "rehabilitation" does not help the "hard-core criminal." Judges should know that sentencing sociopaths to psychotherapy wastes everybody's time. Sociopaths made to enlist in the army can't tolerate the discipline, go AWOL, and are dishonorably discharged. So what can be done? Not much. But consider the following:

1. *Prevention* is the most important intervention mental and medical health professionals can make. Early detection of antisocial behavior in children and young teenagers should be treated promptly before it gets out of hand. Many teen-age gang members are not sociopaths; they want the respect of other members. Sociopaths don't do well in gangs because they try to take advantage of their own fellow members. Getting the non-sociopaths out of gangs and finding alternative ways that they can gain "respect" may prevent them from pursuing a life of crime.

2. *Family counseling* is critical. Therapists may not do much for sociopaths, but they may help their families. Manipulated so often, family members swing from hate to guilt, never knowing what to feel. Because they are so close to the problem, commonsense guidelines by an objective outsider/professional can help them place matters into perspective.
3. *Treating substance misuse* is also critical, since antisocial acts increase during intoxication. Sociopathic behavior has gradations from milder to severe. Drug use may push someone with a milder ASPD into becoming a thief and murderer.
4. *Counseling should be independent of punishment and parole*, whenever possible. If sociopaths know that therapists exert no influence on their sentence, they are a bit more likely to use treatment constructively. Studies in the treatment of rapists and child molesters lend credence to this notion.

BORDERLINE PERSONALITY DISORDER

"Don't leave me, I hate you."
— Title of book on borderlines by Jerold Kreisman, M.D.

In *DSM-IV*, borderline personality disorder (BPD) is characterized by at least five of the following: (a) impulsivity, (b) unstable and intense interpersonal relations, (c) inappropriate or intense anger, (d) identity confusion, (e) affective instability, (f) problems being alone, (g) physically self-destructive acts, and (h) chronic feelings of emptiness and boredom. Table 19–7 lists *DSM-IV* criteria for BPD.

In 1938 the term *borderline* was introduced to describe those patients who straddled the border between neurosis and psychosis. The diagnosis of "borderline schizophrenia," used widely until the mid-1970s, assumed that borderline disorders were a type of "latent schizophrenia." Most authorities now believe that borderline conditions are personality disorders. What nobody disputes is that borderlines *look much better than they are*, a fact which continually deceives professionals as well as laypeople.

Clinical Presentation

Feeling chronically bored and empty, borderlines desperately seek stimulation: They might gamble, sexually act-up, abuse drugs, overdose, instigate brawls, or attempt suicide. Many slash their wrists or douse lit cigarettes on their arms, not to kill or to hurt themselves, but to *feel* something ("I feel so dead, cutting myself is the only way I know I'm alive") or to

TABLE 19-7
DSM-IV* Criteria for Borderline Personality Disorder

A pervasive pattern of instability of interpersonal relationships, self-image, and affects, and marked impulsivity beginning by early adulthood and present in a variety of contexts, as indicated by five (or more) of the following:

(1) frantic efforts to avoid real or imagined abandonment. **Note:** Do not include suicidal or self-mutilating behavior covered in Criterion 5.

(2) a pattern of unstable and intense interpersonal relationships characterized by alternating between extremes of idealization and devaluation

(3) identity disturbance: markedly and persistently unstable self-image or sense of self

(4) impulsivity in at least two areas that are potentially self-damaging (e.g., spending, sex, substance abuse, reckless driving, binge eating). **Note:** Do not include suicidal or self-mutilating behavior covered in Criterion 5.

(5) recurrent suicidal behavior, gestures, or threats, or self-mutilating behavior

(6) affective instability due to a marked reactivity of mood (e.g., intense episodic dysphoria, irritability, or anxiety usually lasting a few hours and only rarely more than a few days)

(7) chronic feelings of emptiness

(8) inappropriate, intense anger or difficulty controlling anger (e.g., frequent displays of temper, constant anger, recurrent physical fights)

(9) transient, stress-related paranoid ideation or severe dissociative symptoms

DSM-IV, p. 654.

relieve tension. Their moods are always reactive, intense, and brief; trivial problems mushroom into calamities. They have been well portrayed in movies such as *Fatal Attraction* and *A Streetcar Named Desire*.

Borderlines' interpersonal relations swing between suffocating dependency and mindless self-assertion. They hate being alone and leach onto others to avoid feeling abandoned. For example, a borderline will call a recently-made friend every day about a "disaster" needing immediate attention. Initially, the friend is flattered by the borderline's "idealization" of him, yet he soon finds himself sucked into a gooey, all-consuming relationship. When he tries to cool things, the borderline denigrates him ("devaluation") with a vengeance: She'll pour ink on his couch, demand money, and accuse him of "being miserly," call him at 3 A.M. to complain that he's a "bastard," etc. The borderline's digs contain just enough truth to fester under the friend's skin, which eventually leads the friend to apologize.

Borderline relationships, be they platonic or romantic, are all-or-nothing. Borderlines are in love with love, not people. Anything less than total love is hate; anything less than total commitment is rejection ("rejection sensitivity"). Borderlines expect—nay, *demand*— that others do for them what they cannot do for themselves. Chronically sad and demoralized, they adopt friends not because they like them, but because they expect the friends to rid them of unhappiness. When they don't, borderlines dump the friends, look for another savior, and repeat the cycle. Unable to figure out who or what they are ("identity diffusion"), they glom onto others so as to acquire an identity by osmosis. A 25-year-old borderline said she dresses like the rock star Madonna "to express my individuality." While she's convinced nobody ever does enough for her, others find her exhausting and draining—an "empty gas tank" in need of constant refueling.

Borderlines are notorious for *splitting*—that is, they view people as *all good* or *all bad*—and then get others to act out these roles. Everywhere borderlines go, they set people against each other, create havoc, and walk away without anybody realizing until later that the "innocent" borderline caused the chaos.

Mary Rae, an inpatient with BPD, superficially slashed her wrist, squeezed the blood, and showed it dripping to her psychiatrist. As anyone would have predicted, he canceled her weekend pass. This infuriated Mary Rae. She then "confided" in nurse Peter:

> You're the only person who understands me. My doctor and everyone else here hates me. . . . When I cut my wrist I realized I should tell my doctor. So I did, and right away. I *thought* that was the right thing to do. So what does Dr. Jerk-ass do? He locks me up. I don't get it: Staff says we're supposed to be open with them. Well, I was! From now on, I keep everything to myself. I wasn't suicidal—I would hardly tell people if I was. Peter, if only *you* would have been here. Then I could have gone to you and never have cut myself at all. As it is, I'm stuck here all weekend: Just thinking about it makes me suicidal. Can't you help me?

Flattered that Mary Rae confided in him, Peter campaigns to restore her weekend pass. He doesn't realize that Mary Rae has similarly "confided" in five other staff members, each thinking they have a "unique and confidential relationship" with her, which must be kept secret. The unit's staff soon splits between those who feel Mary Rae has been victimized for "being honest" and those who think she's a manipulator and should be shipped to a state hospital. Very quickly, both sides cease squabbling about Mary Rae, but attack each other as insensitive or naive. Meanwhile, as if she's an innocent bystander, Mary Rae fiddles while the staff burns.

Borderline patients may have many "neurotic" symptoms—panic attacks, phobias, anxiety, somatic complaints, conversion symptoms, dysthymia. Under stress, some become *briefly* psychotic. Highly characteristic of borderlines is their giving sane answers on structured psychological tests (e.g., WAIS), but bizarre, psychotic responses on unstructured tests (e.g., Rorschach). Where most people might see a bat or a butterfly on a Rorschach inkblot, one borderline saw "the insides of a cow's stomach run over by a car."

BPD has a chronic, fluctuating course which, although it does *not* lead to schizophrenia, nonetheless significantly impairs social and occupational functioning. A five-year follow-up showed that borderlines function at pretty much the same poor level. Those with higher pre-morbid levels of functioning have better prognoses.

Epidemiology

Twice as many borderlines are women than men. Using strict diagnostic criteria, 1.6–4% of the general population has BPD.

Etiology and Pathogenesis

Kernberg (1975) hypothesized that borderlines have a "constitutional" inability to regulate affects, which predisposes them to psychological disorganization under specific adverse conditions during childhood.

BPD runs in families. First-degree relatives of borderlines have 10 times the rate of BPD and three times the rate of alcoholism than do controls. These relatives of borderlines also have higher rates of mood disorders, but normal rates of schizophrenia and bipolar disorder. While the mode of this familial transmission is unclear, most investigations have focused on psychosocial determinants.

Mahler, Pine, and Bergman (1975) proposed that borderline conditions stem from a disturbance in the "rapprochement subphase of the separation-individuation" process—from 18–36 months. During this period, the child, having experimented with separating self from mother, tries returning to mother for approval and emotional "refueling." These mothers, however, have had their own difficulties with separation, and so they resent the child's "clinging," as if to say, "Before you wanted me, now you don't. So get lost!" These mothers experience their child's attempts at autonomy as abandonments (e.g., "How dare you leave me!") As the child grows up, she replays these dependence-independence conflicts with others. This style of parenting sets up a vicious, out-of-control feedback loop. Fear of separation or abandonment is not met with comfort, but rather rejection. Thus, fear becomes a cue for abandonment which leads to more fear, and so on.

Along similar lines, Masterson (1976) contended that the essence of the borderline's dilemma is a conflict between a desire for autonomy and a fear of parental abandonment. He claimed that mothers of borderlines reward their children's regressive behaviors and discourage their individuation.

A majority of borderlines were physically, sexually, and/or emotionally abused by their care-givers at times; at other times these care-givers may have been adequate or even nurturing. This vacillation creates the problem of both hating and loving the care-giver.

Splitting is a healthy and normal defense in 18- to 36-month-old children. For example, a two-and-a-half-year-old boy with a six-month-old sister said to his father, "No like sister's daddy, like *my* daddy." Yes, this was the same daddy, but this splitting permitted the little boy to like his father while still feeling jealous that his sister was getting a lot of attention. Only later, when his mind is able to handle greater complexity, will this good-bad dichotomy diversify into more ambiguous shades of gray in which the good and bad coexist—the stuff of most adult experience. Borderlines don't accomplish this developmental task. Clinicians find themselves worshipped on an altar some days and vilified in an earthly hell on others. The clinician hasn't changed, but the borderline's opinion has.

Strip aside everything borderlines do and say and what remains is an underlying dread, or perhaps a conviction, of being *bad*—or as one patient remarked, "Underneath madness lies badness." Borderlines may disown this badness by projecting it onto others ("projective identification"), act-up to escape feeling this badness, employ reaction-formation (as when romanticizing ideal love—e.g., Blanche DuBois), or behave self-destructively. Similar defenses are used by borderlines who feel they are *nothing* inside, mere shells of humanity, scarecrows masquerading as people.

Differential Diagnosis

Known as the "disorder which doesn't specialize," BPD presents with such variegated symptomatology that it appears in many patients' lists of differential diagnoses. BPD may co-exist with *schizotypal, histrionic, narcissistic*, and *antisocial personality disorders*. What usually distinguishes BPD are chronic feelings of emptiness and anger, self-mutilation, transitory psychoses, manipulative suicide attempts, intensely demanding relationships, and superficial intactness. The sadness common to borderlines is short-lived and highly reactive. Still, *major depression* and *dysthymic disorder* can co-exist with BPD or be confused with it. Because anger and irritability can be a symptom of major depression, some depression patients may look like a borderline. However, they see their reactive behavior as different than usual for them, and friends usually confirm this observation. *Cyclothymic disorder*, like BPD, has roller-coaster mood swings, but borderlines don't have true hypomanic periods. When briefly psychotic, they may be labeled *schizophrenic* but, unlike most schizophrenics, they use logical sentences and have a lot of affect in describing their psychotic experiences.

Management and Treatment

Clinicians working with patients with borderline personality disorder must walk a narrow path between giving support without rescuing and encouraging independence without signaling abandonment. When borderlines are doing better, praise for their improvement is often interpreted as, "You do not need to see me anymore"—another abandonment. With BPD, empathic and supportive statements should be combined: "You still have a lot of pain, but you are handling it better. There is a lot of work still ahead, but I see progress." A lot of structure and consistency is also important. During a crisis, a scheduled phone check-in works much better than waiting for an emergency.

Only well-trained professionals should consider attempting to treat these most difficult of patients. *Long-term, psychodynamic psychotherapy* is the often recommended treatment for BPD, even though no well-controlled studies have demonstrated its efficacy. One approach starts with fostering the patient's trust in treatment so that exploration of unconscious wishes and fantasies can follow. Another approach stresses reality-testing, providing structure, and avoiding overstimulating "depth interpretations" that may induce psychological disorganization. A *cognitive-behavioral approach*, which stresses integrating adaptive coping skills with intense affective reactions and cognitively fusing opposites, has been successful when used over several years (Linehan, 1993).

Drug treatment can involve MAOIs for depression and rejection-sensitivity and low doses of antipsychotics for brief reactive psychoses and irritability (Cornelius, Soloff, Perel, & Ulrich, 1993). Anticonvulsants such as carbamazepine may decrease impulsive self-destructive behavior. Benzodiazepines may disinhibit behavior and create drug dependence and therefore are not usually recommended. Tricyclic antidepressants have a poor record in treating a borderline's depression. SSRIs may share the efficacy of MAOIs.

AVOIDANT PERSONALITY DISORDER

The essential features of avoidant personality disorder (APD) are extreme social discomfort because of a pervasive fear of being judged negatively. More specifically, *DSM-IV* lists these characteristics: (a) hypersensitivity to potential rejection, humiliation, or shame, (b) only entering relationships in which uncritical acceptance is virtually guaranteed, (c) social withdrawal, (d) a desire for affection and acceptance, and (e) low self-esteem. Table 19–8 presents *DSM-IV* criteria for APD.

Schizoid and avoidant personalities are loners, but the *schizoid* person

TABLE 19-8
DSM-IV Criteria for Avoidant Personality Disorder*

A pervasive pattern of social inhibition, feelings of inadequacy, and hypersensitivity to negative evaluation, beginning by early adulthood and present in a variety of contexts, as indicated by four (or more) of the following:

(1) avoids occupational activities that involve significant interpersonal contact, because of fears of criticism, disapproval, or rejection
(2) is unwilling to get involved with people unless certain of being liked
(3) shows restraint within intimate relationships due to the fear of being shamed or ridiculed
(4) is preoccupied with being criticized or rejected in social situations
(5) is inhibited in new interpersonal situations because of feelings of inadequacy
(6) views self as socially inept, personally unappealing, or inferior to others
(7) is unusually reluctant to take personal risks or to engage in any new activities because they may prove embarrassing

DSM-IV, pp. 664-65.

doesn't want friends and the avoidant person does. These are the painfully shy people permeating Garrison Kellor's Lake Wobegon radio show. They want affection, but not as much as they fear rejection. Because they dread the slightest disapproval and will misconstrue people's comments as derogatory, they have few, if any, friends. Angry and upset at their own inability to relate, they'll try to prevent rejection by ingratiating themselves to others.

A friendly, gentle, reassuring approach is the best way to manage people with APD. Most avoidant children and teens can't avoid becoming avoidant adults. Virtually all people with APD have social phobias, but a majority of people with social phobias do not have APD. Social phobias are to *specific* situations (e.g., public speaking), whereas APD pervades all social relations. APD may have started out as a social phobia that kept getting worse and involving more situations. MAOIs are the most effective medication for social phobias and may also be indicated for APD. In one study, 75% of APD patients who were treated for a year with MAOIs were so improved that they no longer qualified for the diagnosis of APD. If this treatment proves to be effective, the diagnosis of APD may become obsolete. After all, part of the definition of personality disorder is an enduring pattern of behavior. Cognitive-behavioral therapies may also be effective when they focus on assertiveness, desensitization in the situations, and cognitive change. Group therapy can also be helpful. Patients with APD tend to be well-liked and get much support in therapy groups.

DEPENDENT PERSONALITY DISORDER

In *DSM-IV*, the essential features of people with dependent personality disorder (DPD) are: (a) passively allowing others to assume responsibility for major areas in their lives because (b) they lack self-confidence or the ability to function independently; (c) they then subordinate their needs to those of others, (d) become dependent on them, (e) and avoid any chance of being self-reliant. Table 19–9 lists the *DSM-IV* criteria for DPD.

Everybody has dependent traits and wishes. What distinguishes the dependent personality is that the dependency is total, pervading all areas of life. Dependents dread autonomy; they may be productive, but only if supervised. They are likely to view themselves as inept or stupid. When pressed to name redeeming qualities, they might reluctantly confess to being good companions, loyal and kind.

Ethel is prototypic. She refers to herself as "man's best friend." Her man is Mitch, a husband who schedules her days, tells her what foods to eat, picks her doctors, chooses her clothes, and selects her friends. Explains Ethel: "He likes to think, and I don't. Why should I decide things, when he'll do it for me?" This arrangement pleased both for years until Mitch announced he was going to China

---

TABLE 19–9
DSM-IV* Criteria for Dependent Personality Disorder

A pervasive and excessive need to be taken care of that leads to submissive and clinging behavior and fears of separation, beginning by early adulthood and present in a variety of contexts, as indicated by five (or more) of the following:

(1) has difficulty making everyday decisions without an excessive amount of advice and reassurance from others

(2) needs others to assume responsibility for most major areas of his or her life

(3) has difficulty expressing disagreement with others because of fear of loss of support or approval. **Note:** Do not include realistic fears of retribution.

(4) has difficulty initiating projects or doing things on his or her own (due to a lack of self-confidence in judgment or abilities rather than to a lack of motivation or energy)

(5) goes to excessive lengths to obtain nurturance and support from others, to the point of volunteering to do things that are unpleasant

(6) feels uncomfortable or helpless when alone because of exaggerated fears of being unable to care for himself or herself

(7) urgently seeks another relationship as a source of care and support when a close relationship ends

(8) unrealistic preoccupation with fears of being left to take care of himself or herself

---

*DSM-IV, pp. 668–69.

for three weeks on business. Ethel was frantic and sought treatment. Like most dependent personalities, she wanted help not for dependency, but for losing it.

Historically, DPD was known as "passive-dependent" personality and dependent personalities were known as "oral characters." This label referred to their most striking clinical feature—the insistence on being "fed" or taken care of; it also suggested the etiology of overindulged or frustrated wishes during the oral stage of psychosexual development. (More recently, the role of maternal deprivation during the oral stage has been stressed.) Oral features include a constant demand for attention, passivity, dependency, a fear of autonomy, a lack of perseverance, dread of decision-making, suggestibility, and oral behaviors (e.g., smoking, drinking, thumb-sucking). Oral traits are common in "normals," but even more so in psychiatric patients.

The 1963 Midtown Manhattan survey showed that 2.5% of the residents had passive-dependent personalities. DPD is more prevalent in women and in the youngest sibling. Prolonged physical illness during childhood may predispose to DPD. *Histrionic, schizotypal, narcissistic, and avoidant personality disorders* often co-exist with DPD, and *dysthymic disorder* and *major depression* are frequent complications. Although dependent traits are common in *agoraphobia*, the agoraphobic will *actively* insist that others assume responsibility, whereas the dependent personality *passively* abdicates control to others.

Management and Treatment

Patients with dependent personalities will call the office incessantly asking for advice or clarifications and regularly to schedule extra appointments. From the start, firm limits—e.g., no calls to home, clear expectations ("Let's schedule an appointment every two weeks")—and information are important. If medications are being started, it is best to give out information sheets to reduce the calls with questions. If "emergency" appointments are happening too regularly, temporarily increase the frequency of scheduled visits. Sometimes knowing an appointment is coming soon is very reassuring to dependents and they won't feel the need to call regularly. If clear limits are not established in the beginning, it is nearly impossible to establish them later without the patient experiencing a lot of anger or hurt.

More insightful patients may benefit from *psychodynamic psychotherapy*. Often addressed are the patient's (in this sequence) (a) low self-esteem and its origins, (b) fears of harming others by seeking autonomy, (c) dependency on the therapist, and (d) the experience of termination as it relates to dependency. Less psychologically-minded patients, or those not wanting psychodynamic therapy, may benefit from supportive *group therapy* or *assertiveness training*.

OBSESSIVE-COMPULSIVE PERSONALITY DISORDER

> "Are you sure there is a hyphen in 'obsessive-compulsive'?"
> — Anonymous medical student

In *DSM-IV*, the essential features of obsessive-compulsive personality disorder (CPD) are: (a) a restricted ability to express warm and tender emotions, (b) a perfectionism that interferes with the ability to grasp "the big picture," (c) an insistence that others submit to his or her way of doing things, (d) an excessive devotion to work and productivity to the exclusion of pleasure, and (e) indecisiveness. Table 19–10 lists *DSM-IV* criteria for OCPD.

Wilhelm Reich called these patients "living machines." Compulsives are highly productive but never enjoy what they produce. Everything is a chore, nothing is effortless. Every decision demands exhaustive analysis. Every-

---

TABLE 19–10
DSM-IV **Criteria for Obsessive-Compulsive Personality Disorder***

A pervasive pattern of preoccupation with orderliness, perfectionism, and mental and interpersonal control, at the expense of flexibility, openness, and efficiency, beginning by early adulthood and present in a variety of contexts, as indicated by four (or more) of the following:

(1) preoccupied with details, rules, lists, order, organization, or schedules to the extent that the major point of the activity is lost

(2) shows perfectionism that interferes with task completion (e.g., is unable to complete a project because his or her own overly strict standards are not met)

(3) is excessively devoted to work and productivity to the exclusion of leisure activities and friendships (not accounted for by obvious economic necessity)

(4) is overconscientious, scrupulous, and inflexible about matters of morality, ethics, or values (not accounted for by cultural or religious identification)

(5) is unable to discard worn-out or worthless objects even when they have no sentimental value

(6) is reluctant to delegate tasks or to work with others unless they submit to exactly his or her way of doing things

(7) adopts a miserly spending style toward both self and others; money is viewed as something to be hoarded for future catastrophes

(8) shows rigidity and stubbornness

DSM-IV, pp. 672–73.

thing must be right and nothing must be left to chance. They won't make hunches, since hunches may be wrong. They are perfectionist: Carrots must be sliced exactly one-quarter wide or a meal is ruined. Cleanliness *is* Godliness. Compulsives excel at concentrating, and they never stop concentrating (Shapiro, 1965). They can't skim a page; they must scrutinize every word. Their focus is sharp, yet narrow; they see the parts, but never the whole. They are interpersonally obtuse, boring and annoying, subject people to endless irrelevant details, refuse to make decisions, are moralistic and hypercritically self-righteous, insist on conformity (from others), and never get to the point.

Harold, a compulsive accountant, spent eight years obsessing over whether to leave his wife and three kids for his mistress-secretary. "I stay only for the kids," he insisted, but in truth, he never saw them. Repeatedly calculating the pros and cons — even devising a mathematical formula — Harold would ask a friend for advice, promptly reject it, criticize the friend for not helping him enough, and cap it off by complaining that his friend doesn't donate enough money to the synagogue. Like most people with OCPD, Harold considered himself an intellectual, while others considered him a rigid.

OCPD is diagnosed more often in men and in the oldest sibling. Although the precise prevalence is unknown, OCPD is probably common. Frequent complications are major depression, dysthymia, and hypochondriasis. Only 6% of patients with obsessive-compulsive disorder also have OCPD (Baer et al., 1990).

Laypeople call these patients "tight-assed"; psychoanalysts call them "anal characters" because, theoretically, they have arrested at the anal stage of psychosexual development. The anal character is known for having problems with control, authority figures, autonomy, shame, and self-doubt. OCPD runs in families, but it's unclear how much this results from the emotionally constipated climate of the anger-suppressing parents who often rear these patients or from heredity, as suggested by several twin and adoption studies.

Management and Treatment

Patients with obsessive-compulsive personality disorder prefer clinicians who are like themselves. To form an alliance with them, clinicians must demonstrate that they are careful and attend to detail. The OCPD patient, like the paranoid, must have complete explanations of what will happen during evaluation and treatment.

Compulsives are tough to treat, largely because their obsessiveness paralyzes therapy. Though bright, they do not use insight to instigate change, only to avoid it. Psychology is abstract, but compulsives are concrete. They swamp therapists with details. Simply asking a compulsive if he's reviewed the want-ads can result in a critique of everyone in the paper. If interrupted, he becomes angry; if allowed to continue, 10 minutes later he will blame the therapist for wasting time. Consequently, therapy should focus on the here-and-now and stress feelings instead of thoughts. Cognitive-behavioral therapy and psychodynamic explorations of the past can become counter-productive. Progress should be measured in terms of changed behavior, not insight. Group therapy may help those with serious interpersonal problems.

CHAPTER 20

Disorders Usually First Diagnosed in Infancy, Childhood, or Adolescence

CHILDREN HAVE MANY DISORDERS already examined, such as depression, eating, and sleep disorders. But kids can have other problems too, and development may complicate their diagnosis. Normal behavior may become confused with psychopathology. Therefore, the best way to minimize this confusion is to watch youngsters grow up; the alternative is to memorize Table 20–1 and become acquainted with childhood conditions.

MENTAL RETARDATION

The diagnosis of mental retardation is not based on IQ alone but includes deficits in adaptive functioning. IQ tests mainly measure potential ability to perform in school and were not specifically developed to measure ability to perform life functions. Mental retardation is not a single disease, syndrome, or symptom, but rather a state of impairment that is identified by the behavior of the individual. Contrary to popular impression, many mentally retarded people are not immediately detectable. They can look, act, and talk normally. Table 20–2 lists the *DSM-IV* criteria for mental retardation. The diagnosis, which is usually made before seven or eight years of age, describes current thinking and behavior, but does not necessarily give an accurate prognosis. People may be classified as retarded at one time during their lives and not at another. How a particular child will

419

TABLE 20–1
Childhood Development*

Age	Motor and Cognitive Functions
1 month	Roots, sucks, and grasps
3 months	Social smile
5 months	Sits and grasps objects
7 months	Crawls (6–8 months)
8 months	Stranger anxiety
9 months	Separation anxiety
10 months	Object permanence
11 months	Walking (10–14 months)
15 months	Imitation
18 months	Talking (few words)
19 months	Preoperational thought
22 months	Toilet training
6 years	Shift to verbal memory
7 years	Concrete operational thought
12 years	Formal operational thought, abstract reasoning

eventually turn out depends more on co-existing handicaps, motivation, educational and training opportunities, and treatment than on the mental retardation itself. Indeed, mentally retarded people frequently have coexisting handicaps that are more incapacitating than the retardation.

The history of mental retardation is a checkered one. In Europe during the 14th and 15th centuries, the mentally retarded were regarded superstitiously as blessed "infants of the good God." However, during the "Enlightenment" Martin Luther

TABLE 20–2
DSM-IV* Criteria for Mental Retardation

A. Significantly subaverage intellectual functioning: an IQ of approximately 70 or below on an individually administered IQ test (for infants, a clinical judgment of significantly subaverage intellectual functioning).

B. Concurrent deficits or impairments in present adaptive functioning (i.e., the person's effectiveness in meeting the standards expected for his or her age by his or her cultural group) in at least two of the following skill areas: communication, self-care, home living, social/interpersonal skills, use of community resources, self-direction, functional academic skills, work, leisure, health, and safety).

C. The onset is before age 18 years.

*DSM-IV, p. 46.

referred to the "feebleminded" as "Godless" and thought society should rid itself of them. It was not until Binet developed psychometric tests so that schools could "track" school children into special programs that the range of human intellectual capacity became evident. In spite of noble intentions, these IQ tests were often used to exclude many children from school and to identify "imbeciles" in need of sterilization so that mental retardation would not be propagated. Only with Foling's discovery in 1934 of phenylketonuria, a treatable cause of mental retardation, did the study of mental retardation become respectable.

Prevalence

The adult prevalence of mental retardation is generally lower than in childhood. Approximately 3% of the U.S. population is mentally retarded. The vast majority are only mildly retarded. Most people with mild retardation can hold a job and live on their own. Table 20-3 lists the prevalence of mental retardation by degree of severity in the adult population.

Different IQ tests are scaled with different standard deviations: This variation is reflected in Table 20-3 by giving IQ *ranges* rather than fixed points. Between 70 and 84 IQ is defined as borderline intelligence and not mental retardation. People with mild mental retardation are considered "educable" and can master some school subjects such as basic reading and simple arithmetic. People with moderate mental retardation are termed "trainable" because they can learn simple basic tasks but usually cannot master school subjects.

Intelligence in the general population does not follow a normal bell-shaped curve; rather, there are a larger number of cases than would be expected at the lower end of the IQ range. Specific pathological processes, such as major genetic abnormalities or brain injuries, probably cause this bulge at the lower end.

TABLE 20-3
Prevalence of Mental Retardation in Adults*

Category	Percent of Mentally Retarded	I.Q.	Mental Age (years)
Mild	89.0	50–55 to 69*	8.5 to 11.0
Moderate	6.0	35–40 to 50–55	6.0 to 8.5
Severe	3.4	20–25 to 35–40	3.75 to 6.0
Profound	1.6	below 20–25	0 to 3.75

*70–85 IQ are called *borderline intelligence* or *borderline mental retardation*—not quite "normal" but not quite mental retardation.

Epidemiology and Etiology

The specific cause of mental retardation can be identified in only 25–50% of children. This estimate varies because at the low end, *cause* means a specific known syndrome, while at the high end it includes obvious genetic disorders that are unnamed, presumed prenatal insults, or very suggestive evidence of birth complications. In general, the more severe the mental retardation, the more likely a specific cause can be found. In mild retardation a mix of cultural and multigenetic factors is usually involved; such kids frequently have parents with borderline intelligence and are raised in unstimulating, barren environments. They may sit in a crib by themselves during most of their infancy.

A cause usually can be established in cases of moderate and severe mental retardation. The general frequencies of the known causes are (1) *prenatal* (includes genetic), 80–85%; (2) *perinatal* (most often asphyxia), 5–10%; and (3) *postnatal*, 5–10%. Public health measures have substantially reduced two main perinatal causes of mental retardation. Testing babies at birth for *hypothyroidism* (1 in 4,000 births) and *phenylketonuria* (PKU, 1 in 12,000), which is an inability to metabolize the amino acid phenylalanine, has essentially eliminated these causes. Hypothyroid babies are treated with thyroid and PKU babies are put on very low phenylalanine diets.

The three most common *chromosomal causes* of mental retardation are *Down's syndrome* (1 in 700), *Fragile X*, (1 in 1,800 males), *Trisomy 18* (1 in 4,000). The most common *genetic causes* are *Prader-Willi syndrome* (1 in 4,000) and *Wilson's disease* (1 in 4,000).

Down's syndrome accounts for approximately 10% of institutionalized mentally retarded individuals. It is usually caused by an extra 21st chromosome, hence trisomy 21. Its risk is higher with increasing maternal age and probably paternal age. While prenatal women under 35 years have only a 0.2% risk of having a Down's baby, this goes up to 0.9% in 35–40-year-old mothers, 1.4% in 40–45-year-olds, and 2.5% in 45-year-olds. People with Down's have a broad IQ range of 0–100, with a mean IQ of 47–50. They share numerous physical characteristics: high cheekbones, flat nasal bridge, large protruding tongue, microcephaly, small round ears, hypotonic muscles, and hyperflexibility. They are very susceptible to infections, particularly respiratory, and 30–50% have congenital heart defects. Many don't survive childhood and few reach 50 years old. They generally have friendly temperaments and love music.

In *Fragile X syndrome*, mental retardation varies from severe to mild, with a few in the borderline IQ range. Children with Fragile X tend to do particularly badly in math and block designs and have a specific developmental language disorder. Females are the carriers and males are affected. Males are short with long ears, a long narrow face, and sunken chest (pectus excavatum).

Almost all of the chromosome and genetic causes of mental retardation are associated with physical anomalies and most with short stature. Some have specific behavioral abnormalities, such as binge-eating in Prader-Willi syndrome. Prenatal brain and head malformations usually result in severe mental retardation. Many of these are caused by autosomal recessive genes. Approximately a third of the population carries one of these genes, but because each is rare, the chances of two people both having the same gene is small. *Brain abnormalities* include *anencephaly,* in which parts of the brain and skull are missing (usually fatal); *hydroencephaly,* in which the cranium is filled with fluid instead of with brain tissue; and *porencephaly,* characterized by large fluid-filled cysts in the brain. (Transillumination of the head can pick up cysts or hydrocephaly. If these are detected and treated before the cranial fontanelles close, mental retardation can be prevented.) *Skull abnormalities* include *microcephaly,* which is an abnormally small head, and *hydrocephalus,* in which pressure from excess cerebrospinal fluid destroys brain tissue. Skull abnormalities can be caused by a variety of sources other than an autosomal dominant gene.

The most common *intrauterine causes* of mental retardation are *fetal alcohol syndrome* (FAS) (estimates as high as 1 in 600 in the United States (Seattle) and France, and as high as 1 in 8 in certain Native Canadian groups); *asphyxia* from maternal hypertension, toxemia, placenta previa, and other causes; and *intrauterine infections*, with cytomegalovirus (CMV) most common, rubella still in second place, and toxoplasmosis (often gotten from cats) probably third.

Fetal alcohol syndrome usually results in mild mental retardation with mean IQs in the sixties and a range of 25–120. The three hallmark signs of FAS are: (1) CNS deficits (most often with lower IQ) and symptoms of attention-deficit/hyperactivity disorder (ADHD); (2) faces with narrow eye slits (cats eyes), flat cheeks, short nose, thin upper lip, and flat filtrum (the two vertical ridges between the upper lip and nose); (3) growth retardation.

Children with FAS are often frustrating to their parents and teachers because they develop adequate verbal skills and sound normal but have serious attention and math deficits. They can often mimic words well, but don't fully understand or comprehend their meaning. They can "talk a good line," but don't understand basic cause-and-effect relationships; hence, behavioral approaches utilizing positive and negative reinforcement don't work. When told to do a task, they may indicate that they fully understand but then perform disastrously because of very poor comprehension, judgment, and attention span. They do best with structure and repetition. Some mothers find that they must put up the same "to do" list every day for their grade-school children or they won't brush their teeth, get dressed, take a shower, and so on.[1] Fetal alcohol effect (FAE), which is a milder variation of FAS, has only two of the three hallmarks and is more common (1 in 200 to 300 births) than FAS; these children have somewhat higher IQs. Very low social drinking levels during pregnancy (e.g., one drink a day) are associated with high frequencies of attention and math deficits.

The most common *postnatal causes* of mental retardation are *meningitis, head trauma, encephalitis,* and *anoxia.* A child with physically abusive parents may be knocked unconscious and suffer enough brain damage to become mentally retarded.

Differential Diagnosis

In general, the more severe the retardation, the earlier the diagnosis is made. Children with mild retardation often do well enough that they aren't detected until they are in kindergarten or first grade. Typically it is a primary physician who makes the first professional assessment. Table 20–4 outlines key areas that should be evaluated.

The following tips are helpful in using Table 20–4:

1. When you see a "funny looking kid," don't immediately assume mental retardation. Check both parents' appearances — you might see a *"funny looking parent"* with a very normal IQ.
2. If the mother of a mentally retarded child has had multiple spontaneous abortions, then the child is more likely to have a chromosome abnormality.
3. If the child has a selective delay in only one area, such as math or reading, it is not mental retardation but a *learning disorder.*
4. If the child progressed normally for some time and then stopped or slowed, a specific *medical cause* is more likely.

The Denver Developmental Screening Test is an excellent screening tool for developmental problems in infants and preschool children. A child with

---

[1] Parents desiring support and information about FAS can contact NOFAS (National Organization on FAS) at 800-66-NOFAS. Two books — *The Broken Cord* by Michael Dorris, a gripping account of raising a FAS child, and *Fantastic Antone Succeeds: Experiences in Educating Children with Fetal Alcohol Syndrome* by Judith Kleinfell and Siobhan Westcott, a more upbeat "how-to" book for parents and educators — are must reading for parents with FAS children.

TABLE 20–4
Assessing a Child With Mental Retardation

Pregnancy   Lack or loss of fetal growth, abnormal weight gain by mother, particularly minimal fetal movement, maternal drug or alcohol ingestion, illness during the pregnancy (particularly rubella, cytomegalic inclusion disease, syphilis, and HIV)

Birth   Low birth weight, birth complications, abnormalities at birth (floppy, unresponsive)

Infancy   Head size or head growth too small or too large; delay in developmental milestones; abnormal muscle tone, reflexes, postures, and movements

---

developmental delays may not be retarded but instead have hearing or visual impairment. If this is suspected, an audiologist or ophthalmologist skilled in the evaluation of infants and difficult children should evaluate the child. *Chromosome studies* should be done if the child with developmental delays has any *congenital defects, multiple minor malformations, or a combination of minor and major defects.* Any child with developmental delays without a known specific diagnosis may have an *inborn error of metabolism* and should undergo appropriate metabolic studies.

Management and Treatment

Attempts should be made to make a diagnosis because the mental retardation may be treatable and, if not, a reasonable prognosis can still be established. If discovered early enough, some cases of mental retardation and its progression can be arrested, slowed, or partially reversed. The most dramatic examples of successful treatment are giving thyroid to a hypothyroid infant, performing a shunt in a case of early hydrocephalus, and introducing a low-phenylalanine diet to a baby with phenylketonuria. Unfortunately, in most cases the mental retardation doesn't have a specific diagnosis or, if it does, it is not specifically treatable.

The clinician's ability to understand and provide direct management for these children and their parents may determine the child's eventual fate. Questions that parents frequently ask clinicians include: (1) Is our child retarded? (2) What caused it? (3) What can we do about it?

When told that their child is retarded, parents might deny the retardation, which often leads to medical shopping—looking for a physician who will disagree with the original diagnosis or who will say the coveted words, "Your child will outgrow it." A second reaction, which is always present to some degree, is guilt. Since guilt is emotionally painful, parents frequently deal with it by projecting blame for the retardation on someone else, such as their spouse, their ancestors, their obstetrician, their pediatrician, or even on an event that occurred during the pregnancy. The guilt often results in frustrations for the parents and may be manifested by hostility directed toward the clinician. A third response is to rid themselves of the problem. Since this is socially unacceptable, parents may hide these feelings from themselves and others by publicly demonstrating the opposite reaction of overprotection and overconcern.

Parents expect their children to develop normally. When parents observe delayed developmental landmarks, they generally seek medical reassurance at some point. Frequently, they receive reassurance that may be unrealistic. As the child's developmental status continues to lag, parents may exert pressure on the child's physician for referral to a center where a medical diagnosis is obtained and considerable advice given. Often, parents seek additional diagnostic opinions, hoping for a different and more optimistic prognosis. Many parents, after exhausting all possible avenues of diagnostic shopping, will pursue therapeutic shopping in the hope of finding a cure. Finally, as the child's developmental lags persist, the parents gradually begin to accept their problem and turn to the physician and clinicians treating the child for advice and counseling. In some areas parent support groups are available.[2]

Clinicians caring for retarded children must recognize the multifaceted problems facing the family and be able to deal with the parents at their level by helping them accept the diagnosis of mental retardation, cope with their feelings of guilt and resentment, and by working with parents to develop and implement a management plan for the child. Clinicians must avoid removing all hope for parents, while at the same time being realistic in terms of expectations for their child. Above all, clinicians should avoid making decisions for parents based on their own reactions and attitudes. For example, even though a clinician may feel that a baby would be better off if he or she succumbed at birth, the parents may not share this feeling. Most mentally retarded children have the best chance of reaching their full potential in a caring, supportive home with realistic expectations and receiving training and care from specialists in mental retardation.

Sedating antipsychotics probably have been overused in mentally retarded children for behavioral control. Specific accompanying diagnoses, such as ADHD, seizures (especially subtle partial seizures), and mood disorders should be vigorously treated. Children with mild retardation usually respond better to stimulants than children with severe retardation (Handen et al., 1992). Clomipramine and SSRIs may be helpful in reducing anxious, obsessional, or self-injurious behavior. Buspirone, starting at low doses 2.5 mg three times a day, has been recommended for agitation and aggression in mentally retarded children (Sylvester, 1993).

---

[2]Parents of children with Down's Syndrome can call the National Down Syndrome Congress, a parent organization, at (800) 232-6372.

LEARNING, MOTOR SKILLS, AND COMMUNICATION DISORDERS

These disorders, with serious deficits in one or even two specific areas, do not imply mental retardation. Children with these disorders can function adequately in other areas. Three specific learning disorders are described in *DSM-IV*: reading, mathematics, and written expression. Criteria for these disorders are listed in Table 20–5.

Reading disorders usually start with difficulties in learning to read before age seven and then include *spelling problems* by age seven and *writing problems* by age eight. From two to eight percent of school children have a reading disorder, and boys have it more often than girls. While treatment can significantly help children with reading disorders, most will still have some problems in adulthood. Children given proper help and treatment can attain careers comparable to their normal classmates with similar IQs.

A *mathematics disorder* is often not detected until rote memorization and primitive counting strategies no longer work. About 6% of school children have this disorder with the boy:girl ratio being 4:1. Some children may be mistakenly diagnosed with this disorder because of poor teaching in their schools. Early signs of a mathematics disorder include a failure to name and count numbers or to use numbers in simple, everyday activities (e.g., give Jim two candies and Jennifer three candies).

TABLE 20–5
DSM-IV Criteria for Learning Disorders:
Disorders of Written Expression, Reading, and Math*

A. The particular area (reading achievement, mathematical ability or written skills) as measured by individually administered standardized tests (or as an alternative to a test for writing skills, functional assessments can be used) is substantially below that expected given the person's chronological age, measured intelligence and age-appropriate education.†

B. The disturbance in Criterion A significantly interferes with academic achievement or activities of daily living that require this skill.

C. If a sensory deficit is present, the learning difficulties are in excess of those usually associated with it.

*DSM-IV, pp. 50, 51, 53.
†The category "Learning Disorder Not Otherwise Specified" is used for those who do not meet Criterion A for a specific learning disorder, but meet Criteria B *and* C. For example, a significant spelling deficit would be classified here.

Management and Treatment

Clinicians untrained is these areas too often assume they can give professional advice about learning disorders. However, the causes of these disorders are myriad. One part of the of the brain may be functioning abnormally and the rest normally. Each of these abilities requires a complex integration of several subsets of abilities. Ideally, a child neuropsychologist or educational psychologist specializing in this area should evaluate children with these disorders to see which subset abilities are intact and which are not. Then a learning program can be prescribed that capitalizes on the child's strengths and circumvents the weaknesses. For example, a child with very good auditory memory and integration skills who has difficulties in complex visual integration might learn reading more easily by reading a book with a tape of the book playing in the background at the same time. Then the correct sounds are systematically paired with the words. More complex problems such as dyslexia (or as one child once said, *lysdexia*) may merit a variety of special interventions. Dyslexia is probably not a unitary disorder but caused by a variety of subdeficits that need to be individually assessed. Current treatment of mathematics disorders focuses on acquiring basic arithmetic skills and speed training. Giving attention primarily to underlying perceptual-motor-cognitive abilities has yielded poorer results.

Motor skills disorder is a separate category in *DSM-IV* and its only listing in this category is "developmental coordination disorder." The very clumsy child typically shows delays in gross motor skills (e.g., sitting and walking) and fine motor skills (e.g., self-feeding, zipping, or buttoning). The reported boy:girl ratio for this disorder varies between 2:1 and 4:1. These children break things often, though accidentally, and are called "destructive" or, refusing to attempt frustrating tasks such as writing, are called "lazy." Their peers have endless insulting names for them (e.g., "spaz," "klutz"). Academic performance is usually normal, but self-esteem is often affected. ADHD kids appear clumsy from excessive motor activity and inattention, and this disorder must be ruled out. The *DSM-IV* criteria for developmental coordination disorder are listed in Table 20–6.

Communication disorders can be very specific and may not involve other areas of function. Unlike the learning disorders, they can be diagnosed accompanying mental retardation if the language difficulties appear to be excessive for the level of retardation. Four main categories are defined: *expressive language disorder, mixed receptive-expressive language disorder* (developmental receptive language disorder), *phonological disorder* (articulation disorder), and *stuttering*.

TABLE 20–6
DSM-IV Criteria for Developmental Coordination Disorder*

A. Performance in daily activities that require motor coordination is substantially below that expected given the person's chronological age and measured intelligence. This may be manifested by marked delays in achieving motor milestones (e.g., walking, crawling, sitting), dropping things, "clumsiness," poor performance in sports, or poor handwriting.

B. The disturbance in Criterion A significantly interferes with academic achievement or activities of daily living.

C. The disturbance is not due to a general medical condition (e.g., cerebral palsy, hemiplegia, or muscular dystrophy) and does not meet criteria for a Pervasive Developmental Disorder.

D. If Mental Retardation is present, the motor difficulties are in excess of those usually associated with it.

DSM-IV, pp. 54–55.

Kids with *expressive language disorder* understand what they are told but can't express what they want to communicate. Those with *mixed receptive-expressive language disorder* have problems with both areas — understanding and communicating. *Phonological disorder* (articulation disorder) creates a problem with speech, but not necessarily a problem in communication or understanding. The cartoon character, Elmer Fudd, demonstrates this disorder when he says, "Where are you, you Wousy Wabbit?" This is not a disorder if it is the child's normal accent or dialect. For example, the "l" sound doesn't exist in Japanese and frequently, when attempted, sounds like an "r"; hence the famous (notorious?) quote, "Rots of ruck in the coming erections." Dropping the "r" in water would be a problem in Seattle but normal in Boston. In *stuttering*, the sounds are accurately made, but the fluency and time patterning is frequently disrupted. Porky Pig's "Be-ya, Be-ya, Be-ya that's all folks" demonstrates both an interjection ("be-ya") and a repetition.

The sooner the more severe forms of these disorders are detected and treated, the better the outcome. Referral to a speech pathologist and therapist specializing in children's speech disorders is essential, and for the language disorders, a psychologist or neuropsychologist. The family and teachers should be told exactly what the problem is so they don't conclude that the child is stupid or oppositional. Frequently, children with receptive language disorders are accused of hearing but "not listening." Table 20–7 lists *DSM-IV* criteria for the communication disorders.

Language disorders affect 3–10% of school-age children, while stuttering and articulation disorders each affects about 5%. Fortunately, these disorders usually are either outgrown or can be successfully treated. About 50%

TABLE 20–7
***DSM-IV* Criteria for Communication Disorders:**
Expressive Language Disorder, Mixed Receptive-Expressive Language Disorder,
Phonological Disorder, and Stuttering

Common Criteria for Expressive and Mixed Receptive-Expressive Language Disorder

A. The difficulties with expressive (also receptive, if mixed receptive-expressive) language interfere with academic or occupational achievement or with social communication.

B. Criteria are not met for a Pervasive Developmental Disorder and, if only expressive, does not meet criteria for a Mixed Receptive-Expressive Language Disorder.

C. If Mental Retardation, a speech-motor or sensory deficit, or environmental deprivation is present, the language difficulties are in excess of those usually associated with these problems.

Additional Criterion for Expressive Language Disorder

D. The scores obtained from standardized individually administered measures of expressive language development are substantially below those obtained from standardized measures of both nonverbal intellectual capacity and receptive language development. The disturbance may be manifest clinically by symptoms that include having a markedly limited vocabulary, making errors in tense, or having difficulty recalling words or producing sentences with developmentally appropriate length or complexity.

Additional Criterion for Mixed Receptive-Expressive Language Disorder

D. The scores obtained from a battery of standardized individually administered measures of both receptive and expressive language development are substantially below those obtained from standardized measures of nonverbal intellectual capacity. Symptoms include those for Expressive Language Disorder as well as difficulty understanding words, sentences, or specific types of words, such as spatial terms.

Phonological Disorder

A. Failure to use developmentally expected speech sounds that are appropriate for age and dialect (e.g., errors in sound production, use, representation, or organization such as, but not limited to, substitutions of one sound for another [use of /t/ for target /k/ sound] or omissions of sounds such as final consonants).

B. The difficulties in speech sound production interfere with academic or occupational achievement or with social communication.

C. If Mental Retardation, a speech-motor or sensory deficit, or environmental deprivation is present, the speech difficulties are in excess of those usually associated with these problems.

(Continued)

TABLE 20–7
(*Continued*)

Stuttering

A. Disturbance in the normal fluency and time patterning of speech (inappropriate for the individual's age), characterized by frequent occurrences of one or more of the following:

1. sound and syllable repetitions
2. sound prolongations
3. interjections
4. broken words (e.g., pauses within a word)
5. audible or silent blocking (filled or unfilled pauses in speech)
6. circumlocutions (word substitutions to avoid problematic words)
7. words produced with an excess of physical tension
8. monosyllabic whole-word repetitions (e.g., I-I-I-I see him)

B. The disturbance in fluency interferes with academic or occupational achievement or with social communication.

C. If a speech-motor or sensory deficit is present, the speech difficulties are in excess of those usually associated with these problems.

*DSM-IV, pp. 58, 60–61, 63, 65.

of children with expressive language disorder catch up to their peers before they reach school and do not need treatment. Those with more severe forms should get treatment before school age. Many children who also have receptive language problems will eventually acquire normal language abilities, but some of the more severely affected do not. Children with language disorders often have other disorders suggesting developmental delay (e.g., enuresis, and/or phonological, coordination, and reading disorders).

With speech therapy almost all children recover from phonological disorder; the milder cases often recover by age eight without speech therapy. Stutterers typically (80%) recover before age 16, 60% spontaneously. While stress may worsen stuttering, the disorder has a strong biological and genetic association, with 50% of first-degree relatives affected and a boy: girl ratio of 3:1.

Children with these disorders and their families often need counseling to help them deal with the social repercussions from peers (teasing) and with low self-esteem from being criticized by parents and teachers (e.g., "I know you're smart enough to do this, but you must be too lazy to try").

PERVASIVE DEVELOPMENTAL DISORDERS: AUTISTIC DISORDER

Clinical Presentation

These totally self-absorbed kids are so impaired by communication, interpersonal, imagination, and behavioral problems that they are distinctly different from everyone else. Of her autistic son, a mother said, "It's like he's the only animal in his own forest." A father observed about his child, "He lives according to a beat, but I have no idea what the beat is." Emerging between six to 30 months after birth, autistic symptoms do *not* include hallucinations, delusions, or paranoia, which partly explains why autism is not classified as schizophrenia but as "pervasive developmental disorder." Originally named after its discoverer, "Kanner's syndrome," this disorder has been called "early infantile autism," "atypical development," and "childhood psychosis" (Volkmar, Bregman, Cohen, & Cicchetti, 1988).

Soon after birth, children with autism develop abnormally. Within the first three to six months of their lives, their parents may note that they do not develop a normal pattern of smiling or responding to cuddling. As they grow older, they do not progress through developmental milestones such as learning to say words or speak sentences. Instead, they are aloof, withdrawn, and detached. Instead of developing patterns of relating warmly to their parents, they may engage in stereotyped behavior such as rocking, clapping, whirling, or head-banging. Children with this disorder are referred to as "autistic" because they appear to be withdrawn and absorbed into themselves. In the movie *Rain Man* Dustin Hoffman brilliantly portrayed most of the characteristics of autistic disorder.

The impairment in social interaction is usually the first obvious sign of the disorder and persists throughout life. These children appear to lack the ability to bond with their parents or others. Interactions, when they occur, have a detached and mechanical quality to them. Displays of love and affection do not usually occur, nor do these children respond to such displays from others. One parent said, "No smiles, no eye contact, no touch, no warmth—he's a human computer." When stressed, their behavior typically becomes weird or overactive. The verbal impairments range from the complete absence of verbal speech to mildly deviant speech and language patterns. Their speech is often odd: These children may exhibit echolalia, misname objects, invoke words only known to family members, hum monotonous sounds, or always end phrases in question marks.

Even children who develop good facility in verbal expression produce speech that has a repetitive, sing-song, and monotonous quality to it. They may become obsessed with counting things or totally absorbed by moving things (e.g., whirling fans, water fountains). There is an intense and rigid commitment to maintaining specific routines and extreme distress if routines are interrupted.

These patients can have special skills (Treffert, 1988). They may display a superb remote memory, remembering lyrics of songs heard years ago. They may recite schedules, TV programs, historical dates, math equations, and restaurant menus. What's annoying is that they regurgitate this material out of context and inappropriately. Their savant skills—those islets of precocity or special capacities—can occur in music, drawing, calculating, and calendar dates. As preschoolers, a few can teach themselves to read (hyperlexia) without comprehending anything.

Autistic children may underreact or overreact to sensory stimuli. Sometimes smells enrapture them; they may ignore people speaking to them, suggesting deafness, but then respond to the tick of a watch or metronome. Because they might experience pain but react minimally, these kids can injure themselves and not cry. Table 20–8 lists *DSM-IV* criteria for autistic disorder.

Most autistic children are mentally retarded: 40% score under 50, 30% between 50–70, and 30% can top 70. Only 20% have a normal nonverbal intelligence. "Elevated" IQs pop up, but often with inconsistent subscores, enormous "scattering," and considerable variation over time. In general, the lower the IQ, the worse the autism. Psychological tests show that verbal sequencing and abstraction are more disturbed than rote memory or visuo-spatial skills. These patients often have primitive neurological reflexes, "soft" neurological signs, mixed laterality of their hands, and physical anomalies.

Clinical Course

Parents may not recognize the first signs of autism, especially if they are without previous children. Parents may blame the unusual behavior on deafness, until they see their child respond to music, echo sounds, or react to softly-spoken words. In desperation, they may point to a particularly irrelevant event, such as a grandfather's death or a neighborhood fire, as the "cause" of their child's problems.

Although autism lasts the lifetime, slow gains can be made. A supportive home certainly helps. Even when socially awkward and egocentric, 15–30% of adult autistics can live alone and work, but only 2% reach a normal status and gainful employment. As autistic children become adolescents, depression may emerge. As the years continue, their speech and understanding may improve, despite continued perserveration, stuttering, and stereotyped pacing. Marriage is extremely rare.

Medical illness, puberty, and major stresses can trigger temporary regression with hallucinations, delusions, or catatonia. Over 25% of these chil-

TABLE 20–8
DSM-IV **Criteria for Autistic Disorder***

A. A total of six or more items from (1), (2), and (3), with at least two from (1), and one each from (2) and (3):

   (1) qualitative impairment in social interaction, as manifested by at least two of the following:

      (a) marked impairment in the use of multiple nonverbal behaviors such as eye-to-eye gaze, facial expression, body postures, and gestures to regulate social interaction

      (b) failure to develop peer relationships appropriate to developmental level

      (c) a lack of spontaneous seeking to share enjoyment, interests, or achievements with other people (e.g., by a lack of showing, bringing, or pointing out objects of interest)

      (d) lack of social or emotional reciprocity

   (2) qualitative impairments in communication as manifested by at least one of the following:

      (a) delay in, or total lack of, the development of spoken language (not accompanied by an attempt to compensate through alternative modes of communication such as gesture or mime)

      (b) in individuals with adequate speech, marked impairment in the ability to initiate or sustain a conversation with others

      (c) stereotyped and repetitive use of language or idiosyncratic language

      (d) lack of varied, spontaneous make-believe play or social imitative play appropriate to developmental level

   (3) restricted repetitive and stereotyped patterns of behavior, interests, and activities, as manifested by at least one of the following:

      (a) encompassing preoccupation with one or more stereotyped and restricted patterns of interest that is abnormal either in intensity or focus

      (b) apparently inflexible adherence to specific, nonfunctional routines or rituals

      (c) stereotyped and repetitive motor mannerisms (e.g., hand or finger flapping or twisting, or complex whole-body movements)

      (d) persistent preoccupation with parts of objects

B. Delays or abnormal functioning in at least one of the following areas, with onset prior to age 3 years: (1) social interaction, (2) language as used in social communication, or (3) symbolic or imaginative play.

C. The disturbance is not better accounted for by Rett's Disorder or Childhood Disintegrative Disorder.

DSM-IV, pp. 70–71.

dren, especially those with IQs below 50, exhibit major or partial complex seizures. From 4–32% develop grand mal seizures in late childhood, which means one thing: poor prognosis.

Epidemiology

Among kids under 15, the prevalence of autism is 0.04–0.05%. Boys have it three times as often as girls. Mild autism outnumbers serious autism. Lower socioeconomic groups may produce more autism, but this finding may actually reflect inadequate research.

Autism is a biological travesty with familial inheritance. MZ twins have 64% concordance rates; DZ twins, 9% concordance rates. Three percent of autistic siblings, which is 50 times the norm, have the disorder; 15% of these siblings are burdened with frequent body defects, mental retardation, or delayed learning, language, or speech (Smalley et al., 1988). Fragile X syndrome may produce 2–5% of autistic kids; polygenetic factors may produce other cases.

At birth, autistic children have more perinatal complications and congenital malformations. Ten percent of autistic conditions may arise from congenital German measles. The disorder can also stem from specific diseases — e.g., tuberous sclerosis, anoxia during birth, postnatal neurological infections, encephalitis, infantile spasms, and untreated phenylketonuria.

Except in the more neurologically impaired, CTs and MRIs of autistic children have generally been in the normal range (Garber & Ritvo, 1992). Abnormalities in both the dopamine and serotonin systems have been reported.

Differential Diagnosis

Mentally retarded children without autism are more extroverted, act more like their age and exhibit more normal language; they also demonstrate a broad intellectual decline without any of the savant's math, music, or other specialized skills. When both mental retardation and autism clearly co-exist, diagnose both. The stereotyped movements that occur in *tic* and *stereotypic movement disorders* lack the autistic's numerous other features.

Unlike autistics, patients with *hearing, language,* and *speech disorders* can read lips, perform sign language, relate to parents and, over time, display emotional and social appropriateness. The deaf, who babble normally at birth and much less by six to 12 months, may respond only to loud sounds; in contrast, autistics usually ignore both loud and normal tones, but they will react to soft and low sounds. Auditory evoked potentials will diagnose deafness. The *visually impaired* actively engage others, despite their poor eye contact and constant staring at people in motion.

The rare *juvenile-onset schizophrenia* generates hallucinations, delusions, and thought disorder. Mental retardation and seizures rarely accompany it. Before age three, when this schizophrenia typically presents itself, these kids seem normal; only later do their mannerisms, stereotypes, and bizarre behavior develop. Even for the most bizarre or shy autistic, do not give adult diagnoses of *schizoid or schizotypal personality disorder.* From inadequate parenting, social isolation, or "hospitalitis," *psychosocial deprivation* can induce apathetic, withdrawn children who display delayed language and motor skills (*reactive attachment disorder*); yet, unlike autism, these patients markedly improve with an improved environment. Contrary to popular belief, the "wolf" children who were purportedly raised by wolves were probably abandoned autistic children. After living in normal human homes, they still never functioned normally.

Management and Treatment

Two related goals guide treatment of autistic disorder: reducing the child's symptoms and supporting constructive efforts. Initially, clinicians should assess their language, cognition, social interactions, inborn metabolic disorders, degenerative diseases, EEGs, chromosomes, and psychological tests.

Medications. Non-sedating neuroleptics (e.g., haloperidol 0.5–4.0 mg/day) may decrease hyperactivity, stereotyped movements, isolation, weird and inappropriate interpersonal contact, anxiety, agitation, labile affect, and sometimes impaired learning. Stopping or lowering the dose causes a quick return of symptoms (Perry et al., 1989). Fenfluramine (Pondimin), which reduces blood serotonin, may help some youngsters, but side effects limit its usefulness (Sylvester, 1993). If the autistic kids are underactive or hyperactive, stimulants might "normalize" them. Anticonvulsants curtail 35–50% of seizures, while lithium may reduce self-inflicted injuries. As with mentally retarded children, clomipramine and SSRIs may reduce anxious, obsessional, and self-injurious behaviors, and buspirone may reduce agitation and aggression. Clomipramine and fluoxetine have also been reported to increase social interaction and eye contact (Sylvester, 1993).

Social therapies. Parents naturally latch onto every "new" therapy, but *laissez-faire* approaches make no sense. Well-controlled studies suggest that structured classrooms and active behavioral programs encourage language, cognition, and appropriate behavior. Parents should become adept at implementing these behavioral techniques and providing highly structured and time-consuming skills at home. In addition, family life will be enhanced if parents pay attention to healthy siblings, collaborate with public agencies, and if necessary, arrange for long-term care. At some point, clinicians may have to evaluate whether well-supervised residential living would be better for the autistic child than living with parents.

Other pervasive developmental disorders (Asperger's, childhood disintegrative, and Rett's Disorders). Each of these rare, poorly understood disorders bares some resemblance to autistic disorder. *Asperger's disorder* is essentially a partial form of autistic disorder. Kids with Asperger's are impaired (although usually less severely) in social interaction and have the restricted, repetitive, and stereotyped behaviors and interests seen in autism, but without autism's delays in cognitive development and language. Parents might fear that their normal child watches TV and plays video games and will never relate to other kids, but this almost never happens. In Asperger's disorder, it does—the child becomes a sad and extreme caricature of a "nerd."

In *childhood disintegrative disorder,* afflicted children are normal in every way for at least two years and then disaster strikes. They become impaired, like the autistic, in at least two major areas: social interaction, communication or restricted receptive language, and stereotyped patterns of behavior. Some also lose bowel or bladder control. In its worse form, children with this disorder closely resemble autistic children. Most, fortunately, are less severely impaired.

In *Rett's disorder,* seen only in girls, everything is normal for six months and then they develop the stereotyped movements, poor social interaction, and impaired communication seen in autism. In contrast to autistic kids, these have marked impairment of expressive and receptive language, severe psychomotor retardation, poorly coordinated gait or trunk movements, and retarded head growth. Unlike autistics, on the positive side, these kids often develop social interaction later.

DISRUPTIVE BEHAVIOR AND ATTENTION-DEFICIT DISORDERS: ATTENTION-DEFICIT/HYPERACTIVITY DISORDER

Clinical Presentation

The cardinal features of attention-deficit/hyperactivity disorder (ADHD) are hyperactivity, short attention span, and impulsivity that is developmentally inappropriate and endures at least six months. Typically, this condition is recognized before or during early elementary school, although it can manifest from birth and perhaps before (some mothers report that their ADHD child was a nonstop womb kicker). Because younger children naturally have more ADHD features, kids diagnosed at age four are more likely to be "the little terrors" that wear their parents out. Historically ADHD was known as "minimal brain dysfunction," "hyperactive syndrome," and "minor cerebral dysfunction." The new name has been chosen because attention difficulties are prominent and virtually always present among children with these diagnoses.

Children with this diagnosis are a caricature of the "active" child. They are physically overactive, distracted, inattentive, impulsive, and hard to manage. In classrooms, these children can't pay attention, fidget and fuss, fall off inanimate objects such as chairs, and disrupt conversations. Some even get expelled and require private tutoring. Their headlong dive into life seems determined *for* them and not *by* them.

Impatient and frustrated, even intelligent children with ADHD may get lower grades. They'll attack an exam, but get bored or distracted after a few questions. They don't wait their turn; answers precede questions. When they zoom into a room, everybody notices them. Their world is a bang, not a whimper. They're constantly interrupting, screaming, and chattering. Minor events become major cataclysms.

ADHD children may exhibit a depressed mood with or without chronic "body anxiety." The constantly tapping foot is not driven by anxiety but rather by overactivity itself; ask the child why he does that and he might say, "I don't know—my legs just gotta move." Many children with ADHD also demonstrate social immaturity and/or impairments in motor, math, or reading skills. Although lacking overt vision or hearing difficulties, their hearing gets tested regularly, only to find that they hear well but listen poorly. They may have subtle impairments in copying age-appropriate figures, executing rapid alternating movements, making left-right discrimination, and show reflex asymmetries, ambidexterity, and numerous "soft" neurological signs. In short, there's something wrong with these children, but nothing *that* wrong. Table 20–9 lists *DSM-IV* criteria for attention-deficit/hyperactivity disorder.

Clinical Course

When ADHD arises during infancy, symptoms most commonly include overreactivity to stimuli (e.g., noise, light, temperature), crying constantly, staying awake, and frequent agitation. However, a minority are exhausted, weak, oversleep, and develop more slowly for the first few months (Kaplan & Sadock, 1991). Half of the youngsters with ADHD present symptoms before age four, while the rest do so in early elementary school. Gross agitation is more frequent in preschool children, finer degrees of restlessness, later on.

ADHD's overall course is unpredictable: Symptoms may continue into adulthood or remit at puberty. About half of ADHD children have a good outcome, completing school on schedule with acceptable grades. If any symptom disappears first, it is usually the disorder's major hallmark: hyperactivity. About half continue to show some problems with attention and impulsivity as adults. If ADHD subsides during adolescence, the kids may become productive, develop relationships, and launch serious adult plans.

TABLE 20–9
DSM-IV **Criteria for Attention-Deficit/Hyperactivity Disorder***

A. Either (1) or (2):

   (1) six (or more) of the following symptoms of inattention have persisted for at least 6 months to a degree that is maladaptive and inconsistent with developmental level:

   Inattention
   (a) often fails to give close attention to details or makes careless mistakes in schoolwork, work, or other activities
   (b) often has difficulty sustaining attention in tasks or play activities
   (c) often does not seem to listen when spoken to directly
   (d) often does not follow through on instructions and fails to finish schoolwork, chores, or duties in the workplace (not due to oppositional behavior or failure to understand instructions)
   (e) often has difficulties organizing tasks and activities
   (f) often avoids, dislikes, or is reluctant to engage in tasks that require sustained mental effort (such as schoolwork or homework)
   (g) often loses things necessary for tasks or activities (e.g., toys, school assignments, pencils, books, or tools)
   (h) is often easily distracted by extraneous stimuli
   (i) often forgetful in daily activities

   (2) six or more of the following symptoms of **hyperactivity-impulsivity** have persisted for at least 6 months to a degree that is maladaptive and inconsistent with developmental level:

   Hyperactivity
   (a) often fidgets with hands or feet or squirms in seat
   (b) often leaves seat in classroom or in other situations in which remaining seated is expected
   (c) often runs about or climbs excessively in situations where it is inappropriate (in adolescents or adults, may be limited to subjective feelings of restlessness)
   (d) often has difficulty playing or engaging in leisure activities quietly
   (e) is often "on the go" or often acts as if "driven by a motor"
   (f) often talks excessively

   Impulsivity
   (g) often blurts out answers before questions have been completed
   (h) often has difficulty awaiting turn
   (i) often interrupts or intrudes on others (e.g., butts into conversations or games)

B. Some hyperactive-impulsive or inattentive symptoms that caused impairment were present before age 7 years.

C. Some impairment from the symptoms is present in two or more settings (e.g., at school [or work] and at home).

TABLE 20–9
Continued

D. There must be clear evidence of clinically significant impairment in social academic, or occupational functioning.

E. The symtoms do not occur exclusively during the course of a Pervasive Developmental Disorder, Schizophrenia, or other Psychotic Disorder and are not better
   accounted for by another mental disorder (e.g., Mood Disorder, Anxiety Disorder,
   Dissociative Disorder, or a Personality Disorder).

DSM-IV, pp. 83–85.

Kids with both ADHD and conduct disorder have a much worse prognosis than those with ADHD alone. Roughly 25% of adolescents with ADHD
in combination with conduct disorder also develop antisocial personality
disorder. These antisocial ADHD adults complete fewer years of school,
have a higher rate of substance abuse, more arrests, more car accidents,
and more suicide attempts. Adults who had ADHD as children are more
prone to mood disorders, perhaps secondary to both biological vulnerability and the constant assaults on self-esteem during childhood.

Case illustration. Hank got to school a little late. Getting ready for school that
morning, he had spilled a glass of milk while gesturing with his hand, had fallen off
the dining room chair twice, and while looking for a school book, had become
distracted by five other things in his bedroom. Then he tripped a girl on the school
bus as she was walking down the aisle because, for a moment, it seemed like a fun
thing to do. He saw, he did, he thought—in that order.
    At last Hank made it into the classroom, whereupon he dumped his books and
homework into his "rats nest" desk. The class clown had arrived. While fidgeting at
his desk, he chatted excitedly with his friend next to him, but the teacher was talking
to the class and told him to stop. He tried paying attention to the teacher, and when
the teacher asked the class a question, Hank answered it in the instant that five
other hands went up. He thought, "Uh-oh, I got to remember to raise my hand next
time," but at the next opportunity he blurted out the answer again. He was a smart
kid who often knew the answer but got C's because he didn't finish assignments, lost
homework, skipped items on exams, did ten other things instead of studying for a
test. The principal's office was all too familiar a place. He was sent there mostly for
talking, but also for the stunts he performed to get laughs—he had learned to
capitalize on his hyperactivity and impulsiveness by getting laughs from his friends.
They liked him but also found him intrusive, annoying, and distracting.
    Hank's parents were worn out by him and were reduced to hollow "don't-do-that-
stop-that" interchanges that almost never netted the desired consequences. They
regarded him like the family labrador retriever: hyper, friendly—and untrainable.
    Hank's fourth-grade teacher finally persuaded the parents to have Hank as-
sessed. ADHD was diagnosed and in a week's time, he was responding to 30 mg/

day of dextroamphetamine. Having feared addiction, his father was stunned by the "speed," although like most ADHD children on stimulants, Hank did not become euphoric or hyperactive on the drug. Even in normal children the euphoric response doesn't come until adolescence. Hank's restlessness diminished, his concentration improved, and he began getting A's and B's. His parents were taught to deliver consistent, appropriate consequences for Hank's behavior. Hank remained the class clown, but slowly discovered that he could get positive attention in other ways — by helping someone out, doing well on a test or homework assignment, and working *with*, not against, other kids on a group project.

Epidemiology

The American prevalence of ADHD ranges from 2–20%, although 3–5% is more likely. In Great Britain, its reported incidence is 1%. Why the difference? In the United States, it only needed to be present in one setting, while in Great Britain it must be present in all settings, a more sensible criteria and one the *DSM-IV* approaches. ADHD afflicts boys far more than girls, even though the precise ratios depend on the study. One investigation indicated that ADHD occurs six to nine times more often in boys than girls, while a community survey found a 3:1 ratio. Firstborn boys are prime targets. Forty to 75% of kids with ADHD also have conduct disorder (Mesco & Cantwell, 1991).

Etiology and Pathogenesis

Despite the absence of specific brain damage, ADHD is mainly a *biologically-caused disorder*. In many cases genetics has a major role. In contrast to normals, the families of these children have more ADHD; their brothers display ADHD three times more often than brothers of normal kids. Other psychiatric disorders tend to travel with ADHD. Their male relatives have a higher incidence of substance abuse, alcoholism, and antisocial personality disorder, whereas their female counterparts have more somatization disorder and histrionic personality disorder. These various disorders are also more frequent in the biological parents of adopted-away ADHD children. Newer evidence indicates that these other disorders may not be *genetically* linked to ADHD, but are nonetheless linked: an ADHD parent is more likely to marry a person with one of these other disorders (Faraone et al., 1991). Similarly, learning disorders (e.g., dyslexia) are more common in ADHD kids and in their first-degree relatives, but this is due to the fact that an ADHD parent is more likely to have married a spouse with a learning disorder (Faraone et al., 1993). Parents with *only* ADHD are more likely to have children with *only* ADHD, unaccompanied by conduct or learning disorder.

Possible *fetal* and *perinatal causes* of ADHD include poor maternal nutrition, maternal substance abuse, viral infections, and exposure to toxins such as lead. There is no specific neurobiological marker. Frontal lobe hypofunction may affect ADHD's disinhibition. Hyperactive parents of hyperactive children metabolize glucose in the brain at a level 8% lower than normal parents. ADHD occurs in 70% of children and 50% of adults with thyroid hormone resistance, an uncommon disorder. When *delayed developmental milestones* generate an ADHD syndrome, by puberty the kid becomes normal. Chaotic families and child abuse worsen ADHD. Some "experts" claim that food additives and sugar cause ADHD; yet after withdrawing these chemicals, in a placebo controlled fashion, their mothers can't see any change. Social class and ADHD appear unrelated.

Differential Diagnosis

Since many children seem fated to have at least some ADHD symptoms (especially high activity or low attention span), careful differential diagnosis becomes crucial. It is important to know what is normal at each age level and how children behave in a variety of environments. Inexperienced parents may conclude that their children's age-appropriate overactivity is highly pathological, but their teachers, who have experience with many children, view their behavior as normal.

Separating ADHD from *conduct disorder* can be tricky. Children with conduct disorder alone are often misdiagnosed as having ADHD. Because they exhibit many bad and unacceptable behaviors, they may be labeled "hyperactive." However, most are no more active than their normal peers. In contrast, most ADHD kids don't specialize in bad behaviors but rather exhibit *all* behaviors at high rates, including positive ones such as petting animals, joking with friends, and helping out little kids. Children with conduct disorders flaunt their meanness to people and animals; they intend bad outcomes and may not repent. Kids with ADHD can act in haste and repent at leisure.

Management and Treatment

Because other conditions frequently occur with ADHD, referral for IQ, psychological, speech, language, and learning disabilities should be made if clinically indicated (AACAP, 1991). Restlessness can also be caused by chronically used medications, including obviously stimulating medications (e.g., anti-asthmatics, sympathomimetics, steroids, and decongestants) and supposedly sedating medications that may cause a paradoxical response in children (e.g., phenobarbital or antihistamines). With most ADHD parents, guilt is an ongoing preoccupation, and so treating the whole family can be sticky. However, medication and counseling can be very effective.

Medications. A child given separate trials of dextroamphetamine (0.6–1.7 mg/kg/qd) and methylphenidate (0.3–0.6 mg/kg/qd) has a greater than 90% chance of responding to one or the other. In trials of a single stimulant, roughly 30% of patients exhibited marked improvement, 40% received some benefit, and 10–30% were unaffected. If both drugs are equal, methylphenidate is preferred because of fewer cardiac effects (Sylvester, C, 1993). Optimal intellectual improvement and adequate behavioral control may be best at lower doses of methylphenidate. Doses over 6 mg/kg risk worsening intellectual performance (Greenhill, 1990). Methylphenidate's effects last from three to six hours. Dextroamphetamine lasts about twice as long. Because it's chewable, some kids prefer the once-a-day stimulant pemoline (0.5–3.0 mg/kg/qd). Doses of 1.0–2.0 mg/kg are usually optimal (Sallee, Stiller, & Perel, 1992). Stimulants diminish overactivity, impulsiveness, irritability, and emotional fluctuations; they increase vigilance, attention span, and general sociability. These medications don't facilitate learning *per se*, but when attention span lengthens and reduced criticism enhances self-esteem, learning accelerates.

These pharmacological agents can work in two days, but often require one to two weeks. Because of the variability of a child's behavior, and the possibility that a child may temporarily respond to placebo, an ADHD child should have comparison trials of placebo and stimulant. ADHD children rarely develop tolerance and drug abuse, although stimulants might temporarily suppress growth slightly. If there is any question that the stimulant being used has little or no effect, the child should be placed on a different stimulant. While on these medications, blood pressure, pulse, height, weight, appetite, mood, and side effects (tics, etc.) should be regularly monitored. Because children can grow out of ADHD, monitored trials of no medication should be conducted one or more times a year to see if they still need it (AACAP, 1991). As alternatives to stimulants, antidepressants (e.g., imipramine, desipramine) help some ADHD kids, particularly with depression, anxiety, and tics. However, these tricyclic antidepressants must be used very cautiously because they are more likely to cause cardiac arrhythmias in kids. In ADHD adults and adolescents who are likely to abuse stimulants, tricyclic antidepressants or clonidine are often tried first.

Environment. Medication, individual tutoring, family counseling, behavior therapy, and educational training are all critical. ADHD children should understand that drug-taking does not mean they're crazy, that *some* impaired behavior does not permit *all* poor behavior, that "unstructured permissiveness" is not good for them, and that genuine praise usually arises from jobs well done. They do best with a consistent, supportive, moderately structured environment.

The American Academy of Child and Adolescent Psychiatry (1991) recommends: (1) family therapy if there is family dysfunction; (2) individual and/or group therapy for poor self-esteem and peer problems; (3) social skills training (including empathy training) and cognitive therapies for attention/impulsivity symptoms (one goal is to have them verbalize/think *before* acting); and (4) parent behavior training to develop appropriate, consistent, limit-setting abilities and behavior modification programs for behavior problems. Too often, parents who are at their wits' end can no longer see anything positive about their children. Books like *Raising Your Spirited Child* by Mary Sheedy Kurcinka (1991) help them recognize and harness their children's energy and "spiritedness" for positive purposes.

CONDUCT DISORDER

Clinical Presentation

Kids with conduct disorder violate norms and the rights of others. It's usually a boy's disorder, with about 9% of boys and 2% of girls having it. They're always into trouble, be it with parents, peers, or teachers. They're often informers on friends to try to place blame on others. Lying and cheating are typical. Some are called "pathological liars." Physical aggression and cruelty to other people or to animals is common, or they may destroy other's properties (e.g., setting fires). Stealing is common and can range from "borrowing" other people's possessions, to shoplifting, to forgery, to breaking into someone's house. These children are often truant from school and may run away from home. Drug use is common, especially tobacco, liquor, or street drugs. They begin sex at an early age and often have multiple partners. Self-esteem is low, despite the image of "toughness" presented to the public. Poor frustration tolerance, irritability, temper outbursts, and recklessness are common. Table 20–10 lists *DSM-IV* Criteria for Conduct Disorder.

Clinical Course

Onset is typically prepubertal, particularly in the "solitary aggressive" type. The group or gang delinquents often start at puberty. They usually show loyalty to the gang's members and norms but to no one else. Postpubertal onset is more common among females than males. Conduct disorder is the forerunner of adult antisocial personality disorder. Fortunately, not

TABLE 20–10
DSM-IV **Criteria for Conduct Disorder***

A. A repetitive and persistent pattern of behavior in which the basic rights of others or major age-appropriate societal norms or rules are violated, as manifested by the presence of three (or more) of the following criteria in the past 12 months, with at least one criterion present in the past 6 months:

Aggression to people and animals
(1) often bullies, threatens, or intimidates others
(2) often initiates physical fights
(3) has used a weapon that can cause serious physical harm to others (e.g., a bat, brick, broken bottle, knife, gun)
(4) has been physically cruel to people
(5) has been physically cruel to animals
(6) has stolen while confronting a victim (e.g., mugging, purse snatching, extortion, armed robbery)
(7) has forced someone into sexual activity

Destruction of property
(8) has deliberately engaged in fire setting with the intention of causing serious damage
(9) has deliberately destroyed others' property (other than by fire setting)

Deceitfulness or theft
(10) has broken into someone else's house, building, or car
(11) often lies to obtain goods or favors or to avoid obligations (i.e., "cons" others)
(12) has stolen items of nontrivial value without confronting a victim (e.g., shoplifting, but without breaking and entering, forgery)

Serious violations or rules
(13) often stays out at night despite parental prohibitions, beginning before 13 years of age
(14) has run away from home overnight at least twice while living in parental or parental surrogate home (or once without returning for a lengthy period)
(15) is often truant from school, beginning before age 13 years

B. The disturbance in behavior causes clinically significant impairment in social, academic, or occupational functioning.

C. If the individual is age 18 years or older, criteria are not met for Antisocial Personality Disorder.

DSM-IV, pp. 90–91.

all children with conduct disorder go on to develop antisocial personality disorder. Those with milder forms, a later start, or simple peer-pleasing motives are less likely to become tomorrow's criminals.

Etiology and Pathogenesis

Some children have cognitive predispositions that lead them to conduct disorder. Despite normal IQs, they are two or more years behind on academic (particularly verbal) skills and have difficulties with abstract reasoning (particularly, understanding complex directions and social interactions). When they are told what to do, they regularly "screw it up" because they didn't understand the instructions. They end up low on the social ladder and may be regarded as weird. However, they often have excellent, manipulative, problem-solving abilities. It is not a coincidence that many a delinquent has failed reading and writing in school but can work magic on cars or in picking a lock. Parents who decide their kid is inherently bad can send him down the road to jail; those who have the forebearance to view this child as having an academic and educational problem can prevent a deteriorating course by working with the child and his school to help him overcome these problems.

Other risk factors include: a family history of antisocial personality disorder or substance dependence; sexual, physical, and emotional abuse; a learning disorder that makes school an ordeal; and/or an immediate environment that offers more temptations to get into trouble. These issues were discussed in more depth in Chapter 19 on antisocial personality disorder.

Differential Diagnosis

Conduct disorder continues over six months or more, so isolated acts of antisocial behavior don't count. Children with *oppositional defiant disorders* may look like a conduct disorder—what with their temper outbursts, violation of curfews, running away, playing hooky, being spiteful and vindictive, and generally showing disobedience and opposition to authority figures. However, they don't violate the basic rights of others or major age-appropriate societal norms or rules, as do kids with conduct disorders. Adolescents with *major depression* can suddenly engage in antisocial behavior, but they will also meet major depression criteria and, when asked why they behaved so badly, they will say for social approval or to distract themselves from pain. Kids with conduct disorders will answer "because it's fun" or "I don't know, I just felt like doing it." Children with *attention-deficit/hyperactivity disorder* or *specific developmental disorders* are more likely to develop conduct disorder. Each of these diagnoses should be given, if present.

Management and Treatment

There are no treatment approaches proven to be effective with conduct disorder, but many are promising. First treat the treatable coexisting problems such as ADHD, major depression, or drug abuse. Medications for aggression, hyperarousal, and behavioral dyscontrol include lithium, carbamazepine, propranolol, and trazodone and are sometimes helpful adjuncts to treatment (Sylvester, 1993). Tutoring for developmental problems may make it easier for these children to progress in school. If possible, remove children from significantly abusive home environments. Help the parent(s) develop realistic rules and consequences and consistently enforce them. Too often these children are rescued from the consequences of their actions or, alternately, beaten and ignored. Commands should be clear but not hostile. When noncompliant, enforcing "time-outs" or loss of T.V. time is appropriate; when compliant and prosocial, give social rewards such as time with a friend or going on a recreational outing with the family. Objects and money (all too easily stolen) should not be the reward, and the punishment should not be too harsh and overwhelming. For example, grounding a child for two months almost never works.

Children who were truly led astray by the boy (gang) "down the block" can be helped to develop prosocial rather than antisocial alternatives, including community programs that structure their time in positive ways. No parent will admit that his or her child is the one who led others astray, but in this situation, even though the prognosis is much grimmer, prosocial programs can be attempted. Variations on "tough love" approaches have been touted to have some success. Ideally, all of these treatments should be implemented as soon as the symptoms appear and not years later, after the symptoms have become ingrained behaviors.

OPPOSITIONAL DEFIANT DISORDER

This is the quintessential angry child who is chronically argumentative, volatile, spiteful, and vindictive. Children with this disorder ignore or openly defy adults' requests and rules, finding 50 ways to annoy others. Some are more passive—"I won't doing anything"—and others more active, "You deserved it, screw you." They'll blame others for their own mistakes or difficulties. In spite of all these behaviors, they do not have a conduct disorder because they don't seriously violate the basic rights of others. They don't steal, destroy property, force people to do things, or engage in cruel activities. Table 20–11 lists *DSM-IV* criteria for oppositional defiant disorder.

These behaviors are almost invariably present in the home, but not always at school or with other adults or peers. In some kids, the behaviors are displayed outside the home from the beginning, while in others, they start at home and later show them outside. Typically, these children reserve their awful behaviors for adults and peers they know well. Without a good history, children with this disorder are hard to diagnose because they often show little or no signs of the disorder in the clinician's office. When asked why they are so oppositional and defiant, they answer that they are merely responding to unreasonable rules, demands, and requests. Sometimes they are very convincing—so convincing that the naive clinician decides that the problem must be with the parents and perhaps a "parentectomy" is in order.

Oppositional defiant disorder (ODD) typically begins by age eight years and usually not later than early adolescence (Rey, 1993). With the right (or

---

TABLE 20–11
DSM-IV* Criteria for Oppositional Defiant Disorder

A. A pattern of negativistic, hostile, and defiant behavior lasting at least 6 months, during which four (or more) of the following are present:

  (1) often loses temper
  (2) often argues with adult
  (3) often actively defies or refuses to comply with adults' requests or rules
  (4) often deliberately annoys people
  (5) often blames others for his or her mistakes or misbehavior
  (6) is often touchy or easily annoyed by others
  (7) is often angry and resentful
  (8) is often spiteful or vindictive

Note: Consider a criterion met only if the behavior occurs more frequently than is typically observed in individuals of comparable age and developmental level.

B. The disturbance in behavior causes clinically significant impairment in social, academic, or occupational functioning.

C. The behaviors do not occur exclusively during the course of a Psychotic or Mood Disorder.

D. Criteria are not met for Conduct Disorder and, if the individual is age 18 years or older, criteria are not met for Antisocial Personality Disorder.

---

*DSM-IV, pp. 93–94.

wrong, depending on how one looks at it) family environment, the child with a "difficult-child" temperament frequently goes on to become ODD (Maziade et al., 1990). Boys more often have this disorder before puberty, but after puberty the sex ratio is equal. These kids often have low self-esteem, mood lability, low frustration tolerance, and temper outbursts; they may abuse psychoactive substances including tobacco, alcohol, and cannabis. Often ADHD is also present. Some kids with ODD later develop a conduct disorder, but most just keep on having oppositional defiant disorder, no matter what happens. The stability of the diagnosis over time is only less than that of autism and similar to ADHD (Cantwell & Baker, 1989).

The symptoms of ODD usually occur in *conduct disorder*, sometimes occur in the prodromal phase of *psychotic disorders*, and during the course of *mood disorders*. When this happens, diagnose these other disorders and not ODD.

Unfortunately, little is known about the cause or effective treatment of ODD, except that the outcome of treatment is usually poor. These kids refuse to get better. If parents really are overly restrictive, the child typically so overreacts that a chronic power struggle ensues. Sometimes family therapy can help break the deadlock. The therapist must work very hard at not assigning blame to the child or parents. Some clinicians have suggested the use of "paradoxical approaches." For example, the therapist assigns the child to have one temper tantrum next week, when asked to go to bed. In order to show defiance toward the therapist, the child may have to *not* have the temper tantrum next week. This approach should only be used by highly trained clinicians. The only systematic study on treatment found that parent training based on social learning is superior to family systems therapy (Wells & Egan, 1988).

SEPARATION ANXIETY DISORDER

Separation is too gentle a word for this disorder—*abandonment* is closer to the real issue. These children are the clingers, scared and miserable when they are away from the important people in their lives and appeased when they are with them. These kids don't fully outgrow normal separation. For them, going to a friend's house or being left with a baby sitter or in a preschool is an ordeal. They can't wait to get back home, even though life at home has its problems too. You never know when Mom, Dad, or Grandma will be snatched by the jaws of death, or kidnappers will come to take the clinging child away from them. The solution is to shadow parents around the house like a puppy, and at bedtime have at least one of them there in the room, preferably with a night light on. Bedtime can turn into one or two hours of nightly misery. Fear of the dark is common. Mythical nighttime monsters may be under the bed or in the closet. Mere mention of a possible separation sets off physical symptoms of anxiety: stomachaches, nausea, vomiting, and headaches are typical. Parents often say that the child is deliberately making up these symptoms to avoid separating. The truth usually lies somewhere in-between. Real anxiety is always there to set off these symptoms, but these children have also learned that reporting symptoms staves off separation. Adolescents, but not usually younger children, may also have cardiovascular symptoms including palpitations, dizziness, and fainting. In short, these children are on their way to panic disorder. Although most are demanding and intrusive, some adapt by being compliant and eager to please.

Most children with separation anxiety are never brought to clinicians unless they develop "school phobia" or "school refusal" and completely stop going to school. They either never leave home or pretend to go to school and, when the parents are gone, sneak home. The symptoms of separation anxiety disorder include two types of worries (harm to, or separation from, major attachment figures), three types of behaviors (school refusal, daytime and bedtime clinging), and three categories of symptoms related to anxiety (anxiety itself, nightmares, and physical symptoms). The *DSM-IV* criteria for separation anxiety disorder are listed in Table 20–12.

Etiology and Pathogenesis

Frequently this disorder manifests after a life stress such as the loss of a relative or a pet, an illness in the child or a relative, or a change in the child's environment (such as a move to a new neighborhood or a school change). It rarely starts in adolescence. Separation anxiety tends to wax and wane throughout childhood with periods of remission. New stresses typically cause flare-ups. Boys and girls have an equal risk for this disorder. It is not a coincidence that kids with this disorder come from close-knit, caring homes. Such an environment is usually positive and creates strong bonds. On the negative side, however, children may have trouble forming bonds elsewhere. A general rule of preschool teachers and day-care workers is that separation anxiety problems are as much the parents' as the child's problem. A mother may have trouble letting go of her "baby" and experience distress at leaving him in the care of others. She may be a little overprotective, not wanting him to experience unpleasant feelings. When he cries, she stays or returns soon to check on him. Even if he had just settled down, he may cry after spotting Mom, reinforcing her belief that she should never have left. Her hovering and attempts to ensure that he never feels distress reinforce his perceptions that something dangerous is always about to happen.

TABLE 20–12
DSM-IV Criteria for Separation Anxiety Disorder*

A. Developmentally inappropriate and excessive anxiety concerning separation from home or from those to whom the individual is attached, as evidenced by three (or more) of the following:

    (1) recurrent excessive distress when separation from home or major attachment figures occurs or is anticipated

    (2) persistent and excessive worry about losing, or possible harm befalling, major attachment figures

    (3) persistent and excessive worry that an untoward event will lead to separation from a major attachment figure (e.g., getting lost or being kidnapped)

    (4) persistent reluctance or refusal to go to school or elsewhere because of fear of separation

    (5) persistently and excessively scared or reluctant to be alone or without major attachment figures at home or without significant adults in other settings

    (6) persistent reluctance or refusal to go to sleep without being near a major attachment figure or to sleep away from home

    (7) repeated nightmares involving the theme of separation

    (8) repeated complaints of physical symptoms (such as headaches, stomachaches, nausea, or vomiting) when separation from major attachment figures occurs or is anticipated

B. The duration of the disturbance is at least 4 weeks.

C. The onset is before age 18 years.

D. The disturbance causes clinically significant distress or impairment in social, academic (occupational), or other important areas of functioning.

E. The disturbance does not occur exclusively during the course of a Pervasive Developmental Disorder, Schizophrenia, or other Psychotic Disorder and, in adolescents and adults, is not better accounted for by Panic Disorder With Agoraphobia.

DSM-IV, p. 113.

Clinical judgment and familiarity with *normal separation anxiety* is necessary to diagnose this disorder. The extreme narrowness of the source of anxiety — *separation* — distinguishes it from other anxiety disorders, such as *general anxiety disorder* and *panic disorder with agoraphobia*, and from disorders in which anxiety is but one symptom, such as *schizophrenia*, *pervasive developmental disorder*, or *major depression*.

A child brought in for school refusal can be asked, "Why don't you want to go to school?" If she has separation anxiety disorder, she will say, "I want to be home with my mommy." The child with conduct disorder might say, "I don't feel like it —

it's not fun"; the child with *oppositional defiant disorder* might say, "Nobody can make me go to school if I don't want to." Kids without a specific disorder might say, "I'm afraid of failing and looking stupid in class."

A variety of approaches are used to treat children who have never successfully separated. Children should be allowed to have transitional objects such as blankets, stuffed animals, and pictures of family members in the setting. Stretching the length of separation very gradually from minutes to hours can help children master the sensations of separation anxiety. Since children pick up their parents' anxieties, counseling parents to help *their* anxiety about separation is often needed.

For children who have successfully separated but are currently experiencing a separation anxiety disorder after the death or illness of a family member, more specialized approaches (such as grief work) are recommended.

ELIMINATION, TIC, AND OTHER DISORDERS OF CHILDHOOD

The elimination disorders are very common and are discussed in most pediatric and child-care books. Tic disorders, reactive attachment disorder, elective mutism, and stereotypic movement disorder are quite rare. Only brief descriptions will accompany the diagnostic criteria for these disorders.

Elimination Disorders

Both *encopresis* and *enuresis* are more common in boys. They should not be diagnosed until the developmental age is four years for encopresis and five years for enuresis. One fourth of children with encopresis also have enuresis. Physical causes for both disorders should be ruled out.

Generally, two types of kids are more prone to *functional encopresis:* the anxious and the oppositional. The anxious ones develop a vicious cycle; they are afraid to use toilets in public places, develop constipation, and then may develop involuntary overflow incontinence. Soiling almost always occurs during waking hours. For them, the encopresis does not feel under control. The oppositional ones do it deliberately, don't usually have constipation, and to rub their defiance in further, may smear their feces. Occasionally the anxious ones smear their feces in a botched attempt to hide their accidents. Table 20-13 lists the *DSM-IV* criteria for functional encopresis. About 1% of five-year-olds have this disorder.

A history of constipation, developmental delays in other areas, ADHD, or coercive or premature bowel training each increases the risk for encopresis. Toilet phobia can also lead to encopresis and may develop if the available facilities are particularly gruesome or if fantasies about the toilet, such as being drowned or bitten by snakes, take over. Secondary encopresis may begin with stressful events, often with separation themes such as birth of a sibling, starting school, or mom starting a full-time job. School-age children can successfully retain feces at school only to soil

TABLE 20-13
DSM-IV Criteria for Encopresis and Enuresis*

Encopresis

A. Repeated passage of feces into inappropriate places (e.g., clothing or floor) whether involuntary or intentional.

B. At least one such event a month for at least 3 months.

C. Chronological age is at least 4 years (or equivalent developmental level).

D. The behavior is not due exclusively to the direct physiological effects of a substance (e.g., laxatives) or a general medical condition except through a mechanism involving constipation.

Enuresis

A. Repeated voiding of urine into bed or clothes (whether involuntary or intentional).

B. The behavior is clinically significant as manifested by either a frequency of twice a week for at least 3 consecutive months or the presence of clinically significant distress or impairment in social, academic (occupational), or other important areas of functioning.

C. Chronological age is at least 5 years (or equivalent developmental level).

D. The behavior is not due to the direct physiological effects of a substance (e.g., a diuretic) or a general medical condition (e.g., diabetes, spina bifida, a seizure disorder).

*DSM-IV, pp. 107, 109–110.

at home. The ones who don't are usually ridiculed by peers. Encopretic children usually can't explain their behavior.

To avoid the retention-leakage cycle laxatives, stool softeners are used to evacuate the colon. Children are then scheduled to have regular periods on the toilet for the purpose of muscle retraining and are given responsibility for cleaning themselves and any soiled clothing. The parents are helped to develop a matter-of-fact approach in helping their children.

Functional enuresis is a more biologically-based disorder: 75% of these children have a first-degree relative who has had it. At age five, 3% of girls and 7% of boys have it. All but 1% of males and almost all females outgrow it by age 18. Nocturnal enuresis is much more common than diurnal (daytime) enuresis. Nocturnal enuresis usually occurs in the first third of the night; children typically awaken with no memory of a dream or of having urinated. Very stressful events can trigger it in children who had been continent.

Children with enuresis should be evaluated for potential medical causes, such as urinary tract infection, minor neurological impairment, structural anomalies, and medical illness. If no medical problems are found, a variety of treatment options are available: (1) In *retention control* training, children drink a large amount of liquid and gradually delay the time to voiding. Token or social reinforcement can be used to amplify the rewards for success. This method works much better for daytime than for nighttime enuresis. (2) *Conditioning devices*, which set off an alarm when urine contacts the bed, can be highly effective, at least initially. Over one to three months, about 75% of children succeed with this approach, but about 35% relapse when it is stopped. Repeat trials are then used. (3) *Tricyclic antidepressants* (usually imipramine or an *antispasmodic* such as oxybutynin [Ditropan]), have also been used to treat this disorder. Although up to two-thirds of children have a reduction in wetting with 25–75 mg of imipramine, almost all relapse when the medication is stopped.

A popular but unproven technique for nocturnal enuresis involves eliminating fluid intake after dinner, having children void before bedtime, and carrying the sleepy child to the toilet once during the night. This may keep the bed dry, but may not lead to enduring results.

Tic Disorders

Although anywhere from 5–24% of school children have some kind of tic, most fortunately don't have a tic disorder. A tic is defined as an involuntary, sudden, rapid, recurrent, nonrhythmic, stereotyped movement or vocalization. If they weren't normal, eyeblinks could be thought of as tics. Tics (like eyeblinks) are automatic, but can be voluntarily suppressed for varying lengths of time. Stress makes them worse; sleep and absorbing activities make them better. *Motor tics* may be simple (e.g., neck jerking, shoulder shrugging) or complex (e.g., facial gestures, grooming behavior). *Verbal tics* can also be simple (e.g., coughing or barking) or complex (e.g., words or whole phrases spoken out of context). The three tic disorders — *Tourette's, chronic motor or vocal tic disorder*, and *transient tic disorder* — are probably variations on the same genetic abnormality. Chronic motor or vocal tic disorder and transient tic disorder are partial forms of Tourette's. Chronic motor or vocal tic disorder meets all of the criteria for Tourette's, except only motor *or* vocal tics are seen, but not both. In transient tic disorder, a child has motor and/or vocal tics for at least four weeks but not longer than 12 consecutive months. Boys have these disorders at least three times more often than girls. Half develop tics by seven years and the majority by age 14. Tourette's, the worst form, is rare: 1 in 2,000. No other neurological or psychiatric disorder has the vocalizations heard in Tourette's and these related tic disorders. Table 20–14 lists *DSM-IV* criteria for Tourette's disorder.

Stereotypic Movement Disorders

Unlike the tic disorders, the repetitive behaviors in this disorder are intentional. It occurs in 10–23% of institutionalized children with moderate or severe mental retardation. It is also more common in deaf or blind children. The child's primary goal may be to use self-stimulation as an antidote to an otherwise impoverished, low-stimulation environment. Table 20–15 lists *DSM-IV* criteria for stereotypic movement disorder.

Selective Mutism

Children with this rare disorder typically talk at home but refuse to speak at school or in social situations. Children who have a speech disorder are socially withdrawn or are oppositional and more prone to this disorder. Selective mutism generally starts before age five and, in most, lasts only a few weeks. Major stresses such as immigration, hospitalization, or traumas

---

TABLE 20–14
DSM-IV* Criteria for Tourette's Disorder

A. Both multiple motor and one or more vocal tics have been present at some time during the illness, although not necessarily concurrently. (A *tic* is an involuntary, sudden, rapid, recurrent, nonrhythmic, stereotyped motor movement or vocalization.)

B. The tics occur many times a day (usually in bouts), nearly every day or intermittently throughout a period of more than 1 year, and during this period, there was never a tic-free period of more than 3 consecutive months.

C. The disturbance causes marked distress or significant impairment in social, occupational, or other important areas of functioning.

D. The onset is before age 18 years.

E. The disturbance is not due to the direct physiological effects of a substance (e.g., stimulants) or a general medical condition (e.g., Huntington's disease or postviral encephalitis).

DSM-IV, p. 103.

TABLE 20–15
DSM-IV **Criteria for Stereotypic Movement Disorder***

A. Repetitive, seemingly driven, and nonfunctional motor behavior (e.g., hand shaking or waving, body rocking, head banging, mouthing of objects, self-biting, picking at skin or bodily orifices, hitting own body).

B. The behavior markedly interferes with normal activities or results in self-inflicted bodily injury that requires medical treatment (or would result in an injury if preventive measures were not used).

C. If Mental Retardation is present, the stereotypic or self-injurious behavior is of sufficient severity to become a focus of treatment.

D. The behavior is not better accounted for by a compulsion (as in Obsessive-Compulsive Disorder), a tic (as in Tic Disorder), a stereotypy that is part of a Pervasive Developmental Disorder, or hair pulling (as in Trichotillomania).

E. The behavior is not due to the direct physiological effects of a substance or a general medical condition.

F. The behavior persists for 4 weeks or longer.

Specify if:
   With Self-Injurious Behavior: if the behavior results in bodily damage that requires specific treatment (or that would result in bodily damage if protective measures were not used)

*DSM-IV, p. 121.

before age three may predispose some children to mutism. Table 20–16 lists *DSM-IV* criteria for selective mutism.

REACTIVE ATTACHMENT DISORDER OF INFANCY OR EARLY CHILDHOOD

This disorder's profound disturbance in social relatedness is usually associated with grossly pathogenic, neglectful care. In young children, social milestones such as smiling with pleasure by four or five months are missed; they typically appear apathetic, staring vacantly and moving little. They often fail to gain weight but do get taller. Older children may exhibit indiscriminate sociability with strangers. Placement in a more positive environment may lead to normal physical growth, but may only partially correct the disturbed social relatedness. Table 20–17 lists *DSM-IV* criteria for reactive attachment disorder of infancy or early childhood.

TABLE 20-16
DSM-IV Criteria for Selective Mutism*

A. Consistent failure to speak in specific social situations (in which there is an expectation for speaking, e.g., at school) despite speaking in other situations.

B. The disturbance interferes with educational or occupational achievement or with social communication.

C. The duration of the disturbance is at least 1 month (not limited to the first month of school).

D. The failure to speak is not due to a lack of knowledge of, or comfort with, the spoken language required in the social situation.

E. The disturbance is not better accounted for by a Communication Disorder (e.g., Stuttering) and does not occur exclusively during the course of a Pervasive Developmental Disorder, Schizophrenia, or other Psychotic Disorder.

*DSM-IV, p. 115.

TABLE 20-17
DSM-IV Criteria for Reactive Attachment Disorder of Infancy or Early Childhood*

A. Markedly disturbed and developmentally inappropriate social relatedness in most contexts, beginning before age 5 years, as evidenced by either (1) or (2):
   (1) persistent failure to initiate or respond in a developmentally appropriate fashion to most social interactions, as manifest by excessively inhibited, hypervigilant, or highly ambivalent and contradictory responses (e.g., the child may respond to caregivers with a mixture of approach, avoidance, and resistance to comforting, or may exhibit frozen watchfulness)
   (2) diffuse attachments as manifested by indiscriminate sociability with marked inability to exhibit appropriate selective attachments (e.g., excessive familiarity with relative strangers or lack of selectivity in choice of attachment figures)

B. The disturbance in Criterion A is not accounted for solely by developmental delay (as in Mental Retardation) and does not meet criteria for a Pervasive Developmental Disorder.

C. Pathogenic care as evidenced by at least one of the following:
   (1) persistent disregard of the child's basic emotional needs for comfort, stimulation, and affection
   (2) persistent disregard of the child's basic physical needs
   (3) repeated changes of primary caregiver that prevent formation of stable attachments (e.g., frequent changes in foster care)

D. There is a presumption that the care in Criterion C is responsible for the disturbed behavior in Criterion A (e.g., the disturbances in Criterion A began following the pathogenic care in Criterion C).

*DSM-IV, p. 118.

CHAPTER 21

Adjustment Disorders

ADJUSTMENT DISORDERS ARE A large part of clinical practice and often the most rewarding conditions to treat. Using *DSM-IV*, clinicians diagnosed adjustment disorders in about 10% of adults and 32% of adolescents. Adjustment disorders can be disruptive and distressing, yet with time and treatment, they resolve; in fact, many patients emerge healthier and wiser.

Adjustment disorders are the most benign of mental disorders, but more severe than "normal" problems in living (e.g., uncomplicated bereavement, marital problems). Thus, adjustment disorders *are* psychopathology and their diagnoses *are* critical: When adjustment disorders are dismissed as normal problems in living, clinicians risk underestimating the seriousness of the patient's difficulties, such as truancy, financial disaster, or suicidal intent. On the other hand, when adjustment disorders are misdiagnosed as a more ominous condition, the patient may receive inappropriate medication, psychotherapy, or even hospitalization.

Clinical Presentation

Adjustment disorders, according to *DSM-IV*, involve maladaptive reactions to psychosocial stressors occurring within the past three months; the disorders are self-limiting (less than six months) and are not due to another mental disorder. In other words, these are relatively benign, transient, but maladaptive situational reactions. Table 21–1 lists *DSM-IV* criteria for adjustment disorders.

To qualify as maladaptive, a reaction must impair function, or it must be stronger or last longer than a "normal" person's reaction to the same stressor. These reactions constitute relatively persisting patterns of behav-

TABLE 21–1
DSM-IV* Criteria for Adjustment Disorders

A. The development of emotional or behavioral symptoms in response to an identifiable stressor(s) occurring within 3 months of the onset of the stressor(s).

B. These symptoms or behaviors are clinically significant as evidenced by either of the following:

    (1) marked distress that is in excess of what would be expected from exposure to the stressor
    (2) significant impairment in social or occupational (academic) functioning

C. The stress-related disturbance does not meet the criteria for another specific Axis I disorder and is not merely an exacerbation of a preexisting Axis I or Axis II disorder.

D. The symptoms do not represent Bereavement.

E. Once the stressor (or its consequences) has terminated, the symptoms do not persist for more than an additional 6 months.
Specify if:
Acute: if the disturbance lasts less than 6 months
Chronic: if the disturbance lasts for 6 months or longer

* *DSM-IV*, pp. 626–27.

iors, not single acts. On watching his house burn down, a frightened man starts smashing his neighbor's windows. His reaction, although excessive, is limited to this outburst; subsequently, he experiences nothing but the expected sadness and frustration. This man does *not* have adjustment disorder.

Steve Walsh did. Extremely bright and bored by school, at 16 Steve began to skip classes and to peddle marijuana and cocaine. Prior to these behaviors, he had been a good student and had never sold drugs. School officials and the police dragged in Steve, who dragged in his parents. While upstairs in his room one evening, Steve overheard one of his parents' many screaming matches. Steve says that his mother yelled at her husband, "My psychiatrist says I need tranquilizers because you're such a bastard," to which his father replied, "At least I didn't breed that delinquent bastard son of yours." Although Mrs. Walsh tried hushing her husband so Steve wouldn't hear, it was too late. Stunned at first, Steve turned up his stereo earphones to blast and empty his mind. At three in the morning, Steve quietly emerged, grabbed his mother's barbiturates, fled Dayton, drove to Cleveland, and began selling the barbiturates on the street. Steve hated living on the street, but had no place to go. He felt unloved and unwanted; Steve wanted his parents, but refused to call them. Five days later, his father tracked him down, scooped him up, and returned him to Dayton on the condition that the entire family would get therapy. Steve desperately wanted to get away from home and attend a challenging private school. The parents agreed, partly for Steve's sake, but also because they wanted to improve their relationship without Steve's acting up constantly (and "conveniently") distracting them. The plan worked.

Adjustment disorders present with *generalized* symptoms (e.g., disruptions of mood or conduct) as opposed to *specific* ones (e.g., hallucinations, delusions, phobias, and panic attacks). Depression and anxiety are the most frequent mood disturbances. Except for suicide attempts, depressive symptoms are more common in adults (87%) than adolescents (64%), whereas conduct (or behavioral) problems are more prevalent in adolescents (77%) than adults (25%). Suicidal thoughts are more often reported by adults (36% versus 29%), but among those having these thoughts, adolescents (86%) attempt suicide more than adults (47%). Conduct problems among adolescents include truancy, drinking, temper outbursts, vandalism, school suspension, persistent lying, and repeated arrests.

The beginning clinician's most common mistake is to diagnose *adjustment disorders* with depressed mood when the person really has a *major depressive disorder*. If a patient meets criteria for major depression following a major stressor like being fired from work, the diagnosis is still major depression. Even if it seems like the depression was entirely caused by the stressor, people with this form of major depression are more likely than normals to have major depression in their families, in their pasts, and in their futures.

The stressor can be just about anything: It may be acute or chronic, single, or multiple, affect individuals or groups; it may be associated with a specific event or a developmental stage. The stressor's impact varies according to its duration, timing, context, and meaning, and so the severity of any particular stressor depends on the particular individual. (Indicate the nature of the stressor on Axis IV.) For adults, the most common stressors are marital problems (25%), separation or divorce (23%), relocation (17%), finances (14%), and work (9%). For adolescents, they are school problems (60%), parental rejection (27%), substance abuse (26%), parental separation or divorce (25%), boyfriend-girlfriend problems (20%), and parental marital problems (18%). Death of a loved one affected a mere 3% of the adults and 11.5% of the adolescents (Andreasen & Wasek, 1980).

As seen in criterion E of Table 21-1, the diagnosis of an adjustment disorder requires an assumption, or a reasonable prediction, that the patient's symptoms will remit within six months after the stressor has ended.

Clinical Course

In most cases, once the precipitating stressor disappears, so does the adjustment disorder. In a study of 2,078 male Navy enlistees hospitalized for adjustment disorders, their average inpatient stay was two weeks, with 90% returning to full active duty. Those who didn't return were young and had fewer occupational skills (Looney & Gunderson, 1978).

In nearly every respect, adults fare better than adolescents. Adjustment disorders in adolescents are more severe, last longer, require more treatment, and have worse outcomes. Three- to five-year follow-ups revealed 59–71% of adults functioning well, but only 44% of adolescents doing so. Among those doing poorly in both groups, mood, antisocial personality, and substance-use disorders were common, but suicide was rare (2–4%).

Overall, the most reliable predictors of poor outcome were the chronicity of the adjustment disorder, being younger, the frequency of misconduct symptoms, and the number of stressors. Depressive symptoms did *not* predict outcome (Andreasen & Hoenk, 1982).

Epidemiology

Although adjustment disorders are common, few epidemiologic studies have been conducted. Adjustment disorders have been diagnosed in 5% of inpatients, 20% of outpatients, and three times as often in adolescents as adults. However, clinicians may overdiagnose adjustment disorders because of their benign connotations. Their prevalence among various sexes, races, and classes is unknown.

Etiology and Pathogenesis

When *normal* responses to stress are intensified, prolonged, or blocked, they produce either (the milder) adjustment disorders or (the more severe) post-traumatic stress disorder. Responses to stress—normal or pathological—evolve in stages, as previously described (see Figure 4–3). A common adjustment disorder that follows this sequence is the classic "mid-life crisis." In *crisis theory*, Caplan (1964) proposed that people may emerge from such a crisis better off than before; they may develop greater maturity, ego-strength, wisdom, or self-confidence.

It's unknown why some patients react to a stressor with an adjustment disorder, some with a post-traumatic stress disorder, and some with no difficulties at all. Only a few clues exist: Neurologic and personality disorders may predispose patients to developing adjustment disorders; however, except for having alcoholic fathers, no other family traits have been associated with these disorders. Vaillant's (1971) lifetime study of Harvard graduates indicated that those who started with more primitive defenses (e.g., denial and projection) fared more poorly with life crises than those with more adaptive defenses (e.g., sublimation).

Differential Diagnosis

Adjustment disorder should not be diagnosed until "normal *problems in living*" and other mental disorders have been ruled out. *DSM-IV* includes these normal problems in living under "Other Conditions That May Be a Focus of Clinical Attention," and they're outlined in Appendix I. Adjustment disorders differ from these conditions either by impairing functioning or by exceeding the normally expected reactions to a particular stressor. These distinctions are relative and require clinical judgment.

Unlike *post-traumatic stress disorder* (PTSD), which has a delayed onset subtype, adjustment disorder must occur within three months of the stressor. The stressors producing adjustment disorder are "typical" (e.g., marital problems, retirement), whereas those that generate PTSD are unusual, often beyond normal human experience, catastrophic, frequently affecting multitudes (e.g., "Jonestown," plane crash, combat experience, earthquake). Adjustment disorder is briefer and less severe than PTSD.

When a psychosocial stress exacerbates a medical illness, instead of adjustment reaction, the preferred diagnosis is *psychological factors affecting physical condition*. If a stressor aggravates a *personality disorder*, an adjustment disorder is diagnosed only when a new symptom appears that is not central to the personality disorder. For example, after her last child leaves home for college, a mother with a histrionic personality disorder becomes uncharacteristically withdrawn.

Management and Treatment

The main controversy concerning the treatment of adjustment disorders is whether to treat them at all. Although most patients recover fully with therapy, many do not. The arguments against treatment are that because (by definition) adjustment disorders are time-limited, treatment wastes the patient's time, money, and effort. Patients may be harmed by interfering with the natural recovery process (at least in theory). Additional problems might be generated: Patients may become "therapy addicts"; or they may be unable to cope with a newly discovered set of difficulties—how much they hate their fathers, how little they love their spouses; or, if therapy is a bust, they may terminate more discouraged than ever.

The arguments in favor of therapy contend that, because clinicians can never really know in advance whether patients will fully recover, if nothing else, treatment can minimize adverse consequences, such as preventing patients from making dumb, spur-of-the-moment, irreversible decisions. Therapy could also hasten recovery, stop patients from blowing matters out of proportion, and enable them to avert similar crises in the future.

Experts generally believe that treatment should be based on Caplan's (1964) crisis intervention model. Accordingly, the primary goal of treatment is to have patients return to baseline; the secondary goal, or possibility, is to capitalize on the emotional turmoil of the crisis to change some longstanding maladaptive patterns into more useful and self-satisfying ones. In this model, treatment is brief, time-limited, and focused exclusively on problems linked to the stressor. (About half the patients who enter brief psychotherapy for adjustment disorders finish in four weeks.)

The most frequently used treatment is *individual psychotherapy*, which identifies the stressor, examines how it affects the patient, and discusses how the patient should deal with it. *Family therapy* is the second most widely used treatment. When the family plays a major role in the adjustment disorder, family treatment can follow the same principles of crisis intervention. *Medications* might be used temporarily as long as there is a clear target symptom (e.g., insomnia, anxiety), which impairs functioning or slows recovery.

APPENDIX A

DSM-IV Classification: Axis I and II Categories and Codes*

*American Psychiatric Association (1994). *Diagnostic and statistical manual of mental disorders (4th ed.)*. Washington, DC: American Psychiatric Press, pp. 13–24.

Note: These codes are preliminary and are subject to further updates and modifications after additional consultations.

DISORDERS USUALLY FIRST DIAGNOSED IN INFANCY, CHILDHOOD, OR ADOLESCENCE

Mental retardation
Note: These are coded on Axis II.
317	Mild mental retardation
318.0	Moderate mental retardation
318.1	Severe mental retardation
318.2	Profound mental retardation
319	Mental retardation, severity un— specified

Learning disorders
315.00	Reading disorder
315.1	Mathematics disorder
315.2	Disorder of written expression
315.9	Learning disorder NOS

Motor skills disorder
315.4	Developmental coordination disorder

Communication disorders
315.31	Expressive language disorder
315.31	Mixed receptive/expressive language disorder
315.39	Phonological disorder
307.0	Stuttering
307.9	Communication disorder NOS

Pervasive developmental disorders
299.00	Autistic disorder
299.80	Rett's disorder
299.10	Childhood disintegrative disorder
299.80	Asperger's disorder
299.80	Pervasive developmental disorder NOS

Attention-deficit and disruptive behavior disorders
314.xx	Attention-deficit/hyperactivity disorder
.01	combined type
.00	predominantly inattentive type
.01	predominantly hyperactive-impulsive type
314.9	Attention-deficit/hyperactivity disorder NOS
313.81	Oppositional defiant disorder

312.8	Conduct disorder
312.9	Disruptive behavior disorder NOS

Feeding and eating disorders of infancy or early childhood
307.52	Pica
307.53	Rumination disorder
307.59	Feeding disorder of infancy or early childhood

Tic disorders
307.23	Tourette's disorder
307.22	Chronic motor or vocal tic disorder
307.21	Transient tic disorder
307.20	Tic disorder NOS

Elimination disorders
787.6	Encopresis with constipation and overflow incontinence
307.7	Encopresis without constipation and overflow incontinence
307.6	Enuresis (not due to a general medical condition)

Other disorders of infancy, childhood, or adolescence
309.21	Separation anxiety disorder
313.23	Selective mutism
313.89	Reactive attachment disorder of infancy or early childhood
307.3	Stereotypic movement disorder
313.9	Disorder of infancy, childhood, or adolescence NOS

DELIRIUM, DEMENTIA, AMNESTIC AND OTHER COGNITIVE DISORDERS

Delirium
293.0	Delirium due to [*indicate general medical condition*]
___.__	Substance-intoxication delirium (*refer to substance-related disorders for substance-specific codes*)
___.__	Substance withdrawal delirium (*refer to substance-related disorders for substance-specific codes*)
___.__	Delirium due to multiple etiologies (*code each of the specific etiologies*)
780.09	Delirium NOS

Dementia
290.xx Dementia of the Alzheimer's type
With Early Onset: at age 65 or before

.10   uncomplicated
.11   with delirium
.12   with delusions
.13   with depressed mood
With late onset: after age 65
.00   uncomplicated
.30   with delirium
.20   with delusions
.21   with depressed mood
Vascular dementia
.40   uncomplicated
.41   with delirium
.42   with delusions
.43   with depressed mood

Dementia due to other general medical conditions

294.9   Dementia due to HIV disease *(also code 043.1 on Axis III)*
294.1   Dementia due to head trauma *(also code 854.00 on Axis III)*
294.1   Dementia due to Parkinson's disease *(also code 332.0 on Axis III)*
294.1   Dementia due to Huntington's disease *(also code 333.4 on Axis III)*
290.10   Dementia due to Pick's disease *(also code 331.1 on Axis III)*
290.10   Dementia due to Creutzfeldt-Jakob disease *(also code 046.1 on Axis III)*
294.1   Dementia due to *[indicate general medical condition not listed above]*
___.__   Substance-induced persisting dementia *(refer to substance-related disorder for substance-specific codes)*
___.__   Dementia due to multiple etiologies *(code each of the specific etiologies)*
294.8   Dementia NOS

Amnestic disorders

294.0   Amnestic disorder due to *[indicate general medical condition]*
___.__   Substance-induced persisting amnestic disorder *(refer to substance-related disorders for specific substance-specific codes)*
294.8   Amnestic disorder NOS

Other cognitive disorders

294.9   Cognitive disorder NOS

MENTAL DISORDERS DUE TO A GENERAL MEDICAL CONDITION NOT ELSEWHERE CLASSIFIED

293.89   Catatonic disorder due to *[indicate general medical condition]*
310.1   Personality change due to *[indicate general medical condition]*
293.9   Mental disorder NOS due to *[indicate general medical condition]*

SUBSTANCE-RELATED DISORDERS

Alcohol use disorders
303.90   Alcohol dependence
305.00   Alcohol abuse

Alcohol-induced disorders
303.00   Alcohol intoxication
291.8   Alcohol withdrawal
291.0   Alcohol intoxication delirium
291.0   Alcohol withdrawal delirium
291.2   Alcohol-induced persisting dementia
291.1   Alcohol-induced persisting amnestic disorder
291.x   Alcohol-induced psychotic disorder
.5   with delusions
.3   with hallucinations
291.8   Alcohol-induced mood disorder
291.8   Alcohol-induced anxiety disorder
291.8   Alcohol-induced sexual dysfunction
291.8   Alcohol-induced sleep disorder
291.9   Alcohol-related disorder NOS

Amphetamine use disorders
304.40   Amphetamine dependence
305.70   Amphetamine abuse

Amphetamine-induced disorders
292.89   Amphetamine intoxication
292.0   Amphetamine withdrawal
292.81   Amphetamine intoxication delirium
292.xx   Amphetamine-induced psychotic disorder
.11   with delusions
.12   with hallucinations
292.84   Amphetamine-induced mood disorder
292.89   Amphetamine-induced anxiety disorder

292.89 Amphetamine-induced sexual dysfunction
292.89 Amphetamine-induced sleep disorder
292.9   Amphetamine-related disorder
NOS

Caffeine-induced disorders
305.90 Caffeine intoxication
292.89 Caffeine-induced anxiety disorder
292.89 Caffeine-induced sleep disorder
292.9   Caffeine-related disorder NOS

Cannabis use disorders
304.30 Cannabis dependence
305.20 Cannabis abuse

Cannabis-induced disorders
292.89 Cannabis intoxication
292.81 Cannabis intoxication delirium
292.xx Cannabis-induced psychotic disorder
 .11   with delusions
 .12   with hallucinations
292.89 Cannabis-induced anxiety disorder
292.9   Cannabis-related disorder NOS

Cocaine use disorders
304.20 Cocaine dependence
305.60 Cocaine abuse

Cocaine-induced disorders
292.89 Cocaine intoxication
292.0   Cocaine withdrawal
292.81 Cocaine intoxication delirium
292.xx Cocaine-induced psychotic disorder
 .11   with delusions
 .12   with hallucinations
292.84 Cocaine-induced mood disorder
292.89 Cocaine-induced anxiety disorder
292.89 Cocaine-induced sexual dysfunction
292.89 Cocaine-induced sleep disorder
292.9   Cocaine-related disorder NOS

Hallucinogen use disorders
304.50 Hallucinogen dependence
305.30 Hallucinogen abuse

Hallucinogen induced disorders
292.89 Hallucinogen intoxication
292.89 Hallucinogen persisting perception
disorder (flashbacks)

292.81 Hallucinogen intoxication delirium
292.xx Hallucinogen-induced psychotic
disorder
 .11   with delusions
 .12   with hallucinations
292.84 Hallucinogen-induced mood disorder
292.89 Hallucinogen-induced anxiety disorder
292.9   Hallucinogen-related disorder
NOS

Inhalant use disorders
304.60 Inhalant dependence
305.90 Inhalant abuse

Inhalant-induced disorders
292.89 Inhalant intoxication
292.81 Inhalant intoxication delirium
292.82 Inhalant-induced persisting dementia
292.xx Inhalant-induced psychotic disorder
 .11   with delusions
 .12   with hallucinations
292.84 Inhalant-induced mood disorder
292.89 Inhalant-induced anxiety disorder
292.9   Inhalant-related disorder NOS

Nicotine use disorders
305.10 Nicotine dependence

Nicotine-induced disorders
292.0   Nicotine withdrawal
292.9   Nicotine-related disorder NOS

Opioid use disorders
304.00 Opioid dependence
305.50 Opioid abuse

Opioid-induced disorders
292.89 Opioid intoxication
292.0   Opioid withdrawal
292.81 Opioid intoxication delirium
292.xx Opioid-induced psychotic
disorder
 .11   with delusions
 .12   with hallucinations
292.84 Opioid-induced mood disorder
292.89 Opioid-induced sexual dysfunction
292.89 Opioid-induced sleep disorder
292.9   Opioid-related disorder NOS

Phencyclidine use disorders
304.90   Phencyclidine dependence
305.90   Phencyclidine abuse

Phencyclidine-induced disorders
292.89   Phencyclidine intoxication
292.81   Phencyclidine intoxication delirium
292.xx   Phencyclidine-induced psychotic disorder
   .11   with delusions
   .12   with hallucinations
292.84   Phencyclidine-induced mood disorder
292.89   Phencyclidine-induced anxiety disorder
292.9   Phencyclidine-related use disorder NOS

Sedative, hypnotic, or anxiolytic use disorders
304.10   Sedative, hypnotic, or anxiolytic dependence
305.40   Sedative, hypnotic, or anxiolytic abuse

Sedative, hypnotic, or anxiolytic use disorders
292.89   Sedative, hypnotic, or anxiolytic intoxication
292.0   Sedative, hypnotic, or anxiolytic withdrawal
292.81   Sedative, hypnotic, or anxiolytic intoxication delirium
292.81   Sedative, hypnotic, or anxiolytic withdrawal delirium
292.82   Sedative-, hypnotic-, or anxiolytic-induced persisting dementia
292.83   Sedative-, hypnotic-, or anxiolytic-induced persisting amnestic disorder
292.xx   Sedative-, hypnotic-, or anxiolytic-induced psychotic disorder
   .11   with delusions
   .12   with hallucinations
292.84   Sedative-, hypnotic-, or anxiolytic-induced mood disorder
292.89   Sedative-, hypnotic-, or anxiolytic-induced anxiety disorder
292.89   Sedative-, hypnotic-, or anxiolytic-induced sexual dysfunction
292.89   Sedative-, hypnotic-, or anxiolytic-induced sleep disorder
292.9   Sedative-, hypnotic-, or anxiolytic-related use disorder NOS

Polysubstance-related disorder
304.80   Polysubstance dependence

Other (or unknown) substance use disorders
304.90   Other (or unknown) substance dependence
305.90   Other (or unknown) substance abuse

Other (or unknown) substance-induced disorders
292.89   Other (or unknown) substance intoxication
292.0   Other (or unknown) substance withdrawal
292.81   Other (or unknown) substance-induced delirium
292.82   Other (or unknown) substance-induced persisting dementia
292.83   Other (or unknown) substance-induced persisting amnestic disorder
292.xx   Other (or unknown) substance-induced psychotic disorder
   .11   with delusions
   .12   with hallucinations
292.84   Other (or unknown) substance-induced mood disorder
292.89   Other (or unknown) substance-induced anxiety disorder
292.89   Other (or unknown) substance-induced sexual dysfunction
292.89   Other (or unknown) substance-induced sleep disorder
292.9   Other (or unknown) substance-induced disorder NOS

SCHIZOPHRENIA AND OTHER PSYCHOTIC DISORDERS

295.xx   Schizophrenia
   .30   paranoid type
   .10   disorganized type
   .20   catatonic type
   .90   undifferentiated type
   .60   residual type
295.40   Schizophreniform disorder
295.70   Schizoaffective disorder
297.1   Delusional disorder
298.8   Brief psychotic disorder
297.3   Shared psychotic disorder

293.xx   Psychotic disorder due to [*indicate general medical condition*]
.81   with delusions
.82   with hallucinations
____.__   Substance-induced psychotic disorder (*refer to substance-related disorders for substance-specific codes*)
298.9   Psychotic disorder NOS

MOOD DISORDERS

Code current state of major depressive disorder or bipolar I disorder in fifth digit:
1 = mild
2 = moderate
3 = severe, without psychotic features
4 = severe, with psychotic features
5 = in partial remission
6 = in full remission
0 = unspecified

Depressive disorders
296.xx   Major depressive disorder
.2x   single episode
.3x   recurrent
300.4   Dysthymic disorder
311   Depressive disorder NOS

Bipolar disorders
296.xx   Bipolar I Disorder
.0x   single manic episode
.40   most recent episode hypomanic
.4x   most recent episode manic
.6x   most recent episode mixed
.5x   most recent episode depressed
.7   most recent episode unspecified
296.89   Bipolar II disorder
301.13   Cyclothymic disorder
296.80   Bipolar disorder NOS
293.83   Mood disorder due to [*indicate general medical condition*]
____.__   Substance-induced mood disorder (*refer to substance-related disorders for substance-specific codes*)
296.90   Mood disorder NOS

ANXIETY DISORDERS

300.01   Panic disorder without agoraphobia

300.21   Panic disorder with agoraphobia
300.22   Agoraphobia without history of panic disorder
300.29   Specific phobia
300.23   Social phobia
300.3   Obsessive-compulsive disorder
309.81   Posttraumatic stress disorder
308.3   Acute stress disorder
300.02   Generalized anxiety disorder
293.89   Anxiety disorder due to [*indicate general medical condition*]
____.__   Substance-induced anxiety disorder (*refer to substance-related disorders for substance-specific codes*)
300.00   Anxiety disorder NOS

SOMATOFORM DISORDERS

300.81   Somatization disorder
300.81   Undifferentiated somatization disorder
300.11   Conversion disorder
307.xx   Pain disorder
.80   associated with psychological factors
.89   associated with both psychological factors and a general medical condition
300.7   Hypochondriasis
300.7   Body dysmorphic disorder
300.81   Somatoform disorder NOS

FACTITIOUS DISORDERS

300.xx   Factitious disorder
.16   with predominantly psychological signs and symptoms
.19   with predominantly physical signs and symptoms
.19   with combined psychological and physical signs and symptoms
300.19   Factitious disorder NOS

DISSOCIATIVE DISORDERS

300.12   Dissociative amnesia
300.13   Dissociative fugue
300.14   Dissociative identity disorder
300.6   Depersonalization disorder
300.15   Dissociative disorder NOS

SEXUAL AND GENDER IDENTITY DISORDERS

Sexual desire disorders
302.71   Hypoactive sexual desire disorder
302.79   Sexual aversion disorder

Sexual arousal disorders
302.72   Female sexual arousal disorder
302.72   Male erectile disorder

Orgasm disorders
302.73   Female orgasmic disorder
302.74   Male orgasmic disorder
302.75   Premature ejaculation

Sexual pain disorders
302.76   Dyspareunia (not due to a general medical condition)
306.51   Vaginismus (not due to a general medical condition)

Sexual dysfunction due to a general medical condition
625.8   Female hypoactive sexual desire disorder due to [indicate general medical condition]
608.89   Male hypoactive sexual desire disorder due to [indicate general medical condition]
607.84   Male erectile disorder due to [indicate general medical condition]
625.0   Female dyspareunia due to [indicate general medical condition]
608.89   Male dyspareunia due to [indicate general medical condition]
625.8   Other female sexual dysfunction due to [indicate general medical condition]
608.89   Other male sexual dysfunction due to [indicate general medical condition]
___.___ Substance-induced sexual dysfunction (refer to substance-related disorders for substance-specific codes)
302.70   Sexual dysfunction NOS

Paraphilias
302.4   Exhibitionism
302.81   Fetishism
302.89   Frotteurism
302.2   Pedophilia

302.83   Sexual masochism
302.84   Sexual sadism
302.3   Transvestic fetishism
302.82   Voyeurism
302.9   Paraphilia NOS

Gender identity disorders
302.xx   Gender identity disorder
   .6   in children
   .85   in adolescents and adults
302.6   Gender identity disorder NOS
302.9   Sexual disorder NOS

EATING DISORDERS

307.1   Anorexia nervosa
307.51   Bulimia nervosa
307.50   Eating disorder NOS

SLEEP DISORDERS

Dyssomnias
307.42   Primary insomnia
307.44   Primary hypersomnia
347   Narcolepsy
780.59   Breathing-related sleep disorder
307.45   Circadian rhythm sleep disorder
307.47   Dyssomnia NOS

Parasomnias
307.47   Nightmare disorder
307.46   Sleep terror disorder
307.46   Sleepwalking disorder
307.47   Parasomnia NOS

Sleep disorders related to another mental disorder
307.42   Insomnia related to [indicate the Axis I or Axis II disorder]
307.44   Hypersomnia related to [Indicate the Axis I or Axis II disorder]

Other sleep disorders
780.xx   Sleep disorder due to [indicate the general medical condition]
   .52   insomnia type
   .54   hypersomnia type
   .59   parasomnia type
   .59   mixed type
___.___ substance-induced sleep disorder (refer to substance-related disorders for substance-specific codes)

IMPULSE-CONTROL DISORDERS NOT ELSEWHERE CLASSIFIED

312.34   Intermittent explosive disorder
312.32   Kleptomania
312.33   Pyromania
312.31   Pathological gambling
312.39   Trichotillomania
312.30   Impulse-control disorder NOS

ADJUSTMENT DISORDERS

309.xx   Adjustment disorder
.0   with depressed mood
.24   with anxiety
.28   with mixed anxiety and de-
         pressed mood
.3   with disturbance of conduct
.4   with mixed disturbance of
         emotions and conduct
.9   unspecified

PERSONALITY DISORDERS

Note: *These are coded on Axis II.*
301.0   Paranoid personality disorder
301.20   Schizoid personality disorder
301.22   Schizotypal personality disorder
301.7   Antisocial personality disorder
301.83   Borderline personality disorder
301.50   Histrionic personality disorder
301.81   Narcissistic personality disorder
301.82   Avoidant personality disorder
301.6   Dependent personality disorder
301.4   Obsessive-compulsive personality
         disorder
301.9   Personality disorder NOS

OTHER CONDITIONS THAT MAY BE A FOCUS OF CLINICAL ATTENTION

Psychological factors affecting medical condition
316   *[Specified psychological factors]*
         affecting *[indicate general medical
         condition]*
Choose name based on nature of factors:
         Mental disorder affecting medical
         condition
         Psychological symptoms affecting
         medical condition
         Personality traits or coping style af-
         fecting medical condition
         Maladaptive health behaviors af-
         fecting medical condition

         Stress-related physiological re-
         sponse affecting medical condi-
         tion
         Other or unspecified psychological
         factors affecting medical condition

Medication-induced movement disorders
332.1   Neuroleptic-induced Parkinsonism
333.92   Neuroleptic malignant syndrome
333.7   Neuroleptic-induced acute dys-
         tonia
333.99   Neuroleptic-induced acute akath-
         isia
333.82   Neuroleptic-induced tardive dyski-
         nesia
333.1   Medication-induced postural
         tremor
333.90   Medication-induced movement
         disorder NOS

Other medication-induced disorder
995.2   Adverse effects of medication
         NOS

Relational problems
V61.9   Relational problem related to a
         mental disorder or general medical
         condition
V61.20   Parent-child relational problem
V61.1   Partner relational problem
V61.8   Sibling relational problem
V62.81   Relational problem NOS

Problems related to abuse or neglect
V61.21   Physical abuse of child
V61.21   Sexual abuse of child
V61.21   Neglect of child
V61.1   Physical abuse of adult
V61.1   Sexual abuse of adult

Additional conditions that may be a focus of clinical attention
V15.81   Noncompliance with treatment
V65.2   Malingering
V71.01   Adult antisocial behavior
V71.02   Childhood or adolescent antisocial
         behavior
V62.89   Borderline intellectual functioning
         Note: *This is coded on Axis II.*
780.9   Age-related cognitive decline
V62.82   Bereavement
V62.3   Academic problem
V62.2   Occupational problem
313.82   Identity problem
V62.89   Religious or spiritual problem

V62.4   Acculturation problem
V62.89 Phase of life problem

ADDITIONAL CODES

300.9   Unspecified mental disorder (non-
        psychotic)

V71.09 No diagnosis or condition on
        Axis I
799.9   Diagnosis or condition deferred on
        Axis I
V71.0   No diagnosis on Axis II
799.9   Diagnosis deferred on Axis II

DSM-IV Axis IV Classification

The following problem categories may be noted on Axis IV; each is followed by a list of examples.

Problems with primary support group such as death of a family member, health problems in family, disruption of family by separation, divorce, or estrangement, removal from the home, remarriage of parent, sexual or physical abuse, parental overprotection, neglect of child, inadequate discipline, discord with siblings, birth of a sibling.

Problems related to the social environment such as death or loss of friend, inadequate social support, living alone, difficulty with acculturation, discrimination, adjustment to life cycle transition (e.g., retirement).

Educational problems such as illiteracy, academic problems, discord with teachers or classmates, inadequate school environment.

Occupational problems such as unemployment, threat of job loss, stressful work schedule, difficult work condition, job dissatisfaction, job change, discord with boss or co-workers.

Housing problems such as homelessness, inadequate housing, unsafe neighborhood, discord with neighbors or landlord.

Economic problems such as extreme poverty, inadequate finances, insufficient welfare support.

Problems with access to health care services such as inadequate health care services, transportation to health care facilities unavailable, inadequate health insurance.

Problems related to interaction with the legal system/crime such as arrest, incarceration, litigation, victim of crime.

Other psychosocial problems such as exposure to disasters, war, or other hostilities, discord with non-family caregivers (e.g., counselor, social worker, physician), unavailability of social service agencies.

APPENDIX C

DSM-IV Axis V Classification: Global Assessment of Functioning (GAF) Scale*

Consider psychological, social, and occupational functioning on a hypothetical continuum of mental health-illness. Do not include impairment in functioning due to physical (or environmental) limitations.

Code (**Note:** Use intermediate codes when appropriate, e.g., 45, 68, 72.)

---

*The GAF Scale is a revision of the GAS (Endicott J., Spitzer R.L., Fleiss, et al. [1976]. The Global Assessment Scale: A procedure for measuring overall severity of psychiatric disturbance. *Archives of General Psychiatry*, *33*, 766–771). This is a revision of the Health-Sickness Rating Scale (Luborsky, L. [1962]. Clinicians' judgments of mental health. *Archives of General Psychiatry*, 7;407-417). In *DSM-IV*, p. 32.

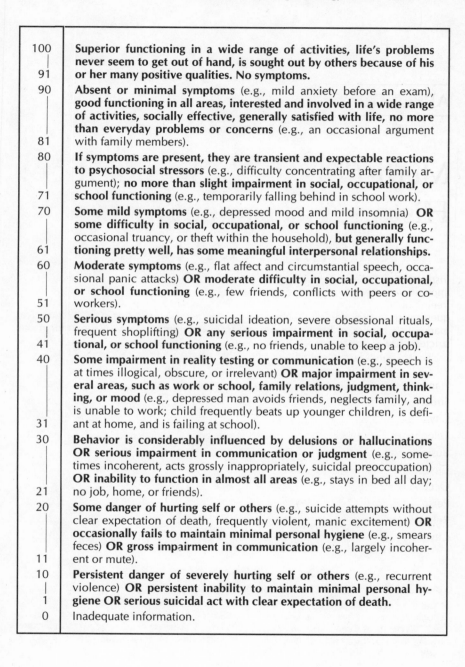

100 | 91	Superior functioning in a wide range of activities, life's problems never seem to get out of hand, is sought out by others because of his or her many positive qualities. No symptoms.
90 | | | 81	Absent or minimal symptoms (e.g., mild anxiety before an exam), good functioning in all areas, interested and involved in a wide range of activities, socially effective, generally satisfied with life, no more than everyday problems or concerns (e.g., an occasional argument with family members).
80 | | 71	If symptoms are present, they are transient and expectable reactions to psychosocial stressors (e.g., difficulty concentrating after family argument); no more than slight impairment in social, occupational, or school functioning (e.g., temporarily falling behind in school work).
70 | | 61	Some mild symptoms (e.g., depressed mood and mild insomnia) OR some difficulty in social, occupational, or school functioning (e.g., occasional truancy, or theft within the household), but generally functioning pretty well, has some meaningful interpersonal relationships.
60 | | 51	Moderate symptoms (e.g., flat affect and circumstantial speech, occasional panic attacks) OR moderate difficulty in social, occupational, or school functioning (e.g., few friends, conflicts with peers or coworkers).
50 | 41	Serious symptoms (e.g., suicidal ideation, severe obsessional rituals, frequent shoplifting) OR any serious impairment in social, occupational, or school functioning (e.g., no friends, unable to keep a job).
40 | | | 31	Some impairment in reality testing or communication (e.g., speech is at times illogical, obscure, or irrelevant) OR major impairment in several areas, such as work or school, family relations, judgment, thinking, or mood (e.g., depressed man avoids friends, neglects family, and is unable to work; child frequently beats up younger children, is defiant at home, and is failing at school).
30 | | 21	Behavior is considerably influenced by delusions or hallucinations OR serious impairment in communication or judgment (e.g., sometimes incoherent, acts grossly inappropriately, suicidal preoccupation) OR inability to function in almost all areas (e.g., stays in bed all day; no job, home, or friends).
20 | | 11	Some danger of hurting self or others (e.g., suicide attempts without clear expectation of death, frequently violent, manic excitement) OR occasionally fails to maintain minimal personal hygiene (e.g., smears feces) OR gross impairment in communication (e.g., largely incoherent or mute).
10 | 1	Persistent danger of severely hurting self or others (e.g., recurrent violence) OR persistent inability to maintain minimal personal hygiene OR serious suicidal act with clear expectation of death.
0	Inadequate information.

Medical-Psychiatric History Form

Instructions: Please complete this form and return it to your therapist at your next appointment. By doing so, you will provide important diagnostic information while freeing-up time with your therapist for other matters. If you are unsure about a question or are unable to answer it, don't worry about it: Simply place a question mark ("?") next to it and move on. Everything you indicate will be held in the strictest confidence.

PATIENT DATA

Name_____ Today's Date_____

Street Address_____

City_____ State_____ Zip_____

Telephone <home>_____ <work>_____

Business Street Address_____

City_____ State_____ Zip_____

Occupation_____ Age_____ Birth Date_____

Person to contact in case of emergency: Name_____

Relation_____ Telephone_____

City_____ State_____ Zip_____

MEDICAL HISTORY

Your Physician's Name_____

Street Address_____ City_____

State_____ Zip_____ Telephone (   )_____

Are you allergic to any drugs? yes ( ) no ( ). If so, to which ones:

_____

Do you have any other allergies? yes ( ) no ( ). If so, to what:

_____

Are you pregnant? yes ( ) no ( ). Do you smoke? yes ( ) no ( ).
When was your last EKG?_____ Was it normal? yes ( ) no ( ).
When did your physician last examine you?_____
Have you been treated for any of the following:

AIDS, or acquired immune deficiency syndrome, or HIV positive ( )
Alcohol abuse ( ), alcoholism ( )
Anemia ( )
Asthma ( ), hay fever ( )
Cancer ( )
Diabetes ( )
Drug abuse or addiction ( )
Epilepsy, seizures, or convulsions ( )
Fainting spells, feeling light-headed, or dizziness ( )
Gastrointestinal problems ( )
Glaucoma ( )
Heart murmur or disease ( )
Hepatitis, liver disease, or jaundice ( )
High blood pressure [hypertension] ( )
Kidney disease ( )
Lung disease, pneumonia ( )
Migraine ( )
Rheumatic fever ( )
Serious injury or accident ( )
Stroke ( )
Thyroid problems ( )
Tuberculosis (TB) ( )
Ulcer ( )
Uncontrolled bleeding ( )
Venereal disease ( )
Other ( ) If so, what? _____

Please list any (prescription or over-the-counter) medication that you are currently
taking and reason.

_____

_____

Please list any street drugs that you have taken in the past.

_____

_____

Have you ever been treated for a psychiatric illness such as anxiety, depression,
insomnia, mania, psychosis? Yes ( ) No ( )

If yes, what were you treated for?_____ Who treated you? (Name and Address)
_____

Have you ever taken any psychiatric medication? Yes ( ) No ( )
If yes, please list them.
_____
_____

Hospitalizaton: List all your hospitalizations for both medical and psychiatric conditions.

Type of Illness/Operation	Hospital	Year

Alcohol use? _____ How many days per month? _____ Average amount in a day? _____
Have people ever annoyed you by criticizing your drinking? _____
Have you ever felt bad or guilty about your drinking? _____
Have you ever tried to cut down on your drinking? _____
Have you ever had a drink first thing in the morning to steady your nerves or get rid of a hangover? _____
Smoking? _____ How much per day? _____
Age began smoking? _____ Age stopped smoking? _____
Usual weight? _____lbs. Recent loss or gain? _____ Weight at age 20 _____
Average hours of sleep at night? _____

SYMPTOM LIST

PLACE A CHECK (✓) in front of any of the following that are or have been a problem for you. DOUBLE CHECK (✓ ✓) the main problems for you.

A. ____ Rashes, color change
____ Itching
____ Warts, moles
____ Eczema, lumps, hives
____ Very dry skin
____ Excessive sweating
____ Bleeding or bruising from minor injury
____ Anemia
____ Lymph node or gland swelling

B. ____ Ear trouble, infection
____ Hearing loss, ringing in your ears
____ Eye problems
____ Nosebleeds
____ Stuffy nose, sinus trouble, hayfever
____ Sore throats
____ Hoarseness
____ Dental or gum problems

C. ____ Enlarged or painful breasts
____ Breast lumps
____ Discharge from nipples

D. ____ Shortness of breath
____ Cough, chest colds
____ Bringing up sputum or blood
____ Wheezing, asthma
____ Chest pain, pleurisy
____ TB or exposure to TB
____ Fever, sweats, chills
____ Pneumonia

E. ____ Chest pain, tightness, pressure
____ Fast or irregular heartbeat
____ Trouble breathing when lying down
____ Waking short of breath
____ Swelling of feet or ankles
____ Previous heart trouble
____ Murmurs or rheumatic fever
____ High blood pressure
____ Poor circulation, varicose veins
____ Blood clots

F. ____ Pain or burning on urinating
____ Trouble starting or stopping urine
____ Blood or pus in urine
____ Frequent urinating
____ Waking to urinate (# of times/ night____)
____ Sores or discharge
____ Gonorrhea or syphilis

G. ____ Trouble swallowing
____ Poor appetite
____ Gas, cramps, pains
____ Heartburn, indigestion
____ Nausea, vomiting
____ Constipation, diarrhea
____ Blood in stool or black stool
____ Yellow jaundice, hepatitis
____ Hemorrhoids
____ Gall bladder problems
____ Hernia

H. ____ Pains in joints, arthritis
____ Swollen joints
____ Back pain, neck pain

I. ____ Head injury, concussion
____ Headaches
____ Dizziness, fainting
____ Convulsions, seizures, fits
____ Shaking, tremor
____ Weakness, paralysis
____ Numbness, tingling
____ Difficulty walking, coordination
____ Depression, anxiety
____ Poor sleeping
____ Nervousness, tension
____ Trouble thinking, remembering
____ Crying, upset, worrying
____ Sexual problems

J. ____ Cancer
____ Diabetes
____ Goiter, thyroid problem

FOR WOMEN ONLY

K. ____ Irregular or frequent periods
____ Very heavy periods
____ Spotting between periods
____ Painful periods
____ Vaginal discharge or itching

Age your first period started_____
Days between one period and start of next _____
Number of pregnancies _____
Living children _____
Number of miscarriages ___ abortions ___
Date of last period_____
Date of last cancer smear (PAP) _____
Did your mother take any hormones while she was pregnant with you?
Yes ( ) No ( ) Don't know ( )

APPENDIX E

Glossary of Psychopathologic Signs and Symptoms

Affect is the instantaneous, observable expression of emotion. It differs from mood (see below), which is a pervasive, subjectively experienced emotion. As the saying goes, "Affect is to mood as weather is to climate." Moods are symptoms; affects are signs. Commonly described affects are:

Blunted, flat, and constricted affects describe (in decreasing order of severity) patients who show almost no emotional lability, appear expressionless, look dulled, and speak in a monotone.

Broad affect is a normal range of affect.

Inappropriate affect is clearly discordant with the content of the patient's speech: A patient giggles while talking about his father's death.

Labile affect shows a range of expression in excess of cultural norms, with repeated, rapid, and abrupt shifts of emotion, as when a patient cries one moment and laughs the next. There are two types of labile affect: With "organic" etiologies, the lability of affect presents as a massive emotional overreaction to external stimuli, which is often part of a catastrophic reaction, and which the interviewer is usually unable to stop. With "functional" etiologies, the lability of affect is an overresponse to internal stimuli, which is less rapid and less extreme.

Alexithymia is a trait (see below) in which the patient has a constricted emotional life, diminished ability to fantasize, and a virtual inability to articulate emotions. Like anhedonia, alexithymia describes the absence of emotion, but in anhedonia, positive emotion seems blocked or stymied, whereas in alexithymia, it's as if no emotion exists. Patients will complain about anhedonia, but not about alexithymia. (See Anhedonia.)

Ambivalence is having two strongly opposite ideas or feelings at the same time, which render the individual virtually unable to respond or decide.

481

Amnesia is a pathological loss of memory. There are two types:

Anterograde amnesia is for events occurring after a significant point in time.

Retrograde amnesia is for events occurring before a significant point in time.

Anhedonia is a mood (see below) in which there is a pervasive inability to perceive and experience pleasure in actions and events that are normally pleasurable or satisfying for the individual or most individuals. Anhedonia often begins with the person trying to carry out the activity, hoping the anticipated pleasure will materialize. When it doesn't, in time the person loses all interest in the activity and tends to avoid it: A football freak ignores the Super Bowl; a devoted father is totally bored by his children; a civil-rights activist no longer cares. (Contrast "anhedonic" with "hedonistic." See Alexithymia).

Anorexia is a loss of appetite.

Anxiety can refer to a symptom or a syndrome. As a symptom, anxiety is a mood (see below) of inner tension, restlessness, uneasiness, or apprehension. As a syndrome, anxiety combines this (internal) mood with (external) physiologic signs, such as tremor, heart-pounding, hypervigilance, dilated pupils, and agitation. Anxiety is pathological only when it chronically interferes with a person's functioning. Whereas anxiety implies the absence of a consciously recognized, external threat, fear implies that such a threat exists. Anxiety focused on an up-coming event is called *anticipatory anxiety*; unfocused anxiety is called *free-floating anxiety*. (See Craving, Panic attack, Phobia.)

Autistic thinking is thought derived from fantasy: The person defines his environment based on internal fantasies instead of on external realities. Autistic thinking also refers to an individual being preoccupied with his own private world; social withdrawal into one's inner world usually results.

Blocking is when a person's train of thought abruptly and unexpectedly stops. Blocking may or may not be pathological, depending on the degree.

Catatonia is extreme psychomotor agitation or retardation. Catatonic patients seem driven, even when motionless; some appear frantic, others fanatical. (See Mutism, Posturing, Stereotypy.) Examples include:

Catatonic excitement is extreme overactivity seemingly unrelated to environmental stimuli.

Catatonic negativism is an apparently motiveless and extreme resistance to all instructions or attempts to be moved. Three manifestations of this negativism are (a) *catatonic posturing*, in which a bizarre position is rigidly held for long periods; (b) *catatonic rigidity*, in which the patient resists all efforts to be moved; and (c) *waxy flexibility*, in which the patient resists having his body moved, but ends up with parts of his body being "molded" into odd positions, as if they were pliable wax.

Cataplexy is a sudden, unexpected, purposeless, generalized, and temporary loss of muscle tone.

Clanging is a type of language in which the sound of a word, instead of its meaning, dictates the course of subsequent associations (e.g., "ding, dong, dell . . . ").

Clouding of consciousness is when the patient is awake and functioning, but has an incomplete or distorted awareness of the environment. It is a higher level of awareness than stupor (see below), in which an awake patient is unaware and unresponsive to the environment.

Circumstantiality is a pattern of speech, which although filled with detours, irrelevant details, and parenthetical remarks, eventually reaches its point; tangentiality (see below) is when the point isn't reached. Circumstantiality may, or may not be, pathological.

Coma is the most impaired end on a continuum of consciousness. Patients may be totally unresponsive to a (painful) stimulus, such as a pinprick, or may twitch, but not display any further evidence of awareness. Slightly better on this continuum is stupor (see below), in which patients may rouse to their name, but their speech is not rational, they show little awareness of their environment, and they may promptly slip back into a coma.

Compulsions are repeated, stereotyped, overtly senseless actions or rituals, which are performed to prevent anxiety. Compulsions are obsessions (see below) expressed in behavior. Obsessions are thoughts, compulsions are deeds. Lady Macbeth's hand-washing is a compulsion to wipe clean her obsession with Duncan's blood.

Concrete thinking is the inability to think abstractly, metaphorically, or hypothetically. Ideas and words are usually limited to a single meaning. Figures of speech are taken literally and nuances of language are missed and not used.

Confabulation is when a patient invents responses, facts, and events to mask an organic impairment.

Craving is a symptom in which the person is consistently preoccupied with, thinks about, or strongly desires a habituating substance or physical activity (e.g., bulimic episodes, gambling, jogging, weight-lifting. Craving only exists when the habituating substance or activity is not in use and is only relieved when it is. Craving is not necessarily associated with physical distress; it may, or may not, coexist with anxiety (see above), but they are different phenomena.

Déjà vu is a sense of familiarity when confronted by a situation or event that has not been experienced previously. Literally = already seen. Although it usually occurs in nonpathological states, it may be pathological.

Delusions are fixed, blatantly false convictions deduced from incorrect inferences about external reality; they are maintained despite enormous, obvious, incontrovertible proof to the contrary, and they are not widely believed in the person's culture or subculture. A false belief that involves an extreme value judgment is a delusion only when it defies credibility. Delusions differ from overvalued ideas (see below), which are unreasonable and persistent beliefs. To various degrees, delusions are systematized or unsystematized. In comparison to *unsystematized* delusions, *systematized* delusions are united by a common theme or event and belong to a complete and relatively well-organized network of beliefs; they develop more insidiously, cause less confusion and impairment, and last longer. (See Folie à deux, Hallucinations, Ideas of reference, Mood-congruent, Mood-incongruent, Paranoia, Schneiderian first-rank symptoms.) Examples:

Bizarre delusions are patently absurd and weird.

Grandiose delusions involve an exaggerated sense of one's own importance, power, ability, or identity. "I am Christ."

Jealousy delusions involve suspicions about a rival (e.g., business rival) or about one's sex partner being unfaithful. Othello.

Nihilistic delusions involve themes of non-existence (not "negativity"), either of the patient, others, or the world. "My insides are gone." "At 1:30 P.M., the world will evaporate."

Persecutory delusions are those in which the person is convinced others are trying to harm, cheat, attack, or conspire against him or her.

Reference delusions are beliefs that external events or people are sending messages or commands of great personal importance to the patient. These delusions are self-referential. A woman insists that a man on TV was speaking to her specifically and instructing her to buy Ajax. (And she did — 1,280 cans!) (See Ideas of reference.)

Somatic delusions pertain to the patient's body and are not consistent with cultural beliefs or with physiology or medicine. "My intestines are rotting." "My brain is turning black."

Depersonalization is when a person perceives her body as unreal, floating, dead, or changing in size. A person's arm may feel like wood or seem detached from her body. Depersonalization differs from derealization (see below), in which a person perceives his environment as unreal. Both phenomena often occur in nonpathological situations, with or without stress.

Derailment is a gradual or sudden deviation in a patient's train of behavior, speech, or thought onto a very different track. It may be hard to distinguish from flight of ideas and looseness of associations (see below). (See Incoherence.)

Derealization is when a person perceives his environment as unreal. The individual feels removed from the world, as if he is viewing it on a movie screen. (See Depersonalization.)

Disorientation is the inability to correctly identify the current time, place, and person's name.

Distractibility is when a patient's attention is frequently drawn to unimportant or irrelevant external stimuli.

Echolalia is a meaningless, persistent, verbal, repetition of words or sounds heard by the patient—often with a mocking, mumbling, staccato, or parrot-like tone. (Greek *echo* = "an echo," and *lalia* = "to babble.") Echolalia is in response to the same stimulus, whereas perseveration (see below) is repeated responses to varied stimuli.

Echopraxia is the repetitive imitation of another person's movements.

Ego-dystonic is a sign, symptom, or experience which the patient finds uncomfortable or doesn't want. For example, obsessions are ego-dystonic.

Ego-syntonic is a sign, symptom, or experience which the patient finds acceptable and consistent with his personality. Many, but not all, delusions, hallucinations, and overvalued ideas are ego-syntonic.

Flight of ideas is accelerated speech with many rapid changes in subject that derive from understandable associations, distracting stimuli, or play on words. In flight of ideas (FOI) the connections linking thoughts are understandable, whereas in looseness of associations (LOA) they are not. Nevertheless, extremely rapid FOI may be indistinguishable from LOA, and when there is a marked cultural gap between patient and interviewer, FOI is often misidentified as LOA. (See Derailment, Incoherence.)

Folie à deux, or "madness for two," is when two closely related persons, usually in the same family, share the same delusions.

Fugue is a sudden, "purposeless," and unexpected flight or wandering away from home or work, during which the person assumes a new identity and has an anterograde amnesia (see above).

Guilt is a painful emotion directed inward, in which the person feels he has violated his own principles or conscience; the individual may feel bad, worthless, or in need of punishment. Whereas guilt is an affective state, conscience is a cognitive state consisting of ideas, beliefs, principles, values, standards, and norms. Both guilt and shame (see below), are emotions, but in shame the person feels embarrassed or ashamed before other people.

Hallucinations are false perceptions in the senses—hearing, seeing, touching, tasting, and smelling—based on no external reality. They differ from illusions (see below) which are false perceptions based on real stimuli. Hallucinations are disorders of perception; delusions (see above) are disorders of thinking. Delusions are always psychotic, hallucinations only sometimes: Some patients know their hallucinations are unreal (e.g., "My mind is playing tricks on me"); those who don't are described as giving a "delusional interpretation" to their hallucinations. Hallucinosis (see below) is a state in which the patient realizes his hallucinations are false. Except for dreams, hallucinations are pathological. *Hypnogogic* and *Hypnopompic* hallucinations are dreams which occur on falling asleep or on waking up, respectively; if unaccompanied by other symptoms, they are merely variants of normal. Pathological hallucinations include:

Auditory hallucinations are false perceptions of sound, usually of a voice or voices.

Gustatory hallucinations are false, usually unpleasant, perceptions of taste. (Metallic tastes may be a side effect of medications or physical illnesses.)

Olfactory hallucinations are false perceptions of smell, such as the patient who kept smelling rotting flesh, as she viewed her "happily dead husband."

Somatic hallucinations are false perceptions of a physical experience inside the body. "I feel an orgasm running in my spleen."

Tactile hallucinations are false perceptions of touch. *Formication*—with an "m"—is a tactile hallucination in which the patient feels that things, often insects, are crawling under his skin; it occurs most during withdrawal from alcohol, cocaine, or hypnosedatives.

Visual hallucinations are false perceptions of sight; they may consist of actual people or flashes of light.

Hallucinosis is when patients hallucinate following cessation or reduction of a substance, usually in a clear (or mildly clouded) consciousness. Most, but not all, hallucinosis is very unpleasant. Knowing these hallucinations are not real, the patient is less likely to act on them than on hallucinations he believes to be genuine.

Hypersomnia is a pattern of excessive sleeping.

Ideas of reference are overvalued ideas in which the patient is virtually, but not totally, convinced that objects, people, or events in his immediate environment have personal significance for him. A man felt whenever a red car parked in front of his home, it probably was a well-disguised message from the FBI that he should be on the alert for dope addicts. With a delusion of reference, all doubt would cease. When they occur in a hypervigilant state, ideas of reference are not necessarily pathological: For instance, a man at a "swinger's bar" says, "All the chicks can't keep their eyes off me."

Illogical thinking involves conclusions that contain clear, internal contradictions or are blatantly erroneous given the initial premises. A patient refuses to go to the movies because the tickets are green. Illogical thinking may, or may not, lead to a delusion, or result from one. "I am a virgin, and therefore, I am the Virgin Mary."

Illusions are misperceptions of real external stimuli. During delirium tremens, alcoholics will misperceive the hair on their arms as bugs: These are illusions, not hallucinations, since they are based on a real stimulus.

Incoherence is a general term to describe incomprehensible speech arising from any kind of psychopathologic thinking.

Insomnia is difficulty sleeping, either as *initial insomnia*, which is trouble falling asleep; *middle insomnia*, which is waking in the middle of the night and eventually falling back to sleep; *terminal insomnia* (also known as "early morning awakening"), in which the person awakes at night and cannot return to sleep; *paninsomnia* refers to difficulty sleeping throughout the night.

Looseness of associations are speech patterns characterized by leaps from subject to subject without the connections being clear or the patient being aware of his rapid shifts. "School is nice. I adore earlobes." (See Derailment, Flight of ideas, Incoherence).

Magical thinking is when a person is convinced that her words, thoughts, feelings, or actions will produce or prevent a specific outcome that defies all laws of cause and effect. Depending on how firmly the magical thinking is held, it may be a delusion or an overvalued idea, as in this example: "I know this seems odd, but when I move my third finger forward, I can make people walk faster; when I move my finger backward, they walk slower." Children, people in primitive cultures, and patients with obsessive-compulsive and schizophrenic-like disorders use magical thinking.

Mood is a pervasive and subjectively experienced feeling state, as opposed to affect (see above), which is transitory and apparent to others. Unlike affect, mood colors the person's view of the world. (See Alexithymia, Anhedonia.) Mood states include:

Apprehensive mood involves worried expectation or anticipation.

Dysphoria is any unpleasant mood, including irritable, apprehensive, and dysthymic moods.

Dysthymia is the mood of depression or pervasive sadness, including a subjective sense of heaviness or feeling "weighted-down," blue, or down-in-the-dumps. Dysthymia implies a mood that is more serious than "run-of-the-mill" unhappiness.

Elevated mood is more cheerful than normal for the person, but is not necessarily psychopathological.

Euphoric mood is an exaggerated sense of well-being and contentment; it implies psychopathology when elevated or expansive. (Elevated moods are "vertical"; expansive moods are "horizontal.") An elevated mood: "I feel wonderful, things are great!" An expansive mood: "I can do anything, bat .400, win every game single-handedly, and have all the fans worship me." A euphoric mood may be elevated and expansive: "I'm flying, I'm on cloud 9, I feel like a god, I'm invincible."

Euthymia is a normal range of mood without dysphoria or elation.

Expansive mood refers to a lack of restraint in expressing feelings and an overvaluation of one's importance; it is often accompanied by an elevated or euphoric mood.

Irritable mood is a feeling of tension or nervousness; one feels prickly, easily annoyed, provoked to anger, or frustrated.

Mood-congruent delusions or hallucinations are consistent with the patient's dominant mood. A mood-congruent delusion in depression might be, "My body's rotting with cancer"; in mania, "I'm the Second Christ."

Mood-incongruent delusions and hallucinations are those that are inconsistent with the patient's dominant mood. Mood-incongruent delusions may be persecutory (e.g., "The Moral Majority is poisoning my tulips") or may involve Schneiderian symptoms (see below).

Mutism is not speaking; it is a frequent feature of catatonia.

Neologisms are distortions of words or new words that a patient invents for psychological reasons; neologisms may also be standard words given idiosyncratic meanings by the patient. A new or misused word is not a neologism when it arises for cultural or educational reasons (e.g., malapropisms).

Obsessions are unwanted and uncomfortable ideas, thoughts, images, or impulses that persistently invade one's consciousness. Unlike people with delusions or overvalued ideas, those with obsessions know their beliefs are absurd and find them ego-dystonic. (See Compulsions.)

Overvalued ideas are unreasonable and persistent beliefs, held with less than delusional intensity, which are not generally held in the patient's subculture. "The mob is tapping my phone—well, I think it is." Patients are more likely to act on delusions (see above) than on overvalued ideas. When patients recover from psychosis, they often go from delusions to overvalued ideas to "normality." Overvalued ideas may have a basis in reality, and some are not pathological, such as preoccupations that one's nose is too big, that only diet can cure cancer, or that "having a baby is the only way I will ever be happy." Ideas of reference (see above) are one type of overvalued idea.

Panic attacks are acute, terrifying, unexpected, and "senseless" attacks of anxiety, in which the person suddenly feels overwhelmed by an imminent sense of doom, despair, and destruction. The attacks include physiologic signs of anxiety (see above) and usually end in several minutes.

Paranoia is not a symptom but a mental disorder characterized by delusions of grandeur and persecution, suspiciousness, jealousy, and resentment.

Paranoid delusion is a delusion of persecution (see above). *DSM-IV* recommends using the term *persecutory delusion* because some patients have delusions of grandeur, believing that people want their money, ideas, etc., but do not feel persecuted.

Paranoid ideation is an overvalued idea (see above) that one is being persecuted.

Paranoid style is a character style in which people are unduly or excessively guarded, jealous, sullen, rigid, humorless, and hypersensitive to injustices allegedly being done to them. When a paranoid style substantially interferes with functioning, it becomes a *paranoid personality disorder*.

Perseveration is a persistent repetition of speech or movement to varied, usually internal, stimuli. It does not include repeated use of stock phrases, such as "you know" or "like." Echolalia (see above) and perseveration are often, but not always, found in dementia and delirium. (See Stereotypy.)

Phobia is undue and irrational anxiety (see above) focused on an avoided object or place.

Posturing is the assumption of relatively fixed bodily positions, usually in catatonia.

Poverty of content of speech, sometimes called "poverty of content," is speech which conveys little information because it is vague, barren, or filled with empty repetitions or obscure phrases.

Poverty of speech is a striking lack of speech, so that replies to questions are brief or monosyllabic; some questions are not answered at all. Poverty of speech refers to an inadequate *quantity*; poverty of content of speech (see above), to inadequate *quality*.

Pressured speech is rapid, virtually nonstop, often loud and emphatic, seemingly driven, and usually hard to interrupt. It typically occurs in mania and in some drug-induced states and in severe anxiety states.

Psychomotor agitation, or simply "agitation," is repetitive, nonproductive motor activity usually associated with feelings of tension—e.g., pacing, fidgeting, constantly standing and sitting.

Psychomotor retardation describes slowed movements, reactions, or speech.

Psychosis is a mental state in which the person is unable to distinguish reality from fantasy.

Reality testing is the ability to distinguish reality from fantasy. The failure to test reality—what Lily Tomlin calls "man's collective hunches"—is the hallmark of psychosis.

Schneiderian First-Rank Symptoms (FRS) are specific types of delusions and hallucinations that involve themes of passivity. In 1939, Kurt Schneider originally claimed that FRS were pathognomonic for schizophrenia, but today, FRS are only deemed as highly suggestive of schizophrenia. Patients with neurological disorders that produce pathological impulses or behaviors (e.g., unprovoked fighting, massive weeping) will commonly say, "This behavior isn't me," yet they will readily admit they are responsible for the behavior. In contrast, patients with FRS deny responsibility for the strange behavior, claiming that "others made me do it." Specific FRS are:

Audible thoughts are auditory hallucinations in which the patient hears his own thoughts being spoken aloud by others. A patient says, "I will think about eating, and then I'll hear a man with a French accent repeat my very own words."

Being controlled (delusions of) reflect the patient's experience of his actions being completely under the control of external influences. He feels like an automaton, a totally passive observer of his own actions. "Andy and Barbara have placed an electronic bug in my brain that makes me run wild through Central Park. Blame them, not me." These are also called "made acts."

"Made" feelings are delusions in which the patient experiences emotions which she insists are not her own, but have been imposed on her by others.

"Made" impulses are delusions in which the patient believes that powerful drives or urges have been forced upon him, compelling him to act. Although he disowns the impulse, he admits that it was he, and not others, who committed the act.

Somatic passivity are somatic hallucinations in which the patient is convinced that an external agent has caused her to be a passive recipient of unwanted bodily sensations.

Thought broadcasting are beliefs that one's inner thoughts are no longer private, have escaped from one's mind, and have become known to everyone. "Everyone in the hospital knows what I'm thinking." Telepathy is not thought broadcasting, since it is culturally sanctioned and, therefore, not delusional.

Thought insertions are ego-alien convictions that thoughts have been placed into one's mind, with the person believing his thoughts are not his own.

Thought withdrawal is a patient's ego-dystonic belief that thoughts are being taken, or stolen from her mind or brain, and that she has fewer thoughts than before. "I was discussing Rome when suddenly my whole brain was sucked empty by the Pope's vacuum cleaner."

Voices arguing are auditory hallucinations in which the patient hears two or more people arguing, typically about the patient, whom they refer to as a third party.

Voices commenting are auditory hallucinations in which the patient hears people commenting on his actions while they are occurring: "He is standing up! He is walking!"

Shame is an emotion in which the person feels embarrassed or dishonored before others. (See Guilt.)

Stereotypy is an isolated, repetitive, and purposeless movement. It appears most often in catatonic and drug-induced states. (See Catatonia, Perseveration.)

Stupor is a state of foggy consciousness and nonalertness in which the patient may respond to noxious stimuli, but otherwise be oblivious to her environment. (See Coma.)

Tangentiality is a disturbance of communication in which the person "goes off on a tangent," but unlike circumstantiality (see above), does not return to the point. Tangentiality may be viewed as repeated derailments (see above), which continually evade a central theme. It may, or may not be, pathological.

Thought disorder is a very general term to describe pathological thinking. Traditionally, thought disorder was divided into *disorders of thought content* (e.g., overvalued ideas, delusions), and *formal thought disorder*, which are abnormalities in the stream and continuity of thought (e.g., blocking, circumstantiality, flight of ideas). Because the boundaries between the form and content of thought are often unclear, *DSM-III* suggested that both terms be avoided and that more specific descriptions and terms be used instead.

Vegetative signs are the biological (or physiologic) signs of depression, such as insomnia, anorexia, weight loss, diurnal mood variation, constipation, and diminished libido. These signs are called *vegetative* because they primarily involve growth and nutrition; they're also called "hypothalamic signs," since they arise from disturbances involving the hypothalamic-pituitary axis.

Word salad is an apparently random and illogical mixture of words and sounds.

Mini-Mental State Exam*

ORIENTATION	Date 1	Date 2	Date 3	Date 4
1. What is the day of the week____? month____? date____? season____? year____? Score 1 for each correct answer. Maximum score = 5.				
2. Where are we: state____, county____, town/city____, residence number____, street name____ (or hospital and floor instead of street and residence number). Score 1 for each correct answer. Maximum score = 5.				
REGISTRATION				
Name 3 unrelated objects slowly (1 second to say each) and clearly (i.e., ball, flag, tree). Ask the client to repeat them. Tell client to remember objects because he/she will be asked to name them in a few minutes. Score first try. Repeat objects until all are learned, up to 6 trials. Maximum score = 3.				

(continued)

*Folstein, M.F., Folstein, S.E., & McHugh, P.R. (1975). Mini-mental state: A practical method for grading cognitive states of patients for the clinician. *Journal of Psychiatric Research*, *12*, 189–198.

ATTENTION AND CALCULATION	Date 1	Date 2	Date 3	Date 4
Ask the client to perform serial 7 subtraction from 100 or serial 3 subtraction from 20. Stop after 5 numbers and score 1 for each number (93, 86, 79, 72, 65) or (17, 14, 11, 8, 5). Maximum score = 5.				
RECALL				
Ask the client to recall the names of the 3 unrelated objects which you asked him/her to repeat above and score 1 for each correct name. Maximum score = 3.				
LANGUAGE				
1. *Naming*: Point to 2 objects and ask client to name them. Score 1 for each correct name (e.g., tie and pencil) Maximum score = 2.				
2. *Repetition*: Ask the client to repeat, "No ifs, ands, or buts." Allow only 1 trial. Score 0 or 1.				
3. *Three-stage command*: Ask the client to, "Take a paper in your right hand, fold it in half, and put it on the floor." Score 1 for each part correctly executed. Maximum score = 3.				
4. *Reading*: Print on a blank card, "Close your eyes" (or use copy below). Ask the client to read the sentence and do what it says. Score 1 if eyes are closed.				
5. *Writing*: Ask the client to write a sentence; do not dictate. It must contain a subject and verb, and make sense. Correct grammar and punctuation are not necessary. Score 0 or 1.				
6. *Copying*: Ask the client to copy the figure below exactly. All 10 angles and intersection must be present to score 1.				
#1 Date: _____ #3 Date: _____ Total #2 Date: _____ #4 Date: _____ (Maximum score 30)				

CLOSE YOUR EYES

WRITE SENTENCE HERE:

WRITE SENTENCE HERE:

WRITE SENTENCE HERE:

WRITE SENTENCE HERE:

Psychiatric Medications: Names & Doses

NAMES		DOSAGE (mg/day)
Generic	Brand	
	ANTIPSYCHOTICS	
Phenothiazines		
Chlorpromazine	Thorazine	50–2,000
Fluphenazine	Prolixin	1–20
Fluphenazine enanthate	Prolixin enanthate	25–75*
Fluphenazine decanoate	Prolixin decanoate	25–75*
Mesoridazine	Serentil	30–400
Perphenazine	Trilafon	8–64
Perphenazine	Etrafon	2/10–24/150
with Amitriptyline	or Triavil	2/10–24/150
Thioridazine	Mellari	150–800
Trifluoperazine	Stelazine	4–40
Butyrophenones		
Haloperidol	Haldol	2–40
Haloperidol decanoate	Haldol decanoate°	25–300°
Thioxanthenes		
Chlorprothixene	Taractan	30–600
Thiothixene	Navane	5–60

NAMES		DOSAGE (mg/day)
Generic	Brand	
Miscellaneous		
Clozapine	Clozari	175–700
Loxapine	Loxitane	20–250
Molindone	Moban	15–225
Risperidone	Risperdal	1–10
MOOD STABILIZERS		
Heterocyclics		
Amitriptyline	Elavil, Endep	75–300
Amoxapine	Asendin	150–600
Clomipramine	Anafranil	100–300
Desipramine	Norpramin, Pertofrane	75–300
Doxepin	Sinequan, Adapin	75–300
Imipramine	Tofranil, Janimine SK-Pramine	75–300
Imipramine pamoate	Tofranil-PM	75–300
Nortriptyline	Pamelor, Aventyl	50–150
Protriptyline	Vivactil	15–60
Trimipramine	Surmontil	75–300
Selective Serotonin Reuptake Inhibitors (SSRIs)		
Fluoxetine	Prozac	20–80
Sertraline	Zoloft	50–200
Paroxetine	Paxil	10–50
Monoamine-Oxidase Inhibitors (MAOIs)		
Isocarboxazid	Marplan†	20–50
Phenelzine	Nardil	30–90
Tranylcypromine	Parnate	30–60
Miscellaneous		
Bupropion	Wellbutrin	100–450
Carbamazepine	Tegretol	400–1,600
Lithium Carbonate	Eskalith, Lithane	600–2,400
Lithium citrate	Cibalith-S	600–2,400
Maprotiline	Ludiomil	75–250
Trazodone	Desyrel	200–600
Venlafaxine	Effexor	75–375

NAMES		SINGLE DOSE (mg)	
Generic	Brand	Daytime Anxiolytic	Nighttime Hypnotic
HYPNOANXIOLYTICS			
Barbiturate-like			
Chloral hydrate	Noctec	—	500–1,000
Ethchlorvynol	Placidyl	—	500–750
Mebrobamate	Equinil, Miltown	400	—
Benzodiazepines (short-acting)			
Alprazolam	Xanax	0.25–2	0.5–2
Estazolam	Prosom	—	0.5–2
Lorazepam	Ativan	0.5–4	2–4
Oxazepam	Serax	10–30	2–30
Temazepam	Restoril	—	15–30
Triazolam	Halcion	—	0.125–0.25
(long-acting)			
Chlordiazepoxide	Librium	5–20	10–30
Clonapazepam	Klonapin	0.25–2	1–2
Clorazepate	Tranxene	3.25–22.50	—
Diazepam	Valium	2–10	5–15
Flurazepam	Dalmane	—	15–30
Prazepam	Centrax	10–20	—
Quazepam	Doral	—	7.5–15
Miscellaneous			
Buspirone	Buspar	10–60	—
Propranolol	Inderal	20–40	—
Zolpidem	Ambien	—	5–20

NAME		DOSAGE (mg/day)	
Generic	Brand	Oral	Intramuscular
ANTIPARKINSONIAN MEDICATION			
Amantadine	Symmetrel	100–300	—
Benztropine	Cogentin	2–6	1–2
Biperidin	Akineton	2–6	1–2
Diphenhydramine	Benedryl	50–100	25–50
Procyclidine	Kemadrin	5–10	—
Trihexyphenidyl	Artane	4–15	—

*Intramuscular dose given every 7–14 days.
°Initial intramuscular dose should be 15–20 times the lowest effective oral dose of haloperidol; injections should be every 3–4 weeks.
†Withdrawn from sale in the United States as of March, 1994.

APPENDIX H

Psychiatric Medications: Side Effects and Their Management

SIDE EFFECT	KEY FACTORS	PRECAUTIONS/ TREATMENT
	I. ANTIPSYCHOTICS	
Allergic		
1. Agranulocytosis; bone marrow suppression.	Only with phenothiazines, thioxanthenes, and clozapine; most often clozopine, and during first 12 weeks of treatment.	Stop all antipsychotics; treat symptomatically; monitor temperature for 2 weeks; periodic blood counts weekly for clozapine.
2. Dermatoses; contact dermatitis.	Most often with chlorpromazine.	Stop drug; may switch to another antipsychotic.
3. Jaundice (cholestatic or hepatocellular).	As with agranulocytosis (#1), except occurs only during first month of treatment.	Stop drug; wait; consider other causes of jaundice.
4. Photosensitivity.	As with dermatoses (#2).	As with dermatoses (#2); avoid sun.

Anticholinergic

5. Blurred vision, for close-up, not distant vision.	More often with less potent antipsychotics (e.g., chlorpromazine, thioridazine); less often with more potent antipsychotics (e.g., fluphenazine, haloperidol).	No longer bothersome in 1–2 weeks; if symptom persists, give total daily dose at bedtime; lower dose, switch to more potent antipsychotic or stop all antipsychotics; use cholinergic drugs; reduce or stop anticholinergic antiparkinsonian drugs, or switch to amantadine.
6. Confusion; toxic delirium.	Related to dose; elderly and brain-damaged are more vulnerable; more common with low potency antipsychotics.	Physostigmine 1–4 mg IV; stop antiparkinsonian agents (or switch to amantadine); stop or reduce or switch to a higher potency antipsychotic.
7. Dry mouth.	As with blurred vision (#5).	As with blurred vision (#5); prevent secondary fungal infection (thrush).
8. Fecal impaction and constipation.	As with blurred vision (#5); more common in elderly.	As with blurred vision (#5); prunes, stool softener, fiber.
9. Narrow angle glaucoma aggravated.	As above (#5/8).	Stop antipsychotics.
10. Paralytic ileus; abdominal distention.	As above (#5/8).	As with blurred vision (#5) and constipation (#8); use cholinergics for acute severe distention; use laxatives if necessary.
11. Tachycardia.	As with blurred vision (#5).	As with blurred vision (#5).
12. Urinary retention.	As with blurred vision (#5), except that enlarged prostrate increases frequency and severity.	As with blurred vision (#5); use cholinergics for acutely severe retention.
13. Hypotension; dizzy or light-headed on standing.	More often on low potency antipsychotics, higher doses, IM/IV routes, and increasing age.	Stand up more slowly; tends to disappear in 1–2 weeks, so if mild, wait; switch to high potency antipsychotic; divide doses; increase fluid intake; consider support hose.
14. Inhibition of ejaculation.	Most often with thioridazine; adrenergic blockade.	Switch from thioridazine (or the offending drug) to another, usually more potent, antipsychotic.

15. Nasal congestion.	Sympathetic depression.	Goes away naturally; if not, try local vasoconstrictors.

Behavioral

16. Oversedation.	More common at first and with less potent antipsychotics; related to dose and to individual tolerance.	Usually decreases in 1–2 weeks; prevent by smaller initial dose or by using more potent antipsychotics.
17. Impaired motor functioning: "slowed reflexes."	As above (#16), especially at first.	Patient must be careful driving, crossing streets, and working near machinery; prevention and remedies as above (#16).

Central Nervous System (other)

18. "Neuroleptic Malignant Syndrome": fever, muscular rigidity, diminished consciousness, autonomic dysfunction.	Unknown cause; often in patients who have taken antipsychotics before without difficulty; more common with IM/IV route, high potency antipsychotics, males, youth, and in dehydrated/exhausted patients.	Withdrawal of all psychotropic drugs; treat symptomatically; stabilize blood pressure, correct fluid and electrolyte balance, treat hyperthermia.
19. Seizures.	Related to dose, drug, prior brain damage, and more sedating antipsychotics. Highest with clozapine.	Reduce dose slowly; might add anticonvulsant.

Endocrine

20. Edema.	Increased antidiuretic hormone secretion.	Wait; goes away naturally.
21. False pregnancy test.	?	Use another test.
22. Lactation; swollen breasts.	Hypothalamic effect; more common with low potency antipsychotics.	Stop or change antipsychotic.
23. Menstrual irregularities.	As above (#22).	As above (#22).
24. Weight gain.	Hypothalamic effect with/without overeating; common with chlorpromazine, clozapine; uncommon with perphenazine and high-potency antipsychotics.	Switch antipsychotic; diet.

Extrapyramidal

25. Akathisia, "the jitters," motor restlessness.	More common with more potent antipsychotics, women, and those in mid-life.	Add antiparkinsonian drug or propranolol, switch to a less potent antipsychotic (especially thioridazine), or stop all antipsychotics.
26. Akinesia, "pseudoparkinsonism," bodily stiffness.	Related to dose, age, genetic predisposition, family history of Parkinson's disease; more common with high potency antipsychotics.	As above (#25).
27. Dystonia, fixed, rigid, bizarre posture.	Idiosyncratic; mildly dose related; more frequent in males, youth, and high potency antipsychotics; occurs between 5 hours and 10 days of taking drug.	Treat acute reaction with IV/IM antiparkinsonian; then do as with #25. Tends to wear off in 10–14 days.
28. Dyskinesia, repeated bizarre movements of face, arms, legs, and hips.	Occurs while on drug; more common in females and with high potency antipsychotics.	Treat as with #25.
29. Tardive dyskinesia; as above, except stops during sleep.	Occurs in patients who stop or greatly reduce dose after being on it for 5 + months (average 2 years); related to lifetime total dose; increased risk with age.	Stop drug and hope dyskinesia disappears; if not, consider "anti-TD" drugs, or suppress TD with more antipsychotic; best treatment is prevention: Only use antipsychotics when mandatory.

Miscellaneous

30. Retinitis pigmentosa.	Only with thioridazine >800 mg/day > 2 months.	Keep thioridazine <800 mg/day.

II. MOOD REGULATORS

Allergic

31. Agranulocytosis.	As with #1; TCAs.	As with #1.
32. Jaundice, as with #3.	As with #3; TCAs.	As with #3.

Anticholinergic

33. Blurred vision as in #5.	More often with TCAs than MAOIs; not with lithium or SS-RIs; common in elderly.	Less or no longer bothersome in 1–2 weeks; if symptom persists, give total daily dose at bedtime; loser dose; switch to

		SSRIs, trazodone, or to secondary TCAs (e.g., desipramine); cholinergic agents.
34. Confusion; toxic delirium.	Related to dose; elderly and brain-damaged especially often with normal doses of TCAs and MAOIs, and during lithium toxicity.	If diagnostic question, give physostigmine 1–4 mg; reduce TCA; stop MAOI, correct lithium toxicity by checking electrolytes, salt intake, renal function, and serum lithium.
35. Dry mouth.	As with blurred vision (#33).	As with blurred vision (#33); prevent secondary fungal infection (thrush).
36. Fecal impaction and constipation.	As with blurred vision (#33).	As with blurred vision (#33).
37. Narrow angle glaucoma aggravated.	As with blurred vision (#33).	Stop TCAs/MAOIs.
38. Paralytic ileus; abdominal distention.	As with #10.	As with #10.
39. Tachycardia.	As with blurred vision (#33).	As with blurred vision (#33); obtain EKG.
40. Urinary retention.	As with #12.	As with #12.
Autonomic Nervous System (other)		
41. Hypotension, as in #13.	TCAs and MAOIs, not lithium, SSRIs or venlafaxine; mechanism unclear.	As in #13.
42. Inhibition of ejaculation.	As above (#41); thioridazine; adrenergic blockade.	Reduce dose, switch to another TCA/MAOI/SSRI.
Behavioral		
43. Excitment, restlessness, initial insomnia.	Mainly with MAOIs, SSRIs, venlafaxine, and protriptyline.	Change drugs.
44. Impaired motor functioning, as in #17.	As in #17; especially common with amitriptyline, doxepin, and trazodone.	As in #17. Use SSRIs, venlafaxine, bupropion.
45. Oversedation.	More common at first and with drugs listed in #44; related to dose and to individual tolerance.	Usually decreases in 1–2 weeks; prevent by smaller initial increases; switch to SSRIs, bupropion, venlafaxine or sec-

		ondary TCAs, especially pro- triptyline or desipramine.
46. Psychosis aggra- vated.	Either an antidepressant- induced "switch phase" into mania or an MAOI-induced psychosis, particularly tranylcy- promine.	If "switch phase," add lithium or stop TCA; if MAOI-induced, change MAOIs or add antipsy- chotic or lithium.
47. Suicide.	Patient may have underesti- mated dangerousness of MAOI or TCA.	Limit quantities; have nurse or relative give drug; ECT? Change to low toxicity agents, SSRIs, bupropion, trazodone, venlafaxine.

Central Nervous System (other)

48. Hypertensive crisis: sudden throbbing frontal headache, pallor, sweats, vom- iting, chills, chest pain.	MAOIs only; induced by tyra- mine-foodstuffs, sympathomi- metic drugs, dextromethor- phan, and meperidine.	Instruct patient on diet; phen- tolamine 5 mg IV in ER or nifed- ipine 10mg po at home.
49. Peripheral neurop- athy.	Seen with TCAs & MAOIs, and with pyridoxine deficiency.	Stop drugs, give vitamins.
50. Seizures.	Related to dose, drug, prior brain damage, and more sedat- ing TCAs. Highest with buprop- ion and clomipramine.	Reduce dose slowly; might add anticonvulsant.
51. Tremors, twitching, ataxia, poor coordi- nation.	Related to age; may occur on normal doses of TCAs, SSRIs, and MAOIs; may occur as lith- ium toxicity.	Reduce or stop TCA, MAOI, SSRI; correct lithium toxicity (#34); reduce lithium.

Endocrine

52. Edema.	Imipramine, probably as in #20.	As in #20.
53. Hypothyroidism, sluggishness, "de- pression."	Secondary to 6 + months of lithium.	Evaluate thyroid function; add thyroid replacement.
54. Menstrual irregulari- ties.	Mainly TCAs.	As with #22.
55. Weight gain.	Hypothalamic effect with/with- out overeating; may result from normalized mood. Seen with	Switch drugs; diet.

phenelzine and all TCAs except desipramine. Not seen
with SSRIs, venlafaxine, or bupropion.

Miscellaneous

56. EKG changes.	Bundle-branch block; mainly due to toxicity from TCAs, but also from lithium.	Reduce dose or stop drug. Switch to SSRI, venlafaxine, or bupropion.
57. GI upset.	Lithium toxicity, but may occur when lithium started. Occurs with SSRIs and venlafaxine at normal doses.	Serum lithium; reduce dose.
58. Polyuria.	Lithium toxicity, but may occur at normal levels.	Check lithium toxicity (#34).
59. Acute tubular ne-crosis.	Lithium toxicity.	Stop lithium; treat symptomatically.

APPENDIX I

Other Conditions That May Be a Focus of Clinical Attention*

Mental and medical health professionals see many clients with emotional or behavioral difficulties that are *not* mental disorders but problems in living. In addition, psychological factors affecting "medical conditions" or "medication induced movement disorders" are also encountered. Though mainly a classification of mental disorders, *DSM-IV* also catalogs and briefly describes these problems. For some problems in living, such as uncomplicated bereavement or occupational problems, clients themselves seek help; for other problems in living, such as malingering or adolescent antisocial behavior, people other than clients request professional consultation. Since an individual can have a mental disorder *and* a problem in living yet only want assistance for the latter, if the problem in living is not a manifestation or consequence of the mental disorder, the problem in living should be specified on Axis I. For instance, an agoraphobic may seek help for academic problems, but not phobia. This appendix names and sketches these *DSM-IV* "other conditions." If the *other condition* is not a primary focus of treatment but is a significant psychosocial or environmental problem, it should be listed under Axis IV. For example, a client may be illiterate but requesting treatment for panic disorder. The illiteracy would be classified under Axis IV as an academic problem.

Abuse or neglect problems refer to severe mistreatment of one individual by another. Subtypes include *physical* or *sexual abuse* of a *child* or *adult* or *neglect of a child*. This is coded differently if the focus of attention is on the perpetrator (use V codes) or on the victim (99.5 for a child, 99.5.81 for an adult).

Academic problem refers to school or learning difficulties not due to a specific

---

DSM-IV, based on material on pp. 675–686.

developmental, mental, or medical disorder. Examples include the student with poor study habits or the serious underachiever.

Acculturation problem refers to a problem involving adjustment to a different culture (e.g., following migration).

Adult antisocial behavior refers to rule-breaking or law-breaking by those without a mental disorder, such as conduct, antisocial personality, and impulse control disorders. Examples include many, but not all, thieves, mobsters, and dope dealers.

Age-related cognitive decline is an objectively identified decline in cognitive functioning consequent to the aging process that is within normal limits given the person's age. Individuals with this condition may report problems remembering names or appointments or may experience difficulty in solving complex problems. This category should be considered only after it has been determined that the cognitive impairment is not attributable to a specific mental disorder or neurological condition.

Bereavement refers to a normal reaction to the death of a loved one. Chapter 10 describes uncomplicated bereavement and how it differs from depression.

Borderline intellectual functioning refers to those seeking help with problems which substantially arise from having IQs of 71–84. Borderline intellectual functioning is easily missed in the presence of another mental disorder, such as schizophrenia or panic disorder, and it may also be hard to distinguish from mental retardation (see Chapter 20).

Childhood or adolescent antisocial behavior refers to isolated acts of rule-breaking or law-breaking by youth; when it is a pattern, the person may have a conduct or impulse-control disorder.

Identity problem refers to uncertaintly about multiple issues relating to identity such as long-term goals, career choice, friendship patterns, sexual orientation and behavior, moral values, and group loyalties.

Malingering refers to the voluntary and deliberate production of false or grossly exaggerated physical or psychological symptoms to achieve a goal; the person wants this goal, and its attainment is understandable in view of the person's circumstances and not just his psychology. Malingering may be evading the draft or playing hooky; it may also serve more respectable ends, such as feigning illness while held by terrorists. Two caveats: First, malingerers do get sick. Second, some malingerers who are ostensibly faking an illness may actually be doing so as a face-saving way to get help with a genuine illness. Malingering should be differentiated from *somatoform* and *factitious disorders*, and should be considered if: (a) medicolegal issues are involved, e.g., workman's compensation, malpractice, "pain and suffering" cases; (b) inconsistent or contradictory information is given in the history; (c) marked discrepancies are noted between history and objective findings; (d) there is lack of cooperation with diagnostic evaluation; (e) patient adamently refuses to be hypnotized or to have an amytal interval; (f) patient demonstrates treatment noncompliance; or (g) there are indications of antisocial personality disorder.

Medication-induced movement disorders include **neuroleptic-induced parkinsonism, dystonia, akathisia** or **tardive dyskinesia, neuroleptic malignant syndrome, medication-induced postural tremor, medication-induced movement disorder NOS** (e.g., movement disorder or malignant syndrome not caused by a neuroleptic or tardive dystonia), and other medication-induced disorders such as **adverse effects of medication NOS,** e.g., hypotension, priapism, and cardiac arrhythmias.

Noncompliance with medical treatment refers to noncompliance with an important aspect of the treatment for a mental disorder or a general medical condition. The reasons for noncompliance may include discomfort resulting from treatment (e.g., medication side effects), expense of treatment, decisions based on personal value judgments or religious or cultural beliefs about the advantages and disadvantages of the proposed treatment, maladaptive personality traits or coping styles (e.g., denial of illness), or the presence of a mental disorder (e.g., schizophrenia, avoidant personality disorder). This category should be used only when the problem is sufficiently severe to warrant independent clinical attention.

Occupational problems refer to work difficulties that do not result from a mental disorder, such as job dissatisfaction or uncertainty in choosing careers.

Phase of life problem refers to difficulties that primarily arise in response to major developmental turning points (i.e., crises, "passages"), such as puberty, separating from parents, starting a career, "mid-life crises," and retirement.

Psychological factors affecting medical condition refers to psychological or behavioral factors that affect a general medical condition by adversely affecting its course (e.g., exacerbations, prolonged recovery), adding a health risk (e.g., overeating in diabetes, high salt intake with hypertension), causing stress-related physiologic responses (e.g., bronchospasm in asthma or chest pain in coronary artery disease), or interfering with treatment (e.g., irregularly taking medication, improper wound care). The psychological factors must have a clinically significant adverse effect on the medical conditions and "there must be reasonable evidence (direct causality is not required) to suggest an association between the psychological factors and the medical condition." Subtypes:

Mental disorder affecting . . . [*indicate the general medical condition*]; includes Axis I or II disorders (e.g., major depressive disorder complicating the treatment of diabetes).

Psychological symptoms affecting . . . [*indicate the general medical condition*]; include psychological symptoms that do not meet full criteria for an Axis I disorder (e.g., anxiety in irritable bowel syndrome or peptic ulcer disease).

Personality traits or coping style affecting . . . [*indicate the medical condition*]; includes traits that are subthreshold for Axis II disorders or represent another pattern that has been demonstrated to be a risk factor for certain illnesses (e.g., type A, pressured, hostile behavior for coronary artery disease).

Maladaptive health behavior affecting . . . [*indicate the general medical condition*] (e.g., a "couch potato" lifestyle, overeating, unsafe sex).

Stress-related physiological response affecting . . . [*indicate the general medical condition*] (e.g., stress-related worsening of blood pressure or coronary pain).

Relational problems refer to a pattern of interaction that is associated with clinically significant impairment in individual or family functioning or the development of symptoms in one or more individuals involved in the relationship. Subtypes include: Parent-child, partner, sibling, or NOS (e.g., co-worker, neighbor, etc.) relational problem, or relational problem related to a mental disorder or general medical condition.

Religious or spiritual problem refers to distressing experiences that involve loss or questioning of faith, problems associated with conversion to a new faith, or questioning of spiritual values that may not necessarily be related to an organized church or religious institution.

References

Abbott, D.W., & Mitchell, J.E. (1993). Antidepressants vs. psychotherapy in the treatment of bulimia nervosa. *Psychopharmacology Bulletin, 29*, 115–119.

Abramson, L.Y., Seligman, M.E., & Teasdale, J. (1978). Learned helplessness in humans: Critique and reformulation. *Journal of Abnormal Psychology, 87*, 49–79.

Abroms, E.M. (1983). Beyond eclectism. *American Journal of Psychiatry, 140*, 740–745.

Agras, W.S. (1991). Nonpharmacologic treatments of bulimia nervosa. *Journal of Clinical Psychiatry, 52*, 29–33.

Allgulander, C., Borg, S., & Vikander, B. (1984). A 4–6 year follow-up of 50 patients with primary dependence on sedative and hypnotic drugs. *American Journal of Psychiatry, 141*, 1580–1582.

Amdur, M.J., Tucker, G.J., Detre, T.D., & Markhus, K. (1969). Anorexia nervosa: An interactional study. *The Journal of Nervous and Mental Diseases, 148*, 559–566.

American Academy of Child and Adolescent Psychiatry (AACAP). (1991). Practice parameters for the assessment and treatment of attention-deficit hyperactivity disorder. *Journal of American Academy of Child Adolescent Psychiatry, 30*(3), I–III.

American Psychiatric Association. (1952). *The diagnostic and statistical manual of mental disorders* (1st ed.). Washington, DC.

American Psychiatric Association. (1968). *The diagnostic and statistical manual of mental disorders* (2nd ed.). Washington, DC.

American Psychiatric Association. (1973). *Task force report 7: Megavitamin and orthomolecular therapy in psychiatry*. Washington, DC.

American Psychiatric Association. (1980). *The diagnostic and statistical manual of mental disorders* (3rd ed.). Washington, DC.

American Psychiatric Association. (1987). *The diagnostic and statistical manual of mental disorders* (3rd ed. rev.). Washington, DC.

Anderson, C.M., Hogarty, G., & Reiss, D.J. (1980). Family treatment of adult schizophrenic patients: A psycho-educational approach. *Schizophrenia Bulletin, 6*, 490–505.

Andreasen, N.C., & Hoenk, P.R. (1982). The predictive value of adjustment disorders: A follow-up study. *American Journal of Psychiatry, 139*, 584–590.

Andreasen, N.C., Rice, J., Endicott, J., Reich, T., & Coryell, W. (1986). The family history approach to diagnosis. *Archives of General Psychiatry, 43*, 421–429.

Andreasen, N.C., & Wasek, P. (1980). Adjustment disorders in adolescents and adults. *Archives of General Psychiatry, 37*, 1166–1170.

Asher, R. (1951). Muchausen's syndrome. *Lancet, 1*, 339–341.

509

Baer, L., Jenike, M.A., Ricciardi, J., Holland, A.D., Seymour, R.J., Minichiello, W.E., & Buttolph, M.L. (1990). Personality disorders in patients with obsessive-compulsive disorders. *Archives of General Psychiatry, 47,* 826–832.

Barlow, D.H., Blanchard, E.B., Vermilyea, J.A., Vermilyea, B.B., & DiNardo, P.A. (1986). Generalized anxiety and generalized anxiety disorder: Description and reconceptualization. *American Journal of Psychiatry, 143,* 40–44.

Barlow, D.H., Cerny, J.A. (1988). *Psychological treatment of panic.* New York: Guilford Press.

Barnes, D.M. (1988). New data intensify the agony over ecstasy. *Science, 239,* 864–866.

Baron, M., Guren, R., Asnis, L., & Lord, S. (1985). Familial transmission of schizotypal and borderline personality disorders. *American Journal of Psychiatry, 142,* 927–934.

Bauer, M.S., & Whybrow, P.C. (1993). Validity of rapid cycling as a modifier for bipolar disorder in *DSM-IV. Depression, 1,* 11–19.

Beck, A.T., Brown, G., Berchick, R.J., Stewart, B.L., & Steer, R.A. (1990). Relationship between hopelessness and ultimate suicide: A replication with psychiatric outpatients. *American Journal of Psychiatry, 147,* 190–195.

Beck, A.T., Rush, A.J., Shaw, B.F., & Emery, G. (1979). *Cognitive therapy of depression: A treatment manual.* New York: Guilford.

Beck, J.C. (1982). Dementia in the elderly, the silent epidemic. *Annuals of Internal Medicine, 97,* 231–241.

Benkelfat, C., Murphy, D.L., Zohar, J., Hill, J.L., Grover, G., & Insel, T.R. (1989). Clomipramine in obsessive-compulsive disorder. *Archives of General Psychiatry, 46,* 23–44.

Beresford, T.P., Blow, F.C., Hill, E., Singer, K., & Lucey, M.R. (1990). Clinical practice: Comparison of CAGE questionnaire and computer-assisted laboratory profiles in screening for covert alcoholism. *Lancet, 336,* 482–485.

Berglund, M. (1984). Suicide in alcoholism: A prospective study of 88 suicides. *Archives of General Psychiatry, 41,* 888–891.

Bird, T.D., Sumi, S.M., Nemens, E.J., Nochlin, D., Shellenberg, G., Lampe, T.H., Sadovnick, A., Chui, H., Minen, G.W., & Tinkleberg, J. (1989). Phenotypic heterogeneity in familial Alzheimer's disease, a study of 24 kindreds. *Annals of Neurology, 25,* 12–25.

Black, D.W., Winokur, G., & Nasrallah, A. (1988). Effect of psychosis on suicide risk in 1,593 patients with unipolar and bipolar affective disorders. *American Journal of Psychiatry, 145,* 849–852.

Black, P.M. (1980). Idiopathic normal pressure hydrocephalus. *Journal of Neural Surgery, 52,* 371–77.

Bleuler, E. (1911/1950). *Dementia praecox, or the group of schizophrenias.* New York: International Universities Press.

Bloch, S., Bond, G., Qualls, B., Yalom, I., & Zimmerman, E. (1976). Patients' expectations of therapeutic improvement and their outcomes. *American Journal of Psychiatry, 133,* 1457–1459.

Bownes, I.T., O'Gorman, E.C., & Sayers, A. (1991). Assault characteristics in post-traumatic stress disorder in rape victims. *Acta Psychiatrica Scandinavica, 83,* 27–30.

Breier, A., & Strauss, J.S. (1984). The role of social relationships in the recovery from psychotic disorders. *American Journal of Psychiatry, 141,* 949–955.

Brown F. (1961). Depression and childhood bereavement. *Journal of Mental Science, 107,* 754–777.

Cannon, W.B. (1932). *The wisdom of the body.* New York: Norton.

Cantwell, D.P., & Baker, L. (1989). Stability and natural history of *DSM-III* childhood diagnoses. *Journal of American Academy of Child and Adolescent Psychiatry, 28,* 691–700.

Caplan, G. (1964). *Principles of preventive psychiatry.* New York: Basic Books.

Caton, C.L.M. (1984). *Management of chronic schizophrenia.* New York: Oxford University Press.

Charatan, F. (1985). Depression and the elderly: Diagnosis and treatment. *Psychiatric Annals, 15,* 313–316.

Charney, D.S, Menkes, D.B., & Heninger, G.R. (1981). Receptor sensitivity and the mechanism of action of antidepressant treatment. *Archives of General Psychiatry, 38,* 1160–1180.

Christenson, G.A., Mackenzie, T.B., & Mitchell, J.E. (1991). Characteristics of 60 adult chronic hair pullers. *American Journal of Psychiatry, 148,* 365–370.

Christie, K.A., Burke, J.D., Jr., Regier, D.A., Rae, D.S., Boyd, J.H., & Locke, B.Z. (1988). Epidemiologic evidence for onset of mental disorders and higher risk of drug abuse in young adults. *American Journal of Psychiatry, 145*(8), 971–975.

Ciraulo, D.A., Barnhill, J.G., Ciraulo, A.M., Greenblatt, D.J., & Shader, R.I. (1989). Parental alcoholism as a risk factor in benzodiazepine abuse: A pilot study. *American Journal of Psychiatry, 146*(10), 1333–1335.

Clayton, P.J., Grove, W.M., Coryell, W., Keller, M., Hirschfeld, R., & Fawcett, J. (1991). Follow-up and family study of anxious depression. *American Journal of Psychiatry, 148,* 1512–1517.

Cohen, M.E., Robins, E., Purtell, J.J., Altmann, M.W., & Reid, D.W. (1953). Excessive surgery in hysteria. *Journal of the American Medical Association, 151,* 977–986.

Coles, R., Brenner, J.H., & Meagher, D. (1970). *Drugs and youth: Medical, psychiatric, and legal facts.* New York: Liveright.

Coombs, G., & Ludwig, A.M. (1982). Dissociative disorders. In J.H. Greist, J.W. Jefferson, & R.L. Spitzer (Eds.), *Treatment of mental disorders* (pp. 309–319). New York: Oxford University Press.

Cooper, J.E., Kendell, R.E., Gurland, B.J., Sharpe, L., Copeland, J.R.M., & Simon, R. (1972). *Psychiatric diagnosis in New York and London.* New York: Oxford University Press.

Cornelius, J.R., Soloff, P.H., Perel, J.M., & Ulrich, R.F. (1993). Continuation pharmacotherapy of borderline personality disorder with haloperidol and phenelzine. *American Journal of Psychiatry, 150,* 1843–1848.

Coryell, W., Endicott, J., Andreasen, N.C., & Keller, M. (1985). Bipolar I, bipolar II, and nonbipolar major depression among the relatives of affectively ill probands. *Americna Journal of Psychiatry, 142,* 817–821.

Cozolino, L.J., Goldstein, M.J., Nuechterlein, K.H., et al. (1988). The impact of education about schizophrenia on relatives varying in expressed emotion. *Schizophrenia Bulletin, 14,* 675–687.

Craske, M.G., Barlow, D.H., & O'Leary, T.O. (1992). *Mastery of your anxiety and worry.* Albany, New York: Graywind Publications.

Cummings, J., & Benson, F. (1992). *Dementia* (2nd ed.). Stoneham, MA: Butterworth Publications.

Custer, R.L. (1979). An overview of compulsive gambling. Paper presented at South Oaks Hospital, Amityville, New York.

Dahl, S. (1989). Acute responses to rape, a PTSD variant. *Acta Psychiatrica Scandinavica, 80*(Supp), 355.

Datlof, S., Coleman, P.D., Forbes, G.B., & Kreipe, R.E. (1986). Ventricular dilation on CAT scans of patients with anorexia nervosa. *American Journal of Psychiatry, 143,* 96–98.

Davis, J.M. (1975). Overview: Maintenance therapy in psychiatry: I. Schizophrenia. *American Journal of Psychiatry, 132,* 1237–1245.

Davis, K.L., Kahn, R.S., Ko, G., & Davidson, M. (1991). Dopamine in schizophrenia: A review and reconceptualization. *American Journal of Psychiatry, 148*(11), 1474–1486.

Dement, W., & Kleitman, N. (1975). Cyclic variations in EEG during sleep and their relation to eye movement, body motility, and dreaming. *Electroencephalography and Clinical Neurophysiology, 9,* 673.

Dement, W., et al. (1985). Changes of sleep and wakefulness with age. In C. Finch & E.L. Schneider (Eds.), *Handbook of the biology of aging* (2nd ed.) (pp. 692–717). New York: Van Nostrand Reinhold.

Den Boer, J.A., Westenberg, H.G.M., & Verhoeven, W.M.A. (1990). Biological aspects of panic anxiety. *Psychiatric Annals, 20,* 494–502.

DeSouza, C., & Othmer, E. (1984). Somatization disorder and Briquet's syndrome: An assessment of their diagnostic concordance. *Archives of General Psychiatry, 41,* 334–336.

Dilsaver, S.C. (1986). Cholinergic mechanisms in affective disorders: Future directions for investigation. *Acta Psychiatrica Scandinavica, 74*, 312–334.

Dole, V.P. (1969). Research on methadone maintenance treatment. *Proceedings of the Second National Conference on Methadone Maintenance*, 359–370.

Dole, V.P., Nyswander, M.E., & Warner, A. (1968). Successful treatment of 750 criminal addicts. *Journal of the American Medical Association, 206*, 2708–2711.

Dorris, M. (1989). *The broken cord*. New York: HarperCollins.

Drake, R.E., Gates, C., Whitaker, A., & Cotton, P.G. (1985). Suicide among schizophrenics: A review. *Comprehensive Psychiatry, 26*, 90–100.

Drye, R.C., Goulding, R.L., & Goulding, M.E. (1973). No-suicide decisions: Patient monitoring of suicidal risk. *American Journal of Psychiatry, 130*(2), 171–174.

Dunner, D.L. (1993). A review of the diagnostic status of "Bipolar II" for the *DSM-IV* work group on mood disorders. *American Journal of Psychiatry, 1*, 2–10.

Emery, V.L., & Oxman, T.E. (1992). Update on the dementia spectrum of depression. *American Journal of Psychiatry, 149*, 305–317.

Engel, G.L. (1977). The need for a new medical model: A challenge for biomedicine. *Science, 196*(4286), 129–136.

Ensel, W.M. (1982). The role of age in the relationship of gender and marital status to depression. *Journal of Nervous and Mental Diseases, 170*, 536–543.

Erikson, E.H. (1968). *Identity: Youth and crisis*. New York: Norton.

Ewing, J.A. (1984). Detecting alcoholism, the CAGE questionnaire. *Journal of the American Medical Association, 252*, 1905–1907.

Fairburn, C.G., et al. (1993). Psychotherapy and bulimia nervosa. *Archives of General Psychiatry, 50*, 419–428.

Fallon, B.A., Liebowitz, M.R., Salman, E., Schneier F., Jusino, C., Hollander, E., & Klein, D. (1993). Fluoxetine for hypochondriacal patients without major depression. *Journal of Clinical Psychopharmacology, 13*, 438–441.

Faraone, S.V., Biederman, J., Keenan, K., & Tsuang, M.T. (1991). Separation of *DSM-III* attention deficit disorder and conduct disorder: Evidence from a family–genetic study of American child psychiatric patients. *Psychology of Medicine, 21*, 109–121.

Faraone, S.V., Biederman, J., Lehman, B.L., Keenan, K., Norman, D., Seidman, L.J., Kolodny, R., Kraus, I., Perrin, J., & Chen, W.J. (1993). Evidence for the independent familial transmission of attention deficit hyperactivity disorder and learning disabilities: Results from a family-genetic study. *American Journal of Psychiatry, 150*(6), 891–895.

Fawcett, J., Clark, D.C., Aagesen, C.A., Pisani, V.D., Tilkin, J.M., Sellers, D., McGuire, M., & Gibbons, R.D. (1987). A double-blind, placebo-controlled trial of lithium carbonate therapy for alcoholism. *Archives of General Psychiatry, 44*, 248–256.

Feighner, J.P., Robins, E., Guze, S.B., Woodruff, R.A., Winokur, G., & Munoz, R. (1972). Diagnostic criteria for use in psychiatric research. *Archives of General Psychiatry, 26*, 57–63.

Fitts, S.N., Gibson, P., Redding, C.A., & Deiter, P.J. (1989). Body dysmorphic disorder: Implications for its validity as a *DMS-III-R* clinical syndrome. *Psychological Reports, 64*, 655–658.

Fordyce, W.E., Fowler, R.S., Lehmann, J.F., DeLateur, B.J., Sand, P.L., & Trieschmann, R.B. (1973). Operant conditioning in the treatment of chronic pain. *Archives of Physical Medicine and Rehabilitation, 54*, 399–408.

Frank, E., Kupfer, D.J., & Perel, J.M. (1989). Early recurrence in unipolar depression. *Archives of General Psychiatry, 46*, 397–400.

Freud, S. (1894/1959). Aetiology of the neuroses (Draft B). In J. Strachey (Ed. and Trans.), *The complete psychological works, the standard edition* (Vol. 1, pp. 179–184). New York: Norton.

Freud, S. (1917). Mourning and melancholia. In E. Jones (Ed.), *Collected papers*. New York: Basic Books.

Freud, S. (1919). Lines of advance in psycho-analytic therapy. In J. Strachey (Ed. and Trans.), *The complete psychological works, the standard edition* (Vol. 17, pp. 157–168). New York: Norton.

Fricchione, G.L., & Vlay, S.C. (1986). Psychiatric aspects of patients with malignant ventricular arrhythmias. *American Journal of Psychiatry, 143*, 1518–1526.

Frischholz, E.J., Lipman, L.S., Braun, B.G., & Sachs, R.G. (1992). Psychopathology, hypnotizability, and dissociation. *American Journal of Psychiatry, 149*, 1521–1525.

Fyer, A.J., Liebowitz, M.R., & Gorman, J.M., Campeas, R., Levin, A., Davies, S.O., Goetz, D., & Klein, D.F. (1987). Discontinuation of alprazolam treatment in panic patients. *American Journal of Psychiatry, 144*, 303–308.

Garber, H.J., & Ritvo, E.R. (1992). Magnetic resonance imaging of the posterior fossa in autistic adults. *American Journal of Psychiatry, 149*(2), 245–247.

Gawin, F.H., Kleber, H.D., Byck, R., Rounsaville, B.J., Kosten, T.R., Jatlow, P.I., & Morgan, C. (1989). Desipramine facilitation of initial cocaine abstinence. *Archives of General Psychiatry, 46*, 117–121.

Gerstley, L.J., Alterman, A.I., McLellan, A.T., & Woody, G.E. (1990). Antisocial personality disorder in patients with substance abuse disorders: A problematic diagnosis. *American Journal of Psychiatry, 147*, 173–178.

Glassman, A.H., Jackson, W.K., Walsh, B.T., & Roose, S.P. (1984). Cigarette craving, smoking withdrawal, and clonidine. *Science, 226*, 864–866.

Glueck, S., & Glueck, E. (1959). *Predicting delinquency and crime.* Cambridge, Mass: Harvard University Press.

Gold, M.S. (1984). *800-Cocaine.* New York: Bantam.

Goldstein, J.M. (1988). Gender differences in the course of schizophrenia. *American Journal of Psychiatry, 145*, 684–689.

Goldstein, M.G., Niaura, R., Follick, M.J., & Abrams, D.B. (1989). Effects of behavioral skills training and schedule of nicotine gum administration on smoking cessation. *American Journal of Psychiatry, 146*(1), 56–60.

Goodwin, D.W. (1985). Alcoholism and genetics: The sins of the father. *Archives of General Psychiatry, 42*, 171–174.

Goodwin, D.W., & Guze, S.B. (1984). *Psychiatric diagnosis* (3rd ed.). New York: Oxford University Press.

Goodwin, D.W, & Guze, S.B. (1989). *Psychiatric diagnosis* (4th ed.). New York: Oxford University Press.

Greenblatt, D.J., Harmatz, J.S., Engelhardt, N., & Shader, R.I. (1989). Pharmacokinetic determinants of dynamic differences among three benzodiazepine hypnotics. *Archives of General Psychiatry, 46*, 326–332.

Greenhill, L. (1990). Attention-deficit hyperactivity disorder in children. In B.D. Garfinkel, G.A. Carlson, & E.B. Weller (Eds.), *Psychiatric disorders in children and adolescents* (pp. 149–192). Philadelphia: W.B. Saunders.

Grinspoon, L., & Bakalar, J. (1985). What is MDMA? *Harvard Medical School Mental Health Letter, 2*(2), 8.

Gualtieri, C.T., Adams, A., Shen, C.D., & Loisells, D. (1982). Minor physical anomalies in alcoholic and schizophrenic adults and hyperactive and autistic children. *American Journal of Psychiatry, 139*(5), 640–643.

Guilleminault, C. (1988). Idiopathic central nervous system hypersomnia. In R.L. Williams, I. Karacan, & C.A. Moore (Eds.), *Sleep disorders: Diagnosis and treatment* (2nd ed.) (pp. 347–350). New York: Wiley.

Guze, S.B., & Robins, E. (1970). Suicide and primary affective disorders. *British Journal of Psychiatry, 117*, 437–438.

Handen, B.L., Breaux, A.M., Janosky, J., McAuliffe, S., Feldman, H., & Gosling, A. (1992). Effects and noneffects of methylphenidate in children with mental retardation and ADHD. *Journal of the American Academy of Child Adolescent Psychiatry, 31*, 455–461.

Hart, K.J., & Ollendick, T.H. (1985). Prevalence of bulimia in working and university women. *American Journal of Psychiatry, 142*, 851–854.

Harvard Medical School Mental Health Letter. (1985). Multiple personality. *1*(10), 1–6, April.

Hauri, P. (1989). Primary insomnia. In M.H. Kryger, T. Roth, & W.C. Dement (Eds.), *Principles and practice of sleep medicine* (pp. 442–447). Philadelphia: W.B. Saunders.

Hauser, P., Zametkin, A.J., Martinez, P., Vitiello, B., Matochik, J.A., Mixson, A.J., & Weintraub, B.D. (1993). Attention deficit–hyperactivity disorder in people with generalized resistance to thyroid hormone. *New England Journal of Medicine, 328*(14), 997–1001.

Hawton, K., Salkovskis, P.M., Kirk, J., & Clark, D.M. (Eds.). (1989). *Cognitive behavior therapy for psychiatric problems – a practical guide.* New York: Oxford University Press.

Hesselbrock, M.N., Meyer, R.E., & Keener, J.J. (1985). Psychopathology in hospitalized alcoholics. *Archives of General Psychiatry, 48,* 1050–1055.

Higgens, S.T., Budney, A.J., Bickel, W.K., Hughes, J.R., Foerg, F., & Badger, G. (1993). Achieving cocaine abstinence with a behavioral approach. *American Journal of Psychiatry, 150*(5), 763–769.

Hirschfeld, R.M.A., Klerman, G.L., Andreasen, N.C., Clayton, P.J., & Keller, M.B. (1985). Situational major depressive disorder. *Archives of General Psychiatry, 42,* 1109–1114.

Hoffman, R.S., & Koran, L.M. (1984). Detecting physical illness in patients with mental disorders. *Psychosomatics, 25,* 654–660.

Hogarty, G.E., Goldberg, S.C., Schooler, N.R., & Ulrich, R.P. (1974). Drugs and sociotherapy in the aftercare of schizophrenic patients: II. Two-year relapse rates. *Archives of General Psychiatry, 31,* 603–608.

Holinger, P.C., Offer, D., & Ostrov, E. (1987). Suicide and homicide in the United States: An epidemiologic study of violent death, population changes, and the potential for prediction. *American Journal of Psychiatry, 144,* 215–219.

Horevitz, R.P., & Braun, B.G. (1984). Are multiple personalities borderline? *Psychiatric Clinics of North America, 7,* 69–87.

Horowitz, M.J. (1985). Disasters and psychological responses to stress. *Psychiatric Annals, 15,* 161–167.

Hser, Y.I., Anglin, M.D., & Powers, K. (1993). A 24-year follow-up of California narcotics addicts. *Archives of General Psychiatry, 50,* 577–584.

Hsiao, K., & Prusiner, S. (1990). Inherited human prion diseases. *Neurology, 40,* 1820.

Hsu, L.K.G. (1980). Outcome of anorexia nervosa: A review of the literature (1954 to 1978). *Archives of General Psychiatry, 37,* 1041–1046.

Hsu, L.K.G. (1986). The treatment of anorexia nervosa. *American Journal of Psychiatry, 143,* 573–581.

Hsu, L.K.G. (1990). *Eating disorders.* New York: Guilford Press.

Hughes, J.R., Oliveto, A.H., Helzer, J.E., Higgens, S.T., & Bickel, W.K. (1992). Should caffeine abuse, dependence, or withdrawal be added to *DSM-IV* and ICD-10? *American Journal of Psychiatry, 149,* 33–40.

Jacobson, N.S., Holtzworth-Munroe, A., & Schaling, K.B. (1989). Marital therapy and spouse involvement in the treatment of depression, agoraphobia, and alcoholism. *Journal of Consulting and Clinical Psychology, 57*(1), 5–10.

James, W. (1893). *The principles of psychology.* New York: H. Hold & Co.

Janis, I.L. (1971). *Stress and frustration.* New York: Harcourt, Brace, Jovanovich.

Janoff-Bulman, R. (1985). The aftermath of victimization: Rebuilding shattered assumptions. In C.R. Figley (Ed.), *Trauma and its wake.* New York: Brunner/Mazel.

Jaspers, K. (1923/1972). *General psychopathology.* Chicago: University of Chicago Press.

Jefferson, J.W., & Ochitill, H. (1982). Factitious disorders. In J.H. Greist, J.W. Jefferson, & R.L. Spitzer (Eds.), *Treatment of mental disorders* (pp. 387–397). New York: Oxford University Press.

Jellinek, E.M. (1952). Phases of alcohol addiction. *Quarterly Journal on Alcohol, 13,* 673–684.

Jenike, M.A. (1992). New developments in treatment of obsessive-compulsive disorder. In *Review of Psychiatry, Vol. II* (pp. 323–346). Washington, DC: American Psychiatric Association.

Jenike, M.A. (1993). Augmentation strategies for treatment-resistant obsessive-compulsive disorder. *Harvard Review Psychiatry, 1,* 17–26.

Jenike, M.A., Baer, L., Ballantine, T., Martuza, R.L., Tynes, S., Giriunas, I., Buttolph, L., & Cassem, N.H. (1991). Cingulotomy for refractory obsessive-compulsive disorder. *Archives of General Psychiatry, 48,* 548–554.

Joachim, C., & Selkoe, D. (1992). The seminal role of β-amyloid in the pathogenesis of Alzheimer's disease. *Alzheimer Disease and Associated Disorders, 6*, 27–34.

Joffe, R.T., Offord, D.R., & Boyle, M.H. (1988). Ontario child health study: Suicidal behavior in youth age 12–16 years. *American Journal of Psychiatry, 145*, 1420–1423.

Johnson, C., & Flach, A. (l985). Family characteristics of 105 patients with bulimia. *American Journal of Psychiatry, 142*, 1321–1324.

Johnston, L.D., Bachman, J.G., & O'Malley, P.M. (1981). Drugs and the nation's high school students. In G.G. Nahas & H.C. Frick (Eds.), *Drug abuse in the modern world: A perspective for the eighties* (pp. 87–98). New York: Pergamon Press.

Kafka, M.P. (1993). Update on paraphilias and paraphilia-related disorders. *Currents in Affective Illness, 12*, 5–13.

Kahana, R.J., & Bibring, G.L. (1964). Personality types in medical management. In N.E. Zinberg (Ed.), *Psychiatry and medical practice* (pp. 108–123). New York: International University Press.

Kandel, D.B., & Raveis, V.H. (1989). Cessation of illicit drug use in young adulthood. *Archives of General Psychiatry, 46*, 109–116.

Kandel, E.R. (1983). From metapsychology to molecular biology: Explorations into the nature of anxiety. *American Journal of Psychiatry, 140*, 1277–1293.

Kang, S.Y., Kleinman, P.H., Woody, G.E., Millman, R.B., Todd, T.C., Kemp, J., & Lipton, D.S. (1991). Outcomes for cocaine abusers after once-a-week psychosocial therapy. *American Journal of Psychiatry, 148*(5), 630–635.

Kaplan, H.I., & Sadock, B.J. (1991). *Synopsis of psychiatry: Behavioral sciences and clinical psychiatry* (6th ed.) (pp. 699–704). Baltimore: Williams & Williams.

Kaplan, H.S. (1974). *The new sex therapy.* New York: Brunner/Mazel.

Kardiner, A. (1977). *My analysis with Freud.* New York: Norton.

Katon, W., Egan, K., & Miller, D. (1985). Chronic pain: Lifetime psychiatric diagnoses and family history. *American Journal of Psychiatry, 142*, 1156–1160.

Katzman, R. (1986). Alzheimer's disease. *New England Journal of Medicine, 314*, 964–973.

Kay, S.R., & Singh, M.M. (1989). The positive-negative distinction in drug-free schizophrenic patients. *Archives of General Psychiatry, 46*, 711–718.

Keller, M.B., Lavori, P.W., Rice, J., Coryell, W., & Hirschfeld, R.M.A. (1986). The persistent risk of chronicity in recurrent episodes of nonbipolar major depressive disorder: A prospective follow-up. *American Journal of Psychiatry, 143*, 24–28.

Kellner R. (1982a). Disorders of impulse control. In J.H. Greist, J.W. Jefferson, & R.L. Spitzer (Eds.), *Treatment of mental disorders* (pp. 398–418). New York: Oxford University Press.

Kellner, R. (1982b). Hypochondriasis and atypical somatoform disorder. In J.H. Greist, J.W. Jefferson, & R.L. Spitzer (Eds.), *Treatment of mental disorders* (pp. 286–303). New York: Oxford University Press.

Kellner, R. (1987). Hypochondriasis and somatization. *Journal of the American Medical Association, 258*, 433–437.

Kendler, K.S., Silberg, J.L., Neale, M.C., Kessler, R.C., Heath, A.C., & Eaves, L.J. (1991). The family history method: Whose psychiatric history is measured? *American Journal of Psychiatry, 148*, 1501–1504.

Kernberg, O. (1975). *Borderline conditions and pathological narcissism.* New York: Jason Aronson.

Kershner, P., & Wang-Cheng, R. (1989). Psychiatric side effects of steroid therapy. *Psychosomatic, 30*(2), 135–139.

Kessler, R.C., Downey, G., Milavsky, J.R., & Horst S. (1988). Clustering of teenage suicides after television news stories about suicides: A reconsideration. *American Journal of Psychiatry, 145*, 1379–1383.

Kessler, R.C., McGonagle, K.A., Ahzo, S., Nelson, C.H., Hughes, M., Eshleman, S., Wittchen, H., & Kendler, K.S. (1994). Lifetime and 12-month prevalence of *DSM-III-R* psychiatric disorders in the United States. Results from the National Comorbidity Survey. *Archives of General Psychiatry, 51*, 8–19.

Khachaturian, Z. (1985). Diagnosis of Alzheimer's disease. *Archives of Neurology, 42*, 1097–1105.

Khan, A., Cohen, S., Stowell, M., Capwell, B., Avery, D., & Dunner, D. (1987). Treatment options in severe psychotic depression. *Convulsive Therapy, 3*(2), 93–99.

Khan, A., Mirolo, M.H., Hughes, D., & Bierut, L. (1993). Electroconvulsive therapy. *Psychiatric Clinics of North America, 16*(2), 497–513.

Khan, A., Noonan, C., & Healey, W. (1991). Is a single tricyclic antidepressant trial an active treatment for psychotic depression? *Progress in Neuro-psychopharmacology and Biological Psychiatry, 15*, 765–770.

Kiersch, T.A. (1962). Amnesia: A clinical study of ninety-eight cases. *American Journal of Psychiatry, 119*, 57–60.

Kinsey, A., Pomeroy, W., & Martin, C. (1948). *Sexual behavior in the human male*. Philadelphia: W. B. Saunders.

Kinsey, A., Pomeroy, W., Martin, C., & Gebhard, P. (1953). *Sexual behavior in the human female*. Philadelphia: W. B. Saunders.

Klein, D.F. (1993). False suffocation alarms, spontaneous panics, and related conditions: An integrative hypothesis. *Archives of General Psychiatry, 50*, 306–317.

Klein, D.N., Taylor, E.B., Harding, K., & Dickstein, S. (1988). Double depression and episodic major depression: Demographic, clinical, familial, personality, and socioenvironmental characteristics and short-term outcome. *American Journal of Psychiatry, 145*, 1226–1231.

Kleinman, A. (1988). *The illness narratives: Suffering, healing, and the human condition*. New York: Basic Books.

Klerman, G.L., Lavori, P.W., Rice, J., Reich, T., Endicott, J., Andreasen, N.C., Keller, M.B., & Hirschield, R.M.A. (1985). Birth-cohort trends in rates of major depressive disorder among relatives of patients with affective disorder. *Archives of General Psychiatry, 42*, 689–693.

Klerman, G.L., Weissman, M.M., Rounsaville, B.J., & Chevron, R.S. (1984). *Interpersonal psychotherapy of depression*. New York: Basic Books.

Kluft, R.P. (1991). Multiple personality disorder. In A. Tasman & S.M. Goldfinger (Eds.), *Review of psychiatry*, vol. 10 (pp. 161–188). Washington, DC: American Psychiatric Association.

Koeningsberg, H.W., Kaplan, R.D., Gilmore, M.M., & Cooper, A.M. (1985). The relationship between syndrome and personality disorder in *DSM-III*: Experience with 2,462 patients. *American Journal of Psychiatry, 142*, 207–212.

Koran, L.M., Sox, H.C., Jr., Marton, K.I., Moltzen, S., Sox, C.H., Kraemer, H.C., Imai, K., Kelsey, T.G., Rose, T.G., Jr., Levin, L.C., & Chandra S. (1989). Medical evaluation of psychiatric patients. *Archives of General Psychiatry, 46*, 733–740.

Kovacs, M., & Beck, A.T. (1976). The communication of suicidal intent: A reexamination. *Archives of General Psychiatry, 33*, 198–201.

Kraepelin, E. (1915/1921). *Clinical psychiatry: A text-book for students and physicians*. Translated and adapted from the 7th German Edition by A. Ross Diefendorf. New York: Macmillan.

Kulk, R.A., Schlenger, W.E., Fairbank, J.A., Hough, R.L., Jordan, B.K., Marmon, C.R., & Weiss, D.S. (1990). *Trauma and the Vietnam War generation*. New York: Brunner/Mazel.

Kurcinka, M.S. (1991). *Raising your spirited child*. New York: HarperCollins.

Kushner, M.G., Sher, K.J., & Bertman, B.D. (1990). The relation between alcohol problems and the anxiety disorders. *American Journal of Psychiatry, 147*(6), 685–695.

Lahey, B.B., Piacentini, J.C., McBurnett, K., Stone, P., Hartdagen, S., & Hynd, G. (1988). Psychopathology in the parents of children with conduct disorder and hyperactivity. *Journal of the American Academy of Child and Adolescent Psychiatry, 27*(2), 163–170.

Levin, E.D., Westman, E.R., Stein, R.M., Carnahan, E., Sanchez, M., Herman, S., Behm, F.M., & Rose, J.E. (1994). Nicotine skin patch treatment increases abstinence, decreases withdrawal symptoms, and attenuates rewarding effects of smoking. *Journal of Clinical Psychopharmacology, 14*, 41–49.

Lewine, R., Burbach, D., & Meltzer, H.Y. (1984). Effect of diagnostic criteria on the ratio of male to female schizophrenic patients. *American Journal of Psychiatry, 141,* 84–87.

Lewinsohn, P.M., Antonuccio, D.A., Steinmetz, J., & Teri, L. (1984). *The coping with depression course: A psychoeducational intervention for unipolar depression.* Eugene, OR: Castalia Publishing.

Ley, P. (1977). Psychological studies of doctor-patient communication. In S. Rachman (Ed.), *Contributions to medical psychology, vol. 1* (pp. 9–42). London: Pergamon Press.

Lieberman, P.B., & Strauss, J.S. (1984). The recurrence of mania: Environmental factors and medical treatment. *American Journal of Psychiatry, 141,* 77–80.

Liebowitz, M.R., Gorman, J.M., Fyer, A.J., & Klein, D.F. (1985). Social phobia: Review of a neglected anxiety disorder. *Archives of General Psychiatry, 42,* 729–736.

Lifton, R.J. (1963). Thought reform and the psychology of totalism: A study of "brainwashing" in China. New York: Norton.

Linehan, M.M. (1993). *Cognitive-behavioral treatment of borderline personality disorder.* New York: Guilford Press.

Lipowski, Z.J. (1980). *Delirium: Acute brain failure in man.* Springfield, IL: C.C. Thomas.

Loewenstein, R.J. (1991). Psychogenic amnesia and psychogenic fugue: A comprehensive review. In A. Tasman & S.M. Goldfinger (Eds.), *Review of psychiatry, vol. 10* (pp. 189–222). Washington, DC: American Psychiatric Association.

Looney, J.G., & Gunderson, E.K.E. (1978). Transient situational disturbances: Course and outcome. *American Journal of Psychiatry, 135,* 660–663.

Luborsky, L. (1984). *Principles of psychoanalytic psychotherapy.* New York: Basic Books.

Lucas, A.R., et al. (1991). Fifty-year trends in the incidence of anorexia nervosa in Rochester, Minn.: A population-based study. *American Journal of Psychiatry, 148,* 917–922.

Ludwig, A.M. (1980). *Principles of clinical psychiatry.* New York: Free Press.

Ludwig, A.M. (1985). *Principles of clinical psychiatry* (2nd ed.). New York: Free Press.

McElroy, S.L., Hudson, J.L., Harrison, G.P., Jr., Keck, P.E., Jr., & Aizley, H.G. (1992). The *DSM-III-R* impulse control disorders not elsewhere classified: Clinical characteristics and relationship to other psychiatric disorders. *American Journal of Psychiatry 149,* 318–327.

McElroy, S.L., Pope, H.G., Jr., Keck, P.E., Jr., & White, K.L. (1991). Kleptomania: A report of 20 cases. *American Journal of Psychiatry, 148,* 652–657.

McGlashan, T.H. (1984). The Chestnut Lodge follow-up study, II. *Archives of General Psychiatry, 41,* 586–601.

McGoldrick, M., & Gerson, R. (1985). *Genograms in family assessment.* New York: Norton.

McKenna, P.J., Kane, J.M., & Parrish, K. (1985). Psychotic syndrome of epilepsy. *American Journal of Psychiatry, 142,* 895–904.

Mahler, M., Pine, F., & Bergman, A. (1975). *The psychotherapy and the science of psychodynamics.* Boston: Butterworth.

Maj, M., Veltro, F., Pirozzi, R., Lobrace, S., & Magliano, L. (1992). Pattern of recurrence of illness after recovery from an episode of major depression: A prospective study. *American Journal of Psychiatry, 149,* 795–800.

Malan, D.H. (1979). *Individual psychotherapy and the science of psychodynamics.* Boston: Butterworth.

Marks, I.M. (1981). Review of behavioral psychotherapy, I: Obsessive-compulsive disorders. *American Journal of Psychiatry, 138,* 584–592.

Marks, I.M., Gray, S., Cohen, D., Hill, R., Mawson, D., Ramm, E., & Stern, R. (1983). Imipramine and brief therapist-aided exposure in agoraphobics having self-exposure homework. *Archives of General Psychiatry, 40,* 153–162.

Marks, R.M., & Sachar, E.J. (1973). Undertreatment of medical inpatients with narcotic analgesics. *Annals of Internal Medicine, 78,* 173–181.

Marmar, C.R., Foy, D., Kagan, B., & Pynoos, R.S. (1993). An integrated approach for treating posttraumatic stress. In J.M. Oldham, M.B. Riba, & A.Tasman (Eds.), *Review of psychiatry, vol. 12.* (pp. 239–272). Washington, DC: American Psychiatric Association Press.

Marmar, C.R., & Freeman, M. (1988). Brief dynamic psychotherapy of post-traumatic stress disorders: Management of narcissistic regression. *Journal of Traumatic Stress, 1,* 323–337.

Marzuk, P.M., Tardiff, K., Leon, A.C., Stajic, M., Morgan, E.B., & Mann, J.J. (1992). Prevalence of cocaine use among residents of New York City who committed suicide during a one-year period. *American Journal of Psychiatry, 149,* 371–375.

Masters, C.L., Harris, C.L., Harris, J.O., Gajdusek, C., Gibbs, C.J., Bernoulli, C., & Asher, D.M. (1979). Jakob-Creutzfeldt disease: Patterns of worldwide occurrence. *Annals of Neurology, 5,* 177–188.

Masters, W.H., & Johnson, V.E. (1970). *Human sexual inadequacy.* Boston: Little, Brown & Co.

Masterson, J.F. (1976). *Psychotherapy of the borderline adult: A developmental approach.* New York: Brunner/Mazel.

Maxmen, J.S. (1991). *Psychotropic drugs: Fast facts.* New York: Norton.

Maxmen, J.S. (1986a). *A good night's sleep.* New York: Norton.

Maxmen, J.S. (1986b). *The new psychiatry: How modern psychiatrists think about their patients, theories, diagnoses, drugs, psychotherapies, power, training, families, and private lives.* New York: Mentor.

Maziade, M., Caron, C., Côté, R., Mérette, C., Bernier, H., Laplante, B., Boutin, P., & Thivierge, J. (1990). Psychiatric status of adolescents who had extreme temperaments at age 7. *American Journal of Psychiatry, 147,* 1531–1536.

Meehan, P.J., Lamb, J.A., Saltzman, L.E., & O'Carroll, P.W. (1992). Attempted suicide among young adults: Progress toward a meaningful estimate of prevalence. *American Journal of Psychiatry, 149,* 41–44.

Mellman, T.A., & Uhde, T.W. (1989). Sleep panic attacks: New clinical findings and theoretical implications. *American Journal of Psychiatry, 146,* 1204–1207.

Menninger, K. (1938). *Man against himself.* New York: Harcourt, Brace & World.

Merikangas, K.R. (1984). Divorce and assortative mating among depressed patients. *American Journal of Psychiatry, 141,* 74–76.

Mesco, R.H., & Cantwell, D.P. (1991). Risk factors outlined in antisocial behaviors in children with ADHD and conduct disorder. *Psychiatric Times,* 34–36, April.

Meyers, N. (1993). *The seven-per-cent solution.* New York: Norton.

Mitchell, J.E., Hatsukami, D., Eckert, E.D., & Pyle, R.L. (1985). Characteristics of 275 patients with bulimia. *American Journal of Psychiatry, 142,* 482–488.

Molnar, G., Feeney, M.G., & Fava, G.A. (1988). Duration and symptoms of bipolar prodomes. *American Journal of Psychiatry, 145,* 1576–1578.

Moran, M.G., Thompson, T.L., & Nies, A.S. (1988). Sleep disorders in the elderly. *American Journal of Psychiatry, 145,* 1369–1378.

Motto, J.A., Heilbron, D.C., & Juster, R.P. (1985). Development of a clinical instrument to estimate suicide risk. *American Journal of Psychiatry, 142,* 680–686.

Mowbray, C.T. (1985). Homelessness in America: Myths and realities. *American Journal of Orthopsychiatry, 55,* 4–8.

Murphy, D.L., & Pigott, T.A. (1990). A comparative examination of a role for serotonin in obsessive-compulsive disorder, panic disorder, and anxiety. *Journal of Clinical Psychiatry, 51*(4, supp.), 53–60.

Murphy, J.M., Monson, R.R., Olivier, D.C., Sobol, A.M., & Leighton, A.H. (1987). Affective disorders and mortality. *American Journal of Psychiatry, 44,* 473–480.

Narrow, W.E., Regier, D.A., Rae, D.S., Marderscheid, R.W., & Locke, B.Z. (1993). Use of services by persons with mental and addictive disorders. *Archives of General Psychiatry, 50*(2), 95–107.

Norman, K. (1984). Eating disorders. In H.H. Goldman (Ed.), *Review of general psychiatry* (pp. 464–480). Los Altos, CA: Lange.

North, C., & Cadoret, R. (1981). Diagnostic discrepancy in personal accounts of patients with 'schizophrenia.' *Archives of General Psychiatry, 38,* 133–137.

Ochitill, H. (1982). Somatoform disorders. In J.H. Greist, J.W. Jefferson, & R.L. Spitzer (Eds.), *Treatment of mental disorders* (pp. 266–286). New York: Oxford University Press.

Othmer, E., & DeSouza, C. (1985). A screening test for somatization disorder (hysteria). *American Journal of Psychiatry, 142*, 1146-1149.

Oxman, T.E., Rosenberg, S.D., Schnurr, P., & Tucker, G.J. (1985). Linguistic dimensions of affect and thought in somatization disorder. *American Journal of Psychiatry, 142*, 1150-1155.

Perley, M., & Guze, S.B. (1962). Hysteria—the stability and usefulness of clinical criteria. *New England Journal of Medicine, 266*, 421-426.

Peroutka, S.J. (1987). Incidence of recreational use of 3,4-methylenedioxymethamphetamine (MDMA, 'Ecstasy') on an undergraduate campus. *New England Journal of Medicine, 817*, 1542-1543.

Perry, J.C., & Cooper, S.H. (1989). An empirical study of defense mechanisms. *Archives of General Psychiatry, 46*, 444-452.

Perry, R., Campbell, M., Adams, P., Lynch, N., Spencer, E., Curren, E., & Overall, J. (1989). Long-term efficacy of haloperidol in autistic children: Continuous versus discontinuous drug administration. *Journal of the American Academy of Child Adolescent Psychiatry, 28*, 87-92.

Perry, S.W. (1984). The undermedication for pain. *Psychiatric Annals, 14*, 808-811.

Peselow, E.D., Sanfilipo, M.P., DiFiglia, C., & Fieve, R.R. (1992). Melancholic/endogenous depression and response to somatic treatment and placebo. *American Journal of Psychiatry, 149*(10), 1324-1334.

Peterson, R.C., Mokri, B., & Laws, E.R. (1985). Surgical treatment of idiopathic hydrocephalus in elderly adults. *Neurology, 35*, 307-311.

Pettinati, H.M., Kogan, L.G., Evans, F.J., Wade, J.H., Horne, R.L., & Staats, J.M. (1990). Hypnotizability of psychiatric inpatients according to two different scales. *American Journal of Psychiatry, 147*, 69-75.

Phillips, M.R., Ward, N.G., & Ries, R.K. (1983). Factitious mourning: Painless patienthood. *American Journal of Psychiatry, 140*, 420-425.

Phillipson, E.A. (1993). Sleep apnea—a major public health problem. *New England Journal of Medicine, 328*, 1271-1273.

Pierce, D.W. (1981). The predictive validation of a suicide intent scale: A five-year follow-up. *British Journal of Psychiatry, 139*, 391-396.

Pilkonis, P.A., & Frank, E. (1988). Personality pathology in relationship to treatment response. *American Journal of Psychiatry, 145*, 435-441.

Pitts, F.N., & McClure, J.N. (1967). Lactate metabolism and anxiety neurosis. *New England Journal of Medicine, 277*, 1329-1336.

Pope, H., Jonas, J.M., & Jones, B. (1982). Factitious psychosis: Phenomenology, family history, and long-term outcome of nine patients. *American Journal of Psychiatry 139*, 1480-1483.

Post, R.M., Rubinow, D.R., Uhde, T.W., Roy-Byrne, P.P., Linnoila, M., Rosoff, A., & Cowdry, R. (1989). Dysphoric mania: Clinical and biological correlates. *Archives of General Psychiatry, 46*, 353-358.

Prien, R.F., & Gelenberg, A.J. (1989). Alternatives to lithium for preventive treatment of bipolar disorder. *American Journal of Psychiatry, 146*, 840-848.

Prien, R.F., & Kupfer, D.J. (1986). Continuation drug therapy for major depressive episodes: How long should it be maintained? *American Journal of Psychiatry, 143*, 18-23.

Ramchandani, D., & Schindler, B. (1993). Evaluation of pseudoseizures: A psychiatric perspective. *Psychosomatics, 34*, 70-79.

Rankin, J.G., Winkenson, P., & Santamaria, J. N. (1970). Factors influencing the prognosis of the alcoholic patient. *Australian Annals of Medicine, 19*, 232-239.

Redmond, D.E., Jr. (1979). New and old evidence for the involvement of a brain norepinephrine system in anxiety. In W.E. Fann, I. Karacan, A.D. Porkorney, & R.L. Williams (Eds.), *Phenomenology and treatment of anxiety* (pp. 153-203). New York: Spectrum.

Regestein, Q.R., & Monk, T.H. (1991). Is the poor sleep of shift workers a disorder? *American Journal of Psychiatry, 148*, 1487-1493.

Reich, W. (1949/1968). *Character analysis* (3rd. ed.). New York: Noonday Press.

Rey, Joseph M. (1993) Oppositional defiant disorder. *American Journal of Psychiatry,* *150*(12), 1769–1778.

Reynolds, C.F., Hoch, C.C., Kupfer, D.J., Buysse, D.J., Houck, P.R., Stack, J.A., & Campbell, D.W. (1988). Bedside differentiation of depressive pseudodementia from dementia. *American Journal of Psychiatry, 145,* 1099–1103.

Ries, R.K. (1985). *DSM-III* implications of the diagnoses of catatonia and bipolar disorder. *American Journal of Psychiatry, 142,* 1471–1474.

Ries, R.K., Roy–Byrne, P.P., Ward, N.G., Neppe, V., & Cullison, S. (1989). Carbamazepine treatment for benzodiazepine withdrawal. *American Journal of Psychiatry, 146*(4), 536–537.

Rittenhouse, J.D. (1982). Drugs in the school: The shape of drug abuse among American youth in the seventies. In G.G. Nahas & H.C. Frick (Eds.), *Drug abuse in the modern world: A perspective for the eighties* (pp. 99–105). New York: Pergamon Press.

Robins, L.N. (1966). *Deviant children grown up.* Baltimore: Williams & Wilkins.

Robins, L.N., Helzer, J.E., Weissman, M.M., Orvaschel, H., Gruenberg, E., Burke, J.D., & Regier, D.A. (1984). Lifetime prevalence of specific psychiatric disorders in three sites. *Archives of General Psychiatry, 41,* 949–958.

Robins, L.N., & Regier, D.A. (Eds.). (1991). *Psychiatric disorders in America: The Epidemiologic Catchment Area study.* New York: Free Press.

Rosenthal, N.E., Sack, D.A., Gillin, J.C., Lewy, A.J., Goodwin, F.K., Davenport, Y., Mueller, P.S., Newsome, D.A., & Wehr, T.A. (1984). Seasonal affective disorder. *Archives of General Psychiatry, 41,* 72–80.

Ross, C.A., Anderson, G., Fleisher, W.P., & Norton, G.R. (1991). The frequency of multiple personality disorder among psychiatric inpatients. *American Journal of Psychiatry, 148,* 1717–1720.

Ross, C.A., Joshi, S., & Currie R. (1990). Dissociative experiences in the general population. *American Journal of Psychiatry, 147,* 1547–1552.

Ross, C.A., Miller, S.D., Reagor, P., Bjornson, L., Fraser, G.A., & Anderson G. (1990). Structured interview data on 102 cases of multiple personality disorder from four centers. *American Journal of Psychiatry, 147,* 596–601.

Ross, H.E., Glaser, F.B., & Germanson, T. (1988). The prevalence of psychiatric disorders in patients with alcohol and other drug problems. *Archives of General Psychiatry, 45,* 1023–1031.

Roy, A. (1985). Early parental separation and adult depression. *Archives of General Psychiatry, 42,* 987–991.

Roy, A., Adinoff, B., Roehrich, L., Lamparski, D., Custer, R., Lorenz, V., Barbaccia, M., Guidotti, A., Costa, E., & Linnoila, M. (1988). Pathological gambling. *Archives of General Psychiatry, 45,* 369–373.

Roy, A., DeJong, J., & Linnoila, M. (1989). Extraversion in pathological gamblers. *Archives of General Psychiatry, 46,* 679–681.

Roy-Byrne, P., Geraci, M., & Uhde, T.W. (1986). Life events and the onset of panic disorder. *American Journal of Psychiatry, 143,* 1424–1427.

Rutter, M. (1981). *Maternal deprivation reassessed* (2nd ed.). London: Penguin Books.

Sallee, F.R., Stiller, R.L., & Perel, J.M. (1992). Pharmacodynamics of pemoline in attention deficit disorder. *Journal of American Academy of Child Adolescent Psychiatry, 31,* 244–251.

Salzman, C. (1985). Benzodiazepine dependence. *The Harvard Medical School Mental Health Letter, 1*(10), 8.

Satel, S.L., & Edell, W.S. (1991). Cocaine-induced paranoia and psychosis proneness. *American Journal of Psychiatry, 148,* 1708–1711.

Schellenberg, G.D., Bird, T.D., Wijsman, E.M., Orr, H.T., Anderson, L., Nemens, E., White, J.A., Bonnycastle, L., Weber, J.L., Alonso, M.E., Potter, H., Heston, L.L., & Martin, G.M. (1992). Genetic linkage evidence for a familial Alzheimer's disease locus on chromosome 14. *Science, 258,* 668.

Schnoll, S.H., & Daghestani, A.N. (1986). Treatment of marijuana abuse. *Psychiatric Annals, 16*(4), 249–244.

Sederer, L.I. (1983). Depression. In L.I. Sederer (Ed.), *Inpatient psychiatry: Diagnosis and treatment* (pp. 2–27). Baltimore: Williams & Wilkins.

Segal, J.H. (1989). Erotomania revisited: From Kraepelin to *DSM-III-R*. *American Journal of Psychiatry, 146*(10), 1261–1266.

Selzer, M.L. (1969). Alcoholics at fault in fatal accidents and hospitalized alcoholics: A comparison. *Quarterly Journal of Studies on Alcohol, 30*(4), 883–887.

Shapiro, D. (1965). *Neurotic styles.* New York: Basic Books.

Shapiro, D. (1979). *Neurotic styles.* New York: Basic Books.

Sifneos, P. (1979). *Short-term dynamic psychotherapy, evaluation, and technique.* New York: Plenum.

Silverstein, B., Peterson, B., & Perdue, L. (1986). Some correlates of the thin standard of bodily attractiveness for women. *International Journal of Eating Disorders, 5*, 895–905.

Skolnick, P., & Paul, S.M. (1983). New concepts in the neurobiology of anxiety. *Journal of Clinical Psychiatry, 44*, 12–19.

Smalley, S.L., Asarnow, R.F., & Spence, M.A. (1988). Autism and genetics. *Archives of General Psychiatry, 45*, 953–961.

Snyder, S. (1981). Dopamine receptors, neuroleptics, and schizophrenia. *American Journal of Psychiatry, 138*, 460–464.

Solomon, S.D., Gerrity, E.T., & Muff, A.M. (1992). Efficacy of treatment for posttraumatic stress disorder. *Journal of the American Medical Association, 268*, 633–638.

Sorensen, T.I.A., Bentsen, K.D., Eghoje, K., Orholm, M., Haybye, G., & Christoffersen, P. (1984). Prospective evaluation of alcohol abuse and alcoholic liver injury in men as predictors of development of cirrhosis. *Lancet*, Aug. 4, 241–244.

Spitzer, R.L. (1976). More on pseudoscience in science and the case for psychiatric diagnosis: A critique of Rosenhan's "On being sane in insane places" and "The contextual nature of psychiatric diagnosis." *Archives of General Psychiatry, 33*, 459–470.

Spitzer, R.L., Williams, J.B.W., & Skodal, A.E. (1980). *DSM-III*: The major achievements and an overview. *American Journal of Psychiatry, 137*, 151–164.

Squire, S. (1983). Is the binge-purge cycle catching? *MS*, October, pp. 41–46.

Steinberg, M. (1991). The spectrum of depersonalization: Assessment and treatment. In A. Tasman & S.M. Goldfinger (Eds.), *Review of psychiatry, vol. 10* (pp. 223–247). Washington, DC: American Psychiatric Association.

Steinberg, M., Rounsaville, B., & Cicchetti, D.V. (1990). The structured clinical interview for *DSM-III-R* dissociative disorders: Preliminary report on a new diagnostic instrument. *American Journal of Psychiatry, 147*, 76–82.

Strangler, R.S., & Printz, A.M. (1980). *DSM-III*: Psychiatric diagnosis in a university population. *American Journal of Psychiatry, 137*, 937–940.

Strober, M.S. (1991). Family-genetic studies of eating disorders. *Journal of Clinical Psychiatry, 52*, 91–112.

Strupp, H.H., & Binder, J.L. (1984). *Psychotherapy in a new key: A guide to time-limited dynamic psychotherapy.* New York: Basic Books.

Sussman, N., & Hyler, S.E. (1985). Factitious disorders. In H.I. Kaplan & B.J. Sadock (Eds.), *Comprehensive textbook of psychiatry* (4th ed.) (pp. 1242–1247). Baltimore: Williams & Wilkins.

Sylvester, C. (1993). Psychopharmacology of disorders in children. *Psychiatric Clinics of North America, 16*(4), 779–791.

Targum, S.D., Dibble, E.D., Davenport, Y.B., & Gershon, E.S. (1981). The family attitudes questionnaire: Patients' and spouses' views of bipolar illness. *Archives of General Psychiatry, 38*, 562–568.

Telner, J.I., & Singhal, R.L. (1984). Psychiatric progress: The learned helplessness model of depression. *Journal of Psychiatric Research, 18*(3), 207–215.

Tennant, F.S., Jr. (1986). The clinical syndrome of marijuana dependence. *Psychiatric Annals, 16*(4), 225–234.

Terr, L. (1991). Childhood traumas: An outline and overview. *American Journal of Psychiatry, 148*, 10–20.

Theander, S. (1985). Outcome and prognosis in anorexia nervosa and bulimia. *Journal of Psychiatric Research, 19*, 493–508.

Treffert, D.A. (1988). The idiot savant: A review of the syndrome. *American Journal of Psychiatry, 145*(5), 563–571.

Tune, L., Carr, S., Hoag, E., & Cooper, T. (1992). Anticholinergic effects of drugs commonly prescribed for the elderly: Potential means for assessing risk of delirium. *American Journal of Psychiatry, 149*, 1393–1394.

Ursano, R.J., & Hales, R.E. (1986). A review of brief individual psychotherapies. *American Journal of Psychiatry, 143*, 1507–1517.

Vaillant, G.E. (1966). A 12-year follow-up of New York narcotic addicts. *Archives of General Psychiatry, 15*, 599.

Vaillant, G.E. (1971). Theoretical hierarchy of adaptive ego mechanisms. *Archives of General Psychiatry, 24*, 107–118.

Vaillant, G.E., Bond, M., & Vaillant, C.O. (1986). An empirically validated hierarchy of defense mechanisms. *Archives of General Psychiatry, 43*, 786–794.

Vaughn, C.E., & Leff, J.P. (1976). The influence of family and social factors on the course of psychiatric illness: A comparison of schizophrenic with depressed neurotic patients. *British Journal of Psychiatry, 129*, 125–137.

Victor, M., & Adams, R.D. (1953). The effect of alcohol on the nervous system. In *Proceedings of the Association for Research in Nervous and Mental Diseases*. Baltimore, MD: Williams & Wilkins.

Victor, M., Adams, R.D., & Collins, G.H. (1971). *The Wernicke-Korsakoff syndrome*. Philadelphia, PA: F.A. Davis.

Victor, M., Adams, R.D., & Collins, G.H. (1989). *The Wernicke-Korsakoff syndrome* (2nd ed.). Philadelphia: F.A. Davis.

Victor, M., & Hope, J.M. (1958). The phenomenon of auditory hallucinations in chronic alcoholism. *Journal of Nervous and Mental Disorders, 126*, 451.

Virkkunen, M., DeJong, J., Bartko, J., & Linnoila, M. (1989). Psychobiological concommitants of history of suicide attempts among violent offenders and impulsive fire setters. *Archives of General Psychiatry, 148*, 652–657.

Volberg, A., & Steadman, H.J. (1988). Refining prevalence estimates of pathological gambling. *American Journal of Psychiatry, 145*, 502–505.

Volkmar, F.R., Bregman, J., Cohen, D.J., & Cicchetti, D.V. (1988). *DSM-III* and *DSM-III-R* diagnoses of autism. *American Journal of Psychiatry, 145*(11), 1404–1408.

Walsh, B.T. (1991). Psychopharmacologic treatment of bulimia nervosa. *Journal of Clinical Psychiatry, 52*, 34–38.

Walsh, B.T., Hadigan, C.M., Devlin, M.J., Gladis, M., & Roose, S.P. (1991). Long-term outcome of antidepressant treatment for bulima nervosa. *American Journal of Psychiatry, 148*, 1206–1212.

Walsh, F. (1982). *Normal family process*. New York: Guilford.

Ward, N.G. (1990). Pain and depression. In J.J. Bonica (Ed.), *The management of pain* (pp. 310–319). Malvern, PA: Lea & Febiger.

Ward, N.G., Rowlett, D.B., & Burke, P. (1986). Sodium amylobarbitone in the differential diagnosis of confusion. *American Journal of Psychiatry, 135*, 75–78.

Weber, J.J., Elinson, J., & Moss, L.M. (1967). Psychoanalysis and change. *Archives of General Psychiatry, 17*, 687–709.

Wehr, T.A., & Rosenthal, N.E. (1989). Seasonality and affective illness. *American Journal of Psychiatry, 146*, 829–839

Weinberger, D.R. (1984). Brain disease and psychiatric illness: When should a psychiatrist order a CAT scan? *American Journal of Psychiatry, 141*, 1521–1527.

Weiner, H. (1985). Schizophrenia: Etiology. In H.I. Kaplan & B.J. Sadock (Eds.), *Comprehensive textbook of psychiatry* (4th ed.) (pp. 651–680). Baltimore: Williams & Wilkins.

Weissman, M.M., Leckman, J.F., Merikangas, K.R., Gammon, G.D., & Prusoff, B.A. (1985). Depression and anxiety disorders in parents and children: Results from the Yale family study. *Archives of General Psychiatry, 41*, 845–852.

Wells, K.B., Stewart, A., Hays, R.D., Burnam, A., Rogers, W., Daniels, M., Berry, S.,

Greenfield, S., & Ware, J. (1989). The functioning and well-being of depressed patients: Results from the medical outcome study. *Journal of the American Medical Association, 262*(7), 914–919.

Wells, C.E., & McEvoy, J.P. (1982). Organic mental disorders. In J.H. Greist, J.W. Jefferson, & R.L. Spitzer (Eds.), *Treatment of mental disorders* (pp. 3–43). New York: Oxford University Press.

Wells, K.C. & Egan, J. (1988). Social learning and systems family therapy for childhood oppositional disorder: Comparative treatment outcome. *Comprehensive Psychiatry, 29,* 138–146.

Wender, P.H., & Klein, D.F. (1981). *Mind, mood, and medicine: A guide to the new biopsychiatry.* New York: Meridan.

Wilkins, W. (1973a). Client's expectancy of therapeutic gain: Evidence for the active role of the therapist. *Psychiatry, 36,* 184–190.

Wilkins, W. (1973b). Expectancy of therapeutic gain: An empirical and conceptual critique. *Journal of Consulting Psychology, 40,* 69–77.

Winokur, G., & Coryell, W. (1992). Familial subtypes of unipolar depression: A prospective study of familial pure depression disease compared to depression spectrum disease. *Biological Psychiatry, 32,* 1012–1018.

Winokur, G., Coryell, W., Endicott, J., & Akiskal, H. (1993). Further distinctions between manic-depressive illness (bipolar disorder) and primary depressive disorder (unipolar depression). *American Journal of Psychiatry, 150,* 1176–1181.

Winokur, G., March, V., & Mendels, J. (1980). Primary affective disorder in relatives of patients with anorexia nervosa. *American Journal of Psychiatry, 137,* 695–698.

Wittgenstein, L. (1958). *Philosophical investigations* (2nd ed.). Translated by G.E.M. Anscomb. New York: Macmillan.

Wolf, M.E., Alavi, A., & Mosnaim, A.D. (1988). Posttraumatic stress disorder in Vietnam veterans: Clinical and EEG findings; possible therapeutic effects of carbamazepine. *Biological Psychiatry, 23,* 642–644.

Wortis, J. (1993). The perennial alcohol problem. *Biological Psychiatry, 34,* 589–590.

Yager, J. et al. (1993). Practice guideline for eating disorders. *American Journal of Psychiatry, 150,* 207–228.

Yalom, I.D. (1975). *The theory and practice of group psychotherapy* (2nd ed.). New York: Basic Books.

Yalom, I.D. (1985). *The theory and practice of group psychotherapy* (3rd ed.). Norton: New York.

Young, T., et al. (1993). The occurrence of sleep-disordered breathing among middle-aged adults. *New England Journal of Medicine, 328,* 1230–1235.

Zimmerman, M. (1994). *Interview guide for evaluating DSM-IV psychiatric disorders and the mental status examination.* Philadelphia: Psychiatric Products Press.

Zisook, S., & Schuchter, S.R. (1991). Depression through the first year after the death of a spouse. *American Journal of Psychiatry, 148,* 1346–1352.

Index